Global Capitalism, FDI and Competitiveness

Global Capitalism, FDI and Competitiveness

The Selected Essays of John H. Dunning, Volume II

John H. Dunning

Emeritus Esmee Fairbairn Professor of International Investment and Business Studies, University of Reading, UK and Emeritus State of New Jersey Professor of International Business, Rutgers University, USA

Edward Elgar

Cheltenham, UK • Northampton, MA, USA

Published by
Edward Elgar Publishing Limited
Glensanda House
Montpellier Parade
Cheltenham
Glos GL50 1UA
UK

Edward Elgar Publishing, Inc.
136 West Street
Suite 202
Northampton
Massachusetts 01060
USA

A catalogue record for this book is available from the British Library

ISBN 1 84064 742 6
Printed and bound in Great Britain by MPG Books Ltd, Bodmin, Cornwall

Contents

Acknowledgements

The author and publisher wish to thank the following who have kindly given permission for the usė of copyright material.

Allen and Unwin for 'Assessing the costs and benefits of multinational enterprises to host countries: A tool kit approach' (1997), in *Conferencenia International Sobre Economici Portugesa*, Lisbon: German Marshall Fund of the US and Fundacao Calouste Gulbenkian, 835–69.

Banco Nazionale del Lavoro for *'International Business in a Changing World Environment'* (1982), *Banco Nazionale del Lavoro*, **143**, November, 351–74.

Blackwell Publishers Ltd for 'The European internal market program and inbound foreign direct investment' (1997), *Journal of Common Market Studies*, **35** (1), 1–30 and (2), 189–223.

Economic and Social Studies Ltd for 'Globalization: The Challenge for National Economic Regimes', in a booklet of the same name, 1994, Dublin, Economic and Social Research Institute.

Journal of International Business Studies for 'Location and the multinational enterprise, a neglected factor?' (1998), *Journal of International Business Studies*, **29** (1), 45–66.

Oxford University Press for 'Globalization, technological change and the spatial organization of economic activity', by John H. Dunning, from *The Dynamic Firm: The Role of Technology, Strategy, Organization and Regions*, edited by Alfred D. Chandler Jr., Peter Hadström, and Örjan Sölvell (1998) and 'Regions, globalization; and the knowledge-based economy: The issues stated'(2000), in Dunning J.H. (ed.), *Regions, Globalization, and the Knowledge-Based Economy*, 8–41.

Routledge for 'Some paradoxes of the emerging global economy. The multinational solution' (1996), Chapter 14 in Dunning, J. H., *Alliance Capitalism in Global Business*, 357–372.

Taylor and Francis for the article 'Governments and the macro-organization of economic activity: a historical and spatial perspective', by Dunning, J.H. (1997), *Review of International Economy*, **4** (1), 42–86: http://www.tandf.co.uk

United Nations Conference on Trade and Development for 'Globalization, Economic Restructuring and Development' (1998), The 6th Raúl Prebisch Lecture Geneva, UNCTAD, 1–39, First delivered as the 6th Raúl Prebisch Lecture, on the occasion of UNCTAD's thirtieth anniversary in October 1994 at the Palais des Nations in Geneva.

United Nations, International Investment *for 'The competitive advantages of countries and MNE activity'* (1992), *Transnational Corporations*, **1** (1), 135–68 and 'The geographical sources of competitiveness', (1996), extracts from *Transnational Corporations*, **5** (3), 1–30 and 'Re-evaluating the benefits of foreign direct investment' (1994), *Transnational Corporations*, **3** (1), 9–22 subsequently reprinted in J.H. Dunning, *Alliance Capitalism and Global Business*, London and New York, Routledge, 1995, 209–223

Unwin and Hyman for 'Multinational enterprises, industrial restructuring and competitiveness: A UK perspective' (1995), in Dunning, J. H., *Multinationals, Technology and Competitiveness,* London and Boston, Unwin Hyman, 1988, pp. 172–202

Every effort has been made to trace and contact the copyright holders but if any have been inadvertently overlooked, the publishers will be pleased to make the necessary arrangements at the first opportunity.

Introduction

This volume and Volume I of the set consists of some of my more substantial and influential contributions to the study of international business (IB), foreign direct investment (FDI) and global capitalism. The contributions stretch over nearly three decades, although the great majority were written in the 1980s and 1990s.

The second volume covers a variety of topics, ranging from the economic and social implications of global capitalism to the rising importance of regional economies in their desire to attract inward foreign direct investment (FDI), to issues of competitiveness and how national governments might best respond to the opportunities and challenges of globalization. The first group of essays – Chapters 1 to 4 – identifies a number of features of the changing world environment which have occurred over the last two decades and their relevance for international business (IB) activity. The comparisons and contrasts between the situation in the early 1980s (Chapter 1) and 2000 (Chapter 2) are both interesting and instructive. Chapter 2 contains some of my recent thoughts on the actions which need to be taken if the global capitalist system, as we know it today, is to survive and prosper. Particular attention is given to the role of the four main institutions of global capitalism, viz. markets, civil society, national governments and supranational agencies. The recent (2001) terrorist attack on the World Trade Center in New York City dramatically emphasizes some of the economic, political and moral imperatives which need to be addressed if global capitalism is to remain the dominant system of wealth creation.

In Chapter 3, we identify and evaluate some of the paradoxes of the emerging global markets, and how national governments and MNEs, faced with a similar group of paradoxes, have overcome and/or reconciled them. Chapter 4 turns more specifically to the challenges of globalization faced by developing – and particularly poorer developing – countries in their attempts to transform and upgrade the structure of their economies. Again, as in Chapter 10 of Volume I, this chapter emphasizes the particular features of alliance capitalism and stresses the need for social and ethical harmony among and between countries of different economic and ideological persuasions.

Chapters 5 to 7 turn to consider some spatial implications of our contemporary global and knowledge-based economy. Chapter 5 (and especially Table 5.1) details some changes in the specific variables affecting MNE activity between the 1970s and 1990s. The rising importance of both macro- and micro-regional governing entities in affecting the siting of mobile innovatory and productive activities is emphasized in Chapter 6. Especial attention is paid in both that chapter and Chapter 7 to the growing significance of the economies of agglomeration of (related) economic activities, and the impact of, and response to, cross-border industrial clusters by MNEs.

Chapters 8 and 9 contain two essays – one written in 1977, the other 17 years later – dealing with the costs and benefits of inbound FDI. Much of the content of these two chapters formed the basis for Part 3 of my book *Multinational Enterprises and a Global Economy* (Dunning, 1993), and have subsequently been explored in more depth and detail in a series of annual *World Investment Reports* prepared by UNCTAD, and published by the United Nations. Certainly, the advent of the global economy has heightened or reduced the existing costs and benefits, and has added new ones. But in general, the price to countries of *not* participating in the global economy has increased over the last two decades, while some of the earlier (perceived) costs have been mitigated by the intensified competition between global firms. At the same time, most national governments have redirected their policies away from FDI *per se* to attempting to secure the maximum net benefits from being part of a global economy.

Chapter 10 looks more specifically at the consequences of the completion of the European internal market (viz. Europe, 1992) – the penultimate stage in the movement towards a fully integrated European community[1] – on both extra- and intra-EC inward FDI. In doing so, it draws upon both the theory of FDI and that of economic integration, and finds that removal of most non-tariff barriers to the movement of goods and services has, indeed, had a positive impact on the flow of new FDI into the EC as well as influencing its industrial and geographical composition.

The next group of essays presents some of my thoughts on the subject of the competitiveness of firms and countries. Chapter 11 extends the well-known Porter diamond of competitive advantage (Porter, 1999) to embrace the impact of both inbound and outbound FDI on the productivity of indigenous resources and capabilities. Chapter 12 looks at some empirical evidence of the extent to which the world's leading industrial MNEs perceive they augment their domestic competitive advantage from foreign sources. This they may do directly as a result of the foreign activities (especially innovatory activities) of their affiliates, and/or indirectly by the ability of these affiliates (or foreign partners in a strategic alliance) to tap into the technological and organizational capabilities of indigenous firms and into the innovatory systems of host countries.

In Chapter 13, we examine the ways in which, and the extent to which, inward and outward MNE activity helped restructure the UK's economy in the 1970s, and, in so doing, upgraded the allocative and technical efficiency of UK industrial firms. *Inter alia*, it shows that the performance of both the UK affiliates of foreign MNEs and the domestic operations of UK MNEs generally record superior performances than other UK-based producers.

The final chapters of this volume set out two of my contributions on the changing role of national governments in the light of the increasingly significant role of cross-border investment technology flows and strategic alliances. Chapter 14 takes a broad look at the historical evolution of the macro-economic and micro-management policies of Western (and especially the UK) governments, and how the widening spatial dimension of economic activity is affecting these policies. Chapter 15 returns to the theme of Chapter 2, but looks more specifically at the challenges posed by globalization to the economic management of both national governments and supranational regimes. In particular, it pays attention to the various forms of government intervention and the transaction costs associated with such intervention. It also examines the extent to which and the form in which the easier mobility of goods, services, assets and people across national boundaries reduces the freedom of national governments to operate independent macroeconomic policies and micro-management strategies.

John H. Dunning
Rutgers and Reading Universities

NOTE

1. The final stage being the adoption of a common currency and monetary system.

REFERENCES

Dunning, J.H. (1993), *Multinational Enterprises and the Global Economy*, Wokingham, Berkshire: Addison-Wesley.
Porter, M.E. (1990), *The Competitive Advantage of Nations*, New York: The Free Press.

1. International business in a changing world environment*

INTRODUCTION

In this chapter, we consider some aspects of the interface between international business – primarily in the guise of the MNE – and the governments of the countries which are host to its activities, within a changing world economic and political scenario. The chapter sets out to examine why, how and in what ways this interface has been shaped by, or has shaped, the events of the past 25 years, and speculates a little about the prospects for the remainder of the twentieth century.

ANTECEDENTS OF THE MNE

The Multi-Plant Enterprise

The MNE is the modern equivalent of the multi-plant domestic enterprise, which dates back more than a century. In particular, the years following the Civil War saw the transformation of many regional American corporations into national corporations, and the emergence of multi-plant establishments, under the same ownership, in different parts of the USA. And it is, perhaps, worth recalling that the spread of Northern US companies into the south was regarded by some observers at the time with almost the same suspicion and unrest as that exhibited more recently by some Southern (developing) countries towards international corporations from the Northern hemisphere.

A useful starting point to any understanding of the modern MNE is to regard it as an extension of the domestic multi-plant firm (Caves, 1982). In both instances, a company seeking to service a market beyond its immediate catchment area must have some kind of advantage, which we shall call an ownership-specific advantage (Dunning, 1981, 1988a) over and above that possessed by its competitors, or potential competitors, producing in that market.

* From *Banco Nazionale del Lavoro*, No. 143 (November 1982): 351–74. Revised and updated, and published as Chapter 1 in *Multinationals, Technology and Competitiveness*, London: Unwin Hyman, 1988.

In both instances, too, it must be more profitable to supply the market from a foreign, rather than a domestic, location, and for the firm possessing the advantage to use it itself rather than sell the right to do so to other firms.

The growth of the multi-plant and/or multi-activity domestic enterprise in the second half of the last century may be explained by a series of separate, but interconnected, events. The first was the introduction – in both Europe and the USA – of the joint-stock company and the principle of limited liability, which, by lessening the risk for entrepreneurial capital, aided the finance of the technological and organizational advances of the time, and paved the way for the growth of the large business corporation (Chandler, 1977). The second event was the emergence of technology, including organizational technology, as the major vehicle of economic development.

From earliest times, economic progress has been conditioned by the availability of human and natural resources, and the efficiency by which these resources are administered to meet man's demands. In the first stage of development, typified by a Robinson Crusoe type economy, technology is primitive, and is freely available or easily copiable; the economic system is elemental, and man's standard of living essentially rests on the abundance of natural resources immediately available and his capacity to convert these resources into finished products. To make progress from such a situation one of two things is normally necessary. First, the economy must obtain the goods it needs but is unable to produce for itself from elsewhere; second, ways must be found of increasing the quality and productivity of its own resources.

Trade, technological advances and improvement in economic management have proved important vehicles of growth in the past, and, in some countries, for example, Japan, have more than compensated for deficiencies in natural resources. What is less obvious is that, as the more accessible non-renewable resources are depleted and the benefits of trade become fully exploited, the role of technology and organization becomes more decisive. Now technology has several unique features. Like natural resources its use has to be organized, but, unlike them, it has to be created in the first place.[1] Moreover, technology is frequently mobile across space, and often assumes the characteristics of a public good (in the sense that once produced it can be made available to additional consumers at a zero or low marginal cost). Because of these properties, society has devised various mechanisms, including the patent system, to allow the generators of some kind of technology privileged rights to its use, at least for a period of time – that is, the technology becomes ownership-specific. Not all types of technology, of course, are patentable or need to be patented. For example, the system- (and often customer-) specific computer technology of a company like IBM requires an extremely costly infrastructure which competitors find difficult to emulate. But it is the gain or erosion of such property rights, and the efficiency of their usage, which explain much of the birth, growth and death of firms in modern industrial society.

There are three main types of ownership (*O*) advantages which give both domestic and multinational firms an edge over their competitors. The first is an exclusive or preferential access to a particular input or market (which might be directly acquired or negotiated with independent buyers or sellers); where the firm owns these rights it may have the option of leasing them to other firms either in its home or a foreign country. The second advantage is the possession of a unique intangible asset, for instance, a patent or a trade mark. Such an asset is locked into the firm and is often the output of its own research and development or marketing department, or the accumulation of managerial expertise. Like the first, however, it is often capable of being transferred to other firms, by way of a technical service agreement, managerial contract and the like.

The third *O*-specific advantage is different from the other two and reflects the ability of hierarchies to organize related productive activities more efficiently than the market. It stems not so much from the possession of a particular asset but from the economizing of transaction costs when such transactions are under the same governance. Such an advantage includes better access to, and ability to assimilate, information flows; the economies of synergy and the spreading of overhead costs; the capacity to practise price discrimination; the diversification of risks; the ability to protect property rights; and the efficient scheduling of production consequent upon internalizing intermediate goods or services markets. For example, a branch plant of an existing firm can benefit from the research and development or marketing facilities of its parent company, which a *de novo* competitor would have to reproduce for itself. Because of their high transaction costs, the rights to these assets cannot be bought and sold, that is, externalized, in the same way as can the first and second kind, for their value depends on their being centrally co-ordinated and controlled. Nevertheless, they often confer an important economic leverage on the firms possessing them, which, according to many economists,[2] is the main *raison d'être* for the existence of large diversified firms, including MNEs.

The last reason for the growth of multi-plant firms over the last century has to do partly with the economies of product or process specialization and partly with the supplying of distant markets from alternative production sites, that is, what we might call location-specific factors. Again there is a parallel between domestic multi-plant and MNE activity; the basic question is the same – where is it best to site a plant to supply a market? The literature on the subject offers three sets of answers. The first is where costs are lowest. Given that technology is firm- rather than branch- (or plant-) specific, then production costs will be determined by spatial differences in the prices and productivity of factor inputs, while transfer costs will vary according to distance, the nature of the product being marketed and government-imposed inducements to, or restrictions on, trade. However, the point worth stressing is that multi-plant operations are likely to be pronounced when the ownership advantages of a firm are of a kind which favours the geographical separation rather than the concentration of production units. The second answer to 'Why multi-plant firms?' is that a physical presence of a firm in a market may improve a firm's competitive viability and may make it more difficult for a prospective competitor to enter that market; a lot of import substituting foreign direct investment, as described in the product cycle literature (Vernon, 1966, 1974, 1979), originates in this way.

Thirdly, firms may produce in different locations to minimize transaction costs over space, and to take advantage of international product and process specialization. In this respect, improvements in transport, initiated by railroads in the nineteenth and aircraft in the twentieth centuries, have had a decisive impact on the location of economic activity. But, no less dramatically, so have advances in communications and data transmitting technology. While, in one way, such innovations have worked alongside new product and process technology to centralize value-adding activity, in another, by reducing obstacles to the movement of goods, people and information, they have contributed to its spatial diversification.

The International Trading Enterprise

Let us now turn to consider another antecedent of the MNE which is still very much a part of international business: the trading company. Trade is usually the first introduction of a firm into the international economic arena; indeed, domestic trade, in the form of exports from a production unit located in one part of the country to a customer in another, tends to precede the establishment of production units in the latter region. The reasons for this are straightforward. Initially, an enterprise, because of its uncertainty about market prospects, or its ability to produce in an unfamiliar environment, is reluctant to incur the heavy setting up and monitoring costs which FDI usually involves. So the first step from a domestic to a foreign market tends to take the form of trade – either of intermediate or of final products. However, trade, like international production, requires a firm to possess one or two types of advantage over a firm in the country to which it is selling. Either it must have access to country-specific resource and organizational mechanisms not available to firms in the buying country and not transferable between the two countries, *or* it must possess ownership-specific advantages which, although they may reflect the economic institutional and cultural characteristics of the country from which they originate, are capable of being deployed in another country. Just as economic growth is increasingly dependent on advances in technology and organizational systems, so the pattern of trade is increasingly reflecting the mobile ownership advantages of firms, rather than the immobile resource endowments of countries. But, whereas in the case of the first kind of trade resources have to be used where they are located, in the second this is not necessary, and trade will be replaced by foreign production, wherever the location-specific endowments (which require to be combined with the ownership advantages of firms) most favour foreign countries.

Driven by purely economic considerations, business corporations would prefer to ignore political boundaries and view the world as a single, integrated market. And it is true that national frontiers do not necessarily herald a discrete change in the amount or disposition of factor endowments. The 49th parallel and many borders in Western Europe make little *economic* sense. Resources are more unevenly distributed within the USA than, for example, between Washington and British Columbia or Michigan and Southern Ontario. In such cases, there may be a greater economic affinity between firms on one side of their national border and markets on the other, than between the same firms and distant parts of the domestic market.

If we interpret economic distance as the cost of overcoming the obstacles of space between an enterprise's place of production and its markets, including the transaction cost of surmounting language, cultural and other barriers, then, given the size and nature of the markets, the enterprise will normally seek to service those nearest to it. Governments may increase or lessen this distance. In the past, economic and political ties and a common legal and commercial system between metropolitan European powers and their colonies helped to lower spatial costs; export-free zones are performing this function today and trade and monetary integration, as it exists within parts of the EEC, has a similar effect. Import controls or political differences, for example, vividly demonstrated between East and West Germany or South and North Korea, work in the opposite direction. Both by the economic systems they operate and the development and other strategies they pursue, governments may exercise a decisive influence on transfer costs and the profitability of international business.

The purpose of government intervention in economic distance is primarily to alter patterns of resource allocation in pursuance of social and strategic objectives. Sometimes the intervention may be directed to encouraging import substitution activities; sometimes to strengthening the competitive viability of indigenous *vis-à-vis* foreign enterprises; and sometimes to gain tax revenue or protect the balance of payments. A great deal of foreign direct investment in the post-war period, especially in developing countries, has been prompted by host government intervention, either in response to penalties imposed on trade or to incentives to local production; likewise, governments, by regulating the conditions for FDI have sometimes fostered non-equity transfers of technology via licensing, management contracts and the like.

Scholars interested in comparative economic systems find it is helpful to classify countries by use of (what is called) the ESP paradigm.[3] Countries differ from each other, for example, in respect of their stage of development or propensity to attract international business, according to their economic *environment* (E), *systems* (S), and *policies* (P). By *environment* is meant the resources, including existing technology, available to a particular country and the ability of its enterprises to use these to service domestic or foreign markets. By *system* is meant the organizational framework within which the use and allocation of these resources is decided. Is it, for example, the market which is the main administrative mechanism or is it some form of government fiat or some combination of the two? What is the role of the government in affecting the transaction costs of different organizational forms? *Inter alia* the answers to these questions will affect the creation of *new* technology, and will be determined, in part at least, by political circumstances and by cultural and social attitudes. By *policy* is meant both the strategic objectives of governments and the measures taken by them or related institutions to implement and advance these objectives, within the system and environment of which they are part.

ENVIRONMENT (*E*)

Components:	*Outcomes:*
• Human resources • Natural resources • Stage of economic development • Cultural/historical background	• Level and structure of output (primary, industrial service, specializations) • Attitudes to work, wealth, foreigners, etc.

SYSTEM (*S*)

• Capitalist (free enterprise) • Socialist • Mixed • Alliance with other countries	• Structure of decision taking • Propensity to engage in international commerce • Resource allocation controlled by market • Nationalization

POLICIES (*P*)

• Macro-economics (fiscal, monetary, exchange rate) • Micro-economics (industry, trade, competition) • General (education, consumer protection) • Specific to FDI	• Extent and form of government interventions • Controls • Performance requirements

Figure 1.1 The ESP paradigm

Figure 1.1 sets out the main attributes of the ESP configuration and their respective outcomes.

Clearly, the three elements of the paradigm are interlinked: each affects and is affected by the other. A change in government policy may dramatically recast the economic system, as, for example, in the cases of Chile and the Republic of China, while over a longer period government involvement in educational and research and development programmes may no less impinge on the environment. A detailed appraisal of the ESP characteristics of countries takes us a long way to understanding the likely interaction between MNEs and the nation-states in which they operate.

Most of the literature on international economics tends to concentrate on the *environmental* influences of trade and foreign direct investment. Certainly, the classical and neo-classical trade models assume a market system in which there is atomistic competition, no government intervention, zero economic distance and technology which is freely and instantaneously transferred across national boundaries. Later theories acknowledge market imperfections and, implicitly at least, by accepting the possibility of ownership-specific advantages – including scale economies – and positive transaction costs, some of the characteristics of a mixed economy. From the start, explanations of international production have more explicitly taken system and policy factors into account. For example, in a survey of the 44 most commonly quoted factors said to determine the investments of firms in developing countries, one half were found to be directly related to system or policy variables and the remainder to environmental variables (Root and Ahmed, 1978). Although the survey was primarily concerned with their locational choice, the ESP paradigm is no less relevant in explaining differences in the ownership advantages of MNEs of different nationalities and the modalities by which these advantages may be used.

Let us recap our thesis up to this point. MNEs possess many of the characteristics of multi-plant domestic firms and of firms engaged in international trade. The fact that a corporation locates part of its income generating activities outside its national boundaries, that is, engages in international production, does not really affect the nature of the beast. It must still possess certain advantages over firms which might seek to serve the same market; it must also be worthwhile to use these itself, rather than lease them to other firms (that is, the net benefits from internalization – which may include risk reduction – are expected to exceed those offered by the market); and it must be profitable to produce at least part of its output in a foreign, rather than a domestic, location. What primarily distinguishes *international* from *domestic* corporations is the configuration of the ESP variables facing the two groups of firms and the way in which this impinges on the OLI (ownership, location, internalization) advantages just described. The form and structure of these OLI advantages then determine the extent and pattern of multi-plant operations. This suggests that any explanatory model of international production must take account of new variables, and particularly those to do with location-specific systems and policies, which do not usually vary between regions *within* a country, for example, those to do with operating in different political, currency and tax regimes; while others, which also influence the siting of domestic economic activity – communication and labour costs etc. – take on different values.

MULTINATIONAL ENTERPRISES AND HOST COUNTRY INTERACTION: THE LAST 30 YEARS

Using this kind of approach, let us now turn to examine some aspects of the interaction between MNEs and the countries in which they have operated in the last 30 years or so. We can identify three fairly distinct stages in this interaction. While the precise timing of each stage may differ between companies and countries, by and large, the first lasted from the early 1950s to the mid-1960s; the second from the mid-1960s to the mid-1970s and the third from the mid-1970s to date. For reasons which will become apparent, we shall call them respectively the honeymoon, the confrontation and the reconciliation phases.

The Honeymoon Phase

Any partnership, and particularly one which is intended to be lasting, starts off with each partner having a great expectancy of what the other can offer, although this is sometimes more a matter of faith than anything else. And certainly, if love is not blind, mutual attraction does tend to wear rose-coloured spectacles, which magnify the good and overlook the less desirable features of one's partner. So it was with the early post-war interface between MNEs – or foreign direct investors as they were then known – and the countries in which they operated. From the viewpoint of both newly emerging developing nations and war-ravaged Europe, the capital, technology, managerial skills and entrepreneurship of US firms were sorely needed. However, owing to a shortage of dollars and an inadequate international market for these assets, these could only be obtained via equity investment, that is, their transfer remained internalized within the transferring firm. During these years, US economic and technological hegemony was at its peak, and American corporations dominated international production just as UK firms had dominated world trade a century and a half before. At the same time, US manufacturers were looking for new markets for their products (particularly in the late 1950s, when some of the steam had gone out of the domestic economy) and new sources of materials to supplement indigenous supplies.

On the face of it, it seemed a perfect partnership between US investors and host countries, although in some cases it was Hobson's choice for the latter, as at the time only MNEs possessed many of the assets or markets they needed. And it was this very monopoly which gave rise to the first signs of discontent in the relationship. Nevertheless, in the 1950s and early 1960s at least, all (or most) was sweetness and light, and with the international economic climate, fashioned at Bretton Woods and Havana in the mid-1940s ensuring exchange rate stability and a well-ordered trading regime, the scenario for international business was more promising than at any time since before the First World War.

One other thing is worth mentioning. Most MNEs in those days were quite small, and involved in many fewer countries than they are today. Most manufacturing affiliates, too, were set up as import-substituting ventures, and were truncated replicas of their parent companies acting independently of each other and closely identified with the interests of the host country. Only in the primary goods sectors had foreign corporations evolved anything approaching a global product or marketing mandate, or was there much intra-firm trading. The main impact of such corporations in these years was, then, in the assets they provided, rather than the way in which these and local resources were allocated.[4]

The Confrontation Stage

As a marriage passes out of its honeymoon stage and becomes more firmly established, the partners are better able to assess how far each is *in fact* able to satisfy the other's aspirations. Sometimes this learning process affects the attitudes and behaviour of one or both of the partners; sometimes the character of the relationship changes; sometimes the balance of influence shifts. One thing is certain, however: after a time, each partner becomes aware of the weaknesses as well as the strengths of the other, and the costs as well as the benefits of the relationship.

The most far reaching changes in the international economic climate of the 1960s and early 1970s stemmed directly from the growing political independence of many developing countries, a better identification of their economic goals and a more realistic perception of their capacity to achieve these goals.

This national self-awareness, coupled with a Keynesian approach to economic management and the setting up of new economic systems and policies, was occurring at a time when MNEs were gaining a substantial foothold in many host countries. As more emphasis began to be given to such developmental goals as satisfying basic needs, advancing self-reliance, improving the balance of payments and raising the level of technological capacity, so FDI became evaluated in these terms – and not surprisingly, in one direction or another, was found wanting. Gradually, it dawned on governments that the kind of contribution which MNEs might make to development was not always or necessarily that which they most needed. To be sure, foreign firms provided technology, but was it always the appropriate kind or at the right price? True, their affiliates might help to save imports, but did they always buy as much from local producers as was socially desirable? Admittedly, they might export part of their output, but was not this restricted to markets designated by their parent company? Agreed that they created employment, but were not their production methods more capital-intensive than those of indigenous firms, and did they always recruit or train local management as well as they might?

On top of this, MNEs were perceived to transmit a way of life which was not always welcomed and, through advertising and other promotional means, to adversely influence social and cultural values. By their presence and behaviour they could drive out, or preclude the entry of, indigenous competitors, while, in refusing to transfer high value-added activities from their home countries, and/or by internalizing knowledge and information transfers, they could lessen the chances of a host country achieving even a modest technological capability. Finally, because of their monopoly power, they were able to earn high economic rents, and so the local net output created by them might be minimal and in some cases even negative.

These were years, too, when the management style and organizational strategy of some of the larger MNEs was changing. As the activities and geographical spread of their foreign affiliates increased, so did the tendency of corporations to adopt a more centralized and multidivisional control structure, while decisions about capital investment, product range, sourcing and markets were more likely to be taken from a regional or global perspective. The trend, too, towards the international standardization of some products, and specialization of processes and markets, placed an increasing premium on quality control, the continuity of output, the protection of proprietary rights and transaction cost economizing, all of which encouraged a more integrated governance structure of MNEs and conferred upon them *O* advantages of the third kind described on p. 3.

In the later 1960s, fixed exchange rates held good, world economic growth continued apace and inflation was generally under control. But the system was under great strain, particularly when the US balance of payments position turned sour and the US dollar lost some of its appeal as a reserve currency. Two events in the early 1970s – the devaluation of the dollar and the huge price rise of oil by the Organization of Petroleum Exporting Countries (OPEC) – heralded a watershed in post-war international economic relations. These events, together with the growing frustration of many developing countries with the inability of the existing economic order to reduce the income gap between themselves and the developed nations, sparked off a period of intensive North/South confrontation. Though much of the debate was rhetorical, it did create an uncongenial climate for international business. In the first half of the 1970s

MNEs came under increasing scrutiny and attack. Not only were they criticized on the grounds of their unacceptable behaviour[5] and uneven contribution to economic development, but also because they were perceived to be an expression of a no longer acceptable international economic system; if the system could not be changed, *inter alia* because of the inadequate bargaining strength of developing countries, then at least some redress might be taken against one of its institutions – the MNE.

This flexing of muscles by many countries, including some developed countries such as Canada and Australia, was both understandable and inevitable, even though the actions taken were often imprudent and counter-productive.

The early 1970s were the 'high noon' of confrontation between several nation-states and MNEs. The measures taken by governments are well known and already part of history:[6] they ranged from outright expropriation of foreign assets of MNEs, through restricting the level and direction of new investment, to laying down comprehensive performance criteria for foreign affiliates, and aiding indigenous firms to compete more effectively against foreign affiliates.

The response of the MNEs – which has not been so well documented – was predictable. Where their subsidiaries were already fully integrated into the local economy (as in the case of many older import-substituting ventures), but were still earning an economic rent, they absorbed the costs of intervention – but thought twice before investing any new capital. In other cases, however, their options were wider: these ranged from restricting the transfer of technology or the introduction of new products to circumventing controls on income flows through transfer pricing manipulation; from switching – or threatening to switch – production to a more congenial environment to trying to persuade their home governments to use their economic or political leverage against offending host governments.

In the main, this kind of reaction further enraged host countries, especially where, in order to compete for the same foreign investment, they were forced to pay even higher economic rents. So harmonized regional action as, for example, taken by the Andean Pact countries and the EEC, and an international consensus in the form of the Commission on Transnational Corporations (TNCs),[7] and other UN bodies, was urged to strengthen the negotiating and bargaining power of host nations, and also to provide more information about MNEs and their role in the development process. Some of us involved in these early discussions saw the Commission on TNCs, in particular, as a kind of marriage guidance counsellor, which might provide a forum for a dialogue between MNEs and governments so that each might be better informed of what the other expected and had to offer and also be more appreciative of the interaction between each other's policies and strategies.

Reconciliation

As often happens, just as one is beginning to find a solution to a particular problem the problem becomes less pressing or ceases to exist. The later 1970s saw governments learning from the experiences of the previous decade, refining, modifying and extending policy instruments better to harness the contribution of foreign direct investment – witness the very sophisticated machinery now used by some Latin American and East Asian countries in their dealings with non-resident companies. At the same time, at an international level, attention has centred on drawing up codes of conduct or guidelines of behaviour for MNEs and improving the flow of information about their activities. There are now encouraging signs that governments have made progress in their understanding not only of the costs and benefits of different types of MNEs and foreign direct investment, but also of the costs and benefits of obtaining resources through alternative routes. If the 1960s and the early 1970s were years of disillusionment regarding the net benefits of international business, the later 1970s brought no less disenchantment with the gains offered by unbundling the package of resources provided by MNEs. However, the result of a sometimes costly learning process has been a more enlightened appraisal of the alternative forms of resource importation, and a more positive and constructive set of policies towards MNEs. At the same time, MNEs have become more cognizant of the ways in which their operations might not always work in the best social interests of the countries in which they operate. A new and better trained breed of managers and civil servants has emerged, and the focus of bargaining has moved to promoting a more harmonious and mutually beneficial relationship between the parties concerned, rather than of extracting the most economic rent out of each other.

These shifts in attitudes have been sparked off and shaped by changes in the ESP configuration of countries and the OLI configuration of firms. We would simply emphasize four such changes. First, and most important, there has been a widening of the sources of many of the assets which, in the 1960s, were largely monopolized by US and some European MNEs. The markets for many kinds of technology, management skills and capital have become less imperfect, and hence the incentive to internalize their sales has lessened. Second, the 1970s and 1980s have witnessed considerably higher levels of unemployment, more competition for the kind of resources which MNEs have to offer and lower rates of growth than the 1960s, and, as a consequence, host countries have become more sympathetically disposed to inward direct investment. Third, and allied to the first, an increasing number of countries are themselves engaging in FDI – South Korea, Brazil, Hong Kong, Singapore and Taiwan are among some recent examples[8] – and, as a result, we see movements in disembodied intangible assets beginning to resemble those of goods embodying these assets, with intra-industry international production developing along the lines of intra-industry trade (Dunning, 1988). Fourth, while we observe a substantial growth of all types of non-equity or contractual resource exchanges, we also see more integration between the activities of some MNEs, which has occurred in spite of the volatility of exchange rates and an unstable monetary environment of the latter 1970s. This has led some countries to ask themselves how far they want to be locked into the kind of international economic order that the division of labour imposed by MNEs seems to require. For the dilemma is that the more unique the contributions of MNEs are to development, the less amenable they are to government control.

There is, of course, a political dimension to what has happened in the last decade. With a few exceptions – the French elections being a notable example – governments have moved to the right, and with this policies have been modified and more emphasis has been placed on the market as an allocative mechanism.[9] Moreover, countries which have grown the fastest in the past decade are generally those which are favourably disposed towards inward direct investment and accept the need to be economically interdependent with the rest of the world. But governments come and go, and policies, and even systems, come and go with them. The scholar evaluating the ESP paradigm from a longer-term perspective has to try to discern broad trends and, with the usual caveats, we would argue that the happenings of the last decade, viewed in this context, do allow us to make certain observations about the likely course of international business.

TOWARDS A NEW UNDERSTANDING BETWEEN MNEs AND GOVERNMENTS

The last few years have seen signs of a more mature and positive relationship emerging between MNEs and governments. Each now knows the conditions under which either may, or may not, be expected to contribute to the other's well being. But because the economic and social goals, the ability to achieve these goals, and the bargaining power of countries differ, it follows that one might expect a wide divergence of policies directed towards the involvement of MNEs. Moreover, there is nothing permanent about an ESP configuration of a particular country; the opening up of some Eastern European countries and mainland China to international business is testimony to this. Similarly, MNEs vary in size and strategy and the OLI values affecting their behaviour will change over time.

One of the lacunae in the literature on international business is a dynamic approach to its role in economic development. What we believe is needed is a reinterpretation of W.W. Rostow's model of the economic growth process –

first presented in the late 1950s (Rostow, 1959) – and an extension of Hollis Chenery's analysis of transitional growth and world industrialization (Chenery, 1977, 1979) explicitly to incorporate the various modalities of international economic involvement. In formulating such an approach, we believe some use can be made of the ESP/OLI paradigms and, that, although the value of the explanatory variables affecting the configuration of each may fluctuate wildly both between countries and over time, some useful hypotheses might be made about the interaction of international business and the stage and direction of economic development.

Elsewhere (Dunning, 1981, 1988a), we have put forward the concept of an international direct investment development cycle (or path). Put in its simplest terms it comes down to this. In the initial stage of economic development there is only a very limited role for foreign business, however rich a country may be in natural resources, basically because of the lack of domestic markets, the inadequacy of its commercial, technological or educational infrastructure, its inferior organizational capacities, and its immature or inappropriate economic policies. In the second stage of development when GNP per head in 1985 values reaches around the $500 mark – but occasionally well before, for example, India – foreign business may be attracted by the prospects of larger domestic markets and better production capabilities, while import-substituting investment may be aided by local governments imposing import controls, and by foreign firms anxious to gain a presence before their competitors. On the other hand, in the case of countries whose prosperity relies more on the export of primary products, then, *ceteris paribus*, improved infrastructure facilities – particularly roads, docks, airports and telecommunication facilities – may be sufficient to lower the costs of production and marketing to an economic level. However, as with import substitution investment, firms may wish to internalize the technology transferred, not only to maintain product quality and protect property rights but also to exploit the gains of integrating new activities into the existing operations, for instance, to guarantee supplies. At this stage of development, information markets are likely to be extremely imperfect, and consequently, the transaction costs of contractual resource flows will be high. Finally, depending on the availability of cheap and well-motivated labour, in some larger industrializing economies MNEs may begin assembling and processing goods for export to industrialized countries.

It is at this point that most explanations for the determinants of international production seem to stop; indeed, their interest is largely confined to discrete acts of investment rather than to the process by which the pattern of foreign involvement is built up (Kogut, 1983). But let us take our examination a step further. When one looks at the role of MNEs in developed countries one observes similar types of import substitution and export oriented investment taking place, although the sectors in which MNEs dominate may be different. One also sees a different type of investment, however, which, like intra-industry trade, is primarily a phenomenon of the advanced industrialized countries; this is rationalized investment – of the Ford, Philips Eindhoven and IBM type – which is geared to exploiting the advantages of product- or process-specialization, scale and scope economies and the economies of synergy. Unlike import-substituting investment, rationalized or efficiency-seeking investment requires to be centrally co-ordinated, and the resulting pattern of resource allocation may not always be consistent with individual host country goals.

The link between the role of MNEs in developing and developed countries lies in the interface between MNEs and the development process via the ESP variables. Ignoring the role of government for the moment, factors such as size of country, structure of resources and economic distance from the main centres of technology and markets play a crucial role in influencing the OLI configuration of both foreign and domestic firms. But we would expect that as a country moves along its development path, its indigenous firms would begin to generate their own ownership advantages in those sectors which required the type of resources in which it has, or is developing, a comparative advantage. At the same time, expanding markets and the changing costs of a country's endowments might increase the demand for new products which required the kind of resources which foreign firms were best able to provide, either by trade or foreign production. On balance, we would anticipate that, as it approaches economic maturity, a country would become *more* rather than less involved in international production, though its *balance* as a net inward or outward direct investor would very much depend on the structure of its resource endowments *vis-à-vis* the rest of the world (for example, Canada compared with that of Japan).

What is perhaps more difficult to predict is the *form* in which the changing advantages of international business will be exploited. The choice between trade and foreign production is not the real issue, although in passing one might suggest that, as countries develop, the case for international production based on differential factor endowments weakens; instead, the options rest increasingly on differences in technology and consumer tastes between countries, and the opportunity for the economies of scale and scope.

We earlier argued that the growth of MNEs – especially in the late 1950s and early 1960s – rested on advances in the technology and organization of intra-firm information flows over space, and on the continued imperfections of markets. The relative decline in the MNE as a resource or rights transferor (that is, its acting as an arbitrager in shifting resources from where they earn less to where they earn more) over the past 15 to 20 years may then be put down either to its reduced efficiency as an organizational unit or to a lowering of the transaction costs of the external market. The evidence strongly supports the latter hypothesis; indeed, advances in intra-firm communication and information technology have continued to favour multinational hierarchies. The widening of alternative sources of technology, however, the decline in the transaction costs of intermediate goods and services, especially some primary products, mature or standardized technology and some kinds of information, have all combined to make licensing agreements, managing contracts, turnkey operation and other non-equity resource flows more viable than once they were.

However, this tendency has not occurred in all countries or in all sectors of activity; indeed, in those sectors in the vanguard of technological progress, for example, fibre optics, telematics, microchips and biotechnology, the markets for new technology remain as imperfect as ever, and MNEs continue to dominate. Moreover, as we have seen, as firms grow they tend to generate the kind of *O*-specific advantages which are not readily marketable. Since the production and trade of products based on these advantages is mainly between developed countries, it is not surprising that the 100 per cent-owned affiliate still flourishes in these areas. It also remains the main mode of involvement in sectors in which the advantages of internalization are strong (for example, Japanese trading companies are 100 per cent owned, even if their manufacturing associates are not, as are most export-platform affiliates).

From this viewpoint, the future of international business – like its past – rests on the extent, pattern and geographical distribution of technological and organizational advances. Recent innovations in data retrieval, storage and dissemination systems – particularly transborder information flows – suggest that the boundaries of large firms will be pushed further out and that hierarchies will be even easier to manage. However, human factors – for example, the huge costs associated with human error and disruptions in large organizations – and government intervention – for example, in breaking up or controlling conglomerates – may have the opposite effect. Innovations of new products and processes will continue, but their direction and rate – as opposed to the dissemination of *existing* technology – may well condition the extent to which contractual resource flow will replace direct investment as the main vehicle of resource transference. At the same time, the likely spread of ownership advantages among firms of different nationalities, and the growth of intra-industry production, suggests that a lot of international subcontracting will be internalized as firms wish to exploit non-marketable advantages.

What, now, of the role of governments in the development process? More than anything, governments have influenced the modality of resource transference across boundaries, and sometimes (and Japan and Korea are classic cases) through their educational, technological and industrial strategies, the ownership advantages of their countries' own firms as well. Governments also affect international business by the economic systems they operate, the work, cultural attitudes and social values they fashion, and the particular policies they pursue. We have seen that these change with the ideologies of governments,[10] and there is only a faint suggestion that S and P variables vary with economic development, with industrial maturity being associated with less rather than more state intervention in trade and investment.

More important, perhaps, is the extent to which countries wish to be interdependent or independent of each other. With so many uncertainties (for instance, economic and political stability and the future of non-renewable resources), but with the growing internationalization of ideas, customs and technology, most countries pursue a schizophrenic course; they want the benefits of cross-border interdependence but not the costs. Most noticeably, they wish to maintain their economic and political sovereignty. The trade-offs vary, too, according to the relative bargaining powers of MNEs and host countries, and the way in which the advantages and disadvantages of interdependence change over time. Thus, regional integration is a recognition of the benefits of large markets, while a self-sufficient energy or science and technology policy suggests that countries also value some degree of economic autonomy.

After a century of unparalleled economic expansion and the acceptance of the benefits of interdependence, the inter-war years saw most countries adopting a much more insulated stance, with governments seeking more control over their own destinies. The post Second World War period up to 1971 tried to capture some of the spirit of the nineteenth century by emulating the conditions which made for its prosperity, but these conditions had their costs, and it was these costs which countries were seeking to minimize in the 1970s as they moved towards a new mercantilism, with economic stability tending to give way to self-reliance as the main driving force in many parts of the developing world.

SOME OBSERVATIONS ON THE FUTURE OF MNE/GOVERNMENT RELATIONSHIPS

Underlying the changes in the international economic climate described above there do seem to be a number of irreversible trends. Governments are much more active in the areas of social programmes, defence and environmental protection schemes and, in spite of political swings, are likely to continue to be so. In the international arena, a policy of controlled geocentricism seems the most probable future scenario, with nations seeking to benefit from economic co-operation with the rest of a shrinking world, and, at the same time, either separately or through sympathetic sectoral or regional groupings, to influence supranational decisions and minimize the adjustment costs of industrial restructuring. Even for very large countries, a policy of economic isolationism will become increasingly difficult to sustain. All this, of course, places an enormous burden on existing regional and international organizations, which are likely to take on board increasing co-ordinative responsibilities, particularly in the energy and environmental fields.

In summary, then, it seems likely that the response to international business from countries and international organizations will increasingly parallel that towards trade, and that, in due course, similar mechanisms will be devised to provide an orderly framework for international production and resource transference, as GATT provides for trade in goods. For the foreseeable future, however, control will continue to be exerted through the unilateral policies of governments – aided by more intensive monitoring of corporate behaviour – codes and guidelines, the goodwill of companies, the actions of organized labour, and, not least, by competition.

Within such a scenario we would expect international business to flourish, but its character to change and its organizational structure to become a lot more diversified. The integrated MNE would remain a dominant force in technology and information-intensive sectors, but probably would not be the typical foreign investor of the future. With the advent of telematics, the opportunities for smaller firms to internationalize their operations will increase. At the same time, there might be an extension of functional internalization based on either equity participation (as exists in banking and import and export merchanting) or through contracts (as exists in the hotel industry). There might be, too, a growth of time-limited equity arrangements, particularly in the less technology-intensive import substituting sectors, with MNEs from Japan and the more advanced developing countries playing an active tutorial role (Kojima, 1978), while MNEs in high-technology sectors from developed countries are likely to display a greater propensity towards strategic alliances and collaborative arrangements, in order to strengthen their global marketing capacities (Ohmae, 1985; Contractor and Lorange, 1987).[11]

At the same time, as mergers and rationalizations are part of domestic economic life – particularly in times of structural change – as long as imperfections remain in international capital and foreign exchange markets, we would foresee an increase both in the exit and entry of MNEs and of transborder acquisitions, with one type of MNE, the multinational conglomerate, behaving more like an institutional portfolio than a direct investor. Finally, we would envisage a greater role for governments as initiators, and the international capital markets as financiers, of projects in which foreign firms will act more as contractors or subcontractors than as entrepreneurs. Gone are the days when foreign companies *own* country-specific natural resources which are the basis of that country's comparative trading advantage with the rest of the world. This indigenization of assets will become more widespread in some manufacturing and service sectors – with the role of the foreign direct investor becoming increasingly that of a catalyst for self-development rather than that of an economic imperialist.

More generally, in many ways, the international economic climate of the last two decades of the twentieth century will be very different from that of the third quarter. Then the emphasis was on technological innovations and productivity improvements, spurred on by the need to cope with rising living standards and manpower shortages; these generated ownership-specific advantages of a capital- or technology-intensive kind. In the foreseeable future, in an industrialized world of limited growth and substantial unemployment, and one which is concerned with environmental factors and the depletion of non-renewable resources, and in a developing world increasingly conscious of its obligation to satisfy basic needs, the innovatory emphasis may well be on materials and energy saving, and on increasing agricultural output.

If this diagnosis is correct, it may be that the type of technological advances of the later 1980s and 1990s will require different organizational forms to exploit them. As some countries move towards a post-industrial stage of development, more innovations will occur in the service sector. Already this has happened in the spheres of banking and finance, insurance, telecommunications, medical services and data provision and transmission (Quinn, 1987). It is by no means certain that the resource endowments needed for these innovations and their development will be those which generated their predecessors, nor that the hierarchical structure of firms evolved during the 1960s and 1970s will be suitable for the remaining years of the twentieth century.

All this suggests a constantly shifting role for MNEs in the world economy and the form of their involvement. This is no less true of the domestic business sector in many countries, however; very few firms supply the same product or markets that they did 50 years ago. Yet whatever the problems of size and diversification, for every firm that cannot manage to cope efficiently, another can – spurred on by some new technology or organizational advance which it can accommodate within its hierarchy. That, perhaps, may prove to be the criterion of change: new innovations, institutions and ideas on the one hand, and the willingness of countries to be economically interdependent on the other.

Twenty years ago, some commentators, notably Howard Perlmutter (1969) were forecasting a world dominated by the leading 200 or 300 MNEs by the 1990s. Today, perceptions of the future of international business are very different. Due to the increasing speed at which technology is disseminated, it may be that some retrenchment or realignment of the multi-plant phenomenon and the ownership of foreign assets is on the cards. Add to this the possibility that the technologies of the future will require a different form of governance for their commercialization, then it is at least possible that some of the giant MNEs of today will be the dinosaurs of tomorrow. This does not necessarily augur a decline in international business. Rather, it suggests that the MNE of the 1960s as a packager and a transmitter of resources may no longer be as unique or appropriate an organizational form as it has been in the past, and that the future will see the ingredients of growth differently bundled and channelled through the market and by co-operative arrangements between independent firms as well as by foreign direct investment.[12]

CONCLUSIONS

We conclude this chapter by observing one particularly disturbing feature of the world economy in the 1980s, which, to a large extent, is a response to the events of the past decade. This is the drift to protectionism by the industrialized developed countries. This drift does not primarily take the form of restrictions or traditional non-tariff barriers, but of domestic interventionist policies by governments which affect the kind and standard of goods and services produced, their means of procurement and the terms on which they are traded.

Such protectionism is reminiscent of the beggar-my-neighbour trade policies of the inter-war years but goes well beyond these. In the 1930s, non-resident companies tried to overcome trade obstacles by setting up local producing facilities. This seems to be recurring in the 1980s, particularly with respect to Japanese penetration of European and North American markets. However, unlike the situation in the inter-war years, governments today are major (in some cases the only) purchasers of goods and services, particularly those supplied by MNEs in high-technology industries.

Now, while GATT rules generally forbid member governments to impose discriminatory import duties, and the OECD guidelines for MNEs endorse the principle of equitable treatment between national and foreign-owned firms, it is not difficult to find ways around their rules and guidelines, particularly where sensitive areas of national security are involved. And it is worth observing that the impact of many of the new technologies, for example, telematics, microchips and biotechnology, straddles both private and public domains, and that commercial and social interests are becoming more difficult to disentangle. While the movement towards deregulation in some service sectors is likely to make for more foreign direct investment, the pressure to mitigate the inroads of competition from Japan, and the newly industrialized countries in manufacturing goods, could lead to governments introducing protectionist policies which might jeopardize the fabric of international production built up by MNEs during the last two decades. Indeed, whereas in the 1960s and 1970s the main battleground of the MNEs was in the developing world, in the 1980s this battleground has removed to Europe, the USA and Japan. Dare one hope that the combined wisdom of individual governments, international agencies and MNEs may be deployed, not only to avoid conflict, but also to promote positive industrial, trade and investment policies which will allow international business to adjust to the economic challenges of the future as it has done so successfully in the past?

NOTES

1. That is to say, technology is the output of natural resources; it is a secondary rather than a primary resource, although once produced it fundamentally affects the efficiency of natural resource usage.

2. For example, Chandler (1977); Williamson (1981); Casson (1987).
3. As developed by Koopman and Montias (1971).
4. See Chapter 3 of Dunning (1988b).
5. The most blatant example being the ITT intervention in Chilean politics.
6. See, for example, the various reports of the UN Centre on Transnational Corporations, especially UNCTC (1978, 1983, 1988), Boarman and Schollhammer (1975) and Lall and Streeten (1977).
7. The UN's preferred nomenclature for MNEs.
8. For an examination of MNEs from developing countries see Wells (1983), Lall (1983) and Khan (1987).
9. Though often within the framework of a well-defined and articulated economic and industrial economic strategy, for example, as in the case of Japan.
10. The relation between country-specific ideologies and national competitiveness is examined by Lodge and Vogel (1987).
11. Which route is chosen depends on how far the benefits of internalization can be captured in a contractual agreement.
12. The increasing relevance of the non-equity forms of resource transference is now being explored by the OECD Development Centre. (See, for example, Oman, 1984.)

REFERENCES

Boarman, P.M. and Schollhammer, H. (eds) (1975), *Multinational Corporations and Governments* (New York: Praeger).

Casson, M.C. (1987), *The Firm and the Market* (Oxford: Basil Blackwell).

Caves, R.E. (1982), *Multinational Enterprises and Economic Analysis* (Cambridge: Cambridge University Press).

Chandler, A.D. Jr. (1977), *The Visible Hand: the Managerial Revolution in American Business* (Cambridge, Mass: Harvard University Press).

Chenery, H. (1977), 'Transitional growth and world industrialization', in B. Ohlin, P. O. Hesselborn and P.M. Wijkmar, *The International Allocation of Economic Activity* (London and Basingstoke: Macmillan).

Chenery, H. (1979), *Structural Change and Development Policy* (Oxford: Oxford University Press).

Contractor, F.J. and Lorange, P. (1988), *Cooperative Strategies in International Business* (Lexington, Mass: D.C. Heath).

Dunning, J.H. (1981), *International Production and the Multinational Enterprise* (London: Allen & Unwin).

Dunning, J.H. (1988a), *Explaining International Production* (London: Allen & Unwin).

Dunning, J.H. (1988b), *Multinationals, Technology and Competitiveness* (London: Allen & Unwin).

Khan, K.M. (ed.) (1987), *Multinationals of the South* (London: Francis Pinter).

Kogut, B. (1993), 'Foreign direct investment as a sequential process', in C.P. Kindleberger and D.B. Audretsch (eds), *The Multinational Corporation in the 1980s* (Cambridge, Mass.: MIT Press).

Kojima, K. (1978), *Direct Foreign Investment* (London: Croom Helm).

Koopman, K. and Montias, J.M. (1971), 'On the description and comparison of economic systems', in A. Eckstein (ed.), *Comparison of Economic Systems* (San Francisco, CA: University of California Press).

Lall, S. (1983), *The New Multinationals* (Chichester and New York: John Wiley).

Lall, S. and Streeten, P. (1977), *Foreign Investment, Transnational and Developing Countries* (London and Basingstoke: Macmillan).
Lodge, G.C. and Vogel, E.F. (eds) (1987), *Ideology and National Competitiveness* (Boston: Harvard Business School Press).
Ohmae, K. (1985), *Triad Power* (New York: The Free Press).
Oman, C. (1984), *Changing International Investment Strategies: The New Forms of Investment in Developing Countries*, OECD, Development Centre, Paris.
Perlmutter, H. (1969), 'The tortuous evolution of the multinational enterprise', *Columbia Journal of World Business*, **4**(1), pp. 9–18.
Quinn, J.B. (1987), The impact of technology in the service sector', in B.R. Guile and H. Brooks (eds), *Technology and Global Industry* (Washington: National Academy Press).
Root, F.R. and Ahmed, A.A. (1978), 'The influence of policy instruments on manufacturing direct investment in developing countries', *Journal of International Business Studies*, **9**, winter, pp. 81–93.
Rostow, W.W. (1959), *The Stages of Economic Growth* (Cambridge: Cambridge University Press).
UNCTC (1978), *Transnational Corporations and World Development. A Re-examination*, New York, UNCTC E78, II, A 5.
UNCTC (1983), *Transnational Corporations and World Development: Third Survey*, New York, UNCTC E83, II, A 19.
UNCTC (1988), *Transnational Corporations and World Development: Fourth Survey*, New York, UNCTC.
Vernon, R. (1966), 'International investment and international trade in the product cycle', *Quarterly Journal of Economics*, **80**, pp. 190–217.
Vernon, R. (1974), 'The location of economic activity', in J.H. Dunning (ed.), *Economic Analysis and the Multinational Enterprise* (London: Allen & Unwin).
Vernon, R. (1979), 'The product cycle hypothesis in the new international environment', *Oxford Bulletin of Economics and Statistics*, **41**, pp. 255–67.
Vernon, R. (1983), 'Organisational and institutional responses to international risk', in R.J. Herring (ed.), *Managing International Risk* (Cambridge: Cambridge University Press).
Williamson, O.E. (1981), 'The modern corporation: origins, evolution, attributes', *Journal of Economic Literature*, **XIX**, December, pp. 1537–68.

2. Whither global capitalism?*

INTRODUCTION

The subject of this chapter has already intrigued scholars, business practitioners and politicians and various interest groups; and, no doubt, will continue to do so well into the twenty-first century. Yet, within the last decade or so, attitudes towards economic globalization, and predictions about its future, have undergone a profound transformation. From the euphoria which followed the fall of the Berlin Wall, and the liberalization of many goods, services and money markets, we are currently experiencing a kind of backlash – not dissimilar to that which followed the first positive reactions to the industrial revolution of the late eighteenth and nineteenth centuries (Kennedy, 1996; Searle, 1998).

For now, as then, a different set of winners and losers is being created, and new social and political concerns are emerging. Titles of books published in the last couple of years, such as: *The Global Trap* (Martin and Schumann, 1997); *The Manic Logic of Global Capitalism* (Greider, 1997); *Has Globalization Gone Too Far?* (Rodrik, 1997); *False Dawn* (Gray, 1998); *Global Capitalism in Crisis* (Soros, 1998); *Turbo-Capitalism* (Luttwak, 1999); *The Lexus and the Olive Tree* (Friedman, 1999) all emphasize some of the (perceived) downsides of globalization, which need to be set against its benefits emphasized by most economists and business strategists. *Globaphobia* (Bartlett and Lawrence, 1998), indeed, may not be an exaggerated word to describe the current and growing disquiet about the future of global capitalism.

Where next, then, one might ask? Will the current round of concerns and anxieties – so dramatically displayed at Seattle in December 1999 at the time of the World Trade Organization (WTO) meetings – escalate and force a back-tracking from the path now being pursued by so many countries; or will the more optimistic view of the future prevail – albeit with a greater emphasis on what Claude Smadja, at the 1999 World Economic Forum in Davos, referred to as 'responsible globality'?

Let me declare my hand straight away as a 'conditional' optimist. What does this mean? Well, it is my belief that global capitalism *can* succeed, but *only* if certain conditions, which are not being currently met, are met. And it is the

* From *Global Economy Quarterly*, **1**(1) (2000): 3–48.

'identification' of these conditions, and of how these might be advanced, on which this chapter focuses.

Two Underlying Paradoxes

I start by offering two paradoxes of global capitalism, then go on to look at its objectives, describe some of its unique features, and examine some of its costs and benefits. I then proceed to discuss on what (I believe) needs to be done if it is to continue as the dominant form of economic organization well into the twenty-first century.

The first paradox is this: the success of global capitalism rests largely on the efficient operation of unfettered cross-border markets. *However, it is a feature of many of these markets – notably knowledge and financial markets – that they incur substantial transaction costs of one kind or another, such as those associated with structural discontinuities, volatility and information asymmetries.* Hence, it follows that the role of both internal and external market governance in helping to reduce these costs, and in setting rules and standards within which transactions take place, is becoming more, rather than less, important than once it was.

The second paradox – or perhaps dilemma would be a better word – is *how best to reconcile the inevitably uneven distributional effects of the global marketplace with the imperatives of social justice, and to do so in the context of a reduced leverage of national governments to compensate those who, through no fault of their own, find themselves especially disadvantaged by globalization.*

The Objectives and Nature of Global Capitalism

But, first, what is global capitalism, and what are its distinctive characteristics? Let me distinguish between 'ideal' and 'actual' global capitalism. By 'ideal' global capitalism I mean the optimal cross-border interaction between, or integration of, the different forms or brands of national or regional capitalism,[1] each of which is designed to meet the specific economic, social and cultural demands of its citizens. By 'actual' capitalism I mean the existing state of the economic and social interconnections between regions and nation states, each of which is committed, in principle at least, to the market system of organizing economic transactions, but each of which embeds, and in some cases influences, the character of the system by its own institutional structures, ideologies, and social and cultural mores.

Let me next rehearse some of the conditions necessary to sustain 'actual' global capitalism, and move it closer to 'ideal' global capitalism. First, it should be concerned with the creation of both tangible *and* intangible wealth;[2] with both the quantity and the quality of assets, goods and services; and with the output of both private and collective (i.e. public) goods and services. Second, global capitalism needs to incorporate a set of appropriate ethical mores, which will fashion the behavior of the participants in the marketplace. Third, it is important that these mores should acknowledge, and, where appropriate, influence, the *unique* characteristics of both global capitalism and its constituent national institutions. Fourth, sustainable global capitalism must rest on the acceptance and promotion of such transcendent moral virtues as social justice, human dignity, respect for basic rights, and the absence of racial and religious discrimination. Its scope and content must also be embedded in democratic regimes.[3]

Let me pause at this point to give a working definition of economic globalization. According to the International Monetary Fund (1997):

> Globalization refers to the growing interdependencies of countries worldwide through the increasing volume and variety of cross-border transactions in goods and services, and of international capital flows; and also through the rapid and widespread diffusion of all kinds of technology.[4]

I might add that this definition takes as axiomatic that these tasks will best be achieved through the workings of the free markets – aided, abetted, and suitably modified by the actions and policies of extra-market institutions.

The Unique Features of Global Capitalism

What, then, is unique and special about global capitalism? Let me highlight just five features; and it is the combination of these which, I believe, sets apart the global economy from the international economy of the last century or more.[5]

1. Cross-border transactions are deeper, more extensive and more interconnected than they have ever been.
2. Resources, capabilities, goods and services are more spatially mobile than they have ever been.
3. Multinational enterprises (MNEs) play a more significant role as creators and disseminators of wealth, than they have ever done before; and they originate from, and produce in, more countries than ever before.
4. There is more real and financial volatility in cross-border markets – and particularly in capital and exchange markets – than there has ever been.
5. The advent of the digital environment and electronic commerce is completely changing the character and locational profile of cross-border transactions – particularly of all kinds of services.

Widening our analysis out a little, we might identify four distinctive features of the present stage of capitalism – of which the spatial dimension is only one. These are set out in Table 2.1. Let us consider each of these. First, in contrast to the earlier stages of capitalism, the main source of contemporary wealth creation is knowledge or intellectual capital of all kinds – be it embodied in human or physical resources, or in tangible or intangible assets. Second, although the production of many enterprises, particularly MNEs, spans the planet, there is a greater spatial concentration of some kinds of economic activity – both between and within countries – than there has ever been.[6] (This is the paradox of 'sticky places' within 'slippery space' (Markusen, 1996).) Third, the world is entering a phase of capitalism in which all forms of alliances and cooperative ventures (e.g. within and between enterprises, between enterprises and non-market institutions and between governments) are playing a more important role. Fourth, I believe that the kind of social and moral virtues which twenty-first century capitalism especially needs to nourish if it is to properly fulfil its functions, are somewhat different from those demanded by industrial, merchant or land-based capitalism.

But, let me make three other points about the nature of global capitalism. First, to reiterate an earlier observation, there are currently many varieties of capitalism in the world economy. That of Japan and Germany is very different from that of the US or Canada; that of Taiwan and Thailand is not the same as that of Korea; that of Chile is totally different from that of China. One of the tasks of 'ideal' global capitalism is then to integrate the rich mosaic of these species of capitalism in a way which acknowledges and respects their unique cultural heritages and institutional frameworks, but internalizes and builds upon their common goods. Second, to some scholars (of which I am one) global capitalism is best regarded as a process; to others it is an accomplished fact. Third, to some commentators, regionalization is part of globalization; to others it is a substitute for it; and, indeed, may impede its progress.[7]

How Does One Measure the Extent of Economic Globalization?

How does one measure the extent and depth of global capitalism? The data set out in Table 2.2 and Appendix Tables A2.1 and A2.2 speak for themselves. Although some of these are a little dated, they all portray a similar picture. In particular we would point to the growing importance of FDI, and all forms of cross-border financial transactions over the last 30 years or so; to the more gradual dispersion of innovatory capacity, at least among the medium- and high-income industrial countries; and to the increased significance of trade, and especially intra-FDI trade as a percentage of world GNP.

But do these figures over-play the uniqueness of globalization? Perhaps they do. A lot depends on the perspective one takes. Certainly, it has only been in

Table 2.1 Features of three stages of market-based capitalism (a Western model)

	Seventeenth–early nineteenth century	Nineteenth century–later twentieth century	Late twentieth century onwards
Primary source of wealth and form of activity	Land based: agriculture and forestry. Some local and international merchant commerce	Machine/finance based: manufacturing	Finance/knowledge based: producer and consumer services
Spatial dimension	Local/regional	Regional/national	Regional/global: but with some national or sub-national clusters
Principal organizational form	Traditional economy: mixture of feudal and entrepreneurial: nation state only in its infancy	Managerial/hierarchical: generally adversarial economic relationships: elements of a command economy	More market-oriented: alliance/heterarchical: more cooperative economic relationships
Moral virtues	Obedience, externally imposed discipline and enforced trust. Some familial and community spirit of cooperation	Hard work, civic responsibility, social justice, entrepreneurship, individualism	Personal responsibility, creativity, spontaneous sociability, trust, reciprocity and compassion

the last 25 years that the significance of trade and FDI as a percentage of GNP of the major industrialized countries has exceeded that of 1913 (Kleinknecht and ter Wengel, 1998). Certainly, too, not all industries, firms, or activities of firms are as globalized as others. Moreover, the majority of wealth in most countries – particularly in large countries such as China, India and the US – continues to be internally generated.

Table 2.2 Some indices of globalization

- *Foreign direct investment*: As a proportion of world gross product the combined stock of outward and inward investment rose from 7.8% in 1967 to 14.0% in 1988 and to 23.6% in 1997. The average value of cross-border M&A sales rose from $25 billion in 1980 to $160 billion in 1990 to $544 billion in 1998.
- *Foreign portfolio investment*: As a proportion of world gross product, the flow of outward and inward foreign portfolio investment rose over 14 times between 1970 and 1996 – from 0.33% in 1970 to 1.94% in 1985 and 4.70% in 1996.
- *The international banking market*: The sales of international banking firms as a percentage of world gross output rose from 1.2% in 1964 to 1995, to close on 50% in 1997.
- *Foreign exchange transactions*: By 1997, the turnover in the foreign exchange markets has risen to over $1.5 trillion each day, 12 times that of its lèvel in 1979 and over 50 times that of world trade.
- *Innovation*: As more countries engage in innovatory activities, the proportion of R&D activities undertaken by the foreign subsidiaries of MNEs is rising, although it is still only one-half that of their sales and assets (in 1994–1995 it was 22% in the case of the world's leading industrial corporations, compared to 10% in 1980).
- *Foreign trade*: The annual average percentage growth of world trade in goods and services rose from 4.0% between 1853 and 1913, to 6.0% between 1950 and 1985 (after declining in the inter-war years) to 7.0% between 1985 and 1997. In 1960, less than 10% of trade conducted by MNEs was intra-firm; in 1997 it was between 35 and 40%.

Sources: A variety of official publications, notably the UN, World Bank and IMF.

But, perhaps most significantly, virtually all national governments still strongly influence the character and content of innovation and corporate governance systems, education and training policies, institutional infrastructures and the entrepreneurial ethos of both institutions and individuals within their sphere of jurisdiction (Doremus, Keller, Pauly and Reich, 1998). In the last resort, too, it is national governments which are the main socializers of the risks of globalization; and it is they – or their representatives at the international negotiating tables – who will determine both the extent and pattern of globalization (or regionalization); and of how many of its costs and benefits are distributed between countries and interest groups.[8]

The Causes of Global Capitalism

In Table 2.3, I set out some of the main driving forces making for contemporary – and particularly – global capitalism. These may be identified as *attracting*, *enabling* and *threatening* forces. Table 2.3 gives examples of each of these. Each, in its various ways, has led to a more *knowledge-based* economy; more *alliance-based organizational* patterns, more *global or regional production and marketing strategies* by firms, and a shift in the *significance or prioritization of particular moral or ethical norms.*

Table 2.3 *Causes of global capitalism*

Attracting	E.g. the renaissance of the market economy, and the liberalization of many markets, several new emerging economies, increasing geographical dispersion of created assets
Enabling	E.g. technological advances, lower barriers to cross-border transactions, decreased cost and improved quality of transport and communication facilities, global capital markets
Threatening	E.g. more intensive global competition, volatility of exchange and financial markets, accelerating rates of technological obsolescence

Source: Investment Canada (1990).

The Costs and Benefits of Global Capitalism

I shall confine my attention to identifying just some of the more important of these. The benefits are primarily – though not entirely – economic. They encompass gains from the specialization of economic activity, and those from market-oriented trade and FDI; speedier rates of innovation and the diffusion of intellectual capital across national boundaries; more inter-firm competition; a revival of entrepreneurship, particularly in the small firm sector; the convergence of growth and income levels – at least among the more open industrial and advanced industrializing economies (Sachs and Warner, 1995);[9] more devolution or subsidiarity in economic decision taking (at least in some cases); and the dissemination of welfare enhancing social, cultural and behavioral mores.

What about the downsides, or – no less importantly – the perceived downsides of global capitalism? These are both economic and non-economic. The former are frequently endemic, and are a consequence of rapid technological and social change. They include a variety of cross-border market and institutional failures, and the increased prevalence of economic shocks, discontinuities and uncertainties. The latter include a continuing spatial unevenness (both between and within countries) of the distribution of higher value-added activities (particularly between the most and least prosperous nations); the costs of structural adjustment; an increase in some kinds of long-term unemployment; widening income gaps (e.g. between skilled and unskilled workers, and between the very rich and very poor); and the challenge to social cohesion and national insurance schemes. Of no less concern is the fact that the growing porosity of national borders is facilitating the cross-border movement of *dis*-benefits like drugs, unsafe products, environmental pollution, crime, and terrorism. Finally, in some cases, globalization is eroding the political sovereignty and weakening the economic autonomy of nation states.

The obvious trick, then – which will determine the form and sustainability of global capitalism – is to minimize its costs while maximizing its benefits. Or, in the words of a communique issued by the Group of 7 in Lyon three years ago:

> In an increasingly interdependent world, we must all recognize that we have an interest in spreading the benefits of economic growth as widely as possible, and diminishing the risk either of excluding individuals or groups in our own economies or of excluding certain countries or regions from the benefits of globalization. (Quoted in Rodrik, 1997)

The Institutions of Global Capitalism

Let us now consider how this objective might be achieved – or at least take the debate a step further. At the moment, three future scenarios are 'on the table'. These are set out in Table 2.4. Although I would like to think option 3 will prevail, I think it more likely that option 2 will win the day – although there is a danger that if one backs away from option 3, option 1 could be forced upon us.

To implement option 3 with any chance of success, and to move towards a more acceptable global capitalism, I believe that a more systemic approach to the organization and governance of international economic activity is needed. It is the purpose of the rest of this chapter to set out the main agenda of such an approach. In so doing, I shall focus on the four key institutions of global capitalism, viz. markets, intermediate associations (IAs), governments and supranational entities. These are presented in Figure 2.1 as points on a diamond. Outside the diamond, but affecting the conduct and performance of these institutions is the social and moral order. It is my contention that the role and functions of each of these needs to be reappraised in the light of the unique features and imperatives of contemporary capitalism earlier described.

Table 2.4 Three possible future scenarios of global capitalism

1	The 'creative' destruction of global capitalism. (NB: Several economists in the past, e.g. Karl Marx, Alfred Marshall and Joseph Schumpeter, expressed considerable doubts on the sustainability of capitalism as it existed in their day and age.)
2	The 'muddling through' or 'Band-Aid' solution; marginal adjustments to the *status quo* of existing markets, extra-market institutions (including governments), social mores and behavioral patterns
3	Proactive measures to recognize the unique characteristics and imperatives of global capitalism, and to minimize its costs and maximize its benefits

This task, I believe, should be primarily accomplished by reconstituting and strengthening the governance of the G.C. diamond. If achieved successfully, this could be the main – unique – public or collective good of global capitalism (Prakash, 1999). Table 2.5 distinguishes between two main forms of governance. The first is *spontaneous* and internal to the institutions in question, and/or represents a voluntary response to the advisory or non-coercive actions taken by higher-order institutions. The second is *coercive*. Freedom can only work within

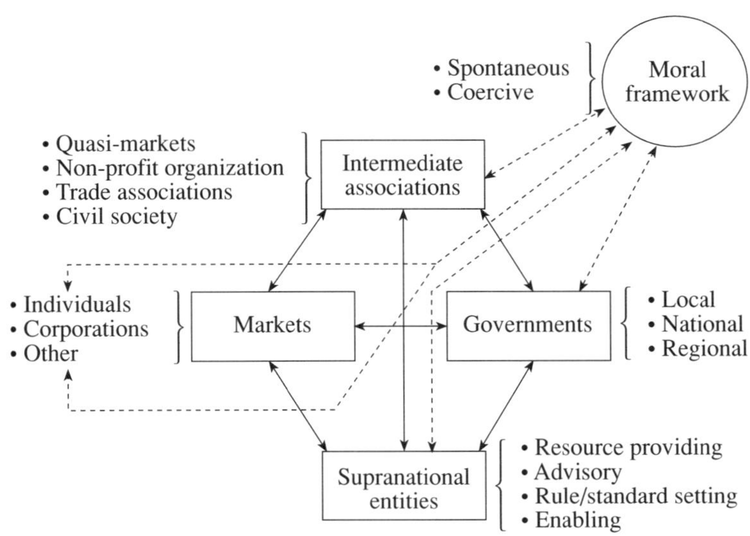

Figure 2.1 The institutions of global capitalism (the G.C. diamond)

the protection of a rules-based system, and the same holds good for each of the institutions of global capitalism. Strong and effective laws, regulations and enforcing agencies are frequently required both to counteract market distortions and the unacceptable behavior of some non-governmental activist groups; and to promote social justice and civil stability. Democratically elected governments and supranational entities are the main rule-setters and enforcers – although they may (and sometimes do) behave in a sub-optimal way. The respective roles of each of these forms of governance is likely to vary between societies, between functions and according to established cultural and ethical mores.

Table 2.5 The governance of global capitalism

- The markets
  Comprising: individuals, groups of individuals, corporations, groups of corporations and, sometimes, intermediate associations and governments
  (Types of governance: self-imposed – spontaneous on part of participants; decreed by agreement with intermediate associations; coercive action and/or macro-economic and organizational policies initiated by governments and/or supranational entities.)
- Intermediate associations
  Comprising: civil society, clubs, non-profit organizations, interest groups and trade associations
  (Types of governance: self-imposed and/or market driven; incentives/penalties and/or coercive action initiated by governments or supranational entities.)
- Governments
  Ranging from sub-national to supranational governments (e.g. EU)
  (Types of governance: policy formation; initiators of incentives/penalties and of regulatory and legal framework for market-related activities.)
- Supra-national
  May be government or independently financed entities
  (Types of governance: advice and guidance to national governments and to market participants, action taken on behalf of national governments; recommendations for actions to be taken by regional and national governments. Initiators of regulatory frameworks on behalf of market participants and extra-market institutions.)

The Market

Consider, first, the market as an institution. Figure 2.2 identifies three main market participants, the different types of markets, why markets might fail, and what might be the possible responses to market failure. Some points worth emphasizing are:

1. In the context of contemporary capitalism, the market should not be regarded as the sole determinant of how scarce resources are utilized, but rather as an institution embedded in a web of interrelated institutions, which, taken as a whole, characterize a society. *It is within this broader context that the performance of markets should be judged.*
2. Markets succeed when they promote the efficient allocation of human, physical and financial resources by maximizing the net benefits of innovation, production and exchange. They fail when they fall short of achieving this objective.
3. The market system, *qua* system, comprises a network of many thousands of individual markets. The fastest growing markets in global capitalism are those involving the production and exchange of intangible assets, goods and services – and particularly all forms of information and intellectual capital.
4. Market imperfections are of two kinds. The first are *structural* imperfections. These arise from the actions of one or other participants of the markets, e.g. natural resource monopolists, or of extra-market institutions such as governments, which inhibit the efficient workings of markets. The second are *endemic* market failures, which usually reflect the intrinsic characteristics of the assets, goods and services being exchanged, and the uncertainties and externalities attached to them. Such failures may affect individual markets differently and the same markets differently over a period of time.

What, then, is the specific impact of global capitalism on markets? We would make three observations.

1. The relative importance of different markets is changing; and those which are growing the fastest are demonstrating the most significant endemic market failure.
2. In one way or another, an increasing proportion of economic transactions are being undertaken across, rather than within, national borders.
3. Goods and services which, at one time, were non-tradable are now tradable across the exchanges. The arrival of electronic markets is likely to add substantially to this tradability – particularly in the case of retailing, financial and professional services.

How do these features – together with the advent of alliance capitalism – affect the likely success of markets? As one might expect, the answer is a mixed one. Those characteristics likely to exacerbate market failure include: more unpredictability and volatility in financial markets, the rising costs of structural adjustment associated with rapid technological change, an increase in the output of collective or public goods, including those designed to reduce the 'bads' of

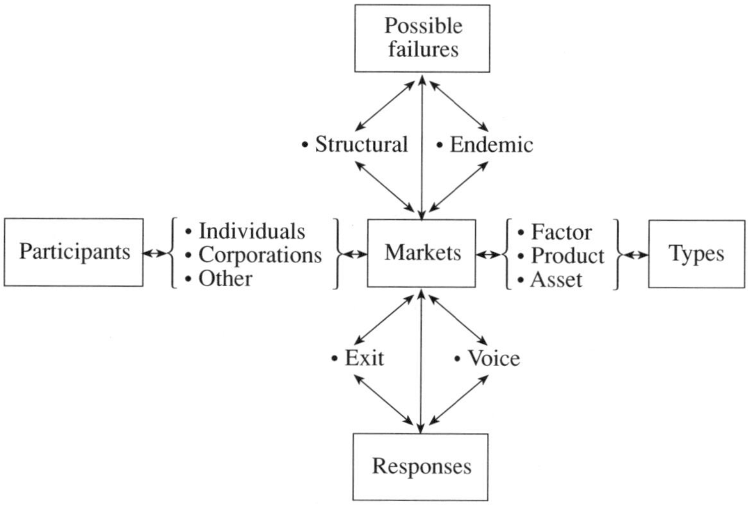

Figure 2.2 Markets and the G.C. diamond

economic activity, new information asymmetries – particularly in the exchange of technologically complex goods – externalities (i.e. the costs and benefits of transactions incurred by non-market participants), new kinds of moral hazard and opportunities arising from the extension of the boundaries of corporations to unfamiliar cultures and political regimes, and, perhaps most important of all, the growing perception that the market mechanism, by itself, cannot ensure the production of those goods and services whose value cannot easily be measured in monetary terms (Sacks, 1999).[10]

At the same time, other features of economic globalization are helping to promote the efficiency of cross-border transactions. These include many technological advances, such as electronic markets and improved cross-border communication facilities, the liberalization and deregulation of many financial and other service markets, more intensive competition among firms, a better appreciation by national governments of the benefits of the market system, the increased flexibility of many labor markets, and an improved capability of market supporting institutions.

How, then, might national or cross-border markets be made more efficient? Using the terminology first introduced by Hirschman (1970), we might identify two kinds of reaction, viz. '*voice*' and '*exit*'. Exit reactions include the bypassing of markets by hierarchies, e.g. MNEs or by the direct intervention of governments.[11] Voice reactions are those designed actively to reduce the imperfections to markets without exiting from them. These reactions may be *spontaneous* or *coercive*. Spontaneous reactions fall into three main groups.

1. Voluntary learning experiences, informal social norms, and self-regulation.
2. The creation of new markets, the specific purpose of which is to lower the transaction costs of existing markets.
3. The facilitation of efficient markets by actions of extra-market institutions, notably by governments providing information, setting standards, upgrading the legal and commercial and financial infrastructure, aiding structural adjustment, and so on.

The type of coercive voice strategies which might be aimed at reducing market failure include formal sanctions, mainly imposed by national governments against the structurally distorting behavior of market participants (particularly corporations), and actions taken to reduce, or cushion the effects of, the volatility associated with some markets.

In brief, for market-based global capitalism to meet the demands expected of it, more effort needs to be directed to increasing the efficiency of those markets which are inherently the most imperfect. These include knowledge-related, alliance-related and distance-related markets; and those transactions which, because of the uncertainty of their outcome, or the information asymmetries between the parties to the exchange, are the most volatile.

Intermediate Associations

Next let us turn to examine the role of extra-market institutions in affecting both 'actual' and 'ideal' global capitalism. The first of these are intermediate associations (IAs) which I believe are destined to play a more important economic and social role in the future. In Figure 2.3 we identify the main kinds of IAs, their distinctive functions and of how they can play a more effective role.

First, what are they? IAs are sometimes called the 'third' sector and comprise the civil society of a democratic capitalist economy. They are by no means a new phenomenon. They are intermediate in the sense they display some of the characteristics of markets and some of those of governments.

IAs are of two main kinds. The first are non-profit organizations (NPOs). These include a variety of clubs and associations which supply goods and services for a price (sometimes a zero price) to their members and/or customers. The second are institutions, usually referred to as non-government organizations (NGOs). For the most part, these act as pressure groups to attain certain economic, political or social objectives on behalf of the interests they represent. In this chapter, I chiefly concern myself with the first kind of IAs. But I do want to make a brief comment on the increasing role of NGOs in the global economy.

NGOs are an extremely heterogeneous collection of institutions – they number many tens of thousands across the globe, of which by 1990 upwards of 2000 were international in scope.[12] Each of these has its own distinctive

Figure 2.3 Intermediate associations and the G.C. diamond

agenda. These include some NPOs, but for the most part, NGOs are policy-oriented advocacy groups whose main purpose is either to affect, by whatever means they deem appropriate, the goals of individuals, interest groups, enterprises and governments, or to influence the ways in which – through the normal course of economic activity – these goals are achieved. Of course, many NGOs, most of which are single-minded in their objectives, have little or nothing to do with global capitalism. But directly or indirectly, many others, e.g. the green or environmental lobby, human rights activists, and those speaking for the poorest sections of the global community certainly do; and their recent influence on the deliberations of the North American Free Trade Agreement (NAFTA), the Rio Earth Summit in 1994, the (aborted) Multilateral Agreement on Investment (MAI), and the WTO in 1999 has been considerable and pervasive.[13]

At their best, NGOs can and do play an important part in the democratic process. In the past, they, rather than markets or governments, have spearheaded important changes in the social attitudes and values of individuals and communities. At the same time, NGOs, because they tend to focus their interests on a specific part of a wider problem; because they ascribe to globalization consequences which though associated with it are not caused by it; because they frequently fail to examine the counterfactual position to that which they are seeking to change; and because they sometimes use anti-social methods to highlight their concerns, can reduce rather than increase economic and/or social welfare. Indeed they are capable of behaving in a thoroughly undemocratic way, in the sense that they are not accountable to the general public for what they do in the way in which both governments and markets are.

To the best of my knowledge, there has been no systematic study on the ways in which NGOs may affect the wealth-creating and welfare-enhancing process in a democratic capitalist economy;[14] nor on the rules of the game or standards of behavior which should underpin their conduct. Such a study is long overdue and is now needed more than ever as NGOs are increasingly organizing themselves across national boundaries, and through the Internet, and other means, are forming a powerful coalition of a variety of interest groups, each of which has its own particular anti-globalization agenda.

Let us now turn to consider NPOs. These are mostly of three types. The first comprise collections of individuals and/or corporations whose main purpose is to gather information, conduct research, provide advice, set standards and monitor the conduct of their members. By and large these act to reduce search and negotiating costs, and to protect the property rights and upgrade the intellectual capital of their members.

The second type of NPOs are quasi-market institutions, which normally supply goods and services at below the full market price. They do not seek to make a profit, and are often subsidized by individuals, corporations, or governments, contributing either money or labor. Examples include museums, art galleries, some educational services, and many recreational activities. The third type of NPO consists of a variety of charitable and philanthropic organizations, and organizations designed to reduce economic and social 'bads', e.g. crime detection and law enforcement agencies. Globalization is requiring these latter organizations to extend their activities beyond their national boundaries, and to engage in cross-border collaborative ventures (e.g. Interpol).

Some other features of NPOs worthy of note are: first, they tend to supply non-tradable services rather than tradable goods; second, they largely engage in labor-intensive activities; and third, their output is primarily geared to meeting the needs of individuals and families, and is largely supplied by small and medium-size enterprises.

There are no comprehensive data on the numbers, value added or employment of NPOs. But, to give just one example, in the US – perhaps the most market-oriented economy in the world – their numbers run into many thousands, and it is reckoned that the assets of the independent sector – and these may include those of some NGOs – are about one-half of those of the federal government; and that this sector accounts for about 10 percent of total national employment. Moreover, these percentages are growing (Van Til, 1998; Ben-Ner and Gui, 1993; Rifkin, 1995; Salamon and Anheier, 1997).

Why then should we concern ourselves with NPOs? Primarily because we believe they offer a wide range of economic and social benefits, not to mention values, which, if nurtured, can help to cushion some of the adverse consequences of global capitalism, and foster communitarism at a national or local level. Let me cite just a few examples of these benefits. First, socialization and voluntarism are worthwhile acts in themselves, and can foster the bonding and communitarism of all groups in society. Second, they can act as useful adjuncts to efficient markets, e.g. by providing information and setting standards to consumers and to small and medium-size enterprises. Third, they help provide quality-of-life enhancing goods and services, which otherwise might not have been supplied or supplied as economically. Fourth, they can create jobs, the quality of which is frequently rewarding to the providers of the services. Fifth, since much of the output of NPOs is not tradable, employment is likely to be less volatile than that in the tradable goods sector. And finally, NPOs may provide a useful 'safety net' of employment for those who either wish to withdraw from the mainstream labor market, or are forced out by technological change, or by other causes.

How might IAs be made more effective and encouraged? They can be made more effective by upgrading the quality of their governance structures, increasing their transparency and accountability, and by better networking. In the case of NGOs, there is a strong case for governments and/or supranational agencies to move clearly the acceptable limits of activist behavior; and where appropriate encourage more dialogue between the NGOs and other institutions. In the case of NPOs their activities might be fostered in three main ways:

1. By tax and related fiscal incentives offered by local or national governments.
2. By direct grants or subsidies, and by appropriate government-supported training schemes.
3. By moral suasion, improving the 'image' of NPOs, and by publicizing and fostering the virtues of social responsibility and voluntarism.

In short, I believe that IAs can, and should, play an important part in the kind of institutional reform and reconfiguration which is needed if some of the current and likely future economic costs and social disharmonies of global capitalism are to be avoided or minimized. Whether they will, or whether the activities of NGOs will 'kill the capitalistic goose that lays the wealth creating golden egg' remains to be seen.

The Role of National and Sub-national Governments

What next of the role of national and sub-national governments? Consider Figure 2.4, which identifies the various levels of governance, the functions of governments, the actions of governments and how governments can perform their duties more effectively.

Figure 2.4 National and sub-national governments and the G.C. diamond

The unique economic tasks of democratic governments are well known.[15] We do, however, sometimes need to remind ourselves of these – particularly when we are tempted to think that the best contribution governments can make to promoting 'ideal' global capitalism is an 'opting out' one – viz. *not* to interfere with the workings of the free market.

What, then, are these functions? First, governments bear the primary responsibility for designing and implementing a variety of macro-economic and macro-organizational policies, each of which are essential to the pursuance of economic goals of the constituents they represent. Second, they are (or should be) enablers of efficient factor, asset and product markets, and as upholders of the legal and commercial institutions underpinning these markets. This task includes – as we have already seen – rule and standard setting, which over-arch market transactions. Third, they are the main providers of most kinds of social capital and public goods. Fourth, it is their duty to ensure that structural distortions and/or an abuse of economic power by market participants (e.g. firms, labor unions, special interest groups, including NGOs) are minimized. Fifth, they are the main initiators of a range of laws, regulations and policies intended to promote a range of non-economic goals, e.g. notably those to do with social justice, environmental protection, health and safety standards, etc. Sixth, they are the primary vehicle for protecting and promoting national economic interests at the international negotiating table (e.g. at the WTO and IMF). Seventh, they bear the responsibility for minimizing the social disruptions of structural change. And lastly, they are, in the last resort, creators and sustainers of a social architecture and upholders of a set of moral values consistent with, and supportive of, democratic capitalism. These are no mean tasks.

What is likely to be the impact of economic globalization on national governments? First and foremost, it is *not* to reduce their role, as several commentators have suggested, but rather to redefine and transform it. For most of the present century, the main micro-management task of governments has been to minimize the (perceived) socially unacceptable effects of market transactions. Today it is to provide the most propitious economic environment for knowledge generation, and for upgrading the productivity of indigenous resources and capabilities; and to equip its citizens with the skills, expertise and motivation they need to face the demands of the global marketplace (Smadja, 1999). But, no less important is the increasing need for national governments to address the social consequences of contemporary economic events, and to find ways of dealing with their uneven, destabilizing or unjust consequences. The penalty for failing in this task is, at least, social unrest and political instability; and, at most, the overthrow of democratic capitalism.

What actions, then, might governments take? I offer the following points.

- Governments need to upgrade their information and statistical data providing services. This is particularly important for small and medium-sized enterprises struggling to compete in a globalizing, knowledge-based economy.
- They need to invoke codes of conduct and/or offer incentives for their constituents to engage in market friendly but socially responsible courses of action; and to reconfigure their institutional structures and behavioral norms to best promote these actions.
- They need to reconsider the allocation of decision-taking among different levels of governance, and to delegate, where appropriate, responsibility to IAs, sub-national authorities and specialized investment agencies for matters specific to their constituents.
- By various policy measures, they need to increase the benefits and reduce the costs of dynamic structural adjustment.
- They need to enact legislation to ensure that the behavior of participants in markets works in the public interest. Some of this legislation, e.g. with respect to restrictive practices, transfer pricing, safety and working conditions, etc., may need to be modified in the light of the growth of cross-border FDI and strategic alliances.
- They need to give more attention to identifying and providing the location bound resources and capabilities sought by foreign investors; and, as far as possible, carve out a set of unique (and non-imitable) competitive advantages, which might encourage the firms and assets they desire to become more embedded within their boundaries.

- They need to pay more attention to the social and economic contributions IAs might make to promoting social capital (Etzioni, 1996), and to counteracting some of the less desirable effects of globalization and technological change. On the other hand, while working together with IAs to better achieve these goals, they need to take firmer measures against NGOs that use undemocratic means to pursue their objectives.
- In a variety of ways, they should foster an ethos and set of moral virtues conducive to the advance of 'ideal' global capitalism, and to ensure that its institutions meet and, where appropriate, enhance, their social obligations.
- They need to participate actively in the decisions of supranational entities. They need to be better informed and more effective in their bargaining and/or mediatory skills at the international negotiating table.
- They need to give more attention to encouraging entrepreneurship and the innovatory and other contributions of small and medium-sized enterprises.
- They need to reconfigure their modes of governance to better respond to the premium placed by the new globality on such qualities as speed, flexibility, versatility and ability to deal with change and insecurity. In the words of Claude Smadja, 'Managing the trade-off between unpredictability associated with flexibility and the desire for security will increasingly present *governments* a challenge' (Smadja, 1999) (my italics).
- Most of all, they need to avoid engaging in 'beggar-my-neighbor' micro-management policies aimed at steering economic activity to their own territories. In the contemporary globalizing economy, both national and sub-national governments may be tempted to offer quite substantial fiscal and other incentives to attract inbound foreign investment. Yet, all too frequently, these result in a series of locational tournaments from which no one benefits except, of course, the investing firms and/or governments (UN, 1998).

Table 2.6 summarizes some of my views about the likely consequences of global capitalism for the role of national and sub-national governments in policy formation. It will be seen that while I believe that, for the most part, the macro-organizational and ethos forming role of national governments is tending to increase or remain about the same, at the same time, at least, some of these functions are being taken over by sub-national administrations. By contrast, the leeway of national governments to pursue independent *macro-economic* policies is being diminished by the increasing cross-border mobility of both financial and real capital.

Supranational Entities

I now turn to consider Figure 2.5. It is generally accepted that economic globalization will increase the role of supranational entities. Such entities

Table 2.6 The impact of global capitalism on the role of national and sub-national governments

Actions	The dimensions of global capitalism			MIR	MF	Level of governance	
	Knowledge	Alliance	Spatial			National	Sub-national
1. Macro-economic policies	0	0	?	–	+	–	0
2. Macro-organizational policies							
Trade	0	0	–	–	+	–	0
Innovation	+	+	0	0	+	+	+
Education	+	+	0	+	+	+	+
FDI	0	+	?	–	+	–	+
Transport and communication	+	0	+	+	+	+	+
Industrial	+	0	–	–	+	–	0
Regional	+	0	0	–	+	+	+
Competition	0	+	–	–	–	–	0
Fiscal	0	0	?	0	+	–	+
Labor	+	0	+	–	+	+	+
Environment	0	0	–	+	+	+	0
3. Ethos forming/encouragement	+	+	+	–	+	+	0

Notes:
+ = Increased role
0 = No change in role
– = Reduced role
? = Uncertain
MIR = Market intervening/replacing
MF = Market facilitating

Source: Author's perception.

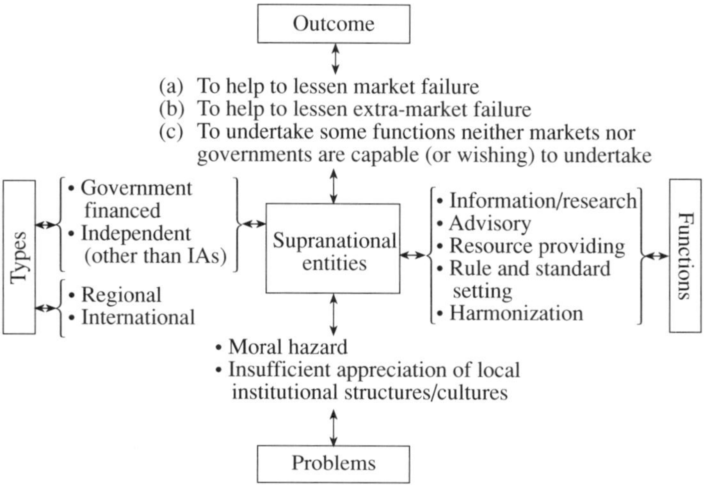

Figure 2.5 Supranational institutions of the G.C. diamond

embrace a wide organizational spectrum, e.g. from formally constituted regional bodies (e.g. EU) to purely advisory institutions, e.g. UNCTAD. Why is this so? Why, in fact, do we need supranational entities? I would suggest there are three main reasons:

1. Because national or sub-national governmental regimes are unable, or unwilling, to deal with various types of market or extra-market failures in cross-border transactions, particularly those which are associated with the activities of MNEs, and/or those of international NGOs.
2. Because national or sub-national governments may themselves behave in a way which: (i) structurally distorts market or extra-market transactions; and/or (ii) creates or exacerbates endemic market failure; and/or (iii) initiates a range of non-economic policies which may have adverse consequences on the efficient operation of markets.
3. Because national or sub-national governments, on their own, may not have the leverage to implement the appropriate social policies to cushion some of the more damaging effects of the global marketplace on the wellbeing of their constituents.

To what extent, then, are supranational entities equipped to meet the demands of an either actual or 'ideal' global capitalism? Can such entities adopt more regionally or globally integrated strategies? Should they? Consider the role of two spatial levels of supranational entities, viz. the regional and the international.[16]

First, regional entities. There are a plethora of these, which vary considerably in their scope and modes of governance. Much has been written on the costs and benefits of regional economic integration;[17] and I will not repeat them here. I would, however, make three points:

1. Essentially any form of regional integration suggests sacrifice of *some* degree of national autonomy in decision-taking. This sacrifice is presumably though a worthwhile price to pay by the participating nations to gain the (perceived) economic and social benefits from the liberalization of intra-regional markets.
2. The costs and benefits of economic globalization I earlier identified no less apply at a regional level. However, the scale, content and distribution of these costs and benefits may be different. So, too, may the form of the governance of regional authorities, and the ease or difficulty with which participating nations can reach agreement on critical issues.
3. Regional integration may be seen either as part of, or a stepping stone towards, global capitalism,[18] or as an alternative to it. Much will depend on the policies pursued by the regional authority in respect of its transactions with the rest of the world. If, taking an extreme case, regional integration leads to the abolition of all intra-regional trade and FDI barriers, but the retention or increase in such barriers against other nations or regions, then, while regionalization may have been advanced, globalization will not have been. (This, incidentally is the scenario which scholars such as Alan Rugman fear will happen in the next decade or so (Rugman, 2002).) If, by contrast, regional economic integration also leads to a reduction in *inter*-regional trade and FDI barriers, then regionalization and globalization may be regarded as complements to each other. In any case, supra-regional authorities may need to treat the actions of regional authorities in exactly the same way as they do with national or sub-national authorities.[19]

Next, then, we examine the likely impact of global capitalism on the role of supranational entities. Here it may be helpful to distinguish between four groups of entities.

1. Those which are primarily *resource providers* and are currently *multi-domestic* in their outlook and policies. Examples include the IMF and the World Bank. Recent experience (e.g. the Asian economic crisis) has demonstrated that these entities would do well to take better account of (a) the distinctive characteristics of national or regional capitalist systems, and (b) the extent to which and the ways in which these systems are converging, or are not converging. To do this, such entities almost certainly need additional resources, which only national governments can provide.

2. Those which are primarily *rule or standard setters*, and which tend to view their functions from a *more global perspective*. But, as yet, only a few such entities exist. The leading example is that of WTO, whose brief may, in due course, be extended to some non-trade areas, e.g. foreign direct investment, intellectual property rights, the environment and competition policy.[20] Is the attention of existing entities likely to be increasingly directed to resolving conflicts of interest between macro regions, as it is between nation states? Does the extension of rules of the game demanded by global capitalism require new entities? In the finance field the answer is probably 'yes'.[21] More generally, is a new umbrella entity, e.g. a World Economic Organization, needed? Is it possible? Is it desirable? Certainly the idea of globalizing the concept of *public* goods (and bads) by encouraging inter-government cooperation, and the setting up of new institutions charged with the task of ensuring that such goods are provided with minimum market and/or institutional failure, is favoured by several economists, notably Amartya Sen, Joseph Stiglitz and Jeffrey Sachs (Kaul, Grunberg and Stern, 1999).
3. Those which are primarily *coordinators of action* pursued by national or regional extra-market institutions. These tend to be issue oriented entities, e.g. those concerned with the environment, intellectual, law and order, health, air traffic control and so on. Here there is some evidence that more globally coordinated strategies are being pursued.
4. Those which act as a *focal point for information gathering, research, dialogue and an exchange of views* among the national participants; and on occasions to take supranational action which affects the global or regional allocation of economic activity. Examples include the UN (and its various agencies) and the OECD, whose role is currently being redefined in the light of contemporary events.

I would assert that each of the four kinds of supranational entities needs to better recognize that those kinds of market or institutional failure which are unique to global capitalism cannot fully be resolved either by spontaneously generated action on the part of the market participants or by more formal norms and rules set down by national governments or regional authorities. This is particularly the case with capital flows which are both huge and subject to extreme volatility. Only by appropriate international macro-stabilization policies, and by the encouragement of national policies designed to reduce short-term speculative capital movements, and to combat the moral hazards inherent in some transactions, can this be achieved. At the same time, there is pressure from many quarters for a greater transparency and accountability (not to mention democratization) of some supranational entities – and particularly those which are re-evaluating their roles in the light of globalization. Finally, as David

Henderson (1999) has observed *à propos* the MAI negotiations, there needs to be much more commitment on the part of national governments to effect the gains of multilateral arrangements; not to mention abiding by the existing rules of the multilateral trading system, e.g. by self-imposed codes of good behavior introduced by multinational enterprises (MNEs).

The Moral Imperatives

Yet, when all is said and done – and even if the main institutions of global capitalism are technically capable of performing efficiently, there remains the issue of social acceptability of the system and its underpinning moral framework. Among others, Ralf Dahrendorf, Hans Küng and Claude Smadja have consistently argued that unrestrained globalization might well tax the social integration mechanisms of societies and lead to the exclusion of a considerable number of people from its benefits. This, in turn, could lead to mounting conflicts between 'the haves' and the 'have nots', and endanger the very social cohesion which proponents of globalization assert that it advances. This, indeed, as I have already pointed out, is one of the – and perhaps *the* – critical challenges of globalization, which not only requires some recognition of existing institutions, but the revitalization and reconstruction of the existing moral order. So let me, finally, turn to Figure 2.6, which shows how I believe

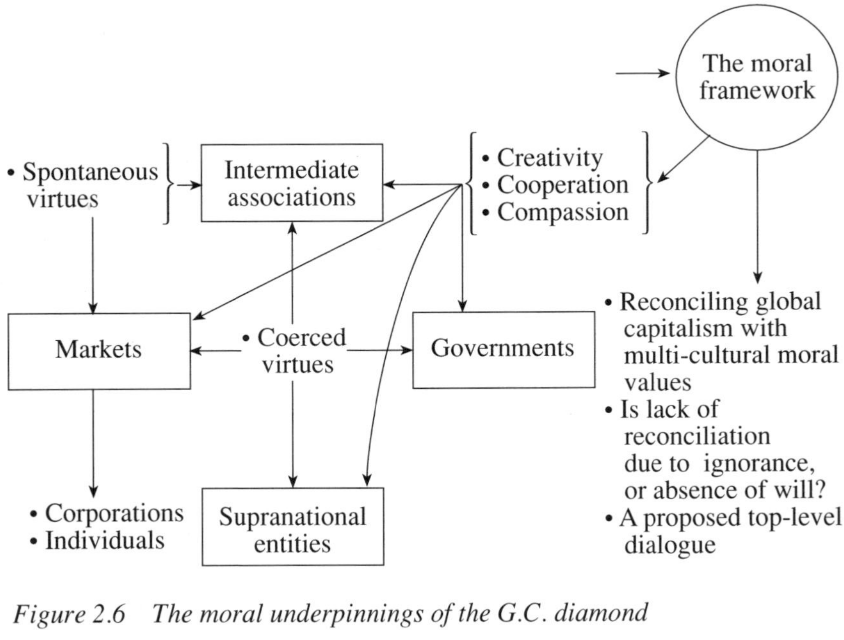

Figure 2.6 The moral underpinnings of the G.C. diamond

the moral dimension can shape the working of the capitalistic system, and the attitude of individuals and institutions to improving it.

In particular, I suggest that the framework should consist of three building blocks, each of which represents the presence or absence of three sets of virtues which are especially germane to global capitalism, viz. *creativity* (essential for the upgrading of intellectual capital), *cooperation* (without which alliance capitalism cannot succeed) and *compassion* (an integral part of the globalization of social justice, and of the stability and cohesiveness of societies). Further details are set out in Table 2.7. It is the extent to which these virtues can be translated into the ideologies and actions of the four main institutions of global capitalism which will ultimately determine its success or failure.[22] The reasoning behind this statement is set out in the following three propositions:

1. Over the long haul, in democratic societies, global capitalism can only work at the suffrage of their electorates. If, however, the majority of the electorate perceive they, or others for whom they feel responsible, do not benefit from global capitalism, in the way they believe they should, they can vote for – or take other action to promote – some alternative social order.
2. It then follows that perceived economic inclusiveness and social justice must be an integral part of the objectives of global capitalism if it is to flourish.
3. But these goals can only be achieved if there is a strong and sympathetic moral ethos pervading all institutions and governance structures.

What is the justification for these propositions? Consider the following points:

- Throughout history, most, if not all, successful economies have been initiated and girded by a strong moral ethos, albeit the contents of which have been country or time specific. And frequently, these same economies collapsed when this moral foundation was undermined.[23]
- In the past, new social orders or new trajectories in economic progress have frequently been preceded by a reconfiguration of a renewed attention on existing moral cultures, as, for example, was the case in biblical times and in nineteenth-century Western Europe. However, as we enter the new millennium it would seem that the (appropriate) order of the social capital of many societies is lagging behind that of scientific, technological and organizational developments.

How might moral virtues – and particularly those germane to the three 'C's – be promoted? Although I would like to think this could be achieved by spontaneous, i.e. voluntary, action on the part of individuals, families and institutions, I am sufficiently a realist to accept that externally imposed codes, rules, laws and sanctions by governments and supranational entities must also play a critical part.[24]

Table 2.7 What are the particular moral virtues which a knowledge- and alliance-based globalizing economy demands?

(a) *Intellectual capital* (Creativity)
Imagination, individual initiative, an entrepreneurial spirit, perseverance, a willingness to learn and upgrade one's intellectual assets, self-discipline, self-confidence and self-respect.

(b) *Alliance capitalism* (Cooperation)
Trust, spontaneous social responsibility, forbearance, probity, reciprocity, an ability to compromise, adaptability, group loyalty, an appreciation of the common good, and a respect for the goals, opinions and judgements of others.

(c) *Global geography* (Compassion)
A sense of fairness and justice, an awareness of, and respect for, the needs and rights of others – particularly those in least developed countries – brotherly love, stewardship, neighborliness, generosity of spirit.

But exactly *who* should be responsible for initiating and practicing moral virtues? Consider two approaches to answering this question: (i) the 'top-down' approach; and (ii) the 'bottom-up' approach. The top-down approach suggests that the responsibility to promote the three 'C's and their ingredients rests primarily with supranational entities and national governments. This approach embraces the direct or indirect promotion of such virtues, and implementation of penalties and sanctions against individuals and institutions behaving in an unvirtuous way. The points in favor of it are that governments and, at least some supranational entities, have the authority, and can acquire the necessary resources to put ethically justifiable social and other programs into action.

But there are also drawbacks to this approach. One is that coercive action is always second best. Another is that incentive and social welfare schemes may encourage moral hazard among their beneficiaries. It may lead to an abrogation of personal responsibility and self-discipline; and, in some cases, lead to libertarianism. It opens up distance, i.e. reduces connectivity, between those who define the moral virtues and those expected to abide by them.[25]

By contrast, a bottom-up approach is based on the presumption that, to be effective, the adoption of moral virtues must be the spontaneous and voluntary decision of individuals, families and institutions. Indeed, some commentators would argue that the market is, itself, a highly moral institution depending as it does on its participants practicing such virtues as honoring promises, respecting property and taking responsibility for their own actions (Barry, 1999).

Others, e.g. Soros (1998) and Sacks (1999) disagree, and contend that without some form of extra-market rules, norms and values, the integrity of a transactional market economy cannot be preserved.[26] These principles stem from various sources, including the teaching and moral suasion of religious and educational leaders, the printed word, familiar structures, corporate values[27] and by the behavioral mores of society as a whole.[28] The main advantage of such an approach is that, in democratic capitalism, voluntarism is normally to be preferred to the imposition of sanctions; while there are few of the cons attributable to the top-down approach.

On the other hand, only so many welfare enhancing goals can be accomplished by voluntarism; there is the 'free rider' problem; and finally, if it is to flourish, individual liberty must be linked to some form of communitarism (Etzioni, 1996). But when all is said and done, does not global capitalism need a global ethic (Küng, 1998)? Is, indeed, such an ethic feasible? Are there fundamental or core values that cross national boundaries and which are acceptable to both Western and non-Western cultural and religious traditions. Tom Donaldson (1996) is certainly one who believes that there are, and that such values should provide a moral compass for business practices (I would add that governments, supranational entities, IAs, consumers, and other market participants no less need such a compass).

As things stand at the moment, the epicenter of global capitalism is the triad of North America, Western Europe and Japan. But they are not the epicenter of the planet's social norms or moral codes. Two issues of related interest then arise. First, to what extent is the integration of multi-domestic capitalism likely to be constrained by differing interpretations of the content and significance of moral free space?[29] Will global capitalism adapt to multiple ethical conventions; or will the latter become more harmonized? And, if so, in what direction?

Second, there is the question as to whether 'ideal' global capitalism can accommodate substantially different religious or ethnic mores (Huntington, 1996). Is it possible to design an overarching global ethic – but one which can accommodate and respect different non-core cultural and other values? For if, instead of uniting nations by a common pursuit of democratically acceptable wealth creation and distribution, it divides nations with different ethical mores, then it is possible such capitalism will be rejected at the global ballot box (or by less democratic means). However, it may well be that insensitive attitudes towards cross-cultural differences arise from ignorance. If this is so, a top-level dialogue between the upholders and practitioners of different religious traditions and moral values may have some merit. The purpose of the dialogue would be to see if it were possible to identify and give operational substance to a universal code of moral virtues; and to examine and perhaps map the contours of moral free space. Moreover, such a dialogue should be a continuing one as the interpretation of the context absolute and contextual moral values and the boundaries between them is constantly changing. After all, since it is human beings – rather than physical assets – who are the main instruments by which new wealth is created, organized and distributed, it is critical to nurture the intellectual, social and spiritual qualities which determine their willingness and ability to best achieve this goal.[30]

CONCLUSIONS

I now briefly summarize the main thrust of my thoughts. Figure 2.7 links the kinds of inadequacies of contemporary markets and institutions, and the moral behavior underlying these, which, in our opinion, need to be tackled if global capitalism is to succeed and be continually upgraded. I believe the contents of this figure are self-explanatory. Table 2.8 further illustrates these points by looking at some of the failures which were brought to light by the recent Asian crisis and which still beset Russia. As can be seen, there is no one single reason why 'actual' capitalism of the late 1990s is not delivering the kinds of benefits expected of it. Rather, there are a multiplicity of interconnected deficiencies in the various ingredients of capitalism, each of which needs to be addressed –

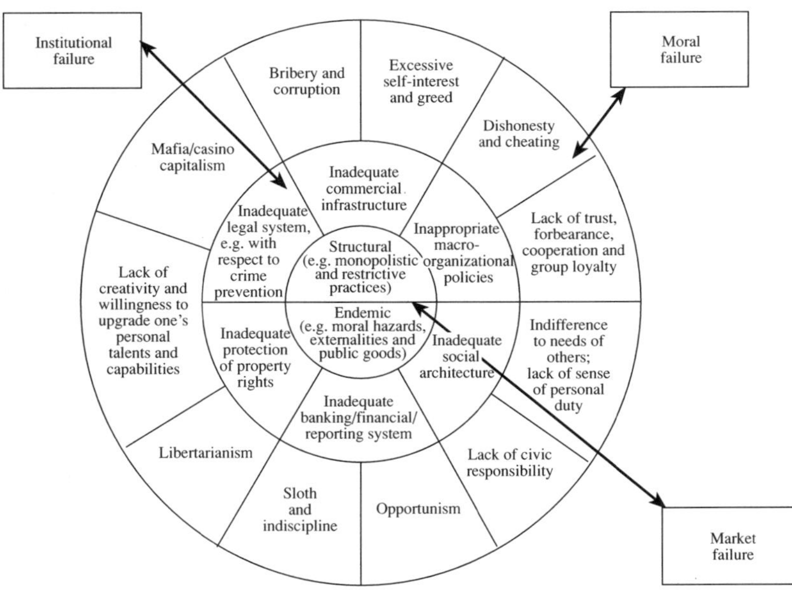

Figure 2.7 Illustrations of three perceived ways in which global capitalism might fail

Table 2.8 Illustrations of four 'failures' of global capitalism as revealed in the case of recent economic events in seven countries

	Japan	Korea	Indonesia	Thailand	Hong Kong	Malaysia	Russia
Managerial failure							
• Imprudent risk management*	X	X	X	X	X	X	X
• Misjudgement of economic conditions/trends	X	X	X	X	X	X	X
Market failure							
• Moral hazard*		X	X	X	X	X	
• Inappropriate macro-economic policies*	X	X	X	X			X
• Excessive speculation (land and stock market)	X				X		
• Overvalued currency/ tied exchange rates*				X			
• Bad timing of short-term debt*		X		X			
• A presence of a strong black market			X				X
• Contagion effect					X	X	
Institutional failure							
• Inappropriate regulatory/supervisory system	X	X	X	X	X	X	X
• Inadequate banking system	X	X		X			X
• Inadequate legal (and other) infrastructure			X			X	X
• Inappropriate financial system*	X	X	X	X			
• Inadequate protection of property rights			X				
• Lack of transparency/inadequate accounting standards	X	X	X	X		X	X
Moral failure							
• Crony/mafia capitalism*	X		X		X	X	X
• Bribery and corruption	X	X	X	X			X
• Lack of trust/social responsibility*			X			X	X
• Excessive greed of investors/institutions*		X			X	X	

* At an international level as well as a domestic level

and addressed as holistically as possible – if anything approaching optimal, or 'ideal,' capitalism is to be reached.

It is, then, my contention that the answer to 'Whither global capitalism?' – or perhaps, more appropriately, 'What must be done if global capitalism is to survive and prosper?' – rests on a number of conditions being fulfilled. First is recognition of the fact that since human beings – rather than physical assets – are the main instruments by which new wealth is created, organized and distributed, it is critical to nurture the intellectual, social and spiritual qualities which determine their willingness and ability to best achieve this goal. Second is that means are found, by both private and public institutions, of overcoming the more deleterious economic and social consequences of global volatility and change.

The third condition is that national governments need to promote the appropriate macro-economic and macro-organizational policies which are consistent with the promotion of efficient and socially acceptable global capitalism. Fourth, suitable adjustments require to be made to the structure and content of institutions – especially financial institutions – which might (i) improve risk management, (ii) foster more efficient, accountable and transparent transactions in the global marketplace, (iii) and reduce moral hazard. Fifth, supranational entities should be given sufficient authority or persuasive powers to encourage, and where appropriate enforce, a minimum standard of institutional infrastructure across nations, and the adoption of 'best practice' macro-economic and management policies on the part of national governments.

Sixth, while applauding the rich mosaic of different capitalist modes throughout the world, such pluralism needs to be directed to ensuring the benefits of the global capitalism are greater than the sum of its parts. And seventh, it is necessary for individual and social moral virtues to be strengthened and reconfigured in a way which is both consistent with a knowledge-intensive, alliance-based, multi-cultural society, and which will best enable markets and extra-market institutions to work together to promote efficient growth and social justice. Only then will the global marketplace be an acceptable servant of individuals and society, and not an unacceptable master.

So, 'Whither global capitalism?' *Is* global capitalism at bay? Is it likely to be? Perhaps the most one can realistically hope for is a step beyond both euphoria and globaphobia; and a real appreciation of the social and moral imperatives which need to be addressed and resolved if what is, perhaps, the most promising form of wealth creation the world has ever known is not to sow the seeds of its own destruction.

APPENDIX

Table A2.1 Indicators of extent to which a country is globally involved: FDI[1] to GDP ratio

Order	Country	1980	1990	1995	1996	1996/1980 (1980 = 100)
1	Singapore	7.1	51.1	52.9	56.2	791.5
2	Hong Kong	3.4	18.6	55.8	43.8	1288.2
3	Netherlands	18.3	33.6	35.0	39.8	217.5
4	Belg/Lux	5.2	23.6	27.1	38.6	742.3
5	Switzerland	18.1	22.0	32.9	33.6	185.6
6	New Zealand	8.2	13.2	28.0	33.2	404.9
7	Malaysia	13.5	19.2	32.4	31.7	234.8
8	UK	13.6	23.0	28.0	25.6	188.2
9	Canada	14.4	16.7	20.0	21.7	150.7
10	Sweden	3.6	13.5	23.6	21.0	583.3
11	Australia	4.9	18.1	21.4	20.7	422.4
12	Chile	1.7	16.9	13.6	16.4	964.7
13	Norway	1.2	10.1	14.4	15.5	1291.7
14	Ireland	9.8	8.5	13.4	14.1	143.9
15	Denmark	4.7	6.4	12.3	13.2	280.9
16	Indonesia	7.1	18.3	12.8	12.9	181.7
17	Spain	2.8	8.3	11.8	12.4	442.9
18	France	3.2	8.2	10.7	11.6	362.5
19	Mexico	2.2	6.7	13.4	11.5	522.7
20	Finland	1.2	6.1	9.5	10.7	891.7
21	Taiwan	3.0	7.1	9.3	9.7	323.3
22	USA	5.8	7.6	8.8	9.4	162.1
23	Germany	5.5	8.8	8.4	9.2	167.3
24	Venezuela	1.3	5.3	6.7	9.1	700.0
25	Italy	1.8	5.2	7.2	9.0	500.0
26	South Africa	13.4	7.6	7.7	8.8	65.7
27	Greece	5.7	9.0	8.5	8.7	152.6
28	Brazil	3.6	4.5	9.5	7.6	211.1
29	Austria	2.6	4.9	6.8	7.2	276.9
30	Thailand	1.5	4.9	5.9	6.8	453.3
31	Portugal	2.5	4.2	5.4	4.9	196.0
32	Japan	1.1	3.7	2.5	3.2	290.9
33	Korea	1.0	1.6	2.2	2.7	270.0
34	Hungary	N/A	3.2	16.4	17.2	N/A
35	China	N/A	2.1	10.3	13.7	N/A
36	Czech Rep.	N/A	0.5	4.6	7.2	N/A
	World	9.7	15.9	20.0	21.4	220.6

N/A-Not available

1 Inward + outward investment as a percentage of GDP

Source: UN, various editions of *World Investment Report* (an annual publication).

Table A2.2 Indicators of extent to which a country is globally involved: trade[1] to GDP ratio

Order	Country	1980	1990	1995	1996	1996/1980 (1980 = 100)
1	Hong Kong	104.1	129.0	151.7	142.3	136.7
2	Singapore	206.9	151.0	142.0	136.3	65.9
3	Malaysia	44.9	81.8	97.4	91.5	203.8
4	Ireland	55.2	57.1	72.8	74.2	134.4
5	Belg/Lux	58.0	67.0	65.0	66.1	114.0
6	Netherlands	44.9	51.9	50.0	50.9	113.4
7	Philippines	26.0	30.4	40.3	46.9	180.4
8	Taiwan	53.1	33.1	46.4	46.4	87.4
9	Thailand	23.5	37.9	44.9	42.2	179.6
10	Austria	27.3	88.1	38.8	41.1	150.5
11	Hungary	40.2	29.8	35.5	39.7	98.8
12	Canada	24.2	25.4	36.3	37.2	153.7
13	Sweden	26.2	29.7	37.7	36.6	139.7
14	Norway	30.9	37.4	35.1	36.3	117.5
15	Korea	34.2	30.0	33.6	34.4	100.6
16	Finland	29.8	23.8	33.5	34.0	114.1
17	Switzerland	32.5	36.0	33.1	34.0	104.6
18	Denmark	27.0	33.3	33.3	33.0	122.2
19	Portugal	32.0	34.5	31.5	31.8	99.4
20	Mexico	10.4	19.2	29.1	31.4	301.9
21	UK	22.5	25.5	28.7	29.6	131.6
22	Chile	24.9	33.0	29.6	29.2	117.3
23	Venezuela	25.5	29.8	24.0	29.0	113.7
24	New Zealand	23.3	27.3	29.1	28.3	121.5
25	South Africa	30.1	22.6	25.1	26.9	89.4
26	Poland	29.7	25.1	24.8	26.2	88.2
27	Indonesia	23.4	26.2	27.0	26.1	111.5
28	Spain	13.8	18.8	23.9	25.1	181.9
29	Germany	23.2	30.8	22.5	23.3	100.4
30	France	18.9	22.6	22.3	22.8	120.6
31	Australia	14.3	17.1	20.1	19.8	138.5
32	Greece	22.0	22.4	20.0	19.4	88.2
33	China	6.3	15.1	19.5	17.4	276.2
34	USA	9.1	10.3	11.9	12.0	131.9
35	India	8.3	8.3	7.5	9.8	118.1
36	Japan	12.7	10.3	8.7	9.7	76.4

[1] Exports + imports as a percentage of GDP

Source: UN, various editions of *Statistical Yearbook*.

ACKNOWLEDGEMENTS

I am most grateful for the comments and constructive suggestions made by H. Peter Gray, Robert Heilbroner, Steve Kobrin and David Robertson on an earlier draft of this chapter.

NOTES

1. For a discussion of the differences between various capitalist systems – and particularly the way in which extra-market institutions exercise control, or adjust to the imperatives of the market system, see Chandler (1990), Lazonick (1991), McCraw (1997), Groenewegen (1997) and Hall and Soskice (2001). Chandler, for example, refers to the US style of capitalism as 'competitive managerial', to the UK style as 'personal' and to the German style as 'cooperative managerial'. Various adjectives have been used to portray Japanese style capitalism. These include 'competitive communitarism', 'human capitalism', and 'relational capitalism'. Taiwan's capitalism has been referred to as 'familial', Korea's as 'statist' and France's as 'Golbertian' or 'hierarchical', and China's as 'socialist'!
2. Intangible wealth includes such products as protection of the environment, the provision of social services, and the reduction of crime. It will be noted that this is a much broader definition of economic welfare than that contained in gross domestic or gross national product (GDP or GNP). Indeed, I suspect that much of the future debate about the merits or demerits of global capitalism will centre on the goals one is seeking to achieve, rather than the best means by which any particular set of goals may be advanced. In other words, any evaluation of the costs and benefits of globalization will increasingly reflect the cultural and ideological perspectives of the evaluators! For some examples, see Levy (1999).
3. Each of these conditions, it will be noted, were emphasized, e.g. by Adam Smith and others, as being necessary for the successful pursuit of market-based (national) capitalism of the late eighteenth and nineteenth centuries.
4. For other, but similar, definitions see, e.g. Kilminster (1997), Kobrin (1997) and Gundlach and Nunnenkamp (1998).
5. For a more skeptical view on the distinctiveness of economic globalization, see Hirst and Thompson (1996) and Kleinknecht and ter Wengel (1998).
6. As set out by several authors in Dunning (2000).
7. In cases where regional trading and investment blocs are formed, and which encourage intra-regional economic transactions but impose tariff or non-tariff barriers on inter-regional transactions, such regionalization is (we would argue) best described as regionalism. For a recent discussion on the trend toward regionalism, see Rugman (2000).
8. As is clearly seen in such regional associations such as the European Union and OECD, and in such international institutions such as the WTO and various UN agencies. Witness, for example, the recent failure of the Multilateral Agreement on Investment (MAI) and the breakdown of the WTO discussions in Seattle.
9. Using data from the World Development Report (1997), it can be shown that those countries classified as *upper middle income* in 1980 increased their GNPs per head at a faster rate than those classified as *high-income* countries in that year.
10. In his own words, 'markets are the best way we know of structuring exchanges – goods to be bought and sold. They are far from the best way of ordering relationships or preserving goods whose value is not identical with their price' (Sacks, 1999, p. 53).
11. By way of 'command' strategies or by intervention in the workings of the market (e.g. by regulatory and other means).
12. Sylvia Ostry (2000) for example writes about international non-governmental organizations or INGOs.

13. See, e.g., Scholte, O'Brien and Williams (1999).
14. For example, one useful exercise might be to examine the effect of NGOs on the flows of FDI following the breakdown of the MAI agreement; at the same time this would best wait until the repercussions of the breakdown of the MAI talks are fully known.
15. For a recent examination of these tasks see various chapters in Dunning (1997).
16. Strictly speaking, I ought also to address the various kinds of bilateral economic arrangements which countries might conclude with each other. However, space precludes me from doing this. Data on the extent and composition of bilateral investment treaties are, for example, given in the annual *World Investment Reports* published by the UN. See, for example, UN (1998).
17. For a comprehensive examination of these, see Jovanovic (1997).
18. For example, as part of their globalization programs, MNEs frequently pursue regional production strategies (Rugman, 2002).
19. Thus it is quite possible (indeed, from recent history, this appears all too likely) that the WTO will be faced with as many dispute cases between the EU and (say) the US and Japan, as it will between the member states of the EU and those countries.
20. Here especially, thorny issues arise. For example, to what extent may the harmonization of environmental standards be perceived to impose a non-tariff barrier to exports from developing countries who may be forced to incur costs in meeting these standards? For an examination of the role of the WTO in helping to promote multilateral investment liberalization, see Brewer and Young (1999). For a discussion of the reasons why the WTO failed to come to an accord on a multilateral investment agreement, see Kobrin (1998).
21. See for example, IMF (1997), Soros (1998), Lloyd (1999) and Messner (1999).
22. It will be observed that different varieties of capitalism possess these virtues to a greater or lesser extent. Thus US style capitalism is relatively strong on creativity, but relatively weak on compassion; European capitalism is relatively stronger on cooperation and compassion; Japanese and Korean capitalism is particularly strong on cooperation but less strong on creativity; Chinese capitalism is also relatively strong on cooperation, but relatively weak on both creativity and compassion, and so on. At the same time, there are suggestions that economic globalization is leading to a convergence of at least some aspects of capitalism practiced by different countries (Jacoby, 1998).
23. For a full analysis of this and related theses see, e.g. Landes (1998).
24. The intrusive use of mobile (cellular) telephones is one!
25. Such a criticism is less directed to sub-national governments and to many IAs.
26. As presupposed by Emile Durkheim many years ago (Durkheim, 1938) and later by Friedrich von Hayek (1988).
27. Hirschman (1970) – referred to earlier – regarded loyalty as an important determinant of success of any voice strategy of firms and states to market failure. We would regard it as an important element of a successful voice response to moral failure.
28. These virtues make up what Francis Fukuyama in his latest book (Fukuyama, 1999) terms, social capital. He defines social capital as 'a set of informal values or norms shared among members of a group which permits cooperation among them' (p. 16). Much of his treatise, which I only came across after completing this chapter, is devoted to explaining how social capital needs to be upgraded and reconstituted if it is to meet the needs, and indeed influence the course, of contemporary economic, political and social events.
29. Another way of thinking of moral free space is that of situational ethical behavior. The real problem, however, is to identify the boundaries between core values, e.g. human dignity, respect for human rights, etc., and those which defy absolute prescriptions for behavior.
30. I am, of course, aware that many other institutions, notably the UN Commission on Human Rights are actively engaged in pursuing many of these issues, but the idea of setting up a group of 7 or 8 (or whatever number) of religious and other leaders is I think worth exploring.

REFERENCES

Barry, N. (1999), 'The Market Still Adequate?' in Sacks, J. (ed.) *Morals and Markets*, London: IEA, Occasional Paper No. 9, pp. 27–34.

Bartlett, G. and Lawrence, B.Z. (1998), *Globaphobia: Confronting Fears about Open Trade*, Washington: The Brookings Institution.

Ben-Ner, A. and Gui, B. (eds) (1993), *The Non-Profit Sector in the Mixed Economy*, Ann Arbor: University of Michigan Press.

Brewer, T. and Young, S. (1999), 'The World Trade Organization: Global Rulemaker', in Hood, N. and Young, S. (eds), *The Globalization of Multinational Enterprise Activity and Economic Development*, Basingstoke: Macmillan Press.

Chandler, A.D. Jr. (1990), *Scale and Scope: The Dynamics of Industrial Capitalism*, Cambridge, MA: Harvard University Press.

Donaldson, T. (1996), 'Values in tension: ethics away from home,' *Harvard Business Review*, Sept.–Oct., pp. 48–62.

Donaldson, T. and Dunfee, T.W. (1994), 'Towards a United Conception of Business Ethics: integrative social contracts theory,' *Academy of Management Review*, April.

Doremus, P.N., Keller, W.W., Pauly, L.W. and Reich, S. (1998), *The Myth of the Global Corporation*, Princeton, NJ: Princeton University Press.

Dunning, J.H. (ed.) (1997), *Governments, Globalization and International Business*, Oxford: Oxford University Press.

Dunning, J.H. (ed.) (2000), *Regions, Globalization and the Knowledge Based Economy*, Oxford: Oxford University Press.

Durkheim, E. (1938), *The Rules of Sociological Method*, Glencoe, IL: Free Press.

Etzioni, A. (1996), *The New Golden Rule*, New York: Basic Books.

Friedman, T.L. (1999), *The Lexus and the Olive Tree*, New York: Farrar, Straus and Giroux.

Fukuyama, F. (1999), *The Great Disruption*, London: Profile Books.

Gray, J. (1998), *False Dawn*, New York: The New Press.

Greider, W. (1997), *One World or Not: Ready or Not: The Manic Logic and Global Capitalism*, New York: Simon and Schuster.

Groenewegen, J. (1997), 'Institutions of Capitalism: American, European and Japanese Systems Compared,' *Journal of Economic Issues* **31** (2), pp. 333–47.

Gunlach, E. and Nunnenkamp, P. (1998), 'Some consequences of globalization for developing countries,' in Dunning, J.H. (ed.), *Globalization, Trade and Foreign Direct Investment*, Amsterdam: Elsevier, pp. 153–74.

Hall, P.A. and Soskice, D. (eds) (2001), *Varieties of Capitalism*, Oxford: Oxford University Press.

Handy, C. (1997), *The Hungry Spirit*, London: Avon Books.

Hayek, F.A. (1988), *The Fatal Conceit: The Errors of Socialism*, Chicago: University of Chicago Press.

Heilbroner, R.L. (1992), *Twenty-first Century Capitalism*, London: UCL Press.

Henderson, D. (1999), *The MAI Affair: A Story and its Lessons*, Melbourne: Melbourne Business School, Felham Paper No. 5.

Himmelfarb, G. (1995), *The De-moralization of Society*, London: IEA Health and Welfare Unit Choice in Welfare No. 22.

Hirschman, A. (1970), *Exit, Voice and Loyalty: International Differences in Work-Related Values*, Cambridge, MA: Harvard University Press.

Hirst, P. and Thompson, G. (1996), *Globalization in Question*, Cambridge: Polity Press.

Huntington, S.P. (1996), *The Clash of Civilizations*, New York: Simon and Schuster.

IMF (1997), *World Economic Outlook: Globalization, Opportunities and Challenges*, Washington: International Monetary Fund, May.

Investment Canada (1990), *The Business Implications of Globalization*, Ottawa: Investment Canada Working Paper No. V.

Jacoby, S.M. (1998), *Welfare Capitalism in Japan and the United States*, Los Angeles, UCLA GIBER Working Papers 98–125.

Jovanovic, M.N. (1997), *International Economic Integration*, London and New York: Routledge, Critical Perspectives on the World Economy (4 volumes).

Kaul, I., Grunberg, I. and Stern, M.A. (1999), *Global Public Goods*, Oxford: Oxford University Press.

Kennedy, P. (1996), *Globalization and its Discontents. The 1996 Analysis Lecture*, London: BBC.

Kilminster, R. (1997), 'Globalization as an emerging concept,' in Scott, A. (ed.), *The Limits of Globalization. Cases and Arguments*, London and New York: Routledge, pp. 257–83.

Kleinknecht, A. and ter Wengel, J. (1998), 'The myth of economic globalization,' *Cambridge Journal of Economics* **22**, pp. 637–47.

Kobrin, S. (1997), 'The architecture of globalization: State sovereignty in a networked global economy,' in Dunning, J.H. (ed.), *Governments, Globalization and International Business*, Oxford: Oxford University Press, pp. 146–71.

Kobrin, S. (1998), 'The MAI and the clash of globalization,' *Foreign Policy* **4**, pp. 93–109.

Küng, H. (1998), *A Global Ethic for Global Politics*, New York and Oxford: Oxford University Press.

Landes, D. (1988), *The Wealth and Poverty of Nations*, London: Little, Brown and Co.

Lazonick, W. (1991), *Business Organization and the Myth of the Market Economy*, Cambridge: Cambridge University Press.

Levy, B. (1999), *Global Good Governance in the Age of Globalization and Issues and Policy Implications*, Ottawa Faculty of Administration Working Paper, 99–30, September.

Lloyd P.J. (1999), 'Economic dynamics and the new millennium: the architecture of the multinational organizations,' *Journal of Asian Economies* **10**, pp. 211–36.

Luttwak, E. (1999), *Turbo-Capitalism*, New York: HarperCollins.

Markusen, A. (1996), 'Sticky places in slippery space: a typology of industrial districts,' *Economic Geography* **72** (3), pp. 293–313.

Martin, H.P. and Schumann, H. (1997), *The Global Trap*, London and New York: Zed Books.

McCraw, T.K. (1997), *Creating Modern Capitalism*, Cambridge, MA: Harvard University Press.

Messner, D. (1999), 'Towards a new Bretton Woods,' *Development and Cooperation* **1**(4–5), 19.

Osborne, D. and Gaebler, T. (1992), *Reinventing Government: How the Entrepreneurial Spirit is Transforming the Public Sector*, Reading, MA: Addison-Wesley.

Ostry, S. (2000), 'Convergence and sovereignty: policy scope for compromise,' in Prakash, A. and Hart, J.A. (eds), *Coping with Globalization*, London and New York: Routledge, pp. 52–76.

Prakash, A. (1999), *Governance and Economic Globalization: Continuities and Discontinuities*, Washington, DC: Washington University, School of Business and Public Management.

Rifkin, J. (1995), *The End of Work*, New York: G.P. Putnam's Sons.

Rodrik, D. (1997), *Has Globalization Gone too Far?*, Washington: Institute for International Economics.
Rugman, A. (2002), 'Multinational enterprises and the end of global strategy,' in Dunning, J.H. and Mucchielli, J.L. (eds), *Multinational Firms: The Global–Local Dilemma*, London and New York: Routledge, pp. 3–17.
Sachs, J. and Warner, A. (1995), *Economic Convergence and Economic Policies*, Cambridge, MA: NBER Working Paper No. 5039.
Sacks, J. (1999), '*Morals and Markets*,' London: IEA Occasional Paper, No. 109.
Salamon, L.M. and Anheier, H.K. (1997), *Defining the Non-Profit Sector*, Manchester (UK): Manchester University Press.
Scholte, J.A., O'Brien, R. and Williams, M. (1999), 'The WTO and Civil Society,' *Journal of World Trade* **33** (1), pp. 107–23.
Searle, G.R. (1998), *Morality and the Market in Victorian Britain*, Oxford: The Clarendon Press.
Smadja, C. (1999), 'Living dangerously,' *Time*, February 22.
Smart, T. (1998), 'Globalization: a dream or a deadly fantasy?,' *International Herald Tribune*, November 10.
Soros, G. (1998), *The Crisis of Global Capitalism*, London: Little Brown and Company.
UN (1998), *World Investment Report 1998: Trends and Determinants*, Geneva and New York: UN.
Van Til, J. (1998), *Mapping the Third Sector – Voluntarism in a Changing Social Economy*, Washington, DC: Foundation Center.
Vernon, R. (1998), *In the Hurricane's Eye: The Troubled Prospects of Multinational Enterprises*, Cambridge, MA: Harvard University Press.
World Bank (1997), *World Development Report 1997*, Oxford: Oxford University Press.

3. Some paradoxes of the emerging global economy: the multinational solution*

INTRODUCTION

In approaching the end of the twentieth century, one cannot but be struck by both the similarities and differences of circumstances to those faced by our forefathers one hundred years ago. Then, as now, was an era of dramatic and widespread technological change.[1] Then, as now, a new generation of telecommunication advances was shrinking the boundaries of economic activity. Then, as now, the organizational structures of firms and the socio-institutional framework of countries were in a state of flux. Then, as now, the cartography of political space was being reconfigured. Then, as now, the jurisdiction of national governments was being questioned, and the locus and composition of civic responsibilities were being redefined. Then, as now, new relationships and alliances were being forged between, and within, private and public institutions, and among different ethnic, religious and social groups.

But, to a more discerning observer, the differences between the two ages are more marked than the similarities. Key among these is that, while the events of the late nineteenth century were taking place *within* a well-established and widely accepted social and political order, those now occurring seem to be challenging long-cherished ideologies and values – and, in some cases, the very institutional fabric of society. At the same time, contemporary events are moulding a very unpredictable future – both for individuals and for institutions – and, more often than not, they are as divisive as they are unifying in their consequences. Our contemporary world is in a state of transition and turmoil. Some may view this as a form of creative destruction – of ideas, of technologies, of institutions and of cultures. Others fear that it is the beginning of an era of social and political unrest, the like of which we have not seen for many generations. The order of hierarchical capitalism which, as a wealth-creating

* From the 6th Tore Browaldh Lecture delivered at the University of Götenborg in 1996 and republished in J.H. Dunning, *Alliance Capitalism in Global Business* (1997), Chapter 14, pp. 357–72, London and New York, Routledge.

system, has served much of the world so well over the past century, is being increasingly questioned, but no one is quite sure what is going to replace it – or indeed what should replace it.

Part of our increasing sense of bewilderment and insecurity, I suggest, arises because many of the events now occurring are paradoxical, if not antithetical, in both their characteristics and implications. Indeed, we may well be moving out of Eric Hobsbawn's 'Age of Extremes'[2] into an 'Age of Paradoxes'. Nowhere is this more clearly seen than in the globalization of economic activity. Surely few can deny that alongside an impressive array of opportunities and benefits offered by deep cross-border economic integration, it is demanding enormous and often painful adjustments, not only of corporations and governments, but of the working lives, leisure pursuits and mind sets of ordinary men and women. One political scientist, in a book published last year, with the intriguing title *Jihad vs McWorld*,[3] writes about our planet simultaneously 'falling apart and coming together', and starkly contrasts the economic and technological forces which are integrating nations into one 'gigantic and homogeneous theme park', and the frightening, but no less widespread, movement towards inter- and intrastate fragmentation along ethnic, tribal and religious lines.

In this chapter, I shall consider just four paradoxes[4] or contradictions of the emerging global economy – or what the Chinese might prefer to call the 'yin' and 'yang' of globalization. I believe that the ways in which these paradoxes are approached and reconciled – if, indeed, they are reconciled – will determine the shape of our planet's political and economic future, and the social well-being of each and every one of us. I shall also suggest that hints of how the paradoxes may be managed by the international community are already contained in the strategies and actions of (successful) multinational enterprises (MNEs), just as, a century ago, the emergence of large national enterprises helped point the way to the macro-economic management of (the then emerging) hierarchical capitalism.

CO-OPERATION AND COMPETITION: THE PARADOX OF RELATIONSHIPS

At the end of the last century, the main form of interface between firms was competition. Most transactions between buyers and sellers were at spot or arm's-length prices, and adversarial in nature. Apart from the conclusion of mergers, combines and other business agreements to restrict competition, rival firms perceived little need to co-operate with each other. In most advanced industrial nations, free enterprise was perceived 'to rule OK', and where markets failed, either firms or non-market entities intervened by internalizing these markets – namely, by an 'exit', rather than a 'voice', response. To the 'yin' of competition there was no counter-balancing 'yang' of co-operation.

By contrast, yet at the same time, the behaviour of national governments was predicated on the assumption that international commerce was beneficial because it enabled each country to produce goods and services which were *complementary* to each other's needs. This, after all, is what the principle of comparative advantage is all about. True, some interventionist actions – particularly by governments of later industrializing nations – were being practised,[5] but the dictum 'Firms compete but countries co-operate – and both obey the dictates of the market' was widely upheld. This was the deeply implanted order of things, which the events of the second industrial revolution of the late nineteenth century did little to disturb.

As we enter the new millennium, interfirm and inter-nation-state relationships are taking on more complex, pluralistic and contradictory forms. The last decade, in particular, has witnessed a spectacular increase in collaborative agreements between firms, both to penetrate new markets and to share the costs and speed up the process of innovation. Paradoxically, at a time of increased competition between firms in the factor and final goods markets, there has been a shedding of non-core activities by firms along and between value chains, and a replacement of them by a range of closely monitored interfirm alliances and networking arrangements. This movement has also led to another paradox – namely, the renaissance of small to medium-size firms – at a time when giant MNEs continue to engage in international mergers and acquisitions (M&As), and dominate the markets for technology-intensive and branded goods and services.

The reasons for the emerging 'yin' and 'yang' of the organization of economic activity are many, but most reduce to the rapidly rising overhead costs of production – at a time when manufacturing methods are becoming more flexible – an accelerating rate of technological obsolescence, a closer interdependence between many cutting-edge technologies, and the growing integration of different stages of the value-added chain (especially between R&D and the manufacturing departments of firms). Such events, together with the growing ease with which firms can co-operate with each other, have encouraged them to specialize in activities based on their core competencies, while, at the same time, to forge new and continuing alliances with firms now supplying inputs into these activities.

National governments, too, are finding that globalization is leading to new, and incongruous, cross-border relationships. Increasingly, in a world in which trade and FDI are within rather than between industrial sectors, unemployment is unacceptably high, human resource development is at a premium, and firm-specific assets are easily transferable across national borders. Governments are increasingly and openly competing with each other for similar resources, as well as seeking to advance their own particular social agendas. As the economic structure of countries tends to converge, so institutional and organizational factors are becoming more important location-specific endowments. Foremost among these are the actions of governments, which I will consider in more detail a little later. For the moment, I would simply note that, in contrast to the late nineteenth-century scenario, where the policies of national governments were either independent of, or tended to complement, each other, those of today are a mixture of the 'yin' of competition and the 'yang' of co-operation.

Even the most cursory review of the now-emerging relationships between firms and governments suggests that, far from being antithetical, co-operation and competition each have a unique and mutually reinforcing role to play in a dynamic market economy. In and of themselves, each is a neutral concept; however, each may be deployed in a market-distorting or a market-facilitating way. There is an unacceptable face of co-operation and an unacceptable face of competition. One of the challenges of the globalizing economy is to manage and resolve the apparent contradictory nature of these two organizational forms. Clearly, the decision of *when*, *with whom* and *how* to co-operate, and *when*, *with whom* and *how* to compete, is partly determined by firm-, industry- and country-specific characteristics. Because of this, it is difficult to lay down any universal guidelines. But, in the last two decades or so, Western firms and nations have learnt a great deal about the 'yin' and 'yang' of commercial relationships and institutional arrangements practised in East Asia. The knowledge so gained is now being assiduously adapted to Western norms and needs – so much so that the expression 'alliance' capitalism is now being used to describe a new trajectory of market-based socio-economic systems. A feature of this trajectory is that it is reconstituting the concepts of competition and co-operation, from being exclusive alternatives to being mutually reinforcing organizational forms.

In seeking to manage or resolve the paradox of relationships, I would like to suggest that nation states have much to learn from MNEs. Such corporations – at least the successful ones – are 'masters of the paradox'. They are well experienced both at translating the horns of dilemma of economic change into virtuous circles of growth and profitability, and of using competition and co-operation and strategies to obtain their long-term objectives (Baden-Fuller and Stopford, 1992). While, in the last resort, most MNEs are subject to the discipline of the global market-place, an increasing number are forming alliances with other firms to develop new products or seek out new markets. The key to achieving the right balance between competition – a 'go it alone strategy' – and co-operation – a 'do it together strategy' – seems to rest on the perception of managers about the nature and strength of their distinctive or core competitive advantages, relative to those of their competitors, and that of the other (i.e. complementary) assets which need to be combined with these critical capabilities if they are to exploit them effectively.[6] Research suggests that firms are most likely to co-operate with each other to reduce their resource commitments in acquiring or enhancing these complementary assets, but that they are more reluctant to do so when this requires sharing knowledge and learning experiences about their critical competencies. Once this balance of options is achieved – and this is a constantly moving target – competition and co-operation are no longer seen to be exclusive alternatives, but reinforcing avenues for advancing competitiveness.

GLOBALIZATION VS LOCALIZATION: THE PARADOX OF SPACE

As the late nineteenth century witnessed the widening of local into national markets, and the emergence of foreign direct investment (FDI) as a significant form of international commerce, so the late twentieth century is seeing the regionalization and globalization of economic activity. The difference, however, between these two events is not just one of the size and character of markets – but the fact that, while a century ago, economic activity was largely conducted between independent buyers and sellers, the unique feature of the contemporary world economy is the deep structural integration and interdependence of cross-border transactions.

The extension of geographical space has not affected all activities to the same extent. While the markets for some goods (e.g. Coca-Cola, fast food, Levi jeans, Gucchi handbags) and some kinds of services (e.g. financial assets, music, television and sports) span the globe, others are restricted by the specificity of local supply capabilities, customs, tastes and government regulations. Similarly, while some parts of the value chain (e.g. those involving the electronic transmission of standardized data) acknowledge few geographical borders, others, in which trust-based relations, personal interface and complex, but non-codifiable, knowledge are at a premium, are having to pay more heed to spatially constrained capabilities and needs. Hence, we have the paradox of what Ann Markusen (1996) has referred to as 'sticky places within slippery space'. At the same time, the imperatives of much of contemporary product and production technology and the lowering of natural and artificial barriers to traversing space have most certainly enabled firms to take a more holistic stance to their foreign and domestic operations.

The liberalization of markets, more outward-looking development policies, and the current attractions of regional economic integration have all helped to push out the territorial boundaries of firms. While FDI is the main route by which this extension is being accomplished, increasingly, as I have already mentioned, cross-border alliances – varying from international subcontracting and *keiretsu*-type relationships to R&D consortia among rival firms – have become more significant in the last decade, and seem likely to be a major feature of the capitalism of the twenty-first century.

If we can think of the spatial widening of economic activity as the 'yin' of globalization, the 'yang' is surely the increasing pressure on individuals, firms, nations and localities to reassert their distinctive traits and values. The paradox of regional economic integration – albeit often market driven – is that it introduces an economic uniformity into people's lives, which they wish to offset by emphasizing other, and more unusual, characteristics of their individuality. In some cases – although we would hesitate to suggest this has been caused by the emergence of the global economy, however much it may facilitate it – it leads to ethnic and ideological schisms and to political disintegration and fragmentation. Just as there can be little doubt that the merger movement among corporations is going on alongside a regeneration in the role and prosperity of small businesses, so as countries group together better to attain their common economic aspirations, they are anxious to reassert their distinctive cultural and ethnic heritages. As John Naisbitt (1994) has put it, there is a rising conflict between universalism and tribalism, and between regional unification and fragmentation.

As the global economy favours the growth of the large MNE, so many of its spatial units are becoming smaller. The same may well be true of the 'body politic'. The concept of subsidiarity is gaining widespread acceptance at all levels of governance, and the role of subnational region, district, city and town in affecting the location of economic activity would appear to be more, rather than less, important. Certainly, this is the view of Kenichi Ohmae, who, in his latest book (Ohmae, 1995) argues persuasively that, in a borderless world, region states may well come to replace nation states as the ports of entry into the global economy and the centrepiece of economic activity.[7]

Once again, however, I would suggest that the contradiction between the globalization and the localization of economic space is more perceived than real, and that this is being amply demonstrated by the activities of the more successful MNEs. They know full well the axiom 'think globally but act locally', and of the need to balance the gains arising from the integration of scale-related technologies with those which stem from adapting world product production markets, techniques and work practices to local situations. They also appreciate that the ability to recognize these latter needs, and to co-ordinate them efficiently, are important competitive advantages in their own right. At the same time, the *kind* and *degree* of adaptation required in the late 1990s is very different from that of a century ago. Then, it was mainly based on the availability (and quality) of natural resources and of national consumer tastes. Now, it is based on the flexible use of created assets (namely, of innovations, production technologies and organizational structures), and on an acceptance of the fact that in a variety of quite subtle ways, the kind of product improvements sought by consumers reflects national and subnational, as well as international, physical and spiritual values.

In short, globalization is leading to a spatial reconfiguration of economic activity – and also the governance of such activity. In some cases, this is resulting in a harmonization, or homogenization, of the functions of firms and of the tastes of consumers the world over. In others, it is increasing the value of close spatial linkages between firms (such as that fostered in business districts and science parks) at a subnational level, while, at the same time, stimulating individuals and nations to differentiate themselves from each other and emphasize their discriminating characteristics. The 'yin' – or slippery space – of economic integration is then going hand in hand with – indeed some would say giving rise to – the 'yang' – or sticky place – of a re-evaluation of national or local cultural, religious and ethnic diversities. As long as these trends of globalization are treated as complementary, rather than substitutable for each other, then there is no real paradox of geographical space. And, as I have already suggested, the more successful MNEs are already demonstrating some of the ways in which spatially related tensions can be minimized and used to promote their global objectives. I accept, of course, that this task is a good deal more challenging for national and regional governments, but grapple with it they must if the full benefits of globalization are not to be destroyed by intercountry social and cultural strife. I shall return to this point towards the end of this chapter.

THE ROLE OF GOVERNMENTS: THE PARADOX OF 'LESS, YET MORE', AND THAT OF 'CENTRALIZATION VS DECENTRALIZATION'

A century ago, there was comparatively little dispute about the role of national administrations – at least in Western economies.[8] The spiritual heritage of Adam Smith and the founding fathers of the American Revolution was very much alive. In economic matters, at least, the invisible hand of the market was thought superior to that of the visible hand of extra-market planning and government intervention. The duties of government were to defend the realm, to maintain internal law and order, to combat the unacceptable face of capitalism, to provide the legal and commercial framework in which property rights were respected and unfettered markets might flourish, and to alleviate unavoidable social distress.

There was no conflict in performing these tasks; they were not even regarded as competitive to those of other organizational forms. The fact that in some countries (e.g. France and Germany) governments pursued more paternalistic policies and were more interventionist than others (e.g. the UK) was accepted to reflect their distinctive institutional heritages, or their particular stages of development, rather than any differences in their economic philosophies. In any event, because of the immobility of resources and absence of any cross-border structural integration of economic activity, national administrations were able to follow largely autonomous economic and social strategies. Even what international commerce there was at the time was largely determined by a world order, namely the gold standard, although restrictions on some kinds of trade, and other forms of government intervention, were beginning to emerge.

Today, the optimum or appropriate role of government is hotly debated. In particular, the last 20 years have seen a blurring of the boundaries of the organizational modes of capitalist economies, while globalization has led to an intensification of the 'yin' and 'yang' of government intervention. On the one hand, as markets have become more liberalized and central planning has become discredited, the interventionist role of governments has lessened. On the other, as the economic prosperity of firms and nations has become more dependent on the continual upgrading of indigenous created assets – notably innovatory capacity, human resources and the commercial and communications infrastructure, many of which are within the power of governments to influence – the role of the state has become more critical.

I believe that, for the most part, globalization is *not* reducing the role of national governments. But it is changing its *raison d'être* and its content. And it is doing so within the context of deepening structural integration; the growing importance of public goods (e.g. crime prevention, health care, education and the environment); and the increasing ease with which corporations can avoid unpopular actions by their national governments by relocating their activities elsewhere (i.e. 'vote' with their feet).[9]

Another feature of globalization and economic change is that it is leading to a greater coincidence of interests between governments and the private sector in market economies. Even the arch-priest of market forces – the World Bank – has recognized this.[10] The 'yin' of a policing and umpiring, but otherwise non-interventionist, stance of governments is being supplemented by the 'yang' of governments as institution builders, facilitators of efficient markets and catalysts of dynamic comparative advantage, and managers of social conflict (Chang and Rowthorn, 1995). Hence the paradox that a free market needs strong government – a paradox which scholars are only able to resolve by constructing a theory of state involvement which 'takes full account of uncertainty and innovation, institutions and political economy' (Chang and Rowthorn, 1995, p. 46).

To date, the need for a reconstituted role of governments in the age of alliance capitalism has only been fully acknowledged – and put into practice – by some East Asian governments (Wade, 1995). The competing or adversarial relationship between governments and private enterprise, which was (and is) a feature of hierarchical capitalism, remains strongly embedded in Western – especially US – cultures. But the phenomenon of the globalizing economy, the growing recognition that a nation's competitiveness rests as much on its ability to supply the location-bound assets necessary to attract or retain firm-specific mobile assets as those assets themselves, and the acceptance that, *de facto*, governments *do* compete with each other for these latter assets, are combining to induce a 'sink or swim together' philosophy among all except the most extreme free market administrations.

Of the three paradoxes so far identified, that of the 'less' or 'more' of governments may be the most difficult to resolve. This is not only because of entrenched ideological views and institutional rigidities, but also because the costs and benefits of non-market intervention are extremely difficult to measure. So, if and when markets do fail, it cannot necessarily be presumed that government intervention will improve the situation, as the costs of such intervention may be greater than the benefits. Such evidence as we have (e.g. Bradford, 1994; Wade, 1995) suggests that the interaction between national governments, fiat governments and markets in countries such as Korea, Taiwan and Malaysia has led to a virtuous circle of growth and efficiency, while that in many parts of Latin America, at least until recently, has led to a vicious circle of low economic growth and social unrest.

Although there has been some research done on the kinds of government action which are most likely to improve economic performance,[11] for the most part our knowledge is woefully inadequate. Once again, however, there are some hints from the responses of MNEs to market failure and to the demands of globalization. In particular, there are major changes now taking place in the organizational structure of firms. Pyramids of hierarchies are being increasingly flattened as more heterarchical (and horizontal) relationships are being forged between decision takers and line managers. Nowhere is this being more clearly demonstrated than in the Swedish/Swiss MNE Asea Brown Boveri (ABB).[12] In this changed organizational scenario, the job of top management is less to control and take decisions, and more to orchestrate a strategic vision and set performance standards, to nurture organizational values and to encourage down-the-line entrepreneurship. The 'yin' of a centralized corporate strategy and the setting of targets is being accompanied by the 'yang' of devolved responsibility for achieving these goals, that is subsidiarity in action. Similarly, one can see globalization leading to a relayering of some of the traditional tasks of national governments to regional states or business districts and local authorities, while others (e.g. the harmonization of trade, FDI and competition policies, and the framing of technical and environmental standards) are increasingly becoming the responsibility of regional or supranational regimes. According to Charles Handy (1995, p. 113), this is leading (and I quote his words) 'to the disappearing middle of national administrations'.

THE HUMAN CONSEQUENCES OF GLOBALIZATION: THE PARADOX OF BENEFITS AND DISBENEFITS

Perhaps the most transparent effect of globalization – or more accurately the economic forces associated with it – is that on the everyday lives of people the world over. While the 'yin' of structural economic interdependence and the liberalization of markets is undisputedly raising average living standards, offering new job opportunities, widening consumer choice, and, in a whole variety of ways, improving the lifestyles of large numbers of people, the 'yang', or downside, of globalization is no less dramatically portrayed in disturbingly high levels of unemployment – particularly among the younger unskilled workers – a personal sense of insecurity and foreboding associated with rapid technological change, the breakdown of traditional social mores, the resurgence of ethnic conflicts, and the easier cross-border movement of tangible or intangible *disbenefits*, for example organized crime, drug trafficking, international terrorism and unacceptable patterns of behaviour. It is downsides such as these which Klaus Schwab and Claude Smadja (1996) – two of the most prominent advocates of global trade and integration – had in mind when, at the Davos Forum in 1996, they referred to a 'mounting backlash against globalization'. Other commentators have gone further by asserting that, unless the less desirable consequences of globalization are tackled and, at least, partially resolved, the utopian vision – and I paraphrase Aldous Huxley's words – of a 'brave new economic world' could quickly be turned into a cauldron of social unrest, political upheaval, cultural fragmentation and ideological conflict between nations, or even civilizations.[13]

Such a stark paradox, I believe, was much less in evidence at the turn of the last century.[14] True, at that time there was much structural change, brought about, *inter alia*, by the advent of electricity, the telephone, the internal combustion engine and the introduction of the Fordist system of production. But economic growth, both in the older and newer capitalist economies of the time, was, in general, able to cope with the less desirable consequences; the jobs created were generally more congenial than those which they replaced, while, for the most part, improvements in education and vocational training were able to keep pace with the needs of the market-place. Moreover, most of the required social adjustments were contained within domestic economies, and it was not until after the First World War that FDI became a significant allocator of economic activity and, hence, jobs between countries.

At that time, too, there were far fewer non-economic claims on the resources and capabilities of countries than there are today. Most social welfare programmes were in their infancy, and very little attention was paid to environmental issues. In the main, the second industrial revolution of the late nineteenth century was accomplished with more observable benefits and fewer observable costs than those resulting from its predecessor of a century earlier, or (so it would appear) its successor a century later. Even the hierarchical system of managerial capitalism, although it had some adverse consequences on the fortunes of small family-owned enterprises, generally offered the ordinary worker more benefits and opportunities than it took away!

Again, the situation is totally different in the emerging global neighbourhood of the 1990s. This is apparent both at the level of the individual firm and that of the nation state. Almost daily, it seems, one reads about huge restructuring and relocation programmes of corporations, which frequently have traumatic effects on people's lives and livelihoods – not just in one country, but in several. Often the slogan 'one person's job is another person's dole' is all too true. Often, too, the benefits – as well as the costs – of McWorld are exploited by ethnic or religious fundamentalists to advance the course of Jihad.[15] There are both losers and winners in the globalization process, and the very pace of economic change often requires major adjustments even in the lives of the winners. Over the last two decades, I would suggest, there has been more reallocation of economic activity involving people-adjustment, both within and between countries, than at any other time since the late eighteenth century.

At the level of the nation state, globalization is requiring one of the basic tenets of comparative advantage – namely, the cross-border immobility of resources – to be questioned. Not only are many firm-specific assets and capabilities mobile across national boundaries, but the demands being made by the owners of these assets and capabilities on those which are locationally bound are changing. Thus, for example, in their choice of investment locations, both between and within countries, MNEs are being increasingly influenced by the presence of agglomeration economies of transport and communications infrastructure, and by the price and productivity of skilled labour.[16] As I have indicated, not only are these assets largely location bound, but their supply is strongly influenced by government action. If these policies are inappropriate, or are not perceived to be as congenial as those offered by other governments, then those assets which have the opportunity to do so will move elsewhere. In such an event, globalization may result in more economic disbenefits than benefits – certainly to the countries and the immobile assets losing the economic activity. Equally, because of differences in age, structures, social policies and the competence of national administrations, the ability of countries to absorb the 'yang' of globalization will vary considerably.

How can one hope to reconcile the conflicting consequences of globalization – which, in the economic arena at least, are mainly distributional? I believe the first essential thing is to recognize that, barring natural or human catastrophes, the globalization of economic activity is largely irreversible. This is because it is the result of technological advances which, themselves, cannot be reversed. However, the pace and form of globalization can be affected, as can the response of governments to some of its less welcome consequences. And, it is the extent to which countries can successfully devise new ways to minimize these costs by effective 'voice' rather than 'exit' strategies which will determine the net benefits they derive from globalization.

Since many of the less welcome effects accompanying the advent of the global village are non-economic, it might be thought that the actions of MNEs can be of only limited relevance to governments. This would be incorrect, and for two reasons. The first is that the more socially responsible MNEs are demonstrating that there need be no real conflict between the achievement of economic and social goals. Nowhere is this more clearly seen than in the area of environmental standards. Far from being exporters of pollution – as was once thought – MNEs are among the trail blazers of environmentally friendly, yet competitiveness-enhancing, innovations, and often set, rather than follow, the dictates of governments. Similarly, in their redeployment, retraining and pension schemes, the more progressive global companies offer a microcosm of the type of policies which governments would do well to study. Second, because they span the globe, many MNEs provide a salutary reminder to national administrations that 'best practice' techniques – particularly in minimizing the social hardships of structural change – are not always 'home grown', and there is much to learn from other cultures and institutional regimes.

I accept, of course, that, by themselves, corporations cannot – and, indeed, should not – be expected to resolve the challenges of globalization, although initiatives such as the *Business Leaders Forum* set up by HRH the Prince of Wales in 1989 to consider the corporate response to the social, cultural and spiritual dimensions of globalization, are to be warmly commended. But the potential for dialogue and collaboration between the main instruments of globalization and the stakeholders affected by it remains largely untapped. In this connection, I particularly welcome the recently published report by the Commission on Global Governance entitled *Our Global Neighbourhood*. The Commission – the brain-child of ex-German Chancellor Willy Brandt – was set up in 1992, under the joint chairmanship of the (then) Prime Minister of Sweden – Ingvar Carlsson – and Shridath Ramphal, the ex-Secretary General of the Commonwealth, and comprised 28 very distinguished statesmen, business leaders, bankers, and presidents of international agencies from throughout the world. In its 'call to action', the report makes many astute recommendations on matters ranging from global security to managing economic interdependence and fostering a global civic ethic. It also urges the UN to convene a *World Conference on Global Governance*, to which (it suggests) should be invited not only the political leaders of the world, but those of 'the wider human constituency' who are 'infused with a sense of caring for others and a sense of responsibility to the global neighbourhood' (Commission on Global Governance, 1995). Such a gathering of men and women of goodwill would, indeed, be an expression of the 'benefits' of international co-operation, which, I would argue, is needed to counter-balance some of the disbenefits of international competition.

CONCLUSIONS

To conclude: as we enter the twenty-first century, we do so with a mixture of optimism and pessimism, and of hope and trepidation. The future seems both more complex and more daunting than that faced by our forefathers a century ago. This, I have suggested, is for four reasons. The first is the increasing dichotomy between the territorial space open to individuals and corporations, and under the jurisdiction of governments. This is leading to a number of paradoxes and dilemmas – particularly as far as the intercountry distribution of the gains and losses of globalization is concerned. The second is the erosion of the boundaries of the leading institutions for organizing economic activities – and particularly those of firms, markets and governments. *Inter alia*, this is resulting in a more intricate and pluralistic network of interinstitutional arrangements, and to a new complementarity between the 'yin of competition and the 'yang' of co-operation.

Third, improvements in standards of living – especially among wealthier nations – are increasingly taking the form of quality-of-life-enhancing goods and services (e.g. computer software, telecommunications, education, health care, environmental protection and the absence of crime, terrorism, etc.), the supply of which governments, by their actions or non-actions, strongly influence. The consequences of globalization are being increasingly evaluated by their effects on the availability, character and distribution of these 'public' products. In so far as communication advances and the cross-border integration of economic activity are being accompanied by a renewal of national or subnational- (e.g. tribal-) specific cultures and values, this is creating a range of interrelational tensions and dilemmas quite different in scale and effect from those arising from the second industrial revolution.

Fourth, while twentieth-century hierarchical capitalism has generally been accompanied by an expansion in the economic role of national governments, twenty-first-century alliance capitalism and the renaissance of the market economy seems likely not only to demand changes in the nature of that role, but to increase and deepen that of both subnational and supranational authorities.

In seeking to reconcile the paradoxes of globalization, I have further suggested that the ways in which successful MNEs have adapted their organizational and economic strategies to the changes demanded of them by recent economic events bear close scrutiny by public authorities as they seek to reformulate their own policies. Moreover, the cross-border activities of firms – notably via FDI and strategic alliances – may, themselves, assist national governments not only to upgrade the competitiveness of their own firms and indigenous resources, but to do so in a way which promotes their longer-term economic and social goals. Of course, the strategies of MNEs, like those of governments, may be protective and result in a vicious circle of market–state interface, and the discouragement of these is as important as any positive competitiveness-enhancing actions which both firms and governments might implement.

Looking further ahead into the twenty-first century, as the Yale historian Paul Kennedy has recently done (Kennedy, 1993), one cannot but be sobered by one final paradox which, in many ways, overarches everything I have been saying here. That is, currently the wealthiest 12 per cent of the world's population owns or controls 85 per cent of the world's stock of created assets, while the rest, that is 88 per cent of the population, owns or controls only 15 per cent of these assets. Moreover, virtually all of the 50 per cent increase in the world's population over the next 30 to 35 years is likely to occur in the less wealthy parts of the world. Clearly, the geographical imbalance between the current technology revolution and the population revolution – to use Kennedy's terminology – is a potential social time bomb. Whether or not the bomb is defused will, I believe, largely rest on two factors. The first is the nature and pace of Indian and Chinese economic development, as, between them, these two super giants are expected to account for between 25 and 30 per cent of the world's population by 2025. The second is whether the peoples of the world and their leaders can summon up enough determination and emotional intelligence to reconcile the growing threat of ideological warfare which is epitomized by the Jihad vs McWorld syndrome. For, I fear, unless this is done, our global dream could so easily turn into a global nightmare!

As a university educator and researcher, I should like to make one final remark. The future shape of our planet is now being fashioned by the decisions taken in the board rooms of larger corporations, in the corridors and chambers of government departments, and around the conference tables of international agencies. Anything we, as international business scholars, can do to provide the decision makers with information about the costs and benefits of globalization, and what requires to be done at various institutional and decision-taking levels, is surely to be applauded. Indeed, it is our duty so to participate and to influence those who guide our destinities and those of our children.

NOTES

1. Some economists (e.g. Carlota Perez, 1983) would go as far as to argue that both the 1880s and the 1980s heralded in a new Kondratiev cycle of techno-economic and socio-institutional change.
2. Eric Hobsbawn is a distinguished historian who has authored several books with titles depicting (what, to him, is) the key characteristic of the period he is writing about. Among these are *The Age of Revolution, 1789–1848*, *The Age of Capital, 1848–1875*, *The Age of Empire, 1875–1914* and *The Age of Extremes, 1914–1991* (1995).
3. Barber (1995). Jihad refers to an ideology of parochial ethnicity, which is often portrayed as extreme ethnic or religious fundamentalism. McWorld is the ideology of the global corporation, which is primarily interested in economic gain and would like to ignore all national or political boundaries.
4. Put more accurately, perceived paradoxes; we believe the paradoxes described are more 'imaginary' than 'real'.
5. And more than is commonly realized. For a contemporary account of the interventionist – albeit catalytic – role of the US government in the development of US industry – agriculture in the nineteenth century, see Kozul-Wright (1995).
6. The concept of core and complementary assets has been explored by several business scholars, but particularly by David Teece (1987).
7. See also a perceptive article on a related theme by Richard Florida (1995).
8. The same might well be true of most Eastern economies, but here the functions of government were viewed in a very different light to those in the West.
9. An expression first coined at the time of the American Revolution to reflect the extent to which firms and/or individuals could escape (through emigration) unacceptable taxes and other fiscal duties imposed by national governments.
10. See especially World Bank (1991).
11. As is reviewed, for example, in Dunning (1994) and Panic (1995).
12. As documented, for example, by Bartlett and Ghoshal (1994).
13. See Barber (1995) and Huntington (1993).
14. But, interestingly enough, it was in the years following the first industrial revolution. Indeed, as Paul Kennedy astutely observes, the disbenefits of the globalizing market economy of the late twentieth century fairly accurately mirror those of the *national* market economy of the first half of the nineteenth century, following the industrial revolution and the *laissez-faire* philosophies of some of the classical economists (Kennedy, 1993).
15. Barber (1995) gives some fascinating examples of how practical applications of the two starkly opposing ideologies often aid and abet each other, and that neither is complete without the other. For example, he points out that modern transportation and communication technologies, and the export to Jihad ideologies and practices, often lead to non-Jihad nations or regimes becoming more dependent on Jihad nations or regions for their economic well-being.
16. For a review of the literature, see Dunning (1993), Braunerhjelm and Svensson (1995) and Mariotti and Piscitello (1995).

REFERENCES

Baden-Fuller, C.W.F. and Stopford, J.M. (1992), *Rejuvenating the Mature Business*, London and New York: Routledge.

Barber, B.R. (1995), *Jihad vs McWorld*, New York: Times Books.

Bartlett, C.G. and Ghoshal, S. (1994), *Beyond the M-Form: Towards a Managerial Theory of the Firm*, Pittsburgh: Carnegie Bosch Institute for Applied Studies on International Management, Working Paper No. 94–6.

Bradford, C.I. (1994), *The New Paradigm of Systemic Competitiveness: Toward More Integrated Policies in Latin America*, Paris: OECD.
Braunerhjelm, P. and Svensson, R. (1995), *Host Country Characteristics and Agglomeration in Foreign Direct Investment*, Stockholm: Industrial Institute for Economic and Social Research (mimeo).
Chang, H.-J. and Rowthorn, R. (eds) (1995), *The Role of the State in Economic Change*, Oxford: Clarendon Press.
Commission on Global Governance (1995), *Our Global Neighbourhood*, Oxford and New York: Oxford University Press.
Dunning, J.H. (1993), *Multinational Enterprises and the Global Economy*, Wokingham, England, and Reading, MA: Addison-Wesley.
Dunning, J.H. (1994), *Globalization: The Challenge for National Economic Regimes*, Dublin: The Economic and Social Research Council.
Florida, R. (1995), 'Towards the learning region', *Futures* **27**(5): 527–36.
Handy, C. (1995), *The Empty Raincoat*, London: Arrow Business Books.
Hobsbawn, E. (1995), *The Age of Extremes 1914–1991*, London: Abacus.
Huntington, S. (1993), 'The clash of civilizations', *Foreign Affairs* **72**, Summer: 22–49.
Kennedy, P.M. (1993), *Preparing for the Twenty-First Century*, New York: Random House.
Kozul-Wright, R. (1995), 'The myth of Anglo-Saxon capitalism: reconstructing the history of the American state', in H.-J. Chang and R. Rowthorn (eds), *The Role of the State in Economic Change*, Oxford: Clarendon Press, pp. 81–113.
Mariotti, S. and Piscitello, L. (1995), 'Information costs and location of FDIs within the host country: empirical evidence from Italy', *Journal of International Business Studies* **26**(4): 815–41.
Markusen, A. (1996), 'Sticky Places in Slippery Spaces: a typology of industrial districts', *Economic Geography* **72**(3): 293–313.
Naisbitt, J. (1994), *Global Paradox: The Bigger the World Economy, the More Political its Smallest Players*, New York: William Morrow.
Ohmae, K. (1995), *The End of the Nation State: The Rise of Regional Economies*, London: HarperCollins.
Panic, M. (1995), 'International economic integration and the changing role of national governments', in H.-J. Chang and R. Rowthorn (eds), *The Role of the State in Economic Change*, Oxford: Clarendon Press, pp. 51–80.
Perez, C. (1983), 'Structural changes and the assimilation of new technologies on the economic and social system', *Futures* **15**: 357–75.
Schwab, K. and Smadja, C. (1996), *Start Taking the Backlash Against Globalization Seriously*, Address given to Davos Forum, January.
Teece, D. (1987), 'Profiting from technological innovation: implications for integration collaboration, licensing and public policy', in *The Competitive Challenge*, Cambridge, MA: Ballinger.
Wade, R. (1995), 'Resolving the state–market dilemma in East Asia', in H.-J. Chang and R. Rowthorn (eds), *The Role of the State in Economic Change*, Oxford: Clarendon Press, pp. 114–36.
World Bank (1991), *The World Development Report 1992*, Oxford and New York: Oxford University Press.

4. Globalization, economic restructuring and development*

INTRODUCTION

On 9 November 1989, just over 75 years after the outbreak of the First World War, the cold war ended. Both events were primarily political landmarks, but each symbolized a turning point in modern economic history. The first marked the end of a period of path-breaking technological advances and unparalleled economic growth. The second signalled not only the full renaissance of the democratic market system, but the beginning of a journey towards a new global economic order, the like of which our grandparents could scarcely have envisaged.

But for most of the present century, the world has been on an economic 'roller coaster'. The 1920s and 1930s were a period of fragile peace and economic instability, and a time when most nations sacrificed the benefits of cross-border trade and commerce for narrow and elusive national interests.

The post-Second World War years started promisingly enough. *Pax Americana* and the international trading and monetary regimes, crafted at Bretton Woods, provided the institutional framework for a period of sustained growth, particularly for developed countries.[1] But the prosperity was short-lived. The 1970s saw the end of US hegemony, and the re-emergence of floating exchange rates. They also witnessed a determination, by many newly self-governing developing countries, to shed the yoke of economic imperialism. In spite of valiant efforts by the United Nations to establish a new international economic order, both the income and ideological gaps between the rich and poor nations widened.

Yet, however understandable, the quest for economic autonomy was already beginning to look unattainable. A fresh wave of technological and organizational advances was starting to weave a new tapestry of economic interdependence. There was also a growing disenchantment about the benefits of inward-looking development strategies and socialist economic policies, although such disenchantment was nothing compared to the political maelstrom about to occur in Central and Eastern Europe and in China. Towards the end of

* The 6th Raúl Prebisch Lecture, Geneva (1998), UNCTAD 1–39.

the 1980s, the wind of liberalization was blowing through almost all nations. Today, the world stands on the threshold of a new era which, while, in some respects, harks back to the golden years of the nineteenth century, is likely to be qualitatively different from it – both in its characteristics and in its consequences.

In this chapter, I wish to suggest that, notwithstanding the dramatic social and political events of the last century, it has been the growth in the world's capacity to innovate new goods and services which has provided the main engine of economic progress. This capacity is epitomized not only by such inventions as the steam engine, electricity, the computer, the micro-chip and the laser, but, no less significantly, by the gradual and continuous upgrading of human skills and experience, and of organizational competences. These developments have been mainly market driven, but the extent to which they have been translated into welfare-enhancing goods and services has been influenced by the actions of national governments and supranational regimes.

In many respects, the globalizing economy of the 1990s is the latest stage in the enlargement of the spatial dimension of economic activity that dates back to pre-industrial times. Essentially, its speed and direction have been conditioned by advances in transport and communications technologies, and by the actions of governments in affecting the creation, management and disposition of physical and human assets. Yet it is only in our lifetime that the role of trade, foreign direct investment (FDI) and cross-border strategic alliances has become such a critical determinant of economic progress. And it has only been in the last 20 years that the world economy has become so structurally interdependent that the use of the world *global*, as distinct from *international*, has become justifiable.

I will explain my reasoning for this statement a little later in this chapter. But first, I would like to set out exactly how the present trajectory of the world economy is different from those that preceded it. I will then go on to discuss some of the likely benefits and costs of globalization – particularly for sustainable development – before considering some of its implications for the macro-governance of economic activity.

I would like to identify three ages, or eras, in the development of capitalist economies. The timing of each age is approximate, and is decided by what I shall call the 'dominant' paradigm of techno-economic organization, and the socio-institutional framework of capitalism prevailing at the time. Each age also has an identifiable spatial dimension, and each is associated with the leadership of a particular country or group of countries. My intention is briefly to describe the characteristics of each age; and to consider their consequences for the governance of economic activity, for sustainable development and for human welfare.

The three techno-economic paradigms, as identified by several authors,[2] are the *craft* or *batch*, *mass* or *scale*, and *flexible* or *innovation-driven systems* of production. The three forms of capitalism are *entrepreneurial*, *hierarchical* and *alliance capitalism*; and the three spatial dimensions related to these systems and stages of capitalism are the *sub-national or national*; the *national or international*; and the *regional or global*.

THE AGE OF ENTREPRENEURIAL CAPITALISM: THE ERA OF CRAFT, OR BATCH, PRODUCTION; FROM LOCAL TO NATIONAL MARKETS, *C*. 1770–1875

The first century following the industrial revolution was dominated by a micro-organizational system which reflected the technical characteristics and spatial limitations of the time. This was the age of the steam engine, of mechanical power and of batch production. It was the age of entrepreneurial capitalism and of the privately owned and managed firm. It was the age in which the UK was the hegemonic nation. It was the age in which the factory system replaced the putting-out system of work, and labour markets became internalized. Yet value chains were short, innovations were largely process driven and capital requirements were modest. It was an age of unitary organizational structures. It was an age when firms enjoyed few economies of scale or scope. It was an age in which inter-firm cooperation was confined to a few sub-national agglomerations of related activities, e.g. the Lancashire cotton textile and textile machine industry. It was the age when, for the most part, firms served only local or national markets.

For most of the nineteenth century, the international allocation of activity was based on the disposition of natural resources, and trade reflected a Ricardian comparative advantage of these resources. Apart from finance capital, there were few cross-border transactions in created assets, although there was a substantial exodus of people and knowledge, especially across the Atlantic. Until the advent of the telephone and telegraph in the 1870s, inter-continental communications were extremely rudimentary. At the beginning of the era, it took days or weeks for a simple message to be transmitted between continents, while the difficulties of cross-border travel were well dramatized by Phineas Fogg in Jules Verne's *Around the World in 80 Days*.

The predominant allocative and signalling device in the craft era was the market, and almost all transactions were 'arm's-length'. The multi-activity – much less the multinational firm – had hardly emerged. There was little vertical integration or horizontal diversification by firms. Neither did governments intervene much in market transactions. Following the dictum of Adam Smith, they viewed their main tasks as the providers of the socio-economic and institutional infrastructure necessary for market-led economic development, the administration of law and justice and the defence of the realm. Domestic macroeconomic policy was largely circumscribed by the discipline of the gold standard. Macro-organizational policy reflected the *laissez-faire* thinking of the time. As the period progressed, some latecomer nations began to protect their infant industries from foreign competition. But, for most of the nineteenth century, the only international coordination of resource deployment was that exercised by market forces.

Although entrepreneurial capitalism was accompanied by a simple division of labour, the distribution of economic power was strongly centripetal. Moreover, even when developing countries were brought into the network of world commerce, the benefits accruing to them rarely spread beyond enclaves, whose sole *raison d'être* was to serve the needs of foreign buyers and customers. Indeed, it was during the craft age that the dual economy was born.

HIERARCHICAL CAPITALISM: THE AGE OF MASS PRODUCTION; FROM NATIONAL TO INTERNATIONAL MARKETS, *C.* 1875–1980

Like its predecessor, the second industrial revolution was heralded in by a series of revolutionary technological discoveries. These stemmed largely from the US, which, during the third quarter of the nineteenth century, assumed the economic leadership from the UK. Although, perhaps, the more conspicuous of the new inventions were the electrical generator, the internal combustion engine, and – often neglected by scholars – the calculating machine,[3] no less far reaching was the introduction of precision machinery and instruments, which helped perfect the interchangeability of components and parts, and which, in turn, made possible the large-scale production of standardized finished goods. It also led to the replacement of entrepreneurial by hierarchical capitalism.

For most of the following century, and fuelled by a series of transport and communications innovations – which dramatically encapsulated the time and cost of traversing space – the mass or scale system of production became the dominant techno-economic system of production, especially in the more dynamic sectors of industrialized economies. The focus of the system was very much directed to the production of goods rather than of services. The factory was the temple of wealth. Its logo – the relentless conveyor belt – was brilliantly satirized in Chaplin's film *Modern Times*.

The dedicated mass production system order was different from that which preceded it in six important ways. First, to effectively exploit scale economies, it required substantial amounts of investment in plant, machinery and equipment, which were often beyond the ability of individual entrepreneurs to finance. Hence the genesis of limited liability and managerial capitalism. The order also required a regular and uninterrupted flow of inputs, large and stable markets, and good distributional facilities.

Second, in contrast to the craft system, the main impacts of the mass production system were felt in the fabricating or assembling, rather than in the processing, sectors. And it was in the former sectors where, in order to better coordinate the stages of production, and to reduce the risk of supply, irregularities and uncertain delivery dates, firms began to internalize intermediate product markets and to engage in vertical integration. This, indeed, was the origin of the multi-product firm, the multidivisional or M form of organizational structure, and of hierarchical capitalism.

Third, the scale system altered the relationship between the managers of firms and the employed labour force. By the time the system had been perfected by Henry Ford in the 1950s – hence the coming of the term 'Fordism' – the factory worker was regarded as a 'cog' in the production process – or a cost to be minimized, and in no way as a contributor to the innovatory or decision taking process. At the same time, the emergence of labour unions increased the vulnerability of the production process to disruptions and strikes. The response of management was two-fold. The first was to replace manpower by machine power wherever it was economic to do so, and the second was to combat the possibility of unwelcome labour practices by paying workers above the average wages (which also helped fuel the market for the goods they produced).[4]

Fourth, the scale system required modifications to the socio-institutional framework which best suited the craft system. In particular, it made more demands on governments as the creation of knowledge became more firm specific, so markets were less able to provide the right signals for socially optimum innovatory activities. This was partly because the market price of technology did not fully capture its extra-market benefits, and partly because it was increasingly taking on the characteristics of a public good – i.e. it was expensive to produce and inexpensive to reproduce. Hence the introduction, by governments, of the patent system. Moreover, to maintain the momentum of economic growth, production processes had to be continually improved and upgraded. This required more scientists, engineers and technicians, and this, in turn, demanded additional expenditure by governments on education and training. Governments also began to accept more responsibility for providing the kind of public goods, e.g. utility, road and rail and communication services, which firms needed to draw upon if they were to be competitive. Finally, the scale system compelled governments to take a more active role in regulating abuses of power by large firms in heavily concentrated industries.

Fifth, as technological advances continued to push out the limits of growth, firms began to look overseas for their inputs and markets. At the same time, as US corporations began to replicate their domestic activities abroad, the scale system became more widely adopted in Europe, Japan, and in some larger developing countries. This further widened the area of competitive space. It also changed the nature of cross-border transactions. Whereas much trade of entrepreneurial capitalism had been between countries with different *natural resource* endowments, an increasing proportion of trade of hierarchical capitalism was directed towards nations with similar patterns of *created* assets; and the specialization of economic activity became less dependent on the distribution of natural resources, and more based on the exploitation of economies of scale and the distinctive needs of consumers located in different countries. This is not to suggest that trade between developed and developing countries was insignificant, but simply that the location of new economic activity began to increasingly favour the more advanced countries.[5]

Sixth, the scale era also led to new organizational forms of international transactions. Throughout the last half-century in particular, trade has become increasingly concentrated in the hands of transnational hierarchies which, as the scope of their foreign operations has widened, have increasingly sought to integrate their global production and marketing systems (UNCTAD, 1993). While generally welcomed by some smaller industrializing nations, for the most part this new international division of labour, until comparatively recently at any rate, was viewed with some scepticism by most larger developing countries – and particularly by those who, in the early post-war period, gained their political independence.

Seventh, when extended beyond its national boundaries, hierarchical capitalism, although leading to a centrifugal distribution of value-added activity, also tended to increase the centralization of economic power. It was precisely the concern that developing countries might be locked into a static international division of labour, which inhibited the upgrading of their indigenous resources and capabilities, that led Raúl Prebisch to advocate the promotion of import substitution policies by such countries, and the formation of economic groups among themselves. While some of his advice was certainly heeded, that part which required governments to pursue efficiency-enhancing macro-economic policies was, to a large extent, ignored. Indeed, it is an irony that it was largely countries from that part of the world about which Prebisch had least to say and write, viz. East Asia – and especially Korea, Taiwan and Singapore – that have been the most successful in turning hierarchical capitalism to their own advantage; and this they have done by a judicious combination of market-led import substitution and export-led development strategies, and sound macro-economic policies.

In summary, then, the combination of US-led hierarchical capitalism, advances in transport and communication technologies, and the emergence of many new, independent nation states has helped fashion the internationalization of economic activity for most of the present century. Yet such internationalization could hardly be called global as it excluded the most populated countries in the world – China and India – and the whole of the Communist bloc. Moreover, although throughout the period the economic structures of countries were becoming increasingly linked by aid, trade and investment, it has only been in the last 20 years or so that hierarchical capitalism – mainly in the guise of TNCs – has fused national economies in such a way that their fortunes have become inextricably bound up with each other.

Finally, to help avoid a recurrence of destructive unilateral trade policies of the inter-war years, the first major international economic regimes were set up in the mid-1940s. These were of two main kinds. The first, typified by GATT, the IMF and the World Bank, established ground rules for trade and a mechanism by which various forms of international market failure might be reduced by a better coordination of domestic macro-economic policies. These international organizations were supplemented by a variety of formal and informal regional arrangements and a bevy of bilateral or multilateral agreements favouring particular sectors or countries.[6] A feature of all these supranational regimes, however, was that they viewed the world as consisting of two major economic blocs – the developed industrial economies led by the US, and a diverse group of developing countries.

The second kind of international organizations set up were less formal, and their main objective was to provide a forum for an exchange of views on a variety of international issues, and, where appropriate, to recommend to national governments specific courses of action. The United Nations is, perhaps, the best example of this kind of organization, and in the 1960s and 1970s, it and its various agencies provided the focal point for discussion and recommended action on matters particularly germane to the interests of developing countries.

THE AGE OF ALLIANCE CAPITALISM: TOWARDS FLEXIBLE PRODUCTION; FROM AN INTERNATIONAL TO A REGIONAL AND GLOBAL ECONOMY, *C.* 1980 AND BEYOND

Quite often, the very success of any organizational structure sows the seeds of its own demise[7] if for no other reason than success breeds inertia and a reluctance to acknowledge and adapt to new situations. While it is too early to record the passing of the mass production age, the last decade has seen the emergence of a new form of economic organization, which may well become the dominant mode in the years to come. The essence of this new paradigm is captured in the techno-economic concept of flexible and innovation-led production, and the socio-institutional concept of alliance capitalism.[8]

The world of the mid-1990s is, indeed, a very different place from the one into which most of us were born. The hegemony of the UK in the nineteenth century and the US in the twentieth century has been replaced by a triarchy of economic power comprising the US, Japan and the European Union. The production of goods is no longer the major focus of economic activity. Services now account for three-fifths of the GDP of developed countries, and nearly one-half of that of developing countries (World Bank, 1993b).

Increasingly – as is most vividly illustrated by Japan and Singapore on the one hand, and Zaire and the old USSR on the other – the economic prosperity of a country is less determined by the natural resources it possesses, and more by its stock of knowledge, the skills and expertise of its people, and the capability of its institutions – both private and public – to efficiently organize these assets. Issues to do with the quality of life and the structure of governance are in the process of a radical rethinking. It is not just competitiveness and development which have risen to the top of the political agenda, but *sustainable* competitiveness and development. And most dramatically of all, the political contours of nations – or more correctly nationhood[9] – and regions, as recognized by most of us, are being redrawn by the fusing forces of economic integration on the one hand, and the ideological schisms and cultural disintegration on the other.

There have already been a plethora of books, articles and newspaper stories written on the nature and extent of globalization. Most recently (1993/4), three volumes with the intriguing titles *Global Embrace*, *Global Dream* and *Global Paradox*[10] have seen the light of day. Of the various definitions of globalization, my preference is for the one given by Anthony McGrew, who in a jointly edited book, *Globalization and the Nation States*, published in 1992 (McGrew and Lewis, 1992), writes

> Globalization refers to the multiplicity of linkages and interconnections between the states and societies which make up the present world system. It describes the process by which events, decisions, and activities in one part of the world come to have significant consequences for individuals and communities in quite distant parts of the globe. Globalization has two distinct phenomena: scope (or stretching) and intensity (or deepening). On the one hand, it defines a set of processes which embrace most of the globe or which operate worldwide; the concept therefore has a spatial connotation. ... On the other hand it also implies an intensification on the levels of interaction, interconnectedness or *interdependence* between the states and societies which constitute the world community. Accordingly, alongside the stretching goes a deepening of global processes. (p. 23)

In short, then, globalization is leading to the structural transformation of firms and nations, and is creating new relationships and new dependencies. Sometimes, the transformation takes place at a regional level; much of the integrated production networks of TNCs is so focused. Sometimes, it occurs at a global level. For example, the contemporary global financial system is one in which national markets throughout the world, though physically separate, operate as if they are in the same place (Stopford and Strange, 1991). One scholar has put it even more dramatically by averring that global financial integration is 'the end of geography'.[11]

The main causes of globalization are well known. I have space to focus on just two.[12] The first is the pressure on firms – by consumers and competitors alike – to continually develop new products and upgrade the quality and/or reduce the price of existing goods and services. At the same time, the escalating costs of research and development, coupled with ever-shortening product life cycles, are compelling firms both to curtail the scope of their value-added activities and to search for wider markets. Moreover, in order to effectively and speedily exploit their core competences, firms are finding they need to combine these with the core competences of other firms, and those of governments. Hence the emergence of strategic alliances and networks to which I shall give more attention later in this chapter.

The second cause of globalization – which in many ways is better described as a removal of an obstacle – is the renaissance of market-supporting policies pursued by national governments; and the growth of market-led regional integration. In the last five years alone, more than 30 countries have abandoned central planning as the main mode of allocating scarce resources; while over 80 have liberalized their inward FDI policies. The privatization of state-owned enterprises, the liberalization and deregulation of markets – especially for services – and the removal of a bevy of structural distortions, have all worked to stimulate cross-border corporate integration, both within TNCs and between independent firms, or groups of firms.

Underlying and reinforcing these two explanations for globalization, and fashioning its character, have been changes in the organization of economic activity, and it is on these that I wish to dwell now. At a micro-level, the changes are best exemplified by the introduction of a more flexible, yet systemic, approach to production, together with a growing appreciation by firms of the need to form close and ongoing relationships with other firms to fully capture the benefits of their own competences. At a macro level, they reflect the changing costs and benefits of alternative systems of allocating scarce resources, and particularly the demands being made by globalization on national governments and supranational regimes.

Since we are in the midst of these techno-economic and socio-institutional changes, it is premature to judge either their extent or their consequences for the world economy.[13] But the clues we have been able to discern so far point to a very different path of economic development than the one we have lived through over the past 20 or 30 years.

First, then, the micro-organization of business activity. There are several forces at work which are leading firms to replace the Fordist or mass production system, which I earlier described. First, improved living standards – particularly in the Triad nations – have caused consumers to reorient their spending habits. Price competition is down-sized; quality and other forms of non-price competition are up-sized. There is a greater expectancy of fault-free products, continuous product improvement and the innovation of new goods and services. At the same time, competitive pressures are demanding that firms should re-examine their cost control procedures from inventories to manning levels and to advertising budgets. Lean production has become the order of the day.

Second, the new technologies of the 1980s and 1990s, such as computer-aided design and manufacturing techniques and the miniaturization of components, are not only enabling firms to exercise more rigorous quality control, but are permitting the use of multi-purpose machinery and equipment.

Third, contemporary technological and organizational advances are demanding a much closer synthesis and interactive learning between the innovatory and production functions of the firm. Indeed, in the words of Kenney and Florida (1993), 'the factory itself is becoming a research laboratory – a setting for both product and process innovation' (p. 303). In this new environment, knowledge and intellectual labour are being mobilized on a collective basis, and the skills and ideas of shop floor workers are being actively tapped to raise product quality and productivity. Such innovation-driven production both facilitates the functional integration of tasks and more explicitly socializes the organization of production (Kenney and Florida, 1993, p. 305).

This more flexible and coordinated approach to value-added activity has considerable 'spin-off' effects – especially in the fabricating sectors – as, more often than not, in order to improve the quality, performance or reliability of the finished product, there has to be a simultaneous improvement in the quality of bought-out components, parts and materials. The design of a new auto, aircraft or word processor is no longer a matter only for the auto, aircraft or word processor assemblers, but involves successive tiers of component and part producers throughout the value chain. Yet the present tendency for firms to shed activities not directly related to their core assets is increasing their dependency on external subcontractors. To ensure that this does not involve unacceptable transaction and coordinating costs, the firms are then having to understand and work closely with these subcontractors. Hence the terms 'relationship' or *filière* enterprises, and that of 'quasi integration' to describe the growth of vertical cooperative arrangements and networks. Hence, too, the growing importance of a 'voice' rather than an 'exit' strategy in customer–supplier relations (Helper, 1993).[14]

This closer inter-firm cooperation on innovation and quality upgrading has also extended to the prompt and reliable delivery if another characteristic of the flexible production system – viz. keeping the costs of inventories down – is to be accomplished. Thus the need for close and timely contact with several suppliers has tended to encourage clusters of firms situated within a few hours' travelling distance of each other.

Inter-firm cooperation has not only been confined to suppliers. As we have seen, the rising costs of innovation, the need for speedy adjustment to technological change, and the fact that technology is becoming increasingly systemic or generic in its character means that firms need to share the costs and risks of R&D, and often to do so with firms who, in many other respects, are their competitors. Indeed, such alliances have been the most rapidly growing form of international business activity over the last decade (Hagedoorn, 1993). Such interactive learning and innovation, achieved by the loose coupling of firms in alliance capitalism, is in marked contrast to the active pursuit of a vertical or horizontal integrated strategy of hierarchical firms.[15]

The growing integration between the innovatory and production functions of firms, the disaggregation of the value chain, the miniaturization of key components and the increasing importance of networks and alliances in knowledge sharing and joint development is having enormous implications for the ecosystems and organizational structures of firms. Increasingly, the way in which a firm manages its assets and combines these with the external economies offered by the system of which it is part is becoming as important a competitive advantage as the possession of the assets themselves. This is why the flexible production system has been called 'organocentric' in contrast to the 'technocentric' or 'machinocentric' production system of the Fordist era and why the 'hierarchical' enterprise is being replaced by the 'alliance' enterprise, and by 'enterprise networks' (Sydow, 1992).

At the same time, the post-Fordism production system is upgrading both the quality and the status of some kinds of labour. Labour is now regarded more as a multifunctional asset than as a cost; and as a critical participant in the wealth-creating process. The *quid pro quo* of industrial relations has also changed. In exchange for job security and more involvement in the decision-taking process, the individual worker has to be prepared to switch jobs on the factory floor, to be continually retrained, and to be part of a team-based organization of work designed to promote the functional integration of tasks. In flexible production, the pyramidal structure of decision taking, which was a hallmark of hierarchical capitalism, is superseded by a flatter and more heterarchical system of governance. The entrepreneurial process is being decentralized to middle and front line management, as top management increasingly sees its function as a creator of organizational purpose and a setter of performance standards (Bartlett and Ghoshal, 1994).

I have described at some length the characteristics of the flexible or innovation-led techno-economic system,[16] because it is likely to have far-reaching implications for the future path of globalization, and, in particular, for sustainable development. These I shall turn to discuss very shortly. But, let me first acknowledge that, although the flexible system is challenging the scale paradigm as the dominant mode of organizing production, different countries, sectors, firms and plants have embraced the principles and procedures of the system to different degrees. It is, for example, no accident that it has taken deepest root in Japan and in the auto industry, as economic, cultural and institutional conditions in that country and that industry particularly favoured its adoption. Today, the name Toyotism is synonymous with the concepts of demand-driven production, pull-through work flow, zero defect components, just in time delivery, total quality management, and with the way in which the flagship, or core firm, in any network of relationships empowers and guides the various activities of the network.

In the last decade, political, economic, technological forces have all combined to encourage the widespread adoption of flexible production systems and alliance capitalism. It is, for example, a system better suited than its predecessor to the production of dynamic goods and of producer services. At the same time, the internationalization of networks and cooperative arrangements would not have been possible without the liberalization of cross-border markets, or without the recognition by anti-trust authorities that some forms of cooperation between firms promote the objectives of a market economy rather than impede them.

In short, the globalization of economic activity, coupled with network-related flexible production systems, is changing the face of capitalism – and in the main, for the good. In the Triad countries, at least, bureaucratic and authoritarian regimes of hierarchical governance are being replaced – albeit sometimes at a very slow pace – by less adversarial relationships between the various participants in the wealth-creating process. The governance of production, itself, relies as much on the discipline of mutual trust, forbearance and consensus, and the readiness to exchange ideas and to share tasks and responsibilities as on legalistic work rules, sanctions and the threat of punitive action.

Alliance capitalism is also reconfiguring the location of production, but how much it decentralizes the key wealth-creating activities of firms depends on the nature of the alliances formed. While some industrial districts and clusters of related activities are mainly made up of small to medium-sized firms, the majority of networks now being formed are comparable to a stellar galaxy in which a central star outlines the rest. According to Bennett Harrison (1994), although small and medium-sized firms are likely to play a more important role in alliance capitalism, most will still be part of networks dominated by large or flagship firms. As examples, he cites the global webs of small firms centred around Benetton – the Italian clothing firm – and Nike, the giant running shoe TNC. Harrison argues that both production systems illustrate the principle of 'concentration without centralization'; and the fact that network relationships may be highly asymmetrical and foster, rather than inhibit, dualism in cross-border labour markets. However, there are exceptions to this rule. The knitwear industry in the province of Modena in Northern Italy comprises over 4000 firms, most of which are extremely small, and comprised of artisans and their families and friends[17] (Lazerson, 1993).

For national governments and socio-institutional systems, the key implications of globalization and alliance capitalism are twofold. The first is that the cross-border mobility of created assets – especially knowledge and information – is widening the locational options of firms – and particularly TNCs. Hence it follows that actions by national governments which affect the profitability and competitiveness of these firms may also influence the former's ability to attract or retain the latter's presence.

The second implication for national governments is that the kind of complementary assets required by firms to create or sustain their own core competences, and to exploit them efficiently, are frequently influenced by the actions of such governments. The assurance of an educated labour force and of telecommunications services of international standards are the most obvious examples. This suggests that if it is to succeed, alliance capitalism needs a less confrontational and more cooperative partnership between the private and public sector than that which existed (and still exists) under hierarchical capitalism.[18]

The net result of these attributes is that the kind of governmental action needed to facilitate an efficient market system in the current phase of internationalization is very different from that of the other two. While accepting the fact that in a market economy, firms are the main wealth creators and that most attempts by government to intervene in the decisions of firms have been counterproductive (and incidentally, the Japanese score card in this respect is no better than the US or European scorecard),[19] it is, nevertheless, the case that governments are being forced to give more attention to ensuring that the economic environment over which they have some influence is conducive to promoting competitiveness. I shall return to this point later.

The new system of flexible production also has important implications for the geography of economic activity. If the competitiveness of firms is advanced by being part of a domestic network of activities – the Japanese *keiretsu* is a classic example – by continuous process improvement (*kaizen*) and by just in time (JIT) system of deliveries, it is reasonable to suppose that these same firms might be reluctant to engage in foreign production. At the same time, I have suggested that, as competition becomes more global, firms cannot avoid extending their territorial horizons to capture new markets, acquire new knowledge, monitor the behaviour of their competitors and secure cheaper sources of supply. This puts the relational firm in a dilemma. While ideally it may prefer to service global markets from a home base, it, more than the hierarchical firm, recognizes the value of establishing ongoing and symbiotic relationships with foreign suppliers, customers, governments and workers. Sometimes, the relational firm may attempt to short-circuit this process by encouraging other members of its domestic network to move abroad with it. This, for example, explains the substantial presence of Japanese-owned auto component affiliates in the US, Asian and European networks of the Japanese auto assemblers.[20]

The importance of combining the global and local dimensions of transnational business strategy is becoming increasingly acknowledged by scholars and practitioners alike. Several years ago, Akita Morita, the Chairman of Sony, coined the expression 'glocalization' to depict a situation in which firms – Janus-like – worked in two dimensions at once – the global and the local. While seeking to reap the benefits of cross-border integration, the glocalizing firm also took care to acknowledge and respect differences in consumer preferences, business customs, cultural values and worker attitudes across countries. This, however, does not mean that adaptation must only be one way. According to Percy Barnevik, the Chief Executive Officer of Asea Brown Boveri (ABB),

> Global managers have exceptionally open minds. They respect how different countries do things and they have the imagination to appreciate why they do them in that way. But, they are also incisive, they push the limits of the culture. Global managers do not passively accept it when someone says you cannot do that in Italy or Spain because of the unions or you cannot do that in Japan because of the Ministry of Finance. They sort through the debris of cultural excuses and find opportunities to innovate.[21]

All this suggests that there are many and diverse spatial implications of the globalizing economy. At the one extreme, we have the example of the integration of the world's financial markets. As Walter Wriston (1992) has observed:

> The new world financial market is not a geographical location to be found on a map, but rather more than 200,000 electronic monitors in trading rooms all over the world that are linked together.[22]

At the other extreme, even the most globalized integrated firm must respond to a range of government laws and regulations which go down to state, county or town level within a country. In between these two extremes is the regional dimension in which, as I have said, most international integration of production by TNCs has, so far, taken place.

I do not wish to get into the debate of whether the structural integration of regions is a building block or a stumbling block towards globalization. As it has so far progressed, it is probably a little of each. The evidence suggests that, while firms initially choose to extend their territorial boundaries by trading with or investing in neighbouring countries, or in countries in which they have language or ethnic ties, the amount of inter-regional trade, investment and alliances in high-technology sectors exceeds that of its intra-regional equivalent. At the same time, there is no denying that there are critical areas of tension and conflict between regions separated by economic or psychic distance which, if not removed, could lead to the formation of regional fortresses. Unfortunately, most of these are a reflection of institutional and structural impediments which cannot easily be resolved within the context of existing international regimes; but, over time, and particularly, if the authority of these regimes could be widened and strengthened, I think it unlikely that regional economic interests will thwart the benefits of globalization. On the other hand, there are other areas of nationhood-related tensions now emerging, which compels me to take a less optimistic view of the future. These I will return to a little later.

I would like to make one other observation before considering some of the effects of globalization: the flexible production system and alliance capitalism are not only reshaping the socio-institutional structure of domestic economic activity; they are also promoting new modalities of cross-border transactions. Clearly, movements towards regional and corporate integration reinforce each other; economic and political forces complement each other; and networks of firms lock nations into regional or global webs of interdependence. On the road to globalization, there are signs that nations, like firms, are reassembling the building blocks of interdependence. This has important implications for both the sovereignty and legitimacy of nation states.

THE CONSEQUENCES OF GLOBALIZATION

I now turn to examine some of the likely consequences of globalization for economic development. In doing so, I propose to argue that just as globalization is qualitatively different from previous stages of internationalization, so its effects on development are distinctive. Indeed, I wish to go further and suggest that the international economic order of the 1970s is no longer appropriate for the 1990s, and that this needs to be replaced by what we might call a global economic order.

So far in this chapter, I have painted an optimistic view of globalization, and it is true that the structural transformation of the world now occurring does hold out great promise for the future. It is also the case that the political changes and technological advances of the last decade have provided a stronger basis for economic growth than at any other time since the mid-1940s. The world has the necessary resources, knowledge and experience. It has the technical means by which these assets can be transmitted between countries. It has the economic systems, policies, institutions and structures capable of translating human and physical resources into the goods and services which people want. Moreover, at first sight, the 'organocentric' production system, with its focus on smaller production runs, multi-purpose machinery, economies of scope, and relational networking; its renewed reliance on the 'putting out' of some value activities; and its greater respect for the individual in the workplace, appears to be particularly well suited to the needs and capabilities of developing countries, and to the linking of these with those of the flagship nations in the global economy.

Already, we see signs of the fruits of alliance capitalism in East Asia, where much of the expansion of cross-border activity has taken the form of networking by small and medium-sized firms. We also see a much greater willingness of the newly emerging TNCs from China, Korea, Mexico and Thailand to collaborate with local firms than was earlier demonstrated by their US and European counterparts. To my mind, one of the great promises for development which ranks at least as highly as regional integration and intra-Southern hemisphere trade and investment is the emergence of a new brand of capitalism which blends the richness of the Confucian ethos of cooperation with that of the staunch individualistic culture of the West.

Unfortunately, however, there are down-sides to globalization. There is, in John Naisbitt's words, 'a global paradox' (Naisbitt, 1994). The most immediate and visible consequences of the down-side – which all countries of the world are currently experiencing – is the increase in structural unemployment brought about by competitive pressures, the implementation of new technologies and the introduction of more market-oriented and, in the long run, I believe, more employment-creating systems of governance. Across the globe, for developed and developing countries alike, change is bringing economic hardship. And it is transforming the lifestyles of people, and their expectations about the future. Nowhere is this more conspicuously seen than in Central and Eastern Europe, and in the dynamic, but internationally mobile, sectors of economic activity.

It has long been recognized that the invisible hand of the market is only acceptable if there is some way that the losers from market forces are compensated by the winners, and this primarily means helping the losers to adjust to political and technological change. And, as I see it, the possible Achilles' heel of globalization and alliance capitalism is that they could so easily become dysfunctional if they cannot accommodate the desires of ordinary men and women looking for and willing to work, and, if they (and I include in they the actions of governments) fail to equip individuals with the skills and talents necessary for the kind of jobs which are now being created.

This, indeed, is one of the most daunting challenges of the 1990s. For there can surely be little doubt that long-term unemployment is one of the most socially divisive and destabilizing forces of modem times. While, as we have seen, the innovation-led production system offers more purposeful, responsible, and rewarding job opportunities for those in work, it does not, in itself, help reduce unemployment – at least not in the short run. This is because the new system requires a different mix of labour skills than the one it is replacing, and to match these needs, not only do labour markets need to be more flexible, but quite huge retraining programmes are needed.

More generally, if global economic interdependence offers the prospects of higher productivity and living standards, it also more closely links national economies to exogenous financial and other disturbances. The world economy of the 1990s is intrinsically more fragile and vulnerable than that of 30, 40 or 50 years ago. No longer is it just the case that if the US sneezes, the world catches a cold. Economic shocks originating in any one of the five or six leading economies are now electronically and instantaneously transmitted across the globe, with possibly devastating effects on nations which may have had nothing to do with the causes of the shocks. Even being part of a micro-network of value-adding activities can bring external costs, as well as external benefits to the participating firms. This is why a much more systemic approach to the management of macro-economic affairs, and a more educated understanding of the spatial implications of economic turbulences, needs to be high on the political agenda of national and regional governments in the next ten years.

If a globalizing economy may lead to greater economic instability, it may also have unacceptable – not to say frightening – implications for national security, social dumping, environmental erosion, the spread of epidemics, drug abuse, terrorism and ethnic violence. Bad news travels just as fast as good news; and crime, disease and war know fewer territorial boundaries than once they did. Other than acknowledge their critical moment, it is not my intention to deal with these non-economic issues of globalization here. In this respect, however, I would like to draw your attention to the *Commission on Global Governance*, set up, two years ago, in Geneva.[23] The purpose of the Commission is to examine the implications of the kind of global integration we have been considering for the governance of the world community. Its task goes well beyond the economic implications of globalization. Indeed its central concern is with issues of peace, security, the environment, poverty and democratic values, and the adequacy, legitimacy and transparency of existing institutions to effectively cope with these issues. I welcome this Commission, and am particularly pleased that the structure of its membership – composed, as it is, of 29 members drawn from every walk of life and from 25 different countries – is, itself, an excellent example of the kind of networking I have been identifying in this chapter.

I would, however, like to make just two brief points. The first is that while the forces of globalization are leading to a convergence of the spending habits of the world's consumers, they are also exposing substantial differences in the way people think and behave. Indeed, not all countries welcome the effects of globalization, as they fear it may erode their traditional lifestyles. As I have observed, this leads to a global dilemma. On the one hand, the universality of such goods as the motor car, the television set, the Sony Walkman, Coca-Cola, hamburgers and jeans, and such services as tourism, sport and pop music, are leading to cultural convergence. On the other, most people want to remain loyal to their distinctive customs and institutions. The task of resolving this dilemma peacefully is, indeed, likely to tax the minds of both scholars and politicians well into the next century. How, for example, does one balance the advantages of sovereignty with those of interdependence, of homogeneity with diversity, of centralization with decentralization, of communitarism with individualism and so on? There is, of course, nothing new in these perplexities, but globalization has put them in a new and starker perspective, and given their resolution a new urgency.

There seems little doubt that the end of the cold war, and the growing pressures towards economic 'at-oneness', are refocusing the attention of people towards cultural and ideological and religious issues, over which – let me remind you – most of the wars in history have been fought. I also sense that the battle lines being drawn are not primarily between the haves and have nots, but between groups of nations with different ways of looking at the world. The picture painted by Samuel Huntington in a recent issue of *Foreign Affairs* (1993) on the future relationships between the major civilizations of the world is not an optimistic one. My own feeling is that there is more in common among the ideologies and religions of these civilizations – at least what they preach about attitudes and conduct – than there are differences, and that a focus on these similarities, rather than on the differences, offers the best hope for the global peace.

My second comment must be even shorter. I have already referred to the dominant organizational system now evolving as that of alliance capitalism. This is because the unit of economic activity – the individual firm – in order to fully promote its own objectives, needs – and needs increasingly to be part of – i.e. allied to – a network or web of related activities. I believe that this concept can be extended to a global level. From the time of the Roman Empire and beyond, history is littered with the debris of once all-powerful nations. For much of the nineteenth century, the UK really did rule the economic waves. The pound sterling was the business currency of the world and the principles of the craft system were practised by all industrial countries. The mantle of economic leadership passed to the US around 1870, and the mass, or scale, production system became the symbol of its hegemony. But today there is no single dominant nation. Instead, as Dr Fred Bergsten (1990) has observed, it is likely that the leadership of the world over the next century will have to be collectively shared by the European Community, Japan and the US. Such an alliance of flagship nations, particularly if widened to embrace China – which, according to some authorities, already has the second largest GNP in the world – will require all the bonding characteristics of inter-firm collaborative schemes – and some more!

THE DEVELOPING ECONOMIES

But what of the developing countries? How and where do they fit into the future? What, indeed, does globalization mean for the trajectory of economic development? I have paid too little attention to the specific problems and needs of the developing world so far in this chapter, this is partly because I believe the opportunities and challenges of globalization cut across the traditional North/South divide, and partly because, over the next 25 years, it is likely that many millions of the descendants of yesterday's impoverished generation will come to enjoy at least the basic creature comforts which we, in the richer countries, so easily take for granted.

But that is in the future, and, notwithstanding the possibility that the East Asian miracle might spread Westwards to India and Northwards to China, and that more developing countries will be drawn into North–South regional integration schemes, I think there is little prospect that most of the poorer countries in the Southern hemisphere will derive much immediate benefit from the new global economic order. Indeed, according to the Division on TNCs and Investment of UNCTAD, the share of new FDI going to the least developed nations in the early 1990s was only one-half that of the 1980s (UNCTAD, 1994).

At the same time, the prospects for economic growth in the 1990s are considerably better than that actually achieved in the 'lost' decade of the 1980s. The World Bank has projected that, on average, the GDP growth rate of developing countries will be 4.7 per cent per annum between 1992 and 2002, and that even in the poorest countries – excluding India and China – the rate of growth will be 3.5 per cent (World Bank, 1993a).

The World Bank offers four main reasons for its cautious optimism. The first is that the macro-economic and organizational reforms introduced in the 1980s are now starting to show results. The second is that internal supply-side sources of growth, e.g. domestic savings rates, incentives to invest and the emergence of a production system less dependent on the economies of scale, are expected to improve. The third is that commodity prices are predicted to stabilize in real terms – a sharp break from their 20-year declining trend. And, the fourth cause for optimism is the increased flow of capital now being directed to the third world. Between 1987 and 1992, for example, developing countries attracted 30 per cent of the new FDI compared with 20 per cent for most of the previous decade. Private portfolio flows rose even more dramatically – from $6 billion per year between 1982 and 1988 to $34 billion in 1992 (World Bank, 1993a). In recent years, too, such investments have been supplemented by new financial instruments, e.g. debt–equity swaps, depository receipts, and also by the setting up of new financial institutions, e.g. the European Development Bank.

Overall, then, I sense that the portent for real growth in the developing world – taken as a whole – are probably better than they have been for many years.

There is a huge untapped reservoir of young and energetic manpower and an equally huge unmet set of consumer needs waiting to be activated; and the example of countries like Japan and Singapore, which lack the natural resources which were the foundation of nineteenth-century development, ought to provide good heart to even the poorest of countries. Increasingly, as we have seen, the key to economic prosperity in the twenty-first century lies in the ability of firms and countries to acquire and create new knowledge – and in the case of smaller developing nations, new markets.

To what extent is economic development currently being led by exogenous – mainly Triad-related – globalizing forces, and to what extent is it being endogenously induced? The answer to these questions will obviously vary from country to country, depending, for example, on the size and structure of the economy, its stage of development, and the government policies it pursues. However, even the larger and most prosperous developing countries now accept that – to paraphrase John Donne – 'no nation in this global age can afford to be an island'. The only question at issue is 'how far', 'with whom', 'in what way' and 'by what means' should developing countries engage in alliance capitalism.

I earlier suggested that the hierarchical production system was centrifugal in as much as it decentralized the production of labour-intensive activities to low-wage countries. This resulted in a scale-related division of labour, with consequences broadly similar to those arising from the resource-based division of labour in the nineteenth century. While this system aided development, it was an uneven development. While it encouraged interdependence, it was an asymmetrical interdependence. All too frequently, the foreign sector was not fully integrated into the host economy; as a result, the syndrome of the dual economy began to emerge.

In both kinds of international specialization, it was the smaller economies which usually benefited the most, although both in Latin America and East Asia, regional integration schemes did lead to some intra-regional alliance capitalism. Most larger developing countries also had trading and investment links with the developed world, but, as the main objective of several of these economies – particularly in the 1970s – was to use these links as a means of advancing their own economic autonomy, there were few genuine cross-border alliances and only a limited transfer of organizational systems.

The embracing of alliance capitalism, at a time when most developing nations are modifying their internal economic strategies to better benefit from economic interdependence, is encouraging such countries to play a more pro-active role in the globalizing economy. At the same time, the extent which alliance capitalism is primarily a phenomena of the Triad nations is yet to be seen. Certainly, outside the apparel and footwear industries, the great majority of joint ventures and networks so far concluded have been between firms in the dynamic industrial or service sectors, and to involve at least one developed nation (Hagedoorn, 1993). Moreover, the experience of smaller European nations, both within and outside the EU, suggests that their counterparts in the developing world may find it extremely difficult to create the sophisticated infrastructure which networks require.

History also suggests that the winners are likely to be those developing countries which can offer the best educational and communication infrastructures to foreign firms, and are geographically close to the industrial heartland of the Triad. However, by the late 1990s, it may be expected that at least the larger and more prosperous developing countries will have built up their own internal networks, and that their firms will have established alliances with firms from developing countries in the same region. In so doing, they will take the first step towards developing-world-led globalization. Indeed, it is already occurring in the Chinese economic space of East Asia, and in the Malaysian–Thailand axis. And, as more Latin American countries adopt outward-looking development strategies, it is likely to happen there too (World Bank, 1993c). By contrast, because of ethnic, religious and cultural differences, the prospects for intra-regional integration in East Asia, the Middle East and much of sub-Saharan Africa would seem less promising.

Although, as we have suggested, there are aspects of flexible production systems and interactive learning which favour the resources and capabilities of developing countries and may lead to a revitalization of the 'putting-out' system of production, there are others, notably the increasing role played by costly created assets in the competitive process, and the need for a physically close and ongoing relationship between firms in dynamic sectors along the value chain,[24] which are centripetal in their effects. Because of this, it follows that, at least for the foreseeable future, and with the possible exception of China and India, developing countries are unlikely to be the flagships of global alliance capitalism. However, there are reasons to suppose that some at least could become hubs of regional alliance capitalism. Singapore is already bidding to be the leading financial and high-technology centre and cruise gateway of South East Asia, while US computer firms are increasingly favouring the Caribbean as a regional centre for their software facilities.

For the poorer developing countries, most of which are far removed from the critical nodes of growth, the impact of globalization and alliance capitalism is likely to be marginal – except in so far as they may benefit from a 'trickle-down' effect of some kinds of subcontracting.[25] This, however, should not be taken to mean that these countries will not benefit from other economic events in the 1990s; but rather that any such gains will be the outcome of internal economic and institutional reforms, and of the higher spending power of the faster-growing nations; and, in the case of resource-rich countries, the stabilization of commodity prices, the direction of resource-related innovation and the emergence of new sources of supply. But, in their attempts to upgrade their wealth-creating abilities, I believe that the least developed nations will continue to have to rely mainly on aid and loans from foreign governments and international institutions. This is simply because their most pressing need is to improve their educational, legal and commercial infrastructures which, in the past at least, private investors have been unwilling to finance.

At the same time, with the introduction of more market-oriented macro-organizational policies, I would expect the threshold at which FDI becomes viable to fall. I would also like to think that such policies – and the kind of technological advances I earlier described – will make it easier for both governments and firms from the poorer nations to explore the possibility of partnerships and cross-border alliances, and the promotion of more regional economic cooperation.

It would be interesting to know what Raúl Prebisch's reactions would have been to flexible production systems and alliance capitalism. On the one hand, as I have suggested, it probably lowers the obstacles facing firms from developing countries in upgrading their competitive advantages, as the *ownership* links with firms from developed countries are no longer as critical as they once were. Moreover, the optimum size of many value-added activities is falling, where the opportunities for out-sourcing to even the smallest firms are opening up. Individual entrepreneurship is also playing a more important role in the 'new' competition (Best, 1990). On the other hand, I have argued that, to be successful, a post-Fordist firm needs to maintain a close and ongoing access to the assets and capabilities of other firms; and it is the extent to which such firms are located in other countries, and/or are dominated by large TNCs, that is likely to determine whether or not developing countries can truly evolve and sustain a path of economic development which best suits their own interests. Prebisch's advocacy of closer networking among firms from developing countries is as appropriate today as it was 25 years ago, as, indeed, was his belief in a strong and supportive role of government in the developmental process, a subject to which I now turn.

THE IMPLICATIONS OF GLOBALIZATION FOR NATIONAL GOVERNMENTS

For the last section of this chapter, I would like to consider some of the consequences of globalization and alliance capitalism for national governments and international economic regimes. Unquestionably, the most significant of these arises from the increasing ease with which competitiveness-enhancing assets can move across national boundaries. This means that any action governments might take which affect the competitiveness of these assets cannot be divorced from the actions taken by other governments. The theory of competing governments suggests that, in the last resort, a country's citizens can respond to high taxation – or any other unacceptable government policies – by 'voting with their feet' (Brennan and Buchanan, 1985), i.e. by emigrating to another country. This idea can readily be extended to explain the locational choices of firms, as they may be affected by tax and macro-organizational policies. No longer can governments assume that the firms, resources and capabilities presently located in their areas of jurisdiction are inextricably bound to those territories, nor that they are impotent to attract resources and capabilities now sited in other countries. Finally, there are suggestions that the actions of governments are becoming increasingly interdependent on each other. Governments – on behalf of their constituents, and like firms – may compete as oligopolists.[26]

Yet, while most large TNCs have responded to the demands of globalization and alliance capitalism by reconfiguring their organizational structures and decision-taking procedures, there is little evidence that governments have elected to do so. The result is that most are singularly ill equipped to deal with the consequences of globalization. Exceptions include some East Asian administrations, which are not only taking a more holistic approach to the organization of their tasks and functions, but are replacing a 'hub and spoke' hierarchical structure of governance by a 'spider's web' network structure, in order to encourage more fruitful interdepartmental exchanges of information and cross-fertilization of ideas.

I believe that the main reason for the reluctance of governments to embrace new structures of governance is the inflexibility and intransigence of established institutional regimes, and the opposition of powerful sectoral interests within the executive branch to changing the *status quo*. It is, I think, no accident that the administrations with the least institutional impedimenta are those which are most successfully adapting to the needs of the global marketplace. To this extent, developing nations could well have a comparative organizational advantage – particularly if their cultures are sympathetic to alliance capitalism.

The second issue I wish to raise concerns the direct impact of government behaviour on the competitiveness of the firms located in their territories. This impact arises because many of the complementary assets needed by firms to create and effectively exploit their core competences are, themselves, government owned or influenced. This suggests that the ability of governments and private firms to work together (e.g. with respect to innovatory activities, retraining, environmental protection and the promotion of inter-firm alliances) might be a competitive advantage in its own right. Again, developing countries would do well to take note of this particular aspect of alliance capitalism as they seek to evolve their unique strengths in a global economy.

The third consequence of globalization is that it requires national governments to reappraise their role as overseers of economic activity. To the economist, the only justification for such a role is that the net benefits arising from it can be achieved at a lower real cost than any other form of organization, such as the market, individual hierarchies or networks of firms. It has long been recognized that, as well as being responsible for the defence of the realm, law and order, and the definition and enforcement of property rights, governments are particularly well equipped to supply – or to organize the supply of – some kinds of public and social goods, and especially those whose benefits accrue as much to the community at large as to the producing institution.

Yet there is nothing fixed or immutable about *which* organizational form is best suited to produce particular products. Yesterday's case for the public ownership of public utilities or transportation systems may no longer hold today. Technological developments, for example, have undermined most of the *raison d'être* for a government monopoly of mail and telephone services. New methods of monitoring and charging for the use of highways have better enabled private firms to supply these products, while the growth of inter-firm networks offers an alternative to government funding of expensive capital projects.

At the same time, it would be wrong to conclude that the renaissance of the market system should reduce the role of government to a minimalist one. It is yet another paradox of globalization and alliance capitalism that, to ensure its efficient functioning, there needs to be a closer cooperation between the public and private sectors. The underlying characteristics of most markets of the 1990s are very different from those of the craft or the scale production eras. There is more uncertainty attached to them. The specificity of assets has enormously increased. There is more information asymmetry between buyers and sellers. There are more opportunities for opportunism. Markets cost more to set up and monitor, and they generate more externalities than once they did. Underlying demand and supply conditions are continually changing; and an increasing number of products are taken on the form of 'public' goods. Moreover, globalization brings with it its own governance costs, such as those which arise from the structural integration of different cultures and institutional regimes. At the same time, the market system is *par excellence* an example of a social good; and it is the government's responsibility to see that this system works to the interests of its constituents.

Too often, I believe, governments, hierarchies and markets are considered as substitutes to each other. This is a fake dichotomy. Today's economy requires a plurality of organizational modes, each working in tandem with the other – each supporting the other. Too often taxation is regarded as a necessary evil, rather than a price which has to be paid for the supply of competitiveness-enhancing public or social goods and services. Too often, too, governments are perceived as regulatory and controlling agencies rather than as facilitators of markets, and as suppliers or stimulators of the appropriate learning systems and mind sets for the upgrading of human and physical assets.

Elsewhere (Dunning, 1994) I have asserted the need for a fundamental rethink of the functions of government, or, if you like, a 'perestroika' of government. This, I believe, is not primarily a question of increasing government expenditure – although the demands of technological change may require large sums of money to be spent on infrastructure (especially in the area of worker retraining and innovatory activities), but of reconstructing the building blocks of governance to achieve a more holistic and integrated set of macro-economic and macro-organizational policies.[27]

In many respects, governments of developing countries are in a good position to meet the demands of the global economy. In almost all countries there is a history of strong interventionist governments, and also an ability to change trajectory speedily. In the last decade, there has not only been a marked realignment in macro-economic policies, but also a movement towards a less confrontational stance between governments and the business community. Some of the actions taken – such as the introduction of the policies I have already identified – normally take several years to have any real effect. Others involve major institutional and attitudinal changes, which could take a generation or more to accomplish.

But as a guide to the principles of modern government, I can do no better than refer to a recently published book by two US scholars, David Osborne and Ted Gaebler (1992) called *Reinventing Government*. While the authors are mainly directing their thoughts to an American audience, I think what they have to say is no less relevant to governments all over the world. Chapter titles such as 'Entrepreneurial Government', 'Competitive Government', 'Catalyst Government', 'Flexible and Adaptable Government', 'Empowering Government', 'Mission Driven Government', 'Market Oriented Government', 'Anticipatory Government', 'Consensus Government' and 'Customer Driven Government' give some of the flavour of what the authors are recommending. But it all comes down to the need for a reconsideration of what government is, or should be, about, and if the discipline of globalization hastens this reconsideration, I welcome it.

INTERNATIONAL REGIMES

I cannot, however, end this chapter without making some reference to the role of supranational forms of governance. Because of space constraints, I will do little more than acknowledge the role of privately sponsored international associations or consortia of firms.

Perhaps the most frequently asked question about globalization is:

> As the globe is becoming more structurally integrated by the activities of large and powerful private corporations, and also by the actions of national governments to protect the interests of their own citizens, does this not require some form of supranational polity to ensure that the behaviour of both corporations and national governments is consistent with global economic welfare?

I propose to answer this question by identifying the circumstances in which supranational economic regimes are likely to be a superior form of governance to markets, hierarchies, networks of firms or individual governments. I hope you have recognized some logical progression in my analysis. I began by discussing the costs and benefits of alternative forms of organizing production and transactions by firms within a market-oriented economy, and how these costs and benefits had changed over time. I then went on to suggest that if they were to properly fulfil their social function, techno-economic production systems – be they made up of individual firms or networks of firms – required a macro-organizational framework which only governments, as custodians of the interests of their citizens, could provide. Again, because of technological advances, changes in economic policies and the opening up of the world economy, this framework itself became increasingly questioned. In particular, I argued that in the contemporary age of alliance capitalism, governments needed not only to take a more systemic approach to their varied economic functions, but also to better recognize that, because of the increased mobility of wealth-creating assets, they are increasingly competing with each other for investment.

There are two main reasons why supranational regimes may be necessary in a global economy. The first is that the unilateral behaviour of governments, which is geared to promote the good of their own citizens, may not be globally welfare maximizing. This is because of the possible adverse effects, i.e. negative externalities, of this behaviour on the citizens of another nation. These might arise, for example, from the pursuance of geo-economic and rent-seeking strategies by one government which might lead to retaliatory action by other governments. The 'beggar-my-neighbour' trade sanctions imposed by governments of industrial countries in the inter-war years are a classic example of welfare-reducing policies, and it was precisely to deter this kind of behaviour that GATT was established in 1946 to draw up the 'rules of the game' for international trade. But, as we have seen, the globalization of the world economy has considerably widened the scope of competition and interdependence among governments. This has, consequently, enlarged the international playing arena, and has made it necessary for more rules to be established if geo-economic conflict is to be avoided, and the game is to be played fairly and to the benefit of all (Luttwak, 1993).

The second reason for supranational regimes is that there are some cross-border market failures which cannot be fully compensated for, or surmounted, either by the actions of hierarchies or by national governments. The presence of international politico-market failure is most dramatically seen in the fields of satellite communications, the exploration of the sea bed, the protection of the ozone layer, environmental pollution and military security. In each of these instances, supra- or inter-governmental action may be necessary either to reduce the coordinating and transaction costs of such activities, or to capture the extra-territorial benefits of inter-country networking. The twenty-first century seems certain to witness a growing number of these international public and social goods, each of which will require pluralist governance structures if they are to work for the global good.[28]

It is, perhaps, worth reminding ourselves that inter-government cooperation on non-economic matters dates back many years. Agreements on technical standards, weights and measures, and meteorological systems were all first concluded in the last century. However, the idea that supranational regimes may be an appropriate means of governing *economic* activity is relatively new, and is still very controversial. But, two things should be said. The first is that it is becoming increasingly difficult to distinguish between what is and is not an economic activity. For example, each of the examples of politico-market failures I have just described affect, in some way of other, the infrastructure of modern economic activity. The second is that the emergence of the global economy, alliance capitalism and the widening competing interface between governments is forcing a reappraisal of our attitudes towards the role of trans-national economic regimes.

There are essentially two ways of implementing supranational governance. The first is by the subordination of the sovereignty of nationhood to some kind of supranational authority. One form of such subordination is a merger of nation states – which, carried to its extreme – leads to world government. While all the evidence seems to point to the disintegration, rather than the integration, of nation states, we are also witnessing – and here there are some interesting parallels with what is happening in the corporate world – the growth of inter-country alliances, or networks. These are usually set up to achieve a specific objective, but they all address problems, challenges and opportunities which can only be effectively dealt with at a supranational level.

In the economics arena, however, supranational control is likely to be primarily exercised at a functional or issue level. In spite of the recent protracted and tortuous GATT negotiations, there is a lot of room for grafting other issues onto the GATT agenda. The indirect ways in which national governments can, for good or bad, affect trade and FDI are growing all the time. Besides the most obvious of below-cost competition, i.e. dumping, price competition, industrial, environmental and social policy can all be used as instruments for tilting the level of the playing fields. Perhaps the newly established World Trade Organization (WTO) (I say newly established, although it was first recommended nearly 50 years ago) will provide the institutional framework for this. I believe that international labour standards have already been placed on the agenda of the WTO.

Alongside the strengthening of global governance systems – particularly at an issue level – regional governance systems are also becoming more important. It is much more likely that national governments will be prepared to surrender parts of their economic jurisdiction to a supranational authority made up of nations with similar institutional, cultural and ideological backgrounds to their own than to one which comprises nations which are widely different in these respects.

At the same time, there is nothing to prevent representatives of regional schemes from getting together to discuss issues of extra-regional interest. This, in fact, is what the G7 is mainly about, and it has had a good deal of success in the past. While I would anticipate that regional integration – of one form or another – is likely to be an increasingly preferred way of supranational governance – particularly where the harmonization of national policies is desired – I can foresee a whole set of new alliances among nations being established in the next few years, and these could pose new problems for the coordination of governance itself. Again, I think there are lessons to be learned from the success and failures of inter-firm networking.

The other main (and complementary) avenue to supranational governance[29] is, in many respects, more in the spirit of alliance capitalism, in that its success rests less on mandates and regulations and more on the sharing of ideas, co-operation, trust, reciprocity and forbearance of its participants. The focal aim of this form of polity is to coordinate the actions of national governments in their response to cross-border market failure.

Such attempts to achieve this objective usually originate in the debating chambers of the United Nations and its various agencies, the OECD, the European Community, ASEAN and similar institutions. But the influence of such bodies should not be taken lightly – particularly as it affects developing countries. I certainly do not see these institutions playing a less important role as globalization proceeds; indeed, I am more sanguine that, with the ending of the cold war, and at least some harmonization of economic policies among governments, in tackling the remaining, but no less serious, problems facing the nations of the world, a spirit of fusion, rather than fission, in the ideas expressed and decisions reached will prevail.

In particular, I believe that Raúl Prebisch would have relished the challenges and opportunities now facing UNCTAD. Far from being constrained in its activities by the initiation of such institutions as the WTO, I can envisage it taking on additional responsibilities. In this respect, the arrival of the erstwhile UN Centre on Transnational Corporations in Geneva is of critical significance. For, as I have indicated, both trade and economic development are being increasingly fashioned by the cross-border equity and non-equity investment relationships forged by TNCs. Moreover, as it seems likely that a higher percentage of TNC activity will be directed to developing countries in the next decade or more, it is entirely appropriate UNCTAD should take this new area of research and advisory work under its wing.

But, more than this, UNCTAD has always taken an eclectic view of its terms of reference, and has studied and given advice on many subject areas which indirectly, rather than directly, affect trade and development. Competition policy and environmental issues are just two examples. As an increasing number of trade-related issues, previously thought to be of purely domestic relevance, now increasingly impact on trade, FDI and so UNCTAD's responsibilities should be widened to embrace these. In particular, I foresee matters to do with the evolving techno-economic structure of production and the socio-institutional framework of nations – and especially those of developing nations – as demanding the highest priority as UNCTAD embarks on its next 30 years of research programmes. I wish it well.

In summary, then, I believe that the twin forces of globalization and the movement toward multi-polar, rather than hegemonic, politics are demanding a reappraisal of the kind of supranational regimes that have dominated world politics over the past half-century. The time has surely come to ask such questions as:

> What aspects of the organization of economic activity are best coordinated at an international level; and how is this changing with the advent of the global economy? In what way do the existing supranational institutions need to be revamped to better accommodate the needs of the structural integration of the world economy? How can newly emerging institutions like the EBRD[30] be accommodated into the existing scheme of things, and what are the appropriate rules or regimes for managing the world economy? Should international coordination aim to promote economic convergence or diversity and specialization? Is the current organizational structure of international institutions suited to the needs of the twenty-first century? What form should policy coordination take and how should it be policed in an age of alliance capitalism? To what extent should there be more jointly shared responsibility between supranational institutions and private firms?

It is questions such as these that should be engaging the minds of our best scholars, of the business community and of governments over the next decade.[31]

CONCLUSIONS

To sum up, then, I believe globalization is requiring the adoption of a new form of capitalism – which I have called alliance capitalism – if it is to be successful in promoting economic welfare and sustainable development. The distinctive feature of alliance capitalism is that its success depends upon the harmonious interaction of the wealth-creating constituents in society. Cooperation and competition go side by side; they are opposite sides of the coin of economic progress.

I have argued that the concept of alliance capitalism has relevance for both the micro- and macro-organization of economic activity. As far as the former is concerned, I believe the continual upgrading of consumer demands, the accumulation of created assets and the learning experiences of human beings are the main vehicles of economic progress; and the way in which these resources and capabilities are organized is likely to become an increasingly important determinant of commercial success in the years to come. In particular, I have suggested that, whereas for most of modern history the interaction between individual firms and markets has been the cornerstone of economic development, progress in the globalizing economy is likely to depend more on the way firms create new competitive advantages and manage these in conjunction with the core assets of related firms, while the efficiency of individual firms and markets is increasingly likely to rest on how these firms and markets interact with others which are part of the same network of production and exchange. I have also argued for a close partnership between the various stakeholders of firms, and between firms and governments, particularly in the building of the human and physical infrastructure for tomorrow's wealth-creating activities.

I have further asserted that, in the formation of their macro-economic and organizational strategies, governments are being forced to interact more closely with each other. Sometimes, this interaction takes the form of competition,[32] and sometimes of voluntary or involuntary cooperation. At the same time, the globalizing economy is demanding a re-examination of the scope and authority of supranational economic regimes, both to minimize the global welfare-reducing actions by national governments, and to encourage the harmonization of these actions whenever they can help reduce the costs of organizing cross-border production and transactions.

Finally, I have argued that the transition from hierarchical to alliance capitalism has very considerable implications for sustainable development. On balance, I believe these implications to be welfare-enhancing, although the extent and form of the benefits is likely to differ between sectors and countries. At the same time, I also believe that it is desirable for developing countries to try to create their own networks of value-added and interactive learning activities, and to do so in a way which promotes their own comparative dynamic advantage. I am less optimistic that, in the near future, the most impoverished nations, and particularly those which are most distant from the hubs of economic power, will gain much from globalization *per se*, although the secondary, or spill-over, effects of other economic and political events may be more positive.

I believe that the success of globalization and alliance capitalism will rest on the extent to which the peoples and governments of the world can learn to live in peace and harmony with each other. For, if Samuel Huntington is right and if our global dream is not to be turned into a global nightmare, the clash of civilizations must be avoided.

Now civilizations are – and always have been – largely differentiated by religious convictions. Today – as in the past – there is much which is different between these beliefs, and certainly I see little prospects – nor would I advocate – that one religion should 'take over' another. Yet, as far as the 'rules of the game' which guide the civilized behaviour of individuals and communities are concerned, I believe there is much more which unites Buddhism, Judaism, Islam and Christianity (to name just four of the great religions) than that which divides. Is it too unrealistic to ask that a G7, 8 – or whatever the appropriate number is – of the world's spiritual leaders be convened; and that their brief be to establish common ground rules for the values and behaviour of their followers? A naive or impossible dream? Perhaps. A useless exercise? Maybe. But I fear without some consensus on spiritual values among people of good will from widely different cultures, any gains in material welfare which global interdependence might bring could be completely destroyed by a clash of civilizations, the like of which is too terrible even to contemplate.

NOTES

1. For a contemporary review of this era in international politics, see Kuttner (1991).
2. Notably Best (1990), Gerlach (1992), Lazonick (1992), Kenney and Florida (1993), Harrison (1994) and Oman (1994). In an earlier contribution, Carlota Perez (1983) presented an evolutionary model of the capitalist economy in which she sought to integrate two sub-systems of development – the techno-economic and the social and institutional. She argued, as we do later in this chapter, that new technological trajectories, characterized by 'quantum jumps in the best practice frontier' (Perez, 1983, p. 358), if they are to be successfully implemented and diffused, require adaptations to existing socio-institutional systems, which, in turn, feed back to technological styles or patterns. Perez, however, dealt with only two of the three models of techno-economic production embraced in our chapter, although she acknowledged that the third – i.e. flexible production – was then (i.e. in the early 1980s) beginning to emerge. See also Perez and Freeman (1988).
3. Charles Babbage was the inventor of the calculating machine in 1856, the direct descendant of which is the modern-day computer. For a recent appreciation of the role of Babbage as an economist, see Rosenberg (1994).
4. In their responses to imperfections in both intermediate product and labour markets, and for most of the present century, firms have preferred to adopt an 'exit' rather than a 'voice' strategy (Hirschman, 1970). The former strategy is one by which a problem is circumvented by finding an alternative solution (e.g. the internalization of markets by hierarchies). The latter is to resolve, rather than escape from, the problem (e.g. by working with suppliers and labour representatives to reduce transaction and communication costs, and enhance a spirit of cooperation and goodwill).
5. To give just a couple of figures, in 1914 about two-thirds of FDI was directed to developing countries, and about four-fifths of TNC activity was of a resource-seeking kind; by 1980, both these proportions had fallen to one-quarter (Dunning, 1993a).
6. Examples include the Lomé Convention, and the Multi-fibre Agreement (MFA).

7. What Schumpeter (1947) has called 'creative destruction'.
8. The concept of flexible production is, perhaps, best articulated by Piore and Sabel (1984), Best (1990), OECD (1992) and Ruigrok and Van Tulder (1995), and that of alliance, or collective, capitalism by Gerlach (1992) and Lazonick (1992).
9. Peter Gray has defined nationhood as 'the desire to preserve national identity'. For an exposition of this concept, see especially Gray (1990, 1992) and Gray and Lundan (1994).
10. See Wendt (1993), Barnett and Cavanagh (1994) and Naisbitt (1994).
11. O'Brien (1992), quoted in Kobrin (1993).
12. For a more extensive treatment see, for example, OECD (1992, 1993), Oman (1994), Ruigrok and Van Tulder (1995) and Dunning (1994).
13. In an examination of some of the changes now taking place in the Baden-Württemberg province of Germany, Herrigel (1993) observes there are tensions between managers from the transforming firms (e.g. Robert Bosch) who believe that the systemic logic of Fordism can no longer reproduce itself in the current economic environment of truncated product cycles, rapid technological change and organizational decoupling; and managers from the traditional firms who argue that turbulent markets are ephemeral, that rapid product change and high development costs are more than balanced by traditional products and markets, and that the well-tried strategies of hierarchical fragmentation are still the best way of protecting firm-specific proprietary assets.
14. In contrast to the situation in hierarchical capitalism; see note 12.
15. An extreme example is quoted by Williamson (1985) of the Ford Motor Company's 'behemoth at River Rouge' where its empire included ore lands, coal mines, 70 000 acres of timberland, saw mills, blast furnaces, glass works, ore and coal barges and a railway.
16. Sometimes also called post-Fordism, the New Competition and Toyotism.
17. The Modena 'network' is an example of the resuscitation of the putting-out system which was largely replaced by the factory system of the nineteenth century. Indeed, a feature of alliance capitalism is that it can accommodate a plurality of organizational forms.
18. This point is further taken up in several chapters of Dunning (1993b).
19. A recently published study by Season and Weinstein (1994) for example, finds that Japanese industrial policy in the 1955–90 period was generally unsuccessful in targeting winning sectors.
20. Banerji and Sambharya (1994) have shown, for example, that 27 per cent of the first-tier suppliers to the major Japanese automobile manufacturers have invested in the US. Of the 130 Japanese firms which have invested, 89.2 per cent were members of vertical *keiretsus* dominated by one or other of the leading automobile manufacturers.
21. Quoted in Wendt (1993) p. 100 and initially in Taylor (1991).
22. As quoted in Kobrin (1993).
23. The Commission is a privately sponsored initiative which has the backing of the Secretary General of the United Nations.
24. The increasing need for close proximity would appear to run counter to the reduction in transaction and coordinating costs arising from telecommunication advances. Yet the example of the City of London is instructive. While many of the routine banking, financial and insurance operations have been decentralized, a network of the core and innovating activities remains firmly embedded in the square mile. This is because the perceived gains from face-to-face contact between the constituents of the network are greater than ever. As manufacturing firms – at least in dynamic sectors – upgrade their R&D and skilled labour, they become more closely interdependent in their informational and technological needs; and as trust and forbearance become a more important component of transactions, then, at least at the top end of the value chain and in the early stages of their production cycles, the need for close physical proximity increases rather than diminishes. This need was recognized nearly 30 years ago by Raymond Vernon (1966). The idea of the factory as a research laboratory also suggests closer physical linkages between R&D and production activities (Kenney and Florida, 1993).
25. For example, in the garment and footwear industry, although the first-tier suppliers of flagship MNEs are usually located in the more advanced developing countries, e.g. Hong Kong and Singapore, these suppliers may, themselves, 'put out' the more labour-intensive production processes to small firms and artisans as far afield as Bangladesh, Sri Lanka and Nigeria.

26. This is particularly the case as between governments of countries of a similar size, economic structure and stage of development.
27. Which may, too, embrace some social policies in so far as the outcome of these may no less affect competitiveness.
28. For a more detailed examination of international regimes and politico-market failure, see Eden and Hampson (1990).
29. In this chapter, I do not intend to deal with the issue of bilateral governance.
30. European Bank for Reconstruction and Development.
31. Some of the questions I have listed are precisely those of a three-year research project about to begin at the London Business School (Currie et al., 1993).
32. As described, for example, by Ostrom (1971), quoted in McKenzie and Lee (1991).

REFERENCES

Banerji, K. and Sambharya R.B. (1994), *Vertical Keiretsu and International Market Entry: The Case of the Japanese Automobile Industry*, West Virginia and Rutgers Universities (mimeo).

Barnett, R.J. and Cavanagh, J. (1994), *Global Dreams*, New York: Simon & Schuster.

Bartlett, C.G. and Ghoshal, S. (1994), *Beyond the M-Form: Towards a Managerial Theory of the Firm*, Pittsburgh: Carnegie Bosch Institute for Applied Studies on International Management, Working Paper No. 94–6.

Beason, R. and Weinstein, D. (1994), *Growth, Economies of Scale and Targeting of Japan 1955–1990*, Boston: Harvard Institute of Economic Research, Discussion Paper 1644.

Bergsten, C.F. (1990), 'The world economy after the cold war', *Foreign Affairs* **69**: 96–112.

Best, M. (1990), *The New Competition. Institutions of Restructuring*, Cambridge, MA: Harvard University Press.

Brennan, G. and Buchanan, J.M. (1985), *The Power to Tax*, Cambridge: Cambridge University Press.

Currie, D.A., Hall, S.G.F. and Whitney, J.D. (1993), *Global Institutions and Economic Policy Coordination*, London: Proposal for a research project submitted to and approved by the Economic and Social Research Council.

Dunning, J.H. (1993a), *Multinational Enterprises and the Global Economy*, Wokingham, Berkshire: Addison-Wesley.

Dunning, J.H. (1993b), *The Globalization of Business*, London and New York: Routledge.

Dunning, J.H. (1994), *Globalization: The Challenge for National Economic Regimes*, Dublin: The Economic and Social Research Council.

Eden, L. and Hampson, P.O. (1990), *Clubs are Trumps: Towards a Taxonomy of International Regimes*, Ottawa Centre for International Trade and Investment Policies, Carleton University, C/TIPS 90–102.

Gerlach, M.L. (1992), *Alliance Capitalism: The Social Organization of Japanese Business*, Oxford: Oxford University Press.

Gray, H.P. (1990), 'Free trade, economic integration and nationhood', *Journal of International Economic Integration*, **V**, Spring, 1–12.

Gray, H.P. (1992), 'Economic integration and nationhood: extension', *Journal of International Economic Integration*, **8**, Spring, 58–67.

Gray, H.P. and Lundan, S. (1994), 'Nationhood, the GATT ideal and a workable international trading system', *Banco Nazionale del Lavoro Quarterly Review*, **188**, March, 99–114.

Hagedoorn, J. (1993), 'Strategic technology alliances and modes of cooperation in high technology industries' in Grabher, G. (ed), *The Embedded Firm*, London and New York: Routledge, pp. 116–38.

Harrison, B. (1994), *Lean and Mean: The Changing Landscape of Power in the Age of Flexibility*, New York: Basic Books.

Helper, S. (1993), 'An exit–voice analysis of supplier relationships' in Grabher, G. (ed.), *The Embedded Firm*, London and New York: Routledge.

Herrigel, G.B. (1993), 'Power and the redefinition of industrial districts' in Grabher, G. (ed.), *The Embedded Firm*, London and New York: Routledge.

Hirschman, A. (1970), *Exit, Voice and Loyalty*, Cambridge, MA: Harvard University Press.

Huntington, S. (1993), 'The clash of civilizations', *Foreign Affairs*, **72**, Summer, 22–49.

Kenney, M. and Florida, R. (1993), *Beyond Mass Production*, Oxford and New York: Oxford University Press.

Kobrin, S.J. (1993), *Beyond Geography: Inter-Firm Networks and the Structural Integration of the Global Economy*, Philadelphia: William H. Wurston Center for International Management Studies, The Wharton School Working Paper 93–10.

Kuttner, R. (1991), *The End of Laissez Faire*, New York: A.A. Knopf.

Lazerson, M. (1993), 'Factory or putting out?: Knitting networks in Modena' in Grabher, G. (ed), *The Embedded Firm*, London and New York: Routledge, pp. 203–26.

Lazonick, W. (1992), 'Business organizational and competitive advantage: capitalist transformations in the twentieth century', in Dosi, G., Gianetti, R. and Toninelli, P.A. (eds), *Technology and Enterprise in Historical Perspective*, Oxford: The Clarendon Press.

Luttwak, E.N. (1993), 'The coming global war for economic power', *The International Economy*, September/October 1993,18–21, 64–7.

McGrew, A.G. (1992), 'Conceptualizing global politics' in McGrew, A.G. and Lewis, P.G. (eds), *Global Politics: Globalization and the Nation State*, Cambridge: The Polity Press.

McKenzie, R.B. and Lee, D.R. (1991), *Quicksilver Capital*, New York: The Free Press.

Naisbitt, J. (1994), *Global Paradox*, New York William Morrow.

O'Brien, R. (1992), *Global Financial Integration: The End of Geography*, London: Pinter Publishers.

OECD (1992), *Technology and the Economy*, Paris: OECD.

OECD (1993), *Globalization of Industrial Activities: Background Synthesis Report*, Paris: OECD, Directorate for Science, Technology and Industry, COM/OSTI/IND/TD 93 109.

Oman, C. (1994), *Globalization and Regionalization: The Challenge for Developing Countries*, Paris: OECD Development Centre.

Osborne, D. and Gaebler, T. (1992), *Reinventing Government*, Reading, MA: Addison-Wesley.

Ostrom, V. (1971), *The Political Economy of the Compound Republic: A Reconstruction of the Logical Foundations of American Democracy*, as presented by the Federalists, Blacksburg, VA: Center for the Study of Public Choice/University Books.

Perez, C. (1983), 'Structural change and assimilation of new technologies in the economic and social systems', *Futures*, **15**, October, 357–75.

Perez, C. and Freeman, C. (1988), 'Structural crises of adjustment, business cycles and investment behavior' in Dosi, G., Freeman, C., Nelson, R., Silverberg, G. and Soete, L. (eds), *Technical Change and Economic Theory*, London: Pinter Publishers, pp. 38–66.

Piore, M. and Sabel, C. (1984), *The Second Industrial Divide: Possibilities for Prosperity*, New York: Basic Books.

Rosenberg, N. (1994), *Exploring the Black Box*, Cambridge: Cambridge University Press.

Ruigrok, W. and Van Tulder, R. (1995), *The Logic of International Restructuring*, London and New York: Routledge.

Stopford, J. and Strange, S. (1991), *Rival States, Rival Firms*, Cambridge: Cambridge University Press.

Sydow, J. (1992), 'Enterprise networks and co-determination: The Case of the Federal Republic of Germany', in ILO (ed.), *Is the Single Firm vanishing? Inter-Enterprise Networks, Labour and Labour Institutions*, Geneva: ILO.

Taylor, W. (1991), 'The logic of global business: An interview with ABB's Percy Barnevik', *Harvard Business Review*, **69**, March/April, 94.

UNCTAD (1994), *World Investment Report 1994: Transnational Corporations, Employment and the Workplace*, Geneva: UNCTAD

Wendt, H. (1993), *Global Embrace*, New York: Harper Business.

Vernon, R. (1966), 'International investment and international trade in the product cycle', *Quarterly Journal of Economics*, **80**: 190–207.

World Bank (1993a), *Global Economic Prospects and the Developing Countries*, Washington: The World Bank.

World Bank (1993b), *World Development Report*, Oxford: Oxford University Press.

World Bank (1993c), *The East Asian Miracle*, Oxford: Oxford University Press.

Wriston, W.B. (1992), *The Twilight of Sovereignty*, New York: Charles Scribner's and Sons.

5. Regions, globalization and the knowledge-based economy: the issues stated*

INTRODUCTION

The purpose of this chapter is to offer an analytical framework for evaluating the implications of recent economic events on the spatial distribution of economic activities; and of the role played by multinational enterprises (MNEs)[1] and cross-border inter-firm coalitions[2] of firms on the international and intra-national division of labor. In particular, we shall be concerned with the parallel, yet apparently antithetical, forces towards the geographical dispersion of asset augmenting and asset exploiting activities,[3] and the concentration of such activities in limited spatial areas; or what Ann Markusen (1996) has referred to as the paradox of 'sticky places within slippery space'.

The theme of this chapter is of increasing interest to businesses practitioners and to policy makers alike; and to the academic community. To business practitioners, research is revealing that, as the core competencies of firms become more knowledge-intensive, yet more mobile across space, so the choice of location in the production, organization and use of those assets is becoming a more critical competitive advantage.[4] To the national or regional policy makers, the challenge is to offer, both to indigenous and foreign-owned firms, the spatially anchored resources and capabilities within their jurisdiction, which are perceived by these firms to be at least as attractive complements to their own ownership specific advantages as those offered by other countries or regions. To the academic scholar, locationally related studies are at the cutting edge of interdisciplinary research, and of the intersection of research being undertaken by trade, FDI and evolutionary economists, by economic geographers, by industrial sociologists and by business strategists.

The chapter proceeds in the following way. First, it identifies and describes the main features of four of the critical events of the past two decades which have affected the global locational options available to firms, and their choice

* From J.H. Dunning (ed.), *Regions, Globalization, and the Knowledge Based Economy*, Oxford: Oxford University Press (2000), pp. 8–41.

between these options. Second, it examines and explains the trend towards the closer and deeper economic interdependence between, and among, countries, which is the critical characteristic of both (macro-) regionalization[5] and globalization. The third section looks more closely at the nature of clustering and agglomeration of related value-added activities; and whether it is possible to offer a paradigm of why particular kinds of asset augmenting and asset exploiting foreign direct investment (FDI) are attracted to certain countries and micro-regions. Fourth, the chapter examines the ways in which the growth of MNE-related activity has affected, and is affecting, both the international and intra-national location of production; and of our thinking about its determinants and effects. Fifth, we shall analyze some of the consequences of our findings and our theorizing both for national and regional policy makers, and for business practitioners. Finally, a concluding section will discuss some of their implications for scholarly research -and particularly that which draws together the different approaches to the issues under discussion.

THE CHANGING WORLD ECONOMIC SCENARIO: THE MID-1970s TO THE LATE 1990s

In this section, we identify four main events of the last two decades which we believe have had a profound impact on both the nature and composition of global economic activity, on its ownership and location, and on its organizational modes. These are:

1. The increasing importance of all forms of intellectual capital in both the asset creating and asset exploiting activities of firms.
2. The growth of co-operative ventures and alliances between, and within, the main wealth creating institutions.
3. The liberalization of both internal and cross-border markets.
4. The emergence of several new major economic players in the world economy.

We shall deal with each of these in turn.

The Knowledge Economy

Over the last three centuries, the main source of wealth[6] in market economies has switched from natural assets (notably land and relatively unskilled labor),[7] through tangible created assets (notably buildings, machinery and equipment and finance), to intangible created assets (notably knowledge and information of all kinds) which may be embodied in human beings, in organizations or in physical assets. It has, for example, been estimated that, whereas in the 1950s, 80 percent of the value added in US manufacturing industry represented primary or processed foodstuffs, materials or mineral products, and 20 percent knowledge, by 1995, these proportions had changed to 30 percent and 70 percent respectively (Stewart, 1997). No less significant, the book value of the tangible assets of corporations is becoming a decreasing component of their market value. One estimate (Handy, 1990) put this at between 25 percent and 33 percent in the mid-1980s, while Leif Edvinson (1997) has more recently calculated that, for most organizations, the ratio of their intellectual capital[8] to that of their physical and financial capital is between 5 to 1 and 16 to 1.

Between 1975 and 1995, expenditure on all kinds of research and development in the OECD economies rose three times the rate of output in manufacturing industry (OECD, 1997). Over the same period, while the number of patents registered in the US increased from 76 800 to 113 600, i.e. by 48 percent, those in the more knowledge-intensive sectors[9] rose from 16 827 to 47 533, i.e. by 182 percent (US Patent and Trademark Office, 1997). The proportion of the age group 15–24 engaged in higher education increased from 35 percent in 1980 to 56 percent in 1993 (World Bank, 1997). Finally, capital spending on information technology, which, in 1965, was only one-third of that on production technology, now exceeds it. Throughout economic activity, created intangible assets are replacing natural or created tangible assets as the main source of wealth augmentation in industrial societies. *Inter alia*, this is demonstrated by the rising contribution of services, relative to goods, in the gross national product (GNP) of most countries.[10]

These data all tell a consistent story, viz. the trend towards the cross-border augmentation of assets by cross-border FDI and strategic alliances as an important instrument for increasing economic wellbeing. They also suggest that, in evaluating the economic prosperity of societies, scholars need to give more attention to the dynamics of asset seeking FDI. Most theories of the firm, of industrial organization and of location are still caught in a static web; and are mainly interested in how existing assets may be deployed – and located – in the most efficient way. The advent of the knowledge-based economy demands that scholars should give at least as much attention to a scenario in which assets, far from being largely fixed and immobile as in bygone days, are now eminently increasable and mobile. This may require a fundamental re-think of the relevance of the leading paradigms and theories of the 1970s and early 1980s in explaining the contemporary spatial distribution of economic activity.

Intellectual capital is different from other forms of capital in its deployment in another way. While, to be effective, one piece of land, or a particular machine, or even 'x' dollars of financial assets, is (or are) largely independent of another piece of land, machine or 'x' dollars of financial assets, this is not the case with a unit of knowledge and other forms of intellectual capital. Not only is knowledge a heterogeneous commodity and can be put to multiple uses; often, one kind of knowledge needs to be combined with several other kinds to produce a particular good or service. With the development of two of the key 'engines' of the knowledge economy, viz. the microchip and the computer, the distinction between 'high' and 'low' technology industries, as proxied by the final output they produce, is becoming less and less meaningful. In their use of knowledge, parts of the textile, food processing, retail construction and health care industries are just as technologically advanced as the electronics, pharmaceutical, financial services and management consultancy sectors.

The intellectual capital needed both to augment and to exploit assets is then complex; and it is rarely the property of only one firm. For a firm to increase or deploy its own knowledge effectively, it may have to complement this knowledge with that of other firms, and, more often than not, by way of some kind of collaborative agreement.[11]

There are, of course, several reasons for the growth of inter-firm collaboration which will be further discussed in the next section. Here we would offer just three observations about the nature of contemporary knowledge. First, it can be highly expensive; the cost of the next generation of micro-chips or a new generic drug frequently runs into billions of dollars. Second, the outcome of much investment in augmenting knowledge, e.g. by research and development (R&D), is highly uncertain. Third, many kinds of knowledge (and particularly those which can be imitated) obsolesce quite speedily. Together with its increasing complexity, these features of intellectual capital – coupled with its competitive protecting or enhancing imperatives – have very considerable implications for both the location and the organization of firms; and, indeed, for the character and composition of micro-regions.

Alliance Capitalism

One of the particularly interesting features of the leading market economies of recent years has been the extent to which the hierarchical form of governance of both private and public organizations has been complemented with, and in some cases replaced by, a variety of inter-organizational co-operative agreements. This has caused scholars to suggest that the present stage of capitalism may best be described as alliance capitalism.[12] These alliances may, and do, take a variety of forms, and involve a large number of institutional entities. They may be between the different stakeholders of the firm and/or between the various operational or functional units, making up a firm's value chain (viz. *intra*-firm alliances). They may be between one firm and another – for example, between a firm and its competitors, suppliers or customers (viz. *inter*-firm alliances).[13] They may be between a private firm and a public institution; between public institutions, notably between regional and national governments. They may also be between various interest groups, e.g. consumers, environmentalists and labor unions and so on.

Inter-corporate alliances may be formed to promote asset augmenting or asset exploiting activities. In the former case, partners are normally sought to access synergistic or complementary knowledge-intensive assets, learning and organizational capabilities, and markets. Technology advancing alliances may also be concluded to share the cost of R&D and to speed up the innovatory process. In the latter case, alliances are usually formed to increase the efficiency of existing asset deployment, by, for example, facilitating economies of scope and scale, and by making better use of existing managerial and marketing capabilities. In such cases, firms may engage in coalitions to protect or strengthen their competitive positions versus other firms; while, unless precluded from doing so by anti-trust legislation, one firm may acquire another to increase its market power and gain additional economic rents.

The growth of knowledge capitalism has led to an explosion of inter-firm alliances. Data on mergers and acquisitions (M&As) and collaborative non-equity coalitions suggest that, whether by FDI or by cross-border licensing, franchising and other agreements, alliances have been most pronounced, and increased the most, in knowledge-intensive sectors (UNCTAD, 2000), and have been predominantly concluded between MNEs and other corporations in advanced industrial countries.[14]

Liberalization of Markets

Perhaps the most dramatic and most transparent economic event of the last two decades has been the growing liberalization of both national and international markets. Though most vividly demonstrated by the removal of the Berlin Wall in 1989, and the opening up of the People's Republic of China to inbound FDI, the reconfiguration of national economic policies of most Latin American countries, India and some African economies, and the move towards closer macro-regional integration in various parts of the world, have all contributed to the renewed vitality of the market system as the main instrument for the harnessing and deployment of scarce resources and capabilities throughout the world.

Since the early 1980s, artificial barriers to trade have tumbled – particularly at the macro-regional level. At the same time, both transport and communication costs have fallen dramatically,[15] as have the intra-firm costs of doing business within and across national boundaries. As a result, the share of trade and FDI, as a proportion of the GNP of the great majority of countries, has risen sharply.[16]

Several other indices of the growing openness of countries to the rest of the world point to the same conclusion. Most dramatic of these has been the spectacular expansion of cross-border financial flows, and of the extent and depth of international financial integration. For example, foreign portfolio investment flows rose from $56.2 billion in 1984 to $412.5 billion in 1995 (IMF, vd), while the increase in international bank loans has consistently outpaced that of both world exports and FDI for most of the 30 years prior to 1994 (Perraton et al., 1997). Relatedly, the average daily trade in the foreign exchange market rose from $15 billion in 1973 to $880 billion in 1992 and $1300 billion in 1995, while cross-border sales and purchases of financial assets rose from less than 10 percent of GDP in 1980 in the US, Germany and Japan to 135 percent, 170 percent and 85 percent respectively in 1993 (Kozul-Wright, 1997).

Even more impressive is the recent increase in the use of cross-border communications media. In 1990, the minutes per capita spent on international telephone calls for all countries in the world was 6.3; by 1998 it was 15.3. In 1990, there were 2.6 million Internet users and 11 million mobile cellular subscribers: by 1999 the corresponding figures were 257 million and 472 million (International Telecommunications Union, 2000).

Finally, we might mention the great increase in cross-border people traffic over the last two decades. Though part of this, e.g. the trebling of tourist expenditure, and the quadrupling of the number of passengers on international airlines[17] cannot be put solely at the door of the liberalization or deregulation of markets, these and other people movements (e.g. migration, employment of foreigners, cross-border travel to work, etc.) have most certainly been aided, directly or indirectly, by the reduction in obstacles to the movement of goods, assets, services and people.

Emerging Markets

The last and most gradual – but by no means the least important – event (or trend is, perhaps, the better word) is the take-off of several developing economies as major players on the world economic scene. Most of these are in Asia and Latin America; and most are commonly referred to as 'newly industrializing' economies. Three, i.e. Hong Kong, Singapore and South Korea, were among the wealthiest 30 countries in the world in 1997 (World Bank, 1998).

The clearest expression of the significance of the emerging economies, both as locations of production and as markets, is their share of the world's GNP. In 1980, Latin American, South East and East Asian developing countries accounted for 24.1 percent of the world's GNP; the corresponding figure for 1995 was 26.8 percent (World Bank, vd). Comparable figures for the share of world exports were 18.4 percent and 28.9 percent; for the share of the world's inward foreign direct investment *stock*, 16.7 percent and 23.5 percent

(UNCTAD, 1998); for the share of the world's inward foreign portfolio investment flows, 1.7 percent and 12.6 percent (IMF, vd);[18] for the share of commercial energy use, 19.2 percent and 29.7 percent; for the share of the world's patents registered in the US, 0.4 percent and 3.5 percent (US Patent and Trademark Office, 1999); and for the share of the world's telephone lines, 17.8 percent and 43.8 percent (UN, vd).

Coupled with the economic events earlier described – all of which are intensifying the competitive pressures between corporations, and are leading to a reconfiguration of their product and innovation strategies – the emergence of new economies is helping to fashion a new North–South and South–South division of labor. However, as they move along their investment development paths (Narula, 1995; Dunning and Narula, 1996), the economic structure of industrializing countries tends to move closer to that of their more advanced industrialized counterparts. The more knowledge-intensive asset augmenting activities tend to remain very heavily concentrated in the latter countries;[19] and, indeed, in micro-regions within these countries.[20] We shall take up this point in 'Localization, clusters and the concept of "sticky" places', below.

GLOBALIZATION: EXTENDING AND DEEPENING THE ECONOMIC INTERDEPENDENCE BETWEEN NATIONS

What then is the impact of the events described on the location of economic activity? Location theory has long since asserted that a profit maximizing firm will site its value-added activities where it perceives this particular goal is best advanced.[21] Such profits represent the differences between revenue (a demand-related variable) and costs (a supply-related variable), plus taxes and duties, less allowances and subsidies. Costs are of four main kinds, viz. design and development, production, transportation and transaction. Taxes, duties, allowances and subsidiaries may be direct or indirect, general or specific. In imperfect – and particularly oligopolistic – markets, firms will also take account of the locational strategies of their competitors.

Each of these broad locational determinants is to some extent product, activity and country (or region) specific. Besides the availability and costs of factor and intermediate inputs, the main supply-related variables influencing whether a firm concentrates or disperses its asset augmenting or asset exploiting activities over space are, on the one hand, the extent to which such activities can benefit from scale economies, and, on the other, the spatially related transaction costs involved. As George Stigler (1951) pointed out many years ago – as did Adam Smith before him – division of labor, i.e. the specialization of economic activity, is limited by the size and geography of the market. Today, we might add to this variable the *character* of the market (and in particular the extent to which it is customized), and the transaction costs of exchanging goods and services between different political and cultural regimes.

We make these fairly obvious introductory points, as it is worth emphasizing that the extent, form and pace of globalization are not uniformly spread across the planet, nor across different value-added activities. Some goods and services, for example, are non-tradable, i.e. they are immobile across space. Some are produced in their entirety in only one or a few countries, and are exported across the globe. Some are replicated in their entirety in several countries, but only sold in their country of production. Some parts of the global activities of firms (e.g. research and development) tend to be concentrated in a few countries and regions, while others are spread more widely.

What then is economic globalization? In Chapter 4 (page 83) we set out Anthony McGrew's interpretation of the term (McGrew, 1992). Suffice it to say here that globalization is a process leading to the structural transformation of firms and nations. It represents a discontinuity in the process of internationalization in the sense that it creates new and deeper cross-border relationships and dependencies. Sometimes, the transformation takes place at a regional level: many of the integrated production networks of MNEs are so focused. Sometimes, it occurs at a global level. For example, the advent of electronic commerce is dramatically truncating distance in financial and foreign exchange markets (Stopford and Strange, 1991). One scholar has gone so far as to aver that the emergence of the Internet and global financial integration is heralding 'the end of geography' (O'Brien, 1992). Sometimes, however, globalization, while facilitating the cross-border movement of intermediate products, notably technology, is also leading to the widespread replication of end products.

Chapter 2 has already identified some of the forces 'pushing' or 'pulling' in the direction of regionalization and globalization. We now set out a few additional facts, particularly as they relate to the growth of MNE-related activity:

1. Over the last decades the growth of world trade has consistently outpaced that of world output – usually by a ratio of 2 to 1; while in 1998 the sales of the foreign affiliates of MNEs exceeded that of world trade by 74 percent (UNCTAD, 1999).
2. The majority of the global sales of MNEs are in knowledge or information sectors, or in sectors supportive of these activities.
3. Between one-third of cross-border trade in non-agricultural goods and services, and between one-half and three-fifths of all capital and technology flows, is now internalized within MNEs.
4. There have been two important trends in MNE-related activity (FDI and alliance formation) over the past two decades. The first is the spectacular growth of asset seeking mergers and acquisitions (M&As) and strategic

alliances within the triad countries, or within regions of the US, Japan and Western Europe.[22] The second has been the no less dramatic growth of asset exploiting FDI in some emerging markets, notably China,[23] an increasing part of which has been supplied from other Asian developing countries.[24]

5. A rising proportion of FDI in both developed and developing countries is in services – particularly information intensive services.[25]
6. An increasing proportion of the total R&D expenditures is accounted for by their foreign subsidiaries.[26] Moreover, it is growing faster than that of other forms of MNE-related production,[27] and also than that of the indigenous firms of the countries in which MNE subsidiaries are located.[28] Furthermore, an increasing proportion of the foreign R&D activities of MNEs is directed to augmenting their home-based intellectual capital – often by tapping into foreign R&D facilities – rather than to more effectively deploying their existing R&D capabilities (Kuemmerle, 1999).

LOCALIZATION, CLUSTERS AND THE CONCEPT OF 'STICKY' PLACES

We have already suggested that globalization does not necessarily mean that all wealth creating activities are dispersed uniformly throughout the world. Far from it. If, indeed, the specialization of economic activity is limited by the size of the market, then it would be proper to hypothesize that globalization will be accompanied by more, rather than less, specialization; and hence, by implication, will lead to further spatial concentration of such activity. Much, of course, will depend on how the production, transportation and transaction costs imposed by artificial barriers to trade vary with size of output produced. The 'where' of concentration will depend on the national and micro-regional specific characteristics influencing such costs, and also on the spatial proximity of related activities (clusters), which generate both static and dynamic external economies.

In examining the proposition that some types of wealth creating activities are becoming more concentrated in sub-national clusters, it may be useful to distinguish between traditional and contemporary trade and location models. Traditional, i.e. Heckscher–Ohlin type, trade models were primarily designed to explain the optimum (i.e. the most efficient) patterns of trade between countries, based on the distribution of immobile factor endowments. Location theories were similarly concerned with the optimum siting of asset exploiting activities, i.e. those designed to maximize the static efficiency of the investing firms; but, unlike trade theories, they explicitly acknowledged the role of the transaction costs (and benefits) of spatially proximate activities.[29]

Contemporary trade and location theories are more contextual than their predecessors.[30] While those just described are still a robust explanation of some kinds of cross-border division of labor – particularly of natural-resource-intensive activities between developed and developing countries – they are less comfortable in explaining the distribution of knowledge-intensive activities, and particularly those between and within advanced countries and under the governance of MNEs. Such activities are not only likely to incur substantial overhead costs, and thus need non-decreasing returns to scale and the necessary volume to cover these; but, as already indicated, they frequently involve multiple and interrelated technological inputs.[31] To minimize distance-related transaction costs, and to maximize the benefits of dynamic learning economies, it frequently pays firms to concentrate their activities within a limited spatial area. Hence the concept of the learning region (Florida, 1995); and with it, the significance of dynamic agglomerative economies as a locational pull to firms – and particularly those seeking to augment their resources and capabilities.

Globalization may then lead to a dispersion of knowledge-intensive production between and within countries; and to a convergence in cross-border economic structures. It may equally lead to a concentration of such production in particular countries, and in micro-regions within those countries, in which case economic structures of the countries and micro-regions will tend to diverge from, rather than converge with, each other.

In fact, both trends are discernible, but it is the contention of this chapter that: (i) the greater the degree of knowledge intensity of a particular activity; (ii) the easier it is for labor to migrate across regions or countries; (iii) the lower the distance-related costs; and (iv) the more firms engage in FDI and alliance-related activities to augment, rather than exploit, their existing assets, then the more likely is it that national and micro-regional economies will develop specialized centers of excellence.[32] At the same time, it is quite evident that the main competitors to some micro-regions in attracting and retaining mobile investment are not other micro-regions in the same country, but micro-regions in other countries.[33]

This observation is consistent with the growing sophistication of both intra-industry trade and intra-industry FDI between countries and/or micro-regions. Such sophistication is not confined to the types of products produced. Rather, it extends to the innovatory milieu of the competing locations, and, in particular, to the opportunities of firms within that milieu to tap into and learn from the resources, capabilities and entrepreneurship of each other, i.e. augment their core competencies.[34]

These opportunities, and the benefits of spatial clustering, clearly vary between industries and firms; and they may be exploited through a variety of organizational routes – e.g. arm's-length markets, non-equity alliances and FDI. Which modality is chosen will depend on the extent and character of the relevant *dynamic* spatially specific transaction costs, e.g. those associated with innovatory activities. In general, one might predict that: (i) the less complex and/or independent the knowledge required for the production of a particular good or service; (ii) the more codifiable (i.e. less tacit) or idiosyncratic that knowledge is; (iii) the less information symmetry there is between the related firms; (iv) the fewer the chances for opportunistic behavior; (v) the less uncertain the outcome of any relationship is; and (vi) the more widely located the customers are, then the lower the spatial transaction costs, and the less the economies of agglomeration are likely to be.[35]

Clustering is, therefore, likely to be strongly activity specific, and to be most marked where the critical decision takers in firms need to be in close physical proximity to exchange, or share, tacit knowledge. The City of London is a classic example of an agglomeration of interdependent firms each producing part of a final product.[36] Globalization and technological change have combined to strengthen such clustering, and also to upgrade the knowledge intensity of the constituent firms. At the same time, the increasing mobility of firm specific assets and the growing complementarity between different kinds of technology has fostered more diversity of economic activity, often with beneficial consequences for innovatory output (Feldman and Audretsch, 1999).

So far, we have tended to concentrate on supply-related reasons why firms cluster. We have argued that while the original Marshallian reasons for clustering[37] still hold good, those to do with a variety of 'soft' locational factors and access to knowledge and learning capabilities have become more important[38] (Florida, 1995; Giersch, 1996). At the same time, clusters may be fashioned by the needs of consumers, and some of these also possess all, or at least most, of the characteristics so far identified. Such clusters are particularly noticeable in the consumer services sectors; they tend to be city oriented and include airline offices, car rental agencies, film distributors, medical services and fast food chains.

THE ROLE OF MNEs IN AFFECTING THE LOCATION OF ECONOMIC ACTIVITY

So far in our analysis, we have not considered the unique role of MNEs in affecting the location of economic activity. To this we now turn. What is distinctive about this particular organizational form? As defined earlier, an MNE is an institution which owns or controls value activities in at least two countries. Many of the larger MNEs own or control value-added activities in a large number of countries, and do so via both FDI and cross-border alliances. To what extent does the locational pattern of such activities differ from what it would be if each of them had been separately and independently owned? Does the common ownership of production in two or more countries affect our theorizing about the geography of asset augmenting or asset exploiting investment, and its tendency to be concentrated or dispersed?

The Multi-domestic MNE

To answer this question, let us consider two types of governance structures of MNEs.[39] The first is the *multi-domestic* or 'stand-alone' structure, which most MNEs outside the natural-resource-based sectors adopted until the 1960s. The main feature of the multi-domestic MNE is that it treats its foreign subsidiaries as autonomous wealth creating units. Each subsidiary tends to replicate – albeit often on a truncated scale – the asset exploiting activities of its mother company, and to supply its products to local and/or closely adjacent markets. Though the parent organization may export intangible assets (e.g. technology, managerial and marketing expertise) and other intermediate products (e.g. materials, components and parts) to its affiliates, for the most part, there is likely to be little trade in finished products between the parent company and its affiliates, or among its affiliates. In short, the multi-domestic MNE engages in little integrated production and little cross-border product or process specialization.

Frequently, in the past, the multi-domestic or 'stand-alone' MNE has been prompted to engage in FDI to overcome tariff barriers and other restrictions to trade, or to be near to critical supply facilities and/or to the special needs of foreign consumers. *De facto*, this kind of defensive market seeking FDI often replaces trade, and does little to promote a more efficient regional or global division of labor. However, there are also some kinds of *aggressive* market seeking MNE activity which, while not replacing trade, do little to promote it. Examples include FDIs in some service sectors, e.g. in fast food chains, building and construction, railroads, public utilities, and the regional offices of MNEs.

Yet, though globally dispersed, multi-domestic MNEs may still favor particular locations *within* a country. Moreover, these are not always the same as those chosen by domestic firms. Several studies on the intra-national distribution of inbound investment from 1958 onwards[40] have shown that foreign affiliates of MNEs tend to be located in or near large conurbations, and/or be adjacent to leading ports. They also tend to favor subnational clusters of related activities, and to be more sensitive to the regional policies of governments[41] (Yannopoulos and Dunning, 1976).

One other frequently voiced need of first-time foreign investors is to reduce the costs of producing in an unfamiliar environment as much as possible. Several country-based studies[42] have shown that in various countries, either the presence of indigenous firms has attracted FDI into the same micro-region, or the establishment and growth of one investor has had a positive signaling effect on other foreign investors (Liu, 1997).[43] On the other hand, there is also some evidence that foreign-owned firms prefer to establish *de novo* clusters of related activities. Examples include the surge of biotechnology investments in California in the 1980s, and major new investments by the Japanese auto companies – Nissan in North East England, Toyota in Derby – in the 1990s (UNCTAD, 1995).

The Globally (or Regionally) Integrated MNE

The main feature of this kind of MNE is that it adopts a systemic and holistic approach towards its global operations, and treats its foreign affiliates as part of a network of interrelated activities, designed to promote the interest of the MNE *in toto*. Where possible, the integrated MNE will take full advantage of the geographical distribution of natural and created assets, of spatially related agglomerative economies, and of liberalized markets. This means it is likely to engage in more rationalized and efficiency seeking FDI than is its multi-domestic counterpart, and to source its inputs and augment its resources and capabilities from across the globe. It is also likely to engage in a good deal of intermediate and final product trade between its parent company and its affiliates, and among its affiliates – especially within regionally integrated areas. The activities of the globally integrated MNE are then likely to promote both trade and FDI.

The globally integrated MNE is very much a creature of the late twentieth century; and each of the events described in 'The changing world economic scenario', above has helped foster such integration. Broadly speaking, the integrated MNE promotes three kinds of cross-border specialization. The first is *horizontal* specialization in which each of the products supplied by the same firm is produced in a different region or country. The primary rationale of this specialization is to take advantage of the economies of scale and differentiated consumer needs, although where the products require a different mix of natural resources and capabilities, it may be of the H–O type. The second is *vertical* specialization where different stages of the value-added chain of a particular product are undertaken in different locations. The main object of this type of specialization – which predominantly (though not exclusively) occurs between developed and developing countries – is to take advantage of differences in factor costs and consumer tastes, although the opportunity to gain scale economies may also be relevant.

The third kind of specialization – asset augmenting specialization – is an amalgam of the first two; but it is different in that it is designed less to advance the static efficiency of the MNE, and more to enhance its future wealth creating capabilities in a cost learning effective way. The geography of this kind of labor is mainly confined to the advanced industrial countries, and geared to either promoting the efficiency of the MNE's global R&D capabilities[44] or gaining access to foreign created assets which will best protect or enhance its competitive advantages.[45] It is this kind of specialization which is being increasingly fashioned by the imperatives of the knowledge-based global economy, and by the need of firms located in one country to complement their core competencies with those of firms located in another country.[46]

To what extent is the globally integrated MNE likely to prefer to locate the three kinds of cross-border specialization in particular micro-regions of host countries? The evidence is mixed. The primary issue with respect to horizontal and vertical FDI is the extent to which 'static' spatial transaction costs favor its proximity to a cluster of related firms, so it can exploit the benefits of 'untraded interdependencies' (Storper, 1995). However, over time, most of these clusters have evolved their own nexus of innovating and learning capabilities; in other words, they also generate dynamic externalities to the participating firms.

Examples of both horizontal and vertical clusters abound.[47] The former include the watch industry of Geneva, the cork industry of Northern Portugal, the woolen textile industry of Prato and Biellia in Northern Italy, the film industry of Hollywood, the diamond industry of Amsterdam, the tomato canning industry of Campania, Southern Italy, the cutlery industry of Solignen, and the financial services industry of the City of London and Wall Street (New York). Examples of vertical clusters include the large number of export zones set up in developing countries – especially in Asia – to house relatively labor-intensive stages of the value chain by MNEs, in such manufacturing sectors as textiles, leather goods and consumer electronics, and, more recently, in services such as insurance, shipping, shared support centers and computer software.[48] In more advanced countries, the Boeing agglomeration of related firms in the Seattle region and the Toyota complex of firms in the Tokyo region are examples of vertically integrated clusters, in which a flagship firm producing an end product, which comprises a large number of components and parts, is surrounded by a satellite of its suppliers.

It is our contention that the dynamic externalities associated with these horizontal and vertical clusters are becoming more important as intellectual capital becomes more sophisticated, idiosyncratic, tacit, complex and context dependent. Furthermore, as the main repositories of such knowledge, and certainly the principal organizing unit for accessing and leveraging geographically dispersed units (Doz, Asakawa, Santos and Williamson, 1997), MNEs are not only drawn to regional clusters, but, by their presence and impact, to influence their character and growth.[49] Historical examples include the chemical and cotton thread industries of New Jersey (Wallace, 1998) and the office machinery industry of mid-Scotland (Dunning, 1958, 1998). More recent cases include clusters of the Japanese consumer electronics affiliates in South Wales (Strange, 1993), and a bevy of MNEs in the Bangalore software sector (Balasubramanyam and Balasubramanyam, 2000).[50]

It is, however, the third type of industrial specialization and clustering which is increasingly engaging the attention of scholars, and it is one, too, in which both national and micro-regional authorities are watching carefully. The spectacular development of business, industrial and science parks, and specialized service sectors, are all testimony to the belief that the asset augmenting activities of firms benefit from being part of a knowledge creating milieu – in which private firms, universities, technical colleges, and government research institutions are all involved. Many of these clusters were initially initiated by micro-regional authorities to help upgrade the resources and capabilities under the jurisdiction; and, sometimes, they were targeted specifically at mobile investors.[51] For the most part, such clusters tend to be concentrated in the Triad regions or nations; and as intellectual capital becomes more geographically diffused and cross-border innovatory competition becomes more intense, firms from one part of the Triad are finding it increasingly desirable to establish an R&D presence, and/or conclude technology enhancing alliances with firms, in another part.[52]

But more than this: as firms increasingly scan the globe for knowledge capital, they are engaging in FDI specifically to tap into, and harness, country and firm specific resources, capabilities and learning experiences.[53] Such assets may be synergistic with their core assets, or complementary to them. They can be harnessed by the acquisition of, or merger with, foreign firms and/or by the conclusion of non-equity coalitions with them. MNEs may also use their foreign affiliates or partners as vehicles for seeking out and monitoring new knowledge and learning experiences; and as a means of tapping into national innovatory or investment systems more conducive to their dynamic competitive advantages (Doremus, Keller, Pauly and Reich, 1998). In such cases, a presence in the innovating heartland of the sectors will help lower the transaction costs involved in such a task. Thus firms are likely to be attracted to pockets of intellectual capital in a foreign economy, and in so far as they are allowed to do so, to participate in joint research and development and collective learning experiences (Florida, 1995).

There is some casual evidence that the R&D activities of firms tend to be more spatially concentrated in a country than are other activities,[54] and are more likely to be drawn to centers of academic excellence and to industrial and science parks. There is also some suggestion that the major metropolitan areas and their surrounding hinterlands are becoming the loci of agglomerative knowledge enhancing activities. Indeed, according to Allen Scott (1998), as sources of new employment, they are not only growing faster than the national average,[55] but are becoming the leading regional motors of technological change.

In summary, then, the changing geography of MNE-related activity is a microcosm of that of the world economy. On the one hand, MNEs are conducting a rising proportion of their value-added activities outside their home countries,[56] and also in more countries.[57] For the most part, too, their affiliates are becoming more embedded in their local environments; and are helping to foster the dispersion of at least some kinds of intellectual capital. MNEs from developing countries also tend to locate their activities away from the large industrial concentrations originally favored by their developed countries' counterparts. For example, FDI in Europe by Korean auto and electronics MNEs has been more concentrated in Central and Eastern Europe and in the less prosperous areas of the UK and other EC countries than has FDI by US and Japanese MNEs (UNCTAD, 1995, 1997, 1998). The numbers of cross-border M&As and strategic alliances have also risen faster than their domestic counterparts (Booz, Allen and Hamilton, 1997).

On the other hand, MNEs and their affiliates are being increasingly drawn to a network of 'sticky' places for their wealth creating activities; and there is a strong suggestion that the events of the last two decades, and particularly the deepening of the knowledge-based economy and the growing interdependence between cutting edge technologies, have increased the spatial costs of related economic transactions. This has prompted MNEs to locate their R&D and production units in a geographical area large enough to accommodate a concentrated nexus of competitors, suppliers, customers, and/or of firms using common support services, but small enough to maximize the benefits of 'untradable interdependencies' (Storper and Scott, 1995).

We may infer then that there is no real paradox of geographical space; and that globalization and localization are opposite sides of the same coin.[58] This section of the chapter has further suggested that, because of their unique characteristics, MNEs are likely to display a different geography of economic activity than that of their uni-national counterparts. In part, this is a reflection of the products they produce; but mostly it arises from their capabilities to harness and utilize resources, capabilities and markets from throughout the world, and to do so within their own governance structures. Such advantages, we believe, make for more globalization and more spatial clustering than would occur if all the cross-border value-added activities, owned and controlled by MNEs, were undertaken by independent firms; and if all trade were conducted at arm's-length prices. But much more research is needed if this suggestion is to be more than just a suggestion!

We would briefly make one further point. There is some evidence (see, for example, OECD, 1996) to suppose that industrial clusters, particularly of small and medium size (SME) firms, tend to generate the kind of external economies which assist at least some of the clustering firms to internationalize their markets and/or production. In particular, several of the country studies in OECD (1996) reveal a close correlation between the export success of firms and their participation in cross-border alliances, and their involvement in domestic networks.

A REGIONAL PERSPECTIVE

We now turn to consider some of the implications of recent economic events for the role of micro-regions as spatial entities, and for the governance of those regions. Is it the case, as some writers (e.g. Ohmae, 1995) have suggested, that micro-regions are replacing the nation state as the principal spatial mode of governance; or is the more temperate view of geographers such as Allen Scott, and business strategists such as Michael Porter, that such regions will become increasingly important milieux for competitiveness enhancing activities of mobile investors, and as engines of national economic growth, a more persuasive one?

Much research has been conducted over the past 30 years on the role of FDI and MNE-related activity in advancing the economic wellbeing of nation states,[59] but relatively little on how it has affected that of micro-regions.[60] In principle, one would expect the results to be very similar, and particularly so when the micro-regions are the size of small countries (cf. the impact of FDI on the economy of Baden Württemberg with that of Belgium, or that of Northern Ireland with that of Denmark). While, traditionally, scholars have always distinguished between intra- and international economic activity, and have generally assumed that the sovereignty of sub-national governments is more constrained than that of national governments, contemporary economic events are demanding a reappraisal of these views. This is particularly so in the case of countries which have become part of macro-regional integration schemes.

Nevertheless, *de facto*, the economic governance of most micro-regions is shared and executed by a range of authorities – micro-regional, national, and supranational. The exact role of each will vary from macro-region to micro-region, country to country and over time. In many respects, the relation of micro-regional to national governance may be likened to that of a subsidiary of a MNE to its parent company. The subsidiary has its own goals and agenda for achieving these goals; so does the parent company. The amount of decision taking responsibility devolved to the subsidiary is likely to depend on such variables as the functions performed by it, its size, age and experience, the respective capabilities of the managers of the parent organization and those of the subsidiary, and the extent to which the managers of the latter, while promoting their own goals, are perceived to advance those of the MNE of which they are a part.

The same principle of 'subsidiarity' may be applied to understanding how much sovereignty is decentralized from national to micro-regional governments.[61] But, from the perspective of the regional government, its economic tasks are clear cut. These are, first, to promote the full and most efficient usage of the resources and capabilities within its jurisdiction; and second – in so far as is within its power – to provide the supportive infrastructure for its existing resources and capabilities to be upgraded, and for its indigenous firm to be competitive in world markets.

The contribution of inbound mobile investment is normally judged by these criteria. However, the questions of particular interest here are: first, whether in the contemporary globalizing, knowledge-based economy, such investment is likely to make a more, or less, significant contribution to regional economic welfare; second, what should be the policies of regional governments to ensure that such a contribution is an optimum one; and third, how far are these policies supported by, or reconcilable with, those pursued by national, and/or supranational, governments, which seek to promote a broader canvass of interests.

The governments of micro-regions are like the managers of firms in another respect. They compete with each other for resources, capabilities and markets. An increasing role of many sub-national authorities, in recent years, has been directed to providing as many cost-effective incentives and as few obstacles as possible to the kind of mobile investment the region perceives it needs to promote its dynamic comparative advantage. Many of these incentives have taken the form of investment grants, tax holidays, free or subsidized land, customized public utilities, the aggressive pursuance of which by some micro-regions, e.g. some states in the US, has led some scholars to refer to them as locational tournaments (Mytelka, 1996).

But no less significant have been the concentrated efforts of some micro-regional governments to provide, or ensure that the private sector provides, the kind of location bound assets which investors – be they from the region or elsewhere – perceive they need if they are to best exploit their more mobile core competencies. However, it is becoming clear that regional authorities need to do more than this, simply because many of these assets (e.g. cost-efficient utilities, educational facilities, transport and communication infrastructure) are either provided, or can be fairly easily replicated, by their competitors.[62] This suggests that they need to offer mobile investors a unique set of spatially fixed competitive advantages, which are either customized to their individual needs (Peck, 1996), or are not easily imitated by other regional governments. There is also need for strategic collaboration between the different levels of sub-national governance to minimize both private and public transaction costs.[63] Finally, local administrations, in conjunction with local co-operative and/or trade associations, educational and innovatory institutions, need to create an environment which not only helps promote the agglomeration of related activities, but one in which mobile investors can accumulate resources and capabilities, yet from which they may find it difficult to exit (Harrison, 1992)![64] This, more often than not, is an extremely difficult thing to do, although some micro-regions, e.g. Silicon Valley in California and some small countries, e.g. Singapore and Hong Kong, have done so very successfully.[65]

What also is becoming increasingly clear is that, to advance their economic objectives, micro-regional governments need to give as much attention to providing the right milieu for asset augmenting activities of their resident firms – be they domestic or foreign – as for asset exploiting activities. Once again, the idea of the dynamic learning region comes to the fore, and, with it, the need for local administrations to adapt their infrastructural systems to best meet the demands of the global economy[66] to work together with the private sector to minimize any structural distortions and transaction costs which might impede both the redeployment and upgrading of local resources and capabilities.

It is within this context that the role of micro-regional clusters needs to be evaluated. To what extent is regional prosperity advanced if the agglomeration of vertically or horizontally related activities is encouraged – or, at least, not inhibited – by regional governments?[67] If such spatial networks are to be facilitated, how best might this be accomplished and what form should the clusters take?

It is possible to identify several kinds of spatial clusters.[68] These are likely to vary according to their scope, density, pattern of activities, growth potential, innovatory capacity and governance structures (Enright, 1998). In this chapter, we shall confine our discussion to six types of clusters. The first of these are 'hub-and-spoke' clusters, in which a hub or nucleus of flagship firms generates a circle of satellite (or spoke) firms. In this case (the Boeing complex around Seattle, the Toyota complex around Tokyo, the Pohang Steel complex around Pohang in Korea, and the newly emerging Jenoptak electronics complex at Jena in Eastern Germany are good examples) the success of the cluster is likely to rest on the capability of the flagship firm to leverage and develop a network development of suppliers and customers which are able to gain external economies not only from the hub firm but also from each other.[69]

The second kind of cluster is that exemplified by the Northern Italian textile industry, the Portuguese cork industry, the Cambridge (New Zealand) horse breeding industry and the Geneva watch industry, and was first identified by Alfred Marshall (1920).[70] It comprises a concentration of enterprises engaged in similar economic activities, so that each can draw from such external economies as the availability of a common pool of natural resources and transportation facilities. The third type of cluster, like the second, consists of a complex of firms producing similar goods and services. The difference is that while, in the former case, the main cluster specific benefits arise from a reduction of static distance-related transaction costs, and from internalizing static external economies, in the latter they primarily take the form of institution building learning economies and the sharing of collective knowledge. The R&D laboratory is, in fact, a major component in the success of the latter, but not the former cluster, as is the interchange of tacit knowledge and ideas between the constituent firms and local universities and technical colleges.

The fourth type of industrial district is that which arises from an agglomeration or of government publicly sponsored institutions. Examples include a congregation of aerospace military and other research establishments which are concentrated around Farnborough and Aldershot in South East England,[71] around Colorado Springs in the US, and around San José dos Campos in Brazil;[72] and which generate a satellite of subcontractors in adjacent regions. The willingness and capacity to create and develop such spatial networks is obviously strongly dependent on national, rather than on regional, priorities and policies. In general, the most regional governments can do is to provide the human and physical infrastructure required to make them a success. State governments in several countries, notably the US, however, have played an important role in encouraging tertiary education. For example, state-funded universities explain much of the growth of cities such as Durham, Chapel Hill, Ann Arbor, Austin and Madison in the US, which rank among the fastest growing US conurbations (Markusen and Gray, 1999).

The fifth type of cluster is that typified by export processing zones in developing countries. Here, often tempted by tax and other incentives offered by national and/or regional governments, foreign MNEs have set up primarily export oriented labor-intensive activities; and, *via* the signaling effect, have encouraged the agglomeration of like firms. However, if such clusters are to be anything but enclaves, and fully benefit the local economy, a national or regional policy which promotes the continuous upgrading of indigenous resources, and the establishment of backward or forward linkages with local firms, is essential (McIntyre, Narula and Trevino, 1996).

The sixth type of cluster is specifically directed at encouraging all forms of asset augmenting activities.[73] Science and technology parks are primary examples of such clusters. To be successful, they need an up to date and sophisticated institutional infrastructure, and an innovative milieu which helps generate the fluidity of knowledge, learning externalities and social capital demanded by the participating firms (Putman, 1993). As we have already indicated, such clusters are usually, though not exclusively, located in the major metropolitan areas or in university towns and cities in advanced industrial countries.

We have suggested that foreign MNEs may, and frequently do, play a major role in the formation, structure and development of the third, fifth and sixth types of cluster; in some cases, too, they may initiate the first type of cluster. In the second and fifth types of cluster, foreign MNEs would normally be expected to engage in resource seeking, market seeking or efficiency seeking investment; in the first, third and sixth kinds, in addition to asset exploiting activities, foreign investors may also be aiming to augment their existing competitive advantages. Some recent research by Birkinshaw and Hood (1997) on Canadian, Scottish and Swedish MNEs suggests that, while, historically, the role and influence of foreign affiliates have been more pronounced in 'branch plant' clusters, in the future they are likely to make a contribution to the character and content of 'leading edge' (i.e. innovating) clusters.

While, as we have already indicated, scholarly research has generally concluded that, in the absence of structural market distortions, the economic welfare of recipient countries has been advanced by asset exploiting FDI, there have been few studies on the effects of asset augmenting FDI on either national or regional economic welfare. Back in the 1960s, there was a good deal of concern in Europe about the possible 'poaching' of intellectual capital by US inbound investors in some knowledge-intensive sectors, notably the pharmaceutical industry. This concern was especially marked as and when US firms acquired European companies and transferred some of their innovatory activities back to the US (Dunning, 1970). Strangely enough, the huge wave of intra-triad M&As which have occurred over the last decade do not seem to have sparked off the same kind of anxiety. It is possible, although we think improbable, that this is because it is perceived that the price paid for such resources and capabilities is a socially acceptable one.[74] A more likely explanation is the fact that the recent spate of cross-border M&As and strategic alliances has been a two-way phenomenon; certainly European and US purchases of foreign firms have been fairly evenly matched by the foreign acquisitions of European and US firms[75] (DeLong, Smith and Walter, 1996; UNCTAD, 1998).

At the same time, there has been some reluctance by national administrations to allow foreign owned firms to participate in domestic R&D consortia – and particularly those publicly funded. Examples include the outlawing or limited participation of foreign owned firms in SEMATECH – a US consortium of semi-conductor firms; and, indeed, the somewhat ethnocentric attitude of successive US governments to the ownership of innovatory activities undertaken in the US.[76] By contrast, the European authorities take a more relaxed attitude to the foreign membership of such consortia, as, indeed, does the Japanese government.

The social benefits of inbound asset augmenting investment deserve further study; and particularly, at a regional level, of the distribution of its benefits between the parent companies (and countries) of the foreign affiliates and the micro-regions in which the latter are located. Case studies of the consequences of such FDI, which is deliberately designed to acquire intellectual capital from the host locations, are sorely needed. In particular, is the price paid by the foreign investor for such capital, compared with that which might have been paid by a domestic firm, sufficient to compensate for any 'leakages' of proprietary knowledge to the investing country? Do the foreign firms bring other benefits to the micro-region; or, should one not be concerned with the issue at all – particularly where host regions to FDI are also home regions to outbound MNEs – and let the market make the appropriate decisions?

SOME MANAGERIAL IMPLICATIONS

The final section of this chapter will identify some of the possible implications of recent economic events for managers of MNEs *à propos* their location decisions. The first point we would emphasize is that making the right location choice for a particular FDI, and attaining the right portfolio of locations for all FDIs by a particular firm, can, itself, be an important competitive advantage. Moreover, as firms become more multinational, as firm specific assets become more mobile, and as the options for locating most kinds of FDI widen, so achieving the optimum mix of locations for the harnessing and deployment of geographically dispersed resources and capabilities, for the procurement of inputs, and for the supplying of their products to end markets, is becoming more critical.

At the same time, this issue has been largely ignored in the managerial literature. My guess is that for every 50 treatises, monographs and papers published on the strategic management of resources and capabilities, and the appropriate entry mode into foreign markets, there has been only one on the impact of locational choice on firm specific competitiveness. Maybe business scholars consider this outside their domain, and that locational decisions are taken only on purely economic grounds.[77] Yet even in the 1920s, it was being postulated that, in oligopolistic industries at least, one firm's locational choice was likely to be influenced not only by the existing location of other firms, but by how the latter might react to its own choice (Hotelling, 1929). And certainly one of the central themes of the Multinational Enterprise Project led by Ray Vernon of Harvard in the 1960s[78] was 'why' and 'where' US, European and Japanese businesses preferred to site their manufacturing business outside their home countries. In 1974, Vernon wrote a classic paper on the 'Location of Economic Activity' (Vernon, 1974), in which he specifically differentiated between the locational strategies of large asset exploiting MNEs at different stages of their product cycles.[79] Though Vernon did not specifically couch his analysis in terms of the locational competitiveness of the investing firms, this, in fact, was his main interest.

For much of the last 30 years, academic interest in the geography of economic activity has been mainly confined to economists and economic geographers. While some of the earlier oligopolistic type models have been extended and refined,[80] they still do not address head-on the locational issues of critical concern to scholars of business strategy. In the last decade or so, however, three new research thrusts have emerged. The first is the influential work of Paul Krugman (1991, 1993, 1995) on the determinants of the geographical concentration of economic activity. The second is the extension of Michael Porter's earlier studies (Porter, 1985, 1990) on the competitive advantage of firms to embrace a spatial dimension (Porter, 1994, 1996, 1998). The third is the growing attention being given by MNEs to the dynamic interaction between the competitive (or ownership specific) advantages of firms and the competitive (or locational) advantages of countries, particularly in respect of asset augmenting FDI (Gray, 1996; UNCTAD, 1996; Dunning, 1997, 1998); and also the acknowledgement by some scholars (e.g. Oliver, 1997) that the resource-based theory of the firm might be usefully widened to incorporate variables external to firms, and, in particular, the local institutional environment in which they operate.

We have already suggested that one of the unique competitive advantages of the large MNE in a knowledge-based, globalizing economy is its ability to identify, access, harness and effectively coordinate and deploy resources and capabilities from throughout the world. This must surely include an explicit and appropriate locational strategy. Such a strategy should embrace not only all the activities of the MNE, but also those of its competitors, suppliers and customers, over which it has some influence and/or control. On the one hand, decisions about the acquisition and use of technology, those about the cross-border sourcing of inputs, the siting of R&D and production, and the servicing of global markets, are becoming increasingly complex. On the other, as the product and production strategies of MNEs in any particular industrial sector are tending to converge,[81] their locational choices could become more critical to their overall competitive advantages. And this applies no less to their search for the right micro-region(s) in which to site their investments as to their search for the right country(ies).

CONCLUSIONS

In this chapter, we have sought to describe and analyze the impact which recent economic events have had on the location of value-added activities, and particularly on those of MNEs. More specifically, we have focussed attention on the centrifugal forces making for the macro-regionalization and globalization of FDI and inter-firm alliances, and on the centripetal forces making for a more concentrated geographical pattern. We have also distinguished between those value-added activities embodying largely location bound resources and capabilities and those embodying mobile resources and capabilities.

The chapter has also identified the differences between the kind of international division of labor fostered by multi-domestic MNEs and globally (or regionally) integrated MNEs; and how each, and the growing significance of micro-specific agglomerative economies, is affecting the intra-national, as well as the cross-border, allocation of innovatory and productive activities.

In our analysis of these issues, we distinguished between the asset augmenting and asset exploiting motives for MNE related activities, and their different locational needs. In particular, we discussed the notion of distance-related transaction costs; and argued that, in the contemporary knowledge-based economy, dynamic transaction costs, e.g. those to do with learning and the coordination of innovation-related tasks, were at least as, if not more, important in influencing locational decisions as were their static counterparts. This led on to an examination of the drawing power of clusters of related firms in micro-regions; and how MNEs have both responded to, and influenced, the form of these clusters. Empirical evidence suggests that, whereas in the case of asset exploiting FDI, MNEs are most active in clusters involving below average knowledge-intensive activities, in the case of asset augmenting FDI they are increasingly gravitating to above average knowledge-intensive activities.[82]

One of the key conclusions of this chapter is that a carefully planned and executed locational strategy of MNEs is becoming an increasingly important factor influencing their global competitiveness. *Inter alia*, such a strategy should comprise the siting of firm specific, but mobile intangible, assets, in countries and/or micro-regions which offer the most congenial complementary immobile assets. This conclusion applies equally to asset seeking and to asset exploiting FDI. Since, too, the distance costs of the more idiosyncratic knowledge-intensive transactions are probably increasing – as are the number and complexity of these transactions – the advantages of the spatial clustering of related activity increase – and this is in spite of the huge advances in telecommunications and distance learning facilities.

A second critical conclusion of our analysis is that the growing mobility of firm specific core competencies is placing increasing responsibility on micro-regional authorities to ensure the availability and quality of location bound complementary assets to attract the right kind of mobile investment. Moreover, as we have said, such a competitive advantage depends not only on the regional provision of general supportive assets (e.g. basic infrastructure), but on the identification and promotion of a set of the specific and unique advantages which cannot be easily imitated by other regions. These latter advantages and the policies of micro-regional authorities necessary to secure and augment them – may well include the promotion of distinctive clusters of related activities which, as shown in 'The role of MNEs' above, may be of very varied forms.

This chapter has also identified various lacunae in our scholarly knowledge about the ways in which MNEs might affect the economic prosperity of host micro-regions – particularly where the objective of the former is to protect or add to their asset base. The changing relationship between micro-regional, national and supranational governmental regimes, as each affects both the competitiveness of micro-regions and the behavior of MNEs investing, or likely to invest, in those regions, is also an under-researched area. More attention, too, needs to be given by students of business strategy to the significance of locational choice as a competitive advantage of firms; and how it may impact on their resource base, learning capabilities, values and entrepreneurial behavior.

Finally, if it is true that micro-regions are increasingly becoming one of the leading motors of economic development (Scott, 1998), and the gateways of countries to the global marketplace (Ohmae 1995), does it not make sense to view the MNE as one of the critical channels for organizing cross-border asset seeking and asset exploiting activities not only between different nation states but also between micro-regions within different nation states. Is it, indeed, not the case that the economic linkages between Silicon Valley in California and Silicon Glen in mid-Scotland, or between the New York and London financial districts, are at least as significant as those between the UK and the US as factors determining the international location of economic activity, and patterns of cross-border trade?

ACKNOWLEDGEMENT

I am grateful to H. Peter Gray for his comments on an earlier draft of this chapter.

NOTES

1. Defined as enterprises which own or control foreign owned value-added activities, and which internalize cross-border intermediate product markets.
2. Such as a variety of non-equity co-operative agreements, e.g. strategic alliances, licensing, franchising, subcontracting, turnkey agreements and so on.
3. By asset augmenting activities we mean those directed to increasing the existing stock of resources and capabilities within the domain of firms or countries; by asset exploiting activities we mean those directed to utilizing existing assets in order to produce added value from them.
4. See, for example, some recent contributions by Michael Porter (Porter, 1994, 1996, 1998) on this subject.
5. Throughout this chapter, we will define macro-regions as a grouping of nation states located in geographically bounded but proximate space. A classification of a macro-region may vary according to the purposes of that classification. Examples of macro-regions include the European Union (EU), the North American Free Trade Agreement (NAFTA), MERCOSUR, APEC and ASEAN. By contrast, we shall use the term micro-regions to embrace sub-national spatial units. These units may be large, e.g. states within the US; or very small, e.g. cities, industrial estates and science parks.
6. We use this expression to embrace all activities, both asset augmenting and asset exploiting which create an income stream.
7. A clear exception must be made of craftsmanship, which dates back to the Middle Ages and beyond.
8. This is a generic expression embracing all kinds of knowledge and competition embodied in both human, physical and organizational capital. For further details, see Edvinson (1997).
9. Chemicals and pharmaceuticals, machinery and electrical equipment, computers and office equipment, industrial and scientific instruments.
10. In 1995, on average, services (excluding those part of primary or secondary production) accounted for 63 percent of the world's GNP compared with 53 percent in 1980 and 45 percent in 1965). For further details see World Bank (1997), Tables 11 and 12.

11. The knowledge content of a firm may be likened to a completed jigsaw puzzle. The central pieces represent its core competencies, which are usually created by itself. However, to obtain the complete picture, these pieces need to be locked into others. These, while representing the resources and capabilities of other firms, have to be shaped so as to fit into the central pieces.
12. Sometimes referred to as 'relational', 'collective', 'collaborative and associational' and 'stakeholder' capitalism. For a review of these and similar concepts, see Dunning (1997a) and Cooke and Morgan (1998).
13. Cooke and Morgan (1998), for example, distinguish between the principal–agent and trustee models of corporate governance; between hierarchical (M form) and heterarchical (N form) modes of organization; between stand-alone, or linear, and integrated approaches to innovation; between coercive and participatory forms of work organization; and between adversarial and collaborative supply chain relationships.
14. Estimates of alliances vary considerably. A recent study by Booz, Allen and Hamilton has put the number of all cross-border alliances and M&As in 1995 and 1996 as high as 15 000 (Booz, Allen and Hamilton, 1997). Another estimate by Hagedoorn (1996) is that between 1980 and 1994 the number of newly established cross-border technology alliances (which are mainly directed at asset augmenting activities) rose by over three times. Finally, the value of international M&As between 1991 and 1997 has increased by four times, and accounted for around three-fifths of all FDI flows over the same period (UNCTAD, 1998).
15. Between 1920 and 1970 average ocean freight and port charges (per short ton of cargo) fell from $25 to $5; the average air transport costs per passenger mile fell from $0.68 to $0.11; while the cost of a three-minute telephone call from New York to London fell from $244.7 to $3.3 (Hufbauer, 1991).
16. For example, between 1980 and 1996 the combined exports and imports as a percentage of GNP × 2 of the US rose from 9.1 percent to 12.0 percent. Corresponding figures for the UK were 22.5 percent and 29.6 percent; for Germany 23.2 percent and 22.2 percent; for Korea 34.2 percent and 34.4 percent; and for Venezuela 25.5 percent and 29.0 percent. The relevant figures for FDI stock as a percent of GNP were 5.8 percent and 9.4 percent for the US, 13.6 percent and 25.6 percent for the UK, 5.5 percent and 9.2 percent for Germany, 1.0 percent and 2.7 percent for Korea and for Venezuela 1.3 percent and 9.1 percent (IMD, 1998).
17. For further details, see UNCTAD (1998).
18. Averaged over the years 1979 and 1994–96.
19. To give just one example, in 1996, of the worldwide research and development expenditure of around $580 billion, 91 percent was concentrated in the advanced industrial countries. (Author's estimate, calculated from data contained in IMD, 1998, Table 7.01.)
20. Some evidence for this assertion in respect of changes in the location of economic activity in the European Community consequential upon the completion of the internal market is given in Dunning (1997b). In a more recent paper, Cantwell and Iammarino (1998) have shown that between 1969 and 1995 some 60.8 percent of the R&D activities by foreign owned firms in the UK was concentrated in the Soudi East of England, compared with 41.7 percent for all large firms.
21. NB usually, but not always, those of its individual value-adding units.
22. Overall, between 1985 and 1997 the value of cross-border M&As, as a proportion of FDI flows, averaged 55 percent, while between the early 1980s and 1996 the number of inter-firm technology agreements increased by 2 to 3 times (UNCTAD, 1998, pp. 19 and 23).
23. The share of new FDI directed to developing countries rose from 19.6 percent in 1983–88 to 29.6 percent in 1989–94 (UNCTAD, 1995).
24. Thus, in 1995 it was estimated that 75 percent of the foreign direct investment stock in China was from other Asian countries.
25. In 1993, 11.7 percent of the sales of US foreign affiliates was in services (other than trade) and 7.9 percent in finance and business services. The corresponding figures for 1982 were 8.1 percent and 4.4 percent (US Dept of Commerce, 1985 and 1995).
26. US Department of Commerce data reveal that, in 1994, the R&D performed by US foreign affiliates amounted to 13.0 percent of that of their parent companies. The corresponding percentage in 1982 was 7 percent and in 1989 9 percent (US Department of Commerce, 1985, 1998; Dunning, 1993).

27. Further details are set out in various articles and books. See especially Granstrand, Håkanson and Sjolander (1992), OECD (1997a, 1997b), Archibugi and Iammarino (1998) and Cantwell and Harding (1998).
28. For example, the share of patents registered in the home countries of OECD member states accounted for by non-resident firms doubled between 1984 and 1994, as did the share of patents registered abroad by firms from those countries.
29. Initially by Adam Smith (1776) and Alfred Marshall (1920) and then by most economic geographers and spatial economists.
30. For a review of some of these see Audretsch (1998) and other papers contained in a special issue of the *Oxford Review of Economic Policy*, **14** (2), Summer, 1998.
31. As acknowledged and explored by James Markusen in his various writings. See especially Markusen (1995).
32. For a summary of the main factors which facilitate intra-national and intra-regional agglomeration, see Ottavinano and Puga (1997). For an analysis of why spatial clustering is more likely to occur *within* countries rather than *between* countries see Davis and Weinstein (1997).
33. Thus, for example, Silicon Valley in California, as well as competing with some other (but not all) regions in the US for mobile knowledge-intensive investment, may also compete with, e.g. Silicon Glen in Scotland and similar micro-regional complexes in Japan, Germany and Italy. The main competitor to the Sheffield cutlery industry is not another UK region, but Solingen in Germany. For other examples see Enright (1998).
34. Such research as has been conducted (see, for example, Baptista and Swann, 1994) suggests that firms which are located in strong clusters in the UK are more likely to innovate than those in other regions.
35. However, a recent study on inter-firm alliances in the US semi-conductor industry suggests that the 'optimum' spatial area associated with such economies may be larger than is commonly supposed (Arita and McCann, 1998).
36. As documented in some detail by Dunning and Morgan (1971).
37. Notably, the access to a pool of flexible skilled labor, common support services and availability of non-tradable specialized inputs, the capturing of information spillovers, a more competitive and/or entrepreneurial environment, and a common set of shared values and ideologies.
38. According to Giersch, as the economic variables affecting production costs in different countries converge, so the non-economic variables affecting transaction costs become a more significant determinant of locational competition. Such variables include the ethics of property and contracts, attitudes to technical progress, and economic and civic morality modes of corporate and individual behavior and cultural assets.
39. As described by Michael Porter (1986). In practice, however, most large modern MNEs exhibit aspects of each of these structures.
40. See, for example, Dunning (1958) (reprinted with a statistical update 1998), Hill and Munday (1992), Mariotti and Piscitello (1995) and Cantwell and Iammarino (1998).
41. Thus in the UK, for example, the proportion of post-World War II FDI located in areas of above average unemployment or below average rates of growth has been considerably higher than that of indigenous firms (Dunning, 1958 (1998)).
42. Notably those of Srinivasan and Mody (1998), and Braunerhjelm and Svensson (1995).
43. A recent example is the 'follow my leader' strategy of Japanese MNEs in the consumer electronics industry in South Wales. Since Sony first invested in a Newport factory, several other Japanese companies have located in the same area.
44. An example in the pharmaceutical industry to undertake R&D on tropical medicines in the tropical countries and advanced biotechnology in the triad countries.
45. As in the case of much of Japanese FDI in the European pharmaceutical sector – an internationally oriented sector in which currently Japanese firms have a competitive *dis*advantage.
46. This is not to deny there may be restrictions placed on foreign owned firms from accessing some kinds of capital. This point is taken up further in the section headed 'A regional perspective'.
47. For a recent catalogue of some of these, see Enright (1998).

48. Note that not all of these clusters are based on semi-skilled labor; for example, the comparative advantage of a Bangalore computer software complex is based on the created availability of highly skilled and professional labor.
49. For example by encouraging 'follow my leader' tactics by other firms (Knickerbocker, 1973). In his study of the inter-state distribution of FDI in the US, Miles Shaver (1996) showed that this was positively correlated to their separate agglomeration measures.
50. However, there are other clusters which have developed without the presence of MNEs. The City of London financial district, the North Italian woolen textile industry, and even (initially at least) the electronics industry, Silicon Valley are all cases in point.
51. In a recent paper, Enright (1998) gives several examples of foreign firms being drawn into spatial clusters by the presence of knowledge enhancing facilities. Nissan, he observes, does a substantial part of its new design work in Southern California, a leading center of auto design. Several European chemical and pharmaceutical companies do the bulk of their biotechnology research in biotechnology clusters in the US. The established financial centers of London, New York and Tokyo, far from losing their competitive advantage in high value activities, seem to be consolidating this advantage. At the same time, banking and financial MNEs are being increasingly drawn to new financial clusters in Hong Kong and Singapore (Enright, 1998, p. 5).
52. For some evidence of the increasing role played by the subsidiaries of MNEs in innovatory activities, see Pearce (1999), Pearce and Papanastassiou (1996) and Papanastassiou and Pearce (1999). In this latter paper, the authors also point to the role played by supportive institutions in the UK, e.g. universities, scientific institutions, etc., in influencing the amount and character of R&D undertaken by foreign affiliates in that country.
53. There is widespread support for this statement. For a summary of the literature, see Dunning (1996, 1998) and Makino (1998). Both authors also offer an interpretation of the theory of asset seeking investment.
54. For example, where in 1993, 68.4 percent of the Japanese owned R&D laboratories were concentrated in four US states, viz. California, Michigan, New Jersey and Massachusetts, only 32.8 percent of Japanese owned manufacturing establishments were so located (Florida and Kenney, 1994). In the UK, between 1969 and 1995 60.8 percent of patents registered by the subsidiaries of foreign firms, were attributable to research undertaken in London and South East England (Cantwell and Iammarino, 1998a). In Italy, over the same period, 67.2 percent of patents registered by such firms were attributable to research undertaken in two districts – Piedmonte and Lombardia (Cantwell and Iammarino, 1998b).
55. In his paper, Scott shows that the growth of the value added in manufacturing in the 40 metropolitan areas in the US with more than one million people was 30.6 percent between 1972 and 1992 (after discounting for inflation) – well above the national average of 20.3 percent. However, he also shows that the fastest rate of growth (81.5 percent) occurred in the 'sunbelt' group of metropolitan areas, which, not only did not have the industrial heritage of the other, e.g. areas in the North East, but made a focussed effort to build their economies on knowledge- and information-intensive manufacturing and service sectors.
56. Clearly this varies between countries and according to the respective investment opportunities offered by home and foreign countries. Over the last decade or so, for example, the proportion of the sales of the foreign affiliates of US corporations has remained around 30 percent; but in the case of several European countries, e.g. UK and Germany and most Asian countries (especially Japan), it has markedly increased (UNCTAD, 1997, 1998).
57. The spread of MNEs into more countries is particularly noticeable in the service sectors.
58. For a more detailed examination of this theme, see Enright (1998).
59. See especially Caves (1996) and Dunning (1997a).
60. One recent exception is that of Wallace (1998), who has recently completed a Ph.D. dissertation on FDI in New Jersey.
61. We recognize, of course, there are many layers of micro-regional governance, e.g. from states, to countries, to districts, to cities, to businesses and other parks.
62. This is not to deny there may be some 'X' inefficiencies in the actions of regional government in providing these services, or in promoting a 'hassle free' business environment; or, indeed, of publicizing the benefits of the resources and capabilities within their jurisdiction to foreign

investors as well, or aggressively, as they might. For a discussion of such policies pursued by US state governments, see Donahue (1998).

63. For an examination of the importance of this kind of collaboration, and of .the need for a reconstruction of some local institutions in the light of the increasing importance of mobile investment, see an interesting case study of the Korean MNE LG in South Wales (Phelps and Tewdwr-Jones, 1998; Phelps, Lovering and Morgan, 1998).
64. Enright (1998), for example, gives details of the specific needs of different kinds of clusters for complementary assets, some of which are under the governance of regional authorities. These include 'effluent treatment facilities for specific industries (Catalan leather), dedicated water (Malaysian electronics) or electricity lines (Venezuelan metals) and specialized port (Hong Kong trading) or airfreight facilities (Dutch flowers), specific training programs in software (Bangalore), motion pictures (Los Angeles), materials science (Sassuolo), wine making (Napa Valley), and electronics (Singapore) among others' (Enright, 1998, p. 7).
65. See, for example, a very interesting paper entitled 'Singapore Incorporated' by Haley, Low and Toh (1996).
66. For a careful analysis of the role of institutional systems in minimizing the transaction costs of economic activity and maximizing the benefits of specialization and the agglomeration of related firms see Kasper and Streit (1998). Although the authors do not address the specific problems and challenges of micro-regional governments, much of what they write is directly relevant to them.
67. Michael Porter, in his 1990 book, argued that the main role of national governments was to do nothing which would prevent, retard or distort cluster formation. In his latest thinking, Porter (1996, 1998) assigns a more positive role for micro-regional governments; and particularly that of promoting 'specialization, upgrading and trade among regions' (Porter 1996, p. 88). Porter goes on to assert that cluster formation can be encouraged by *specialized* infrastructure and institution in areas where factor endowments, past industrial activities, or even historical accidents have resulted in concentration of economic activity.
68. See Park (1996), Markusen (1996) and Markusen and Gray (1998).
69. For a detailed analysis of the Seattle hub-and-spoke district see Gray, Golob and Markusen (1996). In his review of clusters, Park (1998) distinguishes between supplier and customer, and advanced supplier and advanced customer hub-and-spoke clusters.
70. And, indeed, before that by Adam Smith (1776), as recently highlighted by Ozawa (2000).
71. And documented by Hall et al. (1987).
72. As documented by Diniz and Razavi (1997).
73. As viewed from the perception of the micro-region.
74. See Dunning (1970) for a discussion of the social and private price of domestic assets acquired by foreign firms.
75. Between 1990 and 1997 the combined foreign acquisitions by European and US firms amounted to \$1134 billion, while the foreign purchases of European and US firms totaled \$957 billion (UNCTAD, 1998).
76. The relationship between US technology policy and the competitiveness of US firms and inbound foreign direct investment is explored by Ham and Mowery (1997).
77. Sometimes as modified by the personal preferences or prejudices of the main decision taker(s)!
78. Most particular as explored by Knickerbocker (1973) in his 'follow my leader' hypothesis and Graham (1978) in his exchange of threats hypothesis.
79. Most noticeably from the innovatory through the mature to the senescent stage.
80. See, for example, Graham (1990) and Cantwell and Randaccio (1992).
81. Although we accept that firms might continue to differentiate their products from those supplied by their competitors – and, indeed, to do so even more intensively than in the past.
82. See an interesting paper by Birkinshaw and Hood (1997), which distinguishes between two kinds of clusters, viz. 'leading edge' cluster, e.g. Silicon Valley, and a 'branch plant' cluster, e.g. Scotland's electronics industry. They conclude that, historically, FDI has tended to be concentrated and has had the most influence on structure and development of the latter kind of cluster. They accept, however, that the advent of the globalizing economy may lead to more FDI in the leading edge clusters.

REFERENCES

Archibugi, D. and Iammarino, S. (1998), *Innovation and Globalization, Evidence and Implications*, Reading: University of Reading Discussion Papers in International Investment and Business, March.

Arita, T. and McCann, P. (1998), *Industrial Alliances and Firm Location Behavior: Some Evidence From the US Semiconductor Industry*, Reading: University of Reading Discussion Papers in Urban and Regional Economies, No. 130, March.

Audretsch, D.B. (1998), 'Agglomeration and the location of economic activity,' *Oxford Review of Economic Policy* **14** (2), pp. 18–29.

Balasubramanyam, V.N. and Balasubramanyam, A. (2000), 'The software cluster in Bangalore', in Dunning, J.H. (ed.), *Regions, Globalization and the Knowledge-Based Economy*, Oxford: Oxford University Press, pp. 349–63.

Baptista, R. and Swann, P. (1994), *Do Firms in Clusters Innovate More? An Exploratory Study*, London: London Business School (mimeo).

Birkinshaw, J. and Hood, N. (1997), *Foreign Investment and Industry Cluster Development: The Characteristics of Subsidiary Companies in Different Types of National Industry Clusters*, Stockholm School of Economics and Strathclyde University (mimeo).

Booz, Allen and Hamilton (1997), *Cross Border Alliances in the Age of Collaboration*, Los Angeles: Booz, Allen and Hamilton.

Braunerhjelm, P. and Svensson, R. (1995), *Host Country Characteristics and Agglomeration in Foreign Direct Investment*, Stockholm: Industrial Institute for Economic and Social Research (mimeo), October.

Cantwell, J.A. and Harding, R. (1998), 'The internationalization of German companies' R&D,' *National Institute Economic Review* **16** (3), pp. 99–115.

Cantwell, J.A. and Iammarino, S. (1998), *Multinational Corporations and the location of Technological Innovation in the UK Regions*, University of Reading Discussion Papers in International Investment and Management, No. 262, December.

Cantwell, J. and Sanna Radaccio, F. (1992), 'Intra-industry direct investment in the European Community,' in Cantwell, J.C. (ed.), *Multinational Investment in Modern Europe: Strategic Interaction in the Integrated Community*, Aldershot (Hants) and Brookfield (Vermont): Edward Elgar, pp. 71–106.

Caves, R. (1996), *Multinational Firms and Economic Analysis* (Second edition), Cambridge: Cambridge University Press.

Cooke, P. and Morgan, K. (1998), *The Associational Economy*, Oxford: Oxford University Press.

Davis, D.R. and Weinstein, E. (1997), *Economic Geography and Regional Production Structure: An Empirical Investigation*, Cambridge, MA: NBER Working Paper No. 6093.

DeLong, G., Smith, R.C. and Walter, I. (1996), *Global Merger and Acquisition Tables 1995*, New York: Salomon Center (mimeo).

Diniz, C.C. and Razavi, M. (1997), 'State Anchored Dynamos: São José Dos Campos and Campinos, Brazil,' in Markusen, A. and Lee, Yong Sook, *Second Tier Cities: Explaining Rapid Growth in Brazil, Korea, Japan and the United States*, Minneapolis: University of Minnesota Press, pp. 97–123.

Donahue, J.D. (1998), *Disunited States*, New York: Basic Books.

Doremus, P., Keller, W.W., Pauly, L.W. and Reich, S. (1998), *The Myth of the Global Corporation*, Princeton, NJ: Princeton University Press.

Doz, Y.L., Asakawa, K., Santos, J.F.P. and Williamson, P.J. (1998), *The Metanational Corporation*, Fontainebleau, France: INSEAD Working Paper 97/60/SM.

Dunning, J.H. (1958, 1998), *American Investment in British Manufacturing Industry*, London: Allen & Unwin (1998 edition published by Routledge, London and New York).

Dunning, J.H. (1970), *Studies in International Investment*, London: Allen & Unwin.

Dunning, J.H. (1993), *Multinational Enterprises and the Global Economy*, Wokingham, England and Reading, MA: Addison-Wesley.

Dunning, J.H. (1996), 'The geographical sources of competitiveness of firms: the results of a new survey,' *Transnational Corporations* **5** (3), December, pp. 1–30.

Dunning, J.H. (1997a), *Alliance Capitalism and Global Business*, London and New York: Routledge.

Dunning, J. H. (1997b), 'The European internal market program and inbound foreign direct investment,' *Journal of Common Market Studies* **35** (1 and 2), pp. 1–30 and 189–223.

Dunning, J.H. (1998a), 'Globalization and the theory of MNE activity,' paper presented to a conference on *Multinational Enterprise Activity and Economic Development*, Strathclyde, Scotland, May.

Dunning, J.H. (1998b), 'The changing geography of foreign direct investment,' in Kumar, K. (ed.), *Globalization, Foreign Direct Investment and Technology Transfer: Impact and Prospects for Developing Countries*, London and New York: Routledge, pp. 43–90.

Dunning, J.H. and Narula, R. (eds) (1996), *Foreign Direct Investment and Governments*, London and New York: Routledge.

Dunning, J.H. and Morgan, E.V. (eds) (1971), *An Economic Study of the City of London*, London: Allen & Unwin.

Edvinson, L. (1997), *Intellectual Capital Development*, Stockholm: Skandia.

Enright, M.J. (2000), 'The globalization of competition and the localization of competitive advantage: policies toward regional clustering,' in Hood, N. and Young, S. (eds), *Globalization of Economic Activity and Economic Development*, Basingstoke, Hampshire: Macmillan, pp. 303–31.

Feldman, M.P. and Audretsch, D. (1999), 'Innovation in cities: science based diversity, specialization and localized competition,' *European Economic Review* **43**, pp. 409–27.

Florida, R. (1995), 'Towards the learning region,' *Futures* **27** (5), pp. 527–36.

Florida, R. and Kenney, M. (1994), 'The globalization of Japanese R&D: the economic geography of Japanese R&D investment in the United States,' *Economic Geography* **70**, pp. 343–69.

Giersch, H. (1996), 'Economic morality as a competitive asset,' in Hamlin, A., Giersch, H. and Norton, A., *Markets, Morals and Community*, St Leonards, Australia: Center for Independent Studies Occasional Paper No. 59.

Graham, E.M. (1978), 'Transatlantic investment by multinational firms: a rivalistic phenomenon,' *Journal of Post Keynesian Economics* **1**, pp. 82–99.

Graham, E.M. (1990), 'Exchange of threats between multinational firms as an infinitely repeated non-cooperative game,' *International Trade Journal* **4** (3), pp. 259–77.

Granstrand, O., Håkanson, L. and Sjolander, S. (eds) (1992), *Technology, Management and International Business: Internationalization of R&D and Technology*, Chichester (UK): Wiley.

Gray, H.P. (1996), 'The eclectic paradigm: the next generation,' *Transnational Corporations* **5** (2), pp. 51–66.

Gray, M., Golob, E. and Markusen, A. (1996), 'Big firms, long arms, a portrait of a "hub and spoke" industrial district in the Seattle region,' *Regional Studies* **30** (7), pp. 651–66.

Hagedoorn, J. (1996), 'Trends and patterns in strategic technology partnering since the early seventies,' *Review of Industrial Organization* **11**, pp. 601–16.

Haley, U.C.V., Low, L. and Toh, Mun-Heng (1996), 'Singapore Incorporated: reinterpreting Singapore's business environments through a corporate metaphor,' *Management Decision* **34** (9), pp. 17–28.

Hall, P., Breheny, M., McQuaid, R. and Hart, D. (1987), *Western Sunrise*, London and Boston: Allen & Unwin.

Ham, R. and Mowery, D. (1997), 'The United States,' in Dunning, J.H. (ed.), *Governments, Globalization and International Business*, Oxford: Oxford University Press, pp. 283–321.

Handy, C. (1990), *The Age of Unreason*, London: Hutchinson.

Harrison, B. (1992), 'Industrial districts: old wine in new bottles,' *Regional Studies* **26** (5), pp. 469–83.

Hill, S. and Munday, M. (1992), 'The UK regional distribution of foreign direct investment: analysis and determinants,' *Regional Studies* **26**, pp. 534–44.

Hotelling, H. (1929), 'Stability in competition,' *Economic Journal* **29**, pp. 41–57.

Hufbauer, G. (1991), 'World economic integration: the long view,' *Economic Insights* **30**, pp. 26–27.

IMD (1998), *The World Competitive Yearbook 1998*, Lausanne: IMD.

IMF (vd), *Balance of Payments Statistical Yearbook* (annual publication), Washington: IMF.

International Telecommunications Union (2000), *Telecommunications Industry at a Glance: Mobile Driving Growth of Telecommunication Markets*, Geneva: ITU.

Kasper, W. and Streit, M. (1998), *Institutional Economics, Social Order and Public Policy*, Cheltenham, UK: Edward Elgar.

Knickerbocker, F.T. (1973), *Oligopolistic Reaction and the Multinational Enterprise*, Cambridge, MA: Harvard University Press.

Kozul-Wright, R. (1997), 'The size of nations: small economies in a globalizing world,' *Development and International Cooperation* **XIII** (24 and 15), pp. 105–38.

Krugman, P.R. (1991), *Geography and Trade*, Cambridge, MA: MIT Press.

Krugman, P.R. (1993), 'On the relationship between trade theory and location theory,' *Review of International Economics* **1** (2), pp. 110–22.

Krugman, P.R. (1995), *Development, Geography and Economic Theory*, Cambridge, MA: MIT Press.

Kuemmerle, W. (1996), 'The drivers of foreign direct investment into research and development: an empirical investigation', *Journal of International Business Studies* **30** (1), pp. 1–24.

Liu, S.X. (1998), *Foreign Direct Investment and the Multinational Enterprise. A Reexamination Using Signaling Theory*, Westport, CT: Greenwood Publishing.

Makino, S. (1998), *Toward a Theory of Asset Seeking Foreign Direct Investment*, Hong Kong: The Chinese University (mimeo).

Mariotti, S. and Piscitello, L. (1995), 'Information costs and location of FDIs within the host country: empirical evidence from Italy,' *Journal of International Business Studies* **26** (4), pp. 815–41.

Markusen, A. (1996), 'Sticky places in slippery space: a typology of industrial districts,' *Economic Geography* **72** (3), pp. 293–313.

Markusen, A. and Gray, M. (1999), 'Clusters and regional development in New Jersey,' in J.H. Dunning (ed.), *New Jersey in a Globalizing Economy*, Newark: Rutgers University, CIBER.

Markusen, J.R. (1995), 'The boundaries of multinational enterprises and the theory of international trade,' *Journal of Economic Perspectives* **9** (2), pp. 169–89.

Marshall, A. (1920), *Principles of Economics*, London: Macmillan (eighth edition).

McGrew, A.G. (1992), 'Conceptualizing global politics' in McGrew, A.G. and Lewis, P.G. (eds), *Global Politics: Globalization and the Nation State*, Cambridge: The Polity Press.

McIntyre, J.R., Narula, R. and Trevino, L. J. (1996), 'The role of export processing zones for host countries and multinationals: a mutually beneficial relationship?,' *International Trade Journal* **10**, pp. 435–66.

Mytelka, L.K. (1996), *Locational Tournaments, Strategic Partnerships and the State*, Ottawa: Carleton University (mimeo).

Narula, R. (1995), *Multinational Investment and Economic Structure*, London and Boston: Routledge.

National Science Foundation (1997), *Patenting Activity in the US*, Washington: National Science Foundation.

O'Brien, R. (1992), *Global Financial Integration: The End of Geography*, London: Pinter Publishers.

OECD (1996), *Networking Enterprises, Local Development*, Paris: OECD.

OECD (1997a), *Science and Technology Indicators*, Paris: OECD.

OECD (1997b), *Internationalization of Industrial R&D: Patterns and Trends*, Paris: Group of National Experts on Science and Technology Indicators, OECD.

Ohmae, K. (1995), *The End of the Nation State: The Rise of Regional Economies*, London: HarperCollins.

Oliver, C. (1997), 'Sustainable competitive advantage: combining institutional and resource based views,' *Strategic Management Journal* **18** (9), pp. 697–713.

Ottavinano, G. and Puga, D. (1997), *Agglomeration in the Global Economy: A Survey of the New Economic Geography*, London Centre for Economic Performance, Discussion Paper No. 356.

Ozawa, T. (2000), 'Small and medium size MNC, industrial clusters and globalization: the Japanese experience', in Hood, N. and Young, S. (eds), *Globalization of Multinational Enterprise Activity and Economic Development*, Basingstoke, Hampshire: Macmillan.

Papanastossiou, M. and Pearce, R.D. (1999), *Multinationals, Technology and National Competitiveness*, Cheltenham: Edward Elgar.

Park, S.O. (1996), 'Networks and embeddedness in the dynamic types of industrial districts,' *Progress in Human Geography* **20** (4), pp. 476–93.

Pearce, R.D. (1998) 'The evolution of technology in multinational enterprises: the role of creature subsidiaries,' *International Business Review* **8**, pp. 125–48.

Pearce, R.D. and Papanastassiou, M. (1996), 'R&D Networks and Innovation: Decentralized Product Development in Multinational Enterprises,' *R&D Management* **26** (4), pp. 315–33.

Peck, F.W. (1996), 'Regional development and the production of space: the role of infrastructure in the attraction of new inward investment,' *Environment and Planning* **28**: pp. 327–39.

Perraton, J., Goldblatt, D., Held, D. and McGrew, A. (1977), 'The globalisation of economic activity,' *New Political Economy* **2** (2).

Phelps, N.A. and Tewdwr-Jones, M. (1998), 'Institutional capacity building in a strategic vacuum: the case of the Korean company LG in south Wales,' *Environment and Planning C: Government and Policy* **16**, pp. 735–55.

Phelps, N.A., Loverin, J. and Morgan, K. (1998), 'Tying the firm to the region or tying the region to the firm?', *European Urban and Regional Studies* **5** (2), pp. 119–37.

Porter, M.E. (1985), *Competitive Advantage*, New York: The Free Press.

Porter, M.E. (ed.) (1986), *Competition in Global Industries*, Boston: Harvard Business School Press.

Porter, M.E. (1990), *The Competitive Advantage of Nations*, New York: The Free Press.

Porter, M.E. (1994), 'The role of location in competition,' *Journal of Economics of Business* **I** (1), pp. 35–9.

Porter, M.E. (1996), 'Competitive advantage, agglomerative economics and regional policy,' *International Regional Science Review* **19** (1 and 2), pp. 85–94.

Porter, M.E. (1998), 'Location, clusters and the "new" micro-economies of competition,' *Business Economics* **33**, Jan., pp. 7–13.

Putman, R.D. (1993), *Making Democracy Work: Civic Traditions in Modern Italy*, Princeton: Princeton University Press.

Schoenberger, E. (1988), 'Multinational Corporations and the new international division of labor: a critical appraisal,' *International Regional Science Review* **11** (2), pp. 105–19.

Scott, A. (1998), *Regional Motors of the Global Economy*, Newark: Rutgers University, CIBER Distinguished Lecture Series No. 1, March.

Shaver, J.M. (1996), *Industry Agglomeration and Foreign Greenfield Investment Survival in the United States*, New York: Stern School of Business (mimeo).

Smith, A. (1776), *An Inquiry into the Nature and Causes of the Wealth of Nations*, London (reprinted in Cannon, E. (ed.), New York, 1937).

Solvell, O. and Bengtsson, M. (1997), *The Role of Industry Structure Climate of Competition and Cluster Strength*, Stockholm Institute of International Business, Stockholm, School of Economics (mimeo).

Srinivasan, K. and Mody, A. (1998), 'Japanes & US firms as foreign investors: do they march to the same tune?,' *Canadian Journal of Economics* **31** (4), pp. 778–97.

Stewart, T.A. (1997), *Intellectual Capital*, London: Nicholas Brealy.

Stigler, G. (1951), 'The division of labor is limited by the extent of the market,' *Journal of Political Economy* **LIX**, pp. 185–93.

Stopford, J. and Strange, S. (1991), *Rival States, Rival Firms: Competition for World Market Shares*, Cambridge: Cambridge University Press.

Storper, M. (1995), 'The resurgence of region economies: ten years later: the region as a nexus of untraded interdependencies,' *European Urban and Regional Studies* **2** (3), pp. 191–221.

Storper, M. (1997), *The Regional World*, London: Guilford Press.

Storper, M. and Scott, A.J. (1995), 'The wealth of regions,' *Futures* **27** (5), pp. 505–26.

Strange, R. (]993), *Japanese Manufacturing Investment in Europe*, London and New York: Routledge.

UN (vd), *Annual Statistical Yearbook*, New York: UN.

UNCTAD (1993), *World Investment Report 1993: Transnational Corporations and Integrated International Production*, New York and Geneva: UN.

UNCTAD (1995), *World Investment Report 1995: Transnational Corporations and Competitiveness*, New York and Geneva: UN.

UNCTAD (1996), *Investment Incentives*, New York and Geneva: UN.

UNCTAD (1997), *World Investment Report 1997: Transnational Corporations, Market Structure and Competition Policy*, New York and Geneva: UN.
UNCTAD (1998), *World Investment Report 1998: Trends and Determinants*, New York and Geneva: UN.
US Patent and Trademark Office (1997), *Patenting Trends 1997*, Washington: US Patent and Trademark Office.
US Patent and Trademark Office (1999), *Patent Counts by Country/State and Year*, Washington: US Patent and Trademark Office, March.
US Dept. of Commerce (1995), *U.S. Direct Investment Abroad. Provisional Results 1993*, Washington: US Government Printing Office.
US Dept. of Commerce (1985), *U.S. Direct Investment Abroad 1982 Benchmark Survey Data*, Washington: Government Printing Office.
US Dept. of Commerce (1998) *U.S. Direct Investment Abroad 1994 Benchmark Survey Data*, Washington: Government Printing Office.
Vernon, R. (1974), 'The location of economic activity,' in Dunning, J.H. (ed.), *Economic Analysis and the Multinational Enterprise*, London: Allen and Unwin, pp. 84–114.
Wallace, L. (1998), *Foreign Direct Investment and the New Jersey Economy*, Newark, NJ: Ph.D. Thesis, Rutgers University, Faculty of Management.
World Bank (1997), *World Development Report*, Oxford: Oxford University Press.
World Bank (1998), *World Development Report*, Oxford: Oxford University Press.
Yannopoulos, G.N. and Dunning, J.H. (1976), 'MNEs and regional development: an exploratory paper,' *Regional Studies* **10** (5) pp. 389–401.

6. Location and the multinational enterprise: a neglected factor?*

INTRODUCTION

In 1986, the economist Wilfred J. Ethier, in seeking to explain the existence of multinational enterprises (MNEs), concluded that 'internalization appears to be emerging as the Caesar of the OLI triumvirate' (Ethier, 1986, p. 803). I did not agree with this statement then; nor do I do so now. The OLI triad of variables (ownership, location and internalization, discussed below) determining foreign direct investment (FDI) and MNE activity may be likened to a three-legged stool: each leg is supportive of the other, and the stool is only functional if the three legs are evenly balanced. In so far as the third leg completes this balancing it may be regarded as the most important, but there is no reason to suppose one leg performs this task better than another.

In the case of the eclectic paradigm, I would accept that the I component is the critical leg, if, given the O advantages of firms and the L advantages of countries, one is trying to explain why firms internalize the cross-border market for these advantages, rather than sell them or their rights to independent firms. But, I would aver it is no less correct to argue that, given its O-specific advantages, the critical choice of a multi-activity firm is whether it should internalize its intermediate product markets within its home country or in a foreign country; and that the outcome of this choice is primarily determined by the costs and benefits of adding value to these products in the two locations. I say primarily because the geography of international business activity is not independent of its entry mode; nor, indeed, of the competitive advantages of the investing firms. This interdependence is particularly apparent when one examines the dynamics of knowledge-intensive MNE activity.

In the 1960s, scholars such as Raymond Vernon and his colleagues at Harvard (see especially Vernon, 1966, 1974 and Wells, 1972), working on the determinants of FDI, gave pride of place to locational variables, particularly those determining the siting of US market seeking FDI by US firms in advanced industrial countries (see also the work of some European scholars, such as Bandera and White, 1968 and Scaperlanda and Mauer, 1969). In the mid-1970s

* From *Journal of International Business Studies*, **29** (1) (1998): 45–66.

– apart from research on the internationalization process of firms (see, for example, Johanson and Vahlne, 1977) – attention switched from the act of FDI *per se* to the institution making the investment. Here the main focus of interest was why firms should choose to set up or acquire foreign value-adding activities, rather than export the intangible assets (or the right to use these assets) underpinning such activities, directly to foreign firms (see especially the writings of Peter Buckley and Mark Casson, J.C. McManus, Jean-François Hennart, Alan Rugman and Birgitta Swedenborg, all of which are cited in Caves, 1982, 1996).

While I would be the first to acknowledge the value of this approach in advancing our understanding of MNEs *qua* MNEs, I believe that the contribution of the internalization school has done more to explain the existence and growth of the multi-activity firm than that of the MNE *per se*. This is because, with relatively few exceptions,[1] the transaction and coordination costs identified with arm's-length intermediate product markets have not, in general, been specific to cross-border markets, or, indeed, to traversing space.

The emphasis on the firm-specific determinants of international economic activity, while still driving much academic research by scholars in business schools, is now being complemented by a renewed interest in the spatial aspects of FDI; and of how these affect both the competitive advantages of firms and their modes of entry into, and expansion in, foreign markets. We believe there are two main reasons for this. The first is that the changing extent, character and geography of MNE activity over the past two decades – itself a reflection of a series of path-breaking technological, economic and political events – is demanding an explanation by international business scholars. The second is that new research agendas, particularly those of economic geographers, trade theorists and international political economists, are not only paying more attention to the spatial aspects of value-added activity, but are also seeking to incorporate these aspects into the mainstream thinking about the growth and competitiveness of firms, the relationship between trade and FDI, and the economic structure and dynamic comparative advantage of regions and countries.

This chapter seeks to review some of these happenings, most of which come into prominence between the two editions of the publication of Richard Caves, *Multinational Enterprise and Economic Analysis* (1982, 1996). To his credit, Richard Caves acknowledges many of these in his second (1996) edition. But, since much of his analysis relates to the work of scholars in the 1980s,[2] his chapter on the international allocation of economic activity (Chapter 2) does not fully embrace the events and academic research of the last decade or so. It is these which will be the main concern of this contribution. The chapter will proceed in the following way. First if will briefly describe the changing global economic scenario in which MNE activity has been conducted since the mid-1970s, and also the various strands of intellectual thought which have sought to explain this. Second, it will examine how the microlocational determinants of international production have changed; and how the location portfolio of MNEs may itself help promote their dynamic competitive advantages. Third, it will consider how, from a more macroeconomic standpoint, the emergence of the MNE as a leading vehicle of cross-border transactions has affected our thinking about the determinants of trade and other non-MNE-related transactions.

THE CHANGING WORLD SCENARIO FOR INTERNATIONAL BUSINESS ACTIVITY

The last two decades have witnessed a gradual movement towards a world economy characterized by three features. The first is the emergence of intellectual capital as the key wealth-creating asset in most industrial economies. In the 1990s, the market value of industrial corporations has been variously calculated (e.g. by Blair, 1995; Handy, 1989; Edvinson, 1997) at between 2½ and 5 times the value of their tangible assets, compared with 1½ times in 1982. The annual capital expenditure on information technology by US corporations now exceeds that on production technology (Stewart, 1997). The knowledge component of the output of manufacturing goods is estimated to have risen from 20 percent in the 1950s to 70 percent in 1995 (Stewart, 1997), while those workers whose main task is to create new knowledge or disseminate information (viz. professional and technical workers, managers, sales and clerical workers – the so-called 'white collar' workers) increased their share of the American labor force from 42 percent in 1960 to 58 percent in 1990, and this share is expected to rise to more than 60 percent by 2000.

A further indicator of the rising significance of non-material assets as creators or facilitators of wealth is the growth of services, and particularly those which are, themselves, knowledge or information intensive. In 1995, on average, services accounted for 63 percent of the world's gross national product (GNP), compared with 53 percent in 1980 and 45 percent in 1965 (World Bank, 1997). In so far as knowledge-intensive and knowledge-supporting production has its unique spatial needs, and tends to require resources and capabilities which MNEs are particularly well suited to provide, it is not unreasonable to hypothesize that both these features will impinge on the geographical distribution of FDI and related activities.

Secondly, and even more transparent, is the increasing globalization of economic activity, made possible, *inter alia*, by advances in transport and communications technologies and the reduction in trade and investment barriers throughout the world (UNCTAD, various issues and World Bank, various issues). Over the last two decades, the growth of world trade has consistently outstripped that of world output, while in the mid-1990s the sales of the foreign affiliates of MNEs exceeded the value of world trade by 27 percent (UNCTAD, 1997). Moreover, between one-third and one-half of trade in non-agricultural products and between one-half and three-fifths of capital and knowledge flows are currently internalized within MNEs.[3]

At the same time, the ease with which MNEs can transfer intangible assets across national boundaries is being constrained by the fact that the location of the creation and use of these assets is becoming increasingly influenced by the presence of immobile clusters of complementary value-added activities. This is particularly the case where the transaction costs of traversing distance are high, or where the transactional benefits of spatial proximity are significant.[4] Thus while globalization suggests that the location and ownership of production is becoming geographically more dispersed, other economic forces are making for a more pronounced geographical concentration of such activity both within particular regions and within countries.[5] In the words of Ann Markusen (1996), these events are presenting scholars and policy makers with a paradox of 'sticky places within slippery space'.

The third feature of the contemporary global economy is the emergence of what may be called 'alliance' capitalism (sometimes called relational, collective, stakeholder and collaborative capitalism – see Dunning, 1995). While retaining many of the characteristics of hierarchical capitalism, the distinctive feature of alliance capitalism is the growing extent to which, in order to achieve their respective objectives, the main stakeholders in the wealth-seeking process are needing to collaborate more actively and purposefully with each other. Such collaboration includes the conclusion of closer, continuing, and more clearly delineated *intra*-firm relationships, e.g. between functional departments and between management and labor; the growth of a variety of inter-firm co-operative agreements,[6] e.g. between suppliers and customers and among competitors; and the recognition by governments and firms alike of the need to work as partners if the economic goals of society (for which the former are ultimately responsible) are to be best achieved.

Once again, the growing propensity of firms to engage in cross-border alliances has implications not just for the modality by which knowledge and other intangible assets are transferred across national boundaries, but for the location of value-added activities – especially high value asset-augmenting activities.

Underpinning and reinforcing each of the events just described are two other factors which also have had a profound effect on both the macro and micro geography of MNEs. The first is the advent, in the 1980s, of a new generation of technological advances which, according to Alan Greenspan (in a speech given to New York bankers in April 1997) are only now, in the later 1990s, fully bearing fruit.[7] The second factor is the renaissance of the market economy, and the consequential changes in the macroeconomic policies and macro-organizational (micro-management) strategies of many national governments. This is most vividly demonstrated by the happenings in China and Central and Eastern Europe, but, almost as far reaching is the reappraisal of the role of the State and markets in economic development now being played out in India, and in several African and Latin American economies (World Bank, 1997). Both factors have had a major impact on the economic and political risk assessment of FDI by MNEs.

THE CHANGING GEOGRAPHY OF MNE ACTIVITY

The developments just described have all impacted on the geography of FDI and MNE activity (as described in more detail in Dunning, 1998). In the period 1991–1996, 64 percent of global FDI inflows were received by the developed countries, 33 percent by developing countries and 3 percent by Central and Eastern European countries. The corresponding percentages for the period 1975–1980 were 77 percent, 23 percent and less than 0.1 percent (UNCTAD, 1997). No less noticeable have been the changes in the distribution of inbound FDI within these regions. While the shares of Western Europe and the United States compared to all FDI in developed countries, have remained broadly the same,[8] those within developing countries have markedly changed. For example, between 1975–1980 and 1991–1996, South, East and Southeast Asia (including China and India) increased their share of inbound investment to developing countries from 26 percent to 62 percent, while that of Latin America and the Caribbean fell from 53 percent to 34 percent.

It is perhaps worth observing that although the share of inbound FDI to the gross fixed capital formation of the countries more than doubled between the second half of the 1970s and the first half of the 1990s (UNCTAD, 1988, 1996a), the changing geography of FDI parallels reasonably well that of all investment, independently of its ownership. Between 1975 and 1980, and 1990 and 1995, for example, the share of world inbound FDI accounted for by developed countries fell from 78 percent to 70 percent, while that of world gross fixed capital formation (including that part financed by foreign firms) fell from 84 percent to 73 percent. The corresponding figures for all developing economies were 21 percent and 30 percent, and 15 percent and 26 percent; and for Asia 7 percent and 19 percent, and 7 percent and 19 percent. Although there are differences in the geography of FDI which can be specifically attributed to the political or economic conditions in the host country[9] – and it is most certainly the case that the geography of outward FDI is quite strongly country specific[10] – the data suggest that many of the factors which explain the location of FDI may not be unique to its country of origin. We shall not elaborate on this point here; but it is, perhaps, worthy of more attention.

THE MICROECONOMICS OF THE LOCATION OF MNE ACTIVITY

With the caveat of the last paragraph, we now consider how scholarly thinking about the location of MNEs has evolved over the last two decades. Incidentally, we suspect that the fact that this subject has not been given much attention by international business scholars is partly because scholars have believed that the principles underlying the locational decisions of firms within national boundaries can be easily extended to explain their cross-border locational preferences;[11] and partly because economists were either generally satisfied with existing explanations, or just not interested in the subject. Certainly, until the early 1990s, there was little in common between the methodologies of international trade economists and locational economists, excepting the work of Bertil Ohlin (1933) and his successors. This was primarily because the former were concerned with country-specific general equilibrium models or models under very restrictive conditions, whereas the latter were mainly interested in firm or industry-specific partial equilibrium models with fewer constraints (Krugman, 1993).

Earlier in this chapter, we identified three major developments in the global economy which have impinged upon both the capabilities and strategies of MNEs, or potential MNEs, and the locational attractions offered by particular countries to mobile investors. In particular, we emphasized first the growing significance of firm-specific knowledge-intensive assets in the wealth-creating process, and the kind of customized assets, e.g. skilled labor and public infrastructure, which needed to be jointly used with these assets if they were to be effectively harnessed and deployed;[12] secondly, the reduction of many natural and artificial impediments to trade, but the rise of other spatially related transaction costs; and thirdly, the growing need and ease with which firms are able to coordinate their cross-border activities and form alliances with foreign firms.

Some of these factors have led firms to own and concentrate particular types of value-added activities within a limited number of locations; others have led them to disperse such activities across several locations. Some have favored a realignment of MNE activity towards advanced developed economies; others have favored a location in emerging market economies. All are symptomatic of a changing international division of labor, which, because of their increasing role in the world economy, and their need to capture the economies of interdependent activities, MNEs have helped to fashion.

The literature on the locational preferences of foreign direct investors has long acknowledged that these will not depend on the types of activities in which they are engaged, but on the motives for the investment and whether it is a new or a sequential one. Different kinds of investment incentives are needed to attract inbound MNE activity of a natural-resource-seeking compared with that of a market- or efficiency-seeking, kind. Export-oriented FDI is likely to be less influenced by the size of local markets than is import-substituting FDI. Investment in R&D facilities requires a different kind of human and physical infrastructure than investment in assembling or marketing activities, and so on.

But, perhaps, the most significant change in the motives for FDI over the last two decades has been the rapid growth of strategic asset-seeking FDI, which is geared less to exploiting an existing O-specific advantage of an investing firm, and more to protecting, or augmenting, that advantage by the acquisition of new assets, or by a partnering arrangement with a foreign firm. In some ways, such FDI is similar in intent to that of a natural-resource-seeking investment in earlier times but, its locational needs are likely to be quite different. Partly this is because it is frequently motivated by strategic considerations (especially in oligopolistic industries), and partly because the availability of the assets sought, viz. technical knowledge, learning experiences, management expertise and organizational competence, tend to be concentrated in advanced industrial countries, or the larger developing countries. The growth of strategic asset-seeking FDI in recent years is best demonstrated by the increasing role of mergers and acquisitions as modalities of FDI. According to UNCTAD (1997), between 55 percent and 60 percent of FDI flows over the period 1985–1995 was accounted for by mergers and acquisitions. Most of these were concentrated within North America, Europe and Japan, and in knowledge- and information-intensive sectors.

The locational preferences of firms making more traditional forms of FDI have also changed – as, indeed, have the attitudes of recipient countries to these investments. We might mention two of these. First, as foreign affiliates have become more embedded in host countries, this has led to a deepening of their value chains, and a propensity for them to engage in higher-order (e.g. innovatory) activities. This fact has been documented in numerous studies both on the geographical distribution of R&D and on that of patents registered by MNEs (as recent examples of these, see Dalton and Serapio, 1995; Almeida, 1996; Dunning, 1996; Kuemmerle, 1996; Shan and Song, 1997; and various studies of John Cantwell and colleagues, e.g. Cantwell and Harding, 1997; and Bob Pearce and Marina Papanastassiou, e.g. Papanastassiou and Pearce, 1997, of the University of Reading). *Inter alia*, the Cantwell and Harding study showed that between 1991 and 1995, 11 percent of the US registered patents of the world's largest firms were attributable to research locations outside the home country of the parent company. Only in the case of Japan was there no rise in the proportion of patents registered by foreign affiliates since the early 1970s (for a more general discussion on asset-augmenting FDI, see an interesting dissertation by Wesson, 1993). So far, however, this tendency of engaging in higher-order activities has been largely confined to developed countries. In

1994, for example, some 91 percent of the foreign R&D undertaken by US MNEs was located in developed countries, compared with 79 percent of their total foreign sales (Mataloni and Fahim-Nader, 1996).

Second, the location-specific assets which MNEs perceive they need to add value to the competitive advantages they are exporting (via FDI) are changing as their downstream activities are becoming more knowledge intensive. Various surveys have demonstrated that, except for some labor or resource investments in developing countries, MNEs are increasingly seeking locations which offer the best economic and institutional facilities for their core competencies to be efficiently utilized. For example, in a field study by Fabrice Hatem (1997), apart from market access and market growth, economic and institutional facilities were not only valued much higher than traditional criteria of access to raw materials, cost of labor, and fear of protectionism, but in all cases they were also thought to increase in significance over the five-year period 1996–2001. There is a suggestion, too, that the presence of other foreign investors in a particular country is becoming more significant, both as an 'investment-stalk' or signaling effect to other foreign firms less familiar with that country (Srinivasan and Mody, 1998; Liu, 1998), and as an agglomerative magnet by which firms benefit from being part of a geographical network or cluster of related activities and specialized support services. In a study of the location patterns of US MNEs between 1982 and 1988, Wheeler and Mody (1992) identified three agglomeration benefits, viz. infrastructure quality, degree of industrialization, and existing level of FDI. They found that these exhibited a high degree of statistical significance and had large positive impacts on investment (p. 66). In an analysis of Swedish outbound FDI, over the period 1975–1990, Braunerhjelm and Svensson (1995) confirmed a positive and significant statistical relationship between that variable and the presence of pecuniary externalities associated with demand and supply linkages, including the diffusion of knowledge, e.g. spillover effects, resulting from a clustering of related firms.

A more formal examination of the changing nature and significance of external economies, and of how these are leading to a more concentrated pattern of certain kinds of FDI – particularly that of strategic asset-seeking investment in knowledge-intensive sectors – is set out in Krugman (1991). Indeed, it was his study which helped spark off the fruitful dialogue now taking place between industrial geographers, economists and business analysts. Though this dialogue is principally concerned with the role of sub-national spatial units as repositories for mobile investment, it is also offering a number of valuable insights on the changing role of transportation and communication costs as they affect the coordination and supply of end products from existing agglomerations, and the decentralization of intermediate production;[13] and also on the changing competitive advantages of regions – particularly as they impinge upon spatial transaction costs and dynamic external economies, such as those to do with complex technologies, uncertain or unpredictable markets, interactive learning, face-to-face discussions and the exchange of uncodifiable knowledge (Florida, 1995; Storper and Scott, 1995).

Certainly the incentives offered by regional authorities within the European Union (EU) and of states within the United States have been shown to be a decisive factor in influencing the intraregional location of inbound MNE activity (for some interesting case studies, see, for example, Donahue, 1997; Ohmae, 1995). There is also a good deal of casual evidence to suggest that the promotional campaigns and incentives – in the form of the speedy processing of planning applications, land grants, subsidized rents, tax holidays and generous investment allowances – offered by local or regional development agencies to attract FDI tend to resemble those of 'location tournaments'[14] (Taylor, 1993; UNCTAD, 1996b). Again, the experiences of the United States and the EU – or, indeed, of some of the larger countries in the EU, e.g. the United Kingdom – are salutary in this respect.

In Table 6.1, we attempt to summarize some of the differences between the kind of variables posited to influence the locational decisions of MNEs in the 1970s – most of which are well documented in Chapter 2 of *Multinational Enterprise and Economic Analysis* – and those which scholars are hypothesizing, and field research is showing to influence these same decisions of MNEs in the 1990s. In doing so, we have separately classified the four main kinds of FDI identified earlier. However, we readily accept that other contextual variables, e.g. size of firm, degree of multinationality, country or region of origin and destination and industry, insofar as these have different situational needs, may be no less significant.

The contents of the table are largely self-explanatory, but we would highlight just four main findings. The first is the changing role of *spatial transaction costs*, which reflect both the liberalization of cross-border markets and the changing characteristics of economic activity. While, in general, the reduction of these costs has led to more aggressive market-seeking FDI, and has promoted a welfare-enhancing international division of labor, it has also favored the spatial bunching of firms engaged in related activities, so that each may benefit from the presence of the other, and of having access to localized support facilities, shared service centers, distribution networks, customized demand patterns and specialized factor inputs (Maskell, 1996; Rees and McLean, 1997).

The second finding is that the complementary foreign assets and capabilities sought by MNEs wishing to add value to their core competitive advantages are increasingly of a *knowledge-facilitating* kind, and that this is particularly the case as their affiliates become more firmly rooted in host economies (Grabher, 1993). Examples include the deepening of value-added activities by Japanese manufacturing subsidiaries in Europe and North America. An

Table 6.1 Some variables influencing the location of value-added activities by MNEs in the 1970s and 1990s

Type of FDI	In the 1970s	In the 1990s
A. Resource-seeking	1. Availability, price and quality of natural resources. 2. Infrastructure to enable resources to be exploited, and products arising from them to be exported. 3. Government restrictions on FDI and/or on capital and dividend remissions. 4. Investment incentives, e.g. tax holidays.	1. As in the 1970s, but local opportunities for upgrading quality of resources and the processing and transportation of their output is a more important locational incentive. 2. Availability of local partners to jointly promote knowledge and/or capital-intensive resource exploitation.
B. Market-seeking	1. Mainly domestic, and occasionally (e.g. in Europe) adjacent regional markets. 2. Real wage costs; material costs. 3. Transport costs; tariff and non-tariff trade barriers. 4. As A3 above, but also (where relevant) privileged access to import licenses.	1. Mostly large and growing domestic markets, and adjacent regional markets (e.g. NAFTA, EU etc.). 2. Availability and price of skilled and professional labor. 3. Presence and competitiveness of related firms, e.g. leading industrial suppliers. 4. Quality of national and local infrastructure, and institutional competence. 5. Less spatially related market distortions, but increased role of agglomerative spatial economies and local service support facilities. 6. Macroeconomic and macro-organizational policies as pursued by host governments. 7. Increased need for presence close to users in knowledge-intensive sectors. 8. Growing importance of promotional activities by regional or local development agencies.

Table 6.1 continued

Type of FDI	In the 1970s	In the 1990s
C. Efficiency-seeking	1. Mainly production cost related (e.g. labor, materials, machinery, etc.). 2. Freedom to engage in trade in intermediate and final products. 3. Presence of agglomerative economies, e.g. export processing zones. 4. Investment incentives, e.g. tax breaks, accelerated depreciation, grants, subsidized land.	1. As in the 1970s, but more emphasis placed on B2, 3, 4, 5 and 7 above, especially for knowledge-intensive and integrated MNE activities, e.g. R&D and some office functions. 2. Increased role of governments in removing obstacles to restructuring economic activity, and facilitating the upgrading of human resources by appropriate educational and training programs. 3. Availability of specialized spatial clusters, e.g. science and industrial parks, service support systems etc.; and of specialized factor inputs. Opportunities for new initiatives by investing firms; an entrepreneurial environment, and one which encourages competitiveness-enhancing cooperation within and between firms.
D. Strategic-asset-seeking	1. Availability of knowledge-related assets and markets necessary to protect or enhance O-specific advantages of investing firms – and at the right price. 2. Institutional and other variables influencing ease or difficulty at which such assets can be acquired by foreign firms.	1. As in the 1970s, but growing geographical dispersion of knowledge-based assets, and need of firms to harness such assets from foreign locations, makes this a more important motive for FDI. 2. The price and availability of 'synergistic' assets to foreign investors. 3. Opportunities offered (often by particular sub-national spatial units) for exchange of localized tacit knowledge, ideas and interactive learning. 4. Access to different cultures, institutions and systems; and different consumer demands and preferences.

exception to this finding is some low value-adding activities in the least developed areas of the world.

The third finding is that as strategic-asset-acquiring investment has become more important, the locational needs of corporations have shifted from those to do with access to markets, or to natural resources, to those to do with access to knowledge-intensive assets and learning experiences, which augment their existing O-specific advantages.

The fourth finding is that much of the recent FDI in developing countries is prompted either by traditional market-seeking motives (e.g. as in China, Indonesia and India), or by the desire to take advantage of lower (real) labor costs, and/or the availability and price of natural resources. Yet, even there, where firms have a choice, the physical and human infrastructure, together with the macroeconomic environment and institutional framework of the host country, tend to play a more decisive role than they once did.

MACROECONOMIC ASPECTS OF THE CHANGING INTERNATIONAL ALLOCATION OF ECONOMIC ACTIVITY

In the previous section, we set out some of the reasons for the changing locational patterns of MNE activity over the past two decades. We concluded that developments in the global economy over these years had not only opened up or enlarged markets for products normally supplied by MNEs, but, by affecting the production and transaction costs of FDI, had markedly influenced its industrial structure and geography. In general, the 1990s are witnessing a closer integration in the international value-added activities of MNEs. In the case of some kinds of FDI, falling material, transportation and communication costs, and rising transactional benefits arising from the common governance of interdependent activities have made for a more concentrated pattern of FDI, both between and within regions and/or countries. In other cases, however, the emergence of new – and often important – markets, and the lowering of tariff and non-tariff barriers have made for a more dispersed pattern of FDI.

We now turn to consider some macroeconomic, or country-specific, issues. In particular, we wish to address two questions. First, to what extent is the changing locational pattern of FDI affecting our understanding about the determinants of the optimal international allocation of economic activity; and second, how far, in light of the growing significance and integration of MNE, does one need to reconsider the policy implications for national and regional governments as they seek to advance their particular economic and social objectives?

Until the 1950s, most explanations of the allocation of economic activity were based on the distribution of natural resources – especially labor, land and finance capital. The principle of comparative advantage advocated that countries should specialize in the production of those products which required the resources and capabilities in which they were relatively the best endowed; and trade these for those which required resources and capabilities in which they were relatively poorly endowed. This was the basis for a general equilibrium model of trade. Its restrictive assumptions – viz. perfect competition, the immobility of factors, homogeneity of traded products, constant returns to scale and zero transportation costs – as recently reiterated by Krugman (1993), are well known. In that model, there was little or no room for innovatory activities, or for the deployment of such created assets as intellectual capital, organizational expertise, entrepreneurship and interactive learning, either by countries or firms; and even less for the distinctive characteristics of MNEs.

Over the last four decades, these restrictions have been gradually relaxed in three main ways. First, independently of the work of scholars on FDI and MNE activity, there has been a growing appreciation by trade economists of the need to incorporate such variables as economies of scale, fabricated assets, learning experiences and market structure into their models, and to recognize that the role of these varies with types of economic activity. It is, for example, now generally accepted that different parts of the value chain may be distributed between countries, or regions within countries, according to their knowledge, capital, natural resource and labor content, and to the geography of these inputs. Second, more attention is now being paid to the extent to which the external economies which arise from the clustering of related activities may lead to a concentration of economic activity in certain countries or regions. Third, more recognition has been given to the differences in consumer tastes between countries, while, very gradually, institutional factors, such as those specific to the multi-activity or multi-firm, and to the role of governments have begun to be acknowledged.

In incorporating these changes into their thinking, the proponents of the positive theory of trade are now able to offer a more realistic explanation of the international allocation of economic activity, while, from a normative viewpoint, though dented, the principle of comparative advantage still has much going for it as a guiding light as to how best to allocate scarce resources between countries (Wood, 1993). This is particularly the case when it is widened to embrace created assets, including those which are institutional, policy and culturally related (Lipsey, 1997).

However, a second intellectual lacuna remains, which makes it difficult to reconcile the approaches of location theorists and international trade economists in explaining the international allocation of production. This is the presence – and the increasing presence – of the MNE, whose central feature is its common ownership of cross-border value-adding activities. Here we need to turn once again to the work of the internalization scholars. For to explain how MNEs *qua* MNEs affect the international location of economic activity, we need to consider how they differ from uni-national firms. Otherwise, one should be able to use the tenets of contemporary trade and/or location theory to explain such activity. It is here that research by international business scholars is particularly relevant.

An earlier section of this chapter suggested that the changes in the geography of FDI over the last two decades have been broadly in line with those of the capital expenditures of all firms. This could mean that the ownership or multinationality of firms was not a significant variable in explaining such changes; and that trade in intermediate or final products internalized, and/or controlled, by MNEs, is no differently determined than trade between independent firms, i.e. arm's-length trade.

However, as copious research shows (as reviewed, e.g. in Caves, 1996; Dunning, 1993), the main impact of the foreign-ness, or multinationality, of firms has not been on the *level* of economic activity and/or trade of the countries in which they operate, but on the *structure* of these variables. From the very earliest of studies on FDI, scholars have shown that the foreign affiliates of MNEs tend to be concentrated in different industrial sectors than do their indigenous counterparts. Since each sector is likely to have its distinctive locational and trading propensities, it follows that FDI will have a differential impact on the geography of economic activity. Sometimes, this impact will reflect the characteristics of the country of the investing firms, e.g. Japanese FDI in the European auto and electronics industries in the 1980s; sometimes a very unique competitive advantage, or set of advantages; and sometimes their pattern and degree of multinationality. For it is the geographical diversity of asset-agmenting and asset-exploiting FDI, and the costs and benefits associated with their common governance, which is one of the singular features of contemporary MNE activity – especially in developed countries.

Scholars such as Bruce Kogut recognized these specific attributes of MNEs many years ago (see, for example, Kogut, 1983, 1985), but as the degree, scope and intensity of the foreign operations of firms has increased over the last decade (as demonstrated, for example, in the annual *World Investment Reports* of UNCTAD), and as these are now used to harness new resources, capabilities and markets, as well as to exploit the existing O advantages of firms, so have these particular qualities of multinationality become more prominent.

Though such qualities can be readily embraced into location theory, they are less easily incorporated into general equilibrium trade models. Primarily, this is because, unlike industrial organization theory, trade theory has not come to grips with the multi-activity firm, or multi-plant production, or has embraced innovation into its thinking (one notable exception is that of Grossman and Helpman, 1991). Recent papers by James Markusen (1995) and Markusen and Venables (1995) have made a brave attempt to integrate the OLI framework paradigm of international production and the newer models of trade (i.e. those embracing firm-specific economies of scale, product differentiation and imperfect competition), but they tend to concentrate on how the cross-border specialization of specific knowledge-intensive activities may differ from that predicated by traditional trade theory. In a similar vein, research by Brainard (1993) and Horstman and Markusen (1992) has concluded that MNE-related production will be in equilibrium when firm-level fixed costs and spatial transaction costs are large relative to plant-level economies.[15] None of these approaches, however, fully takes account the key properties of multinationality, as distinct from the foreign ownership of firms. While embracing some of the characteristics of internalized markets for O-specific assets, they ignore others – and especially those which elsewhere we have referred to as transaction-cost-minimizing O advantages.[16]

Considering the normative implications of the work of Markusen and others, and using the language of traditional trade theory, we might say that it will be to the benefit of countries if their firms engage in outward FDI in two very different situations. The first is where the utilization of their O-specific advantages, the production of which is relatively well suited to the resources and capabilities of the home countries, is best undertaken in a foreign country (or countries)[17] *and within the same firm* (i.e. the benefits of 'first-best' internalized intermediate product markets exceed those of 'first-best' arm's-length transactions). The second is when to protect or augment their global competitive advantages, firms engage in buying assets in a foreign country (or countries) more favorable to their creation, but not to their deployment. By contrast, a country will benefit from inward direct investment when it has a comparative advantage in adding value to the services of the imported created assets – again within the investing entity – rather than producing these assets itself, or where a foreign firm chooses to buy assets created in the country (at the right price) and utilize these assets in a foreign country (or countries).

In most cases, given the presence of MNEs, the recipe for an optimal allocation of economic activity between countries is quite similar to that in a world in which there is no FDI. But the relative roles of markets, hierarchies and governments in this recipe are likely to be different. In conditions other than that of perfect competition, hierarchies, or heterarchies – in the guise of multi-activity and/or multinational firms – may be a more efficient coordinator of resources and capabilities than arm's-length markets (Caves, 1996). This is particularly likely to be so in a dynamic knowledge-based economy in which some of the ingredients of endemic market failure, and particularly those of uncertainty, irregularity, complexity, externalities, scale economies, vertical integration, and the interdependence of markets, are present, as it is these which tend to generate the kind of value-added activities which can be coordinated more efficiently under a single governance. In such cases, and providing that the final goods' markets served by MNEs are contestable, and national governments pursue positive and non-distorting market-facilitating macro-organizational policies (Dunning, 1997b), MNEs may act as surrogates for markets. By internalizing intermediate product markets, they may help protect or enhance, rather than inhibit, the efficiency of final goods' markets.

While not wishing to undervalue the role of governments in curtailing the anti-competitive behavior of firms, and in pursuing market friendly macro-organizational strategies, we believe that contemporary changes in the ways in which resources and capabilities are managed are facilitating a more appropriate balance between cross-border hierarchical (i.e. internalized) and external market transactions. Perhaps the one area for potential concern is the widespread growth of international mergers and acquisitions and strategic alliances (UNCTAD, 1997). In so far as these may assist firms to be more innovatory, entrepreneurial and competitive in global markets, they are to the good; but, where they make it easier for companies to engage in structurally distorting business practices, they need to be carefully monitored.

The unique impact of MNEs on the international allocation of production rests on the extent to which the internalization of cross-border intermediate product markets produces a different and more efficient structure of economic activity than would otherwise have occurred. Herein lies an interesting paradox. On the one hand, the liberalization of markets and the reduction of some kinds of spatial costs are easing the trans-border movement of goods, intangible assets and services. On the other, technological and organizational change, whenever it enhances the interdependence of value-added activity, is encouraging international production to be undertaken within plants and firms under the same ownership, and for at least some of this production to be spatially concentrated. It would seem that as fast as structural and distance-related market failures are removed, others, making for internalized intermediate product markets and untraded spatial interdependencies, are becoming more important.

Hints of this 'new' international division of labor are shown not only by the growing participation of MNEs in global production – as described earlier in this chapter – but also by their increasing share of world export markets, at least in the manufacturing sector (documented by, *inter alia*, Dunning, 1993; UNCTAD, 1996a; Caves, 1996). Other data also suggest that the export propensity of MNEs, or their affiliates, in the sectors in which they are most active exceeds that of indigenous competitors. Except in the case of a few countries, notably Japan, the payments for the services of knowledge-intensive assets received by US MNEs from their foreign affiliates, expressed as a proportion of their total exports, is considerably greater than the equivalent proportion between US and independently owned firms. For example, in 1996, royalties and fees received by US firms from their foreign affiliates amounted to 6 percent of their exports to these affiliates. The corresponding proportion of non-affiliation royalties and fees received by all US firms as a proportion of total US exports was 3 percent (US Department of Commerce, 1997).

Furthermore, of all royalties and fees received by US firms from foreign-based firms in the years 1993 to 1996, 79 percent were internal to US MNEs.[18]

The extent to which MNEs promote, or gravitate to, spatial clusters within a country or region is an under-researched area. Clearly, some older clusters, e.g. the Portuguese cork industry, the Swiss watch industry, the North Italy textile industry and the City of London financial district, developed without much MNE participation. But many of the newly established clusters, which are geared more to accessing the external economies of knowledge creation, interactive learning and the upgrading of the competitive advantage of the constituent firms, are influenced by a rather different set of costs and benefits; and a casual examination of the membership of science and technology parks, export processing zones, research and development consortia and service support centers would certainly suggest that MNEs are actively involved – often as flagship firms. Certainly among developed regions (e.g. the European Union) and countries (e.g. United States), knowledge-intensive and export-oriented activities tend to be more geographically concentrated than other kinds of activities (see, for example, illustrations given in Porter, 1990; Dunning, 1997b, Chap. 3; and Dunning, 1997c).

Any modern theory of international economic activity must then take account of how the common ownership of cross-border production and transactions may result in a different value added and spatial configuration than that which would arise if such functions were separately undertaken by uni-national firms. *Inter alia*, the extra attributes comprise the spreading of firm-specific overheads and risks; the intra-firm sharing and transference of knowledge, experience and markets; and the external economies arising from jointly organized innovatory, production and marketing activities. For many of these activities, there is no external market; the output of one part of the firm can only be sold as an input to another part of the same firm. However, these interdependent activities may not need to be undertaken in the same region or country. For other activities, internal markets may offer more coordinating benefits and/or less transactional costs than arm's-length markets. In both cases, however, it may be preferable to think of the MNE not as a second-best substitute for the market, but as a partner with the market to promote first-best allocative efficiency throughout and across value chains.

The notion of efficiency-promoting internal markets needs to be more formally built into both positive and normative macro models of international economic activity. In addition to acknowledging the different geographical needs of asset-producing and asset-exploiting activities, models of trade need to incorporate the benefits of organizing the two sets of activity under common ownership *vis-à-vis* that of the external market. This, in principle, is not a difficult thing to do. Essentially, it comes down to an identification and evaluation of the country, activity and firm-specific variables which determine whether the different transactional and coordinating functions are best organized within market friendly hierarchies, or by the market *per se*. We have already argued that markets for created assets, and for the goods and services arising from them, are likely to be intrinsically more imperfect than those for natural assets and for the goods and services arising from them. In some instances, too, it may be efficiency enhancing for these markets to be internalized. We also contend, with Behrman and Grosse (1990) and Meyer (1998), that most cross-border markets are likely to be more imperfect than their domestic equivalents, and that, because of this, MNE activity *may* be more welfare enhancing than multi-plant activity within an economy. We say 'most' cross-border markets, because some domestic markets, particularly in emerging developing economies, are likely to be more imperfect than those in developed countries. But issues such as foreign-exchange uncertainty, institutional and cultural differences, and the differential role of governments are obviously likely to play a more important role in affecting the workings of cross-border than domestic markets. And we say 'may' be more welfare enhancing, because much will depend upon the conditions under which foreign investment takes place.

At the same time, the extent to which cross-border markets are internalized via MNE activity will itself depend on the characteristics of the trading partners and the countries involved, as well as on the types of assets, goods and services being exchanged. In their attempts to explain the alternative forms of trans-border trade, and to advance both the positive and normative theories of trade, international economists need to delve deeper into the structure of country-specific advantages in organizing trade (particularly in knowledge-related products), through FDI and inter-firm alliances, as compared with arm's-length markets.

CONCLUSIONS

The previous two sections of this chapter have examined how changes in the global economy over the past two decades are affecting scholarly thinking about both the microeconomic geography of FDI and MNE activity, and the more macroeconomic explanations of the international allocation of all value-added activity. In particular, we focused on three points. The first is the growing importance of intangible assets – and particularly intellectual capital – in the wealth-creating process, and of the need of companies to harness, as well as to exploit, these assets from a variety of locations. Secondly, we emphasized the changing role of location-bound assets, which mobile investors look for as complements to their own core competencies. In doing so, we again underscored the increasing significance of created assets (and particularly those which governments, in their macro-organizational policies, can and do influence), and, also, the benefits which spatial clusters offer whenever distance-related transactions and coordination costs are high.

Thirdly, we argued that, to adequately incorporate the activities of MNEs within existing trade-type theories of the international allocation of economic activity, more attention needs to be given both to the specific motives, determinants and consequences of the common governance of related cross-border activities, and to the conditions in which internalizing intermediate product markets might make for a more efficient (in the sense of the 'next-best' realistic alternative, assuming that all cross-border avoidable structural market imperfection have been removed) spatial configuration of economic activity in the contemporary global and innovatory economy. We have also suggested that any paradigm of the geography of FDI, as contrasted to that of the investments of all firms, needs to be constructed on similar lines.

What are the implications of our analysis and findings for future international business research? First, to return to the starting point of this chapter, and in line with the thinking of Michael Porter (1994, 1996), I believe more attention needs to be given to the importance of location *per se* as a variable affecting the global competitiveness of firms. That is to say, the locational configuration of a firm's activities may itself be an O-specific advantage, as well as affect the modality by which it augments, or exploits, its existing O advantages. With the gradual geographical dispersion of created assets, and as firms become more multinational by deepening or widening their cross-border value chains, then, both from the viewpoint of harnessing new competitive advantages and more efficiently deploying their home-based assets, the structure and content of the location portfolio of firms becomes more critical to their global competitive positions.

Second, in seeking to make an optimal use of the existing location-bound assets within this jurisdiction, and to promote the dynamic comparative advantage of their resource capabilities, governments need to give more attention to ensuring that their actions help fashion, support and complement those of efficient hierarchies and markets. This involves a greater appreciation both of the changing locational requirements of mobile investments, and of how, in the case of those markets where endemic failure is the most widespread, governments may work in partnership with firms either to improve markets (i.e. by a 'voice' strategy[19]), or to replace these markets (by an 'exit' strategy). With the growing importance of knowledge-related infrastructure, and accepting the idea of sub-national spatial units as nexus of untraded interdependencies (Storper, 1995),[20] this presents both new challenges and opportunities to both national and regional governments in their macro-organizational and competitive enhancing policies.

NOTES

1. Such international-specific transaction costs have recently been explicitly identified by Klaus Meyer in a volume (Meyer, 1998) based upon his doctoral dissertation at the London Business School.
2. For example, of the 1150 or so publications cited in his volume, only 13 percent are to monographs or articles published after 1990.
3. Author's estimate, based on data on the royalties paid for managerial know-how; and of the relationship between foreign portfolio and foreign direct investment.
4. There have been only a few attempts to use transaction cost analysis to explain the spatial distribution of economic activity. One example is that of the industrial geographers Michael Storper and Allen Scott. See, for example, Storper (1995), Storper and Scott (1995) and Scott (1996). Yet such analysis offers a powerful tool for explaining why firms requiring idiosyncratic inputs, e.g. tacit knowledge of various kinds, and/or those supplying idiosyncratic and uncertain markets tend to value proximity with their suppliers and/or customers. Perhaps the best illustration of a spatial cluster, or agglomeration, of related activities to minimize distance-related transaction costs, and to exploit the external economies associated with the close presence of related firms, is the Square Mile of the City of London.
5. Scott (1996) gives some examples, including the growing concentration and specialization of both manufacturing and service activities in large metropolitan areas within both developed and developing countries. In an interesting recent paper, Davis and Weinstein (1997) conclude that intra-national concentration of value-added activity is likely to obey the dictates of economic geography more than that of the international concentration of such activity.
6. Estimates of such ventures vary enormously. A recent study by Booz, Allen and Hamilton (1997) has put the number of cross-border alliances (including mergers and acquisitions) formed in 1995 and 1996 to be as high as 15 000. Another assessment by Hagedoorn (1996) suggests that between 1980 and 1994, the number of newly established cross-border technology-related inter-firm agreements rose by over three times. Finally, the value of international mergers and acquisitions over the same period was estimated to have accounted for between 50 percent and 60 percent of all new FDI (UNCTAD, 1997).
7. For a detailed exposition of the development of a new trajectory of technological advances, see Lipsey (1997) and Ruigrok and Van Tulder (1995).
8. Though there have been marked fluctuations in the shares within and between these periods, which reflect, *inter alia*, changes in exchange rates and the positioning of countries in their cycles of economic development. For example, during 1975–1980, the United States attracted 32 percent of FDI received by developed countries; by 1985–1990 that share had risen to 42 percent. However, it fell again to 18 percent in 1991 and 1992; but since then it has recovered, and in 1995–1996 it stood at 35 percent.
9. Japan is a classic case in point. In the period 1990–1994 it accounted for 29 percent of the world's gross fixed capital formation, but only 0.8 percent of inbound FDI flows.
10. To give just one example: in the period 1990–1994, 49 percent of US direct investment flows were directed to Western Europe, 10 percent to Asia and 25 percent to Latin America. The corresponding percentages for Japanese direct investment flows were 20 percent, 19 percent and 10 percent (UNCTAD, 1997; Dunning, 1998).
11. Unlike the theory of the firm; although if there had been a well-developed theory of the multi-activity firm prior to the work of scholars such as Buckley, Casson and Hennart, one wonders if this aspect of international business activity would have attracted so much attention!
12. We use the word 'customized' deliberately, following the contention of Peck (1996) that host governments may sometimes need to individualize or customize the upgrading of their physical and human infrastructure both to meet the specific needs of mobile investors, and promote the competitive dynamic advantage of the location-bound resources within their jurisdiction.
13. I am indebted to the reviewer of this chapter for making this point.
14. An expression first used in David (1984), and since taken up by Wheeler and Mody (1992) and Mytelka (1996).

15. In Markusen's words 'multinational enterprises in this framework are exporters of the services of firm-specific assets ... subsidiaries import these assets' (Markusen, 1995, p. 175).
16. Abbreviated, Ot transaction (or coordinating) cost-minimizing advantages, cf. Oa = asset-specific advantages.
17. Which foreign country, or countries, is decided by the normal locational criteria.
18. Other data on royalties and management fees received by US firms from foreign firms are regularly published by the United States Department of Commerce in the *Survey of Current Business*, and in the *Benchmark Surveys of U.S. Direct Investment Abroad*. See also UNCTAD (1995, 1996a, 1997).
19. The concepts of 'voice' and 'exit' strategies as applied to MNE-related activity are explained in Dunning (1997a).
20. The idea of a region as a spatial unit which internalizes distance-related transaction costs which otherwise would fall upon its constituent firms is an interesting notion worth pursuing by international business scholars. For, like a firm, the strategies pursued by a region to provide a set of unique, non-mobile and non-imitable locational advantages for its firms may well determine its own competitive advantages relative to those of other regions. At the same time, regions, like firms, may decline as well as prosper; but our knowledge about the focus leading to the spatial dis-agglomeration of related activities is woefully inadequate.

REFERENCES

Almeida, P. (1996), 'Knowledge sourcing by foreign multinationals: patent citation analysis in the U.S. semi-conductor industry', *Strategic Management Journal*, **17** (Winter): 155–65.

Bandera, V.N. and J.T. White (1968), 'U.S. direct investments and domestic markets in Europe', *Economic Internazionale*, **21** (February): 117–33.

Behrman, J.N. and Robert Grosse (1990), *International business and governments*, Columbia, South Carolina: University of South Carolina Press.

Blair, M.M. (1995), *Ownership and control: rethinking corporate governance for the 21st century*, Washington, DC: The Brookings Institution.

Booz, Allen and Hamilton (1997), *Cross border alliances in the age of collaboration*, Los Angeles, CA: Booz, Allen and Hamilton.

Brainard, S.L. (1993), 'A simple theory of multinational corporations and trade with a trade-off between proximity and concentration', Cambridge, MA: NBER Working Paper No. 4269, February.

Braunerhjelm, P. and R. Svensson (1995), 'Host country characteristics and agglomeration in foreign direct investment', Stockholm: Industrial Institute for EC and Social Research (mimeo), October.

Cantwell, J. and R. Harding (1997), 'The internationalization of German companies' R&D'. Discussion Paper in International Investment and Management, No. 233, University of Reading.

Caves, R. (1982 and 1996), *Multinational firms and economic analysis*, Cambridge: Cambridge University Press. First and second editions.

Dalton, D.H. and M.G. Serapio (1995), *Globalizing industrial research and development*, U.S. Department of Commerce, Office of Technology Policy, Washington, DC: U.S. Department of Commerce.

David, P. (1984), 'High technology centers and the economics of locational tournaments', Stanford, CA: Stanford University (mimeo).

Davidson, W. (1970), 'The location of foreign direct investment activity: country characteristics and experience effects', *Journal of International Business Studies*, **11**(2): 9–22.

Davis, D.R. and D.E. Weinstein (1997), 'Economic geography and regional production structure: An empirical investigation', Cambridge, MA: National Bureau of Economic Research, Working Paper Series No. 6093 (July).

Donahue, J.D. (1996), *Disunited States*, New York: Basic Books.

Dunning, J.H. (1993), *Multinational enterprises and the global economy*, Wokingham, England and Reading, MA: Addison-Wesley.

Dunning, J.H. (1995), 'What's wrong – and right – with trade theory', *International Trade Journal*, **9**(2): 153–202.

Dunning, J.H. (1996), 'The geographical sources of competitiveness of firms: some results of a new survey', *Transnational Corporations*, **5**(3): 1–30.

Dunning, J.H. (1997a), *Alliance capitalism and global business*, London and New York: Routledge.

Dunning, J.H. (ed.) (1997b), *Governments, globalization and international business*, Oxford: Oxford University Press.

Dunning, J.H. (1997c), 'The European internal market program and inbound foreign direct investment', *Journal of Common Market Studies*, **35**(1 and 2): 1–30 and 189–223.

Dunning, J.H. (1998), 'The changing geography of foreign direct investment', in N. Kumar (ed.), *Globalization, foreign direct investment and technology transfer: Impact and prospects for developing countries*, London and New York: Routledge, pp. 43–90.

Edvinson, L. (1997), *Intellectual Capital Development*, Stockholm: Skandia.

Ethier, W.J. (1986), 'The multinational firm', *Quarterly Journal of Economics*, **101**: 806–33.

Florida, R. (1995), 'Towards the learning region', *Futures*, **27**(5): 527–36.

Fujita, M. and J.R. Thisse (1996), 'Economics of agglomeration, Kyoto: Kyoto University', Institute of Economic Research Discussion Paper No. 430, January.

Grabher, G., (ed.), (1993), *The embedded firm*, London and New York: Routledge.

Grossman, G.M. and E. Helpman (1991), *Innovation and growth in the global economy*, Cambridge, MA: MIT Press.

Hagedoorn, J. (1996), 'Trends and patterns in strategic technology partnering since the early seventies', *Review of Industrial Organization*, **11**: 601–16.

Handy, C. (1989), *The age of unreason*, London: Hutchinson.

Hatem, F. (1997), *International investment: Towards the year 2001*, Geneva: United Nations.

Helpman, E. and P.R. Krugman (1985), *Market structure and foreign trade*, Cambridge, MA: MIT Press.

Horstman, I.J. and J.R. Markusen (1992), 'Endogenous market structures in international trade', *Journal of International Economics*, **32**: 109–29.

Johanson, J. and J.E. Vahlne (1977), 'The internationalization process of the firm – a model of knowledge development and increasing market commitments', *Journal of International Business Studies*, **8**: 23–32.

Kogut, B. (1983), 'Foreign direct investment as a sequential process', in Kindleberger, C.P. and D. Audretsch (eds), *The multinational corporation in the 1980s*, Cambridge, MA: MIT Press, pp. 38–56.

Kogut, B. (1985), 'Designing global strategies: corporate and competitive value added chains', *Sloan Management Review*, **25**: 15–28.

Krugman, P. (ed.) (1986), *Strategic trade policy and the new international economics*, Cambridge, MA: MIT Press.

Krugman, P.R. (1991), *Geography and trade*, Cambridge, MA: MIT Press.

Krugman, P.R. (1993), 'On the relationship between trade theory and location theory', *Review of International Economics*, **1**(2): 110–22.

Kuemmerle, W. (1996), 'The drivers of foreign direct investment into research and development: An empirical investigation', Boston, Harvard Business School Working Paper No. 96: 062.

Lipsey, R.G. (1997), 'Globalization and national government policies: An economist's view', in John H. Dunning (ed.), *Governments, globalization and international business*, Oxford: Oxford University Press, pp. 73–113.

Liu, S.X. (1998), *Foreign direct investment and the multinational enterprise. A re-examination using signaling theory*, Westport, CT: Greenwood Publishing.

Loree, D.W. and S.E. Guisinger (1995), 'Policy and nonpolicy determinants of U.S. equity foreign direct investment', *Journal of International Business Studies*, **26**(2): 281–300.

Malmberg, A., O. Slovell and I. Zander (1996), 'Spatial clustering, local accumulation of knowledge and firm competitiveness', *Geografiska Annaler Series B, Human Geography*, **78**(2): 85–97.

Markusen, A. (1996), 'Sticky places in slippery space: A typology of industrial districts', *Economic Geography*, **72**(3): 293–313.

Markusen, J.R. (1995), 'The boundaries of multinational enterprises and the theory of international trade', *Journal of Economic Perspectives*, **9**(2): 169–89.

Markusen, J.R. and A. Venables (1995), 'Multinational firms and the New Trade Theory', Cambridge, MA: NBER Working Paper No. 5036, February.

Maskell, P. (1996), 'Local embeddedness and patterns of international specialization', Copenhagen, Copenhagen Business School (mimeo).

Mataloni, R. and M. Fahim-Nader (1996), 'Operations of U.S. multinational companies: preliminary results from the 1994 benchmark survey', *Survey of Current Business* (December): 11–37.

Meyer, K. (1998), *Direct investment in economies in transition*, Cheltenham, UK and Lyme, U.S.: Edward Elgar.

Mytelka, L.K. (1996), 'Locational tournaments, strategic partnerships and the state', Ottawa: Carleton University (mimeo).

Ohlin, B. (1933), *Inter-regional and international trade*, Cambridge, MA: Harvard University Press, revised edition 1967.

Ohmae, K. (1995), *The end of the nation state: The rise of regional economies*, London: Harper.

Papanastassiou, Marina and Robert Pearce (1997), 'Technology sourcing and the strategic role of manufacturing subsidiaries in the UK: local competencies and global competitions', *Management International Review*, **37**(1): 5–25.

Peck, F.W. (1996), 'Regional development and the production of space: the role of infrastructure in the attraction of new inward investment', *Environment and Planning*, **28**: 327–39.

Porter, M.E. (1990), *The competitive advantage of nations*, New York: The Free Press.

Porter, M.E. (1994), 'The role of location in competition', *Journal of Economics of Business*, **1**(1): 35–9.

Porter, M.E. (1996), 'Competitive advantage, agglomerative economies and regional policy', *International Regional Science Review*, **19**(1 and 2): 85–94.

Rees, D. and T. McLean (1997), 'Trends in location choice', in A. Jolly (ed.), *European Business Handbook 1997*, London: Kogan Page (for CBI).
Ruigrok, W. and R. Van Tulder (1995), *The logic of international restructuring*, London and New York: Routledge.
Scaperlanda, A. and L.J. Mauer (1969), 'The determinants of U.S. direct investment in the EEC', *American Economic Review*, **59** (September): 558–68.
Scott, A.J. (1996), 'Regional motors of the global economy', *Futures*, **28**(5): 391–411.
Shan, W. and J. Song (1997), 'Foreign direct investment and the sourcing of technological advantage: evidence from the biotechnology industry', *Journal of International Business Studies*, **28**(2): 267–84.
Srinivasan, K. and Ashoka Mody (1998), 'Japanese and US firms as foreign investors: do they march to the same tune?', *Canadian Journal of Economics*, **31**(4): 778–99.
Stewart, T.A. (1997), *Intellectual capital*, London: Nicholas Brealy.
Storper, M. (1995), 'The resurgence of region economies: ten years later: the region as a nexus of untraded interdependencies', *European Urban and Regional Studies*, **2**(3): 191–221.
Storper, M. and A.J. Scott (1995), 'The wealth of regions', *Futures*, **27**(5): 505–26.
Taylor, J. (1993), 'An analysis of the factors determining the geographical distribution of Japanese manufacturing investment in the UK, 1984–91', *Urban Studies*, **30**(7): 1209–24.
US Department of Commerce (1997), 'U.S. international sales and purchases of private services', *Survey of Current Business*, October: 95–138.
UNCTC (1988), *Transnational corporations and world development*, New York: UN.
UNCTAD (1995), *World investment report 1995: Transnational corporations and competitiveness*, New York and Geneva: UN.
UNCTAD (1996a), *World investment report 1996: Transnational corporations, investment, trade and international policy arrangements*, New York and Geneva: UN.
UNCTAD (1996b), *Incentives and foreign direct investment*. Geneva and New York: UN.
UNCTAD (1997), *World investment report 1997: Transnational corporations, market structure and competition policy*, Geneva and New York: UN.
Vernon, Raymond (1966), 'International investment and international trade in the product cycle', *Quarterly Journal of Economics*, **80**: 190–207.
Vernon, Raymond (1974), 'The location of economic activity', in John H. Dunning (ed.), *Economic analysis and the multinational enterprise*, London: Allen and Unwin, pp. 89–114.
Wells, L.T. (ed.) (1972), *The product life cycle and international trade*, Cambridge, MA: Harvard University Press.
Wesson, T.J. (1993), 'An alternative motivation for foreign direct investment', Ph.D. dissertation, Harvard University.
Wheeler, K. and Ashoka Mody (1992), 'International investment and location decisions: the case of U.S. firms', *Journal of International Economics*, **33**: 57–76.
Wood, A. (1993), 'Give Heckscher and Ohlin a chance', Sussex: University of Sussex, Institute of Development Studies (mimeo).
World Bank (1997), *World development report: The state in a changing world*, Oxford and New York: Oxford University Press.

7. Globalization, technological change and the spatial organization of economic activity*

INTRODUCTION

One of the most distinctive features of the globalizing economy of the early 1990s is the extent to which the cross-border movement of created assets is internalized either within multinational hierarchies or between two or more separately owned, but interrelated, firms[1] located in different countries. It is the contention of this chapter that the resulting international division of labour, and the nature of the competitive advantages of both firms and countries, is fundamentally different from that determined by the disposition of locationally immobile assets and the transactions between independent buyers and sellers.

For much of the past century, most of the explanations for the international specialization of value-added activity have been based upon the uneven spatial distribution of natural resources. But, today, the competitive and comparative advantages of countries are increasingly determined by the ability of governments and firms to create and organize the deployment of created assets, and from the trade in foreign direct investment (FDI) arising from these assets. At the same time, the significance of intrafirm and interfirm alliance trade is also increasing.

The metamorphosis in the organization of natural and created assets, and of international transactions, is having critical implications for both the ownership and location of economic activity. This is most conspicuously shown by the increasing role of multinational enterprises (MNEs) in global production and trade (UNCTAD, 1995). It is true that new organizational systems are favouring the participation of small firms, but there are strong suggestions that those involved in the most dynamic sectors of the international economy are most likely to be part of a business district or cross-border network of activities, in which the pivotal role is played by large multi-activity and multi-locational corporations (Harrison, 1994).

* From A.D. Chandler, F. Hagström and O. Sölvell, *The Dynamic Firm: The Role of Technology, Strategy, Organization and Regions*, Oxford: Oxford University Press (1998), pp. 289–314.

EXPLAINING CHANGES IN THE SPATIAL ALLOCATION OF ECONOMIC ACTIVITY

Under classical and neo-classical theories of trade, the international division of labour was determined entirely by the geographical disposition of natural resources and the stock of capital. Changes in economic activity were presumed only to occur as a result of the increase or depletion of such resources. Trade in capital and intermediate products, like that of finished goods and services, was assumed to be arm's length; otherwise assets were perceived to be completely location bound. There was no reason for FDI to exist, as there were no incentives for firms to internalize cross-border markets. Neither was there any necessity for firms to engage in cross-border alliances or networks.[2]

The treatment of technology in neo-classical theory was ambiguous. Either it was ignored altogether or it was assumed to be freely available to all firms, and instantaneously transferable across national boundaries. The transborder locational consequences of technological change were rarely considered in the literature, although, in part, this deficiency was partly remedied by the neo-technology theories of trade of the 1950s.[3]

A central feature of received trade theory was the complete disregard of the firm, or interfirm alliances, as institutional entities and of the costs of organizing economic activity. The competitiveness of a country was judged by the ability of its economic system to allocate resources in a way that maximized its comparative advantage. It is, perhaps, worth emphasizing that *international economics* – as a distinctive discipline – originated because of the presumed differences in the determinants and outcomes of the allocation of resources *within* a nation as compared with those *between* nations. In turn, these were postulated to arise because, beyond the jurisdictional boundaries of nations, all resources were perceived to be completely immobile. It was also assumed that each country processed a distinctive pattern of resource endowments.

In the neo-classical tradition, trade economists gave little attention to the distribution of international economic activity *within* countries. This lacuna was taken up by locational economists. However, their focus of interest was rather different. Rather than asking the question 'What determines the optimum mix of activities for a subnational location?', they asked the question 'What determines the optimum location for a particular mix of activities?' Partly, this lack of concern with issues central to international economics is reflected in the fact that resources were assumed to be fully mobile within countries. Consequently, the dominant paradigm of locational economics became the principle of *absolute* competitive advantage, rather than that of *comparative* competitive advantage.

In contrast to trade theory, the unit of analysis in locational economics was the firm, and most of the neo-classical models constructed, for example by Von Thunen (1876), Weber (1929), Hotelling (1929), Lösch (1940) and Hoover (1948), were extensions of the profit-maximizing theory of the firm. Given a particular market, the optimum location was that which minimized production plus transport costs. In imperfect markets, firms had to balance the spatial implications for maximizing revenue with those of minimizing costs. No such spatial choice was allowed firms between a domestic and foreign location.

For the most part, the dichotomy between intra- and intercountry spatial economics remains. One notable exception is the work of Bertil Ohlin, who, perhaps, more than any other economist, tried to bridge the gap[4] between the two intellectual strands. In 1976, he organized a symposium in Stockholm to which he invited some leading economists, geographers and regional scientists to share their thoughts on the determinants of the international allocation of economic activity. However, for the most part, the papers presented, and the ensuing discussion (later published in book form by Ohlin et al., 1977), proceeded on parallel lines with few interdisciplinary bridges being built. Trade economists stuck to their last and apart from my own contribution, which gave birth to the eclectic paradigm of international production, there was no attempt to take on board either organizational issues or the implications of the growing mobility of intangible assets.[5]

Over the past two decades, there has been a gradual shift of emphasis away from *country*- to *firm*-specific considerations in exploring the territorial spread of business activity. Indeed, with a few notable exceptions, which are detailed elsewhere in this chapter, the main advances in our understanding of this phenomenon have come not from scholars versed in extant international economics, but from those working on the boundaries of that subject of institutional and technological economics, organizational theory and business strategy.

At the same time, most of the mainstream thinking scholars from these disciplines have not embraced an international dimension and, as a result, our understanding of the way resources are organized and distributed across national boundaries has been constricted.[6] But the globalization of economic activity is likely to force scholars, working both in traditional trade and locational economics and those in a variety of business-oriented disciplines, to search for a more common paradigmatic approach.

What then might be the intellectual components of any future explanation of the spatial organization of economic activity? In this chapter, we propose to examine a number of features of the globalizing economy and how they are affecting the extant paradigms and theories of a variety of disciplines – and also to speculate a little on the future direction of both uni- and interdisciplinary research in the later 1990s.

THE ROLE OF CREATED ASSETS IN TRADITIONAL THINKING

As countries move along their development paths, the role of *created*, relative to *natural*, assets as the main generators of future income increases. As their name implies, created assets embrace all forms of wealth produced from natural resources. More particularly, they include accumulated knowledge, skills, learning and experience, and organizational competence, which are embodied in human beings, proprietary rights, institutions and physical capacity. Some scholars may add to these other 'softer' assets, such as an entrepreneurial spirit, an ability to benefit from co-operative alliances and networking, and a mentality which favours wealth creation, and a continual upgrading in quality and efficiency of existing assets. Unlike natural resources – notably land, power sources and climate – many, but not all, created assets are transportable over space, although the precise way in which they are packaged may not be.[7] Unlike natural assets, too, most created assets are likely to be the privileged possession of particular private or public institutions. These two characteristics of created assets – namely, their mobility and their ownership specificity – cut right across the assumptions of neo-classical international economics[8] and are forcing scholars to reappraise their explanations of spatial activity.

For the most part, *organizational scholars* have paid only limited attention to the underlying characteristics of created assets. Two notable exceptions are Alfred Chandler and David Teece, who, in their various writings,[9] have distinguished between the competitive advantages of firms arising from their possession of a core asset, for example a patent, brand name or the exclusive access to a market, and those which arise from the efficient co-ordination of these assets with complementary assets owned by other firms. In Chandler's view, it is the access to and efficient deployment of the latter kind of competence which has been one of the key components of corporate success over the past century, and, by inference, that of nations as well. However, while examining some of the country-specific features which might lead to the creation of co-ordinating assets, neither Chandler nor Teece has given much attention to the spatial implications of the governance of interrelated assets, except, perhaps, to suggest that these might aid, rather than inhibit, industrial clustering and the concentration of economic activity.[10]

In contrast to organizational scholars, *scholars in the Schumpterian tradition* have placed rather more emphasis on the possession and accumulation of technological assets as a firm-specific advantage, and of the role of innovatory systems as a country-specific advantage. More recently, as attention has become focused on the learning experiences, technological trajectories and innovatory strategies of firms, the interests of the neo-Schumpterians, such as Antonelli,

Chesnais, Dosi, Freeman and Pavitt, and those of the organizational and business strategists, such as Teece, Hedlund, Bartlett and Ghoshal, have begun to converge. Both approaches have paid some attention to the spatial implications of technological innovation. In particular, building on the work of Ray Vernon (1970) and Gary Hufbauer (1965, 1970), Dosi et al. (1990) have incorporated this variable, at a *country* level, into extant trade theory. Several Italian scholars, notably Cainarca et al. (1988), Antonelli (1991) and Archibugi and Pianta (1993), have examined the international and intraregional diffusion of technological activity, while Bartlett and Ghoshal (1989) have argued that MNEs which successfully co-ordinated and integrated their technological strategies are those most likely to record the most creditable performances as international direct investors.

For their part, until recently, *international economists* have tended to treat created assets as a country-, rather than a firm-, specific competitive advantage. Using such indices as R&D expenditure as a proxy for created assets, and patents or technology-intensive products as the output of such assets, they have sought to incorporate this variable into H–O-type models – and undertake some evaluation of its importance.[11] In his explanation of Japanese direct investment abroad, Kojima (1978, 1990) argued that *countries* which had a comparative advantage in the *creation* of technological assets, but not in their *use*, should export technology as an intermediate product, and import those products which required other created, or natural, assets in which they were comparatively disadvantaged. Only in his more recent writings (e.g. Kojima, 1992) has Kojima considered the mode by which technology is exported as a factor influencing the spatial distribution of economic activity.[12]

Until the 1970s, relatively little attention was given to the competitive advantages of firms by *micro-economists*. In the heritage of Edward Chamberlin (1933), Joan Robinson (1933) and Joe Bain (1956), any advantage one firm was supposed to have over another was presumed to reflect the form and degree of its monopoly power. Only in the last 20 years or so has the emphasis on firm-specific advantages switched to the firm's ability to create to acquire assets which yield competitive enhancing results. The work of Michael Porter (1980, 1985), following in the tradition of industrial economics, and that of Barney (1986), Dierickx and Cool (1989) and Rumelt (1984), which has helped refocus attention on the resource-based theory of the firm (Penrose, 1959), are examples of two schools of thought which specifically address the question of why some firms are more successful at creating and sustaining core competencies than others.

To what extent is it possible – or indeed desirable – to integrate these various approaches? Our own preference is first to accept that, at any given moment of time, each firm possesses a unique portfolio of accumulated assets – including those which may be located outside its national boundaries – and that the way these assets are organized is determined by the trajectory chosen by the management of the firm to advance its time-related objectives and its position on that path. These assets we term ownership-specific (O) for, in the last resort, it is ownership which determines the jurisdictional boundaries of a firm. In turn, however, the fecundity of assets may be influenced by the extent and type of activity in which a firm engages, the region or country in which it operates and the characteristics of the firm, other than its ownership.

In its explanation of the international allocation of economic activity, neoclassical trade theory treats all firms as 'black boxes', and only immobile country-specific assets are taken to determine the trading patterns of nations. Both the asset portfolios and the products supplied by competing firms are assumed to be homogeneous, and all firms are presumed to engage in only a single activity, and to be price takers. Even the concept of dynamic comparative advantage pays little attention to the growth of the firm. However, in practice, we know that the propensity of firms, within a particular sector and of a particular nationality, to engage in intra- and international activity varies a great deal, and this is because of their distinctive asset portfolios and/or the way in which they organize and manage such assets.

Now, if it were possible to identify a 'best practice' asset structure and a 'best practice' usage of a dynamic firm, normalizing for such variables as its nationality, size and product range, one could presumably incorporate these ownership-specific characteristics into any macro-model of spatial activity. The problem is to define what *is* the 'best practice' firm, when each firm is moving along a different trajectory of innovatory activity, product specialization or spatial diversification.[13] In an uncertain world, only with hindsight can the optimum behaviour of a firm be identified and, most certainly, yesterday's 'best practice' firm is not necessarily a guide to tomorrow's 'best practice' firm. This makes the incorporation of firm-specific behaviour into any *normative* theory of the spatial allocation of economic activity a very difficult thing to do.[14] Indeed, it may be questionable how productive such an effort might be!

Yet, in explaining the spatial activity of resources as it *is*, as opposed to how it *ought* to be, it is surely incumbent on scholars at least to identify – if not to evaluate – the way in which the O-specific asset portfolios of firms affect both their ability to compete in spatial markets and their preference for siting their value-added activities in different locations. But, for the most part, this has not been done. For example, while it is generally acknowledged that patent protection may confer an O advantage on the patenting firm, without a knowledge of the asset portfolios, production functions, interfirm relationships and strategies of that firm and those of its competitors, it is impossible to gauge the consequences of that patent protection for either the industry of that firm or the country in which it is domiciled. Thus, for example, the impact of patent protection on the competitiveness of an auto firm engaging in scale production may be very different from that on one pursuing a more flexible manufacturing strategy. On the other hand, it may be reasonable to hypothesize that, in the absence of patent protection, there would be less incentive to engage in research and development in the first place, and, if and when countries differ in their national innovatory systems, this could have considerable spatial consequences.

It is possible to analyse the spatial consequences of other O-specific advantages in a similar way. However, it may be conceptually useful to distinguish between those advantages which arise from the privileged access to specific assets and those which stem from the way in which such assets, and those which are more generally available, are organized. We shall consider the spatial implications of these latter assets in our next section.

We would, however, make one further point about firm-specific assets. Much of received spatial economics rests on the assumptions that the sole objective of firms is to maximize profits and that there is minimal market failure. In practice, neither assumption is legitimate. However, where competitive pressures exist, then, as the theory suggests, firms are forced to look more closely at ways and means of lowering production costs and/or increasing revenues, and of organizing their assets in a way which minimizes transaction costs. A similar argument applies to reaping economies of scale. To overcome the costs of market failure, it may be inevitable that some concentration of competitive advantages among firms arises. So long as the privileged firms are not protected, that is, markets are contestable, this may be an optimum solution as the most analogous to the perfect market model which is assumed by received theory.

So far in our analysis of the spatial implications of firm-specific advantages, we have been concerned with those which, independently, arise directly from a firm's *own* asset portfolio and management. But, sometimes, these advantages may, themselves, be influenced by its participation in interfirm networks and its locational choices. The gains to be derived from the geographical concentration, agglomeration or clustering of related activities have been well acknowledged by industrial and locational economists, at least since the time of Alfred Marshall.[15] By contrast, until recently they had been largely ignored by trade economists, mainly, we suspect, because of the latter's narrow interpretation of the boundaries of a firm and their reluctance to embrace endemic market failure (in this case arising from externalities) into their models or theories.

However, over the last decade, a systemic approach to the dynamics of the firm, and its interaction with related firms located in close proximity to each other, has gained increasing attention by scholars from economics, organization theory, business strategy, geography and sociology.[16] Owing to the increased ease with which products, assets and people can move across national boundaries, the traditional paradigms of the micro-organization of business activity, and their spatial implications, are becoming increasingly inappropriate. In particular, as flexible and network-related production systems tend to place Fordist-type hierarchies as the dominant systems of value-added activity, the concept of 'neo-Marshallian' subnational spatial areas, for example the business or industrial district as a critical unit of economic organization, is gaining ground. We have already alluded to the main feature of the globalizing economy as the replacement of an 'arm's-length' international division of labour by one largely characterized by trading and production relationships between related parties.[17] It is also evident that this leads both to some clustering of value-added activities by foreign direct investors in particular countries – very much on the lines earlier observed by Knickerbocker (1973)[18] – and to an increasing spatial concentration of such activities – and particularly innovatory activities – between countries.

The renaissance of the Marshallian agglomerative economies has been acknowledged by several scholars, including Michael Porter (1990) and Paul Krugman (1991), both of whom assign it considerable importance in affecting the competitive advantages both of the participating firms and of the regions and countries of which they are a part. The point at issue here is the extent to which firms with O-specific assets, and particularly those which advance global competitiveness, need to be in close proximity to other firms supplying complementary assets in order to minimize their transaction and co-ordination costs.

It is not difficult to find historical or contemporary examples of the way in which agglomerative economies have added to the O advantages of the participating firms; and also to the competitiveness of the regions and countries. Among the best known are the square mile (= City) of London and Silicon Valley in California, the Geneva watch and the Solingen cutlery industries.[19] However, there are strong suggestions that, in spite of (or perhaps it is because of) advances in transportation and communication technologies, the value of agglomerative economies is increasing.[20] This is especially so in the more dynamic and service-intensive industrial sectors, in which there is usually an above-average representation of smaller and entrepreneurial firms, which are likely to gain particular benefit from networking with other firms, and the near presence of diverse, yet complementary, assets.[21] It also reflects the increasing need of firms producing or using complementary assets at the top end of the value chain to keep in close touch with each other,[22] and is encouraged by various facets of innovatory-led production, including the desire of firms to keep inventories to the minimum. One of the fastest-growing sectors of economic activity is that of industrial and science parks. Here, too, there is a good deal of intraindustry FDI in research and development activity, as the major MNEs seek to acquire, as well as to exploit, already existing knowledge.[23]

It is difficult, if not impossible, to define an optimum space of a regional cluster, as this will critically depend on the composition of the activities making up the cluster. But, one noticeable result of European integration is the realignment of the geography of agglomeration, which, *inter alia*, is leading to the emergence of new cross-border networks. Examples include those parts of the Low Countries and Germany adjacent to the Ruhr Valley, and along the borders of Northern Italy and France. It is most conspicuous in sectors no longer encumbered by non-tariff barriers; in those which gain most benefit from labour pooling and the common availability of specialized inputs and services; in those which comprise activities which are technologically or organizationally synergistic to each other; and in those which are faced with relatively insignificant transport and communications costs.

Trade liberalization has also affected the location of economic activity in other regions of the world. In his study of the Mexican economy, for example, Hanson (1994) found that the introduction of more market-oriented policies of the Mexican government has led to a relocation of the geographical clustering of manufacturing activity from Mexico City to the US border region. Trade liberalization has also tended to compress regional wage differentials.

THE GROWING SIGNIFICANCE OF THE CO-ORDINATING AND TRANSACTION FUNCTIONS OF FIRMS

We have already observed that neo-classical economists regarded the firm solely as a production unit, and markets to be the optimal modality for the exchange of inputs and outputs relevant to that production. Prior to Knight (1921), Schumpeter (1947) and Penrose (1959), the co-ordinating role of the entrepreneur was given little attention, except that it was generally accepted by micro-economists that, in conditions of perfect competition, the eventual limit to the size of firms was the rising costs of co-ordination.

Yet, as several scholars from a wide range of disciplines have demonstrated, the relative significance of the transaction and co-ordinating costs (cf. e.g. production costs) of economic activity tends to increase with economic development.[24] This is essentially because, as the division of labour becomes more specialized, the likelihood of learning constraints, information asymmetries and opportunism between independent transacting parties increases. Where it is perceived that these costs are higher than those of internal, or quasi-internal,[25] organizational mechanisms, then individual hierarchies, or groups of related firms, will replace the market as an organizational mode. Hence, the growth of multi-activity firms and networks is directly correlated with the growth of market-related transaction and co-ordination costs, and also with advances in organizational and communications technology.

The geographical specialization of economic activities across space is likely to lead to additional transport and co-ordinating costs, both of the market and of firms. Sometimes – as in the case of some service-intensive activities, for example R&D and merchant banking, where face-to-face contact between producers and users is imperative – such costs are infinite. Initially, economists measured distance costs entirely by the direct costs of traversing space. But again, owing to technological advances and a more complex division of labour, these costs, relative to market-related transaction and co-ordinating costs, have fallen. Increasingly, the locational preferences of firms are being set by their ability to organize spatially dispersed or spatially concentrated activities.

Although *international economists* have largely ignored them, *international business* (IB) scholars have long recognized that the distinction between cross-border and domestic value-added activities lies in the presence of transnational market failures. These include not only the most obvious co-ordinating costs and learning and information constraints firms have to incur when they commence production in a less familiar, and perhaps riskier, economic and political environment, but also those to do with establishing and fostering relationships between individuals and institutions in countries with different historical and institutional backgrounds, legal systems, lifestyles, political and religious ideologies and business customs.

Historically, cultural distance[26] has been one of the key variables determining the geographical pattern of economic activity, notably between metropolitan countries and their colonies, and between countries with comparable legal systems and commercial practices. Almost certainly, the globalizing economy is eroding some types of cultural distance and causing a realignment of spatial preferences among firms. On the other hand, where, to acquire the intermediate products or complementary assets necessary to protect or advance their own competitive advantages, firms perceive a need to be part of a subnational network, this could add to their spatial specific co-ordination and transaction costs. Whether the resulting spatial realignment is predominantly centripetal or centrifugal will obviously reflect a balance between the production, transaction and co-ordinating costs of clustering particular kinds of economic activities, and those of decentralizing such activities.

While scholars have long since recognized that the gains to be derived from agglomerative economies are activity specific, rather less attention has been paid to the role of subnational or country-specific variables in determining such clusters. To some extent, Michael Porter (1990) rectifies this deficiency, and correctly points to the growing importance of subnational clusters as a variable influencing the competitiveness of firms and countries. Building on Porter's analysis, we would like to suggest that the capability of countries to develop and sustain efficient clusters rests, first, on the macro-economic and organizational policies of governments; second, on the innovating and marketing strategies of the participating firms; third, on the willingness and ability of those firms to capture the benefits and minimize the costs of clustering; and fourth, on the availability and quality of complementary assets – notably R&D, transport and communication infrastructure and a flexible labour market. Such a capability may well become one of the most important location-bound and country-specific characteristics determining the competitive advantages of particular activities and the composition of a country's economic activities in the emerging age of alliance capitalism.[27]

To what extent, then, have scholars embraced the spatial consequences of the inability of arm's-length markets to maximize the net benefits of the co-ordinating and transaction functions of a market economy? As far as much of extant *international trade* theory is concerned, the answer is very little,[28] although there have been some brave attempts to integrate theories of trade and international production.[29] As for *international direct investment* theory, the record is much better. Indeed, perhaps the critical contribution of international business scholars over the past two decades has been to develop a firm-level theory of international direct investment, by explaining the situations in which firms will internalize cross-border intermediate product markets – the so-called internalization (I) paradigm[30] – and also why firms should opt to undertake the value-added activities arising from such internalization from one location rather than another.

At the same time, IB scholars have paid much less attention to the ways in which the intracountry allocation of economic activity might affect the competitive advantages of firms or nations; or indeed to the significance of agglomerative economies in explaining the intracountry distribution of FDI.[31] This deficiency is in the process of being partially corrected by economic geographers,[32] and by economists interested in the spatial distribution of technological innovation.[33] We say 'partially' for although this group of scholars has sought to identify the reasons why particular activities tend to agglomerate together, there has been little rigorous evaluation either of the origins or the significance of systemic market failure leading to the clusters, or to how these failures may differ between industrial sectors.[34] And, although *organizational scholars* have considerably advanced our knowledge about the nature and determinants of networks or related activities,[35] and of the management of innovatory systems,[36] they, too, have been slow to embrace the spatial dimension in their models.

Business analysts, notably Chandler (1977, 1990) and Porter (1990), have, in general, confined their attention to examining the attributes of industrial clusters of activities within a country, although, in his work, Porter has made some attempt to relate the location-bound characteristics of countries to the kind of subnational clusters they generate. Porter, however, does not draw much on the market failure paradigm for his explanation of why a group of firms with synergistic O assets may wish to be clustered in one region or country rather than another; nor how this clustering may vary, according to country-specific characteristics, and to the asset management strategy of the participating firms.

What, then, can one glean from these rather diffuse disciplinary perspectives? To what extent is it possible to evaluate the role of organizational structures as they affect the competitiveness of firms and countries and the location of economic activity? We would suggest a three-pronged approach. The first, drawing mainly on organizational theory and industrial economics, is to identify which kinds of co-ordination and transaction costs are most likely to be space related, and how far these costs are likely to vary between different types of activities and/or countries. The second, which combines the work of scholars on the dynamics of the firm, technological accumulation and business strategy, is to look more closely at the determinants of the asset portfolios of firms, and the strategic management of these portfolios, so as to identify the critical firm-specific characteristics influencing the location of activity.

The third prong is to relate the findings of the first two prongs to the received theories of trade and location, and to see whether country- and firm-specific co-ordinating and transaction costs can be incorporated into these theories. This, like the inclusion of created assets – and particularly firm-specific mobile assets – into existing explanations of the spatial allocation of resources is a tall order!

THE ROLE OF GOVERNMENTS IN AFFECTING THE SPATIAL ORGANIZATION OF ACTIVITY

We now consider the consequences of globalization for the actions of national and subnational governments,[37] and of supranational institutions and regimes, in so far as they affect the locational choices of the dynamic firm – or groups of firms. Again, historically, *international economics* – and neo-classical economics in particular – has ignored the macro-organizational (as opposed to the macro-economic)[38] role of government. This is mainly because in a Pareto-optimal world, markets are assumed not to fail, and only where structural distortions occur is any government intervention considered necessary.[39]

More recently, this analytical lacuna has, at least partly, been overcome by the work of two groups of scholars. The first – typified by the writings of Paul Krugman (1986, 1994) – has injected new life into international trade theory by extending the tools of industrial economics to explain how strategic trade policy by governments might affect the location of economic activity. The second is the ongoing research of a group of mainly US scholars, notably Ray Vernon, Fred Bergsten, Gary Hufbauer and Monty Graham, on the changing interface between trade, FDI and global business activity, and its implications for a whole range of domestic economic and other issues. Nevertheless, neither group of scholars has given much attention to the ways in which governments might interact with firms and markets to lessen or circumvent the endemic failure of different organizational forms of economic activity, and how these, in turn, might affect the international and intranational disposition of national and created assets.

Turning to *locational economics* and *geography* – including that part of it concerned with the extranational activities of firms – we see a much greater willingness of scholars to tackle head-on the role of government-related variables, notably fiscal penalties and incentives. Indeed, in recent work on the determinants of the locational preferences of MNEs,[40] the role of host governments, and particularly their ability to affect the co-ordinating and transaction costs[41] of economic activity, has been shown to be a critical one. Much of this latter research has been undertaken by *economic geographers*, *regional scientists*, *urban economists* and *international business specialists*, but it is, perhaps, the international marketing scholars[42] who have gone furthest in their attempts to embrace psychic distance (which includes non-economic spatial market failures, many of which are government influenced) into their thinking. Economists interested in the interaction between MNE activity and the pattern and path of technological accumulation are increasingly acknowledging the decisive role of national innovatory systems as a competitive enhancing instrument of governments (Chesnais, 1993; Nelson, 1993).

By contrast, *organization theory* has generally neglected government-related and other exogenous variables in its examination of the decision-making practices of firms. The same charge may also be levelled at much of the strategic management literature,[43] notwithstanding a copious volume of research which has sought to analyse the way in which business strategy may be affected by a firm's external environment. Since, in the past, both organization and management theory has been geared towards explaining the internal functioning of firms operating largely within their national boundaries, this neglect is, perhaps, understandable. But in today's globalizing economy, where governments exercise so much influence on the extent and pattern of cross-border market failure,[44] this neglect – even at the most micro level of analysis – is quite unacceptable.

It is difficult to conclude from the above paragraphs that the role of government as an organizer and co-ordinator of economic activity has, in the past, been given the attention it deserves.[45] There are signs that this is changing and this, we believe, is primarily due to the effect the globalizing economy is having on the costs and benefits of alternative organizational modes – and particularly on the role of governments as facilitators of efficient markets.

The concept of government as a superintendent of the organization of economic activity, and the instruments which government may use to facilitate an efficient market system, are now being much more closely examined by *political scientists*, *economists*, *organizational scholars* and *business strategists* alike.[46] This, as we have already said, is because the kind of co-ordination and transaction costs most influenced by the actions of governments are exercising a more important part in the locational decision process of firms and networks than once they did. This, in turn, reflects the convergence of many kinds of production costs across national boundaries – particularly among advanced industrialized countries – and the increasing role of created assets in the production process.

The macro-organizational actions of government – and elsewhere (Dunning, 1994b) we have explored the situations in which government action to reduce market failure is likely to be the most cost-effective[47] – are clearly likely to be discriminatory in their impact, both between firms and types of economic activity. Of the former, those most likely to be affected are those whose competitiveness rests on continuous product innovation and improvement; new ventures, especially in relatively high-risk sectors; those whose assets are most spatially mobile; and those most dependent on the kind of complementary assets, which are critically influenced by government actions. Viewed from a functional or strategic perspective, the influence of government is most likely to affect the decisions of firms about expenditure on R&D and training, the extent of vertical integration or horizontal diversification and the locational configuration of high-value-added activities.

The subject matter of this chapter embraces several of these areas and the ways in which they interact with each other. To tackle these effectively, government action must be more explicitly considered as a critical explanatory variable, and much more rigorous work needs to be done on the consequences of collective and specific macro-organizational strategies on the ownership, organization and competitiveness of firms, and on the location of different types of economic activity.

CONCLUDING REMARKS

The key message of this chapter is that globalization – and more particularly the forces driving it and its consequences – is affecting the costs and benefits of the four main modalities of organizing economic activity in capitalist economies, namely markets, hierarchies, interfirm alliances and governments. It further argues that, while in the past these modalities have largely been viewed as alternatives to each other, the growing economic interdependence of domestic and cross-border activities and the increasing significance of co-operative ventures, both between firms and between firms and governments, are requiring scholars to search for a more macro-systemic approach to the organization of resources and capabilities in which markets, hierarchies, networks and governments each have complementary roles to play.

Such a macro-systemic approach is especially relevant when considering the interaction between the dynamic firm and its external environment, and especially between the former and firms supplying goods and services, the price and quality of which influences its own competitiveness. The chapter has further suggested that the introduction of flexible production systems and alliance capitalism is causing firms to reorganize their asset portfolios, *inter alia*, by externalizing some of their internal markets, but, at the same time, reinternalizing them among a network of related firms. Finally, we have argued that both the intra- and international locations of economic activity are being increasingly guided by the desire of firms to reduce the costs of market failure and/or to capture the synergies offered by business districts and other spatially related networks of firms, and by the actions of governments designed to promote the competitiveness of their location-bound assets and that of their own MNEs.

None of the traditional disciplines analysing the behaviour of firms has yet fully embraced the features and consequences of globalization in their paradigms and theories. In particular, the significance of firm-specific competencies and management strategies, not to mention the growing cross-border mobility of assets, has still not engaged the attention of mainstream economists. On the other hand, the need for a more systemic approach in addressing issues relating to the growth of firms and groups of firms, the role of governments and the organization and management of a complex bundle of assets, is forcing a reassessment of our ideas about the very nature of economic activity, and the relationships between the major institutional entities.

While it seems probable that, barring catastrophes, the forces currently driving globalization will continue in the foreseeable future, it is less certain how these will affect the organization of created assets between and within firms, the dynamics of technological accumulation and the location of economic activity. As far as the leading global players are concerned, there are suggestions of a flattening of organizational structures and a divestment of activities which do not directly enhance their core competences. At the same time, firms are becoming increasingly aware of the need to balance the advantages of a centralized control of financial assets, R&D and of markets, with those of the decentralization of entrepreneurial initiative and managerial competence, and the need to adapt asset usage to local needs and customs.

While lean and flexible organizational structures are likely to follow – and sometimes lead – the techno-economic system of flexible production and the socio-institutional system of alliance capitalism, and some of the advantages of hierarchical capitalism may disappear, it is probably premature to predict that today's successful large corporations will become tomorrow's dinosaurs. At the same time, as well as studying the production and co-ordinating functions of individual firms, economists should give more attention to the concept of a systemic group or network of firms as a unit of analysis,[48] and of the positioning of individual firms in that grouping or network. It is, indeed, quite possible that some of the economies of scope and co-ordination enjoyed by independent firms will be transferred to the 'flagship' or lead firms in a network, while, concurrently, some of the erstwhile functions of large firms will be contracted out to medium and small-sized firms in the network.

The impact of future technological and organizational advances on the location of economic activity is also unclear. While there is some indication that the leading MNEs are decentralizing some of their production and innovatory activities, this is largely taking place in the same countries or regions from which other MNEs, namely Japan, the United States and the EC, are decentralizing their activities. Moreover, as we have seen, despite advances in telematics, the need for close, if not face-to-face, contact between the managers, administrators, scientists and technologists of interrelated firms – particularly at the top end of the value-added chain and between the factory and the research laboratory – is encouraging centripetal tendencies. Across countries and regions, too, there are suggestions that the principle of comparative advantage may be applied to explaining different clusters or networks of activities;[49] the willingness and ability of firms to embrace alliance capitalism, and the macro-organizational policies of national and regional governments come into play.

There are also suggestions that the forces affecting the geography of innovatory activities are also encouraging similar networks or firms producing at different stages of the same value-added chain. There is nothing particularly new in this phenomenon. What, perhaps, is new is the extent to which the composition and character of such clusters has been affected by inward and outward direct investment. Indeed, one especially interesting feature of networks in the auto and electronics sectors, as for example fashioned by Japanese MNE activity in the EC and the United States, is the extent to which horizontal cross-border linkages have been formed between particular component manufacturers in the host countries and their opposite numbers in Japan.

What of the role of the developing economies in the emerging global economy? This could easily be a subject for a separate volume, although we have touched upon some of the relevant issues in Chapters 3 and 4. But, just as the presence of created complementary assets – and particularly in those which are government induced – and a market-facilitating environment are becoming increasingly important determinants of both domestic and inbound investment in developed countries, so these location-bound characteristics are also the prerequisites for the upgrading of economic activity in most developing countries – especially in those which compete with each other. But, as Porter (1990) and others have shown, because of the limited size of their domestic markets, it is much more difficult for the poorer nations to create the educational and infrastructure needed to participate in global trade and investment. While the examples of Singapore and Hong Kong are salutary, it is difficult to perceive how the smaller developing nations, especially in sub-Saharan Africa and Latin America, can expect to experience the benefits of their counterparts in Europe, either by forging networks with foreign firms or by participating in regional integration schemes.

In conclusion, there are several indications that alliance capitalism is requiring a reappraisal of the appropriate or optimum spatial unit of organizational governance, and that the economic transformation now being fashioned by globalization is likely to upgrade the role of subnational units of governance, and downgrade that of national governments.

Certainly, scholars from a variety of disciplines are beginning to explore or re-explore issues such as regional business cultures, regional institutional building, the learning or intelligent region, regional competitiveness, regional industrial policy, and interregional policy co-ordination (Storper and Scott, 1995; Florida, 1995). Increasingly, regions are being perceived as mini-states.[50] Indeed, Kenichi Ohmae (1993, 1995) has gone as far as to suggest that (what he calls) region states may supplant nation states as the core unit of spatial governance. To quote directly,

> The nation state has become an unnatural, even dysfunctional unit for organizing human activity and managing economic endeavor in a borderless world. It represents no genuine, shared community of economic interests; it defines no meaningful flows of economic activity ... On the global economic map the lines that now matter are those defining what may be called 'region states.' ... Region states are natural economic zones. They may or may not fall within the geographic limits of a particular nation – whether they do is an accident of history. Sometimes these distinct economic units are formed by parts of states ... At other times they may be formed by economic patterns that overlap existing national boundaries ... In today's borderless world, these are natural economic zones and what matters is that each possesses, in one or another combination, the key ingredients for successful participation in the global economy. (Ohmae, 1993, pp. 78–9)

Whether Ohmae's vision is realized remains to be seen. What is, however, already occurring is a realignment of the geography both of the activities of individual and networks of business units and of the jurisdiction of governments. *A propos* the former, Amin and Thrift (1994, p. 13) refer to centres of geographical agglomeration as becoming 'centres of representation, interaction and innovation within global production filiers'. This, they argue, is leading to a spatial reconfiguration of territorial embeddedness based upon the ability of regions to exploit their location-specific advantages. Certainly the idea that geography is dead, as avowed by some scholars (e.g. O'Brien, 1992), with respect to the operation of global financial markets, is more than counterbalanced by the emergence of new localized industrial clusters bound together by the need to minimize distant-sensitive transaction costs, such as those associated with irregular idiocyncratic, uncertain and time-dependent transactions (Storper and Scott, 1995).

Yet the appropriate form of spatial networking remains a matter of debate among scholars. As Chapter 5 has shown, Ann Markusen (1996), has distinguished between four ways of organizing regional business activity, each of which is likely to make a different contribution to the prosperity of the 'sticky' places[51] of which they are a part.[52] These are (i) the *flexible specialization* rubric, as exampled by the Italian textile industry in Prato, Northern Italy, and the watch industry of Switzerland; (ii), the *hub and spoke* industrial districts where the pattern of economic activity is centred on a number of 'flagship' corporations or strategic centres, for example, Toyota City in Japan and the Seattle industrial district (Gray et al., 1996); (iii) the *satellite industrial platform*, which is mainly made up of the affiliates of extra-regional firms, such as in export-processing zones in developing countries; and (iv) the *non-market-centred district* where the local economy revolves around either a group of top-ranking educational institutions or a number of major government-owned administrative or research installations, as along Route 128 in the United States and the M4 corridor in the United Kingdom.

A propos the latter, scholarly opinions vary from those of political scientists who predict an increasing 'squeezing' or 'hollowing out' of national governments as both subnational and supranational administrative structures become more important to those that believe that, however much their functions may be reconstructed, national governments will continue to be the dominant fashioners and monitors of economic systems.[53]

NOTES

1. Interrelated in the sense that the participating firms incur certain costs and enjoy certain benefits which are internal to the relationship, for example a strategic alliance or network, but external to their own activities.
2. Although the presence of intranational networks has long been acknowledged, for example by Alfred Marshall (1919).
3. For a review of these and other trade theories of the time, see Hufbauer (1970) and Stern (1975).
4. See especially his classic volume on interregional and international trade (Ohlin, 1933).
5. Although, in his paper, Hla Myint (1977) did discuss the role of institutional factors in economic development.
6. There are, of course, notable exceptions, including the work of James Markusen, Bruce Kogut, David Teece, Gunner Hedlund, Yves Doz, Sumantra Ghoshal and Christopher Bartlett.
7. One example of a package of assets which is not transportable is the macro-organizational strategies of domestic governments.
8. Although not necessarily of the predictions of international economics. See Dunning (1994a).
9. See, for example, Chandler (1962, 1977, 1990) and Teece (1986, 1992a).
10. Teece, however, has written on the implications of cross-border transfer of technology to the competitive advantages of the transferring firms (Teece 1977).

11. See, for example, Vernon (1966), Keesing (1966) and Gruber et al. (1970).
12. See also the next section of this chapter.
13. The problem is composed when the unit of analysis is extended to an alliance or network of firms.
14. There are other areas of imperfect competition and the appropriate behaviour of strategic oligopolists which cloud the issue even further!
15. See especially Marshall (1919).
16. See, for example, Piore and Sabel (1984), Best (1990), Casson (1991), Gerlach (1992), Patel and Pavitt (1992), Cantwell (1992), Archibugi and Pianta (1993), Harrison et al. (1993), Enright (1944), Harrison (1994), Scott (1994), and various contributions to an edited volume by Grabher (1993).
17. The relationship might be by non-equity ownership, or by some form of cooperative agreement.
18. More recent examples include the 'follow my leader' behaviour by Japanese consumer electronics and auto MNEs into the United States and Europe.
19. Other examples are given by Enright (1994).
20. Venables (1994) has demonstrated that the forces of agglomeration in vertically linked industries are likely to be most pronounced at intermediate levels of transport costs. He suggests that beyond a certain point, lower transport costs will cause industries to operate in multiple locations, which will lead to a spatial convergence, rather than a concentration, of economic activity.
21. In a study on employment growth of industrial sectors in major US cities and counties, Henderson (1994) found that employment gains from dynamic externalities were most marked in cities and counties which offered the most diversified range of complementary assets to their core activities.
22. The kind of face-to-face contact which has always characterized transactions in the City of London (which, in its square mile, probably comprises the most intimate network of firms in the world) seems now to be increasingly valued by firms in the dynamic manufacturing sectors, and particularly those whose technologies and organizational competencies are complementary to each other. In a recent paper, dealing with intra-US geographical clustering and using employment data for three two-digit industrial sectors and four US cities, Hagen and Hammond (1994) found that asset sharing produces significant localization economies, while the economies of labour pooling tend to be most significant in rapidly growing labour markets.
23. Archibugi and Michie (1993) refer to technological acquirers as 'polyp' firms which 'acquire from each country its excellence in research rather than to decentralize their brains'.
24. Notably, Emile Durkheim (1964) from sociology, Douglass North (1990) from economic history, Alfred Chandler (1990) from business strategy, Oliver Williamson (1975, 1990) from organizational theory and Ronald Coase (1937, 1960), Edith Penrose (1959) and Kenneth Arrow (1969, 1974) from economics. An interesting collection of cross-disciplinary essays on the nature of the firm is contained in Gustafsson and Williamson (1990) and Williamson and Winter (1991).
25. Quasi-internal embraces relationships between related parties other than those arising from the ownership of one party by the other. These include non-equity co-operative agreements and networks.
26. The concept of business-related cultural distance is broadly similar to that of psychic differences between countries.
27. See Dunning (1997b), chapters 1 and 2.
28. This is not to say trade economists, notably Paul Krugman, have not concerned themselves with market imperfections and the strategic behaviour of firms; but to the best of our knowledge, they have not embraced transaction and co-ordination costs in their analyses.
29. Notably by Ethier (1986), Horstman and Markusen (1987) and Gray (1992).
30. See especially the various writings of Peter Buckley and Mark Casson, of Alan Rugman and of Jean François Hennart, as set out in Dunning (1993).
31. There are some exceptions, noticeably Teece (1992b) in his study of FDI in California, and Wilkins (1979) in a study of FDI in Florida.

32. See, for example, the various contributions of Allen Scott, that of Malecki (1985), Thwaites and Oakey (1985), Hall et al. (1987), Howells (1990) and Feldman (1993). See also several of the contributions to Krugman and Venables (1994) and especially those of Audretsch and Feldman, Hagen and Hammond, Henderson, and Venables.
33. See especially references set out in note 16 and in OECD (1992) and Kenney and Florida (1994). In their contribution to the Krugman and Venables volume, David Audretsch and Maryann Feldman (1994) found that the propensity of innovatory activity to cluster spatially was greater in industries in which the creation of knowledge spillovers is important, and in which university researchers provide important inputs for such knowledge.
34. The concept of hierarchical failure is rarely discussed in the literature. Yet it seems to us that the existence of networks rests on the failure of both markets and industrial hierarchies to generate the relational or agglomerative economies which networks provide. The more significant these benefits are to protecting or advancing the core competencies of firms, and the greater the costs of engaging in vertical or horizontal integration, the more networks and/or bilateral alliances are likely to replace or supplement hierarchies and markets as an organizational form.
35. See especially the work of the Uppsala scholars (e.g. Johanson and Mattson, 1987).
36. See, for example, Bartlett and Ghoshal (1990).
37. We are using action of governments as a proxy for all actions affecting the allocations which are not taken by the constituents of a market system.
38. The macro-economic role is concerned with the level of economic activity, unemployment, prices, exchange rates; the macro-organizational (sometimes called micro-economic) role is concerned with the allocation of economic activity via industrial, trade, innovation, education, transport, fiscal, environment, etc., policies, and the response of such activity to changes in demand and supply conditions. For a contemporary examination of the macro-organizational role of government see Dunning (1992, 1994b), Stopford (1994) and Stopford and Strange (1991).
39. In other words, governments act to correct market imperfections rather than to prevent market imperfections.
40. As, for example, described in Dunning (1993) and Loree and Guisinger (1995).
41. Or what I have elsewhere described as the 'hassle' costs of doing business (Dunning, 1992).
42. See, for example, Johanson and Vahlne (1977, 1990), Nordström (1991), Reid (1984), Welch and Luostarinen (1988) and Vahlne and Nordström (1992).
43. Although, in some thinking (e.g. Teece, 1986), more stress is being given to the ways in which governments may affect the provision of complementary assets necessary to the efficient exploitation of the O advantages of firms. A recent paper by Kobrin (1993) also tackles the interface between networks and government behaviour.
44. Illustrations include the strategic trade policies of individual governments; the formation of regional economic blocs; and the role of GATT in setting the rules of the game for international commerce.
45. This may seem a strange statement, as governments have always acted as regulatory agencies, as well as initiating and monitoring the economic system, which is responsible for the allocation of scarce resources. But, rarely have governments attempted to optimally coordinate the alternative modes of organization of economic activity. Perhaps this is an impossible dream!
46. See, for example, Krueger (1990), Stopford and Strange (1991), Audretsch (1989), McKenzie and Lee (1991), Wolf (1988) and Osborne and Gaebler (1992).
47. The costs of government intervention have been extensively discussed in the literature; see especially Wolf (1988), Audretsch (1989) and Krueger (1990). For a more in-depth analysis of the comparative advantage of governments as organizing mechanisms (cf. unaided markets and hierarchies) see Wade (1988), World Bank (1993) and Hämäläinen (1994).
48. Of course, there have been various attempts by economists in the past to classify firms into groups, and for various reasons. Yet such terms as 'industry', 'strategic groups' and 'clusters' do not encompass the idea that firms become part of a larger entity in order to capture the external economies which are internal to the entity, and that they perceive this as a preferable way to advance their competitiveness than by engaging in vertical or horizontal integration.

Marshall's concept of 'agglomerative economies' and the Japanese *keiretsu* system of relational enterprises come closest to what we have in mind.
49. To this extent, we do not agree with Porter (1990) that his analysis negates the validity of the concept of comparative advantage; but rather that it suggests that the components and determinants of that advantage have changed.
50. A good example is Richard Florida's analysis of the refashioning of the dominant micro-production system from mass production to knowledge production based (Florida, 1995).
51. So called because particular spatial units have flourished despite the increasing mobility of firm-specific assets. Such mobility, however, needs to be set against the rising need of firms to use a group of complementary but regional-specific immobile assets. This makes for spatial embeddedness or stickiness.
52. For an alternative classification of relational structures, see Storper and Harrison (1991) and Miles and Snow (1992).
53. For a discussion of these views, see various chapters – and particularly the one by John Stopford in Dunning (1997a).

REFERENCES

Amin, A. and Thrift, N. (eds) (1994), *Globalization, Institutions and Regional Development in Europe*, Oxford: Oxford University Press.
Antonelli, C. (1991), *The Diffusion of Advanced Telecommunications in Developing Countries*, Paris: OECD Development Centre.
Archibugi, D. and Michie, J. (1993), *The Globalization of Technology: Myths and Realities*, Cambridge: Judge Institute of Management Studies, 1992–3, No. 18, May.
Archibugi, D. and Pianta, M. (1993), 'Patterns of technological specialization and growth of innovatory activities in advanced countries', in K. Hughes (ed.), *European Competitiveness*, Cambridge: Cambridge University Press.
Arrow, K.J. (1969), *The Organization of Economic Activity: Issues Pertinent to the Choice of Market versus Non-market Allocation*. Testimony presented to the Joint Economic Committee, 31st Congress, 1st Session, 'The analysis and evolution of public expenditures: the PPB system', Washington: US Government Printing Office.
Arrow, K.J. (1974), *The Limits of Organization*, New York: W.W. Norton.
Audretsch, D.B. (1989), *The State and the Market*, New York and London: Harvester Wheatsheaf.
Audretsch, D.B. and Feldman, M.P. (1994), 'External economies and spatial clustering', in P. Krugman and A. Venables (eds), *The Location of Economic Activity: New Theories and Evidence*, London: Centre of Economic Policy Research (CEPR).
Bain, J. (1956), *Barriers to Competition*, Cambridge, MA: Harvard University Press.
Barney, J.B. (1986), 'Strategic factor markets: expectations, luck and business strategy', *Management Science* **32**: 1232–41.
Bartlett, C.G. and Ghoshal, S. (1989), *Managing Across Borders: The Transnational Solution*, Boston: Harvard Business School Press, pp. 215–55.
Bartlett, C.G. and Ghoshal, S. (1990), 'Managing innovation in the transnational corporation', in C.A. Bartlett, Y. Doz and G. Hedlund (eds), *Managing the Global Firm*, London and New York: Routledge.
Best, M. (1990), *The New Competition: Institutions of Restructuring*, Cambridge, MA: Harvard University Press.
Cainarca, G.C., Colombo, M.G. and Mariotti, S. (1988), *Cooperative Agreements in the Information and Communication Industrial System*, Milan: Politecnico de Milano.

Cantwell, J.A. (1992), 'The internationalization of technological activity and its implications for competitiveness', in O. Granstrand, L. Hakanson and S. Sjölander (eds) *Technology, Management and International Business: Internationalization of R&-D and Technology*, Chichester: John Wiley, pp. 75–96.

Casson, M. (1991), 'Internalization theory and beyond', in P.J. Buckley (ed.) *Recent Research on the Multinational Enterprise*, Cheltenham: Edward Elgar, pp. 4–27.

Chamberlin, E. (1933), *The Theory of Monopolistic Competition*, Cambridge, MA: MIT Press.

Chandler, A.D. Jr (1962), *Strategy and Structure: The History of American Industrial Enterprise*, Cambridge, MA: MIT Press.

Chandler, A.D. Jr (1977), *The Invisible Hand: The Managerial Revolution in American Business*, Cambridge, MA: Harvard University Press.

Chandler, A.D. Jr (1990), *Scale and Scope: The Dynamics of Industrial Capitalism*, Cambridge, MA: Harvard University Press.

Chesnais, F. (1993), *National Systems of Innovation, Foreign Direct Investment and the Operations of Multinational Enterprises* (mimeo).

Coase, R.H. (1937), 'The nature of the firm', *Economica* (New Series) **4**, November: 386–405.

Coase, R.H. (1960), 'The problem of social cost', *Journal of Law and Economics* **3**: 1–10.

Dierckx, I. and Cool, K. (1989), 'Assets, stock accumulation and sustainability of competitive advantage', *Management Science* **35**: 1504–11.

Dosi, G., Pavitt, K. and Soete, L. (1990), *Technical Change and International Trade*, New York: Harvester Wheatsheaf.

Dunning, J.H. (1992), The global economy, domestic governance, strategies and transnational corporations; interactions and policy recommendations', *Transnational Corporations* **1**, December: 7–45.

Dunning, J.H. (1993), *Multinational Enterprises and the Global Economy*, Wokingham: Addison-Wesley.

Dunning, J.H. (1994a), 'What's wrong – and right – with trade theory?', *International Trade Journal* **IX**(2): 153–202.

Dunning, J.H. (1994b), *Globalization: The Challenge for National Economic Regimes*, Dublin: The Economic and Social Research Council.

Dunning, J.H. (1997a), *Governments, Globalization and International Business*, Oxford: Oxford University Press.

Dunning, J.H. (1997b), *Alliance, Capitalism and Global Business*, London and New York: Routledge.

Durkheim E. (1964), *The Division of Labor in Society*, New York: The Free Press (originally published in German in 1893).

Enright, M.J. (1994), 'Regional Clusters and Firm Strategy', Paper presented to Prince Bertil Symposium on *The Dynamic Firm, The Role of Regions, Technology Strategy and Organization*, Stockholm, June.

Ethier, W.J. (1986), 'The multinational firm', *Quarterly Journal of Economics* **101**: 806–33.

Feldman, M.P. (1993), 'An examination of the geography of innovation', *Industrial and Corporate Change* **2**: 451–70.

Florida, R. (1995), Towards the learning region,' *Futures* **27**(5): 527–36.

Gerlach, M.L. (1992), *Alliance Capitalism: The Social Organization of Japanese Business*, Oxford: Oxford University Press.

Grabher, G. (ed.) (1993), *The Embedded Firm*, London and New York: Routledge.

Gray, H.P. (1992), 'The interface between the theories of trade and production' in P.J. Buckley and M. Casson (eds), *Multinational Enterprises in the World Economy*, Brookfield, VT and Aldershot: Edward Elgar, pp. 41–53.

Gray, M., Golob, E. and Markusen, A. (1996), 'Big firms, long arms, wide shoulders. The "hub and spoke" industrial district of the Seattle region', *Regional Studies*.

Gruber, W., Mehta, D. and Vernon, R. (1967), 'The R&D factor in international trade and international investment of United States industries', in R. Vernon (ed.), *The Technology Factor in International Trade*, New York: Columbia University Press

Gustafsson, B. and Williamson, O.E. (1990), *The Firm as a Nexus of Treaties*, London and Newbury Park, CA: Sage.

Hagen, Jürgen von and Hammond, G. (1994), 'An empirical test of the Marshall/Krugman hypothesis', in P. Krugman and A. Venables (eds), *The Location of Economic Activity: New Theories and Evidence*, London: Centre of Economic Policy Research (CEPR).

Hall, B., Breheny, M., McQuaid, R. and Hart, D. (1987), *Western Sunrise*, Hemel Hempstead: Allen & Unwin.

Hämäläinen, T. (1994), *The Evolving Role of Government in Economic Organization*, Newark, NJ: Rutgers University (mimeo).

Hanson, G.H. (1994), 'Increasing returns and regional structure of wages', in P. Krugman and A. Venables (eds), *The Location of Economic Activity: New Theories and Evidence*, London: Centre of Economic Policy Research (CEPR).

Harrison, B. (1994), *Lean and Mean: The Changing Landscape of Corporate Power in the Age of Flexibility*, New York: Basic Books.

Harrison, B., Kelley, M. and Appold, S.J. (1993), *Spatially Distributed and Proximate Interorganizational Networks, Agglomeration and Technological Performance in US Manufacturing*, Pittsburgh: Heinz School of Public Policy and Management Congress, Mellon University Working Paper 93–120.

Henderson, V. (1994), 'Externalities and industrial development', in P. Krugman and A. Venables (eds), *The Location of Economic Activity: New Theories and Evidence*, London: Centre of Economic Policy Research (CEPR).

Hoover, E.M. (1948), *The Location of Economic Activity*, New York: McGraw-Hill.

Horstman, I. and Markusen, J.R. (1987), 'Strategic investments and the development of multinationals', *International Economic Review* **28**: 109–21.

Hotelling, H. (1929), 'Stability in competition', *Economic Journal* **29**: 41–57.

Howells, J. (1990), 'The location and organization of research and development: new horizons', *Research Policy* **19**: 133–46.

Hufbauer, G. (1965), *Synthetic Materials and International Trade*, London: Duckworth, pp. 145–232.

Hufbauer, G. (1970), 'The impact of national characteristics and technology on the commodity composition of trade in manufactured goods', in R. Vernon (ed.), *The Technology Factor in International Trade*, New York: Columbia University Press.

Johanson, J. and Mattson, L.G. (1987), 'Internationalization in industrial systems: a network approach', in N. Hood and J.E. Vahlne (eds), *Strategies in Global Competition*, Chichester and New York: John Wiley.

Johanson, J. and Vahlne, J.E. (1977), 'The internationalization process of the firm: a model for knowledge development and increasing market commitments', *Journal of International Business Studies* **8**: 23–32.

Johanson, J. and Vahlne, J.E. (1990), 'Management of foreign market entry', *Scandinavian International Business Review* **1**(3): 9–27.

Keesing, D.B. (1966), 'Labor skills and comparative advantage', *American Economic Review*, Papers and Proceedings 1965 Annual Meeting.
Kenney, M. and Florida, R. (1994), 'The organization and geography of Japanese R&D: results from a survey of Japanese electronics and biotechnology firms', *Research Policy* **23**: 305–23.
Knickerbocker, F.T. (1973), *Oligopolistic Reaction and the Multinational Enterprise*, Cambridge, MA: Harvard University Press.
Knight, F. (1921), *Risk, Uncertainty and Profit*, Chicago: University of Chicago Press.
Kobrin, S.J. (1993), *Beyond Geography: Inter-Firm Networks and the Structural Integration of the Global Economy*, Philadelphia: William H. Wurston Center for International Management Studies, The Wharton School Working Paper 93–10.
Kojima, K. (1978), *Direct Foreign Investment: A Japanese Model of Multinational Business Operations*, London: Croom Helm.
Kojima, K. (1990), *Japanese Direct Investment Abroad, Tokyo: International Christian University, Social Science Research Institute, Monograph series 1.*
Kojima, K. (1992), 'Internalization vs international business approach to foreign direct investment', *Hitosubashi Journal of Economics* **23**: 630–40.
Krueger, A. (1990), 'Economists' changing perception of government', *Weltwirtschaftliches Archiv* **126**(3): 417–31.
Krugman, P. (ed.) (1986), *Strategic Trade Policy and the New International Economics*, Cambridge, MA: MIT Press.
Krugman, P. (1991), *Geography and Trade*, Cambridge, MA: MIT Press.
Krugman, P. (1994), 'Competitiveness: a dangerous obsession', *Foreign Affairs* **73**(2), March/April: 28–44.
Krugman, P. and Venables, A. (eds) (1994), *The Location of Economic Activity: New Theories and Evidence*, London: Centre of Economic Policy Research (CEPR).
Loree, D.W. and Guisinger, S.E. (1995), 'Policy and non-policy determinants of US equity foreign direct investment,' *Journal of International Business Studies* **26**(2): 281–300.
Lösch, A. (1940), *Die Raumliche Ordnung der Wirtchaft*, trans. *The Economics of Location*, New Haven, CT: Yale University Press, 1954.
Malecki, E.J. (1985), 'Industrial location and corporate organization in high technology industries', *Economic Geography* **61**(4): 345–69.
Markusen, A.R. (1996), 'Sticky Places in Slippery Space: a typology of industrial districts', *Economic Geography* **12**(3): 293–313.
Marshall, A. (1919), *Industry and Trade*, London: Macmillan.
McKenzie, R.B. and Lee, D.R. (1991), *Quicksilver Capital*, New York: The Free Press.
Miles, R.E. and Snow, C.C. (1992), 'Causes of failure in network organization', *California Management Review* **34**: 53–72.
Myint, H. (1977), 'The place of institutional change in international trade theory in the setting of the underdeveloped economies', in B. Ohlin, P.O. Hesselborn and P.M. Wijkman (eds), *The International Allocation of Economic Activity*, London: Macmillan, pp. 367–86.
Nelson, R.R. (ed.) (1993), *National Innovation Systems*, New York and Oxford: Oxford University Press.
Nordström, R. (1991), *The Internationalization Process of the Firm: Search for New Patterns and Explanations*, Stockholm: Stockholm School of Business, IIB, Dissertation.
North, D. (1990), *Institutions, International Change and Economic Performance*, Cambridge: Cambridge University Press.

O'Brien, R. (1992), *Global Financial Integration: The End of Geography*, London: Pinter.

OECD (1992), *Technology and the Economy*, Paris: OECD.

Ohlin, B. (1933), *Inter-regional and International Trade*, Cambridge, MA: Harvard University Press (Revised Edition 1967).

Ohlin, B., Hesselborn, P.O. and Wijkman, P.M. (eds) (1977), *The International Allocation of Economic Activity*, London: Macmillan.

Ohmae, K. (1993), 'The rise of the region state', *Foreign Affairs* **72**(2): 78–87.

Ohmae, K. (1995), *The End of the Nation State: The Rise of Regional Economies*, London: HarperCollins.

Osborne, D. and Gaebler, T. (1992), *Reinventing Government*, Reading, MA: Addison-Wesley.

Patel, P. and Pavitt, K. (1992), 'The innovatory performance of the world's largest firms: some new evidence', *Economic Innovation and New Technology* **2**: 91–102.

Penrose, E. (1959), *The Theory of the Growth of the Firm*, Oxford, Basil Blackwell.

Piore, M. and Sabel, C. (1984), *The Second Industrial Divide: Possibilities for Prosperity*, New York: Basic Books.

Porter, M. (1980), *Competitive Behavior*, New York: The Free Press.

Porter, M. (1985), *Competitive Advantage*, New York: The Free Press.

Porter, M. (1990), *The Competitive Advantage of Nations*, New York: The Free Press.

Reid, S.D. (1984), 'Market expansion and firm internationalization', in E. Kaynak (ed.), *International Marketing Management*, New York: Praeger, pp. 197–206.

Robinson, J. (1933), *The Economics of Imperfect Competition*, London: Macmillan.

Rumelt, R.P. (1984), Towards a strategic theory of the firm', in R.B. Lamb (ed.) *Competitive Strategic Management*, Englewood Cliffs, NJ: Prentice Hall, pp. 556–70.

Schumpeter, J.A. (1947), *Capitalism, Socialism and Democracy*, New York: Harper & Row.

Scott, A.J. (1994), 'The geographic foundations of industrial performance', Paper presented to the Prince Bertil Symposium on *The Dynamic Firm, the Role of Regions, Technology Strategy and Organization*, Stockholm, June.

Stern, R.M. (1975), 'Testing trade theories', in P.B. Kenen (ed.), *International Trade and Finance*, Cambridge: Cambridge University Press.

Stopford, J. (1994), 'The growing interdependence between transnational corporations and governments', *Transnational Corporations* **3**(1): 53–76.

Stopford, J. and Strange, S. (1991), *Rival States, Rival Firms: Competition for World Market Shares*, Cambridge: Cambridge University Press.

Storper, M. and Harrison, B. (1991), 'Flexibility, hierarchy and regional development: the changing structure of industrial production systems and their forms of governance in the 1990s', *Research Policy* **20**: 207–422.

Storper, M. and Scott, A.J. (1995), The wealth of regions', *Futures* **27**(5): 505–26.

Teece, D.J. (1977), *The Multinational Corporation and the Resource Cost of International Technology Transfer*, Cambridge, MA: Ballinger.

Teece, D.J. (1986), *Profiting from Technological Innovation Research Policy* **15**(6): 286–305.

Teece, D.J. (1992a), 'Competition, cooperation and innovation', *Journal of Economic Behavior and Organization* **18**: 1–25.

Teece, D.J. (1992b), 'Foreign investment and technological development in Silicon Valley', *California Management Review*, Winter: 88–106.

Thwaites, A.T. and Oakey, R.P. (eds) (1985), *The Regional Economic Impact of Technological Change*, New York: St Martin's Press.

UNCTAD (1995), *World Investment Report 1995: Transnational Corporations and Competitiveness*, New York and Geneva: UN.
Vahlne, J.E. and Nordström, K.A. (1992), *Is the Globe Shrinking? Psychic Distance and the Establishment of Swedish Sales Subsidiaries During the Last 100 Years*, Stockholm (mimeo).
Venables, A. (1994), 'Equilibrium locations of vertically linked industries', in P. Krugman and A. Venables (eds), *The Location of Economic Activity: New Theories and Evidence*, London: Centre of Economic Policy Research (CEPR).
Vernon, R. (1966), 'International investment and international trade in the product cycle', *Quarterly Journal of Economics* **80**: 190–207.
Vernon, R. (ed.) (1970), *The Technology Factor in International Trade*, New York: Columbia University Press.
Von Thunen, J.H. (1876), 'Der Isolierte Staat', English trans, in P. Hall (ed.), *Von Thunen's Isolated State*, Oxford: Oxford University Press.
Wade, R. (1988), 'The role of government in overcoming market failure in Taiwan, Republic of Korea and Japan', in H. Hughes (ed.), *Achieving Industrialization in East Asia*, Cambridge: Cambridge University Press.
Weber, A. (1929), *Über den Standort der Industrien*, trans. *The Theory of Location of Industries*, Chicago: University of Chicago Press.
Welch, L.S. and Luostarinen, R. (1988), 'Internationalization: evolution of a concept', *Journal of General Management* **14**(2), Winter: 34–55.
Wilkins, M. (1979), *Foreign Enterprise in Florida*, Gainesville: University of Florida Press.
Williamson, O.E. (1975), *Markets and Hierarchies, Analysis and Antitrust Implications*, New York: The Free Press.
Williamson, O.E. (1990), *Organization Theory*, New York: The Free Press.
Williamson, O.E. and Winter, S.G. (eds) (1991), *The Nature of the Firm*, Oxford: Oxford University Press.
Wolf, C. (1988), *Markets or Governments*, Cambridge, MA: MIT Press.
World Bank (1993), *The East Asian Miracle*, Oxford: Oxford University Press.

8. Evaluating the costs and benefits of multinational enterprises to host countries: a 'tool-kit' approach*

INTRODUCTION

Studies undertaken on the consequences and policy implications of the activities of foreign owned MNEs in host countries usually fall into two groups. These are, first, those which attempt, by way of field studies or use of published material, to evaluate the effects of inward direct investment and/or suggest policies which should be pursued in the light of such effects. Known as 'because ... then' type studies, to be successful they require:

1. a clearly defined set of criteria by which the contribution of foreign direct investment (FDI) is to be appraised;
2. precisely identified assumptions about what would have happened to the resources deployed in the absence of FDI;
3. comprehensive data on the operations of foreign affiliates of MNEs and also those of their parent companies, which might affect the contribution of their affiliates to the local economy.

Studies of the 'because ... then' kind may be macro- or micro-oriented; they may attempt to examine a broad range of issues or limit themselves to particular effects of FDI, for example, on the transfer of technology, exports, employment, etc. Illustrative of this approach are the writings of Reddaway et al. (1968), Steuer et al. (1973) and Streeten and Lall (1973).

The second group of studies concerns itself less with appraising the effects of FDI on MNEs as with providing a framework or tool-kit to assist those who

* This chapter is based upon a paper presented at a Conference on the Portuguese Economy held at Lisbon in 1977. The author was asked to write on the effects of foreign direct investment on the Portuguese economy, but because of the paucity of data, he was compelled to write a more conceptual essay. Published in *Conferencia International sobre Economici Portuguesa*, Lisbon: German Marshall Fund of the US and Fundacao Calouste Gulbenkian (1977), pp. 835–69. Reprinted as Chapter 13 in J.H. Dunning, *International Production and the Multinational Enterprise*, London: Allen and Unwin (1981), pp. 357–84.

may wish to do so. Here attempts are made to theorise about the possible effects of direct investment and other economic variables, and to suggest possible courses of policy which might be pursued if and when such relationships are established. Such studies are essentially of an 'if ... then' type; *inter alia* they seek to identify the conditions under which MNEs are most likely to contribute to the goals of host countries. Research by Bos et al. (1974) typifies this kind of study, though more often than not, the first group of studies, implicitly or explicitly, assumes some kind of model.

A hybrid of the two approaches begins with second, and then tries to marry up theory with known facts in comparable situations. For example, a study on the impact of FDI on employment in West Germany may be used, within a particular theoretical framework, to suggest the likely effects of FDI on employment in the UK. In our current context, we may hypothesise certain similarities between the structure of the Portuguese and Greek economies, and suggest that some of the known consequences of FDI in Greece may guide Portuguese policy towards foreign affiliates in its economy. Similarly, data on the effects of FDI in the recent past may be used and applied to assist current economic policy. The limitations of this approach are well known and need no elaboration.

Mainly because there are few data on the operations of MNEs in the Portuguese economy, this chapter must be of the second kind. It will summarise, in the following pages, attempts so far made to evaluate the costs and benefits of FDI and formulate a positive policy towards it. In so doing, it will bear in mind two of the questions uppermost in the mind of policy makers, viz. to what extent and under what circumstances can FDI advance a country's welfare? and how can policy best be framed to accomplish this objective? As far as possible, this analysis will be related to the economic situation in Portugal, particularly in the context of its development planning.

CRITERIA FOR ASSESSING THE CONTRIBUTION OF FDI

In attempting to measure and evaluate the contribution of FDI to host countries, three important points arise which are not always given the attention they warrant. The first is to identify the criteria by which one should assess the contribution of FDI. This may seem obvious, but all too rarely does it appear explicitly in policy statements about FDI. Clearly the criteria, in the sense of what comprises a country's welfare, will vary between countries, in the same country over time, and between different sectors within any country. Without a clear basis for comparison, one can never be sure that when differences arise about the costs and benefits of FDI one is not using different yardsticks to

Table 8.1 Patterns of foreign direct investment regulation in selected developing countries, 1978

Parameter	Pattern I (mostly Asia, excluding India, Africa, CACM)	Pattern II (mostly Middle East, North Africa)	Pattern III (mostly South America)
I Administration	Case-by-case screening largely restricted to award of 'incentives' (non-discriminatory).	Case-by-case screening at establishment (degree of discrimination varies).	Separate administration for foreign investment. Screening at establishment.
II Investment screening criteria	Emphasis on functional contributions of investment. Little indication of extensive cost/benefit analysis. Screening largely for award of incentives.	Emphasis on functional contributions and conditions of investment. Little indication of extensive cost/benefit analysis.	Criteria formulated for cost/benefit analysis, often extensive. Includes social cost criteria in some cases.
III Ownership	Few requirements. Few sectors closed to foreign investment.	Joint ventures prevalent.	Strict regulations on ownership and investment (excl. Brazil). A large number of closed sectors.
IV Finance	Few repatriation limitations.	Few repatriation limitations.	Repatriation ceilings in most areas (excl. Mexico). Screening of foreign loans. Special control of payments to parent company.
V Employment and training	Announced indigenisation policies but little headway in practice.	Local quotas for work force. Few local quotas for management.	Specific across-the-board indigenisation requirements.
VI Technology transfer	No controls.	No controls.	Screening and registration of all technology imported.
VII Investment incentives	Long-term tax incentives for establishment.	Establishment incentives limited to five years – in most cases non-renewable.	Incentives tied to specific contributions, but incentives may be curtailed for foreign owned firms.
VIII International dispute settlement	Adherence to international dispute regulation. Regional investment regulation.	Same as pattern I. Regional investment regulation: Arab Economic Union.	Local adjudication and regional harmonisation of investment regulation.

appraise it. Certainly the same effects of foreign owned companies may give rise to different policies in the USA, Taiwan, Mexico and India simply because the criteria by which governments in these countries judge FDI differ. What is good for the UK need not necessarily be good for Portugal; what was good for Portugal in 1950 need not necessarily be good for Portugal in 1976. This would suggest that empirical studies should recognise that host or host/home country-specific factors are as important in evaluating FDI as the characteristics of FDI itself or the behaviour of particular foreign affiliates. Among these one might mention the stage of economic development, cultural values, size, resource and technological capacity, administrative efficiency, political ideology, international involvement (including the extent of FDI), economic expertise, etc. Only now are these factors being explicitly incorporated in models designed to formulate general principles towards FDI. Certainly, the pattern of regulatory action by some developing countries, as set out in Table 8.1, suggests that country-specific variables are as important in determining these as the characteristics of FDI itself.[1]

Attempts to formulate general criteria for gauging the effects of FDI abound in literature. Four groups of host country goals are usually identified: (1) economic (which relates to the type and quantity of products supplied); (2) equity (which concerns the distribution of income and assets); (3) sovereignty (which refers to the right to control one's own destiny); and (4) participation (which suggests the need of people to be involved in the decision taking process). Not always may each of these goals be simultaneously attained, and each must be set within the context of the broadest goal of all, viz. advancing a certain way of life. For example, the volume of certain goods and services might be increased, but only at the cost of more pollution, a change in culture and living habits, and some loss of control over decision taking. On the other hand, economic autarky might rob a country of the main benefits of the international division of labour. It is now being increasingly recognised that the cost/benefit equation of FDI is a very complex thing indeed. But prior to any assessment, a country must try to identify its goals, translate these into operational terms, and decide upon its priorities. Ideally, policies should wait until the trade-offs between the achievement of mutually exclusive goals are known. But if there is one thing which countries, particularly developing countries, have learnt in their experiences with FDI, it is that, in the initial policy forming stage they grossly underestimated the pervading influence of such investment and its wider implications.

While sometimes adding to a country's resource capabilities, FDI may at the same time lock the country into a pattern of economic interdependence, the costs and benefits of which are only later transparent. Foreign investment transmits a way of life from the investing country to the host country, and strengthens the economic order of which it is part, an order which may not be perceived to be in the best interests of the host country. To argue *ad hominem*, that is, against the conduit of FDI (viz. the MNE) though understandable, is not always helpful; the beast is only a creature of its, environment. A better appreciation of the goals of host countries and the way in which foreign companies may impinge on these goals, through the technology (including the technology of choice) they transmit and the decisions they take, is badly needed.

The second major methodological issue, which is particularly troublesome to research workers, and which policy makers are too often apt to ignore, is the problem of evaluating the effects of FDI net of those effects that would have occurred if the resources used by the investing companies had been differently deployed. To illustrate, the effect on UK exports which directly results from the presence of US affiliates in the UK is the actual exports of such affiliates (plus or minus the exports of other companies generated by their activities), minus the exports that would have occurred had not those affiliates been present in the UK. Frequently, it is implicitly assumed that there is no opportunity cost of FDI, that is, in the above case, exports in the absence of US affiliates would have been zero. But rarely is this the actual alternative position; if US firms had not invested in the UK, UK companies may well have invested more, if not in the same sector then in a different one, although admittedly it may have taken a change in government policy to bring this about. And it may make a world of difference which alternative position one chooses. Change the position assumed or the consequences of the same, then, as with changing the criteria by which FDI is appraised, its net contribution to welfare will be different.

It is becoming increasingly recognised that, except for estimating broad macroeconomic effects, the most realistic alternative position will vary between countries, industries and over time. What might happen to the production of computers in the UK in the absence of IBM may be very different to what might happen to the production of petroleum products in the absence of British Petroleum in the USA. The effects of a takeover investment are different from a greenfield investment; those arising from an investment by a well established and integrated MNE are not the same as from a new medium sized investor. A sectoral approach is the only way out of this difficulty; alternatively, it may be desirable to classify FDI by origin (is it marketing or cost oriented?) or by the strategies of investing firms. We shall return to this point later.

A final methodological issue concerns policy prescription. Suppose that it has been possible to measure the contribution of MNEs to employment in a particular country (either generally or within a particular sector); and that, in the light of the criteria established, this contribution can be evaluated. The questions that now arise are: (1) is this the best possible contribution and (2) assuming it is, and it is beneficial, does this mean one should encourage the inflow of direct investment? Whatever the answers, there is a great temptation among policy makers to direct any change perceived necessary as a result of FDI to the foreign investor. If the employment effect of inward investment is negative, how can the foreign firm be made to employ more people? If the balance-of-payments contribution is negative, how can policy be directed to persuading foreign affiliates to export more or import less, or, failing that, to reduce their capital stake? In some cases, such policies may be the correct ones, particularly where it can be established that the MNE is behaving in a less than optimum fashion (e.g. by not maximising its efficiency). But in others it may not be so, for two reasons. The first is that there may be a trade-off between achieving one national goal and another. Insist that the MNE should employ more labour intensive (but more costly) production methods, and exports may suffer; limit the share of an industry's output an affiliate can supply, and its costs of production may be higher than they might otherwise be; insist on more local research and development and the MNE may be reluctant to relinquish 100 per cent ownership, and so on. This comes back to the first of the methodological problems discussed above. The second reason is that the consequences of FDI reflect the government policies which give rise to it. If these are not what is desired, this may be because the signals given to MNEs are inappropriate. A monopoly rent earned by foreign affiliates may be the direct result of tariff policy which curtails competition from abroad; a capital intensive technology could reflect an unsuitable monetary policy or that labour is overpriced; an ability of companies to juggle transfer prices may be prompted by an overvalued or undervalued exchange rate. Faulty government policies provoke reactions by foreign firms which may themselves generate undesirable effects. In these cases, the remedy may not be to force firms to behave in accordance with the policies but to change the policies themselves.

Moreover, government policies which may have been appropriate in the absence of FDI may require modifications because of it. Just because FDI may cause a balance-of-payments deficit, it does not mean that curbing such investment is the best way to remedy such a deficit. Other options, for example, altering the exchange rate, may be less expensive in terms of the country's primary goals. There is a great temptation to blame or praise MNEs because of the outcome of their operations; but, often, to put right any unwanted results requires macro-policy measures, or measures directed towards other firms which make a lower contribution towards the country's primary goals.

Enough has been written to suggest that the evaluation of the activities of foreign owned firms is a difficult business. Which goals are to be met and in what order of priority and over what time period? In terms of what alternatives are the results of MNEs to be evaluated? Where action by governments is required, to what extent should it be specifically directed to FDI and to what extent to affecting the disposition of resources as a whole?

ASSESSING THE IMPACT OF FDI

We now turn to the problems of assessing the operational impact of FDI, and will concentrate on the economic consequences. These can be readily identified as they are those by which the contribution of all enterprises may be assessed. They are basically concerned with levels of output, productivity, output stability, long-term growth and structural efficiency. Sometimes more specific goals may be sought, for example, the employment of particular types of labour, a balance-of-payments surplus, or increasing research and development capacity, which may sometimes complement and sometimes compete with general goals.

To measure the contribution of foreign affiliates, information is needed about their activities. Sometimes, this has already been collected from all enterprises independently of their nationality. Examples (in most economies) include data on output employment and wages (suitably classified by skills and industry); exports, imports, R&D expenditures, capital expenditure, sources of finance, profits, advertising, origin of purchases, and so on. The assembling and classification of such basic information by nationality of enterprise is the first priority. In addition, there are data special to foreign affiliates which need collecting. Foremost among these are the transactions of affiliates across national boundaries and between different parts of the same organisation. Statistics on the inflow of capital and technology need to be supplemented by information on profits, royalties and payments for other factor services made to or by parent companies or other parts of the organisation. Separate data on goods and assets traded between the affiliate and other parts of the MNE should be collected to assist the host government in estimating the extent to which transfer pricing manipulations, and the use of leads and lags, etc., are possible and/or likely. Other relevant facts may only be obtained direct from the parent companies of affiliates, for example, the geographical disposition of its capital and R&D disbursements; here the host government is at present reliant on the goodwill of the companies.[2]

In addition to the quantitative data, qualitative information is needed about the relationships between parent and affiliate, for example, with respect to the strategy of the MNE towards product development, marketing, technology transfer, location of R&D, employment of local nationals, and on particular project appraisals. This is especially important in the case of the larger investments and a regular monitoring service may be necessary to alert government to any marked change in strategy. Some kind of permanent liaison with the 100 or so largest investors in a country and/or with those in the most sensitive sectors would help enormously.[3] In some cases, existing machinery might be extended to accommodate these needs, for example, the case of planning agreements in the UK. The important thing is for the host country to be as knowledgeable as possible about everything that goes on in foreign MNEs, which may significantly impinge on the local affiliates' activities.[4]

Given the information, what does one then do with it? Here some kind of model of how foreign investment may impinge on domestic economic goals is necessary. Models may vary from the extreme macroeconomic (i.e. national economic) to the microeconomic (i.e. the project) level; they may be general or partial; they may be static or dynamic and of varying degrees of econometric sophistication. Most researchers have contented themselves with measuring the contribution of FDI to fairly specific goals, for example, its effect on employment, balance of payments, output, and so on. Illustrative of the more ambitious macro models is that of Bos and his colleagues (Bos et al., 1974) which both researchers and policy makers are using; somewhat less embracing have been those of Steuer et al. (1973) and Streeten and Lall (1973). At a project level, the work of Little and Mirrlees (1974) stands supreme.[5]

Measuring the (gross) economic effects of FDI is essentially an exercise in estimating the local value added and/or employment generated by it, and, in the long run, its contribution to the growth and development of the host economy. Its impact on the balance of payments may affect the extent or speed at which these objectives might be achieved, while the possibility of FDI leading to employment, output or price instability is a risk which must be taken into account. Each of these consequences is measurable, though both the primary and secondary indirect effects of FDI need to be considered. Local value added (LVA) equals the gross output of foreign affiliates (= quantity of goods sold multiplied by price) less all imports, less payments made from net output to foreigners (e.g. dividends, royalties, etc.). LVA is thus affected by (1) the technical efficiency of affiliates, and that of indigenous firms from which they purchase, (2) their ability (through market power) to influence price (or inputs and output) and the level of output, and (3) the quantity and price of imported goods and services. The amount of employment necessary to create that LVA will be determined by the capital/labour ratio and the efficiency of producing firms. The extent to which the balance of payments (on current account) is affected will be related to the affiliates' export/import ratio, which, in turn, will depend on the investing strategy of the parent company; and also the ability of the affiliate to trade across boundaries at other than arm's-length prices. Employment, technology, prices, competitive structure and balance of payments are then the main magnitudes affecting LVA; in what way and to what extent, as we have written earlier, will depend on the industrial sector, type of firm investing and government policy.

Expressed in purely economic terms, the (gross) cost of FDI is the loss in value added caused either by the inefficiency of the foreign affiliates and/or the interest, profits, royalties, etc., remitted to the investing company.

Inefficiency might be due to foreign companies investing in the wrong sort of industries, purchasing at less than minimum prices or from the wrong firms, or producing at below technical price or scale efficiency. In turn, such inefficiencies may stem from a protected market structure, entrepreneurial deficiencies, technical or managerial inadequacies, or inappropriate government policies. Usually, since it is the most dynamic and efficient foreign firms which venture abroad, the costs are most likely allied to the domestic or international market conditions which allow foreign affiliates to earn higher than competitive profits, or the strategy of the parent company which requires foreign affiliates to operate in a way that does not optimise their local net output.[6]

It is important to trace through and measure the secondary effects of FDI, for example, their impact on the local value added of suppliers, customers and competitors; and, through the normal course of labour and managerial turnover, information dissemination, etc., their effects on the economy as a whole. In the longer run, their impact on competitive and industrial structure and patterns of development are of key importance. Often the employment impact of FDI may be less in terms of the numbers employed by the foreign affiliate than the additional employment of indigenous firms supplying to it. This is why policy makers try to insist on forward (domestic) linkages in the case of extractive industries and backward (domestic) linkages in the case of final stage manufacturing industries, for example, motor vehicle assembling for foreign investors. Sometimes, as has been suggested, there is a trade-off between (short-run) goals. The most efficient technology may be necessary to penetrate foreign markets; but it may do little to increase employment. A competitive market structure may only be obtained at the price of fragmenting output among firms, such that none is able to produce efficiently. Insisting upon too high a local equity participation may rob indigenous firms of much needed capital.

Throughout the assessment process, a distinction needs to be made between social and private costs and benefits. The problem basically arises because of the different goals of MNEs and the host nations in which they operate and the fact that domestic prices do not always properly reflect the true opportunity cost of the resources involved. While the pursuance of these goals by MNEs may, and often does, advance those of host countries, clashes inevitably occur. These are of three kinds. First, those which are shared by all privately owned firms, independent of their nationality. Since the attainment of private profit and growth does not always advance public welfare, governments must take actions which are not necessarily welcome by such firms; monopoly legislation is the key case in point. Because of their parentage, however, foreign affiliates may create additional problems for governments. Second, the price extracted by the foreign company from the host country in the form of loss of value added may be both destabilising and contain an element of economic rent, part of which may not be easily identifiable. Third, and most difficult both to measure and evaluate, is where an affiliate is locked into a regional or globally oriented production and marketing strategy of the MNE; and decisions are taken, not on the basis of what is best for the affiliate, but on what is the most profitable deployment of resources for the group as a whole.[7] In turn, this strategy may be affected by international market forces or rules and regulations, which, themselves, may not always operate in the interests of individual host countries.

Another problem, explored in depth by Little and Mirrlees (1974) in their work on project appraisal for the OECD, is that the domestic prices which foreign investors face, and sometimes influence, may not accurately reflect the social value of the resources used, either because of market distortions (tariffs, subsidies, inappropriate exchange rates) or because of implicit or explicit price control (e.g. in the labour market, where there is much unemployment, wage rates may exceed the opportunity cost of labour). This means that to properly calculate the costs and benefits of FDI, shadow prices have to be imputed to domestic inputs and outputs which reflect the social cost of resources deployed.

Although the maximisation of local value added per unit of resources used is a convenient yardstick to measure economic welfare, for many purposes it is deficient. Even in purely economic terms it is possible, in any one period of time, to produce more consumption goods but only at the expense of investment goods (including investment in human capital) and, in consequence, future levels of output. If foreign firms diverted resources from investment to consumption activities, LVA might be increased in the short run (if productivity were greater in the latter sector) but it would be lower or not rise as fast in the long run. The effect of FDI on the composition of output produced must then also be taken into account.

From a longer-term viewpoint, an economy's development rests on its rate of increase of output per capita. This, in turn, depends on the quality and productivity of its material and human resources and the amount it is prepared to invest to add to these resources, or make them more productive. Productivity increases result essentially from the deployment of more efficient technologies and from improving human skills, assuming other obstacles or disincentives, for example, market distortions, penal tax rates, etc., are removed. Small wonder that most host countries view the main benefit of FDI as increasing their technological and scientific capacities and narrowing any technological or managerial gap which may exist between them and other countries. Small wonder either that the transfer of technology is a crucial issue in the foreign investment debate, particularly as it appertains to the terms of that transfer.

There have been many studies on the technological impact of foreign firms on host countries.[8] The general conclusion is that, while they often introduce technologically advanced products and/or new processes of production (particularly at the raw material extraction or final stages of manufacturing), they rarely find it profitable to transfer technologically advanced or skill intensive manufacturing activities or to establish R&D laboratories. Sometimes this is because of an inadequate technological infrastructure in host economies, although in some countries, at least, this may be remedied over time by appropriate education and training programmes. In other cases, it may reflect the strategy of the MNE to centralise technology intensive activities in the home or in a few host countries (Behrman and Fischer, 1980).

It may be argued that this, in itself, is not important as long as local firms are encouraged by FDI to increase their own technological capacity. Indeed, this may be preferable as the ownership of the capacity remains domestic. Here, the evidence is mixed. To take one industry – the pharmaceutical industry – in the larger developed countries, foreign companies, particularly the Swiss and American MNEs, have, through competition and example, stimulated local firms in their R&D efforts. Certainly this has been the case in the UK. On the other hand, due to the inability of small countries to finance other than a very limited amount of technological capacity, foreign enterprises in such countries as Sweden, Australia, Canada and Ireland have tended to dominate the supply of local technology and inhibit indigenous R&D effort.[9] Moreover, where foreign affiliates have established R&D facilities, these have usually been either for purely development programmes or as part of integrated R&D strategy of the MNE. Even though this may not necessarily be to the host country's best interest in reducing dependence on foreign technology, it may still be preferable to any feasible alternative.

The question of how far a country should invest in its own technological capacity is rarely decided on economic grounds alone. At the one extreme, it depends on the extent to which it wishes to be involved in international trade and investment, with all its consequential costs and benefits, and on what terms.

Some of the broader costs of FDI are those of other forms of economic interdependence. But since FDI involves domestic resources being directly controlled by non-resident companies – unlike trade, which involves the exchange of goods at arm's-length prices between independent domestic and foreign firms – apart from enforcing a change in ownership, there is no way of escaping the fact that *de jure* the locus of decision taking rests outside the country which is most affected by the decisions. And the more global the investing firm is in its activities, outlook and strategy, the more the pattern of output and growth of its affiliates will be determined by forces outside their control. Classically, the fear of many developing countries that they may become permanent satellites to the major investing countries rests on the proposition that the MNEs of these countries find it in their interests to retain their main repositories of knowledge and human capital at home; and that this policy is encouraged by the existing international economic order and the patent system. Be that as it may, in their dealings with foreign investors, host countries are becoming increasingly interested in asking such questions as: what kind of output is to be produced? What is its local content? Who takes the decisions which will determine the affiliate's growth path? What linkages are affiliates likely to have with other economic agents within and outside the host country? Do they aid or inhibit economic or technological independence?

While it is less easy to measure the contribution of FDI to economic growth than to GNP, it is possible to get a fairly good idea of its impact on the capacity for growth, and, given data on its productivity, a reasonable estimate of its contribution to growth itself. It is also possible to assess its effect on economic stability, by examining, for example, trends in output and employment, the export/import ratios of foreign affiliates and their sectoral distribution (are they more or less susceptible to cyclical movements?). The possible destabilising effects of FDI due, for example, to the alleged ability of foreign affiliates to better circumvent national economic controls than domestic firms, and the fact that affiliates are sometimes tied in to a global decision taking system, and their response options are often wider than domestic firms, needs also to be appraised. Such research that has been undertaken suggests that while national economic policies are made more vulnerable by the presence of foreign firms, particularly those which are set up to supply foreign markets, no generalisations are possible on the extent to which FDI makes macroeconomic policy more difficult to implement. While they may sometimes be better equipped than domestic firms to ride over economic difficulties and/or minimise the impact of some government policies, they are often more sensitive to local government needs and subject to government persuasion. Perhaps the best example here is in the field of regional policy.

Moving away from economic to sociological or political questions, it is worth mentioning a number of possible effects of FDI which may or may not concern host countries, according to their goals, ideologies and values. Foremost among these are:

1. Equity considerations, reflected *inter alia* in the effects of FDI on the distribution of wealth and income, both between capital and labour and between different labour groups. The received literature suggests that inward investment lowers the marginal productivity of capital and raises that of labour, but empirical studies do not generally support this contention. Certainly within the wage sector, it tends to skew the distribution of earnings. And what of its effects on the distribution of economic power? Does it make for a more or less concentrated distribution of output and decision taking?
2. Cultural considerations, reflected *inter alia* in the type and quality of goods and services produced by foreign affiliates; the way of life reflected in their business practices, dealings with labour, marketing and advertising, respect for the environment; and the value placed upon alternative uses of resources.

Does foreign investment erode cultural identity? This is certainly one of the anxieties of countries like Canada, dwarfed by their immediate neighbours, and of developing countries in which there is substantial FDI from advanced economies with very different forms of culture.

3. Participatory considerations, reflected *inter alia* in the desire of a country's citizens to participate in the making of decisions which affect their own welfare. The cog-in-wheel syndrome is not unique to people working in the branch plants of foreign affiliates. It is as much the fate of the individual worker in any large organisation, publicly as well as privately owned; it is, however, shown in its extreme form in large MNEs, partly because of their intricate organisational hierarchies, partly because they are foreign and partly because of the geographical distance between the decision takers and those affected by the decisions. This anxiety is especially demonstrated at the floor level, and is voiced vociferously by organised labour. But it may apply no less at a government level, as portrayed most vividly by the disquiet of the UK government in 1974 and 1975 in being insufficiently consulted by the Ford and Chrysler car companies about their plans for future investment in the UK.
4. Political considerations, reflected *inter alia* in any attempt by foreign investors to interfere with the political fabric of host countries – the Chilean case is the most spectacular example; and, at the other extreme, day-to-day attempts by MNEs to influence domestic economic policies to their advantage.
5. Ethical considerations, seen *inter alia* by several bribery scandals; the more relaxed policies on the part of some foreign companies to safety standards, for example, in product content and labelling, and in labour practices; in inappropriate advertising and sales techniques, for example, in the case of powdered milk.
6. Environmental considerations, seen *inter alia* by the effect of MNEs on pollution. Many of these considerations may be common to all large firms, but MNEs are especially spotlighted when they arc seen to export certain practices which are banned in their home countries.

It is some of the above factors which many countries consider especially necessary to control in the pursuit of their development goals, and which, it is believed, are affected in a very specific way by FDI. Sometimes host countries are unaware of these costs (or benefits) prior to FDI; in other cases, FDI brings to the attention of host countries differences in practices and standards between themselves and other countries.

A final effect, which we will do no more than mention, concerns the MNE as an agent or even undertaker of the foreign policy of the home government. The whole question of extraterritoriality is an exceedingly complex one; more significant are the various ways, through both legitimate and other means, that the network of interrelationships between governments and companies of the same nationality may be used, where both are in the interests of the home country but not necessarily in those of the host country. Some of these power relationships have been comprehensively identified in a paper by Vaitsos (1976).

EVALUATING THE COSTS AND BENEFITS OF FDI

So much for measuring the costs and benefits of FDI. Already the issue is seen to be highly complicated, partly because of the myriad of goals which may be advanced or retarded by FDI, partly because of the difference in objectives between the foreign investor and the host country, and partly because the costs and benefits of FDI are often so intertwined that action taken to reduce one kind of cost may be counterproductive simply because benefits elsewhere are reduced even more. Yet the policy makers must try to identify the key issues and relate the contribution or potential contribution of FDI to these. Where there are clashes in objectives within the host country, these must be accepted as such, and the responsibility for reconciling them placed upon the host government and not on the foreign investor.

The question of evaluating, as opposed to measuring, the costs and benefits of FDI is an even more hazardous task. Basically it comes down to the problem of attribution. It is one thing to associate costs and benefits with FDI. It is another to attribute these costs and benefits to FDI. Put another way, to what extent would the costs and benefits associated with FDI be different if there were no FDI? Questions like this can only be answered by making some assumptions about the alternative position to FDI, that is, what would have happened in its absence? Only by deducting the costs from the benefits of the alternative position can one assess the net contribution of FDI to a country's welfare.

Economists have approached this particular problem in a variety of ways. One has been able to identify the unique features of FDI, that is, those that can be attributed to its nationality, and measure the contribution of these compared to that associated with FDI as a whole. For example, in evaluating the export performance of foreign affiliates, their actual exports might be compared with those of domestic firms, and any difference attributed to the nationality of their ownership. Illustrative of this approach is a study by Cohen (1975) of the export performance of foreign affiliates in selected Asian countries, and one by Abdel-Malek (1974) of the export orientation of foreign affiliates and domestic firms in Canada. Though attractive, its usefulness depends heavily on the choice of sample firms. Ideally, everything affecting performance, apart from that which can be attributed to nationality of ownership, should be identical. But this may be asking too much. Even within the same industries, firms have different product or process structures; age and size can rarely be perfectly matched, marketing strategies may reflect the personalities of decision takers, and so on. Moreover, in this kind of exercise one is usually forced to compare the operations of one part of an organisation with those of the whole of another. There is, then, a branch plant effect of FDI, which may no less influence its performance than its nationality. Finally, in some cases, it is the degree of foreignness which may be as important as the foreignness itself. In other words, the costs and benefits of foreign affiliates may as much reflect differences in the multinationality of their parent companies as the fact that they are foreign owned. Research on UK owned firms in developing countries suggests that differences between the strategies of UK parent companies are as important in explaining the behaviour of their affiliates in host countries as their foreign ownership (Dunning, 1977). Some affiliates were hardly distinguishable from local firms; others were part of a highly integrated network of international activities.

Treated carefully, however, the differential approach can be a useful device for evaluating the contribution of FDI at a micro or sectoral level. More ambitious, though analytically much more difficult, is the alternative situation approach, which is favoured by economists undertaking more macro-oriented assessments of the effects of FDI. The main features of this approach and some of its limitations have already been outlined. Suffice to remind ourselves that the most comprehensive of the macroeconomic models is that prepared by Bos and his colleagues (Bos et al., 1974), which has been used by Perrakis (1977) to assess the results of FDI on a number of variables in the Greek, Spanish and Turkish economies. Since, in many ways, the Greek economy has a number of structural similarities to that of other parts of Southern Europe, the results of this research are not without interest to the Portuguese authorities.

The other studies have been mainly more specific in objective but they all serve to illustrate the tremendous difference the assumptions make to the outcome of the exercise. Tables 8.2 and 8.3 summarise some results of a selection of studies on the balance-of-payments and employment effects of FDI. They serve to underline the fact that the choice of the most plausible alternative situation, and estimating its costs and benefits, are as relevant as measuring the actual costs and benefits of the operation of foreign affiliates when evaluating the specific contribution of FDI. One difficulty here, to which we shall return in the next section, is to know what are the possible alternative situations that might be pursued. Much depends on government policy, the technology of which is a subject about which little is known. Yet, constraints on the options of governments, through lack of knowledge or understanding, may vitally affect the nature of the alternative situation and hence the answer to the question: Does foreign investment pay?

Table 8.2 Best guess estimates of selected balance-of-payments return of UK and US direct foreign investment in manufacturing industry

	Reddaway data (UK, 1956/63) % of net operating assets controlled by UK firms abroad		Hufbauer/Adler data (US, 1957/64) % of total assets controlled by US firms from abroad	
	Anti-classical model	Reverse classical model	Anti-classical model	Reverse classical model
Initial effect				
1 Capital equipment exports	14	10	27	3
2 Immediate 'multiplier' effect[a]	na	na	2.5	3
Specific recurrent effect				
1 Exports of parts and components	6	4.5	5	1
2 Exports of finished goods (export displacement effect)	–20	–3	–51	2.5
3 Trade propensity effect[b]	na	na	6	–
4 Profits and interest	7.5	7.5	12	12
5 Royalties, fees and services	0.5	0.5	1.5	1.5
6 Imports by investing country from subsidiaries	na	na	–5	–4.5
	–6	9.5	–31.5	12.5
Non-specific recurrent effect				
1 Sustained multiplier effect[c]	na	na	7	–3
	–6	9.5	–24.5	9.5
Recoupment period (approximate years)	Never	8	Never	8

[a] Attempts to measure the balance-of-payments repercussions (to investing country) of an increase in income in the host country consequent upon the capital transfer (see Hufbauer and Adler, 1968, pp. 52ff).

[b] This effect acknowledges the more general trade effects which accompany any expansion of overseas sales. Under anti-classical assumptions it is simply measured by marginal propensity to import from the USA expressed as a percentage of the capital outflow (see Hufbauer and Adler, 1968, p. 47).

[c] The sustained multiplier effect estimates the multiplier effect of the continuing influence of the various specific balance-of-payments effects on income flows in the host country. For the method of calculation see Hufbauer and Adler (1968, pp. 46ff and Table 4.3).

Source: Reddaway et al. (1968) and Hufbauer and Adler (1968).

Table 8.3 Summary of studies relating to employment effects of US MNEs

Study	Type of analysis or source of data	Estimate of % of foreign production which could have been retained in USA	Employment effects				
			US production displacement	Export stimulus	US parent employment	Support firm employment	Net employment
Emergency Committee on American Trade	Sample survey of 74 companies	Not precisely estimated; can be inferred to be low	Not explicitly estimated	+ 300 000	+ 250 000	Not considered	Substantially positive
Ruttenberg, AFL–CIO Study	Aggregate official data	Not dealt with explicitly; can be inferred to be high	500 000 jobs lost due to adverse trade movements, 1966–69, of which MNEs account for an 'important part'		Not considered	Not considered	Negative by an 'important part' of 500 000
Stobaugh and Associates	Combination of 9 case studies of individual investment decisions and aggregate data	Dealt with explicitly in the case studies; was low or zero in the long run in every case	Negligible	+ 250 000	+ 250 000	+ 100 000	+ 600 000
US Chamber of Commerce	Sample survey of 158 companies	Not precisely estimated; can be inferred to be low or zero	Not explicitly estimated	+ 311 245 (based on net trade)	Not considered	Not considered	Positive

Source: Hawkins (1972).

A third way of approaching the specific contribution of FDI is to try to estimate the costs of obtaining the benefits provided by FDI in other ways. This essentially reduces to unbundling the package of resources supplied *in toto* by FDI and estimating both the costs of obtaining the ingredients separately and of putting them together differently. Instead of capital, technology, management and entrepreneurship being supplied (and controlled) from a common source, may it not be better for a particular host nation to import capital from (say) the oil states, technology from (say) the Germans, management from (say) the USA, and combine these with indigenous public and private entrepreneurship and control? It is surprising that so little research has been done on the costs and benefits of unbundling and repackaging the package of resources provided by FDI. At one time, it was widely believed that the unique package of FDI produced special benefits over and above those which the ingredients would give if supplied separately. This may still be true in many cases, but it is now also felt that the special costs associated with FDI may exceed those of the ingredients if supplied separately. Yet countries which have expropriated the assets of foreign companies have not always found that they could subsequently import management and technology more cheaply; and that they may have underestimated the advantages of being host to part of a large integrated MNE. It is not too difficult to point to the conditions under which FDI might be an expensive way (relative to other modalities) of importing resources; for example, where high monopoly rents are earned, where there is little attempt at local integration, and where the MNE may be perpetuating a division of labour between home and host country which is not in the latter's long-term interests. But, in other situations, FDI is likely to be the most beneficial way of obtaining capital and know-how; where, for example, the intricate interrelationships between the ingredients of the package of resources confer special benefits, and where there is sufficient competition to prevent the foreign affiliate from making excessive profits. We need much more research about the particular costs and benefits associated with alternative forms of resource transfer. This is especially so as new modalities in the exchange of capital, knowledge and management are opening up.

SOME NORMATIVE ISSUES

So far in our argument, we have been concerned with measuring the effects of FDI and evaluating it net of what might have happened in its absence. We have considered the alternative situation primarily from an economic viewpoint; but, again, the exercise is no less relevant for appraising cultural, political, etc., impacts. How often is FDI held responsible for something which is not unique to it? Accusations about the export of certain advertising practices or of corruption may apply equally to firms exporting to the country in question or to indigenous firms.

We now come to more normative issues, namely, how best to relate the costs and benefits of FDI to the goals or strategies of host countries. To do this, it is not sufficient to assess whether FDI does promote, or is promoting, national welfare more than some alternative use of resources, though this would, indeed, be a great step forward. It is not sufficient because the actual contribution of FDI may not be the maximum it could make; while the most realistic alternative position may be constrained by lack of local resources or management expertise. To illustrate, a negative contribution by FDI to GNP might suggest that it should be reduced; but it could equally mean that FDI is not efficient, or it is extracting too high a rent from the host country. Increase efficiency and/or reduce economic rent and FDI might become highly desirable. To give another example, the most reasonable alternative situation to FDI in Japan in 1979 is very different from that open to say Peru, Nigeria or Mexico in 1979. Yet a generation ago, Japan had virtually no indigenous industry to compete with the Americans and Europeans. Now, as a result of its development and foreign investment strategy of the 1950s and 1960s, the country is able to profit from importing the ingredients of FDI through non-equity participation quite easily. In other words, a country, by its own policies, can affect its alternative position over time.

The first question prior to the formation of a policy towards (future) FDI is then: are the benefits of existing FDI being maximised? If not, why not and what can be done about it and at what cost? Policies directed to improving the efficiency of foreign affiliates, their fuller integration with the local economy, adapting product technologies or products to better suit local resource endowments, curbing restrictive practices, for example, on exports and the transfer of technology, eliminating tax evasions by a strong policy towards transfer pricing and payment of royalties and fees, a selective encouragement of local equity participation, or gradual divestment of equity interests, ensuring that the behaviour of foreign affiliates towards employees, consumers and suppliers conforms to local customs (or if preferred, the customs of the investing country) – all these options may be implemented to increase the benefits or reduce the costs of FDI. As has been pointed out, this may be easier said than done, partly because increasing benefits in one direction may increase costs in another, and partly because if the benefits are tilted too far in favour of the host country, there is a danger that future investment might be reduced or cease altogether. The factors which determine the bargaining power of countries and companies is a subject in itself (Streeten, 1974); it is certainly difficult to make any broad generalisations, except that, assuming a range of bargaining points acceptable to both parties, much depends on the options open to the two parties.

The second normative question is the extent to which indigenous resources could be better deployed to do the job at present done by FDI. If they can, these policies should be directed to restructuring local industry, and a conscious and selective industrial development programme and/or technological strategy aimed at strengthening the capacity of indigenous firms. To give just one example, it may be that, in a particular economy, foreign owned motor car companies are more efficient than locally owned motor companies, because the latter are too numerous and far too small to employ the most efficient production techniques. Yet, because they are too small, they may not be able to finance their own rationalisation. Government support may then be needed to promote a viable industry which, ultimately, may yield a higher social benefit than FDI. This belief underlay the UK government's financial involvement in the merger between British Motors and Leyland some years ago. More successful has been the French government's investment in the modernisation of the Renault plants. In the promotion of science and technology, the problem facing economies like Portugal is even greater. Take the pharmaceutical industry again. To what extent should policy be directed to (1) encouraging foreign affiliates to undertake fabricating the processing operations, (2) encouraging them also to produce the chemical ingredients, (3) encouraging them to set up R&D laboratories, or (4) encouraging local firms (sometimes under licence to foreign firms) to undertake (1)–(3)? Again, the decision may not be as easy as it may seem. Certainly, it should not be taken on only technological grounds. Only by relating a micro-technological decision in the context of macro-industrial strategy and an appreciation of its effects on the total costs and benefits of FDI – with a reasoned assumption about future trends and policy – can a sensible policy be framed.

The third normative question addresses itself to alternative modes of importing resources for development. This was touched upon in the previous section. All that need be added here is that the current stock of knowledge about the options open to host countries in acquiring the resources they need is very inadequate, as, even more so, is that on the costs and benefits of these options. We might suggest similarly that MNEs are not always as aware as they should be of the benefits of forms of foreign involvement other than a 100 per cent equity holding. There is much ignorance and prejudice here, but I believe there is a general tendency for MNEs to overvalue the benefits of a 100 per cent or even a controlling equity stake in their affiliates, while governments assign too high a priority to acquiring the ingredients of FDI by contractual routes. Again, a good deal more study is required on this question, even to establish broad principles of the conditions under which, and to whom, which form of international arrangement is likely to be most beneficial.[10]

This section has emphasised that it is not only what is, but also what could be, that ought to be taken into account in evaluating the costs and benefits of FDI. Besides the specific considerations outlined here, there are more general questions relating to the investment climate and government policy of the host country.

POLICY TOWARDS INBOUND FDI

We turn finally to policy towards FDI, for at the end of the day, this is what governments are seeking guidance about. The approach in this chapter has been to identify the special ingredients of FDI, pinpoint its main costs and benefits, and then compare these with both the actual and potential benefits of acquiring the same resources, or producing the same or similar output in alternative ways. Policy would then be based upon these findings. It may, however, be argued that, whatever its merits, this procedure would take too much time to give useful results, particularly where there are few or no existing data on the activities of foreign companies. Perhaps a more practical approach would be simply to design policy in such a way as to influence the behaviour of foreign affiliates in the right direction. For example, rather than commission studies to estimate the actual employment effects of FDI, should not policy be directed to ensuring that, as far as possible, FDI does advance manpower goals? Rather than evaluate the extent to which foreign affiliates do earn economic rent, should not steps be taken to minimise the possibility of rent being earned? Rather than set up an inquiry into the extent to which foreign affiliates do engage in adverse transfer pricing manipulation, should not efforts be directed to outlawing this practice? And so on.

This 'if ... then' approach is likely to be successful when one can reasonably appraise the contribution of FDI to national goals. For example, one may be very clear that one does not wish foreigners to have an equity participation in certain industries, or to allow them to control more than a certain percentage of the output of others. It is also more likely to work where one can draw upon the experience of other countries who have already done some research on the actual costs and benefits of FDI. But it is less satisfactory in helping to formulate long-term strategy towards FDI, or of comparing its contribution to national goals with some alternative uses of resources.

In practice, all countries, explicitly or implicitly, adopt some stance towards FDI; this may range from no policy, or a *laissez-faire* approach to it, to the other extreme of completely outlawing it. Even within a country responses may differ by region (according, for example, to extent of unemployment), institutions (cf. those of trade unions, with those of suppliers to or competitors of foreign affiliates), industrial sector, nationality of investor and extent of foreign participation. It has been suggested that it is possible to identify attitudes of countries towards FDI by such variables as size, stage of development, culture, political ideology. In the past, changes in governments have induced far more dramatic changes in policy towards FDI than any action on the part of MNEs.

It is thus impossible to advise on any definitive policy for all countries to follow at all times towards FDI. Policy needs to be regularly reviewed in the light of changes in a country's goals; its capabilities to meet these goals from indigenous resources; and any changes in the actual or potential costs and benefits of FDI. This suggests the need for a regular monitoring of information about the activities of foreign affiliates, and an acceptance by government that if FDI is to make its best contribution, policies which might have been appropriate in its absence may require modification in its presence. For example, the more a country is internationally involved, the more important it is for its exchange rate and trade policy to be right. If FDI should cause the structure of industry to become more concentrated, the more reason for the government to operate an effective competition policy. The greater the involvement of foreign affiliates in technologically advanced industries, the greater the need for a well-defined source and technology policy. Observe that these are all general policies, that is, not especially directed to foreign affiliates, but which may need modification because of their presence.

When one speaks about policy towards FDI, however, one usually means policies that will specifically affect the behaviour of existing or prospective foreign investors. Yet almost all the surveys done on factors influencing FDI stress the importance of the general economic and political environment of the recipient countries. Tax incentives, tariffs, subsidies, controls on profit remittances, and insistence on local equity participation all matter, but it is the overall environment and market prospects that count in the long run. Most MNEs are risk averse; economic and political instability are risks which such companies are only prepared to undertake (if at all) if the prospective returns are higher (i.e. the benefits accruing to the host country are lower). One way for host countries to increase their share of the benefits of FDI is to create a low risk profile so that foreign firms are content with a lower rate of profit on the capital invested.

A full discussion of the gamut of specific and particular policies towards foreign affiliates which might be pursued by a host country is outside the scope of this chapter.[11] But in the context of a cost/benefit exercise, they range from the provision of information to foreign investors about the objectives of host countries (such information may be general or very specific) to outright mandatory control over types of foreign firms admitted, forms of investment, the behaviour of firms once admitted and divestment procedures. In between the 'min–max' extremes are a host of policies open to governments, the appropriateness of which will vary according to circumstances and their likely effect on foreign investors. Guidelines to behaviour are one option which has been endorsed by such bodies as the International Chamber of Commerce, and more recently (with somewhat different intent) by OECD. Several countries and companies have also produced their own guidelines; essentially they are gentlemen's agreements, the success of which depends on the goodwill and co-operation of the parties concerned. One step (but an important step) removed from guidelines are Codes of Conduct, which are more binding on character, and to which sanctions are usually attached. The International Code of Conduct on the Transfer of Technology, promoted by UNCTAD, and the Code of Conduct on TNCs being considered by the Commission on Transnational Corporations (UN, 1976, 1979) are of this kind. From codes, one moves to general economic inducements or constraints, to which foreign investors may or may not respond; and then to very specific rules and regulations which foreign firms must follow, for example, with respect to proportion of equity capital of local enterprises they may own, employment of indigenous labour, import quotas, information and reporting procedures, dividend remissions, and so on. Then, finally, there are more embracing policies directed specifically to foreign companies, for example, those operated by Mexican and Indian governments.

Beyond these unilateral policies are bilateral or multilateral schemes, in which more than one government is involved. These range from a bilateral exchange of information about specific activities of MNEs, or policies adopted towards them, to multilateral treaties on international investment of the GATT variety. Most commentators believe, however, that such generalised agreements, if they ever come about, are a long way in the future. The point of mentioning them here is that multilateral policies – between home and host or host and host or home and home governments – and the action of such bodies as UNCTAD, OECD, EEC, are likely to become more important in affecting the behaviour of foreign investors. Such a transition from unilateral to multilateral action is not without its costs to individual nation states. Though multilateral policies may increase the benefits of FDI for the participating nations considered, taken as a whole they do not ensure that each and every country will benefit from them. Indeed, in some cases the national sovereignty which countries arc seeking to preserve by harmonising their actions may simply be transferred from foreign enterprises to the strongest of the group of countries framing the multilateral action.

Like the FDI they are intended to influence, each of these policy options has its own particular costs and benefits. Once again, what is needed is a model or framework for evaluating such options, and some idea of the conditions under which each of the various options is most likely to be effective.

CONCLUSIONS

For reasons stated at the outset, this chapter is not on a subject of the author's choosing. What has been set down is neither directed specifically to the Portuguese situation, nor, except in a very rough and ready sense, does it answer many of the questions which are the concern of all countries. Indeed it poses more questions than it provides answers. In the Portuguese context, when so little is known about FDI, this may not be a bad thing. What is needed by all governments is a kind of tool-kit, from which it would be possible – given the data or a reasonable estimate of same – to build a policy framework.

But the chapter does make a number of quite important general points. If I had to pick out the most important I would choose five. First, it argues for a sectoral approach to FDI. It really is extraordinarily difficult to generalise about the costs and benefits of FDI. The contribution of foreign affiliates in the extractive industries may be completely different from that in the manufacturing and service industries. Within manufacturing, a distinction needs to be made between import-substituting and export-generating industries, and between the foreign affiliates of MNEs which pursue a global and regional strategy and those which do not. True, if it were found that, *in toto*, FDI had a negative income effect, this might suggest FDI should be restricted; but this policy could be wholly wasteful if, for example, the whole of the negative effect were explained by the behaviour of (say) one large petroleum firm.

Second, arguments have been presented against a series of problem-oriented policy measures towards FDI. The contribution of foreign firms must be looked at as a whole, once one's criteria for evaluating their contribution, with all their implicit trade-offs, have been established. Even if FDI does little to contribute towards a country's technological goals, it does not follow that policies should be implemented to bring this about. For it may be that this can only be accomplished at the expense of the employment and other goals, and, in the end, the country may be worse off than before. There is an interdependence between costs and benefits which requires a macro approach to their evaluation.

Third, it has been stressed that the results of FDI are determined as much by general host government policy and the local economic environment as anything to do with the behaviour of the foreign firms. Once a substantial foreign owned sector exists, governments have a responsibility to reappraise policies implemented in the absence of foreign investment to see whether they are still appropriate. This, of course, governments do not look favourably upon. It is much easier (if not always in the best interests of national welfare) to force the foreign firm to mould itself to existing policies, rather than change the policies so that it can make the best possible contributions. To give an example: if a balance-of-payments deficit appears to be associated with FDI it is tempting to force foreign firms to reduce their investments or to operate in such a way as to eliminate the deficit. But the end result may be a fall in LVA. A more sensible reaction might be to try and eliminate the deficit by other means, for example, a change in the exchange rate, or a reduction in the activity of firms which contribute less to LVA.

The fourth point is that governments, while evaluating alternative routes of obtaining the benefits of FDI, should not presuppose these routes are necessarily preferable. Many a government has nationalised a foreign investment with the expectancy of getting rid of the control exercised by the foreign investor, only to find that the heart of control was not in the possession of equity capital but of technology, which it had not relinquished. The coming years are likely to witness many new forms of international involvement, and governments seeking to formulate policies should very much be aware of these.

A final point concerns negotiating procedures. There is still a very large gap of understanding between governments and enterprises over the goals each is legitimately seeking to pursue, as there is also over the extent to which FDI can advance these goals. This is especially evident once one moves away from the purely economic consequences (as traditionally conceived) to consider social and cultural effects, where goals and values between investing companies and recipient countries may diverge even more. So often one finds that politicians and businessmen are either not talking about the same thing or disagree with each other because their perceptions are different. Admittedly, some value systems of developing countries have only been consciously identified as a result of FDI, which, if it has done nothing else, has helped them know what they do not want. All too easily, it has been assumed either that FDI has no real impact on the social and cultural habitat of recipient nations or that it is good for them to be inculcated with the economic ethic and aspirations of the home country. But, in many cases, it is clear that FDI has been a conduit of a way of life, which, for perfectly good reasons, recipient countries do not necessarily wish to embrace. No one enterprise is to blame for this, but the fact remains that it might not have occurred, or occurred to the same extent, in the absence of FDI. On the other hand, host countries do not always appreciate the intricacies of the kind of global set-up which may give FDI the very advantages which are sought by it; and to force it to behave like a local firm might rob the MNE of its distinctive contribution. Clearly, the concerns of host countries are not of the same order as those of the MNEs, and there is much to be learned by both parties before full headway can be made on harnessing the benefits of FDI to advance economic and social welfare.

NOTES

1. For further details see UNCTC (1978).
2. It is our belief that this kind of information may be more important for host countries to obtain in the future as the activities of MNEs become increasingly integrated.
3. One suggestion here is for government appointed representatives to be in attendance at the board meetings of affiliates.
4. Other kinds of data include those relating to the activities of MNEs in other countries, including the terms of contracts made.
5. For a discussion of evaluating international projects from a firm's viewpoint see Lessard (1979).
6. Note that even maximising LVA does not imply that foreign affiliates should be encouraged to buy from local firms, where it is cheaper to import the inputs and to use the resources saved to produce other goods.

7. Although, in the end, the host country may be better off than if decisions were taken independently in the interests of each affiliate.
8. For a summary of some of the more significant of these, see Moxon (1979).
9. For further details see Dunning, Burstall and Lake (1981).
10. A subject to which the OECD Development Centre is currently (September 1980) devoting some attention. See Oman (1980).
11. For a description of these, see UN (1978) and Hawkins and Walter (1979).

REFERENCES

Abdel-Malek, T. (1974), 'Foreign ownership and export performance', *Journal of International Business Studies*, vol. V (Fall).

Behrman, J., and Fischer, W.A. (1980), Overseas *R and D Activities of Transnational Corporations* (Cambridge, Mass.: Oelgeschlager, Gunn and Hain).

Bos, H.C., Saunders, M., and Secchi, C. (1974), *Private Foreign Investment in Developing Countries. A Quantitative Study on the Evaluation of Macro-Economic Effects*, International Studies in Economics and Econometrics, Vol. 1 (Boston: Reidel).

Cohen, B.I. (1975), *Multinational Firms and Asian Exports* (New Haven, Conn., and London: Yale University Press).

Dunning, J.H. (1977), *UK Transnational Enterprises in Manufacturing and Resource Based Industries and Trade Flows of Developing Countries*, UNCTAD/ST/MD 18 (Geneva: UNCTAD).

Dunning, J.H., Burstall, M., and Lake, A. (1981), *The impact of MNEs on the Technological and Scientific Capacities of OECD Countries: The Pharmaceutical Industry* (Paris: OECD).

Hawkins, R. (1972), *Job Displacement and the Multinational Firm: A Methodological Review*, Occasional Paper No. 3 (Washington, DC: Center for Multinational Studies).

Hawkins, R., and Walter, I. (1979), *Multinational Corporations: Current Trends and Future Prospects*, New York University Graduate School of Business Administration, Working Paper No. 79–110 (November).

Hufbauer, G.C., and Adler, F.M. (1968), *US Manufacturing Investment and Balance of Payments*, Tax Policy Research Study No. 1 (Washington, DC: US Treasury Department).

Lessard, D.R. (ed.) (1979), *International Financial Management* (New York: Warren, Gorham and Lamont).

Little, I.M.D., and Mirrlees, J.A. (1974), *Project Appraisal and Planning for Developing Countries* (London: Heinemann).

Moxon, R.W. (1979), 'The costs, conditions and adaptation of MNC technology in developing countries', in R.G. Hawkins (ed.), *The Economic Effects of Multinational Corporations* (Greenwich, Conn.: JAI Press).

Oman, C. (1980), *Changing International Investment Strategies: The 'New Forms' of Investment in Developing Countries*, mimeo (Paris: OECD Development Centre).

Perrakis, C.I. (1977), 'Output, balance of payments and employment effects of private foreign investment in developing countries: an empirical evaluation of the effects of private foreign investment in the manufacturing sector of Southern Europe, Greece, Spain and Turkey', PhD thesis, University of Reading.

Reddaway, W.B., Potter, S.J., and Taylor, C.T. (1968), *Effects of UK Direct Investment Overseas, Interim Report (1967) and Final Report*, Cambridge Department of Applied Economics (Cambridge: Cambridge University Press).

Steuer, M.D., Abell, A., Gennard, J., Perlman, M., Rees, R., Scott, B., and Wallis, K. (1973), *The Impact of Foreign Direct Investment on the United Kingdom*, Department of Trade and Industry (London: HMSO).

Streeten, P.P. (1974), 'The theory of development policy', in J.H. Dunning (ed.), *Economic Analysis and the Multinational Enterprise* (London: Allen & Unwin), pp. 252–79.

Streeten, P.P., and Lall, S. (1973), *Summary of Methods and Findings of a Study of Private Foreign Manufacturing Investment in Six Less-Developed Countries* (in three parts) 1. *Methodology Used in Studies on Private Foreign Investment in Selected Developing Countries*, Document No. TD/B/3 (VI) Misc.6.2. *Some Reflections on Government Policies Concerning Private Foreign Investment*, Document No. TD/B/C.3(VI)/Misc.7. 3. *Main Findings of a Study of Private Foreign Investment in Selected Developing Countries*, Document No. TD/B/C.3/111 (Geneva: UNCTAD).

UN (1976), *Transnational Corporations: Issues involved in the formulation of a Code of Conduct*, Economic and Social Council E/C 10/17 July (New York: UN).

UN (1978), *National Legislation and Regulations Relating to Transnational Corporations*, Sales No. E 78 II A3 (New York: UN).

UNCTC (1979), 'The code of conduct: latest progress', *CTC Reporter*, vol. 1, no. 6 (April).

Vaitsos, C.V. (1976), 'Power, knowledge and development policy: relations between transnational enterprises and developing countries', in G.K. Helleiner (ed.), *A World Divided* (Cambridge: Cambridge University Press), pp. 113–46.

9. Re-evaluating the benefits of foreign direct investment*

INTRODUCTION

Thirty-eight years ago, the first comprehensive analysis on the consequences of inbound foreign direct investment (FDI) for a host country was published (Dunning, 1958). The subject of study was the UK; since that date, similar investigations have been undertaken – with varying degrees of sophistication – for almost every country in the world.[1] Hundreds of books, theses and government reports, and thousands of papers in academic and professional journals have been written on the topic,[2] and scarcely a day goes by without some newspaper or magazine article lauding or denigrating the globalization of business activity.

Why, then, do we need to revisit the subject? Hasn't everything worth while already been said or written about the role of MNEs in economic development? Well, quite apart from its spectacular growth over the past decade,[3] we would offer two sets of reasons for the current resurgence of interest. Each reflects the changes in attitudes towards the costs and benefits of FDI which have occurred over the past 20 years: the first is by *countries* and the second by *firms* – and particularly by MNEs.[4]

THE CHANGING ATTITUDES OF COUNTRIES

In the mid-1990s, most governments are acclaiming FDI as 'good news', after a period of being highly critical – if not downright hostile – to it in the 1970s and early 1980s. There are a number of possible explanations for this change of heart. Some of these are set out in Exhibit 9.1. The first is the renewed faith of most countries in the workings of the market economy, as demonstrated, for example, by the wholesale privatization of state-owned assets, and the deregulation and liberalization of markets over the last 8–10 years. While these events are being most vividly played out in Central and Eastern Europe and in China,

* From *Transnational Corporations*, **3**(1) (1994): 9–22. Reprinted in J.H. Dunning, *Alliance Capitalism and Global Business*, London and New York: Routledge (1995), pp. 209–33.

the need to remove structural market distortions has also been acknowledged in many other parts of the world – notably in the European Community, India, Mexico and Vietnam.

The second explanation is the increasing globalization of economic activity and the integration of international production and cross-border markets by MNEs (UNCTAD, 1993). The third reason is that the key ingredients of contemporary economic growth of created assets, such as technology, intellectual capital, learning experience and organizational competence, are not only becoming more mobile across national boundaries, but becoming increasingly housed in MNE systems.[5]

Exhibit 9.1 The changing world of foreign direct investment

(a) *From a country's perspective*

- Renaissance of the market system.
- Globalization of economic activity.
- Enhanced mobility of wealth-creating assets.
- Increasing number of countries approaching 'take-off' stage in development.
- Convergence of economic structures among advanced countries, and some industrializing countries.
- Changing criteria by which governments evaluate FDI.
- Better appreciation by governments of the costs and benefits of FDI.

(b) *From a firm's perspective*

- Increasing need to exploit global markets (e.g. to cover escalating R&D costs).
- Competitive pressures to procure inputs (raw materials, components, etc.) from cheapest possible source.
- Regional integration has prompted more efficiency-seeking investment.
- Growing ease of transborder communications and reduced transport costs.
- Heightened oligopolistic competition among leading firms.
- Opening up new territorial opportunities for FDI.
- Need to 'tap into' foreign sources of technology and organizational capabilities; and to exploit economies of agglomeration.
- New incentives to conclude alliances with foreign firms.
- Changes in significance of particular locational costs and benefits.
- Need to balance better the advantages of globalization with those of localization.

The fourth reason why governments are modifying their attitudes towards FDI is that a growing number of economies – especially in East Asia – are now approaching the 'take-off' stage in their economic development, and that, as a result, the competition for the world's scarce resources of capital, technology and organizational skills is becoming increasingly intensive. The fifth is that the economic structures of the major industrialized nations are converging, one result of which is that competition between firms from these nations is becoming both more intraindustry and more pronounced.

The sixth explanation is that the criterion for judging the success of FDI by host governments has changed over the years, and changed in a way which has made for a less confrontational and a more co-operative stance between themselves and foreign investors. More particularly, the emphasis of evaluating inbound MNE activity over the past two decades has switched from the direct contribution of foreign affiliates to its wider impact on the upgrading of the competitiveness of a host country's indigenous capabilities and the promotion of its dynamic comparative advantage. And the last reason is that the learning experience of countries about what MNEs can and cannot do for host countries has enabled their governments better to understand and assess its consequences, and to take action to ensure that it more efficiently promotes their economic and social goals.

The world economy in the mid-1990s is, indeed, a very different place from that of even a decade ago, and the changes which have occurred have had implications both for the responses of individual nation states to FDI and for the very character of FDI itself.

THE CHANGING BEHAVIOUR OF FIRMS

The events just outlined have also affected the attitudes, organizational structures and behaviour of business corporations. Such enterprises, for example, have found it increasingly necessary to capture new markets to finance the escalating costs of their research and development and marketing activities, both of which are considered essential to preserve or advance their competitiveness.[6] Cross-border strategic alliances and networks have been prompted for similar reasons, and to encapsulate the time it takes to innovate and learn about new products, processes and management cultures. Firms have no less been pressured to reduce the cost and improve the quality of their raw materials and components. As a growing number of countries are building their own arsenals of skilled labour and technological capacity, foreign investors are finding it more and more desirable to diversify geographically their information-gathering and learning capabilities. Competition in internationally oriented industries has become increasingly oligopolistic, while – as is described in more detail later – the nature of the competitive advantages of firms, and the factors influencing their locational choices, are very different in the early 1990s to those only a decade or so ago.

Finally, in the more complex global environment of the 1990s, MNEs are being forced to pay more attention to achieving the optimal balance between the forces making for the global integration of their activities, and those requiring them to be more oriented to, and sensitive of, localized supply capabilities and consumer tastes and needs – what Akio Norita of Sony has referred to as 'glocalization'. For, alongside the acknowledged benefits of globalization, there is a growing awareness, particularly among the citizens of smaller countries, of the need to preserve – and indeed promote, as a comparative advantage – their distinctive cultures, institutional structures, lifestyles, working relationships and consumption preferences. MNEs ignore these country-specific differences – which many observers (e.g. Naisbitt, 1994) believe will become important in the future – at their peril.[7]

At one time, firms used to engage in international transactions primarily through arm's-length exporting and importing. Today, the main vehicle is FDI and co-operative alliances. Initially, these latter forms of cross-border commerce were driven by trade; today, they largely determine trade. Outside the primary sector, upwards of two-thirds of the world's exports of goods and services are accounted for by MNEs, and 30–40 per cent of these take place within these same institutions – 60–70 per cent in the case of intangible assets such as technology and organizational skills (Dunning, 1993a; UNCTAD, 1993, 1994).

In the 1990s, MNEs are the main producers and organizers of the knowledge-based assets now primarily responsible for advancing global economic prosperity, and they are the principal cross-border disseminators of the fruits of these assets. It is true that the ambience of innovatory activities, the availability of risk capital and the educational infrastructure are strongly influenced by the actions of governments. It is true, too, that a myriad of small firms and individual entrepreneurs are significant seed-beds of new ideas and inventions. However, increasingly, economic progress is being shaped by the way new knowledge and organizational techniques are systematized and disseminated. Sometimes, the market system is able to perform this task satisfactorily by itself, but, because many emerging innovations are both generic and multi-purpose, and have to be co-ordinated with other assets to be fully productive, firms frequently find it beneficial to supplement or supplant external markets by their own governance systems. Sometimes, too, the efficient production and use of created assets requires firms to co-operate with each other, and even to be located in close proximity to each other.[8]

To some extent, this has always been the case. One of the earliest definitions of a business enterprise was that it was a 'coordinated unit of decision taking',[9] but, today, the firm is better described as 'a coordinator of a network of interrelated value-added activities' (Dunning, 1993b). At one time, the boundaries of the firm were firmly determined by its ownership. Nowadays, they are much fuzzier, as their sphere of influence over the way resources may be used is being extended to embrace a variety of co-operative arrangements and networking agreements.[10] The more activities a firm pursues, the greater the number of coalitions it concludes with other firms, and the more countries in which it produces, then the more its global competitiveness is likely to rest on its ability to integrate these activities systemically.

The 'systemic' view of the MNE implies very different governance structures from those implemented by traditional foreign investors. Rather than acting as an owner of a number of fairly autonomous or 'stand-alone' foreign affiliates, each of which is expected to earn the maximum economic rent on the resources invested in it, the systemic MNE aims to manage its portfolio of spatially diffused human and physical assets – including those owned by other firms over which it has some property rights – as a holistic production, sourcing, financial and marketing system. Of course, there are costs of co-ordinating intra- and interfirm cross-border activities, and these will ultimately determine the extent and diversity of a firm's territorial expansion. But recent advances in international transport and telecommunication technology have pushed out these limits. In cases where corporations have shed some of their foreign assets, this has been mainly done to reduce the scope or range, rather than the geography, of their activities.

A final feature of the FDI of the 1980s and 1990s, which accords with the systemic view of MNE activity, is that probably as much as 90 per cent of it is currently undertaken by already established MNEs; that is, it is *sequential* rather than *initial* investment. This is not to deny that new MNEs are emerging all the time – probably at the rate of 4000 to 5000 a year,[11] and increasingly from developing countries, notably China – but, as yet, the total foreign capital stake of these companies is thought to be quite small. Now, research has established that *sequential* FDI – which, as far as a particular country is concerned, might be a first-time investment – is likely not only to be more geared to the interests of the rest of the investing company's value activities, but to generate its own unique costs and benefits – that is, over and above those generated by an initial investment (Kogut, 1983; Buckley and Casson, 1985). These essentially arise from the consequences of multinationality *per se*. They embrace such gains as those arising from the diversification of exchange risk and economic uncertainty, the spreading of environmental volatility, and the opportunity to exploit better the economies of geographical scope and specialization. They also include the costs of co-ordinating the activities and markets of foreign affiliates in widely different business cultures and political regimes (Kogut and Kulatihala, 1988), and those associated with the setting up and sustaining of a cross-border network of intra- and interfirm relationships.

TYPES OF FDI AND COUNTRIES

Global economic events of the last decade or so, and particularly those driven by technological advances, regional integration and the refashioning of economic systems and policies, have fundamentally altered the perception of governments of host countries about how FDI may contribute towards their economic and social goals. These same events have also caused a reappraisal by firms of *why* and *how* – and, indeed, *where* – they need to engage in international transactions. It is for these reasons that the current generation of scholars – not to mention governments and firms – continue to want to know more about the benefits (and costs!) of FDI. To what extent and in what way is the global economy causing these to change; and what may national and regional administrations do to ensure that inward MNE activity contributes the most benefits it possibly can to their economic and social needs and aspirations?[12]

With these introductory remarks in mind, let us go on to make two very simple statements, which are probably as timely today as they were 20 years ago, and which policy makers concerned with assessing the benefits of FDI would do well to bear in mind constantly. We shall then proceed to elaborate on both of these statements:

The first statement is:

> History and geography matter. Policy makers should seek to learn from their successes and failures of the past, and from those of other countries. But, they should not be slaves to these successes and failures. In the light of the perceived contribution of FDI, they should devise and implement the macro-organizational strategies most suited to their own unique situations and needs.

The second statement is:

> Policy makers should be cautious about expecting easy generalizations about the consequences of FDI. Not only will its effects vary according to the kinds of FDI undertaken, but they will depend on the economic and other objectives set by governments, the economic policies pursued by them, and the alternatives to FDI open to them.

In order to focus better the rest of this chapter, let us assume that the principal criterion by which national administrations evaluate inbound FDI in the 1990s is by *its perceived contribution to the improvement of the competitiveness of the resources and asset-creating capabilities located within their areas of jurisdiction.*[13] This, indeed, is probably the single most important medium- to long-term economic objective of governments of most nations, and particularly of those which are most dependent on foreign-owned created assets and foreign markets for their prosperity.

How, then, might competitiveness of a country be advanced? Exhibit 9.2 identifies five main ways. The first is for a country's firms to produce more efficiently whatever they are currently producing, for example by reducing organizational costs and/or raising labour or capital productivity. The second is by the innovation of new, or the continuous improvement of the quality of existing, products, production processes, and of organizational structures and procedures. The third is by the reallocation of resources and capabilities to produce goods and services which are in better accord with the country's dynamic comparative advantage. The fourth is by capturing new foreign markets – providing this is cost-effective. And the fifth is by reducing the costs, or speeding up the process, of structural adjustment to changes in global demand and supply conditions.

Exhibit 9.2 The five ways for a nation to upgrade the productivity and comparative advantage of its resources and capabilities

1 *Increase efficiency of its existing asset deployment by more effective quality control procedures*, e.g. by networking with other firms; by more cost-effective sourcing; by reducing lead times; by raising labour and capital productivity.
2 *Innovate new products, processes and organizational structures*, e.g. by improving national innovatory systems; by better exploiting the economies of the spatial clustering of related activities; by ensuring risk capital is available for start-up firms.
3 *Improve the allocation of its resources and capabilities*, e.g. from less productive to more productive activities, and towards those in which perceived dynamic comparative advantage is increasing.
4 *Capture new markets*, e.g. by improving knowledge about foreign markets and about customer needs and by better marketing and distribution techniques.
5 *Reduce the costs and/or increase the speed of structural adjustment*, e.g. by encouraging flexible labour markets; by enhancing the quality of retraining programmes; by minimizing bureaucratic inefficiencies; by appropriate fiscal and other incentives for industrial restructuring; by a greater willingness to accept, and adjust to, change.

The potential contribution of inbound FDI to each of these ways or vectors of upgrading competitiveness is fairly self-evident. It may provide resources or capabilities otherwise unattainable or only attainable at a higher cost. It may steer economic activity towards the production of goods and services deemed most appropriate by domestic and international markets. It may boost R&D, and introduce new organizational techniques. It may accelerate the learning process of indigenous firms. It may stimulate the efficiency of suppliers and competitors, raise quality standards, introduce new working practices, and open up new and cheaper sources of procurement. It may provide additional markets. It may better enable a host country to tap into, or monitor, the competitive advantages of other nations. It may inject new managerial skills, profession excellence and entrepreneurial initiatives and work cultures. It may encourage the formation of cross-border co-operative alliances, technological systems and inter-firm networking. It may foster the geographical clustering of related activities that generate their own agglomerative economies. In short, it may interact with the *existing* competitive advantages of host nations and affect their *future* competitive advantages in a variety of ways.

Some of these ways are summarized in a schema set out in Figure 9.1. This figure is an adaptation and extension of Michael Porter's diamond of competitive advantage (Porter, 1990).[14] It suggests that inbound FDI may affect not only the four facets of the diamond, but the actions of host governments, and the mentality of competitiveness of the constituents in the host country. This it may do, for example, by injecting more market-oriented beliefs and practices by encouraging more harmonious labour relations, raising the quality standards expected by consumers.

It is worth noting that the significance of the individual attributes of the 'diamond' of competitive advantage may vary not only between countries, but within a particular country over time. Thus, for example, the relative importance of the production and efficient deployment of created assets, and the means by which these are transmitted over space, has increased as the world economy has become more globalized. Similarly, there are suggestions that the ways in which complementary activities are organized along the value-added chain, and the agglomerative economies to be derived from a spatial clustering of these and other related activities, are becoming more significant. By contrast, the optimum number of domestic firms competing in their home market is probably falling as the geographical focus of competition becomes more regional or global, while, with a few exceptions (e.g. oil-rich Middle Eastern states), the availability of domestic natural resources is probably a less critical competitive advantage than once it was.

We would be the first to accept that most of the competitive advantages just described are also available to domestic firms, but it is our contention that the unique attributes of FDI – and especially those which arise from the multinationality of the investing firms – offer financial, production, marketing and organizational benefits over and above those which indigenous firms may posses or can acquire.

At the same time, there are costs to a host country of inbound MNE activity. These can be divided into two groups. The first comprises various payments (e.g. profits, interest, dividends, royalties, management fees) which have to be

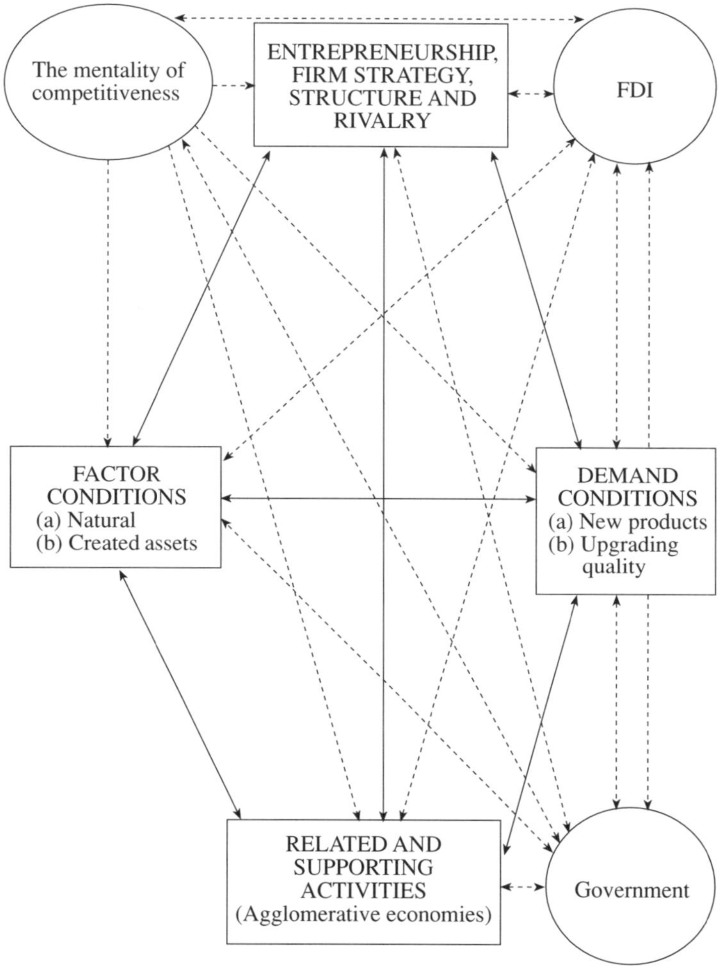

Note: See also Chapter 11, Figures 11.1 and 11.5.

Source: Porter (1990), as modified by the author.

Figure 9.1 The diamond of competitive advantage

made to attract the foreign investor or maintain the FDI. These will vary along a continuum. At one extreme, there are the payments below which a non-resident firm is unwilling to invest; and at the other, the payments above which a country is not prepared to accept the investment. The payments *actually* made will depend on the bargaining skills and negotiating power of the MNEs and of the recipient governments. These, in turn, will depend on the price which a host country would have to pay to acquire the benefits of FDI by alternative means, and the options open to the investing companies to locate their activities elsewhere. In the 1960s and 1970s, the main anxiety of host governments was that the monopoly power of foreign MNEs would enable the latter to extract unacceptably high shares of the value added by their affiliates. Today, the greater concern is that, without the inbound investment, host countries might be deprived of the advantages of being part of an integrated international production and marketing system (UNCTAD, 1993).

The second type of cost associated with FDI arises whenever the behaviour of the investing firms, which is typically geared to advance their global objectives, is perceived to produce unwelcome consequences for the host country. These include the restrictions which a parent company may impose on the sourcing of raw materials and components by its affiliates, and the markets these affiliates may serve. The affiliates may also be limited in the range of products they produce, the production processes they employ, the amount and kind of research and development (R&D) they undertake, and the pattern of their networking with indigenous firms. Through transfer pricing manipulation, it is also possible that income earned in the host country might be syphoned off to the home (or some tax haven) country.

SOME DETERMINANTS OF THE BENEFITS OF FDI

What determines the net benefits of inbound FDI? What can national (and regional) governments do to ensure that such investment best contributes to the upgrading of the indigenous resources and capabilities within their jurisdiction? The short – but hardly satisfactory – answer is that it all depends on the kind of FDI, the conditions which prompted it, the existing competitive advantages of the host country, and the economic policies pursued by the host and other governments. But, fortunately, the economist can go a little further than this by identifying the situations in which a specific host country – or region within a host country[15] – is likely to gain the most from FDI, and, in suboptimal situations, what that country might do to increase this gain. In particular, we will argue that the benefits to be reaped from FDI critically depend on, first, the types and age of the investment, second, the economic characteristics of the host countries (or regions), and third, the macro-economic and organizational strategies pursued by host governments.

Types of FDI

Table 9.1 sets out the main types of FDI, the classification being based on the *raison d'être* for the investment. The first two, namely *resource-seeking* and *market-seeking* investments, represent the two main motives for an initial foreign entry by a firm – be it in the primary, secondary or tertiary sectors. The latter two embrace the two main modes of expansion by established foreign investors. These 'sequential' investments are frequently aimed at increasing the efficiency of the regional or global activities of MNEs by the integration of its assets, production and markets; these are called *efficiency-seeking* investments. However, sequential, and occasionally first-time, investments are increasingly taking the form of *strategic-asset-seeking* investments, the main purpose of which is to acquire resources and capabilities which the investing firms believe will sustain or augment their core competencies in regional or global markets. These assets may range from innovatory capabilities, managerial expertise and organizational procedures, to accessing foreign distribution channels and a better appreciation of the needs of consumers in unfamiliar markets. Strategic-asset-seeking investment is frequently the most expeditious way of acquiring these kinds of competitive advantages (Wendt, 1993).

Table 9.1 Four main types of foreign direct investment

1 *(Natural) resource-seeking* (a) Physical resources (b) Human resources 2 *Market-seeking* (a) Domestic markets (b) Adjacent (e.g. regional) markets	Mainly motives for *initial* FDI
3 *Efficiency-seeking* Rationalization of production to exploit economies of specialization and scope (a) Across value chains (i.e. product specialization) (b) Along value chains (i.e. process specialization) 4 *Strategic- (created-)asset-seeking* To advance regional or global strategy (a) Technology (b) Organizational capabilities (c) Markets	Mainly motives for *sequential* FDI

In the 1960s and 1970s, most FDI was of the first or second types, although regional integration in Europe and Latin America was beginning to lead to some efficiency-seeking (or rationalized) FDI, particularly by large US MNEs in sectors like autos, consumer electronics and office equipment. There was also a small amount of strategic-asset-seeking investment – usually by US firms which had not been among the first of their industry to invest in Europe, but, encouraged by the prospects of market growth, were seeking a speedy means of catching up with their rivals.

In the 1980s and early 1990s, FDI has been increasingly of the third and fourth type. Exceptions include first-time investments by MNEs from developing countries and a new generation of small and medium-sized MNEs from the First World. But, upwards of 75 per cent of all intra-Triad MNE activity since the mid-1980s has been by established European or US MNEs, and by Japanese companies, that, from the start of their internationalizing programmes, have sought to co-ordinate the deployment of their domestic and foreign assets. These firms have viewed each of their foreign affiliates, and frequently their associated suppliers and industrial customers, not as self-contained entities, but as part of a regional or global network of activities.

While FDI in developing countries – which in the period 1988–93 accounted for about one-third (UNCTAD, 1994) of all new FDI (UNCTAD, 1995) – remains primarily of a market- or resource-seeking kind, this, too, is changing. Increasingly, the liberalization of markets and regional integration in Asia and Latin America is enabling foreign MNEs to view their production and sourcing strategies from a regional, rather than a national, perspective. The subregion comprising the eastern coastline of China, Hong Kong, Taiwan and Indo-China is a case in point. More and more, too, many developing countries are being drawn into the hinterland of the globalizing firms from First World countries, as, in their bid to remain competitive, these firms are continually seeking new markets and cheaper, better-quality and more stable sources of supply.

However, unlike the 1960s and 1970s, most investments now taking place in developing countries by First World MNEs are not autonomous investments. Rather, they are part of an integrated network of activities (UNCTAD, 1993). This means that the decisions of an MNE of *what to* produce in a particular country, *where to* source its inputs from and *who* to sell its output to, are based not only on the locational attractions of that country, *vis-à-vis* other countries, but on what is perceived to advance best the global interests of the corporation, rather than the interests of one of its foreign affiliates, or group of affiliates. *Inter alia*, and we shall return to this point later, this requires governments of host countries, in the formation and implementation of their domestic macro-economic strategies – and especially those which affect the decisions of foreign direct investors – to be cognizant of the strategies of governments of other countries whose firms are competing for the same resources and markets.

In Table 9.2, we identify some of the attributes of each type of inbound direct investment which are most likely to enhance the competitive advantages of recipient countries. In practice, the precise contribution of each type of investment will be both activity and firm specific. It is also likely to vary according to age of the investment – generally speaking, the local value added of a foreign affiliate is positively correlated with its age – and, perhaps most important of all, it will depend on the organizational strategies and economic policies adopted by the host government. We shall examine some of these strategies and policies later in this chapter, but, in compiling Table 9.2, we have assumed that they are broadly consistent with the dictates of the international market-place, and that they are primarily directed towards enhancing the dynamic competitive and comparative advantages of the resources and capabilities within their jurisdiction.

Table 9.2 Some likely contributions of different kinds of FDI to the upgrading of competitiveness of host countries

1 Natural-resource-seeking	(a) Provides complementary assets (technology, management and organizational competence)
	(b) Provides access to foreign markets
	(c) May or may not lead to local 'spin-off effects on industrial customers, e.g. secondary processing activities
	(d) Raises standards of product quality
	(e) May or may not foster clusters of resource-based-related activities
2 Market-seeking	(a) As 1(a) above
	(b) Fosters backward supply linkages and clusters of specialized labour markets and agglomerative economies
	(c) As 1(d) and also raises domestic consumers' expectations of indigenous competitors
	(d) Stimulates local entrepreneurship and domestic rivalry
3 Efficiency-seeking	(a) Improves international division of labour and cross-border networking; entices comparative advantage of host country
	(b) Provides access to foreign markets and/or sources of supply
	(c) As 2(b) above
	(d) As 1(d) and 2(e) above
	(e) Aids structural adjustment
4 Strategic-asset-seeking	(a) Provides new finance capital and complementary assets
	(b) As 1(b) above
	(c) As 2(d) above
	(d) As 3(a) above

The conclusions of the tables, which summarize the research findings of scholars,[16] and the experience of national authorities, are self-evident. Each type of FDI has its own particular contribution to make to the five ways of upgrading competitiveness, identified in Exhibit 9.2 and the four facets of Porter's diamond illustrated in Figure 9.1. For example, by the resources and capabilities they transfer, and their transactions with domestic firms, both market- and resource-seeking FDI have the potential to raise the productivity of indigenous resources and capabilities, improve quality standards and stimulate economic growth. In the right circumstances, efficiency-seeking FDI can assist the host country to restructure its economic activities more in line with their dynamic comparative advantage; it can reduce the costs of structural adjustment; and it can foster more demanding purchasing standards both by industrial and personal consumers. Strategic asset-seeking investment may help integrate the competitive advantages of the acquired firm with those of the acquiring firm, and make for additional rivalry between domestic firms. However, this type of FDI, unlike the other three, may be undertaken with the specific purpose of transferring the assets acquired from the host to the home country, and this may work to the disadvantage of the competitiveness of the former country.[17]

The contribution of each type of MNE activity will also vary according to the part, or parts, of the value chain in which it is undertaken. In turn, investment in each part may be differently motivated. For example, some kinds of foreign-owned research and development (R&D) activities are truncated replicas of those of the parent companies; some are akin to efficiency-seeking foreign production; and some are designed to gain an insight into the innovatory advantages of the host country, and, where permitted, to participate in foreign research consortia.[18] This latter motive explains the presence of foreign MNEs in regional clusters of R&D activities in the United States, the EC and Japan. However, in general, inbound investment, providing it helps advance the dynamic comparative advantage of the host country, is likely to have its most beneficial effects where it is directed to those stages of the value chain where the potential for upgrading productivity is the greatest.

Spatial and Country Influences

What, then, are the important factors determining the location of MNE activity in the 1990s? How do they differ from those of 20 years ago? What determines the kind of competitive advantages offered by countries seeking to attract FDI? What should be the attitude and policies of national governments or regional authorities towards FDI in the light of globalization? And, how do these attitudes and policies differ from those displayed in the 1960s and 1970s?

In answer to the first question, Exhibit 9.3 sets out some generic spatial characteristics which scholarly research has shown to most affect the geography of MNE activity. These characteristics – each of which embraces a number of more specific cost- or revenue-determining variables – will impact differently on each of the kinds of FDI just described.[19] They are also likely to vary according to the industry[20] of, and the asset portfolios and strategies pursued by, the investing firms.[21] And, their significance as inbound FDI determinants will also depend on the attributes of particular host countries, such as their size, stage of economic development, industrial structure, degree of economic interdependence with the rest of the world, and the physical and psychic distance from the main investing countries.

Most of these spatial characteristics and the industry-, firm- and the country-specific contextual variables which influence them are well known both to scholars and to business enterprises alike. Yet, in the past, the expectations of governments – and particularly governments of low-income countries – have been shattered because they have not sufficiently taken into account the uniqueness of their own resources and organizational capabilities. The benefits of inward FDI for Nigeria or Taiwan are unlikely to be the same as those for India; those now experienced by Chile and Vietnam are quite different from what they were ten to fifteen years ago; those currently gained in Malaysia and Botswana from efficiency-seeking FDI are scarcely comparable with each other; while those which result from market- and resource-seeking FDI are likely to be highly dependent on the development and macro-organizational policies of host governments, relative to those implemented by other governments competing for the same FDI.

With respect to the second question, the significance of the spatially related variables set out in Exhibit 9.3 has changed considerably over the last two decades. As their share of total production costs has declined, the drawing power of natural resources and unskilled labour has declined while that of created assets and the opportunities of networking with local firms has risen.[22] As the unique competitive advantages of MNEs have become both more mobile and systemic, so such firms have increasingly chosen to locate their value-added activities in countries which can offer the most cost-effective complementary assets, and the quality of infrastructural support which an integrated international production or marketing strategy requires. In this connection, intending investors usually place their need for state-of-the-art facilities for the cross-border transmission of information, technology and finance at the top of their locational priorities. An effective and trustworthy legal framework – particularly in its ability to enforce property rights and resolve contractual disputes – comes a close second. At higher levels of economic development, the quality of a country's educational and technological infrastructure becomes more critical.

Exhibit 9.3 Some country-specific attributes affecting FDI by firms

1 THOSE WHICH CHIEFLY IMPACT ON DIRECT PRODUCTION COSTS AND BENEFITS

- Spatial distribution of natural resources, created assets and markets.
- Input prices, quality and productivity (e.g. labour, energy, materials, components, semi-finished goods).
- Investment incentives and disincentives (including performance requirements etc.).
- Comparative economies of centralization versus decentralization of different segments of value chain (e.g. R&D, production and marketing).

2 THOSE WHICH CHIEFLY IMPACT ON TRANSACTION AND CO-ORDINATING COSTS AND BENEFITS

- Cross-border transport and communication costs.
- Artificial barriers (e.g. import controls) to trade in goods and services.
- Societal and infrastructural provisions (commercial, legal, educational, transport and communication).
- Differences in cross-country political ideologies, language, culture, business, customs and the ethos of competitiveness.
- Economic system and policies of host governments. The organizational and institutional framework for resource allocation.
- The opportunities to exploit the agglomerative economies of industrial districts.

Source: Adapted from Table 4.1 in Dunning (1993a).

More generally, as the organizational and transaction costs of economic activity have become relatively more important – and there is some evidence (Stiglitz, 1989; Wallis and North, 1986) that these are also positively related to the complexity of a nation's industrial structure – countries which can offer a business environment that is conducive to minimizing these costs are, *ceteris paribus*, likely to gain an increasing share of inbound investment. In the early 1990s, two surveys were conducted – one on the determinants of Japanese direct investment in UK manufacturing and the other on the location of international offices (Dunning, 1991). In both surveys, variables related to transaction and co-ordinating costs, for example those to do with interpersonal relations, information asymmetries, language and culture, searching for and dealing with subcontractors, learning about the quality of communications and adapting to local business practices and customer needs, and bureaucratic controls were ranked considerably higher as investment determinants than were traditional variables related to production costs.[23]

Host Government Policies

The literature on FDI is replete with examples on the ways in which the actions of national governments might influence – for good or bad – the location and structure of MNE activities. In this chapter, we shall focus only on the main changes in host government organizational strategies, over the past two decades, which have most affected the level and distribution of FDI.

Foremost among these changes has been a softening in the attitudes of governments towards FDI. This has resulted in a widespread liberalization of policies which previously constrained FDI. These arc described in UNCTAD (1995).[24] In addition, as we have already mentioned, the criterion by which most countries evaluate inbound MNE activity has shifted from its direct contribution to local value added to its longer-term consequences for the competitiveness of indigenous resources and capabilities. This reassessment has occurred at a time when governments – both of developed and developing countries – have been rethinking their own economic functions in the light of political changes and the globalization of the world economy. The most obvious manifestation of this rethinking has been a widespread deregulation and liberalization of markets and the privatization of many state-owned sectors, and the removal, or reduction of, a wide range of government-imposed market imperfections, for example subsidies, tariff and non-tariff barriers, price controls and all manner of rules and regulations.

However, the fact that governments have lessened their direct intervention in markets does not mean that they have abdicated – or indeed should abdicate – their responsibility as *catalysts* and *steerers* and monitors of wealth-creating activities, or as *facilitators* of the private enterprise system. Indeed, as firm-specific assets become more internationally mobile, while others increasingly take on the form of public goods,[25] the role of government as a co-ordinator of markets and hierarchies is becoming a more, rather than a less, critical one. Moreover, because of the demands of modern technology and competitive pressures, the organization of economic activity has become more pluralistic. This places additional responsibilities on governments to ensure the synergistic benefits from alliance or co-operative capitalism are fully exploited.

To a large extent, this reconstructed role of governments – be they subnational, national or supranational – reflects the changes now taking place in the relative efficiency of the different modes of organizing economic activity. The market – as a systemic organizational entity – has been reinstated and upgraded, except in the case of public goods and strategically sensitive products. The current philosophy is that decisions on what is to be produced in a particular country, and how it is produced, are best left to the collective will of thousands of firms and hundreds of thousands, or millions, of consumers. At the same time, this philosophy also presumes that, underpinning and sustaining the market as a resource allocative mechanism, is the visible hand of government. For without the complementary assets of an efficient and up-to-date legal, financial and commercial infrastructure, an educated labour force, an adequate transportation and telecommunications network, a strong anti-monopoly policy, a sound macro-economic policy, and a wealth-creating culture, the market cannot do the job expected of it. We believe that besides its various social and strategic responsibilities, it is the government's task to cultivate and support – though not necessarily undertake – all of these market-enabling activities.

Possibly, what we have so far written is not contentious. Indeed, the policy implications may seem all too familiar. However, the real challenge facing governments is how best to implement these policies. The particular point we wish to emphasize is that the globalizing economy of the 1990s is forcing national governments – be they large or small – developed or developing – to re-examine their domestic economic strategies, in the light of the fact that they are increasingly competing for competitiveness-enhancing assets which are much more footloose than they used to be.[26] Macro-organizational policies which, at one time, only affected the domestic allocation and use of resources, are now as likely to affect trade, FDI and cross-border alliances as much as any tariff, exchange rate change or interest rate hike. If nothing else, the world economy of the 1990s is obliging governments to realign their domestic economic strategies more closely to the needs of the international market-place.

It is our strong contention that governments which are successful in reducing – or helping hierarchies to reduce – the transaction and co-ordinating costs of economic activity, and which best enable their firms to surmount the obstacles to structural change, are, *ceteris paribus*, likely to be the most successful, not only in attracting the right kind of FDI, but to do so at the least real costs. It is surely no accident that the countries which have recorded the most impressive economic performances over the last two decades are also those which have (i) designed and implemented a macro-organizational strategy consistent with upgrading the competitiveness and the dynamic comparative advantage of their location-bound resources, and (ii) ensured that the kind of inward FDI, which best advanced these objectives,[27] was attracted to their midst.

One final difference between the domestic economic policies now being required of governments in a world of increasingly mobile firm-specific assets,[28] and those practised in the 1960s and 1970s, is that, except for cultural or strategic reasons, there is little case for discriminatory action by governments, either in favour of, or against, inbound MNE activity. Though not always admitted, and except for particular types of incentives and performance requirements, most governments have downgraded the significance of FDI policies *per se*. Instead, they are preferring to re-examine the appropriateness of their general macro-economic and macro-organizational strategies *in the light of the globalization of the economic activity and the growing mobility of the critical wealth-creating assets, and on the understanding that FDI and FDI-related trade are the chief modalities by which countries are linked together.* It is, then, the interaction between these policies and the strategies pursued by MNEs that will determine the extent to which inbound FDI is able to upgrade a particular country's competitive advantage.

CONCLUSIONS; AND SOME CAVEATS

This chapter has sought to identify the main contributions which inbound FDI can make to the competitiveness of host countries, and the conditions which must prevail if that contribution is to be optimized. It has also reviewed the changes which have taken place over the past 20 years, in both the determinants affecting MNE activity and the attitudes of governments towards it.

Among the most important of these changes has been the emergence of the global economy, and the deeper structural integration of the world's markets and production systems. This new international division of labour, an integral part of which is the growing mobility of intrafirm intermediate products between countries, is demanding a reappraisal of the economic philosophies and policies of national governments. In particular, the widening locational options of MNEs and the convergence of the industrial structures and trade patterns of advanced countries are forcing national administrations to pay more attention to ensuring that the quality of their location-bound resources and capabilities do not fall behind those of their competitors.

In pursuance of these goals, governments have other critical roles to play, including the elimination of structural and institutional impediments to efficient resource usage; the active promotion of market-facilitating measures; and the encouragement of an ethos of competitiveness among their constitutents. It is the administrations which have gone the furthest in implementing these changes which have been the most successful, not only in attracting inbound FDI, but – much more important – in using it in a way which best advances its national interests in a globalizing economy.

However, we feel it is necessary to conclude this chapter by offering a couple of caveats to what has been written. The first caveat takes us back to some of the possible costs of FDI as a competitiveness-enhancing vehicle. There is a saying, much beloved by Western economists, that there is no such thing as a free lunch. That means all good things have to be paid for; there is a price. This is certainly true of FDI; the only question is whether the price attached to it is a fair and reasonable one. One difficulty faced by many governments in formulating and implementing policies which affect the costs and benefits of inbound FDI is that they either do not have the knowledge, or are uncertain, about what these costs and benefits actually are. This is partly because most decisions, the outcome of which affects the behaviour of foreign-owned

Exhibit 9.4 Some possible contributions of inbound FDI: the upgrading of the competitive advantages of host countries

Positive	Negative	Host country characteristics which favour positive effects
1 By providing additional resources and capabilities, i.e. capital, technology management skills, access to markets.	May provide too few, or the wrong kind of, resources and assets. Can cut off foreign markets, cf. those serviced by domestic firms. Can fail to adjust to localized capabilities and needs.	Availability of local resources and capabilities at low real cost, particularly those complementary to those provided by foreign firms. Minimal structural distortions or institutional impediments to upgrading of indigenous assets. Development strategies which help promote dynamic comparative advantage.
2 By injecting new entrepreneurship, management styles, work cultures and more dynamic competitive practices.	An inability of foreign entrepreneurship, management styles and working practices to accommodate to, or where appropriate, change, local business cultures. The introduction of foreign industrial relations procedures may lead to industrial unrest. By the pursuance of anti-competitive practices, it may lead to an unacceptable degree of market concentration.	The policies pursued by host governments to promote local entrepreneurship and a keen and customer-driven work ethic; the character and efficiency of capital markets; the effectiveness of appropriate market-facilitating policies. Larger countries may find it easier to introduce some of these conditions than smaller countries.
3 By a more efficient resource allocation, competitive stimulus and spill-over effects on suppliers and/or customers, it can help upgrade domestic resources and capabilities, and the productivity of indigenous firms; it can also foster clusters of related activities to he benefit of the participating firms.	Can limit the upgrading of indigenous resources and capabilities by restricting local production to low-value activities, and importing the major proportion of higher-value intermediate products. It may also reduce the opportunities for domestic agglomerative economies by confining its linkages to foreign suppliers and industrial customers.	The form and efficiency of macro-organizational policies and administrative regimes. In particular, the benefits likely to be derived from FDI rest on host governments providing an adequate legal, commercial and assigning priority to policies which help upgrade human and technological capabilities, and encouraging regional clusters of related activities, e.g. science and industrial parks.

4 By adding to the host nation's gross domestic product (GDP), via 1–3 above, and by providing additional tax revenue for government.	By restricting the growth of GDP via 1–3 above, and by transfer pricing (TP) other devices to lower taxes paid by host governments.	See 1–3 above, and by suitable policies by the tax authorities of host governments to minimize TP abuse. Countries which have most to offer MNEs are likely to be more successful in implementing these policies.
5 By improving the balance of payments (b of p), through import substitution, export generating or FDI efficiency-seeking investment.	By worsening the b of p, through limiting exports and promoting imports and outcompeting indigenous firms which export more and import less.	Need to take a long view of importing and exporting behaviour of foreign affiliates. The key issue is not the b of p *per se*, but the contribution of FDI to economic efficiency, growth and stability. However, countries with a chronic b of p deficit may find it difficult to completely liberalize their b of p policies.
6 By better linking the host economy with the global market-place, and helping to advance economic growth by fostering a more efficient international division of labour (d of 1).	By promoting a d of 1 based on what the investing firm perceives to be in its global interests, which may be inconsistent with dynamic comparative advantage, as perceived by host country.	As 3 above – and in particular the extent to which host country governments can pursue policies which encourage investing firms to upgrade their value-adding activities, and invest in activities which enhance the dynamic comparative advantage of indigenous resources. The gains from 6 are particularly important for smaller countries.
7 By more directly exposing the host economy to the political and economic systems of other countries; the values and demand structures of foreign households; to the attitudes to work practices, incentives and industrial relations and foreign workers; and to the many different customs and behavioural norms of foreign societies.	By causing political, social and cultural unrest or divisiveness; by the introduction of unacceptable values (e.g. with respect to advertising, business customs, labour practices and environmental standards); and by the direct interference of foreign companies in the political regime or electoral process of the host country.	Extent to which society is strong and stable enough to adjust smoothly to technological and political change. Also, the strength and quality of government-determined regulations and norms; the nature of the host country's goals and its perceived trade-off between (e.g.) economic growth, political sovereignty and cultural autonomy. The difficulties in optimizing the benefits of the openness induced by FDI are likely to be greatest in countries which are most culturally distinct from their trading or investing partners.

affiliates, are taken by their parent companies on the basis of information and expectations known only to them. This is not to say that these globally oriented decisions necessarily work against the interests of host countries, but it does make life more difficult for a government seeking to optimize the level and pattern of inward FDI and its effects on domestic competitiveness.

We might summarize the main points made in this chapter by reference to Exhibit 9.4, which sets out the main costs and benefits of FDI as have been experienced by host countries over the past two decades or more. The balance between the costs and benefits of each kind of contribution will vary according to the types of investment identified in Exhibit 9.1, to a variety of *firm*- and *industry*-specific features, some of which we have identified in this chapter, and to the age and nationality of the FDI. It will also depend on the characteristics of host countries – and especially, as we have seen, the policies of host governments. Some of these latter characteristics are set out in the third column of the exhibit.

A second caveat we wish to make relates to the nature of a country's competitiveness. As is generally accepted, the term competitiveness is a relative concept and it is used by analysts to compare the economic performance between firms, industries or countries, or that of the same firm, industry or country over time. However, whether a country whose firms are uncompetitive in the production of a particular range of goods or services should encourage inbound FDI to upgrade that competitiveness is a debatable point. Very rarely – if ever – can one country expect to be competitive in the production of all goods and services. Obvious examples include growing bananas in Iceland and producing sophisticated electronic equipment in Chad. One of the tasks of the international market-place – backed by the appropriate government policies – is to allocate resources and capabilities such that each country engages in the kind of economic activities to which it is *comparatively* best suited. FDI can play a useful – and sometimes a decisive – part in this process. What, however, it should not be used for is to 'prop up' activities which can never be internationally competitive. Resources must be directed to where they can be most productively used. After all, one of the functions of trade is to allow a country to import products which it is relatively unsuited to produce for itself and pay for these with products which other countries are relatively unsuited to produce. The success or otherwise of FDI in upgrading the *competitive* advantage of a country's resources and its *comparative* advantage in the international market-place should also be judged by this criterion.

NOTES

1. Of the more substantive studies, we might mention those for Canada (Safarian, 1966), Australia (Brash, 1966), Norway (Stonehill, 1965), New Zealand (Deane, 1970), the Netherlands (Stubenitsky, 1970), Kenya (Langdon, 1981), Singapore (Mirza, 1986), the United

States (Graham and Krugman, 1989), India (Kumar, 1990), Mexico (Peres-Nuñez, 1990) and Central and Eastern Europe (Artisien et al., 1993).

2. In 1991, the Center on Transnational Corporations (as it was then called) identified over 3000 books, reports and articles published between 1988 and 1990 alone (UNCTC, 1991).
3. As documented, for example, in various editions of *World Investment Report*, published annually by UNCTAD.
4. Some of these changes in attitudes and values are reflected in the publications of the UN Center on Transnational Corporations (now the Transnational Corporations and Management Division of UNCTAD in Geneva), since its inception in 1974. In particular, the initial focus on the actions of MNEs, which might constrain the sovereignty of national governments, has gradually been replaced by an examination of the ways in which host governments and foreign direct investors can work together to promote sustainable economic development and the competitiveness of domestic resources and capabilities. The contemporary mood which stresses the complementarity between governments, firms and markets is also echoed in several of the reports of the World Bank (see especially World Bank, 1991, 1993).
5. The expression 'MNE systems' is used deliberately, because although there is a good deal of evidence that uninational – and particularly small to medium-sized uninational – firms continue to play an important role in the generation of created assets, sooner or later these firms are forced into a network of complementary activities in which the larger MNEs act as the lead or flagship firms. This idea is further explored in Van Tulder and Junne (1988), Gugler and Dunning (1993), D'Cruz and Rugman (1993) and Harrison (1994).
6. This is especially so in the case of dynamic industries where product life cycles are shortening and the urgency to innovate new products and introduce more cost-effective production techniques is particularly intense.
7. For some illustrations of the failures of MNEs to acknowledge the significance of inter-country cultural differences, and for some ways in which MNEs may, themselves, build upon these differences to their advantage, see an excellent book by the ex-chairman of Smith Kline Beecham (Wendt, 1993).
8. The gains of spatial agglomeration or clustering of related industries are one of the four critical variables influencing the competitiveness of firms and countries, as identified by Michael Porter (1990).
9. This definition was popularized in the 1930s, when the nature of the firm as an organizational unit was hotly debated among British economists.
10. These include strategic alliances and long-term contractual relations with suppliers. The widening scope of firms to control at least partially the use of resources and capabilities of other firms in which they have no ownership, and vice versa, is encouraging scholars to return to the idea of *groups* of related firms as a critical unit of micro-economic analysis.
11. Estimates of the universe of MNEs, and their affiliates, are constantly being revised upwards. The latest estimates by UNCTAD are that, in the early 1990s, there were at least 39 000 MNEs and 250 000 foreign affiliates (UNCTAD, 1995).
12. While this chapter concentrates on the relations to inbound direct investment, an increasing number of governments are also reassessing the benefits of outbound direct investment. Indeed, as we have frequently stressed, the globalizing economy is forcing governments to take a more integrated view of outward and inward MNE activity, in exactly the way they do of international trade.
13. As, for example, usually measured by gross national product (GNP) per head or rate of increase in GNP.
14. For further details, see Dunning (1992). In our diagram, we have replaced Porter's 'chance' variable by a 'mentality of competitiveness' variable, as we believe this to be a more critically important country-specific factor, which not only is exogenous to each of the four attributes of the diamond, but is closely linked to the government and FDI variables.
15. Much of what is written in this chapter applies equally to the regional dimension of economic activity as to the national dimension. See Chapter 5 of this volume.
16. For a summary of these, see Dunning (1993a). For a more recent empirical investigation into the impact of FDI on the manufacturing productivity of 15 advanced industrial nations, see OECD (1994). This study showed that foreign-owned firms in these countries were typically

more efficient than domestic firms in both absolute levels and in rates of productivity growth. The study also revealed that in ten out of the fifteen countries studied, foreign affiliates created new employment more rapidly than did their domestically owned counterparts.

17. But not necessarily, as much would depend on how the owners of the acquired firm spend the proceeds of the transaction, and how the location-bound resources released by the acquired firm are subsequently deployed.
18. For a recent examination of the structure of FDI in US R&D facilities, see Dunning and Narula (1995).
19. Thus, for example, artificial barriers to trade might encourage defensive market-seeking FDI, but deter efficiency-seeking FDI. Both resource- and efficiency-seeking investors are less interested in the size and character of the local market, which is the main concern of market-seeking investors. Investment incentives and disincentives have been found to be most significant in influencing efficiency-seeking FDI, while sequential investors are less likely to be concerned about cross-country ideological, language and cultural differences than first-time market-seeking investors. Strategic-asset-seeking investors are unlikely to be influenced by input prices or cross-border consumer transport costs to the same extent as are efficiency-seeking investors, while the opportunity to exploit scale economies is likely to be positively correlated with efficiency-seeking FDI, and negatively correlated with market-seeking FDI.
20. According, for example, to differences in input requirements, costs of transporting intermediate and final products, the extent to which products need to be adapted to local customer requirements, the advantages offered by networking with local firms, the behaviour of competitors, and the need to be sensitive to government mandates and policies.
21. Asset portfolios are the accumulated tangible and intangible assets which a firm owns, or to which it has privileged access. It is these portfolios, and the firm's strategic response to them, which will determine the kind and range of products it produces, the extent to which it is vertically integrated, the number and character of its associations with other firms, and the geographical distribution of its activities. In turn, the strategy of a firm will be affected by its age, size, organizational competences and long-term objectives.
22. Exceptions include some resource-seeking and manufacturing assembling investments in the poorer developing countries.
23. See especially Dunning (1991, 1992, 1993b, 1994).
24. Especially interesting are the policies now being introduced by the Indian government, although, of the larger developing economies, India still remains reluctant to embrace fully the FDI strategies of her eastern neighbours.
25. Examples include many capital- and knowledge-intensive products and those which, in their exchange, yield external costs and benefits, that is to non-market participants.
26. The idea of 'competing' governments has a very respectable intellectual heritage. It has, so far, been used by public choice economists to explain how individuals by 'voting with their feet' can act as a constraint to governments in the tax policies, and in the services they offer their tax payers. See, for example, Brennan and Buchanan (1985). But, the idea could be easily extended to explain how a whole range of actions by governments which affect the profitability of firms may also influence their locational preferences.
27. There are examples of countries which have attracted FDI, but have not grown, and vice versa. But, sensible macro-economic and macro-organizational policies have led to FDI being attracted to most competitive sections of the economy or those which are potentially the most competitive.
28. The fact that many firm-specific assets are increasingly mobile does not deny the fact that other vital created assets to economic prosperity are becoming less mobile, for example an efficient domestic and cross-border telecommunications infrastructure.

REFERENCES

Artisien, P.M., Rojec, M. and Svetlicic, M. (eds) (1993), *Foreign Investment in Central and Eastern Europe*, New York: St Martin's Press.

Brash, D.T. (1966), *American Investment in Australian Industry*, Canberra: Australian University Press.

Brennan, G. and Buchanan, J.M. (1985), *The Power to Tax*, Cambridge: Cambridge University Press.

Buckley, P.J. and Casson, M.C. (1985), *The Economic Theory of the Multinational Enterprise*, London: Macmillan.

D'Cruz, J.R. and Rugman, A.M. (1993), 'Business networks, telecommunications and international competitiveness', *Development and International Cooperation* **IX**, December: 223–61.

Deane, R.S. (1970), *Foreign Investment in New Zealand Manufacturing*, Wellington: Sweet & Maxwell.

Dunning, J.H. (1958), *American Investment in British Manufacturing Industry*, London: George Allen & Unwin, reprinted by Arno Press, New York.

Dunning, J.H. (1991), 'Governments, economic organization and international competitiveness', in L.G. Mattson and B. Stymne (eds) *Corporate and Industry Strategies for Europe*, Rotterdam: Elsevier Science, pp. 41–74.

Dunning, J.H. (1992), 'The competitive advantage of nations and MNE activities', *Transnational Corporations*, **1**, February: 135–68.

Dunning, J.H. (1993a), *Multinational Enterprises and the Global Economy*, Wokingham, England, and Reading, MA: Addison-Wesley.

Dunning, J.H. (1993b), *The Globalization of Business*, London and New York: Routledge.

Dunning, J.H. (1994), *Globalization: The Challenge for National Economic Regimes* (The Geary Lecture for 1993), Dublin: Economic and Social Council.

Dunning, J.H. and Narula, R. (1995), 'The R&D activities of foreign firms in the US', *International Studies of Management and Organization* **25**: 39–74.

Gerlach, M. (1992), *Alliance Capitalism*, Oxford and New York: Oxford University Press.

Graham, E.M. and Krugman, P.R. (1991), *Foreign Direct Investment in the United States*, 2nd Edition, Washington, Institute for International Economics.

Gugler, P. and Dunning, J.H. (1993) 'Technology based cross-border alliances', in R. Culpan (ed.), *Multinational Strategic Alliances*, Binghamton, NY: International Business Press, pp. 123–65.

Harrison, B. (1994), *Lean and Mean: The Changing Landscape of Power in the Age of Flexibility*, New York: Basic Books.

Kogut, B. (1983), 'Foreign direct investment as a sequential process', in C.P. Kindleberger and D. Audretsch (eds), *The Multinational Corporation in the 1980s*, Cambridge, MA: MIT Press.

Kogut, B. and Kulatihala, N. (1988), *Multinational Flexibility and the Theory of Foreign Direct Investment*, Philadelphia: Reginald H. Jones Center for Management Policy, University of Pennsylvania (mimeo).

Kumar, N. (1990), *Multinational Enterprises in India*, London: Routledge.

Langdon, S.W. (1981), *Multinational Corporations in the Political Economy of Kenya*, London: Macmillan.

Mirza, H. (1986), *Multinationals and the Growth of the Singapore Economy*, New York: St Martin's Press.

Naisbitt, J. (1994), *Global Paradox*, New York: William Morrow.

OECD (1994), *The Performance of Foreign Affiliates in the OECD Countries*, Paris: OECD.

Peres-Nuñez, N. (1990), *Foreign Direct Investments and International Development in Mexico*, Paris: OECD Development Centre.
Porter, M.E. (1990), *The Competitive Advantage of Nations*, New York: The Free Press.
Safarian, A.E. (1966), *Foreign Ownership of Canadian Industry*, Toronto: University of Toronto Press.
Stiglitz, J. (1989), *The Economic Role of the State*, Oxford: Basil Blackwell.
Stonehill, A. (1965), *Foreign Ownership in Norwegian Enterprises*, Oslo: Central Bureau of Statistics.
Stubenitsky, F. (1970), *American Direct Investment in Netherlands Industry*, Rotterdam: Rotterdam University Press.
UNCTAD (1993), *World Investment Report 1993: Transnational Corporations and Integrated International Production*, New York and Geneva: UN.
UNCTAD (1994), *World Investment Report 1994: Transnational Corporations, Employment and the Workplace*, New York and Geneva: UN.
UNCTAD (1995), *World Investment Report 1995: Transnational Corporations and Competitiveness*, New York and Geneva: UN.
UNCTC (1991), *Transnational Corporations: A Select Bibliography*, New York: UN.
Van Tulder, R. and Junne, G. (1988), *European Multinationals in Core Technologies*, Chichester: John Wiley/IRM.
Wallis, J.J. and North, D.C. (1986), 'Measuring the transaction sector in the American economy 1870–1970', in S.L. Engerman and R.E. Gallman (eds), *Long Term Factors in American Economic Growth*, Chicago: University of Chicago Press, pp. 95–164.
Wendt, H. (1993), *Global Embrace*, New York: Harper Business.
World Bank (1992), *World Development Report*, Oxford and New York: Oxford University Press.
World Bank (1993), *The East Asian Miracle*, Oxford and New York: Oxford University Press.

10. The European Internal Market Program and inbound foreign direct investment*

INTRODUCTION

This chapter considers the impact of the completion of the European Internal Market Program (IMP) on the geographical distribution of economic activity within the European Community (EC).[1] More particularly, it assesses the empirical validity of a number of hypotheses, drawn from FDI theory on the likely effect of the removal of tariff barriers on intra-EC and extra-EC trade and FDI flows, and the relationship between the two. The evidence strongly suggest that the twin forces of regionalization and localization identified in Chapter 3 have been accelerated as a result of recent European integration; and that the balance between the two is strongly determined by the knowledge intensity and mobility of the economic activities involved.

EUROPEAN INTEGRATION PRIOR TO 1985

During the late 1960s and 1970s, there were several scholarly attempts to assess the impact of the European Common Market (ECM) – the first phase of macro-economic regional integration within the European Community (EC), on foreign direct investment (FDI).[2] Although their results were sensitive to the data and the econometric models chosen, all the studies supported the proposition that, while the removal of intra-tariffs, and the establishment of a common external tariff, increased both intra- and extra-FDI – and sometimes significantly so[3] – other determinants of FDI (e.g. market size, market growth, relative factor costs, agglomeration economies, etc.) were at least as, if not more, important, particularly once the initial (and sometimes once-for-all) effects of the ECM had worn off.[4]

Furthermore, the studies showed that the impact of European integration (hereafter called Mark 1 integration) on FDI was strongly conditional on the

* From *Journal of Common Market Studies*, **35** (1) (1997): 1–30 and (2): 189–223..

motives for such investment; and on the time frame of the analysis. Thus, while the direct, or first order, impact of the removal of tariffs was to reduce *defensive import substituting* FDI, and to replace it by exports from the investing country, it also led to the restructuring of existing intra-European FDI wherever its trade creating consequences led to a geographical concentration of production in those activities in which foreign owned firms had a competitive advantage. The indirect, or second order, effects of integration (e.g. increased competitiveness of local firms, augmented income levels and market growth) were shown to lead to more *rationalized* (or efficiency) seeking and *offensive* market seeking. While the former was also associated with an increase in trade (particularly intra-EC trade), the effects of the latter were more ambiguous.

An examination of the FDI data for the period 1957–1985[5] reveals the following main points:

1. Although, as a proportion of their total outbound FDI, that of both EC countries and of non-EC countries – particularly the US – rose quite substantially, non-EC MNEs continued to account for the majority of FDI in the EC.[6]
2. Around 90 percent of inbound extra- and intra-EC FDI prior to 1985 was concentrated in the 'core' countries of the EC,[7] and, much of this (a rough estimate would be about three-fifths) was within a 500-mile radius of Frankfurt. This geographical pattern of economic activity was broadly similar for both extra- and intra-EC FDI; although the latter tended to favor the UK and Germany relatively less, and Belgium and France relatively more.
3. In the early 1980s, about one-third of all FDI from EC countries was directed to *other* EC countries; this compared with 35 percent of US FDI and 15 percent of Japanese FDI to *all* EC countries. The total share of the inbound FDI stock in the EC originating from other EC countries (i.e. the EC's *FDI-intensity* ratio) was generally higher than its share of worldwide FDI (excluding the FDI stock of the investor country).[8] Corresponding *trade-intensity* ratios for intra- and extra-EC transactions for the same year were very similar, although a little higher for intra-EC transactions (UNCTAD, 1994; EAG, 1998).
4. There are few reliable data on the impact of Mark 1 integration on the sectoral distribution of FDI in the EC. The best we have relate to the sales of US manufacturing subsidiaries in the EC. Here, there is some suggestion that the growth of such sales between 1972 (the year before the UK acceded to the Community) and 1985 was most pronounced in those manufacturing sectors subject to plant economies of scale; where the US firms had the most marked competitive (or ownership specific) advantages; where the pre-EC, intra-EC tariffs were highest; and where the post-EC barriers to US–EC trade were the most severe.

5. There is some casual evidence that, apart from some extra-EC defensive import substituting FDI, most intra- and extra-EC FDI was either trade neutral or trade enhancing. Molle and Morsink (1991) found that, over the period 1973–1983, there was a direct correlation between the intensity of intra-EC trade and FDI flows, once the trade intensity index had reached a certain level. US data suggest that the ratio between the sales of US manufacturing affiliates in the EC and exports from the US to the EC increased markedly in the 1960s – and much more so than in the UK, which did not join the EC until 1973. Thereafter, this ratio fell from a peak of 5.8 to 4.9 in 1977 and to 4.0 in 1985 (UN, 1993a).

However, perhaps the most dramatic affect of Mark 1 integration was on intra-EC trade between the affiliates of US firms. In 1957, 85 percent of all sales by such affiliates were to domestic purchasers, and 1 percent were exported to the US; almost all of the rest, viz. 14 percent, were to other EC countries or the UK. By 1966, the exports to countries other than the US had risen to 26.7 percent, by 1977 to 38.3 percent and by 1982 to 45.7 percent (UN. 1993a); and in both 1977 and 1982, 69 percent of these exports were between US affiliates (i.e. intra-firm exports). Other data suggest that intra-EC trade was most pronounced between the core European countries, and was particularly concentrated in sectors characterized by plant economies of scale and (relatively) low or declining transport costs.

In short, the first phase of macro-regional integration in Europe was accompanied by a substantial net increase in EC related FDI and trade flows. However, the largest increases in FDI were from countries outside the EC; and the evidence strongly suggests US (and later Japanese) MNEs were able to take advantage of the removal of tariff barriers, and surmount the transaction costs of the remaining non-tariff barriers better than their EC equivalents.[9] Although, during the period 1958 to 1985, there was a sizeable increase in intra-EC FDI,[10] intra-EC trade grew much faster – and the great majority of this was between, rather than within firms. By contrast, US FDI in the EC increased more rapidly than US exports for the first 20 years of the ECM, after which (until 1985 at least) exports rose more rapidly.

EUROPEAN INTEGRATION: 1985 TO DATE

Some Theoretical Insights

In 1985, the Internal Market Program (IMP) was initiated by the European Commission in Brussels. The intention of the program was to eliminate all remaining non-tariff barriers to trade in goods, services and assets between the member countries of the EC by the mid-1990s. These barriers were classified into four main groups, viz. discriminatory purchasing procedures, border controls, differences in technical standards and differences in fiscal duties. Between 1985 and the late 1990s, it was anticipated that some 319 directives, intended to remove or drastically reduce these barriers, would have been in effect by the (then) 12 member states.

Like the eradication of tariff barriers, that of the non-tariff barriers was expected to have different consequences for individual countries, industrial sectors and firms; and for the modalities of production and servicing markets. For example, the principal consequences of Mark 1 integration was to allow member countries to better exploit their dynamic trading advantages, based both on their natural and created resource endowments and economies of scale. It also helped promote the common ownership of cross-border activities in FDI intensive sectors (Markusen, 1995). In so far as the transaction costs of non-tariff barriers are different from those of tariff barriers[11] and differentially affect countries, sectors and firms, it may be expected that their impact on the modalities of production and servicing markets may also be different.

However, before proceeding to consider how EC 1992 has affected, and is affecting, FDI in the EC, it might be helpful to rehearse the kind of expectations suggested by received economic analysis. As shown in EAG (1998), economists normally draw upon two sets of analytical tools to analyze the consequence of economic integration, viz. the theory of trade and the theory of FDI, or more especially the theory of international production.[12] These should be regarded as complementary, rather than competing, theories. The theory of trade is essentially concerned with the effects of economic integration on the *location* of economic activity, and the extent to which particular markets in the integrated area are serviced by exports or by local production. However, for the most part, received trade theory pays little attention either to the nationality of ownership of economic activity, or to the possibility that such activity might be part of a diversified or multinational firm.[13]

By contrast, the theory of FDI is primarily interested in the impact of macro-regional integration on FDI, either into or out of the member states. While, in so doing, it draws upon the theory of trade, it is also concerned with identifying the consequences of the *foreign* ownership of economic activity within the integrated region on the structure and location of that activity. In other words, FDI theory examines the impact of integration on the competitive advantages of firms of different nationalities, the location of activities associated with these advantages, and the way in which these advantages are organized jointly with the resource capabilities of the host countries.[14]

There is, of course, much in common between these two approaches, if for no other reason than many of the factors which influence the location of economic activity are likely to be independent of the nationality of ownership.

However, in most cases, the consequences of economic integration for trade and FDI are less predictable. For example, the increased competitive pressures arising from the removal of trade barriers, together with the improved opportunities to exploit plant economies of scale, might lead to *strategic asset augmenting FDI*. In this case, there may be a change in the *ownership* of economic activity (e.g. an investment *diversion* effect) but not its location; as a result, the consequences of trade flows – initially at least – may be quite trivial. Similarly, where integration leads MNEs to rationalize the existing value-added activities of foreign subsidiaries, this may lead to both a geographical concentration of scale related production, and an increase in intra-EC trade, over and above that which might be expected to occur between independently owned EC firms.

To keep this chapter to manageable proportions, while attempting to address the more important economic consequences of the IMP, we shall concentrate on four generic hypotheses suggested by the trade and FDI literature.

Hypothesis 1
The first hypothesis is that the IMP will have a positive effect on *intra*-EC trade, and an ambivalent effect on *intra*-EC FDI. Depending on the form and height of existing non-tariff barriers, it is likely to have an ambivalent effect on *extra*-EC trade, but a positive effect on *extra*-FDI and on the *intra*-EC trade by the foreign affiliates of non-EC MNEs.

Both trade and FDI theory suggest that intra-EC trade *creation* will arise as a result of more efficient resource allocation within the EC; and will be most pronounced in those sectors which supply products subject to *plant* economies of scale, and which cost little to transport. At the same time, depending on the level of the external tariff, extra-EC defensive FDI will be relatively unaffected or increased, depending on the competitive enhancing effects of integration, efficiency seeking FDI may increase.[15] The IMP is also likely to affect the value of at least some of the variables determining FDI. It might, for example, be hypothesized that demand related variables, e.g. market size and growth, will become less important for integrated, cf. stand alone, EC affiliates; while supply related variables, e.g. infrastructure and agglomerative economies, may become relatively more important.

Hypothesis 2
The second hypothesis is that the IMP will have an ambivalent effect on the geographical distribution of FDI *within* the EC, both by EC and non-EC MNEs.

However, while the literature suggests that the locational response of foreign investors will vary according to the country of origin of the parent companies, there is no obvious reason why the site specific factors affecting the allocation of activity between a MNE's home country and an EC country (or, in the case of intra-EC FDI, another EC country) will be very different from that as between two separately owned firms in the two countries. At the same time, Markusen and Venables (1995) have shown that, as countries become similar in size, factor endowments and technical efficiency, cross-border activity will become increasingly dominated by MNEs, which will displace trade, provided that transport costs are not insignificant. More generally, they, and other trade economists (e.g. Helpman and Krugman, 1985; Krugman, 1990) suggest that macro-regional integration will lead to a greater concentration of economic activity in knowledge intensive sectors in which plant economies of scale, relative to transport costs, are important, but less concentration in sectors which are more dependent on natural resource endowments for their competitiveness. A corollary to this hypothesis is that the FDI/trade ratio among the high income and more industrialized countries of the EC (or between them and wealthier external investors, e.g. US, Japan and Switzerland) is likely to be higher than that between these countries and the medium income and/or less industrialized countries (Markusen and Venables, 1995, p. 26).

Hypothesis 3

The third hypothesis is that, depending on both country and sector specific factors, the IMP will have an ambivalent effect on the *ownership* of production in the EC. Both the trade and FDI literature suggest that perhaps the most critical component explaining the presence of FDI between and among industrialized countries is the juxtaposition between firm level economies of scale and scope, e.g. such as those that arise from the spreading of various headquarter activities and research and development; plant level economies of scale; the costs of co-ordinating cross-border activities and spatially related costs. MNEs are likely to dominate those sectors where the first and last ingredients are significant, relative to intra-firm co-ordination costs and plant-level scale economies (Markusen, 1995; Caves, 1996).

If it could be shown that those sectors that are the most sensitive to the effects of the IMP were more FDI intensive than the non-sensitive sectors, *and* that integration enhances the kind of ownership advantages specific to MNEs, then it might be reasonably hypothesized that the IMP would lead to an increased share of the foreign ownership of activities in the EC in those sectors.

Hypothesis 4

This hypothesis naturally follows on from Hypothesis 3. Since, as the European Commission has suggested, some sectors are likely to be affected more by the IMP than others, it follows that its consequences for trade and FDI will, at least to some extent, be sector specific. Moreover, both the extant literature and empirical data on FDI clearly demonstrate that MNEs tend to concentrate in sectors which demonstrate one or more of the following characteristics: (i) a high level of R&D relative to sales; (ii) supply intermediate products that are either technically advanced and complex, or offer opportunities for scale economies in their production; (iii) supply end products which are highly differentiated and income-elastic in demand; (iv) are trade and/or FDI supporting; and (v) where the cross-border intra-firm co-ordinating costs of MNE activities are low, relative to the cross-border transport of the goods and services being produced by their foreign affiliates (Hirsch, 1976).

As it happens, most of the sensitive goods and services sectors identified by the European Commission possess one or other of these attributes. Therefore, it is reasonable to hypothesize that FDI in these sectors, or in countries in which these sectors tend to concentrate, will be more affected by EC 1992 than the less sensitive sectors and countries in which the FDI is less well concentrated.

Some Stylized Facts

Before proceeding to analyze the evidence for and against these hypotheses, let us first briefly outline the main trends in intra- and extra-FDI in the EC since 1985, and its distribution between member states. The experience of Mark 1 integration (the completion of which took longer to accomplish than is intended for Mark 2 integration[16]), and our knowledge about FDI trends prior to the prescribed date for market unification (viz. 1 January 1993[17]), suggest that the first five to eight years after the start of the implementation of economic integration are (for most sectors at least) the most critical.

The geography of FDI

Table 10.1 gives details of the changing share of the EC as a host region to foreign direct investors between 1980 and 1995. It shows that in 1980, the stock of FDI directed to the EC[18] was 36.7 percent of that of all recipient economies, and 47.4 percent of that of developed economies. Over the five years immediately *prior to* the announcement of the IMP, these shares *declined* to 29.4 percent and 40.0 percent respectively. However, by the end of five years after its announcement, the EC's shares had *risen* to 40.0 percent of all economies and 49.8 percent of all developed economies. Thereafter, the EC's share of FDI directed to all developed economies stabilized, and by 1996 it was 48.3 percent (a slight *decrease* over 1993 of 51.3 percent). At the same time, because of the increasing attractiveness of developing economies, and particularly China to foreign investors, the EC's share of the worldwide FDI stock in that year was even less than 1980, 33.5 percent cf. 36.7 percent (UNCTAD, 1998).

Table 10.1 Changing share of inward foreign direct investment stock by host region and economy, 1980–1996 (percentages)

Host region/economy	1980	1985	1990	1993	1996
Developed economies	77.5	73.5	80.3	75.2	69.2
Western Europe	41.4	33.3	44.4	42.5	37.9
European Community (12)	36.7	29.3	40.0	38.6	34.9[a]
Core countries	32.8	25.7	34.2	31.5	27.9
Non-core countries	3.9	3.6	5.8	7.1	7.0
Other Western Europe	4.7	4.0	4.4	3.9	3.0
North America	28.6	34.3	29.7	26.5	24.7
Canada	11.3	8.9	6.6	5.1	4.2
United States	17.3	25.4	23.1	21.4	20.5
Other developed economies	7.5	5.9	6.2	6.2	6.6
Australia and New Zealand	3.4	3.7	4.9	4.8	4.9
Japan	0.7	0.7	0.6	0.8	1.0
South Africa	3.4	1.5	0.7	0.6	0.4
Israel	–	–	–	–	0.3
Developing economies	22.5	26.5	19.6	24.1	29.2
Africa	4.3	3.7	2.4	2.4	2.0
Latin America & the Caribbean	10.0	10.0	6.8	8.1	10.5
Asia	7.9	12.6	10.2	13.4	16.5
Other developing economies	0.3	0.2	0.2	0.2	0.2
Central and Eastern Europe	0.0	0.0	0.1	0.7	1.5
Total inward stock	100.0	100.0	100.0	100.0	100.0
Total inward stock value (in millions of US dollars)	480 611	727 902	1 709 299	2 079 538	2 732 649

Note:
[a] Excludes Austria, Finland and Sweden, which joined the European Union (previously called the European Community) in 1995.

Source: UNCTAD (1998). All figures obtained directly from official sources by UNCTAD have been converted into US dollars at the average exchange rate for the year in question.

Whatever else these data show, they reveal a substantial increase in the activity of foreign investors in the EC in the latter part of the 1980s. Normalizing for differences in the growth of GNP between the EC and the rest of the world does not affect this conclusion.[19] However, what *is* of interest (and we shall explore this in more detail later in the chapter) is that at least part of this increase in inbound FDI may have been at the expense of the capital formation of indigenous firms. For example, while gross fixed capital formation (GFCF) in the EC hovered around one-fifth of gross domestic product between 1981 and

1995, the contribution of FDI inflows to that capital formation rose from 2.6 percent in the 1981–1985 period to 5.9 percent in the 1986–1990 period.[20] Between 1991 and 1993 it ranged from 5.5 percent to 5.7 percent, but by 1995 it had risen to 7.2 percent (UNCTAD 1998).[21]

Table 10.2 The geographical distribution of changes in the inward foreign direct investment stock within the EC, end of year 1980–1985 to 1991–1996[a]

	1980–1985 %	1986–1990 %	1991–1996 %
(1) Core countries			
Belgium and Luxembourg	4.1	5.9	21.6
France	28.6	11.3	20.6
Germany	0.8	15.8	8.0
Italy	26.8	8.3	5.1
Netherlands	15.4	10.4	13.5
UK	2.7	32.8	10.0
Total	78.4	84.5	78.8
(2) Non-core countries			
Denmark	–1.5	1.2	4.2
Greece	10.1	1.2	1.9
Ireland	2.4	0.1	2.6
Portugal	0.6	0.8	0.5
Spain	10.1	12.2	11.9
Total	21.7	15.5	21.2
All EC countries	100.0	100.0	100.0

Note:
[a] Excluding Austria, Finland and Sweden, which joined the European Union (previously the European Community) in 1995.

Source: As for Table 10.1.

Table 10.2 gives some details on changes in the distribution of the FDI stock[22] within the EC between 1980 and 1995. We have chosen to divide such countries into two groups, viz. the six core countries of the EC, which are also the high income countries, and the non-core or largely medium income countries.[23] Table 10.2 shows that, between 1980 and 1985, the core countries accounted for 78.4 percent of the increase in FDI stock. In the following five years (1986–1990), this ratio increased marginally to 84.5 percent; but, in the following six years (1991–1996), mainly due to a fall in the dollar value of

UK inbound FDI stocks, it fell back again to 78.8 percent. Even allowing for the country specific differences in the compilation of data, they do not point to any increases to the *overall* geographical concentration of FDI in the EC, but this point will be further investigated later in the chapter.

We now turn to consider similarities and differences between the extra- and intra-EC FDI in the EC over the past decade or so.

Table 10.3 presents data on the distribution of inbound FDI in the EC by the leading source regions and countries since the mid-1980s; and Table 10.4 looks at the significance of the EC as a host region from the perspective of the three largest source countries or regions. The main conclusion to be drawn from Table 10.3 is that the EC countries[24] have attracted a rising share of FDI since the mid-1980s, although part of the reason for this was the sharp retrenchment of MNE activity in the US in the late 1980s and early 1990s.[25] Within the EC, the *stock* of FDI directed to the core countries decreased slightly from around 90 percent in 1995 to nearer 85 percent in 1993.

Table 10.3 Source of FDI flows and FDI stocks in European Community, 1984–1987 to 1990–1993

	Flows – % of total[a]			Stocks – % of total[b]		
	1984–1987	1988–1990	1991–1993	1985	1990	1993
1. North America,	21.7	13.8	18.7	34.6	32.2	29.7
of which US	19.6	12.6	15.7	33.4	30.3	28.0
2. Western Europe,	58.5	68.3	69.2	53.3	55.4	57.4
of which EC	45.0	52.9	59.4	40.4	39.2	43.5
3. Other OECD,	7.3	10.2	5.7	3.0	7.6	7.3
of which Japan	5.3	7.3	2.8	2.7	4.7	4.6
4. Other countries,	12.5	7.7	6.4	9.1	4.8	5.6
Total:	**100.0**	**100.0**	**100.0**	**100.0**	**100.0**	**100.0**
Total amount in US$ million:	**72 325**	**214 025**	**180 145**	**173 832**	**498 561**	**586 012**

Notes:
[a] Annual average.
[b] Included countries: France, Germany, Italy, Netherlands and UK.

Source: OECD (1995).

By contrast, Table 10.4 shows that the intra-EC share of FDI by EC countries (excluding Ireland and Greece) more than doubled between the mid-1980s and the early 1990s. These data immediately suggest that EC specific factors – such as the IMP – may have had a considerably greater impact on intra-EC FDI than

Table 10.4 *Japanese, US and EC foreign direct investment by regions and countries, 1985–1993 (percent of world total)*

	Japan (annual average)			United States (annual average)			European Community (annual average)		
Host region/economy	1985–1987	1988–1998	1991–1993	1985–1987	1988–1990	1991–1993	1985–1987	1988–1990	1991–1993
Developed economies	68.2	77.3	71.3	64.3	68.7	61.7	88.1	89.3	82.0
European Community (12)	17.0	20.9	20.3	38.8	44.6	44.2	30.6	50.8	57.7
Core countries	15.9	20.1	18.8	33.5	38.9	40.1	26.4	42.9	45.1
Belgium and Luxembourg	5.0	1.4	1.0	1.2	3.0	2.9	2.7	8.3	8.6
France	0.8	1.7	1.6	4.0	5.7	4.7	3.7	6.8	6.7
Germany	1.2	1.6	2.4	3.2	2.9	8.9	1.4	6.4	8.8
Italy	0.2	0.4	0.7	1.9	4.4	3.2	2.4	3.0	3.6
Netherlands	3.1	5.7	5.0	9.9	3.1	0.7	8.1	9.4	9.7
UK	5.7	9.4	8.2	13.4	19.8	19.7	8.2	9.1	7.7
Non-core countries	1.0	0.8	1.5	5.3	5.7	4.1	4.2	7.8	12.5
Denmark	0.0	0.0	0.0	–0.7	0.2	0.3	0.1	0.3	0.5
Ireland	0.3	0.1	0.6	3.6	3.0	2.8	0.7	1.8	4.0
Southern periphery*	0.7	0.7	0.9	2.4	2.5	1.0	3.4	5.7	8.0
Other Western Europe†	0.7	1.3	1.1	5.5	6.7	7.8	2.8	4.0	5.4
United States	44.8	47.0	41.9	0.0	0.0	0.0	48.1	27.9	15.9
Canada	1.5	1.8	1.9	14.6	9.8	4.8	3.2	2.7	0.9
Japan	0.0	0.0	0.0	3.1	2.9	1.8	0.6	0.9	–0.1
Australia and New Zealand	4.2	6.3	6.2	2.4	4.8	3.3	2.8	2.9	2.2
Developing economies	31.8	22.7	28.3	35.8	31.3	37.0	11.8	10.5	15.3
Africa	1.1	1.1	1.4	–0.1	–2.0	0.7	0.7	1.1	1.1
Latin America	17.5	8.8	8.2	33.0	26.4	23.1	5.3	4.9	3.8
Middle East	0.2	0.2	0.9	0.4	–0.3	1.7	0.7	0.6	0.6
Asia	12.8	12.2	17.1	3.6	6.9	11.1	2.3	1.8	3.5
Other developing economies‡	0.2	0.4	0.7	–1.1	0.4	0.4	2.9	2.2	6.3
Central and Eastern Europe	0.0	0.1	0.4	0.0	0.0	1.3	0.1	0.2	2.6
Total	100.0	100.0	100.0	100.0	100.0	100.0	100.0	100.0	100.0
World total (million US$)	67497	170922	111212	59405	79771	124910	125876	268431	268352

Notes:
* Greece, Spain, Portugal.
† Austria, Finland, Norway, Sweden, Switzerland.
‡ Includes Malta and Cyprus and other countries not reporting separately.

Source: Japanese Ministry of Finance, US Department of Commerce (various issues), OECD (1995).

on extra-EC FDI, a conclusion quite the opposite from the one we drew about the effects of Mark 1 economic integration.

Throughout the late 1980s and early 1990s, a somewhat higher proportion of intra-EC FDI was attracted to the non-core countries than in the case of Japanese and US FDI; while, over the period as a whole, there is some suggestion of a decentralization of intra-EC FDI, particularly to Southern Europe.[26] However, *within* the core countries, a noticeable difference between extra- and intra-EC FDI is the considerably lower attraction of the UK as an investment outlet in the former than in the latter case.[27] The closer linguistic, cultural. legal and institutional ties between the UK and the US, relative to that of the other core countries of the EC and the US, might have something to do with this.

To what extent does FDI tend to cluster in particular regions or countries; and how far has such clustering, e.g. to take advantage of agglomerative economies, increased in recent years? Table 10.5 compares the FDI intensity ratios[28] of EC countries in selected host regions in the late 1980s or early 1990s, with the respective ratios in the early 1980s. Looking, first, at intra-EC FDI intensities, Table 10.5 reveals that, in all countries except the UK, these intensities were greater than 1.00 in the latter period, although, again, apart from the UK, they were even more pronounced for the 'other' Western Europe region. Second, in the five EC countries for which we have data, the intra-EC intensity ratios increased in the 1980s. Third, the FDI intensity ratios of EC countries in non-European countries were generally less than 1.00 in 1990 (an exception is the above average UK/US ratio); and that, except in the case of FDI in Japan, these ratios generally fell in the previous decade. Fourth, the FDI intensity ratios of both the US and Japan in the EC rose in the 1980s, in spite of the attractions of other parts of the world (notably East Asia) for US investors and the US for Japanese investors.

The sectoral distribution of FDI

Data on the changing sectoral distribution of extra- and intra-EC FDI are only available for a few countries. Perhaps the best statistics are those compiled by the US Department of Commerce. Unfortunately, such data are only published for selected years.[29] In Table 10.6, we set out the increases in the sales of US affiliates in Europe[30] between 1982 and 1989 (which embrace the years before and immediately after the announcement of the IMP), and between 1989 and 1993. The sectors are classified into three groups according to their likely sensitivity (as perceived by the European Commission) to the IMP.[31] We also present similar data for the rest of the world (ROW). The difference between the Europe and the ROW indices might be interpreted as reflecting, in part at least, the 'European' (including the IMP) effect.

Table 10.5 *FDI intensity ratios of selected foreign investing countries by host region, early 1980s–1992*

Investor country	Year	European Community	Other Western Europe	North America	United States	Canada	Japan	Rest of the world
European Community								
Belgium and	1980	1.65	2.18	–0.14	–0.31	0.09	0.29	1.26
Luxembourg	1988	n.a.	n.a.	n.a.	n.a.	n.a.	n.a.	n.a.
Denmark	1982	1.31	3.68	0.86	0.86	n.a.	0.01	0.62
	1991	1.42	5.45	0.38	0.36	0.45	0.77	0.40
France	1982	1.00	1.88	1.15	1.99	–0.21	0.11	0.79
	1991	1.37	1.63	0.62	0.72	0.30	0.16	0.49
Germany	1980	1.02	2.44	0.84	1.21	0.25	0.17	0.84
	1992	1.19	2.60	0.79	0.91	0.27	0.84	0.38
Italy	1980	n.a.	n.a.	n.a.	n.a.	n.a.	n.a.	n.a.
	1992	1.52	2.84	0.31	0.37	0.12	0.41	0.59
Netherlands	1984	0.89	1.65	1.19	1.44	0.43	0.15	0.44
	1992	1.03	2.27	0.99	n.a.	n.a.	0.48	0.52
United	1981	0.50	0.52	1.09	1.43	0.55	0.09	1.25
Kingdom	1992	0.58	0.80	1.32	1.52	0.65	0.61	0.89
Portugal	1985	1.23	0.04	0.49	0.65	0.01	–	1.27
	1988	n.a.	n.a.	n.a.	n.a.	n.a.	n.a.	n.a.
Spain	1984	n.a.	n.a.	n.a.	n.a.	n.a.	n.a.	n.a.
	1989	1.39	1.02	0.31	0.39	0.06	0.18	1.13
Other countries								
United States	1980	0.60	1.05	0.47	–	1.14	0.26	0.63
	1990	0.73	1.34	0.41	–	1.80	1.74	0.73
Canada	1980	0.45	0.45	2.24	3.63	–	0.06	0.66
	1990	0.45	0.38	1.91	2.44	–	0.40	0.62
Japan	1980	0.30	0.26	0.98	1.44	0.24	–	2.13
	1990	0.38	0.24	1.26	1.54	0.24	–	1.28

Ratios are derived from data on stock of foreign direct investment using formula set out in note 28.

Source: Based on UN (1993a) and a variety of national statistical sources.

The data clearly reveal two things. First, the sales of US affiliates in the highly and moderately sensitive sectors rose distinctly faster than those in other sectors between 1982 and 1989 but only marginally so between 1989 and 1993.[32] Second, the average rate of growth in sales for all sectors – but particularly for some of the most sensitive sectors between 1982 and 1989 in Europe, have consistently outstripped that of the ROW.

Other data published by Eurostat (1994) demonstrate an increasing concentration of FDI by both EC and non-EC investors in the tertiary sector, and particularly in finance, banking and insurance, telecommunications and business

Table 10.6 Growth of sales by US affiliates in Europe and the rest of the world by sectors, 1982–1993

Sector	1982–1989 (1982 = 100)			1989–1993 (1989 = 100)			1982–1993 (1982 = 100)		
	All countries	Europe	Rest of world	All countries	Europe	Rest of world	All countries	Europe	Rest of world
High impact									
Beverages	173.9	162.2	183.3	170.1	204.3	147.2	295.8	331.4	269.9
Drugs	182.0	214.8	141.3	167.3	168.6	164.7	304.5	362.2	232.7
Office/computing	324.3	296.4	400.2	116.1	101.7	145.0	376.6	301.5	581.4
Radio, TV communications	80.5	98.2	84.7	132.4	96.9	143.2	106.6	95.2	121.3
Electronic components	229.5	203.5	244.6	147.5	154.9	143.9	338.5	315.2	352.2
Instruments	195.6	181.2	247.6	125.3	125.1	125.6	245.1	226.7	311.1
Finance, except banking	247.8	555.8	164.6	159.5	206.2	98.8	372.7	1146.1	162.6
Insurance	182.4	183.0	182.1	143.7	138.8	153.0	262.1	254.0	278.6
Total high impact	219.9	255.0	187.4	138.2	145.3	131.8	289.6	370.5	247.0
Moderate impact									
Other food products	164.5	218.0	112.8	154.1	155.1	152.4	253.5	338.1	175.0
Other chemical products	145.6	193.6	100.4	115.1	114.3	116.4	167.6	221.3	114.8
Other machinery	127.9	124.2	132.3	92.5	99.8	78.6	118.3	124.0	104.0
Household appliances	321.1	311.5	328.8	119.0	151.5	94.4	382.1	472.0	310.4
Transportation equipment	200.0	218.8	185.1	115.2	186.5	114.2	230.3	253.4	211.4
Textile products and apparel	148.9	140.6	158.7	142.4	160.6	123.8	212.1	225.8	196.5
Rubber products	144.5	237.8	101.9	110.4	102.5	118.8	159.5	243.7	121.1
Glass products	187.0	180.0	200.2	95.4	115.7	61.6	178.4	208.2	123.3
Wholesale trade	179.8	174.5	192.4	120.7	112.4	138.4	217.0	196.1	266.3
Business services	158.1	152.9	171.4	194.4	201.5	178.2	307.4	308.1	305.4
Total moderate impact	177.2	185.6	165.5	120.7	119.0	123.4	213.9	220.9	204.2
Total low impact	161.9	168.0	155.8	122.8	135.1	112.7	198.8	227.0	175.6
All industries (less petroleum)	181.1	193.0	167.3	126.0	125.5	126.7	228.3	242.2	212.0

Source: US Department of Commerce Department Benchmark Surveys (various) since 1989.

services.[33] How much this is due to the IMP *per se* and how much to the deregulation and liberalization of service related markets in general, it is difficult to say. But, it is, perhaps, worth noting that the sectoral composition of intra-EC foreign direct investment flows, and that of non-EC countries in the EC between 1984 and 1992, is broadly similar.

This conclusion is supported by a study by Agarwal, Hiemenz and Nunnenkamp (1995), which shows that the industrial composition of post-1985 French, German, Dutch and UK FDI in the EC has been very similar to that in other industrialized countries. Their work also reveals that only very modest changes have occurred in the sectoral composition of intra- and extra-EC FDI by these same countries between the mid-1980s and the early 1990s;[34] while there is no real evidence that the growth of extra-EC FDI in the sectors in which intra-EC trade has expanded the most rapidly has been at the expense of extra-EC FDI in other developed countries.[35] The only exception may be in some service sectors – notably in finance, insurance, telecommunications and data processing services, where the gains from IMP have been higher simply because the earlier barriers to intra-EC trade or investment were so high.

The share of FDI in EC capital formation

While much of our previous discussion has been concerned with the *locational* competitiveness of the EC, and that of its member states, it is possible that part of any increase in FDI (or sales by foreign firms) might represent an increased *share* of the total investment (or sales) of all EC located firms. Such an increase in the foreign ownership of production might occur either as a result of the improved competitiveness of established foreign affiliates, or through foreign firms acquiring or merging with domestic firms in individual European countries.[36] As an earlier section has shown, the received literature would regard such M&As as a means of sustaining or increasing the ownership (O) advantages of the acquiring firms. However, while in some cases the location of the acquired company may be relevant, in others it may have no significance at all.

Table 10.7 reveals that the share of foreign direct inflows to GFCF in the world economy increased in the second half of the 1980s, but that this increase was mainly confined to the EC and North America. By contrast, in the 1990s, the rise in the foreign share of GFCF was most marked in the case of developing economies and in others in Western Europe; and particularly so in the case of Sweden, which, in 1995, along with Finland and Austria, joined the EU. The increased participation of foreign owned firms in the EC (which is confirmed by other data[37]) is entirely consistent with our knowledge about M&As. Both intra-EC and M&As, and cross-border acquisitions of EC firms by non-EC purchasers'[38] corporations, increased more than ten-fold between 1985–1986 and 1989–1990, before dropping back in the early 1990s to nearer their 1986–1987 levels, since when they have increased again isolating the effects of the IMP (DeLong, Smith and Walter, 1996).

Table 10.7 The ratio of foreign direct investment inflows to gross fixed domestic capital formation, 1981–1995 (percent)

Host region/economy	1981–1985 (Annual average)	1986–1991 (Annual average)	1991	1992	1993	1995
All economies	2.3	3.6	3.5	3.3	4.4	5.6
Developed economies	2.2	3.5	3.3	3.0	3.0	3.9
Western Europe	2.6	5.6	5.4	5.3	6.1	7.2
European Community (12)	2.7	5.7	5.7	5.5	6.0	7.0
Belgium and Luxembourg	7.6	17.5	22.8	25.2	26.1	20.4
Denmark	0.4	3.8	7.3	4.6	8.4	15.3
France	2.0	4.5	5.9	8.2	9.0	8.6
Germany	1.2	1.1	1.2	0.6	0.5	2.6
Greece	6.0	5.9	8.7	5.5	5.2	4.8
Ireland	4.0	5.9	1.3	17.0	15.3	14.2
Italy	1.1	2.0	1.0	1.7	2.6	2.6
Netherlands	6.1	12.8	10.7	12.2	14.2	14.8
Portugal	3.0	9.9	13.7	8.3	7.9	2.7
Spain	5.3	9.6	10.0	10.5	8.6	5.4
United Kingdom	17.6	13.6	9.5	9.8	11.0	13.1
Other Western Europe	1.7	4.3	4.0	2.5	3.9	6.2
North America	2.8	6.3	2.9	2.7	8.4	14.1
Canada	1.0	5.8	2.4	2.4	5.1	11.0
United States	2.9	6.5	3.0	5.0	8.8	5.8
Other developed economies	0.7	0.9	0.7	0.9	0.5	1.2
Developing economies	3.3	3.4	4.0	4.2	6.1	7.4
Africa	2.3	3.9	4.2	5.2	6.1	7.9
Latin America and the Caribbean	4.1	5.3	5.2	7.6	6.4	9.8
Asia	3.1	2.8	3.4	3.2	6.0	6.6
Central and Eastern Europe	neg.	0.1	0.4	1.1	7.4	10.2

Source: UNCTAD (1995, 1996, 1998).

ISOLATING THE EFFECTS OF THE IMP

So much for some stylized facts about recent FDI into the EC, which lend some support to the four hypotheses set out earlier in this chapter. We now turn to examine more rigorously the empirical evidence for these hypotheses, and also some related work of other scholars on the effect of IMP on extra- and intra-EC FDI and trade. In doing so, we are faced with a difficult – indeed, almost an intractable – problem, viz. how to isolate the specific impact of the IMP from the other variables which might influence the level and pattern of extra- and intra-FDI in the EC? For, even if all the data were available (which they are not), the answer would be conditional on: (a) the kind of FDI being discussed; (b) particular country and industry specific factors; (c) how one measures the IMP effect; and (d) what assumptions one makes about what would have happened in the absence of the IMP, viz. the *anti-monde* or *alternative* position.

Basically, there are two main ways of proceeding. One is to construct a model in which an IMP variable is added to the usual determinants of FDI hypothesized by received FDI, and/or trade theory; and then attempt to estimate the significance of that variable. In principle, such an exercise could be conducted for extra- and intra-EC FDI, and for different kinds of FDI. In practice, the data on FDI only allow us to travel this path to a limited extent. We shall, however, review the research which has recently been conducted on this issue.

The second approach is more deductive and predictive, and seeks to test a number of specific hypotheses about the likely effects of economic integration on FDI. The particular hypotheses we shall examine in this chapter were set out earlier in this chapter.

In practice, the two approaches are quite similar, and use almost identical statistical procedures. They also confront the same analytical and measurement problems. Both, for example, need to construct a quantifiable proxy for what is essentially a non-quantifiable phenomenon, viz. the removal of non-tariff barriers to intra-EC trade. Both, too, in the design and specification of their chosen models face the difficulty that many of the other variables hypothesized to influence FDI are, themselves, likely to be affected by die IMP. Introducing leads and lags may help resolve this latter problem, but only to a limited extent.

Since, up to now, most attempts to explain recent movements in FDI into the EC have followed the first approach, we will give most of our attention to these.

INCORPORATING IMP INTO TRADITIONAL FDI MODELS

We are aware of only two attempts to do this, viz. Clegg (1995) and Pain and Lansbury (1996), although other models have identified the significance of non-IMP variables influencing FDI in the EC (or Western Europe[39]). In such cases, it *could* be argued that the value of the residual (i.e. unexplained) variables might be taken as a proxy for the IMP,[40] or, at least, a reflection of its importance, *apart* from its effects on the value of the other variables. An alternative procedure would be to estimate the impact of the IMP on the non-IMP variables and then to credit the IMP with that impact in any explanation of FDI. Thus, for example, if it could be shown that, over the five-year period 1987–1992, the IMP had raised GNP by 6 percent (the most optimistic forecast of the Cecchini report (Cecchini et al., 1988)); then, using the estimates of Julius (1990) and the UNCTAD (1993a), of the elasticities of FDI with respect to changes in the GNP – viz. between 3.5 percent and 4.5 percent – one could then infer that between 21 percent and 27 percent of any increase in FDI over those years was due to the IMP.

Of the more recently published research which has sought to evaluate the determinants of FDI in the EC, those of UNCTAD (1993a), Buigues and Jacquemin (1994), Srinivasan and Mody (1998), Clegg (1995) and Pain and Lansbury (1996) are worthy of special attention. We will now briefly summarize the results of their work in the following paragraphs.[41]

UNCTAD (1993)

The UNCTAD study regressed the annual flows (at times 't') of FDI (both intra- and extra-EC) into the EC and other developed countries, over the period 1972–1988, against five explanatory variables, viz. the level of GNP in year t–1, the change in GNP between t–1 and t, the ratio of *domestic* investment to GNP in year t–1, the exchange rate at year t (defined as the ratio of the domestic currency to the US dollar) and the squared deviation of the exchange rate from its mean over the period 1972–1988. The authors found that, apart from the exchange rate variable, which was insignificant, the remaining four factors explained about 90 percent of the fluctuations in FDI in *both* the EC and other developed countries; and that the coefficients of the explanatory variables always had the correct size. Of these variables, GNP was consistently found to be the most significant, with its coefficient being much larger for the EC than for the other developed countries. The share of domestic investment in GNP was also positively and significantly associated with FDI for both the EC and other developed countries. The variance in the exchange rate was seen to have had a significant negative effect on FDI inflows.

The UNCTAD study also estimated the elasticity of the response of FDI to changes in the value of the independent variables. It found that an increase in both the level of GNP and the ratio of domestic investment to GNP in the EC in one year coincided with an increase in the inflow of FDI of 4 percent in the following year; while a 1 percent change in the variance of the exchange rate would have a relatively small negative (but statistically significant) impact on FDI inflows of $37 million.

Unfortunately, the data in the UNCTAD study do not go up beyond 1988; nor do the authors split their analysis into a pre- and post-IMP timeframe. But, some estimates for the period 1989–1995, made from a variety of sources, including the IMF and World Bank – and which implicitly take account of the IMP – predicted that the annual rate of growth of FDI flows in the EC would outpace that of other developed nations, except Japan.[42] Primarily, this was because the projected growth of GNP and the ratio of domestic investment to GNP was higher in the EC[43] than in other regions of the world. Although the UNCTAD study did not specifically incorporate an IMP variable into their model, the results do suggest that the *indirect* approach to evaluating its significance, viz. by its effects on GNP, domestic investment and the exchange rate, might offer a promising line for further research.

Srinivasan, K. and Mody, A. (1998)

This study was confined to US and Japanese FDI for the period 1977 to 1992. It embraced 35 countries, including 10 EC countries. One of its main purposes was to evaluate the significance of four rather different groups of factors which the literature has suggested influence FDI. These are:

1. *Classical factors* – which the authors proxied by host country market size, and labor and capital costs.
2. *Agglomeration factors* – proxied by the previous level of FDI and the quality of supportive infrastructure to FDI.
3. *Trade restricting factors* – proxied (in reverse) by the degree of openness of an economy; and a dummy for the IMP variable.
4. *Risk factors* – proxied by information provided by various corporate data banks on country risk assessment.

The authors compiled a number of multi-regression equations, using mainly log linear estimates of the FDI function for all developed countries, and for the EC separately.[44] They found that, for each group of countries, both the size of market and cost of labor were significant explanatory variables – but not the cost of capital in the case of the EC. Agglomeration factors, measured in this instance by the production of electricity *per capita*, and the number of telephone lines *per capita*, were significantly related to FDI in the case of the EC, but not for developed countries as a whole.[45] As might be expected, and in contrast to the situation in developing countries, country risk was of only trivial importance, but openness (or negative trade restrictions) was positively and significantly signed in both groups. Eliminating country risk, these three groups of factors explained about 70 percent of the variation in FDI in the EC (and rather less in the case of FDI in all developed countries).

In some additional (unpublished) calculations undertaken by the authors, Srinivasan and Mody found that, when they split their data into three time periods, viz. 1977–1981, 1982–1986 and 1987–1992, there was no evidence that the formation of the IM significantly improved the EC's share of either US or Japanese FDI. Indeed, the case of Japanese FDI, assuming East Asia to be the benchmark group of countries, the share of FDI directed to the EC fell in the period 1987–1992.

Clegg J. (1995)

In a long-range longitudinal study, Clegg attempted to model the determinants of US FDI in the original six member countries of the EC between 1951 (seven years before the European Common Market (ECM) came into effect) and 1990. The unique characteristics of his model were: first, an attempt to incorporate both real and financial variables into three multiple regression equations (one embracing the whole and one each for two sub-periods, 1951–1972 and 1973–1990); and second, in the latter sub-period, the introduction of a dummy variable for the IMP.[46]

Clegg found that of the 10 or 11 explanatory variables included in his equations, market size (proxied by GNP or GDP deflated to constant prices) market growth, a trade discrimination variable, the exchange rate (of the dollar against the six EC currencies) and relative interest rates were all significantly and correctly signed for one or other of the sub-periods, and for the 40-year period as a whole. However, contrary to expectations, for the longer period, market size was shown to be negatively associated with FDI – and significantly so – although, for the first two decades, the two variables were positively correlated. Clegg suggested the reasons for this was that, whereas in the 1950s and early 1960s, most US FDI was defensive and was directed to the larger local markets in Europe, in the later years, particularly after the UK joined the EC, it was more of an efficiency or strategic asset-seeking kind, and geared to exploiting the EC market as a whole.[47]

Clegg's insertion of a dummy variable for the IMP (set to unity for the period 1987–1990) gave inconclusive results. For the period 1951–1990, the variable was positively but insignificantly associated with FDI; but for the sub-period 1973–1990, it was negatively associated. Part of the reason for the apparent conflict in these findings may be that the significance of the other variables in the equation (e.g. market size) quite dramatically changed in the 1980s. At the same time, as Clegg himself recognized, the use of an *aggregate* dummy for the IMP inevitably fails to capture the industry-specific effects of the program.

Buigues, P. and Jacquemin, A. (1994)

One of the distinctive features of this study was its attempt both to evaluate the relationship between extra-EC FDI in the EC and exports to the EC, and to estimate the significance of trade barriers as a determinant of FDI. Taking the share of global FDI directed to seven or nine manufacturing sectors in the EC by US and Japanese MNEs as the dependent variable, the authors regressed its value against that of four independent variables, viz. the share of total US and Japanese exports directed to the EC, intra-EC non-tariff barriers, the sectoral growth in demand in the EC divided by the growth in demand in the US and Japan, and the Community's sectoral specialization, which they defined as the EC's exports for sectors in the total EC exports of manufactured goods divided by the same index for all OECD countries.[48]

The relevant linear regression produced results which were generally supportive of expectations. In particular, extra-EC FDI and trade were seen to be significantly complementary to each other (see Hypothesis 1, above). Second, while non-tariff barriers to trade were a significant determinant of Japanese FDI, they played only a minor role in influencing US FDI.[49] For US sectoral demand growth and EC sectoral specialization, the results were different for US and Japanese investors. In the Japanese case, both variables were shown to have a significant positive association with FDI, while, for the US, only the sectoral specialization variables were significantly related. Although the authors did not include an agglomeration variable in their analysis, they found that both US and Japanese firms tended to strengthen their share of FDI and exports in those sectors in which they already had a comparative advantage in 1980, while they contracted their share of FDI and exports in the sectors in which they had an initial comparative disadvantage.

Pain and Lansbury (1996)[50]

Since, as we have seen, the effects of the IMP are unlikely to be evenly distributed between industries, it is only by incorporating sector specific variables that one can properly evaluate the impact of the IMP. Moreover, apart from our own estimates presented later in this chapter, the Pain and Lansbury study is the only one we know which has made a formal attempt to incorporate *discriminate* dummy variables to proxy the IMP.

The Pain and Lansbury study is unique in another respect, in that it examined the impact of the IMP on the *outward* intra-EC FDI[51] of two of the core EC countries, viz. the UK and Germany.[52] In doing so, it used received FDI theory to test three hypotheses. These are:

1. That intra-EC FDI by UK and German firms has risen more rapidly than it would have done in the absence of the IMP.
2. That intra-EC by UK and German firms has risen either more rapidly than that outside the EC or at the expense of such investment.
3. That the IMP has had a more marked effect on the growth of FDI by UK and German firms in the less trade intensive sectors, notably financial services, since, in the past, non-tariff barriers have constrained both FDI and trade in these sectors relative to that in the more trade intensive sectors.

The econometric model devised by Pain and Lansbury consisted of both location and internalization specific explanatory variables.[53] Of the former, they included the size of the sectoral output in the host country, relative factor costs, currency variability, the extent of trade barriers and the corporate financial conditions in the home country.[54] Of the latter, they used data on the US registered patents of UK and German firms as proxy for their preferences for FDI, rather than cross-border licensing, the idea being that firms would be more likely to internalize the markets for their technology and organizational expertise in high value-added sectors than in low value-added sectors.[55] Estimates of the non-tariff barriers – ranging along an ordinal scale of 1 to 3 – as they were perceived to affect particular sectors – were obtained from Buigues, Ilzkovitz and Lebrun (1990) and Sapir (1993).

The sample period taken for the dependent and explanatory variables apart from the IMP was 1981–1992 in the UK case and 1980–1992 in the German case. For each country, the authors first calculated a (log linear) multi-regression equation *excluding* the IMP variable. In each case, the results were similar and broadly consistent with those of other studies. Host country output was shown to be positively and significantly correlated with UK and German FDI in the EC, although the (sectoral) output elasticities (1.54 and 0.84) were considerably lower than that recorded for GNP by the UNCTAD study (4.34).

Both the UK and German equations recorded a positive, but insignificant, relationship between relative unit labor costs and FDI. This finding is consistent with the notion that high labor costs may reflect the availability and productivity of high-skill labor, and be associated with agglomeration economies, rather than with low (real) labor productivity. Both the corporate gearing ratios and the proxy variable used to capture the currency variability were correctly signed, but insignificant. Taking a three-year cumulative measure of patents registered by the two groups of firms in the US, they found that in equations the coefficients were correctly signed and significant. Overall, Pain and Lansbury estimated that the coefficient between the dependent and the five explanatory variables was very high at 0.972, although, almost certainly, there was some auto correlation between the explanatory variables.

The authors then produced two equations embodying the IMP indicator ordinally ranked according to perceived sensitivity (3 = high, 1 = low). This variable was shown to be positively and significantly related to FDI in the case of both the UK and Germany, i.e. it led directly to an increased level of FDI in the EC, although the coefficient was somewhat higher for the UK. The effect of the inclusion of this variable was to reduce the elasticities on output (in the UK case) and patents (in the UK and German cases), which confirms an earlier point made in this chapter that, in the absence of a specific IMP variable, some of its effects are captured by other variables.

The next part of the Pain and Lansbury exercise was to estimate the difference made to the *value* of FDI in the EC as a result of the IMP. The authors calculated that, by the end of 1992, the IMP may have raised the constant price stock of UK FDI by $15 billion (or 31 percent of the capital stake at that date) and the stock of German FDI by $5 billion (or 6 percent of the aggregate stock level). In both instances, the prime gainers were shown to be the financial and other service sectors and the electronics sector (which includes telecommunications equipment). For the UK, major gains were also recorded in the distribution and food, drink and tobacco sectors, in both of which the UK has a comparative advantage.

Because of the differences in the industrial structure of individual EC countries, the impact of the IMP on UK and German intra-EC FDI investment is likely to be country specific – at least to some extent. Thus, according to Pain and Lansbury, the primary beneficiary of the IMP, in so far as it has affected German outward FDI, has been in the UK, in which it is estimated that the German stake in 1992 was $4.3 billion, or a third higher than it might otherwise have been. Other gainers appear to be Italy, the Netherlands and Portugal; but France and Belgium are both shown to have lost German investment as a result of the IMP, mainly, it would seem, because of the size of German chemicals and distribution investment there. Overall, the study offers little support for the proposition that the IMP has led to a more pronounced intra-EC concentration of economic activity.

FORMULATING SPECIFIC HYPOTHESES ABOUT THE EFFICIENCY OF THE IMP

So much for an examination of a selection of studies which have sought to add an IMP dimension to the explanation of extra- or intra-FDI in the EC; or which help shed light on that dimension if its impact on other explanatory variables could be assessed. The following paragraphs return to consider more specifically the hypotheses set out earlier in this chapter, and to examine first how far the studies so far described throw light on these, and second to present some new findings of our own.

Hypothesis 1

While the Barrell and Pain study showed that Japanese FDI in the EC was significantly and positively related to non-tariff barriers, the Buigues and Jacquemin and Clegg studies supported the proposition that the IMP is leading to an increase in extra-EC FDI, as the US and Japan seek to be 'insiders' in a market favoring the production of firms located in that market.[56] At the same time, research by Agarwal, Hiemenz and Nunnenkamp (1995) and Pain and Lansbury (1996) would appear to refute the hypothesis that intra-EC FDI will fall as a result of deeper economic integration. On the relationship between FDI and trade, the Buigues and Jacquemin research confirmed that US and Japanese exports to the EC were likely to be complementary to, rather than substitute for, US and Japanese FDI in the EC. Another study conducted by ourselves (to be considered later in the chapter) shows a positive relationship exists between these variables and intra-EC transactions, although, consistent with trade theory, the ratio between exports and FDI flows is higher in intra-, than in extra-, EC transactions.

Other evidence on the relationship between intra- and extra-trade and FDI is more casual, although none the less instructive. Data on both extra-and intra-FDI in the EC suggest that the growth in downstream services (notably wholesale trade and business services) is closely correlated with exports from the investing country. For example, the gross product (= value added) of EC based wholesale trading affiliates of US firms rose by 102.9 percent between 1982 and 1989, and by 9.6 percent in the following three years; while over the same time periods, the exports of the US MNEs shipped to their European affiliates rose by 73.7 percent and 28.2 percent. Over the period 1982 and 1989, the rank correlation coefficient between changes in the stock of US assets in EC wholesaling affiliates and US exports to EC countries about which data are available was +0.53, but for that of 1989–1993 it was –0.08.[57]

How far do the above conclusions hold for intra-EC trade and FDI, and to what extent are they country and industry specific? Certainly, as shown by both Eurostat and national data, there appears to be a significantly positive correlation between the recent growth in intra-EC FDI in trade related activities and exports from the investing countries, although the former have tended to outpace the latter.[58] Since, in their more general model, Pain and Lansbury calculated that the IMP raised intra-EC UK and German FDI in distribution by 27 percent and 2 percent of the 1992 stock of FDI, so it may be concluded that, in part at least, the rise in intra-EC trade is also the result of the IMP.[59]

What next of the interface between trade and FDI in particular industrial sectors? In their analysis of the changing share of US and Japanese FDI in, and exports to, the EC for the period 1984–1990, by two-digit manufacturing sectors, Buigues and Jacquemin (1994) found a Pearson coefficient of +0.10 for the former and +0.64 for the latter. (The respective coefficients which related the share of exports and of FDI for 1990 were +0.75 and +0.28.) However, a more detailed industrial breakdown between changes in the sales of US affiliates in Europe and exports shipped by parent companies to their European affiliates between 1982 and 1989 reveals less impressive correlation coefficients of +0.15 in the case of 22 sensitive sectors and a +0.08 in the case of 12 'non-sensitive sectors'.

Details on the relationship between the sectoral distribution of *intra*-EC FDI and trade are hardly better! We have drawn on two sources of information. The first is that contained in a study by Davies and Lyons (1996), which examined changes in intra- and extra-EC FDI penetration ratios and the export shares of German, French and Spanish industries, between 1987 and 1992.[60] The authors showed there was little systematic relationship between the level of foreign ownership, or changes in that ownership, and the level and change in either intra- or extra-EC trade. While, for example, trade and FDI appeared to closely parallel each other in computers, this was not so in the aerospace and the more traditional sectors, while in the Spanish telecommunications sectors and German electrical machinery sectors, a *decrease* in foreign ownership was associated with an increase in the significance of both intra- and extra-EC trade flows.

The second source of data is that of intra-EC FDI and intra-EC trade, published by Eurostat (or related agencies) for the years 1984 to 1992; these data are only available for some two digit industrial groups. In Table 10.8 we set out a comparison between the changing share of intra-EC FDI flows and intra-EC trade; and, in Table 10.9, the changing trade/FDI ratios over this period.

Three particularly interesting features emerge from these tables. The first is the increasing share of intra-EC FDI flows directed to the less technology intensive sectors particularly in the 1980s; this is in marked contrast to the industrial pattern of US and Japanese direct investment in the EC. However – and second – as shown by the changing share of trade flows, it would seem that the intra-EC exports of EC countries are also becoming less technology intensive. Since the more technology intensive sectors are also those which tend to be more integrated across national boundaries, these data suggest that, even by the early 1990s, the European MNEs had still not fully geared their European operations to meet the needs of the internal market. Third, as revealed by Table 10.9, the trade/FDI ratios have fallen substantially over the last decade, although there is no distinct sectoral pattern which emerges.

Table 10.8 Comparisons between share of intra-EC FDI and trade by broad industrial sector, 1984–1992 (percent)

	1984–1986		1987–1989		1990–1992	
	FDI	Trade	FDI	Trade	FDI	Trade
More technology intensive	73.0	59.9	47.0	61.3	50.6	62.1
Chemicals	30.8	18.4	28.4	16.6	9.9	15.9
Non-electrical machinery	15.7	10.6	3.2	11.4	10.1	11.1
Electrical and electronic equipment	18.4	14.8	13.3	15.4	15.3	15.6
Transport equipment	8.1	16.1	2.1	18.0	15.3	19.5
Less technology intensive	26.9	40.1	43.0	38.7	49.5	37.9
Primary and processed food products	9.6	12.5	22.7	11.3	27.2	10.8
Metal and metal products	0.7	3.6	6.4	3.8	3.5	4.1
Other industries	16.5	23.9	23.9	23.7	18.8	23.1
All industries	100.0	100.0	100.0	100.0	100.0	100.0
ECUs (billion)	1.33	319.9	6.67	424.2	9.02	547.2

Table 10.9 Intra-EC trade/FDI ratios, 1984–1992

	1984–1986	1987–1989	1990–1992
More technology intensive	196.4	82.9	74.4
Chemicals	142.7	37.1	97.2
Non-electrical machinery	160.8	325.5	66.5
Electrical and electronic equipment	192.9	73.8	61.9
Transport equipment	478.1	540.3	77.5
Less technology intensive	355.6	46.4	46.6
Primary and processed food products	312.2	31.5	24.1
Metal and metal products	1047.2	37.7	69.7
Other industries	346.5	62.9	74.6
All industries	239.5	63.5	60.7

Note: Annual average: intra-EC FDI is defined as inward investment flows into all Member States of the EC from other Member States of the EC; and intra-EC trade as value of exports between members of the Community.

Source: Eurostat (1994).

Hypothesis 2

We set out some of the changes in the geographical distribution of both extra- and intra-FDI in the EC over the past decade or so. Overall, the share of all FDI by the major EC countries directed to the EC increased in almost all manufacturing and service sectors between the mid-1980s and mid-1990s. However, there seems little to suggest that there has been any general increase in the geographical concentration or agglomeration of FDI *within* the EC, except in a few technology or information intensive sectors thought likely to be the most responsive to the IMP. For example, the UK, which already had a revealed comparative FDI advantage in financial services, has continued to maintain that advantage. In the pharmaceutical sector, there has been further concentration of both intra- and extra-EC FDI in the UK and France. The six core countries accounted for more than four-fifths of the EC related cross-border M&A transactions between 1989 and 1994 (UNCTAD, 1998). However, if anything, the data – fragmentary as they are – suggest that there has been a modest decrease in concentration of FDI in the electronic components, office and computing machines, industrial instruments and business services in the four most populated EC countries.

Outside the knowledge intensive sectors, we observe that, while the core EC countries have continued to attract the bulk of new FDI and cross-border M&A activity, in auto components and in auto assembling, Spain has become a major new production outlet and has attracted both Japanese auto companies and joint ventures of EC and US MNEs. In chemicals, too, there has been some geographical restructuring of new FDI, particularly from Germany and the UK towards the Netherlands and Spain. At the same time, all the major EC chemical MNEs have increased their share of production both elsewhere in the EC (and, outside the EC, in the US) since the IMP was first announced. This pattern of localization and globalization going hand and hand is also repeated in the textile and clothing industry; but, in spite of the increased Europeanization of this sector, imports from outside the EC continued to rise at the expense of the output of indigenous firms (Agarwal, Hiemenz and Nunnenkamp, 1995).

A related hypothesis to the one stated at the beginning of this section is that the lowering or removal of non-tariff barriers will reduce the growth of *extra*-EC FDI in those sectors in which *intra*-EC FDI expands the most rapidly. But, according to Agarwal, Hiemenz and Nunnenkamp (1995), this has not happened. By considering up to nine sectors for each of four countries, viz. France, Germany, the Netherlands and the UK, the authors secured bivariate correlation coefficients between changes in the intra- and extra-FDI between 1985 and 1992, which were generally positive, rather than negative as might be predicted. This, in the words of the authors, suggests that the 'globalization strategies of the major EC investors were largely independent of integration in Europe' (Agarwal, Hiemenz and Nunnenkamp, 1995, p. 12).

Hypothesis 3 (Country effects)

Earlier in this chapter we showed that the share of FDI inflows to the GFCF of all EC countries, except Ireland, increased markedly in the five years immediately following the announcement of the IMP, since when it has fluctuated between 5.3 percent and 7.2 percent. It may be further noted that, although the share of inbound FDI flows to GFCF varies between member states (in 1995 it varied from 2.6 percent in Germany and Italy to 20.4 percent in Belgium), the same or similar rate of increase between the first and second half of the 1980s was experienced by most countries.

When the foreign participation ratio of the EC is compared with that of other developed countries, including the rest of Europe, it can be seen that, in the early 1990s, there was some relative retrenchment of FDI in North America, although, in 1994, the ratios for both Canada and the US were nearer their level of the late 1980s. The buoyancy of the foreign participation ratio in the EC in the 1990s is entirely consistent with the increased share of intra-EC cross-border M&As in all cross-border M&As.

Although we only have piecemeal evidence about the *changing* share of the foreign ownership of particular sectors in EC countries, we do know that, during the 1980s, the share of foreign enterprises in the manufacturing production of five EC countries, viz. France, Germany, Ireland, Italy and the UK, increased in all cases except for Germany where it remained the same. We also know the sectors in which MNEs or their affiliates tend to concentrate, viz. computers, motor vehicles, pharmaceuticals, electronic equipment and industrial instruments (OECD, 1993; Dunning, 1993a). If one, then, examines the industrial composition of the sales of US affiliates in the EC manufacturing in 1993, one sees that between 70 percent and 75 percent were in one or the other sensitive sectors identified by the Commission; and that this percentage has hardly changed since 1982.[61] This percentage compares with a figure between 50 percent and 55 percent of the value added in all manufacturing by *both* indigenous and foreign owned firms in the Community (Buigues, Ilzkovitz and Lebrun, 1990). Since the pattern of FDI by the other major European countries in the EC is broadly similar to that of the US, it may be reasonably concluded that, relative to locally owned firms, the affiliates of foreign MNEs are more concentrated in IMP sensitive sectors; and, excepting for medical instruments, that their share of the output of the *most* sensitive sectors has increased – at least marginally – since the early or mid-1980s.[62]

To some extent, then, these data are further corroboration that, since the mid-1980s, quite a substantial part of FDI in both North America and Europe has been undertaken as part of a deliberate strategy of MNEs designed to maintain or advance their global competitive positions. In so far, too, as economic integration increases inter-firm rivalry, and reduces the transaction costs of engaging in cross-border M&As, it may lead to a change in the ownership of firms, without there being any change in the location of production or trading patterns.

Again, such fragmentary evidence as we have points to M&As being concentrated in the sectors which have been most affected by the IMP. Using data on M&As involving US and European companies[63] between 1985 and 1991 and classified by 19 industrial sectors, it can be shown that 69 percent of the value of the transactions, in which US firms were the buyers and 75 percent of those in which European firms were the buyers, were in the sensitive sectors. For this chapter, we conducted an additional econometric exercise which attempted to test the proposition that changes in the sectoral distribution of US FDI in the leading EC countries would be related to the sensitivity of the sectors to the IMP. The proposition here, derived from the trade and FDI literature, is that the FDI directed to the EC, both absolutely and relative to trade, will be positively correlated to the removal of the trade barriers as US firms seek to become 'insiders' in a more liberalized EC market.

In testing this hypothesis, we compared (by use of pooled data for two time periods, viz. 1982 to 1989 and 1989 to 1993), the change in the sales of US affiliates in Europe, in 31 industrial sectors between 1982 and 1993 to five explanatory variables, viz. (1) the sales of established US affiliates in 1982 and 1989 (this we took to be a proxy for agglomeration economies and a 'familiarity' index for new investors),[64] (2) changes in market size of the EC, (3) changes in the value added per person employed in the EC (as a measure of labor productivity), (4) changes in exports of US MNEs to their European affiliates, and (5) a dummy variable for the IMP, which we relate to the perceived sensitivity of the sectors on a scale of 1 (little sensitivity) to 3 (high sensitivity).[65]

We calculated two equations: one with and one without an IMP variable. The results of the former are set out in Table 10.10. Only the market size variable was statistically significant at the 5 percent level for a one-tailed test. The perceived impact of the IMP was shown to be negatively (although not significantly) related to the sectoral increases in the sales of US subsidiaries.

Inadequate sectoral statistics preclude us from conducting such a detailed exercise for intra-EC FDI. The best we can do is to use the Eurostat data on the sectoral composition of intra-EC FDI flows for the period 1985 to 1992, and see how far these are related to the kind of variables identified in the earlier exercise. However, we did not, in this instance, calculate an agglomeration variable, partly because there are no data on the stock of intra-EC FDI in the early 1980s; and partly because the sectoral breakdown is too broad to calculate a meaningful index. Also, in place of variable (4) in the previous exercise, we computed an index of intra-EC trade published by DEBA (vd). However, because Eurostat FDI data are only available for seven industrial sectors – and there are no sectoral breakdowns by countries – we have divided the period into six three-year intervals[66] to obtain an acceptable number of observations. All FDI data are then expressed as a ratio of the three-year average flow to the average FDI flow for 1984 and 1985. For the first three explanatory variables, viz. change in market size, labor productivity and intra-EC trade, we adopt a similar procedure. However, instead of introducing a dummy variable for the IMP of 1–3, we ranked each of the seven sectors according to their perceived sensitivity of that to the removal of non-tariff barriers (1 = high and 7 = low).[67]

Table 10.10 The determinants of changes in sales of US industrial affiliates in Europe classified by industrial sector, 1982–1993

	Δ Sales[a]
Constant	0.5317 (0.7407)
Actual sales[b]	–0.0171 (1.0563)
Change in market size[c]	0.6500* (0.3694)
Change in productivity[d]	0.4444 (0.7065)
Change in exports[e]	–0.0298 (0.0688)
Dummy[f]	–0.1175 (0.1360)
Adjusted R^2	0.1020
F statistic	1.976

Notes:
[a] Change in sales of US affiliates in Europe 1982–1983 and 1989–1993. These are treated as pooled data.
[b] Actual sales of US affiliates in Europe 1982, 1989.
[c] Change in EC market size 1982–1989 and 1989–1993.
[d] Change in EC labor productivity 1982–1989 and 1989–1993.
[e] Change in exports of US MNEs to Europe 1982–1989 and 1989–1993.
[f] Dummy variable on a scale of 1 to 3 to reflect perceived sensitivity of the sector to IMP.
* Significance level 5% (one-tailed test).

Sources: US Department of Commerce (1985, 1992, 1995), Eurostat (1994), Buigues, Ilzkovitz and Lebrun (1990).

We again formulated two regression equations: one with and one without the IMP variable. The results of the former are set out in Table 10.11. Although these should be treated with even greater caution than the previous exercise, they suggest that the negative effect of IMP on defensive market seeking FDI was outweighed by its positive effect on other forms of FDI – including strategic asset seeking FDI; productivity was also significant at the 1 percent level and correctly signed.

Table 10.11 The determinants of changes in intra-EC FDI flows

	Δ Intra-EC FDI[a]
Constant	–28.4742 (8.9720)
Change in market size[b]	–2.0322 (19.5751)
Change in productivity[c]	36.0070* (9.4544)
Change in intra-EC trade[d]	–0.3782 (14.8770)
Dummy[e]	1.3865* (0.2225)
Adjusted R^2	0.6521
F statistic	15.244

Notes:
[a] Intra-EC FDI flows, expressed as 3-year moving averages from 1985 to 1992, as a percentage of an average of the base years 1984 and 1985.
[b] Change in EC market size by industrial sector; 3-year moving averages (apparent consumption).
[c] Change in EC labor productivity by industrial sector; 3-year moving averages.
[d] Change in intra-EC trade by industrial sector; 3-year moving averages
[e] Dummy variable on a scale of 1 to 7 to reflect perceived sensitivity of the sector to IMP.
* Significance level 1%.

Sources: As for Table 10.10.

Hypothesis 3 (Sector effects)

Previous sections of this chapter have, in fact, touched upon this hypothesis indirectly in as much as we have shown that many of the effects of the IMP have been sector specific. Moreover, we have indicated the types of sectors in which the foreignness or multinationality of enterprises is perceived to confer a competitive advantage. However, it is worth recalling that the main indigenous competitors to foreign firms investing in the EC are significant MNEs in their own right. Moreover, for the most part, the MNEs for Europe are from the same industrial sectors in which inbound FDI is concentrated.[68]

Hypothesis 4

We decided to sidestep the issue of the distinctive characteristics of MNEs – and, indeed, that of the intra-firm co-ordination and transaction costs – by estimating the revealed employment advantage (REA) of foreign, in this case the US, affiliates in the EC. This we did by calculating the share of *total* EC employment in the EC accounted for by US affiliates in each of some 30 industrial sectors in 1993 and then dividing that share by the share of all EC industrial employment accounted for by all US affiliates. A ratio above 1 would indicate US firms had a comparative REA in that sector; and a ratio below 1 that they had a comparative disadvantage.

The REA is the first of the explanatory variables we relate to the dependent variable, which, again, is the increase in the sales of US affiliates in Europe between 1982 and 1993. The other independent variables are export/local sales (FDI) ratios of US MNEs, which we use as a proxy for the preference of US firms to satisfy their European markets from a US cf. a European location, and a dummy variable (on a scale of 1 to 3) which measures the perceived sensitivity of the sector to the IMP.

The results, which are also set out in Table 10.12, explain almost 30 percent of the sales growth of US affiliates. Both the REA and export/local sales ratios are significant at the 5 percent level; however, the IMP variable adds little explanatory value. The REA variable is positively related and the export/FDI ratio is negatively related to the increase in the sales of US subsidiaries in Europe.

Table 10.12 Some determinants of change in sales of US affiliates in the EC classified by industrial sector

	Δ Sales[a]
Constant	0.9814** (0.3258)
REA[b]	0.7227* (0.2776)
Log export/FDI intensity[c]	–0.3891** (0.1389)
DUM[d]	–0.0309 (0.1182)
Adjusted R^2	0.2827
F Statistic	7.174

Notes:

[a] Change in the sales of US affiliates in Europe, 1989/1982 and 1993/1989. These are treated as pooled data.

[b] Revealed employment advantage (REA) of US affiliates in Europe (EU). The first step was to calculate year values for each of the years 1982, 1989 and 1993. The numerator here is the ratio of the percentage of employment in US affiliates of all employment in the EC for each industrial sector, and the denominator is the percentage of the employment in US affiliates of all employment in the EC for all industrial sectors. The second step was to use these values to calculate changes in the REA ratio between 1982 and 1989, 1989 and 1993.

[c] Export/FDI intensity is the ratio of the growth of exports of US MNEs to their European affiliates (1989/1982 to 1993/1989), the growth of sales of the EC affiliates of US firms (1989/1982 and 1993/1989).

[d] Dummy variables (on a scale of 1 to 3) perceived sensitivity of the sector to the IMP.

* Significance level 5%.

** Significance level 1%.

Sources: As for Table 10.10.

CONCLUSIONS

The preparation of this chapter has been like doing a difficult jigsaw puzzle with many pieces missing! Only very faintly and imperfectly is one able to see the full picture.

We have used most of the statistical evidence at our disposal to examine changes in the extent and pattern of extra- and intra-FDI in the EC (or Western Europe) since the early 1980s. That part of the jigsaw is reasonably clear. FDI in the EC has risen faster than in most other parts of the world (save for Japanese FDI in parts of East Asia); but there is little reason to suppose that this has been at the expense of non-EC FDI.

Within the EC, there have been some discernible changes, both in industrial structure and in the geography of economic activity. Of the former, the relative growth of FDI in knowledge intensive activities is, perhaps, the most significant trend – although this is by no means confined to Europe. Of the latter, the access of Greece, Portugal and Spain – and particularly Spain – has led to a modest decentralization of other than the most technology and information intensive activities from the six core EC countries.

Our analysis also confirms that the growth of intra-EC and Japanese FDI has outpaced that of the US over the last decade or more. However, whereas the proportion of goods exported from US subsidiaries in the EC has remained about the same since 1982, other forms of intra-EC trade – including that of European MNEs, have risen quite rapidly.

When trying to isolate the significance of the possible explanation for these events, one is faced with the most challenging conceptual and data problems; and our conclusions must be extremely tentative. We would, however, make five observations:

1. While regionalization and globalization are distinct spatial concepts, it is difficult to perceive how globalization could have had the consequences it has in Europe if the IMP (or something like it) had not come about. This is particularly the case in sectors which are the most internationalized, although it is worth recalling that even the most globally oriented MNEs tend to practice regional, rather than global R&D and production strategies (UNCTAD, 1993b).
2. Almost all the studies examined in this chapter point to the fact that the main dynamic impact of the IMP on FDI flows has been through its effects on other variables affecting FDI – and noticeably market size, income levels, the structure of economic activity and agglomeration economies. *Inter alia*, this makes it very difficult – and indeed, of questionable value – to consider IMP (or a proxy for same) as an independent variable, except perhaps, in the years immediately following 1985, when FDI was influenced more by

the expectations of the program's outcome. But, even considering the IMP as an independent variable, the few studies – including some new ones presented in this chapter – all generally agree that it has stimulated both extra- and intra-EC FDI, but the former more than the latter – but not as significantly so as have other variables.

3. It seems clear that the effects of IMP are sector specific, and there is some evidence that, as hypothesized by trade and FDI theory, extra-EC FDI has increased more in sensitive than in non-sensitive sectors since the early 1980s – and equally important – more in these sectors than elsewhere in the developed world. The Pain and Lansbury study also reveals that, within the IMP, both UK and German FDI in either EC countries would have been less – and particularly so in some of the more sensitive sectors, e.g. finance and insurance.
4. This chapter has examined the validity of several propositions which emerge from trade and FDI theory. First, it has shown that there is only limited evidence that the geographical concentration of economic activity has increased, even in the sectors which benefit from the substantial plant economies of scale. At the same time, the fact that higher-value, e.g. innovatory, activities have remained so highly embedded in the core countries, while the markets for the products has increased substantially, is testimony to the continuing drawing power of the economies of agglomeration in these sectors. Again, consistent with the predictions of neo-classical trade theory, the IMP may well have helped disperse resource based and/or lower-value activities; and, in part, this is documented by the changing structure of intra-EC FDI and trade.

   Second, we have found that there is a complementarity between FDI and trade in most of (but not all) industrial sectors, and that the IMP has done nothing to lessen this complementarity. However, this relationship is less strong for intra-EC than for extra-EC FDI. Third, as predicted by FDI theory, the most significant growth in the *share* of sales of foreign affiliates has occurred in those sectors and countries in which the competitive advantages of these – relative to their indigenous rivals – firms are the most marked. Such fragmentary evidence as we have gives no support to the proposition that non-MNEs have improved their competitive positions *vis-à-vis* MNEs; though, in some sensitive sectors, EC based MNEs have improved their competitive position *vis-à-vis* US and Japanese MNEs; and it is highly likely the IMP has contributed towards this improvement.
5. A substantial proportion of the extra- and intra-EC FDI in the EC since the mid-1980s has taken the form of M&As; and part of the rationale for this has been to acquire strategic assets to advance the regional and/or global competitiveness of the acquiring firm. Although such M&As are essentially a global phenomenon (Walter, 1993), those involving EC firms as sellers

have undoubtedly been facilitated by the IMP. The effect of these M&As on the intra-EC location (cf. the ownership) of economic activity is ambiguous; but, in the majority of cases, there has been some restructuring of activity of the acquired firm; and this, as well as the distinctive sourcing and exporting policies of the acquiring firms may well effect both intra- and extra-EC trade.

Our final observation is that, while for some sectors and for some foreign investors, the dynamic effects of the IMP have already largely materialized, for others – and especially for the service sectors and for Japanese (and possibly some European) investors – these consequences have yet to work themselves out. It is hoped that the next few years will help us fit some new pieces into the jigsaw portraying the effects of the IMP, although these will become increasingly difficult to isolate from the consequences of European monetary integration – mark 3 – in the ever deepening integration of Europe.

NOTES

1. Now called the European Union (EU). However, as most of the analysis contained in this chapter predates the formation of the European Union, we shall use the expression European Community (EC) throughout.
2. For a review of these studies, see UN (1993a).
3. Particularly in the Irish case, where intra- and extra-EC inward investment increased dramatically in the decade after Ireland joined the EC in 1973.
4. A good example is provided by Spain and Portugal. In the five years after their accession to the EC, the average annual increase in the stock of extra- and intra-EC FDI into Portugal was 56.7 percent and into Spain 128.3 percent. In the period 1990–1996, the corresponding increases were 5.7 percent and 10.2 percent (UNCTAD, 1998). Moreover, a serious deficiency of multi-variate studies is that they rarely consider the second-order effects of FDI on the other variables – notably market size and GNP per head – which are usually included in the regression equations.
5. The year prior to the announcement of the Internal Market Program (IMP).
6. Estimates by scholars vary. Yannopoulos (1992) calculated that, for the period 1980–1984, extra-EC FDI *flows* were two-thirds of all inbound FDI; this compared with an estimate made by Molle and Morsink (1991) for the years 1975–1983 of 75 percent; and that by Pelkmans of the percentage of extra-FDI stocks for 1978 of total FDI in the EC of 57 percent (Pelkmans, 1984).
7. Defined both in terms of their GNP per head, and the proximity of their industrial and commercial heartlands to Central Western Europe, viz. Belgium, Luxembourg, France, Germany, Italy, Netherlands and the United Kingdom. We accept, of course, that *parts* of industrial France, the UK and Italy are as far removed from the Ruhr Valley as is Southern Denmark!
8. The ratio is a kind of revealed comparative advantage of the EC in attracting FDI from other EC countries. In 1980 the ratio for German/EC FDI was 1.06; for France 1.00; for Belgium/Luxembourg 1.65; for Denmark 1.31; for the Netherlands 0.89; and for the UK 0.50. The below average figures for the Netherlands and the UK reflected the above average share of North American FDI attracted to these countries. By contrast, the US/EC intensity ratio was 0.60 and the Japanese/US ratio was 0.30.

9. Obviously there were exceptions to this rule. Philips of Eindhoven is one example of an EC MNE which totally restructured its European activities in the first 20 years of the ECM.
10. The most noticeable increase was, perhaps, recorded by the UK where the share of its outward stock directed to the EC rose from 7 percent in 1960 to 15 percent in 1971 and 21 percent in 1985.
11. The transaction costs of tariff barriers primarily represent an addition to the transport costs of exporting or importing goods and services. Those of non-tariff barriers represent a whole range of cost-enhancing measures which affect not only the plant specific costs for production of goods and services, but firm specific costs of transacting and co-ordinating the various extra-plant activities, including the procurement of inputs and the marketing and distribution of outputs. It is only very recently that economists have paid serious attention to the effects of economic integration on these latter costs – and on how integration may help upgrade the competitive advantages of multi-product firms whose activities spread across national boundaries.
12. The theory of international production attempts to explain the extent and pattern of the foreign owned value activities of firms (i.e. production financed by FDI). Like trade, the unit of account is the output of firms and countries, as distinct from FDI, which is an input measure. At the same time, FDI is often taken to be a proxy for foreign production.
13. As, for example, determined by most articles in a Special edition of the *Oxford Review of Economic Policy* (Vol. 14, No. 2) 1998 on 'Trade and Location'. Exceptions include the work of trade theorists, such as Helpman and Krugman (1985), Markusen (1995) and Markusen and Venables (1998).
14. For a survey of the current state of FDI theory, see Dunning (1993a) and Caves (1996). For a recent examination of the impact of MNEs on the geography of international production, see Dunning (1998) and Kozul-Wright and Rowthorn, 1998).
15. This it may do for two reasons. First, the IMP is likely to improve the efficiency of 'insider' relative to 'outsider' firms (this, after all, is one of its main intentions) . Second, it will encourage the restructuring of activities by foreign firms in so much as the unified market enables a more efficient disposition of resources.
16. Although the Common Market came into being on 1 January 1958, it was not until the late 1960s that a tariff-free zone in the EC was finally accomplished.
17. Although between 1985 and 31 December 1992, the majority of directives designed to remove non-tariff barriers had already been put into effect.
18. Throughout, we consider the 12 countries. These include Spain, Portugal and Greece, which joined the EC in the early 1980s, but exclude Austria, Finland and Sweden, which acceded to the EU in 1995.
19. There are, of course, other normalizing factors which one should consider, e.g. changes in exchange rates. Most data in this chapter are expressed in US dollars and there have been some noticeable fluctuations in the value of that currency relative to European countries over the past 15 years – and particularly in the £/$ rate.
20. Of course, for individual sectors of the EC, the share of FDI was considerably higher. For further details see UN (1993b).
21. Before dipping again in 1996 to 5.9 percent.
22. Broadly equivalent to flows, except that changes in stock are more likely to incorporate reinvested profits than the flow data.
23. For the purposes of this exercise, we have included Denmark in the non-core countries.
24. Greece joined the 9 EC countries in 1981 and Portugal and Spain in 1985.
25. For further details, see the various annual surveys on foreign direct investment in the US, published in the Survey of Current Business (US Department of Commerce).
26. These two countries alone increased their share of intra-EC FDI from 3.3 percent in 1985–1987 to 8.6 percent in 1992–1993.
27. Particularly – and rather surprisingly – in the financial services sector. While, for example, in the period 1989–1994, 56.9 percent of all extra EC mergers and acquisitions (M&As) involved UK target firms, the corresponding UK proportion for intra-EC M&As was 15.4 percent.

28. Defined as the ratio of the share of a recipient (host) country (or region) (b) of the total FDI from another (= home) country (or region) (a) to the share of the former country (or region) of the total FDI from all countries, excluding that of the investor country. Expressed algebraically, qab = Iab/Ia*/[I*b/I*–I*a], where qab = intensity of a's investment in b, Iab = investment by a (home country) in b (host country) and * = summation of FDI across all countries (world). See Petri (1994).
29. In 1990, the European Commission identified 40 industrial (e.g. goods-producing) sectors which, prior to the announcement of the IMP, were subject to high or moderate non-tariff barriers. To this list may be added some service sectors, notably finance, insurance, business services and wholesale trade in the service sector. See Buigues, Ilzkovitz and Lebrun (1990), and Sapir (1993).
30. Namely the years of the benchmark surveys of US foreign direct investment (1977, 1982 and 1989) and for each year from 1991 onwards.
31. Unfortunately, there are no recent separate data for the EC itself, but, since the sales of FDI in the EC in 1992 were 90 percent of those in all Western Europe, these data serve as a good proxy for those of the EC.
32. One exception is the business services sector. Particularly impressive was an increase in sales of computer and data processing services of US affiliates in Europe of 399.6 percent between 1989 and 1993.
33. Which includes business services.
34. The authors note some exceptions to the rule, e.g. German FDI in all developing countries and in Asia, and UK FDI in Asia.
35. Contrary to the investment diversion hypothesis, the authors found that the correlation coefficients (again for France, Germany, Netherlands and the UK) between trade and investment were shown to be positive and significant.
36. Notably where agglomerative economies are present, e.g. in some high technology sectors.
37. When expressed as a proportion of the GNP of EC countries, the stock of inbound FDI increased from 4.8 percent in 1980 to 10.6 percent in 1990 and 12.2 percent in 1993, and to 15.2 percent in 1997 (UNCTAD, 2000).
38. Mainly US. According to Walter (1993), the value of cross-border M&As involving EC firms (but excluding extra-EC M&As, where EC were the buyers) rose from $11 526 million in 1985 to $139 033 million in 1989–1990.
39. Often taken as a proxy for EC when separate data on the EC are not available.
40. And, of course, of other determinants not identified by the other variables.
41. For a more detailed specification and formal results of these models, see Dunning (1997a, 1997b).
42. In fact, the growth of the FDI stock into the EC between 1990 and 1995 was almost exactly the same as that into other developed countries (excepting Japan), viz. 37.7 percent compared with 37.9 percent (UNCTAD, 1998).
43. A prediction which seems unlikely to be borne out by the facts!
44. For US FDI only. The study also included an analysis of FDI in developing countries, but we are not concerned with these results here.
45. A study on Swedish FDI, covering the period 1975–1990, confirmed the significance of agglomerative effects, particularly in high technology sectors, but finds that market size and the availability of skilled labor are generally more important locational determinants (Braunerhjelm and Svensson, 1995).
46. A dummy variable of 1 was included for each year from 1986 onwards and 0 for 1985 and previous years.
47. The size of which was, itself, increasing as a result of more intra-EC trade and FDI. This idea is confirmed in a study by Yanawaki (1993) on the intra-EC distribution of employment in 236 Japanese manufacturing subsidiaries in 1988. Yanawaki found that the most significant explanatory variables were relative labor costs, market size and the quality of indigenous technological capacity. His regression analysis supports the predictions of trade theory that inbound FDI will be attracted by the advantaged factor endowments of host countries.
48. As set out by Buigues, Ilzkovitz and Lebrun (1990).
49. This is also the conclusion of Barrell and Pain (1993), in a study of trade barriers (proxied by anti-dumping measures) to Japanese FDI in Europe.

50. The following paragraphs set out some of the results of a study by the authors, commissioned by the Economists' Advisory Group (EAG). Full results appear in EAG (1998). For a more general analysis of the interaction between FDI, technological change and economic growth in Europe, see Barrell and Pain (1997).
51. Apart from that in Ireland.
52. These two countries accounted for 45 percent of the outward FDI stock of EC countries in 1994.
53. As identified in the FDI literature. See Dunning (1993a).
54. These were predicated to affect the availability of finance for foreign investment.
55. Perhaps an even more telling statistic might have been the share of US registered patents by firms of particular countries attributable to research undertaken by their foreign affiliates. See, for example, Cantwell and Hodson (1991).
56. Swedenborg and Agmon and Hirsch came to a similar conclusion in respect of Swedish and Israeli FDI in the EC (Swedenborg, 1990; Agmon and Hirsch, 1995).
57. Viz. share of total US exports directed to EC growth of demand in EC divided by growth of demand in the US/European market and non-tariff barriers.
58. Between 1984–1986 and 1990–1992 intra-EC FDI in manufacturing industry rose by 239.4 percent, and inter-EC exports of manufactured goods by 70–79 percent (Eurostat, 1994).
59. Presumably it would be possible to test this hypothesis directly by replacing the FDI related dependent variable by a trade related variable.
60. For the pharmaceuticals, computers, electrical machinery, telecommunications, aerospace, medical instruments, boilers and containers, shipbuilding and rail stock sectors.
61. These and other data are derived from the periodic benchmark surveys of US foreign direct investment published by the US Department of Commerce. More exact estimates are not possible due to differences in the industrial classification used by the Department of Commerce and the European Commission.
62. In their estimates of the changing foreign ownership ratios of nine sensitive sectors in three countries, viz. France, Germany and Spain (27 observations), Davies and Lyons (1996) found that in 18 of these the ratio had increased or remained the same.
63. As derived by the Securities Data Corporation Merger and Corporate Transactions database.
64. See also a discussion on the relationship between information costs and FDI; see Mariotti and Piscitello (1995).
65. Again, as derived from the European Commission.
66. These are (i) 1985, 1986, 1987, (ii) 1986, 1987, 1988, (iii) 1987, 1988, 1989, (iv) 1988, 1989, 1990, (v) 1989, 1990, 1991, (vi) 1990, 1991, 1992.
67. We did this by expressing employment in the three-digit sensitive sectors – as identified by the Commission as a proportion of the employment in the seven two-digit sectors, and ranked these latter sectors by the size of the percentages we obtained.
68. In other words, the EC is involved in a good deal of intra-industry FDI (as well as intra-industry trade).

REFERENCES

Agarwal, J.P., Hiemenz, U. and Nunnenkamp, P. (1995), *European integration: a threat to foreign investment in developing countries*, Kiel Institut für Weltwirtschaft an der Universität Kiel, Discussion Paper No. 246.

Agmon, T. and Hirsch, S. (1995), 'Outsiders and insiders: competitive responses to the internal market,' *Journal of International Business Studies* **26** (2), pp. 1–18.

Barrell, R. and Pain, N. (1993), *Trade Restraints and Japanese Direct Investment Flows*, London: NIESR (mimeo).

Barrell, R. and Pain, N. (1997), 'Foreign direct investment, technological change and economic growth within Europe,' *Economic Journal* **107**, pp. 1170–97.

Braunerhjelm, P. and Svensson, R. (1995), *Host Country Characteristics and Agglomeration in Foreign Direct Investment*, Stockholm: Industrial Institute for EC and Social Research (mimeo), October.

Buigues, P. and Jacquemin, A. (1994), 'Foreign investment and exports to the European Community,' in Mason, M. and Encarnation, D. (eds), *Does Ownership Matter?*, Oxford: Clarendon Press.

Buigues, P., Ilzkovitz, F. and Lebrun, J. (1990), 'The impact of the internal market by industrial sector; the challenge of member states,' *European Economy*, Special Edition, pp. 1–114.

Cantwell, J. and Hodson, C. (1991), 'Global R&D and UK competitiveness,' in Casson, M.C. (ed.), *Global Research Strategy and International Competitiveness*, Oxford: Basil Blackwell, pp. 133–82.

Caves, R. (1996), *Multinational Firms and Economic Analysis*, Cambridge: Cambridge University Press.

Cecchini, P., Catinat, M. and Jacquemin, A. (1988), *The European Challenge 1992. The Benefits of a Single Market*, Aldershot, Hants: Wildwood House.

Clegg, J. (1995), 'The determinants of United States foreign direct investment in the European Community: a critical appraisal,' Bath: University of Bath (mimeo).

Davies, S. and Lyons, B. (1996), *Industrial Organization in the EC*, Oxford: Oxford University Press.

DEBA (vd) (Data for European Business Analysis), Various statistics on EC trade, production and employment issues, Brussels: European Commission.

DeLong, G., Smith, R.C. and Walter, I. (1996), *Global Merger and Acquisition Tables 1995*, New York: Salomon Center (mimeo).

Dunning, J.H. (1993a), *Multinational Enterprises and the Global Economy*, Wokingham, England and Reading, MA: Addison-Wesley.

Dunning, J.H. (1993b), *The Globalization of Business*, London and New York: Routledge.

Dunning, J.H. (1997a and b), 'The European internal market program and inbound foreign direct investment,' *Journal of Common Market Studies* **35** (1 and 2), pp. 1–30 and pp. 189–224.

Dunning, J.H. (1998), 'Globalization and the new geography of foreign direct investment,' *Oxford Development Studies* **26** (1), pp. 47–69.

EAG (1998), 'The single market review sub-series IV,' *Impact on Trade and Investment, Vol. 1, Foreign Direct Investment*, Brussels: The European Commission.

Eurostat (1994), *EU Direct Investment 1984–1992*, Luxembourg: The European Commission.

Helpman, E. and Krugman, P.R. (1985), *Market Structure and Foreign Trade*, Cambridge, MA: MIT Press.

Hirsch, S. (1976), 'An international trade and investment theory of the firm,' *Oxford Economic Papers* **28**, pp. 258–70.

Julius, DeAnne (1990), *Global Companies and Public Policy*, London: Royal Institute of International Affairs.

Kozul-Wright, R. and Rowthorn, R. (1998), 'Spoilt for choice? Multinational corporations and the geography of international production,' *Oxford Review of Economic Policy* **14**, pp. 274–92.

Krugman, P. (1990), *Rethinking International Trade*, Cambridge, MA: MIT Press.

Mariotti, S. and Piscitello, L. (1995), 'Information costs and location of FDIs within the host country: empirical evidence from Italy,' *Journal of International Business Studies* **26** (4), pp. 815–41.

Markusen, J.R. (1995), 'The boundaries of multinational enterprises and the theory of international trade,' *Journal of Economic Perspectives* **9** (2), pp. 169–89.

Markusen, J.R. and Venables, A. (1998), 'Multinational firms and the new trade theory,' *Journal of International Economics* **46**, pp. 185–203.

Molle, W.T.M. and Morsink, R.L.A. (1991), 'Intra-European direct investment,' in Bürgenmeier, B. and Mucchielli, J.L. (eds), *Multinationals and Europe 1992*, London: Routledge.

OECD (1993), *The Contribution of FDI to the Productivity of OECD Nations*, Paris: OECD.

Pain, N. and Lansbury, M. (1996), 'The impact of the internal market on the evolution of European direct investment,' London: NIESR (mimeo).

Pelkmans, J. (1984), *Market Integration in the European Community*, The Hague: Martinus Nijhoff.

Petri, P.A. (1994), 'The regional clustering of foreign direct investment and trade,' *Transnational Corporations* **3** (3), pp. 1–24.

Sapir, A. (1993), 'Sectoral dimension in market services and European integration,' *European Economy* **3**, pp. 23–40.

Srinivasan, K. and Mody, A. (1998), 'Japanese and US firms as foreign investors. Do they march to the same tune?', *Canadian Journal of Economics* **31** (4), pp. 778–97.

Swedenborg, B. (1990), 'The EC and the locational choice of Swedish multinational companies,' Stockholm: Industrial Institute for Economic Social Research, Working Paper No. 284.

UN (1993a), *From the. Common Market to EC*, New York: UN Transnational Corporations and Management Division, Department of Economic and Social Development.

UN (1993b), *World Investment Directory, 1992. Vol. III Developed Countries*, New York: UN Transnational Corporations and Management Division, Department of Economic and Social Development.

UNCTAD (1993a), *Explaining and Forecasting Regional Flows of Foreign Direct Investment*, New York: UN.

UNCTAD (1993b), *World Investment Report 1993: Transnational Corporations and Integrated International Production*, New York and Geneva: UN.

UNCTAD (1994), *World Investment Report 1994: Transnational Corporations, Employment and the Workplace*, New York and Geneva: UN.

UNCTAD (1998), *World Investment Report 1998: Trends and Determinants*, New York and Geneva: UN.

UNCTAD (2000), *World Investment Report 2000: Cross Border Mergers and Acquisitions and Development*, New York and Geneva: UN.

US Department of Commerce (vd) *US Direct Investment Abroad*, Washington, DC: US Government Printing Office.

Walter, I. (1993), 'The role of mergers and acquisitions on foreign direct investment,' in Oxelheim, L. (ed.), *The Global Race for Foreign Direct Investment*, Berlin and New York: Springer-Verlag, pp. 151–76.

Yamawaki, H. (1993), 'Location decisions of Japanese multinational firms in European manufacturing industries,' in Hughes, K. (ed.), *European Competitiveness*, Cambridge: Cambridge University Press, pp. 11–28.

Yannopoulos, G. N. (1992), 'Multinational corporations and the single European market,' in Cantwell, J.C. (ed.), *Multinational Investment in Modern Europe: Strategic Interaction in the Integrated Community*, Aldershot, Hants and Brookfield, VT: Edward Elgar, pp. 329–48.

11. The competitive advantages of countries and MNE activity*

INTRODUCTION

The dynamic interplay between the competitive advantages of countries and those enterprises of a particular nationality is a subject commanding the increasing attention by students of the MNE. Indeed, it has been suggested that a fuller understanding of the nature, content and determinants of this interaction, as it affects the globalization of production and markets, may provide the basis for one of the next advances in the theory of foreign value-added activity[1] (Dunning, 1990).

Since the mid-1970s, the focus of scholars interested in explaining the existence and growth of the MNE has been directed to identifying and evaluating the relative costs and benefits of organizing the cross-border transactions of intermediate products by hierarchies or markets. In the early 1990s, however, renewed attention[2] is being given to explaining the origin and composition of the resources and capabilities[3] of corporations to engage in production outside their national boundaries and to the determinants of their success in managing and organizing the international portfolio of resources rather than ownership or control. Faced with the same economic conditions and prospects, why are some firms significant global players and others are not? Why is the share of international direct investment accounted for by Japanese companies rising so rapidly? Why is Europe claiming a larger share of US based MNE activity than it used to? What explains the rapid growth of the participation of foreign owned firms in the United States? What determines which developing countries will emerge as important international investors? Why do firms conclude strategic alliances with some firms, but avoid them with others? Why is foreign direct investment (FDI) in services rising more rapidly than that in goods?

These are just some of the questions now demanding answers by MNE researchers. What is their response? Well, one response by the scholar of the MNE *qua* MNE[4] is that only part of the explanation for the growth of foreign

* From *Transnational Corporations*, **1**(1) (1992): 135–68. Reprinted as Chapter 5 in J.H. Dunning, *The Globalization of Business*, London and New York: Routledge (1993), pp. 102–27.

owned production may have to do with the increasing propensity of firms to internalize their cross-border transactions. For example, a particular competitive advantage which may help to explain the capability of a firm to supply a particular market, or set of markets, is not, in itself, a sufficient reason for that firm to create, or add value to, that advantage from a foreign located facility.

Take, for example, a pharmaceutical patent as a competitive advantage of a UK MNE. The *origin* of that advantage is likely to be determined by a combination of factors, including the amount of resources the company allocates to innovatory activities, the quality and motivation of R&D personnel, the organization and technical efficiency of the R&D department, and the successful commercialization of that R&D. The *outcome* of that advantage is that it may enable the UK firm to increase its penetration of the world drug market. Is the possession of this advantage an explanation for any increase in foreign production, which might directly arise from such an advantage; or, is it simply to be taken as an exogenous variable which may or may not lead to such production?

Supposing, next, it can be shown that it pays the UK firm to produce the new pharmaceutical product for worldwide distribution from its German plant rather than to export it from its UK plant. Is this an explanation of international production; or is it rather an explanation of the location of economic activity, *given* its ownership? Or, is the explanation of MNE activity concerned only with the circumstances in which a firm engages in foreign value-added activity rather than the next best option open to it, *given* its resources and capabilities and the locational opportunities open to it?

If this latter is thought to be the main focus of interest, then Michael Porter's book *The Competitive Advantage of Nations* will be of limited appeal.[5] If, however, it is perceived that, for example, part of Japanese direct investment in the US car industry is due to the success of Japanese owned firms in producing highly saleable motor vehicles, irrespective of the mode by which this advantage is exploited, and that the reasons for such a success are, themselves, part of the explanation for their foreign activities, then much of the Porter monograph is highly relevant to the student of the MNE.

Our own view is that Michael Porter has rendered a very considerable service in identifying many of the explanatory variables which help us better appreciate some *country specific* explanations of the changing pattern of international production by MNEs. In particular, his extensive field research has advanced our knowledge of why corporations domiciled in some countries have been successful in penetrating foreign markets in some product areas but not in others; and also why some countries have been able to attract inbound MNE activity in some value-added activities but not in others. The book also offers a penetrating insight as to why, in some countries and sectors, the activities of MNEs help stimulate the technological and organizational efficiency of local firms, and why, in other cases, they inhibit it. More generally, many of the ideas and concepts articulated by Porter help enrich our understanding of the dynamic interplay between the strategy of MNEs and the competitive advantages of countries in which they operate.

THE 'DIAMOND' OF COMPETITIVE ADVANTAGE

By now, most readers of this volume will be familiar with the main analytical tools used by Porter in his 1990 book, viz. the diamond of competitive advantage. By competitive advantage, Porter means the ability of a country – or more specifically indigenous firms of a country – to use its location-bound resources in a way which will enable it (them) to be competitive in international markets. Porter likens the determinants of this ability to a diamond which comprises a set of attributes which 'shape the environment in which local firms compete, and which promote or impede the creation of competitive market' (Porter, 1990, p. 71). He goes on to argue that the diamond is a naturally re-inforcing system, with each of its determinants being contingent on the state of the other (ibid., p. 72).

According to Porter, the strength, composition and sustainability of a nation's competitive advantage will be demonstrated by the value of its national product[6] and/or the rate of growth of that product, *relative to that of its leading competitors*. The extent to which a country is successful in achieving this goal then depends on the kind of goods and services produced by its enterprises, and the efficiency at which they are supplied. This, in turn, Porter suggests, rests on the extent and quality of, and the interaction between, four sets of attributes:

1. The quantity and quality of demand for goods and services by its domestic consumers.
2. The level and composition of its natural resources and created factor capabilities.[7]
3. The domestic rivalry of wealth producing agencies, i.e. the nature and extent of interfirm competition.
4. The extent to which its firms are able to benefit from agglomerative or external economies by being spatially grouped in clusters of related activities.

Surrounding and influencing these variables are two others, viz. the role of government and chance. Excluding the MBA component (to be discussed later), Figure 11.1 sets out Porter's depiction of the 'structure' of the diamond.

The main objective of Porter's work is twofold. First, it is to show that these facets of the diamond, and the way in which they interact, will vary between

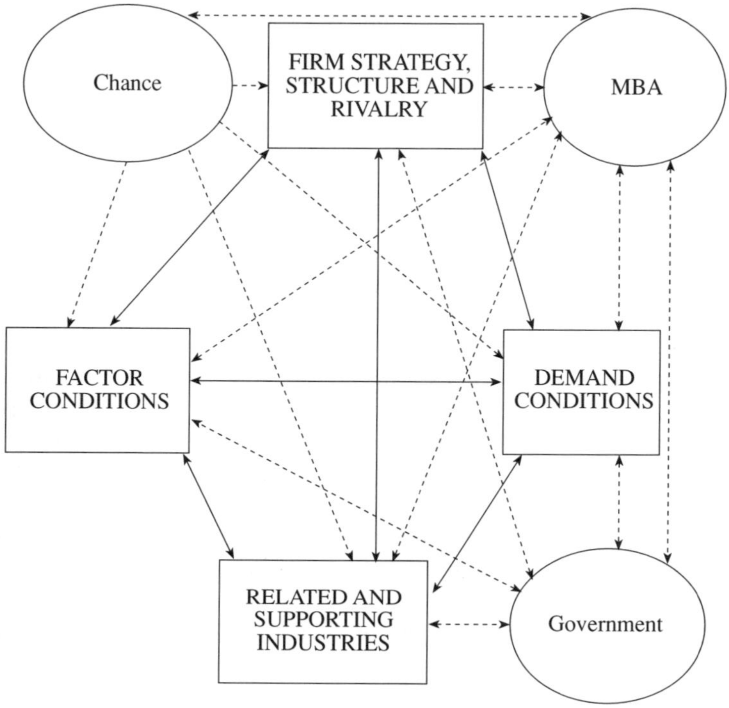

Figure 11.1 The Porter diamond: the complete system

(NB. This figure is basically the same as that portrayed in Figure 9.1, but the latter represents a modification of my earlier emendation to Porter's diamond)

countries. Second, it is to suggest that the principal ways in which countries may improve their competitiveness are to upgrade the quantity or quality of their resources and capabilities and/or to utilize their existing resources and capabilities more efficiently.

Much of Michael Porter's treatise, which extends to over 800 pages, is directed to providing the reader with examples of the ways in which the various facets of the diamond are systemically interrelated. Indeed, one of the author's main contentions is that the efficiency at which the facets of the diamond are coordinated with each other is an important competitive advantage in its own right. To this extent, there is, in Porter's mind, a parallel between the efficiency of the governance of resources and competencies by firms, and that by the governments of countries.

In one sense, there is nothing original in Porter's analysis. Throughout history, a succession of scholars have attempted to identify and evaluate the supply and demand conditions necessary for a country to be competitive in world markets.

Indeed, most have been more comprehensive than Porter, who identifies only four sources of competitive advantage and pays little or no attention to such variables as investment and entrepreneurship.[8] The scholars include those who focus on the so called ESP paradigm, which suggests that an economic prosperity of a country rests on its environment (factor endowments) and markets (E), its economic system (S) and the economic and social policies pursued by its government (P).[9] Most of Porter's analysis can be subsumed under one or other of these headings.

However, what Porter does do, and, we think, does very successfully, is first to set out a paradigm within which the determinants of national competitiveness may be identified, and the way in which they interrelate with each other, and second to offer some hypotheses as to why the significance of these parameters may vary between countries and sectors. The monograph contains eight country case studies[10] and four industry case studies – each of which is addressed to these issues.

The Competitive Advantage of Nations is full of short case studies, persuasive illustrations and intriguing anecdotes of why the structure of competitive advantage, e.g. as between industrial sectors, differs between countries, although Porter makes no attempt to substantiate his propositions by any formal econometric (or for that matter any other) testing! Indeed, on several occasions, the reader feels that the author comes near to rationalizing his arguments, and that, had he chosen to do so, he could have provided illustrations which point to the opposite of the conclusions he draws.

One of the most interesting chapters of the book concerns the role of governments. Porter prefers to consider government not as an attribute of the diamond, but as a fashioner of its structure and efficiency. This makes sense! Although, as producers and consumers, governments may directly affect the supply and demand of both immobile and mobile resources and capabilities affecting competitiveness, they alone have the ultimate responsibility for shaping the framework, or system, under which these resources and capabilities are organized. They set the 'rules of the game' and set the signals, which trigger a response by firms, which determine whether national competitiveness is advanced or not. Moreover, in a variety of ways, they affect the ability and motivation of a nation's citizens and firms, for example to save, to be entrepreneurial, to work efficiently, to accept new ideas and attitudes and to upgrade human and technological capacity. By affecting exchange rates, by participating (or not) in supra-national trading schemes, and by their policies and regulations towards FDI, they may influence the extent to which, and the form in which, a country is involved in international commerce.

It is not the purpose of this chapter to give a detailed critique of Porter's work, but rather to examine its relevance to our understanding of international business activity. In several places, the author addresses himself to the ways in which outward and inward direct investment by MNEs may affect both their own competitiveness and that of the countries in which they operate. In general, however, he seems to believe that the main thrust to improving national competitiveness must come from a better use of indigenous resources and capabilities by domestic corporations. Indeed, Porter frequently cautions governments from relying too much on the affiliates of foreign MNEs to fulfil this task.

While, in principle, we would not wish to take issue with Porter on this point, the fact that between 30 per cent and 40 per cent of the sales of the leading industrial MNEs are now produced outside their national boundaries, and that the value of these sales now considerably exceeds that of international trade, suggests to us that more explicit attention should be given to the ways in which the transnationalization of business activity could affect the nature and character of the diamond of competitive advantage of the countries involved. Certainly, there is ample evidence that the technological and organizational assets of MNEs are influenced by the configuration of the diamonds of the foreign countries in which they produce, and that this, in turn, may impinge upon the competitiveness of the resources and capabilities of their home countries.[11]

Indeed, we would submit that in the global economy of the 1990s, it is entirely appropriate to consider a country's involvement in foreign trade and commerce as a separate exogenous variable affecting the facets of the diamond in the same way in which Porter treats the role of government. However, for the purpose of this chapter, we shall consider only the foreign production of domestic owned firms and the domestic production of foreign based MNEs as they affect the shape of particular national diamonds.

THE ACTIVITIES OF MNEs AS AN ADDITIONAL EXOGENOUS VARIABLE AFFECTING THE DIAMOND

Let us then treat the foreign business activities of MNEs, i.e. the foreign output of domestic MNEs and the domestic output of foreign non-resident owned companies, as an exogenous factor, along with chance and government, affecting the diamond of competitive advantage. Figure 11.2 introduces this new component, i.e. multinational business activity (MBA) into the Porter schema. How might this affect the strength and composition of a nation's competitive advantage?

First, let us briefly remind ourselves of the distinctive features of MNEs, i.e. those which might be attributed specifically to their transnationality. Consider, for example, some of the unique characteristics of *inward* direct investment. First, it is likely to provide a different package of resources and capabilities (e.g. finance capital, technology, management skills, etc.) than that provided by domestic investors. This is partly because these are being imported from a country which has a different combination of competitive advantages, and partly because some of these assets, at least, are likely to be specific to the firm which owns them. Japanese owned subsidiaries in the UK, for example, draw upon a different set of resources and capabilities (or the same resources and capabilities at different prices) than do UK owned firms. Put another way, the sourcing

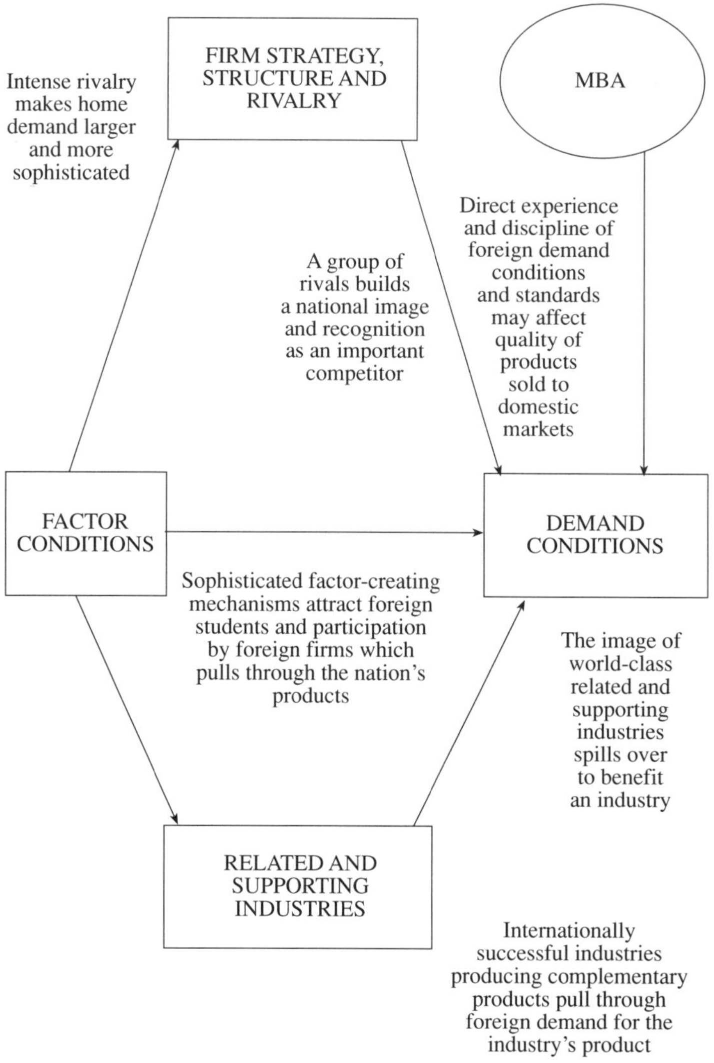

Figure 11.2 Influences on home demand conditions

and marketing opportunities and the production and organizational capabilities of the two groups of firms are likely to be different.

Second, the use made of these assets is likely to be different, partly because the firm is foreign owned, and partly because of the distinctive characteristics of multinationality *per se*, for example, those to do with the international arbitraging of resources and capabilities and the spreading of risks of environmental volatility (Kogut, 1985). *Inter alia*, this suggests that decisions taken by the local subsidiary of an MNE might be different than if it were domestically owned, and that a decision on local resource allocation by a uninational firm might be different than if that firm operated a global network of subsidiaries.

It is the balance between the asset transfer and the control of the use of these assets that is the essence of the uniqueness of MNE activity; although, depending upon the macro-economic situation in the home and host country and the assumptions made about government macro-organizational policies, it is possible that inward investment might also affect the *level* of economic activity.

Consider next some unique features of *outward* direct investment. There are at least three distinguishing attributes of MNEs compared with uninational (or international trading) firms. The first is the additional options to the former in the geographical configuration of their value-added activities. Second, MNEs have more opportunity to diversify their assets and economic activity to reduce exchange and other risks of producing in different countries. Third, MNEs find it easier to gain access to foreign resources, markets, economic systems, business relationships, infrastructure and forms of competition. Indeed (borrowing from Porter's terminology), an important competitive advantage of MNEs is their unique ability to draw upon and make use of different national diamonds of competitive advantage.

Given these (and other) distinguishing characteristics of cross-border business activity, how might it affect the competitiveness of countries? The answer will mainly rest on the values of three contextual variables. The first relates to the *nature* of the MNE activity. Here, the relevant questions include: Is it market seeking, resource seeking, efficiency seeking (e.g. cost reducing) or strategic asset seeking in its intent? Is it primarily to protect or exploit an existing competitive advantage or to acquire a new advantage? Is the investment a greenfield investment or an acquisition of existing assets? Is it a 100 per cent subsidiary or a joint venture? Is it an initial or sequential investment? Is it a stand alone or an integrated investment?

The second group of variables relate to the content and structure of the *existing* competitive advantages of a country. Is domestic rivalry, prior to outward or inward investment, weak or strong? Are its factor endowments plentiful or not? Are domestic consumers demanding more differentiated products or not? What role do governments play in upgrading or standardizing product quality? And so on.

The third main variable, which affects and is affected by the second, are the economic signals provided by governments. To what extent, and in what way, might (or do) governments, directly or indirectly, influence both the competitiveness of the resources and capabilities within their jurisdiction, and the actions of their own, and/or foreign, MNEs?

Clearly, the significance of each of these three variables will depend on (home and host) *country* (or region), *firm* and *activity* specific circumstances; and while, at any given moment of time, they might be independent of each other, over time they are closely interlinked. For example, FDI may both impact on the technological capabilities of rival domestic firms and be affected by them. However, for the purpose of our analysis, it may be appropriate to consider the impact of a change of inward or outward investment on *the existing competitive advantages of firms and industries.*

We would make one other general point. In most analyses of the impact of MBA on national competitiveness, inward and outward direct investment are considered independently of each other. Although each kind of investment has its distinctive consequences, there is some merit in considering these as opposite sides of the same coin. This is especially so when looking at the macro-organizational dynamics of competitiveness. Though there is no necessary connection between a change in inward investment and the propensity of domestic firms to engage in outward investment (i.e. it may affect only domestic resource allocation), in practice, in a world in which four-fifths of MNE activity is within the advanced industrial countries, and is primarily intra-industry in character, the volume and structure of outward and inward direct investment are likely to be closely interwoven, and governed by broadly similar factors.

The evidence suggests, however, that the relationship between the two is not straightforward (Dunning, 1985). Indeed, a fascinating topic for additional research (and one not really tackled at all by Porter) is the identification of the circumstances in which changes in the level and/or structure of outward and inward MBA move in similar directions (i.e. are complementary to each other), and those in which they move in opposite directions (i.e. are substitutable for each other).[12]

For the purpose of this chapter, however, we will try to analyse some of the implications of a spontaneous or induced change in outward and inward MNE activity on each of the four facets of the diamond of competitive advantage, both directly and indirectly through their repercussions on the actions of government. Again, we shall concentrate on just one or two aspects of each of the four facets. We would also reiterate that the facets are closely interlinked and that the more one takes a dynamic perspective of the impact of MNE activity, the less useful it is to consider each competitive-related variable separately.

The Conditions of Demand (see Figure 11.2)

Porter argues that the *structure* of domestic demand may affect the competitiveness of firms in the international market by providing an impetus for domestic firms to produce high quality, well designed, reliable and differentiated goods, relative to those supplied by their foreign competitors. Assuming that such an emphasis on product consistency or differentiation, rather than on a cost-reducing strategy, is the most effective strategy for firms to pursue,[13] to what extent is MNE activity likely to affect, or be affected by, such demand conditions?

Consider first the likely interaction between local patterns of demand and *inward* investment. Here the impact of such investment is likely to depend on the pattern and quality of the existing demand, and how it compares with that of the investing nation and that of other countries in which the MNE produces. It is also likely to depend on the product strategy of the investing firms and the extent to which they perceive product quality and reliability, themselves, to be critical competitive advantages. Another relevant variable is the extent to which a country's citizens have been previously exposed to the products of the investing company (e.g. through exports), and/or how far the products have been produced for export markets by indigenous companies. Much will also rest on whether the FDI takes the form of an acquisition of, or merger with, an existing firm, or a greenfield venture. Finally, over time, the effect on demand quality will rest on the impact of FDI on other facets of the diamond, e.g. domestic rivalry and indigenous technological capability.

It is possible to conceive of a number of possible scenarios. Take, for example, the case of a foreign chocolate producer which acquires a domestic firm in the same line of business, with the aim of gaining access to the local market. Assume, next, that the acquired firm produces high quality chocolate, but that the acquiring firm's competitive advantage lies in producing standardized low cost chocolate. Assume, too, that the acquiring firm has chocolate producing facilities elsewhere in the world, and that it does not intend exporting from the country of the acquired firm. Then, in such cases – unless the acquiring firm simply adds to the product range of the acquired firm – there could be a *lowering* of the standards of demand by the citizens of the host country.[14]

Consider next a scenario in which an investing firm perceives its main competitive advantage to be consistency of the quality of its colour television sets. Assume that some impact on domestic consumer demand (via informing consumers about defect-free products and raising their purchasing standards) may have been made by the exports of the investing country, but that the presence of local production facilities increases this awareness. Then, given the other facets of the diamond, the upgrading of consumer expectations might force other firms to improve the quality, or lower the costs, of their products, which might, in turn, advance their competitiveness. This, in fact, is what appears to have happened as a result of Japanese direct investment in the European and US motor vehicles and consumer electronics industries.

Earlier, we suggested that the impact of inward investment on the diamond of competitive advantage may depend on the purposes of that investment. As far as the impact on *domestic* demand is concerned, this is clearly most likely to be felt where the intention of the investment is to service the domestic, and sometimes adjacent, markets, i.e. import substituting investment, although whether or not this is the case depends, in part at least, on the extent to which the host government may influence the conditions of demand.[15]

Indirectly, demand conditions in the home country, including the influence of the host government over them (e.g. via the level and structure of direct and indirect taxation, their control over the quality of public goods and services, the harmonization and upgrading of technical standards, such as in the procurement of telecommunication systems, and the imposition of rigorous safety, health and environmental regulations) may influence the extent to which foreign firms are willing to invest in the host country, and hence their contribution to other parts of the diamond.

Consider next the way in which foreign activities of domestic MNEs affect, or may be affected by, the structure and content of domestic demand. Take the case of foreign investment by a company from a country in which either intermediate or final product consumers are relatively unsophisticated (perhaps because they are protected from foreign competition) operating in a country in which consumers are highly demanding. Assume, for the moment, that such an investment is possible because the investing companies have some kind of technological or marketing advantage over competitive firms in the recipient country. Then, in so far as consumer expectations and requirements in the foreign market affect the comparability, quality or cost of the product supplied to that market they may, in turn, influence the kinds of products sold in the domestic market. Alternatively, 'easy pickings' in an important foreign market could make a firm less aware of, or less willing to cater to, the more stringent demands of domestic consumers and, indeed, even lower the product quality and reliability of its locally produced output.

On the other hand, the ability of a firm to become an outward investor may be influenced by the extent to which domestic consumers have forced indigenous firms to provide more differentiated or higher quality products than those normally accepted by foreign consumers. A classic case is that of Japanese outward investment in the motor vehicles and consumer electronics sectors;[16] while, similarly, Japanese component suppliers faced with the rigorous demands of their industrial customers in these same sectors are in a better position to supply the latter's competitors in the international market.

So much for extremes and generalities. To what extent can one identify the conditions necessary for MNE activity to act as a vehicle for upgrading consumer demand?[17] We would suggest that the answer is comparatively simple. Consider first the demand conditions of the home country of the inward investor, or the host country of the outward investor, and compare these with those of the countries in which the inward or outward MNE already produces. Second, consider whether or not such knowledge about these conditions, and/or the impetus to create them, could be, or are, being achieved at lower cost, through alternative means. Third, consider whether or not consumers are likely to embrace such conditions. How sensitive are they, for example, to foreign purchasing customs and standards? Fourth, consider the *power* of consumers to influence the quality of products supplied by competitive firms. For example, how significant are they in relation to the purchases of similar products?

Finally, consumer awareness, or pressure for quality improvement, is not always a necessary (and rarely is it a sufficient) condition for the upgrading of consumer demand. Nor is it necessarily desirable if it results in a reduction of economic welfare in other directions.[18] One of the best examples which comes to mind is the quality of in-flight facilities provided by international airlines. Customers, irrespective of their nationality, applaud the quality of food and in-flight service offered by such airlines as Singapore, Thai, Cathay Pacific and Swiss Air, and almost unanimously believe that the calibre of the equivalent amenities provided by many US airlines is inferior. Why, then, it might be asked, don't US air travellers insist upon higher quality from their own airlines?

The answer seems to be twofold. First, the US airlines tend to compete on the basis of (indirect) price reductions, e.g. through generous frequent flyer mileage programmes, which may appeal even to the most discerning business traveller. Second, there is no competition from the best foreign airlines on *domestic* US routes, which still account for the majority of business by US airlines. Thus, whether inward or outward investment raises quality standards very much depends on variables apart from consumer reaction *per se*, although it would be difficult to deny that such foreign investment offers options to consumers which might otherwise not be available.[19]

The Level and Structure of Natural Endowments and Created Capabilities (see Figure 11.3)

Traditionally, the main benefit of inward direct investment has been perceived as the resources and competences it provides – at lower real cost than by the next best alternative modality – and its distinctive impact on the productivity of indigenous resources. This may be achieved in two main ways. First, by the redirection of intermediate products (both along and between value added chains) to where they can be more productively employed. Second, by improving the quality of existing assets and capabilities, or by putting them to

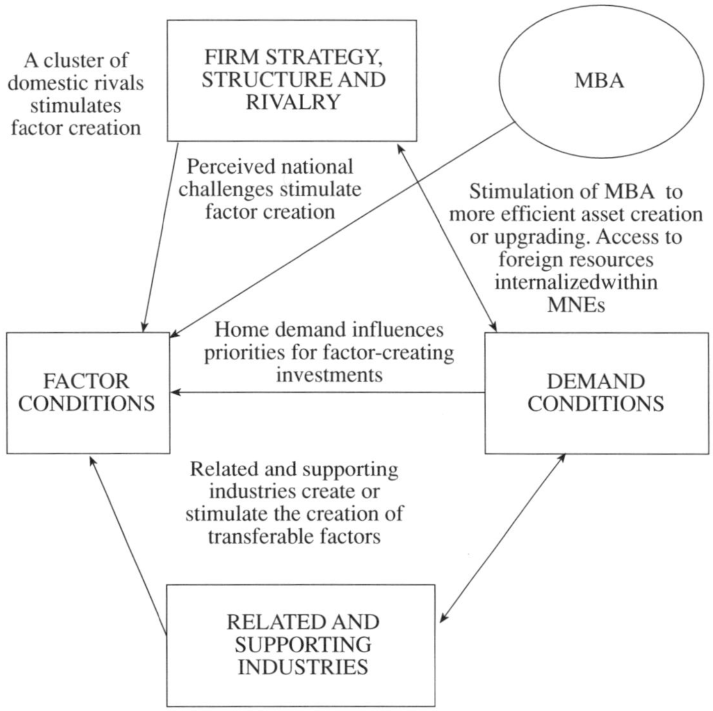

Figure 11.3 Influences on factor creation

more effective use. This latter objective may be accomplished through the injection of more dynamic and successful entrepreneurship and/or by the provision of superior technology and organizational skills. At the same time, inward direct investment has been criticized on the grounds that it may lead to a lowering of the value of indigenous resources and capabilities, e.g. by means of a socially unacceptable rate of depletion of natural resources, or by the repatriation of assets, e.g. R&D facilities, which a foreign firm might have acquired from a domestic firm at a socially unacceptable price.

Outward direct investment may also be viewed in two ways. On the one hand, it may extend the traditional boundaries of the assets owned by the investing companies, and, by opening up new markets, or protecting existing markets, enable domestic resources and capabilities to be used more efficiently. On the other hand, it may transfer such resources and capabilities, notably finance capital and technology, which might have been deployed more productively in the domestic market.

Again, the balance of these costs and benefits, and the interaction between them, will depend on the motives for, and types of, MNE activity; the existing level, pattern and productivity of indigenous resources; and the economic environment in which the investment is made.[20] It will also rest on the alternatives to acquiring resources by FDI.[21] For example, throughout most of the post-war period, Japan has managed to obtain many of the benefits which inward investment might have provided by way of non-equity transfers of technology and human skills (including the conclusion of strategic alliances with foreign firms) and by importing knowledge intensive products. Smaller European countries like The Netherlands, Switzerland and Sweden could not have improved or retained their competitive positions without their companies producing much of their output outside their home countries. By contrast, some commentators (Gilpin, 1975, 1982) have argued that, by exporting advanced technology through outward direct investment, the US has eroded its competitive position, and reduced the capability of its own companies to maintain their innovating capabilities *vis-à-vis* their European and Japanese counterparts.[22]

The distinctive impact of MNEs on the international allocation of natural resources and created capabilities depends not only on ability and desire of such companies to internally transfer such assets between countries but also on the control exerted over the deployment of these and other intermediate products under their control. This is mainly reflected in the type of economic activity undertaken, which, in turn, will affect the kind and productivity of resources used, and the ability of the economy to adapt to changes in world supply and demand conditions. Moreover, in so far as foreign firms may affect both the sourcing of inputs and the destination of outputs, they may also have consequences for the stability of domestic resource deployment.

In examining the specific impact of FDI, it is important to distinguish between short and long run consequences. It is quite possible that in the short run, by producing more efficiently than its indigenous competitors, over a limited range of the value-added chain, a foreign firm may increase domestic output. However, if, in so doing, it competes out of existence a domestic firm that, taking the value added chain as a whole, has a higher domestic value added per resource used, this may lead to a less efficient use of resources and capabilities in the long run.

Such a consequence, however, might be acceptable to the host country if the actions of the foreign firm were in response to competitive market signals and the resources released could be redeployed more productively elsewhere in the economy. To this extent, it is important not to take a partial approach in examining the consequences of FDI. Let us give two examples. Take first a situation in which outward investment is directed either to activities which require resources and capabilities in which the investing country is comparatively disadvantaged, or is losing its comparative advantage, or where the purpose of the investment is to acquire resources and capabilities, which will add to the competitiveness of the existing assets of the investing company.

Suppose, next, that, due to appropriate structural adjustment policies and the willingness of firms to reallocate resources, the resources released were taken over by foreign investors, who, by combining these with other foreign assets, e.g. entrepreneurship, technology, organizational capability, were able to use them more productively. Then, in such a case, MBA is likely both to increase and upgrade indigenous competences.

Consider now a second example. Assume that a foreign firm responds to import controls imposed by the host government, or takes defensive oligopolist reaction to produce goods which require resources, valued at international market prices, in which the home country has a comparative advantage. Suppose, too, that, to avoid unwelcome industrial or penal fiscal policies pursued by their own government, domestic firms choose to increase their foreign, rather than their home, investments. Then, in such cases, although overseas production might be a second or third best solution, the first best solution, in terms of domestic factor endowments, might be for the government to modify its macro-economic policies so that the prices of domestic inputs and outputs more accurately reflect their true opportunity cost.

Finally, the net effect on factor endowments and created capabilities of MNE activity is likely to rest on the price paid for the inward investment and the gains accruing from outward investment to the investing country. For example, a takeover of a domestic firm might reduce the competitiveness of the resources used by the acquired firm (although it may help to improve the competitiveness of those used by the acquiring firm). However, from the perspective of the host country, the takeover would be undesirable only if the agreed price was insufficient to compensate for these (possible) adverse affects. Here the distinction between the social and private price of an acquisition is of critical importance (Dunning and Steuer, 1969).

Similarly, the returns from outward investment should include not only the foreign income earned by the affiliate, but all the other benefits existing from its presence, e.g. the feedback of technological or managerial know-how and the increased market it makes possible for domestic resources. Various studies have shown that, in some sectors, and by some countries, MBA has made a significant contribution to the restructuring and upgrading of domestic resources.[23] Indeed, the foreign activities of Japanese MNEs have played an integral part in the restructuring and upgrading of the Japanese economy since the mid-1960s (Ozawa, 1989)

Domestic Rivalry (see Figure 11.4)

Porter also argues that the extent and degree of competition between domestic rivals is an important variable affecting national competitiveness. In particular, he points to the larger number of firms competing with each other in Japan than

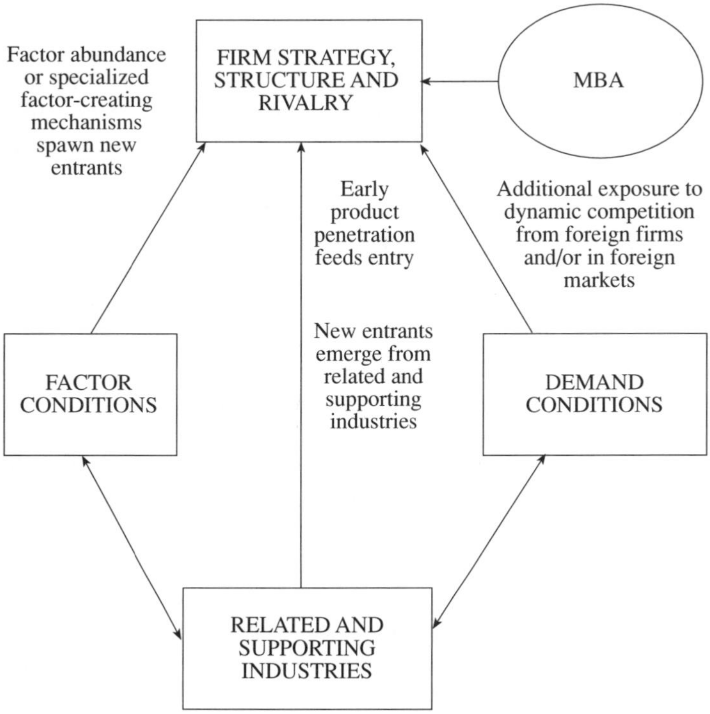

Figure 11.4 Influences on domestic rivalry

in the US as a factor making for the higher industrial competitiveness of the former country.

The optimum structure of a market for competitive and innovatory stimulus has always been a matter for debate. Certainly, it would be erroneous to argue that a greater population of firms necessarily means more *effective* competition. The Canadian experience – and that of other countries with small markets – completely belies this. However, there can be little doubt that the number and type of competitors is an important variable affecting the strategic conduct of firms, and that some forms of market structure are more conducive to the promotion of short or long term competitiveness than others. Lawrence (1987), for example, views an optimum market structure as one which allows neither cut-throat or destructive competition on the one hand nor lethargy on the other, on the part of the constituent firms.[24]

The literature also suggests that MNEs are likely to impact on domestic market structure both by the resources, capabilities and/or markets they can provide and by the control exerted over these assets, and any others germane to their jurisdiction. In turn, these effects may impinge on the behaviour of their competitors and the structure of the industry in which they operate.

Again, it may be helpful to illustrate from two extreme scenarios. The first is where a foreign firm takes over an existing producer and uses its global power to drive out local competitors. Furthermore, assume that this power is being used not to advance efficiency, but to promote a monopoly position. In such a case, it is likely that domestic rivalry will be adversely affected by such investment – although whether or not this lowers overall economic competitiveness will depend upon the other consequences of the takeover. The second scenario is where a foreign firm injects a new element of competition into a market supplied by a local monopolist, or where, as a result of an acquisition, it revitalizes an industry which might otherwise have perished because of insufficient or inappropriate competition.

A major drawback of most attempts to identify the optimum market structure of firms is that they tend to limit their attention to domestic or national markets. In a world in which the bulk of activity in many sectors is dominated by MNEs, this is unacceptable. Competition between the major pharmaceutical, consumer electronics, banking, oil, tyre and motor vehicle companies is not mainly played out in national, but in world, markets. Michael Porter cites the greater number of Japanese firms in several industries as an illustration of competitive rivalry. Yet, at the time of Porter's research, the Japanese market was largely closed to foreign competition. Not only this: until recently, the majority of the output of Japanese companies was sold to domestic consumers.

The situation is very different in the case of some smaller advanced industrialized or industrializing countries, which are also well up in the competitiveness league table, notably Switzerland, Sweden, The Netherlands, Singapore and Hong Kong. We think it unlikely that the Chief Executives of Nestlé', Philips or SKF would accept that the competition they encounter is any the less intense than that faced by their Japanese or US equivalents. The difference is that the former is almost exclusively provided by foreign competitors. What is more important is that, as markets become globalized, and cross-border trading barriers are relaxed, the international dimension of inter-firm rivalry is likely to increase.

Indeed, it is possible to go further and argue that a persuasive case can be made out that, in the right circumstances, rivalry by foreign firms might offer greater benefits than that between domestic firms. At the same time, domestic firms, which also produce outside their national boundaries, are, for the most part, likely to face tougher competition than those which supply only domestic markets – particularly where the latter markets are protected.

Our conclusion is, then, that there are consequences on domestic rivalry which are distinctive to MBA. We accept that, a priori, it may be difficult to predict whether or not, in the long run, these are likely to be beneficial or not.

But, it is possible to argue that both inward and outward direct investment do have the potential for increasing healthy domestic rivalry, and hence improving this particular facet of the diamond of competitive advantage. Whether the potential is translated into reality depends on the existing domestic and international market structure, the type and form of FDI and its impact on the market structure,[25] and the role played by national governments in setting the appropriate signals for rivalry.

Agglomerative Economies and the Clustering of Related Industries (see Figure 11.5)

The presence of economies external to the firm but internal to a network or cluster of firms located in a particular geographical area is a familiar competitive advantage articulated by economists since the time of Alfred Marshall. The fact that clusters of related activities do exist and confer considerable benefits to the participating firms has been spelled out in various regional studies, notably those on the City of London (Dunning and Morgan, 1971), California's Silicon Valley (Scott and Angel, 1987), the location of government research establishments in south east England (Hall et al., 1987), the Greater Grenoble area in France (Boisgontier and de Bernardy, 1986), several districts in Northern Italy (Malerba, 1990) and the Ibaragi Prefecture in Japan.[26] Moreover, these studies suggest that the need for firms to draw on resources and capabilities, which have to be geographically concentrated to be efficiently supplied, is increasing.

The advantages of clusters, as described by Porter, is that firms benefit from a shared culture and learning experience, supply capabilities and local infrastructure, which gives them a competitive edge in both domestic and international markets.

Geographical clusters or networks of economic activity may take various forms. They may be between firms producing different products across value-added chains, or between firms producing similar products at different stages of the same chain. The related presence is assumed to benefit all firms within the cluster and, hence, protect or advance competitiveness.

In his book, Porter does not attempt to measure the significance of clusters as a facet of the diamond, nor whether or not this particular advantage has become more important with the passage of time. Nor does he give much attention to the conditions which make for successful clusters. Clearly, not all firms need to be part of a network of vertical or horizontal linkages. Moreover, not all linkages need to be in the same or similar locations.

Let us now consider the extent to which efficient clustering is likely to be affected by the MBA in either home or host countries. In what way does it respond to, or affect, the propensity of firms to cluster differently than that conducted by non-MNEs?

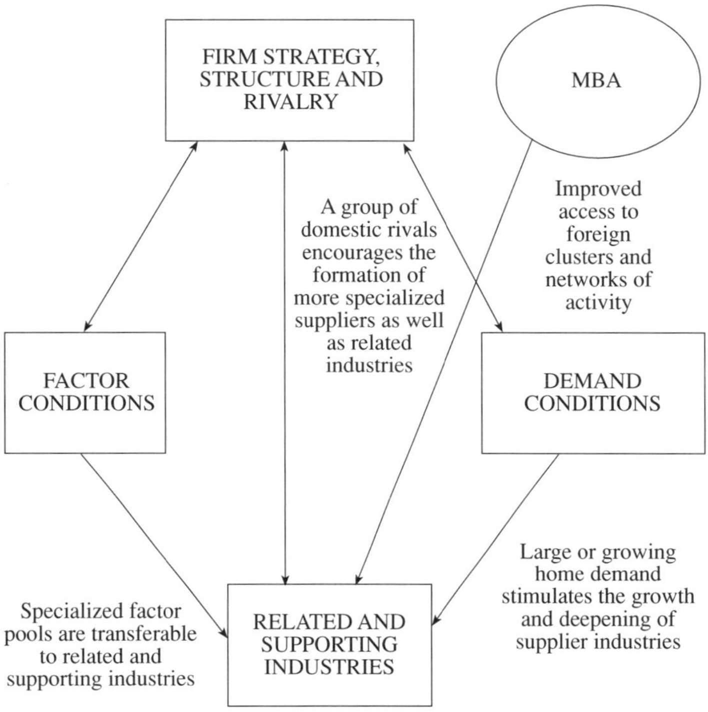

Figure 11.5 Influences on the development of related and supporting industries

Perhaps the first point worth making is that the MNE (and, more especially, the large diversified MNE) is *par excellence* a network of interrelated activities. Indeed, one of its strengths derives from the external economies associated with particular types of activities, which it, as a coordinator of these activities, can capture. Corporate integration makes possible the economies of common governance. Sometimes, these economies are best exploited in the same location, and sometimes in different locations.

At the same time, there is some suggestion that MNEs may create their own clusters of foreign based activity. Indeed, Knickerbocker observed this as a phenomenon of MNE activity two decades ago (Knickerbocker, 1973), while, in the 1980s and 1990s, there is ample evidence that Japanese motor vehicle consumer electronics, rubber tyre and chemical firms are pursuing a 'follow my leader' strategy in investing in Europe and the US. More than this, the presence of such firms is encouraging investment by Japanese component suppliers and subcontractors, and new intra-industry value chain networks are being established.

However, the data are inconclusive on the geographical distribution of these activities. Currently, 75 per cent of output of colour television sets of Japanese affiliates produced in the UK are from factories located in South Wales. The Midlothian industrial conurbation in Scotland attracts two-thirds of all foreign owned firms producing semi-conductors in the UK. More than one-half of Japanese direct investment in German manufacturing industry is sited in the Düsseldorf area. And, there are suggestions that north-east England may become an important new centre for the production of motor vehicles and their components. At the same time, the Japanese investors were not initially attracted by a strong cluster of existing activities; indeed, they have helped create their own clusters.

But, there are other examples which point to the contrary conclusion. The examples of clustering centres cited earlier in this chapter have all attracted foreign based companies which have generally reinforced the value of existing agglomerations of activity. On the other hand, outward investment might be expected to lead to a reduction in the intensity of domestic galaxies. An exception, perhaps, is in R&D and other high value activities of MNEs which tend to be concentrated in their home countries. The critical issue is to identify the optimum grouping of firms to gain the maximum external net economies at the lowest cost; for after a point, diseconomies of agglomeration arise. Such evidence as we have on the effect of foreign firms on clustering does not permit us to come to any generalized conclusion.

Again, however, it is not difficult to point to cases where foreign owned firms might enhance or inhibit particular types of clusters. For example, if such firms replace domestic firms and transfer their R&D activities to their home countries, this could reduce the agglomerative economies of R&D. If, on the other hand, affiliates upgraded factor endowments and the quality of output by increasing the demand for the products of the host country, this could lead to an increase in new kinds of clustering economies. Much would seem to depend upon the type of activities in which a foreign affiliate engages (cf. domestic firms) and the extent to which it buys from local suppliers or sells to local consumers.

The effect of outward investment on the domestic networking of activities is equally ambiguous. There is some suggestion that the Continental European investment of UK motor vehicle component firms was prompted by the better agglomerative economies offered by concentrations of industrial activity in the Ruhr Valley and in Belgium, and that this investment decreased the viability of the corresponding clusters in the UK (Cowling, 1986). At the same time, the competitiveness of the investing firms may well be improved by their investments in foreign clusters, and this may have other beneficial affects on the home economy.

MNEs, GOVERNMENTS AND COMPETITIVENESS

Although Porter addresses a whole chapter to the role of government as a shaper and monitor of economic activity, he has very little to say about the extent and way to which government policy is, itself, influenced by global economic forces, and, in particular, to those which are the result of the internationalization of production.

The interaction between MNEs, governments and competitiveness is a complex subject which is only now being addressed seriously by scholars.[27] Yet it is known to be extremely important, particularly in some developing and smaller developed economies. For the purpose of this chapter, however, we will confine our remarks to just two issues which we believe need to be incorporated into any analysis of the competitive advantages of nation states.

First, one of the distinguishing features of MNEs is their ability to shift value-added activities across national borders more easily than can uninational firms; indeed, this is a *sine qua non* for their existence. In the past, the spatial strategies of MNEs have been primarily based on the size of domestic markets and the relative competitiveness of national resources. In today's global economy, where international sourcing and markets are as, if not more, important as their domestic equivalents, the configuration of MNE activity (particularly within the Triad) is less dependent upon the availability and cost of unimproved natural resources, and more on the knowledge base and infrastructure facilities of economies in which they are producing or contemplating producing.

At the same time, governments can and do strongly influence the extent, quality and cost of these factors by their education, science and technology, industrial, trade, environmental, transport and communications and fiscal policies. Indeed, in a variety of ways, nation states are increasingly competing for resources and capabilities offered by MNEs.[28] The combination of the footloose nature of much modern industry (especially within integrated regions such as the EC) and the increasing significance of government influence on the transaction costs of such activity – and especially of high value activities in which MNEs tend to have a competitive advantage – is something which deserves the attention of scholars.

Second, MNEs can, themselves, influence government behavior, including that which directly impinges on the diamond of competitive advantage. In most industrial economies, MNEs are accounting for an increasing proportion of value-added activity. Egged on by the recent wave of cross-border acquisitions and mergers (A&Ms), such activity is also being concentrated in the largest 'x' per cent of firms. In their emphasis on wealth creating activities and competitiveness, governments are being forced to acknowledge the views of the leading wealth creators.

At the same time, such firms do not always (or solely) have their home country's interests at heart, as an increasing proportion of their sales and profits are earned outside their national boundaries (Dunning, 1993). So, governments may be prompted to take action which may affect the competitiveness of their location bound assets in a variety of ways, as described by Porter. In some instances, this can lead to more competitiveness and a synergy of goals between the long run interests of corporations and those of nation states; a good example is the initiative taken by some leading European MNEs to push forward the completion of the EC's internal market programme. In others, the interest of MNEs may be best served (or perceived to be best served) by urging governments to adopt policies which, far from promoting dynamic competitiveness, may inhibit it by giving shelter to inefficient or non-innovatory firms.[29]

There can be little doubt that policy rivalry between nation states is a feature of the late twentieth century, and is likely to continue to be so for the foreseeable future. Up to now, most attention has been paid to the merits and demerits of strategic trade policy.[30] However, the real issue is one of competitive strategy, which embraces not only the facets of the diamond identified by Porter, but also the ability of firms to reallocate and upgrade their human and physical capabilities to the changing needs of the marketplace at minimum adjustment cost. In each of these areas, as Porter acknowledges, governments have a critical role to play both in setting the framework within which market forces and/or hierarchies can operate, and in counteracting any efforts, either by the participants of the market, or by other governments, to rig the workings of market to their own benefit.

However, in analysing the behaviour of particular national governments, an understanding both of the international forces affecting that behaviour, and of the likely consequences of their actions on the goals of other governments is essential. In their role as instruments of the globalization of economic activity and as links between the strategic policies of the governments of the countries in which they operate, MNEs are likely to have a distinctive impact on the shaping of a whole range of government related actions which, directly or indirectly, affect the shape and quality of national diamonds of competitive advantage.

CONCLUSIONS

In answer to the question, 'Is foreign inward and outward direct investment likely to affect the diamond of competitive advantage?' our answer must surely be 'yes'. Multinationality does confer its own unique characteristics and bring about a distinctive impact on resource allocation and usage. Similarly, the evidence set out in this chapter suggests that the significance of this impact, particularly in the sectors in which the industrialized nations are seeking to promote their competitive advantages, is sufficiently noteworthy for the transnational business variable to be considered as a separate factor affecting the configuration of these advantages.

In answer to the question, 'Will foreign inward and outward investment improve the competitive advantage of host or home countries?' – the answer that is all too frequently (but justifiably) given by economists is 'it all depends'. The most (but this should not be belittled) an economist can do is first to set out the conditions under which, and the ways in which, domestic or foreign MNEs are likely to benefit national competitiveness (either in an industry or an economy) in the short and/or long run, and second to indicate what might be done (and at what cost) to optimize the impact of outward and inward investment (and associated activities, e.g. strategic alliances) on that competitiveness.

The interaction between the globalization of economic activity and national competitiveness provides a rich agenda for the scholar of the MNE. This chapter has sought to identify the ways in which national diamonds of competitive advantages are linked to each other by the operation of transnational enterprises. While Michael Porter provides a useful paradigm in identifying the main determinants of national competitiveness, his lack of attention to the ways in which such competitiveness may be affected by the ownership structure of firms and the way cross-border markets are organized weakens both the content and force of his thesis. But, the good news is that Porter has left the IB scholar plenty of interesting research to do![31]

NOTES

1. Defined as production financed by foreign direct investment or controlled by foreign owned multinational firms.
2. We say renewed attention as some of the earlier explanations of the foreign value-added activity of firms focused largely on their ability to engage in such activities (e.g. Vernon, 1966; Caves, 1971).
3. Amit and Schoemaker (1990) distinguish between resources and capabilities in the following way.

   > Resources consist of proprietary know-how (e.g. patents and trade secrets), financial or physical assets (e.g. property, plant and equipment), human capital, government licenses, etc. Capabilities, in contrast, are tangible or intangible (invisible) assets that are firm-specific and are created over time through complex interactions among the firm's resources. They can be thought of as 'intermediate goods' generated by the firm to provide enhanced productivity of its resources as well as flexibility and protection for its final product or service. Capabilities are based on developing, carrying, and exchanging information through the firm's human capital.

4. For a distinction between the theory of the MNE and the theory of MNE activity see Dunning (1992).
5. At least as an explanation of the growth of the MNE.
6. More particularly that part which enters into international transactions.

7. Natural factor endowments are defined as the stock of unimproved resources and the uneducated labour force of a country. *Created* factor endowments or capabilities are the difference between these and the actual wealth creating assets of a community. These include not only its *ability* to create wealth, but also its *willingness* to do so.
8. Even though Porter's approach is essentially Schumpeterian.
9. For an elaboration of the ESP paradigm see, for example, Koopmans and Montias (1971).
10. Seven from developed and one from a relatively advanced developing country (Korea). It is interesting to speculate on the relevance of Porter's analysis and conclusions to the great majority of developing economies. For a recent analysis of the interaction between the international competitiveness of developing country firms and government policies, see Agarwal and Agmon (1990).
11. To give one (admittedly a rather extreme) example, 95 per cent of the sales of Nestlé is accounted for by their foreign subsidiaries. It follows that the diamond(s) of competitive advantage of foreign countries within which Nestlé operates may be more important to determining the contribution of Nestlé to the Swiss GNP than the equivalent diamond within which Nestlé operates in Switzerland. The point is further explored in an MNE detailed study of the competitive advantages of Sweden (Solvell, Porter and Zander, 1991).
12. To give an illustration, first at an industry level, inward investment in the UK motor industry might rise (fall) with outward investment, or inward investment might rise (fall) as outward investment falls (rises). Second, at a meso-level, inward investment in the UK industry might rise (fall) with outward investment in *other* sectors, or the total outward investment might fall (rise) in sympathy with outward investment. The net effect on competitiveness of all these movements is highly ambiguous and dependent upon the precise configuration of the components of the UK's diamond of competitive advantage.
13. Although the two are not necessarily exclusive alternatives.
14. This is not to say that the investment may not be beneficial as it could stimulate domestic rivalry and raise efficiency in the production of low cost chocolates!
15. Either directly or by affecting the demand of consumers. In India, for example, the priority of the Indian government has been to encourage self-sufficiency of output rather than raise the quality of domestic demand.
16. We accept that part of the stimulus to foreign demand may come from exports.
17. Rather than indirectly by domestic rivalry or innovation.
18. For example, by driving out competition and making possible monopoly pricing.
19. Similarly, if the US airways were open to foreign competition, almost certainly the quality of air travel would improve.
20. For further details, see Dunning (1993).
21. For example, is it prompted by market distortions, or a response to market forces? Is it part of a defensive oligopolistic reaction or a result of the increased efficiency of cross-border hierarchies?
22. A somewhat more sophisticated argument is that, rather than investing overseas to protect or advance their competition in high technology products, it might have more productivity in the long run if the US firms had devoted more resources to product innovation or improving production efficiency in their domestic plants.
23. See especially those contained in Dunning (1985) and Reddaway, Potter and Taylor (1968).
24. To quote from Lawrence: 'An industry needs to experience rigorous competition if it is to be economically strong. Either too little or too much competitive pressure can lead an industry to a predictably weak economic performance characterized by its becoming inefficient and/or non-innovative' (Lawrence, 1987, p. 102).
25. For example, it is possible to envisage multinationalization leading to international cartelization, or helping to inject competition into markets dominated by a single or few producers.
26. Where a new science city at Tsukuba already has the reputation as a world-class centre for R&D (*Japan Update*, 1990).
27. For an analysis of this interaction, see Chapters 14 and 15 of this volume and Behrman and Grosse (1990).

28. Witness, for example, the strenuous efforts by state legislatures in the US to attract inward direct investment. On the interaction between the strategy of resource usage by governments and MNEs, see an interesting paper by Stopford (1990).
29. For an analysis of the interaction between the politically oriented strategies of firms and the likely response of governments, see Rugman and Verbeke (1990).
30. See Stegemann (1989) for a review of the literature on this subject.
31. Some further thoughts on the appropriateness of Porter's focus on a country's 'domestic' diamond of competitive advantage are contained in a special issue of Management International Review, edited by Alan Rugman, spring, 1993.

REFERENCES

Agarwal, R. and Agmon, T. (1990), 'The international success of developing country firms' role of government-directed comparative advantage', *Management International Review* **30**.

Amit, R. and Schoemaker, P.J. (1990), *Key Success Factors: Their Foundation and Application*, Evanston, Ill.: Northwestern University Working Paper.

Aydalot, P. and Keeble D. (eds) (1988), *High Technology and Industry and Innovatory Environment: The European Experience*, London: Routledge.

Behrman, J. and Grosse, R. (1990), *International Business and Governments*, Columbia: University of Carolina Press.

Boisgontier, P. and de Bernardy, M. (1986), *Les Entreprises de 'micro' et la Technopole*, Grenoble CEPS: Université de Grenoble.

Buckley, P. and Casson, M. (1985), *The Economic Theory of the Multinational Enterprise*, London and Basingstoke: Macmillan.

Caves, R.E. (1971), 'International corporations: the industrial economics of foreign investment', *Economica* **38**: 1–27.

Cowling, K. (1986), 'The internationalization of production and deindustrialization', in Amin, A. and Goddard, J. (eds), *Technological Change, Industrial Restructuring and Regional Development*, London: Allen and Unwin.

Dunning, J.H. (ed.) (1985), *Multinational Enterprises, Economic Structure and International Competitiveness*, Chichester: John Wiley.

Dunning, J.H. (1990), *The Globalization of Firms and the Competitiveness of Countries: Some Implications for the Theory of International Production*, Lund: Institute of Economic Research, Lund University.

Dunning, J.H. (1991a), 'Governments, economic organization and international competitiveness', in Mattson, L.G. and Stymne, B. (eds), *Corporate and Industry Strategies for Europe*, Amsterdam: Elsevier Science Publishers, B.V., pp. 41–74.

Dunning, J.H. (1991b), 'Governments and multinational enterprises: from confrontation to cooperation?', *Millennium (Journal of International Studies)* **20**: 225–43.

Dunning, J.H. (1992), 'The theory of transnational corporations', in UNCTC Library on Transnational Corporations, London and New York: Routledge.

Dunning, J.H. (1993), *Multinational Enterprise and the Global Economy*, Wokingham, Berks: Addison-Wesley.

Dunning, J.H. and Morgan, E.V. (1971), *An Economic Study of the City of London*, London: Allen and Unwin.

Dunning, J.H. and Steuer, M. (1969), 'The effects of US direct investment on British technology', *Moorgate and Wall Street*, Autumn: 1–30.

Gilpin, R. (1975), *US Power and the Multinational Corporation*, London: Macmillan.

Gilpin, R. (1982), 'Trade investment and technology policy', in Giersch, H. (ed.), *Emerging Technologies: Consequences for Economic Growth, Structural Change and Employment*, Tübingen: J.C.B. Mohr, pp. 381–409.

Hall, P., Breheny, M., McQuaid, D. and Hart, D. (1987), *Western Sunrise*, London: Allen and Unwin.

Japan Update (1990), 'Direct investment in Japan: new developments', *Japan Update*, Winter: 12–15.

Julius DeAnne (1989), *Global Companies and Public Policies: The Challenge of the New Economic Linkages*, London: Chatham House.

Knickerbocker, F.T. (1973), *Oligopolistic Reaction and the Multinational Enterprise*, Cambridge, Mass.: MIT Press.

Kogut, B. (1985), 'Designing global strategies: profiting from operational flexibility', *Sloan Management Review* **26**, Fall: 27–38.

Koopman, K. and Montias, J.M. (1971), 'On the description and comparison of economic systems', in Eckstein, A. (ed.), *Comparison of Economic Systems*, San Francisco, CA: University of California Press.

Lawrence, P.R. (1987), 'Competition: a renewed focus for industrial policy', in Teece, D.J. (ed.), *The Competition Challenge*, Cambridge, Mass.: Ballinger.

Lipsey, R. and Dobson, W. (1987), *Shaping Comparative Advantage*, Ontario: Prentice Hall for C.D. Howe Institute.

Malerba, F. (1990), 'The Italian system of innovation', Paper presented at the Workshop on The Organization of International Competitiveness, Brussels, May–June.

Ozawa, T. (1989), *Japan's Strategic Policy Towards Outward Direct Investment*, Fort Collins: Colorado State University (mimeo).

Porter, M.E. (1990), *The Competitive Advantage of Nations*, New York: Free Press.

Reddaway, W.B., Potter, S.T. and Taylor, C.T. (1968), *The Effects of UK Direct Investment Overseas*, Cambridge: Cambridge University Press.

Rugman, A. and Verbeke, A. (1990), *Global Corporate Strategy and Trade Policy*, London and New York: Routledge.

Safarian, A.E. (1989), 'Firm and government strategies in the context of economic integration', Paper presented to a round-table on *Multinational Firms and European Integration*, Geneva, May.

Scott, A.J. and Angel, D.P. (1987), 'The US semi-conductor industry: a locational analysis', *Environment and Planning A* **19**: 875–912.

Solvell, O., Porter, M.E. and Zander, I. (1991), *Advantage Sweden*, Stockholm: Norstedts.

Stegemann, K. (1989), 'Policy rivalry among industrial states: what can we learn from models of strategic trade policy?', *International Organization* **43**, Winter: 73–100.

Stopford, J. (1990), 'Global strategic change and resource usage', Paper presented at International Symposium on *MNEs and 21st Century Scenarios*, organized for the studies of Multinational Enterprise, Tokyo.

Vernon, R. (1966), 'International investment and international trade in the product cycle', *Quarterly Journal of Economics* **80**: 190–207.

12. The geographical sources of the competitiveness of firms*

INTRODUCTION

This chapter presents some of the results of a new field study on the geographical sources of firm-specific competitiveness,[1] as perceived by executives of 144 of the world's 500 largest industrial corporations.[2] Full details of the sample and the way in which the survey was organized are set out in the appendix to this chapter.

In 1993, the sample firms were responsible for two-fifths of the global sales of the largest 500 industrial corporations and nearly two-fifths of the foreign direct investment (FDI) stake in all primary and secondary economic activity. For some sectors (e.g. autos, petroleum refining, tobacco, electronics and computers) and for some countries (e.g. Japan, Sweden and the United Kingdom), our coverage is particularly good; for others, it is less so, but from the country and sector groups presented in this chapter, it is entirely acceptable.

The purpose of the field survey was to gain the opinions of senior business executives[3] about the geographical origin of the kind of firm-specific competitive advantages or core competencies[4] identified by the literature.[5] There has been much debate, in recent years, over the extent to which the competitive advantages of firms stem from the location-bound characteristics of their home countries – some of which may be internalized by the firms themselves – or whether, as FDI and strategic alliances have become increasingly directed to acquiring created assets,[6] and as firms (and, particularly, the larger and established MNEs) have been increasing their degree of multinationality,[7] competitive advantages have been increasingly sourced from outside their home countries, or in Michael Porter's terminology, 'multiple home bases'.

As the analytical basis for our study, we shall use the concept of the 'double' diamond of competitive advantage, as developed by Alan Rugman and his colleagues over the past three or four years.[8] Essentially, the Rugman approach extends the concept of Porter's 'single' diamond of competitive advantage[9] – which argues that a firm's competitive advantages are essentially a function of

* From *Transnational Corporations*, **5**(3) (1996): 1–30.

the domestic economic environment – whether or not the attributes of this environment are owned by the firm or available to it. Rugman and others, including the author of this chapter,[10] have argued that the deepening structural integration of the world economy and the burgeoning of alliance capitalism are widening the geographical scope for creating or acquiring competitive advantages, and that any attempt to identify the geographical sources of such advantages must embrace the diamonds of other countries, and particularly those with which the home country firms have the most dealings, by way of trade, FDI and non-equity co-operative ventures.

Our field study aims to offer some new evidence to that recorded by a number of country case studies[11] which, in the main, have confirmed the Rugman/Dunning hypothesis. The uniqueness of the present contribution lies in six directions. First, it obtains the information directly from firms themselves.[12] Second, it attempts to classify the competitive advantages identified in the literature into a number of groups, and, in doing so, uses the four components of Porter's diamond as its framework. Third, our study attempts to relate its findings to a number of critical firm-specific variables, namely size of firm, degree of multinationality, country (or region) of origin and industrial sector. Fourth, it seeks to identify which foreign countries provide the main access to non-domestic competitive advantages which complement those offered by the home country. Fifth, it ranks the significance of the three main modes of involvement of the sample firms in acquiring competitive advantages from a foreign location. And lastly, it sets out the perceptions of the sample firms about the positive or negative influences of different components of home government policy on their global competitiveness.

To contain this chapter to manageable dimensions, we shall adopt a threefold classification of industries, based upon their degree of R&D intensity in the United States. Thus, we define high-technology (HT) sectors as those which recorded an average R&D expenditure as a percentage of sales of 4 per cent or more where scientists and engineers employed in R&D were 2 per cent or more of total employment.[13] Medium-technology (MT) sectors cover those where the corresponding ratios vary between 2 and 3.9 per cent and 1 and 1.9 per cent; and low-technology (LT) sectors embrace those ratios under 2 per cent and under 1 per cent. As to home country or region of origin, we shall consider six main groups, namely large European countries,[14] smaller European countries,[15] the United States, Japan, developing countries,[16] and other countries.[17]

We shall also group our sample firms by their degrees of multinationality. This was obtained by averaging out (for each firm) the percentage of their global assets and global employment,[18] accounted for by their foreign affiliates[19] and then classifying firms into four groups, namely under 15 per cent (low), 15–29 per cent (medium–low), 30–59 per cent (medium–high) and 60 per cent and over (high).

Finally, although all of our sample firms were large companies, their global sales in 1993 varied from $0.22 billion to $138.2 billion. For the purposes of our analysis, we shall categorize our firms into four size groups, namely medium-size firms defined as those with sales of under $5 billion in 1993; large firms: $5 billion to $24.9 billion of sales; very large firms: $25 billion to 49 billion of sales; and mega firms: $50 billion and over of sales.

In later research, we intend to undertake some econometric analysis on the relationship between these four contextual variables and the competitive advantages of firms as, with few exceptions, we have data for each of the 144 firms. In this chapter, we shall confine ourselves to identifying and exploring a number of possible bivariant (and occasionally trivariant) relationships between the sources of competitiveness and firms and/or country-specific characteristics, which – at the very least – may help point the way to more rigorous statistical evaluation.

THE SAMPLE FIRMS: SOME DETAILS

Tables 12.1 to 12.3 set out some details about the characteristics of the sample firms. In general, they mirror our knowledge about the industrial and geographical composition, and the size and degree of multinationality of MNEs as, for example, has been set out in various publications of the UNCTAD (DTCI) (previously UNCTC).[20] For the most part, too, the data set out in the tables are self-explanatory. We would, however, highlight just three points:

1. Although 82 per cent of the sales of our sample firms were within the HT or MT sectors, the degree of technological intensity would not appear to affect significantly the extent of their multinationality. There were, indeed, as wide differences between industries in the three broad sectors identified (compare, for example, aerospace with chemicals in Table 12.1) as between the sectors.
2. The degree to which firms undertake R&D activities in their foreign affiliates is on average about one-half that of their overall activities, although this does vary between sectors (see Table 12.1). Table 12.2, however, shows that the R&D multinationality ratio varies very considerably between countries (compare, for example, Japan and developing countries with the United Kingdom and Sweden).
3. Table 12.3 shows that size of firm does not appear to be a significant influence on the degree of multinationality.[21] Somewhat surprisingly, however, the mega firms – although the most multinational in terms of their sales and assets – were the least multinational in terms of their R&D expenditures.

Table 12.1 Industrial distribution and extent of multinationality of sample firms (1993)

Sector	N	Sales ($ billion)	Sales (%)	Extent of multinationality %		
				Assets	Employment	R&D
High technology	53	892.02	35.99	38.20	39.79	22.74
of which: Aerospace	5	73.10	2.95	6.50	6.25	2.00
Chemicals and pharm.	19	215.91	8.71	51.28	54.18	26.61
Computers	9	213.90	8.63	28.87	28.67	9.60
Electronics	20	389.11	15.70	38.84	39.22	27.52
Medium technology	34	1,152.20	46.48	39.65	39.42	15.44
of which:						
Industrial equipment	8	73.80	2.98	28.00	39.13	12.70
Motor vehicles	12	580.00	23.40	32.20	35.47	7.50
Petroleum refining	14	498.40	20.11	49.75	42.92	24.33
Low technology	57	434.55	17.53	41.70	45.51	28.46
of which:						
Food, drink and tobacco	20	244.30	9.86	50.42	58.14	32.53
Paper	10	38.96	1.57	22.44	20.89	8.14
Building materials	5	16.43	0.66	49.60	46.40	39.67
Metals and metal production	14	107.30	4.33	35.01	38.00	24.65
Other	8	27.56	1.11	53.50	59.57	45.60
Total	144	2478.77	100.00	40.01	41.80	23.34

Source: All data contained in this and subsequent tables are derived from our field survey.

Table 12.2 Distribution of sample firms by region or country of origin and extent of multinationality (1993)

Region/country	N	Sales ($ billion)	Sales (%)	Extent of multinationality %		
				Assets	Employment	R&D
Large European	44	922.87	37.23	49.13	49.95	32.05
of which:						
Germany	13	359.55	14.51	39.71	45.99	23.11
UK + UK/Neth.	23	400.32	16.15	57.28	57.95	38.58
Other	8	163.00	6.58	28.83	32.14	27.78
Small European	21	164.46	6.63	55.24	56.81	32.72
of which:						
Sweden	7	31.96	1.29	70.00	70.29	53.00
Switzerland	5	68.90	2.78	58.00	61.80	33.20
Other	9	63.60	2.57	46.13	43.56	19.75
United States	31	710.20	28.65	36.12	34.48	14.67
Japan	26	606.35	24.46	19.48	28.69	5.99
Developing countries	14	42.49	1.71	27.22	25.42	15.63
Other countries	8	32.40	1.31	30.50	30.57	18.33
Total	144	2478.77	100.00	40.01	41.80	23.34

Table 12.3 Distribution of sample firms by size and extent of multinationality (1993)

Size (sales)	N	Sales ($ billion)	Sales (%)	Extent of multinationality %		
				Assets	Employment	R&D
Medium (<5 billion)	56	141.62	5.71	40.60	39.68	20.10
Large (5–24.9 billion)	58	706.20	28.49	37.30	41.12	26.55
Very large (25–49.9 billion)	16	561.55	22.65	46.09	45.00	29.00
Mega (>50 billion)	14	1069.40	43.14	42.31	49.54	12.80
Total	144	2478.77	100.00	40.01	41.80	23.34

THE GEOGRAPHICAL SOURCES OF COMPETITIVENESS

The next set of tables (Tables 12.4–12.7) presents the views of the respondents of the sample firms of the extent to which they currently derive a number of identified specific competitive advantages as a direct result of their FDIs and/or strategic alliances with foreign firms. They were asked to use a scale of 1 to 7 in their evaluations. They were informed that a rank of 1 would indicate that their competitive advantages were *entirely* derived from the resources, capabilities, markets and interfirm rivalries specific to their home countries, while a rank of 7 would indicate that such advantages were derived entirely from the location-specific attributes of foreign countries. A rank of 4 would suggest that, in the firm's opinion, the origin of the competitive advantages stemmed equally from home and foreign locations.[22]

Sector-specific Differences

Table 12.4 considers four groups of competitive advantages which broadly correspond to Michael Porter's fourfold diamond of the competitive advantages of nations.[23] We have further subdivided three of these four groups into a number of more specific advantages, identified by other scholars. In this table, we have classified our firms into high-, medium- and low-technology-intensity sectors. Economic theory would suggest that firms should seek to acquire competitive assets from those locations which provide these assets at lowest cost and with the greatest security.

Essentially, the Porter hypothesis is that HT firms will create (obtain) their core assets (e.g. innovatory capacity) (Group 1 [iv]) in their home countries, and that MT or LT firms (which, in general, are more likely to be natural resource intensive, or influenced by the characteristics of consumer demand) will tend to assign lower rankings to these and related variables. Such firms will also

Table 12.4 The sourcing of competitive advantages classified by technological intensity of sample firms (1993)

	All	HT	MT	LT
Group 1	3.54	3.46	3.48	3.65
Access to resources and assets	(1.39)	(1.20)	(1.03)	(1.71)
(i) Natural resources	4.24	3.67	4.44	4.62
	(1.70)	(1.36)	(1.67)	(1.88)
(ii) Unskilled labour	3.98	4.10	3.79	3.99
	(1.70)	(1.55)	(1.65)	(1.89)
(iii) Skilled and professional labour	2.98	2.98	2.76	3.12
	(1.27)	(1.06)	(1.17)	(1.50)
(iv) Innovatory capacity	2.88	2.75	2.71	3.11
	(1.40)	(1.16)	(1.17)	(1.70)
(v) Organizational capacity	3.12	3.21	2.88	3.18
	(1.32)	(1.13)	(1.04)	(1.61)
(vi) Managerial expertise	3.24	3.19	3.12	3.38
	(1.42)	(1.32)	(1.37)	(1.56)
(vii) Relational skills	3.75	4.00	3.41	3.71
	(1.62)	(1.64)	(1.33)	(1.73)
Group 2	3.94	4.06	3.37	4.15
Consumer demand	(1.59)	(1.36)	(1.50)	(1.81)
(i) Upgrading of product quality	3.31	3.40	2.94	3.44
	(1.37)	(1.36)	(1.14)	(1.49)
(ii) Making for more product innovation	3.44	3.40	3.06	3.71
	(1.45)	(1.26)	(1.50)	(1.55)
Group 3	4.60	4.68	4.56	4.55
Interfirm competition/rivalry	(1.67)	(1.61)	(1.65)	(1.75)
Group 4	4.10	4.19	3.68	4.29
Linkages with foreign or domestic firms and institutions	(1.37)	(1.32)	(1.12)	(1.52)

Note: Unless otherwise indicated, in all subsequent tables the figures reported are mean responses with standard deviations in parentheses.

Table 12.5 The sourcing of competitive advantages classified by region or country of origin of sample firms (1993)

	All	Large European	Small European	USA	Japan	Other developed	Developing
Group 1	3.54	3.80	3.90	3.61	3.21	2.63	3.21
Access to resources and assets	(1.39)	(1.25)	(1.41)	(1.43)	(1.35)	(1.30)	(1.63)
(i) Natural resources	4.24	4.26	3.65	4.03	4.87	3.39	4.86
	(1.70)	(1.58)	(1.81)	(1.61)	(1.63)	(2.14)	(1.66)
(ii) Unskilled labour	3.98	3.81	4.10	4.37	3.75	4.00	3.92
	(1.70)	(1.63)	(1.77)	(1.50)	(1.80)	(1.91)	(2.10)
(iii) Skilled and	2.98	3.18	3.30	3.27	2.46	3.00	2.21
professional labour	(1.27)	(1.22)	(1.45)	(1.15)	(1.26)	(1.26)	(1.01)
(iv) Innovatory	2.88	2.95	3.38	2.94	2.23	3.29	2.79
capacity	(1.40)	(1.31)	(1.56)	(1.39)	(1.34)	(1.25)	(1.37)
(v) Organizational	3.12	3.30	3.43	3.35	2.85	2.43	2.43
capacity	(1.32)	(1.37)	(1.12)	(1.05)	(1.54)	(1.27)	(1.28)
(vi) Managerial	3.24	3.30	3.86	3.29	3.12	3.14	2.36
expertise	(1.42)	(1.49)	(1.39)	(1.10)	(1.70)	(0.90)	(1.22)
(vii) Relational skills	3.75	3.98	4.43	3.90	3.46	3.29	2.43
	(1.62)	(1.56)	(1.69)	(1.35)	(1.70)	(1.70)	(1.28)
Group 2	3.94	4.39	4.22	3.78	2.96	5.20	3.83
Consumer demand	(1.59)	(1.64)	(1.73)	(1.53)	(1.19)	(1.10)	(1.40)
(i) Upgrading of	3.31	3.65	3.67	3.20	2.36	4.29	3.14
product quality	(1.37)	(1.46)	(1.53)	(1.16)	(1.04)	(0.95)	(1.17)
(ii) Making for more	3.44	3.58	3.90	3.33	2.76	4.14	3.43
product innovation	(1.45)	(1.48)	(1.30)	(1.37)	(1.48)	(1.07)	(1.50)
Group 3	4.60	5.43	5.38	4.23	3.23	4.29	4.36
Interfirm competition/ rivalry	(1.67)	(1.34)	(1.72)	(1.23)	(1.45)	(0.49)	(2.17)
Group 4	4.10	4.41	4.95	3.84	3.65	3.86	3.43
Linkages with foreign or domestic firms and institutions	(1.37)	(1.39)	(1.36)	(1.07)	(1.29)	(1.46)	(1.40)

Table 12.6 The sourcing of competitive advantages classified by extent of multinationality of sample firms (1993)*

	All	Low	Medium–Low	Medium–High	High
Group 1	3.54	2.33	2.83	3.76	4.50
Access to resources and assets	(1.39)	(1.28)	(1.13)	(1.00)	(1.31)
(i) Natural resources	4.24	3.82	3.90	4.21	4.62
	(1.70)	(2.01)	(1.84)	(1.34)	(1.84)
(ii) Unskilled labour	3.98	2.26	3.57	4.38	4.52
	(1.70)	(1.58)	(1.80)	(1.44)	(1.60)
(iii) Skilled and professional	2.98	2.06	2.48	3.33	3.48
labour	(1.27)	(1.18)	(0.90)	(1.19)	(1.20)
(iv) Innovatory capacity	2.88	2.82	2.67	2.80	3.43
	(1.40)	(1.81)	(1.20)	(1.32)	(1.22)
(v) Organizational capacity	3.12	1.94	2.88	3.37	3.57
	(1.32)	(1.25)	(1.26)	(1.09)	(1.19)
(vi) Managerial expertise	3.24	2.35	2.71	3.55	3.73
	(1.42)	(1.27)	(1.30)	(1.29)	(1.28)
(vii) Relational skills	3.75	2.35	3.21	4.13	4.43
	(1.62)	(1.84)	(1.38)	(1.29)	(1.48)
Group 2	3.94	3.27	3.32	3.98	4.96
Consumer demand	(1.59)	(1.98)	(1.39)	(1.43)	(1.49)
(i) Upgrading of product	3.31	3.00	2.79	3.34	4.18
quality	(1.37)	(1.80)	(1.28)	(1.11)	(1.33)
(ii) Making for more	3.44	2.94	3.17	3.49	4.04
product innovation	(1.45)	(1.48)	(1.46)	(1.36)	(1.32)
Group 3	4.60	4.29	4.08	4.68	5.37
Interfirm competition/rivalry	(1.67)	(1.79)	(1.67)	(1.56)	(1.43)
Group 4	4.10	3.06	3.50	4.27	4.87
Linkages with foreign or domestic firms and institutions	(1.37)	(1.48)	(1.25)	(1.25)	(1.14)

* For more precise definitions of extent of multinationality see the introduction.

Table 12.7 Bivariate correlation coefficients between perceived competitive advantages derived from foreign activities by extent of multinationality of sample firms (1993)

	A	B
(a) Natural assets (Group 1 [i–iii])	0.31982	0.18998
(b) Created assets (technological) (Group 1 [iii–v])	0.36478	0.37895
(c) Created assets (managerial) (Group 1 [vi–viii])	0.43228	0.39619
(d) Consumer demand (Group 2)	0.36339	0.35007
(e) Interfirm rivalry (Group 3)	0.27146	0.28016
(f) Linkages with related firms (Group 4 [i])	0.46452	0.39511

A: Extent of multinationality = average share of foreign employment and assets to all employment assets.
B: Extent of multinationality = average share of foreign in all R&D.

tend to be more internationally oriented; hence their predicted higher ranking of cross-border, *vis-à-vis* domestic, competition. The contrasting hypothesis, set out by Rugman, Dunning and other scholars researching into the behaviour of MNEs, is that, as firms become more multinational and globally integrated in their value-added activities, they are likely to derive an increasing proportion of their core assets from outside national boundaries, and, indeed, may deliberately seek out foreign assets which they perceive to be supportive of, or help augment, their own core competencies.

The data in Table 12.4 reveal a mixed picture, although, taken as a whole, they do suggest that the sample firms derive an important part of their competitive advantages – on average between 40 and 50 per cent[24] – from their presence in foreign countries, either by way of FDI or by strategic alliances. The access provided by a foreign location (cf. a domestic location) to natural resources (including unskilled labour), linkages with suppliers, industrial competitors and other foreign producers, and the benefits of larger markets and more stringent consumer demands, were all ranked particularly high (3.44 or above). By contrast, and in line with received theory and the data on innovatory activity, the sample firms perceived that their domestic operations and/or the indigenous resources and capabilities of their home countries continued to provide the main source of competitiveness – and especially so in the case of technological capacity and of skilled and professional labour.

Predictably, there were some differences in the perceptions of firms according to the technological intensity of their main activities. Most noticeably, the LT firms claimed to obtain a higher proportion of their created assets (Group 1 [iii–vii]) from foreign sources than did MT or HT firms, particularly so in the case of innovatory capacity. *Inter alia*, this finding tends to support the proposition that at least part of the competitive advantages of firms obtained from foreign sources is likely to be different from (and complementary to) those obtained from domestic sources. Nevertheless, the table strongly suggests that for each of the advantages identified, a multiple (or at least a dual) location of value-added activities was perceived to yield positive gains.[25] It thus seems reasonable to conclude that, in the opinion of the leading industrial companies, FDI and/or cross-border strategic alliances *do* provide an entry to significant competitive advantages.[26]

Country-specific Differences

Table 12.5 reclassifies the data set out in Table 12.4 by the source region or country of the sample firms. The data reveal few significant differences in the perceptions among the sample firms. As might be reasonably predicted, firms from high-wage economies (e.g. the United States and smaller European countries),[27] rank the foreign sourcing of unskilled labour relatively more highly than those from low-wage and, particularly, developing countries. Likewise, and consistent with the principle of comparative advantage, is the above-average reliance of Japanese firms on foreign natural resources, and the below-average reliance of 'other' developed country firms (in our sample survey, these were all from resource-rich countries[28]) on such resources. Relative to Japanese firms, too, European and US firms appear to value the access to foreign-based created assets (e.g. organizational capacity, management, expertise and relational skills) more highly, although, in general, the competitive advantages of Japanese firms were perceived to be more home specific than those of their major competitors. (This also reflects their lower degree of multinationality; see the next section.)

In respect of each of the other three components of Porter's diamond, European-owned firms appear to rely more on foreign, than on domestic, sources of competitiveness than do their US and Japanese counterparts. This is especially seen to be so in respect of interfirm competition, and, for smaller European firms, of linkages with related firms.

Notwithstanding the below-average significance attached by the sample firms to the acquisition of, or access to, foreign created assets, the rankings – even for MNEs from countries such as Germany and the United States, which record a comparative patenting advantage in HT products (Cantwell and Hodson, 1991) – suggest that large MNEs in the HT and MT sectors are increasingly seeking a technology-related presence[29] in each of the main Triad countries or regions, for example US firms in the European Community (EU) and Japan; Japanese firms in the EU and the United States; and EU firms in Japan and the United States.

Degrees of Multinationality

Perhaps the most frequently cited hypothesis about the propensity of firms to derive competitive advantages from their foreign operations is that the former will be positively related to the extent and the depth of the latter, relative to that of their domestic operations. In this part of our chapter, we attempt two exercises. One is to group the data already presented according to the four bands of multinationality set out earlier. The second is to relate the extent of the two measures of multinationality earlier identified (i.e. (i) the average percentage of global assets and employment employed outside the home country and (ii) the average percentage of global R&D expenditure undertaken outside the home country) to the values placed on Porter's four facets of competitive advantages (our groups 1 to 4), in a series of bivariate relationships.

Table 12.6 shows quite clearly that a greater degree of multinationality of firms is likely to be associated with the perception that an increasing proportion of global competitive advantages is derived from foreign sources. This, of all the tables presented in this chapter, is the most striking in its findings. It would also appear that for created assets (i.e. Group 1 [iii–vii]) the biggest rise in the significance of foreign operations for global competitiveness occurs when the average degree of multinationality (of assets and employment) is 30 per cent or above. However, for innovatory capacity, it is only where the degree of multinationality exceeds 60 per cent that the (average) ranking exceeds 3.00, while, as far as the influence of consumer demand and interfirm rivalry is concerned, it exceeds 5.00. The distinction between the sources of competitive advantages perceived to be derived from FDI and cross-border strategic alliances is particularly noticeable in the case of firms with low and high degrees of multinationality.

Table 12.7 sets out some bivariate correlation coefficients between the two measures of multinationality and six indices of competitive advantage. It suggests that for the main measure of multinationality (A in Table 12.7), the coefficients are positive and significant at a 99 per cent level or above, and that the most likely benefits of increased multinationality are likely to arise from an access to foreign organizational capacity and managerial expertise, and the linkages forged with foreign firms.

The results for the second measure of multinationality, the foreign R&D ratio (B in Table 12.7) are virtually identical to the results obtained for the first measure. Except for the correlation with natural assets (Group 1 [i–ii]), all of the coefficients are positive and significant at the 99 per cent level or above. Not surprisingly, the two measures of multinationality are also significantly positively correlated with each other (0.69, $p < 0.0001$), confirming that they essentially measure aspects of the same phenomenon.[30]

Size of Firm

The final contextual variable – which to some extent is correlated with the degree of multinationality[31] – is size of firm. While it is not obvious why size, itself, should be related to the geographical sourcing of competitiveness-enhancing assets, the literature[32] does suggest that large firms are more likely to engage in FDI than smaller firms, and that multinationality, itself, helps a corporation to maintain, or increase, its share of global markets.

At the same time, it might be hypothesized that medium-size firms are likely to be more specialized in their portfolio of global assets, and, hence, more reliant on foreign sources to enhance or complement this portfolio. However, in recent years, the evidence suggests that very large firms are just as likely to engage in merger and acquisition (M&A) activities as are their smaller competitors. Finally, it might be predicted that the portfolio of foreign competitive-enhancing assets sought by medium-size firms,[33] relative to larger firms, may have more to do with gaining access to specialized resources, capabilities and markets, and/or establishing linkages with local foreign firms, although they may be expected to engage in less competition with foreign-owned firms than their larger counterparts.

Table 12.8 presents the results of our survey. It shows that size of firm is only of marginal importance in affecting the sourcing of most categories of competitive advantage.

WHICH FOREIGN COUNTRIES PROVIDE THE MOST VALUABLE ASSETS TO UPGRADING COMPETITIVENESS?

The next part of this chapter gives some details of the foreign countries most frequently identified by the sample firms as sources of competitiveness-enhancing assets. Here, it is not possible to evaluate the importance of one source country relative to another; instead, we have chosen to identify which kind of competitive advantage is likely to be most closely associated with each country.

What would the received theories of trade and investment predict in this respect? The answer is that much will depend on the type of FDI undertaken (e.g. is it market seeking, resource seeking, efficiency seeking, or strategic asset seeking?), and on the static and dynamic competitive advantages of the home and host countries. Also, like trade, FDI and alliance formation might be either inter- or intraindustry. If the former, then one might expect the countries recipient to FDI to provide assets in which the home country is deficient; if the

Table 12.8 The sourcing of competitive advantages (classified by size of sample firms 1993)

	All	Medium	Large (<5–24.9 bn)	very large (25–49.9 bn)	Mega (>50 bn)
Group 1	3.54	3.58	3.53	3.57	3.43
Access to resources and assets	(1.39)	(1.54)	(1.44)	(1.09)	(0.94)
(i) Natural resources	4.24	3.96	4.41	4.20	4.69
	(1.70)	(1.79)	(1.76)	(1.61)	(1.03)
(ii) Unskilled labour	3.98	4.03	3.89	4.25	3.86
	(1.70)	(1.68)	(1.92)	(1.39)	(1.17)
(iii) Skilled and professional	2.98	2.96	3.06	2.88	2.86
labour	(1.27)	(1.28)	(1.41)	(1.12)	(0.77)
(iv) Innovatory capacity	2.88	2.71	2.98	3.25	2.71
	(1.40)	(1.41)	(1.49)	(1.13)	(1.20)
(v) Organizational capacity	3.12	3.13	3.22	3.00	2.79
	(1.32)	(1.39)	(1.39)	(1.15)	(0.89)
(vi) Managerial expertise	3.24	3.45	3.09	3.19	3.14
	(1.42)	(1.56)	(1.38)	(1.42)	(0.95)
(vii) Relational skills	3.75	3.82	3.78	3.50	3.64
	(1.62)	(1.66)	(1.72)	(1.59)	(1.08)
Group 2	3.94	4.07	3.90	3.93	3.67
Consumer demand	(1.59)	(1.68)	(1.63)	(1.58)	(1.15)
(i) Upgrading of product	3.31	3.30	3.40	3.13	3.14
quality	(1.37)	(1.38)	(1.46)	(1.25)	(1.17)
(ii) Making for more product	3.44	3.57	3.33	3.53	3.29
innovation	(1.45)	(1.46)	(1.48)	(1.46)	(1.33)
Group 3	4.60	4.58	4.72	4.50	4.29
Interfirm competition/rivalry	(1.67)	(1.85)	(1.60)	(1.26)	(1.68)
Group 4	4.10	4.24	4.07	4.25	3.57
Linkages with foreign or domestic firms and institutions	(1.37)	(1.36)	(1.45)	(1.29)	(1.16)

latter, then FDI is likely to be more efficiency enhancing and strategic asset seeking, in which case the foreign country will tend to provide assets similar to those in which the investing firm (or country) has a competitive edge.

In the course of our survey, every respondent was asked to name (up to) three foreign countries which were host to their affiliates, and which they perceived had the most positive impact on their own competitiveness. Table 12.9 presents some of the results by relating each of the competitive advantages identified to the number of times a particular host country was mentioned.

Table 12.9 The sourcing of competitive advantages classified by region or country (number of times countries mentioned among three most important sources of advantages, 1993)

	Europe				North America		Japan	Rest of world		Totals
	France	Germany	UK	Other	USA	Canada		Developed	Developing	
Group 1 Access to resources Natural assets	0.50	2.00	5.00	4.00	6.00	2.00	0.50	2.50	30.00	52.50
Created assets (technological)	1.33	12.33	6.67	9.00	18.00	1.33	7.33	1.67	7.67	65.33
Created assets (managerial)	1.00	4.33	6.00	3.67	10.00	2.67	3.33	1.33	6.33	38.66
Group 2 Consumer demand	0.00	4.00	4.00	0.00	8.00	0.00	0.00	0.00	3.00	19.00
Group 3 Interfirm rivalry	2.00	4.00	4.00	5.00	16.00	1.00	2.00	1.00	4.00	39.00
Group 4 Linkages with related firms	6.00	8.00	7.00	4.00	17.00	1.00	9.00	0.00	4.00	56.00
Totals	10.83	34.66	32.67	25.67	75.00	8.00	22.16	6.50	55.00	270.49
(*n*)	(139)	(131)	(125)	(116)	(113)	(138)	(118)	(142)	(130)	

(*n*) = number of firms in the sample excluding firms from the host country.

The data in the table confirm most of our predictions. Thus, developing countries clearly have a competitive advantage in affording access to natural resources, while Germany and Japan provided more than the average share of technological assets, and the United States more than the average share of managerial assets and consumer demand conditions favouring competitiveness (e.g. large markets). US firms were also perceived to offer relatively more competitive stimulus than other firms, while relative to other countries, Germany, Japan and the United States were perceived as good locations for establishing linkages with other firms.

One surprise of our survey was the frequency with which developing countries were identified as providing access to created assets and to Group 3 and 4 competitive advantage. Although mostly this is the result of pooling a number of countries at different stages of development into the same group, China and Brazil were both mentioned a number of times as providing a locale for more efficient production via economies of scale.[34] As might be expected, the host countries named varied with both the industry of the investing MNEs and their home countries. Thus, for example, firms in HT sectors accounted for 45–57 per cent of all mentions in the HT countries, for example the United States, Germany, Japan and the United Kingdom. Taking European-, US- and Japanese-owned firms as a group, 25.3 per cent of the countries mentioned by the respondents were located elsewhere in the Triad. (Or, alternatively, nearly three-quarters of their advantages were derived from within the Triad.)

THE MODES OF FOREIGN ENTRY MOST LIKELY TO ADVANCE COMPETITIVE ADVANTAGES

The respondents of our sample firms was asked to rank on a scale of 1 to 7 the importance of each of three modes of acquiring and/or tapping into the resources and capabilities of foreign countries, that is foreign diamonds of competitive advantage. These modes were (a) foreign direct investment, (b) non-equity co-operative agreements (e.g. strategic alliances, management contracts, licensing and franchising agreements, etc.) and (c) arm's-length transactions (in both intermediate and final goods and services).

The hypothesis here is that 'deeper' forms of cross-border structural integration, for example (a) and (b), are more likely to result in an addition of competitive advantages to the home company (and country) than 'shallower' forms of transactions, for example arm's-length trade. It might also be predicted that firms are more likely to wish to internalize their assets in sectors which are technology intensive, than those which are not. A related hypothesis is that non-equity co-operative ventures are likely to be ranked higher as a modality for acquiring competitive advantages by firms in low-technology-intensive sectors. Because of their needs to integrate their global operations, it might be expected that the most multinational of firms may be expected to rank FDI relatively higher than firms whose foreign operations are less significant to their overall prosperity. Finally, it might be supposed that firms from countries (e.g. the United States, whose domestic institutions are organized on hierarchical lines are more likely to rank FDI as a (foreign) asset-acquiring route than their counterparts from countries (e.g. Japan) whose institutions practise a more co-operative mode of governance.

Tables 12.10 and 12.11 offer evidence to assess these hypotheses. Overall, it is clearly true that the 'deeper' forms of integration are perceived to offer the most benefits as regards the acquisition of competitive advantages abroad. In Table 12.10, the average rankings for each of the three modalities are classified according to the technological intensity of the firm. While the LT and MT firms behaved as expected, in other words FDI was perceived to offer the most advantages while arm's-length transactions would offer the least, and that arm's-length trade would be relatively more important to LT firms and FDI to MT firms, the HT firms actually derived more advantages from co-operative alliances than from FDI.

Table 12.10 Perceptions of the importance of the mode of foreign involvement of sample firms by technological intensity, extent of multinationality and size (1993)

	(a) FDI	(b) Non-equity	(c) Arm's-length
All firms	5.22 (1.63)	4.66 (1.46)	3.96 (1.45)
High technology	5.23 (1.63)	5.31 (1.08)	4.27 (1.59)
Medium technology	5.53 (1.42)	4.62 (1.41)	3.55 (1.28)
Low technology	5.02 (1.74)	4.07 (1.57)	3.92 (1.36)
Low multinationality	4.06 (2.19)	4.71 (1.69)	3.59 (1.62)
Medium–low multinationality	5.46 (1.67)	5.25 (1.07)	4.25 (1.26)
Medium–high multinationality	5.44 (1.38)	4.83 (1.28)	4.12 (1.53)
High multinationality	5.28 (1.67)	3.93 (1.65)	3.55 (1.21)
Medium size	4.83 (1.84)	4.48 (1.50)	4.00 (1.41)
Large	5.19 (1.61)	4.69 (1.31)	3.95 (1.46)
Very large	6.07 (0.80)	5.07 (1.79)	4.13 (1.46)
Mega	5.93 (0.92)	4.79 (1.58)	3.71 (1.64)

Table 12.11 Perceptions of the importance of the mode of foreign involvement of sample firms by region or country of origin (1993)

	(a) FDI	(b) Non-equity	(c) Arm's-length
All firms	5.22 (1.63)	4.66 (1.46)	3.96 (1.45)
Large European	5.47 (1.42)	4.60 (1.45)	3.81 (1.24)
Small European	4.70 (1.95)	4.81 (1.63)	4.32 (1.34)
United States	4.97 (1.80)	4.58 (1.26)	3.29 (1.64)
Japan	5.96 (1.17)	5.36 (1.41)	4.88 (1.26)
Developing countries	4.79 (1.37)	4.29 (1.14)	4.21 (1.25)
Other countries	4.57 (2.15)	3.14 (1.57)	3.29 (1.38)

Also somewhat contrary to our expectations, the medium–low and medium–high multinationalization firms actually derived more advantages from all three modalities of foreign involvement than did firms in the high multinationalization group. Whether this is another manifestation of the law of diminishing returns or of the differences in the first-mover vs. late-mover experiences, remains to be seen. More in line with our expectations, the connection between internationalization and size was confirmed, as the figures in Table 12.10 would seem to indicate that the gains from FDI accrue predominantly to the largest firms, whereas the benefits from co-operative alliances or trade do not exhibit any obvious pattern.

Finally, Table 12.11 sheds some light on the advantages derived from the different modalities classified by the nationality of the firm. The results here contradict the hypothesis that firms from countries with typically hierarchical organizational structures would prefer FDI, as the Japanese firms stand out in their perception of the advantages derived not only from FDI, but from co-operative ventures and arm's-length trade as well. In summary, although FDI is most likely to be the preferred route by which the domestic and foreign diamonds of competitive advantage are linked, the relative significance of this route is greatest in the case of (large) firms which are (i) medium to high technology and (ii) moderately to highly multinational.

THE DYNAMICS OF THE GEOGRAPHICAL SOURCING OF COMPETITIVE ADVANTAGE

To what extent do firms perceive that their access to foreign diamonds of competitive advantage is becoming a more important contribution to their overall competitive advantages? It might be reasonably hypothesized that, as firms increase their degree of multinationality, they will derive increasingly more competitive advantages from their FDIs or strategic alliances. Of course, the reverse may also be the case. In the course of our survey, firms were asked to rank, on a scale of –3 to +3, whether they perceived their competitive advantages were becoming less (–) or more (+) dependent on their foreign operations.

The results presented in Table 12.12 essentially confirm the impressions already gained from Tables 12.10 and 12.11 concerning the benefits derived from internationalization. Although, overall, the firms perceived that the foreign sourcing of competitive advantages had become more important over time, MT and HT firms were clearly the most positive, as were the very large and mega firms. When classified by their region of origin, firms from small European countries were the most positive in their responses, which may reflect in part the aftermath of the wave of investment created by the perceived threat of a 'Fortress Europe' in 1992 for the countries outside of the Union. Not surprisingly, the firms that were the most multinational also saw the foreign sourcing of competitive advantages as being relatively more important.

Table 12.12 Perceptions of firms as to whether foreign sourcing of competitive advantages has become relatively more important in recent years (1993)

All	1.50 (1.36)
High technology	1.69 (1.35)
Medium technology	1.79 (0.95)
Low technology	1.16 (1.51)
Large European	1.64 (1.27)
Small European	1.90 (1.04)
United States	1.26 (1.53)
Japan	1.62 (1.39)
Developing	1.43 (0.85)
Other	0.38 (2.00)
Medium size	1.47 (1.32)
Large	1.31 (1.55)
Very large	1.87 (0.83)
Mega	2.00 (0.96)
Low multinationality	0.94 (1.55)
Medium–low	1.29 (1.37)
Medium–high	1.62 (1.44)
High	1.96 (0.92)

HOME GOVERNMENTS AND COMPETITIVENESS

The role of governments in affecting the competitiveness of firms is a subject which has long been of fascination to economists and other scholars.[35] In the present context, we are interested in the perceived influences of home governments on the ability and willingness of our sample firms to be globally competitive. In our questionnaire, we identified eighteen possible ways in which governments might exert such an influence. For each of these ways, we asked the firms to assign a figure ranging from –3 to +3, according to whether, in their opinion, home governments had influenced their *global* competitiveness negatively or positively between 1988 and 1993 (0 = no influence at all). Table 12.13 presents our findings classified by the three groups of industrial sectors identified in this chapter. Table 12.14 does the same for firms classified by different nationalities and Table 12.15 for firms classified by their degree of multinationality.

Table 12.13 Perceived influence of home governments on the competitive advantages of the sample firms by technological intensity (1993)

	All	HT	MT	LT
1 Provision and upgrading of infrastructure	0.52	0.48	0.60	0.51
	(1.00)	(1.08)	(1.00)	(0.93)
2 Social policies	–0.13	–0.10	–0.31	–0.05
	(1.44)	(1.47)	(1.42)	(1.43)
3 Monetary and exchange rate policies	–0.11	–0.04	–0.73	0.20
	(2.16)	(1.94)	(2.00)	(2.40)
4 Trade policies	0.35	0.26	–0.12	0.70
	(1.45)	(1.40)	(1.52)	(1.39)
5 Industrial and technology policies	0.36	0.35	0.06	0.54
	(2.08)	(2.11)	(2.46)	(1.80)
6 Education and training policies	0.09	0.15	0.03	0.07
	(1.25)	(1.43)	(1.29)	(1.04)
7 Environmental policies	–0.06	–0.34	0.09	0.13
	(1.24)	(1.22)	(1.33)	(1.16)
8 Market-facilitating policies	–0.37	–0.38	–0.55	–0.25
	(1.99)	(2.05)	(2.15)	(1.85)
9 Promoting an ethos of competitiveness	0.28	0.53	0.13	0.13
	(2.91)	(3.57)	(2.72)	(2.30)
10 Promoting a culture of investment and saving	0.18	0.51	–0.09	0.04
	(1.91)	(2.12)	(2.07)	(1.56)

Table 12.14 Perceived influence of home governments on the competitive advantages of the sample firms by region or country of origin (1993)

	All	Large European	Small European	USA	Japan	Other developed	Developing
1 Provision and upgrading of infrastructure	0.52 (1.00)	0.68 (1.03)	0.81 (0.96)	–0.08 (0.85)	0.44 (0.96)	0.67 (0.67)	1.00 (0.99)
2 Social policies	–0.13 (1.44)	–0.45 (1.50)	0.38 (1.50)	–0.74 (1.37)	0.20 (1.00)	–0.13 (1.55)	0.92 (1.12)
3 Monetary and exchange rate policies	–0.11 (2.16)	0.21 (2.33)	0.52 (2.46)	0.29 (1.44)	–1.62 (1.77)	–0.13 (1.81)	–0.08 (2.43)
4 Trade policies	0.35 (1.45)	0.30 (1.15)	0.29 (1.95)	0.19 (1.49)	–0.19 (1.47)	1.13 (0.64)	1.54 (0.88)
5 Industrial and technology policies	0.36 (2.08)	–0.12 (1.87)	1.19 (2.40)	–0.53 (1.96)	0.72 (2.03)	0.13 (1.46)	2.08 (1.38)
6 Education and training policies	0.09 (1.25)	0.07 (1.32)	0.81 (1.47)	–0.58 (0.81)	0.12 (0.95)	0.00 (0.93)	0.62 (1.50)
7 Environmental policies	–0.06 (1.24)	–0.14 (1.32)	0.00 (1.00)	–0.55 (1.36)	0.50 (0.86)	–0.25 (1.39)	0.31 (1.18)
8 Market-facilitating policies	–0.37 (1.99)	–0.37 (2.02)	–0.14 (2.31)	–1.13 (1.87)	–0.54 (1.79)	–0.25 (1.39)	1.31 (1.38)
9 Promoting an ethos of competitiveness	0.28 (2.91)	0.21 (3.00)	0.57 (3.65)	0.10 (3.28)	0.19 (1.30)	–0.50 (2.20)	1.17 (3.41)
10 Promoting a culture of investment and saving	0.18 (1.91)	0.29 (2.00)	0.38 (1.72)	–0.77 (1.81)	0.84 (1.70)	–0.50 (1.07)	0.85 (2.19)

Table 12.13 shows that, on average, the sample firms thought that actions by their home governments had had either a marginally beneficial effect on their global competitiveness (e.g. provision of infrastructure, trade and industrial and technology policies) or a marginally adverse effect on market-facilitating and social policies. There were few consistent differences between sectors, except that LT firms thought more favourably of most government actions (notably trade, industrial, technology, monetary and exchange rate policies) than either HT or MT firms.

Table 12.15 Perceived influence of home governments on the competitive advantages of the sample firms by extent of multinationality (1993)

	All	Low	Medium–low	Medium–high	High
1 Provision and upgrading of infrastructure	0.52 (1.00)	0.67 (1.12)	0.67 (0.87)	0.37 (1.03)	0.61 (0.87)
2 Social policies	–0.13 (1.44)	–0.39 (1.20)	0.10 (1.64)	–0.27 (1.39)	0.03 (1.59)
3 Monetary and exchange rate policies	–0.11 (2.16)	–0.39 (2.35)	–0.68 (1.89)	–0.03 (2.09)	0.83 (2.19)
4 Trade policies	0.35 (1.45)	0.50 (1.62)	0.32 (1–5?)	0.27 (1.41)	0.60 (1.38)
5 Industrial and technology policies	0.36 (2.08)	1.33 (1.97)	0.59 (2.17)	0.17 (1.96)	–0.13 (2.13)
6 Education and training policies	0.09 (1.25)	0.28 (1.49)	–0.09 (1.06)	0.17 (1.15)	–0.10 (1.45)
7 Environmental policies	–0.06 (1.24)	–0.06 (1.43)	0.00 (0.98)	–0.08 (1.39)	–0.07 (1.08)
8 Market-facilitating policies	–0.37 (1.99)	–0.06 (1.66)	–0.41 (1.44)	–0.53 (2.18)	–0.40 (2.03)
9 Promoting an ethos of competitiveness	0.28 (2.91)	0.24 (2.25)	0.32 (2.93)	0.33 (2.79)	0.13 (3.73)
10 Promoting a culture of investment and saving	0.18 (1.91)	0.72 (1.84)	0.23 (2.43)	–0.02 (1.59)	0.03 (2.18)

More interesting differences are revealed in Table 12.14. While US and European firms perceived that their home governments pursued macro-economic and trade policies marginally favourable to their competitiveness, Japanese firms considered these same policies of their government to work to their disadvantage. By contrast, Japanese firms believed that most macro-organizational policies of their government (e.g. environmental, industrial and technology policies), together with the promotion of a culture of investment and saving, aided their global competitiveness, while US respondents generally thought their government worked to the detriment of their competitiveness. Respondents of firms from small European and developing countries were generally more favourably disposed to the actions of their home governments than those of firms from other countries. Rather surprisingly, while firms from all the major investing countries believed their governments did little to facilitate the efficient operation of markets, firms from developing countries were noticeably more appreciative of the role of governments.

Table 12.15 suggests that there is no consistent pattern in the reactions of firms to their own government's actions according to the degree of multinationality of the former. Thus, while the least multinational of firms regarded the impact of industrial and technology policies, and the promotion of an investment and savings culture, more favourably than did the most multinational firms, the reverse appeared to be the case for macro-economic and social policies. Here, however, bivariant comparisons of this kind tend to break down as it so happens that Japanese firms are the least multinational, and it could be (and most likely is) that the country of the respondent firms is the more important determinant of the role of government than the degree of their multinationality. It is precisely for this and related reasons why a multivariant approach is necessary to complement the descriptive interpretation of the data set out in this chapter.

SUMMARY AND CONCLUSIONS

This chapter has shown that a not insignificant part of the competitive advantages of some of the world's leading industrial corporations is derived from their foreign-based activities. It has also revealed that the extent to which a firm's competitive advantages are so derived is dependent on (i) the kind of competitive advantages and the types of FDI and/or cross-border alliances engaged in by firms, (ii) the technology intensity of the sectors in which they are engaged, (iii) the countries from which they emanate, and (iv) – most particularly – on the degree of their multinationality.

Our data also reveal that an overwhelming majority of firms from all sectors and countries believed that the importance of the foreign sourcing of their competitive advantages had increased in recent years, and that FDI was the favoured modality (followed by that of interfirm co-operative agreements) for acquiring such advantages.

A final section of the chapter touched on the role of home governments in influencing the global competitive advantages of the sample firms. In general, this was not perceived to be of critical significance, but there were noticeable differences observed by firms of different nationalities, which, *inter alia*, reflect some very distinctive country-specific philosophies of the role of governments, hierarchies and markets between larger Western nations (particularly the United States) and Eastern nations (particularly Japan) and some smaller European nations (particularly Sweden).

APPENDIX: CHARACTERISTICS OF THE SAMPLE

The sample consists of a total of 144 responses, which come from 131 different firms. For those firms that provided multiple responses, the statistics on size and degree of multinationality, as well as industry classification, follow those of the largest corporate unit. Outside of these classification variables, all of the multiple responses received are unique, and are treated as individual responses in the analyses.

Of the 144 responses to the survey, 110 come from firms that are ranked in the *Fortune* 500 (based on 1993 sales). The remaining firms were contacted to improve the industrial and/or geographical representativeness of the data, and they are all among the largest multinationals of their respective home countries.

One firm in the sample could not be classified by industry sector, as the identity of the firm was concealed; however, values for the other classification variables were obtained.

NOTES

1. This is the first of three papers which resulted from the survey. Readers interested in a more rigorous testing of the propositions contained in this chapter are invited to consult Dunning and Lundan (1998) and Dunning and Wymbs (1999). This latter contribution also considers some industry-specific characteristics of the foreign sourcing of competitive advantage.
2. As identified by *Fortune* magazine, 25 July 1994.
3. Mainly vice-presidents or directors of foreign operations.
4. Sometimes called ownership-specific advantages of firms.
5. For a summary of the competitive advantages identified by economists, see, for example, Dunning (1993a, Chap. 4), and for those identified by business strategists, for example, see Porter (1990) and Peteraf (1993).
6. The aim of strategic asset-acquiring FDI is to gain access to assets which protect or advance the acquiring firm's competitive advantages and/or reduce the competitive advantages of its rivals. In the language of the eclectic paradigm, firms engage in FDI not to exploit existing ownership (O) advantages, but to acquire such advantages, which, when deployed with their existing O advantages, help sustain or further their global competitive advantages.
7. As documented, for example, in the various editions of the *World Investment Reports* (UNCTAD). The most recent US data (Mataloni, 1995) show that in 1993 the foreign affiliate sales of non-bank US MNEs were 45.0 per cent of their parent sales. This figure compares with a 1983 figure of 37.3 per cent.
8. See especially a special issue of *Management International Review* (No. 33, 1993) edited by Alan Rugman (Rugman et al., 1995).
9. First set out in Porter (1990).
10. See, for example, Dunning (1993b).
11. Including those of Australia, Canada, Denmark, Korea, Mexico and New Zealand. See Rugman (1993).
12. We fully recognize the drawbacks of such a procedure and, in particular, the inevitable subjectivity of the opinions expressed.
13. More specifically, HT sectors include aerospace, chemicals, computers, electronics and pharmaceuticals; MT sectors include industrial equipment, motor vehicles, petroleum refining,

soap and cosmetics; and LT sectors include beverages, building materials, food, metal products, paper, publishing and printing, rubber and plastics, textiles and tobacco.

14. These include France, Germany, Italy, Spain, the United Kingdom and UK/Netherlands.
15. These include Belgium, Denmark, Finland, the Netherlands, Sweden and Switzerland.
16. These include Brazil, Chile, Hong Kong, South Korea and Taiwan.
17. These include Canada, Australia and New Zealand.
18. Or one of these when data on either employment or assets were given. Additionally, for some firms sales data from Worldscope/Disclosure was used.
19. As defined by the firms themselves.
20. See especially their annual *World Investment Reports* (1991–5) and the *World Investment Directory* (4 volumes, 1992–3).
21. But, again, we would remind the reader that all the firms in the sample are large, compared with the great majority of the 38 000 firms identified by UNCTAD as having foreign direct investments. See its *World Investment Report* (1995).
22. The comparison in this exercise is between advantages thought to emanate from the portfolio of assets located in the home country and that in all other countries.
23. Namely, factor conditions, demand conditions, firm strategy, structure and rivalry, and related and supporting industries (see Porter, 1990).
24. Each ranking being expressed as a percentage of 7 (which would suggest that all their advantages were derived from outside their national boundaries).
25. A later paper will attempt to relate the performance of the sample firms to the sources of their competencies.
26. We accept that these data do not, in themselves, indicate whether, if the FDI had *not* taken place, or the alliances had *not* been formed, the overall competitive position of the respondent firms would have been better or worse.
27. Notably Sweden and Switzerland.
28. Namely, Canada, Australia and New Zealand.
29. By this is meant either the pursuance of R&D-related activities by the foreign subsidiaries and/or alliances with foreign firms, or the monitoring of the innovatory activities of foreign firms.
30. Since the Group 1–4 variables are not continuous, the significance levels reported here should be taken as indicators of a possible relationship (to be investigated further in a later paper) rather than any form of final analysis.
31. Although the (Pearson) correlation coefficient between size and multinationality is not significantly different from zero.
32. See, for example, Dunning (1993a, Chap. 6).
33. Remembering that all the firms in our sample are large, relative to the universe of firms, but that some are much larger than others!
34. The figures in Table 12.9 somewhat understate the importance of scale economies, as the figure for Group 2 indicates the overall importance of consumer demand conditions, and not scale economies specifically.
35. For a recent appraisal, see various contributions to Dunning (1997).

REFERENCES

Cantwell, J. and Hodson, C. (1991), 'Global R&D and UK competitiveness', in M. Casson (ed.), *Global Research Strategy and International Competitiveness*, Oxford: Basil Blackwell, pp. 133–82.

Dunning, J.H. (1993a), *Multinational Enterprises and the Global Economy*, Wokingham: Addison-Wesley.

Dunning, J.H. (1993b), 'Internationalizing Porter's Diamond', *Management International Review* **33**, Special Issue No. 2: 7–15.

Dunning, J.H. (ed.) (1997), *Governments, Globalization and International Business*, Oxford: Oxford University Press.

Dunning, J.H. and Lundan, J. (1998), 'The geographical sources of competitiveness of multilateral enterprises: an econometric analysis', *International Business Review* **7**: 115–33.

Dunning, J.H. and Wymbs, C. (1999), 'The geographical sourcing of technology-based assets by multinational enterprises', in D. Archibugi, J. Howells and J. Michie (eds), *Innovation Policy in a Global Economy*, Cambridge: Cambridge University Press, pp. 185–224.

Mataloni, R. (1995), 'U.S. multinational companies: operations in 1993', *Survey of Current Business* June: 31–51.

Peteraf, M. (1993), The cornerstones of competitive advantage: a resource based view', *Strategic Management Journal* **14**: 179–91.

Porter, M.E. (1990), *The Competitive Advantage of Nations*, New York: The Free Press.

Rugman, A.M. (ed.) (1993), *Management International Review* **33**, spring, No. 2 (Special Edition on Michael Porter's 'Diamond of competitive advantage').

Rugman, A.M., Van den Broeck, J. and Verbeke, A. (eds) (1995), *Beyond the Diamond: Research in Global Management*, Vol. 5, Greenwich, CT: JAI Press.

UNCTAD (1991–5), *World Investment Reports 1991–95* (annual publication), Geneva and New York: UN.

UNCTAD (1992–3), *World Investment Directory* (4 vols, 1992–3).

UNCTAD (1995), *World Investment Report 1995: Transnational Corporations and Competitiveness*, Geneva and New York: UN.

13. Multinational enterprises, industrial restructuring and competitiveness: a UK perspective*

INTRODUCTION

Since 1970, the world has experienced a series of events which have had, and are having, a most profound effect on the allocation of economic activity, both between and within countries. Among those of greatest long-term significance are the rising economic stature of some NICs, particularly those from the Far East, and a series of technological breakthroughs, especially in the areas of information and telecommunications, and biotechnology. Of more immediate and pervasive impact has been a deceleration in world economic growth, coupled with a swing to neo-liberal policies of most governments and a more realistic appreciation of the costs and gains of economic interdependence.

These events have affected countries differently, according, for example, to their stage of development and economic structure, and to the way in which central authorities have adjusted to them. Most advanced industrial societies have found the repercussions both painful and destabilizing. While we should not minimize the impact of inflation and cyclical unemployment and the supply-oriented managerial policies to combat these, a more powerful impetus to industrial restructuring has been the dramatic cuts in price–cost margins. These, together with new technologies and growing international competition, have caused sweeping reappraisals of product, process and marketing strategies, and the location of production facilities. This has resulted in a good deal of structural unemployment, and has severely tested governments in their adjustment policies. Indeed, it is the combination of the pattern, pace and extent of these developments which has created so many of the problems of recent years.

This chapter examines the role of MNEs as engines of structural change and transmitters of change across national boundaries, and also as influences on the way in which the international community adapts to change. We shall consider these issues from a UK perspective and concern ourselves with the

* From J.H. Dunning, *Multinationals, Technology and Competitiveness*, London and Boston, MA: Unwin Hyman (1988), pp. 172–202.

impact of the overseas operations of UK MNEs and of the UK affiliates of foreign-based MNEs on the allocation of economic activity, both between the UK and the rest of the world and within the UK.

In particular, we shall bear in mind two commonly held, but very different views; first that MNEs, by their favoured access to human and financial resources and their ability to move them across national boundaries and between industrial sectors, play a positive role in the structural modernization and the transformation of the UK economy; and second that MNEs' decisions regarding resource allocation, taken from a global perspective, may be detrimental to the long-term interests of the UK economy by locking it into an unacceptable international division of labour, by weakening its economic sovereignty and by frustrating its efforts to revitalize its industrial base and develop new technological initiatives.

HISTORICAL BACKGROUND

There can be no doubt that Britain's close involvement in trade and foreign investment has caused it to be particularly vulnerable to fluctuations in world economic events. Only at the time of the first Industrial Revolution can it be said that Britain was in control of its economic destiny; since then, partly because the country already had an industrial heritage, and partly because of the erosion of its technological supremacy, Britain has adjusted to, rather than been the prime mover in, structural change; that is, it has been dominated by exogenous rather than endogenous forces.

For example, in the years before the First World War, the second generation of technological advances based upon the internal combustion engine and electrical power were first commercialized in the USA, even though they often originated from Europe. Initially suited to the American economy and best exploited by large firms, they were transmitted back to the UK by the first wave of American multinational entrepreneurs. During the inter-war years, the new industries they generated, for example, motor vehicles, electrical engineering, etc., helped to compensate for the loss of some traditional markets, for example, textiles, shipbuilding, to the then industrializing countries, for instance, India and Japan. In this way, inward investment performed a useful restructuring role, while outward investment was mainly directed to resource-exploitative ventures in the Commonwealth.

The process of US technical hegemony was accelerated in the Second World War, reaching its peak shortly afterwards, and in the 1950s much of Europe's recovery was aided by US direct investment. At this point in time, the maturing MNEs were the main private repositories of technological innovation; they were also the main organizational route by which such innovations were transferred across boundaries, often aided by barriers to trade and lack of suitable licensees in host countries. In the early post-war years, there was some foreign investment by UK firms in industries in which the UK has lost, or was losing, her comparative advantage, but, by and large, this continued to be directed to resource-based activities or to service markets which were difficult or costly to supply from the UK.

Studies in the 1950s and 1960s on inward and outward investment found that it had a favourable impact on the post-war restructuring of the UK economy.[1] The evidence presented at the time strongly suggested that the UK's economic structure had been tilted more towards high technology and growth manufacturing sectors as a result of inward investment, while the foreign activities of UK MNEs were mainly directed to the primary and more traditional secondary sectors. In 1964, for example, some 71 per cent of the net foreign assets owned by the leading UK manufacturing MNEs were in the less technology-intensive sectors of food, drink and tobacco, household products, paper, metal products, building materials and textiles, and 29 per cent in the more technology-intensive sectors of chemicals, engineering, electronics, and vehicles (Reddaway, Potter and Taylor, 1968). By contrast, in 1965, 67 per cent of the net assets of foreign – mainly US – firms in UK manufacturing were in the more technology-intensive sectors and only 33 per cent in the former industries in less technology-intensive sectors. The data set out in Table 13.1 clearly show that while the foreign activities of UK MNEs in the 1960s were more oriented towards the traditional sectors than those of UK industry in general, the activities of foreign subsidiaries in the UK were more oriented to the high technology sectors.

To some extent, the pattern of activity by MNEs in the 1960s reflected their geographical destination or origin. Britain's past imperialistic ties steered investment towards those sectors in which it had a comparative trading advantage. In 1960, 61 per cent of the net foreign assets owned by UK MNEs outside oil, banking, and insurance was invested in Commonwealth countries. Over the last 20 years, the growing importance of the involvement by UK MNEs in Europe has shifted the sectoral distribution towards more high technology sectors. At the same time, these investments, like those of foreign MNEs in the UK, reflect the changing locational attractions of countries. Some foreign governments, for example, by nationalization or other deterrents, have virtually outlawed some kinds of MNE activity; much of the vertical disinvestment by UK firms since 1960 can be explained in these terms. Changing locational advantages also explain a lot of import-substituting investment in the inter-war years. Tariff barriers and other import controls induced US firms to set up factories in the UK, as did the shortage of US dollars after the Second World War. In the 1980s, European and US protectionism against Japanese imports was prompting Japanese MNEs to follow a similar strategy. Natural or artificially

Table 13.1 The industrial structure of UK inward and outward direct investment in the 1960s

	Inward (capital stake end 1965)		All UK firms (net output 1963)		Outward (capital stake end 1964)	
	£m	%	£m	%	£m	%
Food, drink and tobacco	207.9	12.7	1,292.0	12.5	537.6	39.3
Chemicals and allied industries	211.9	13.0	949.9	9.2	194.5	14.2
Metal manufacturing	134.4	8.2	1,500.2	14.5	132.2	9.7
Mechanical engineering	336.7	20.7	1,435.8	13.9	19.9	1.5
Electrical engineering	185.1	11.4	954.0	9.2	67.5	4.9
Motor vehicles	303.5	18.6	1,184.4	11.5	51.8	3.8
Textiles, clothing and footwear	34.9	2.1	1,234.1	12.0	94.1	6.9
Paper and allied products	46.2	2.8	845.6	8.2	118.8	8.6
Rubber products	58.4	3.6	167.7	1.6	74.3	5.4
Other manufacturing industries	110.4	6.8	755.3	7.3	76.2	5.6
All manufacturing	1629.4	100.0	10,319.0	100.0	1366.7	100.0

Sources: Inward capital stake, *Board of Trade Journal*, 26 January 1968; all UK firms net output, *Census of Production*, 1963; outward capital stake, Reddaway, Potter and Taylor (1968).

induced shifts in the locational pull of countries both affect, and may be affected by, the extent and balance of international direct investment; in other words, the structure of foreign direct investment – and hence its impact on the economy – is influenced by the disposition of immobile resource endowments, including government policy, as well as that of more mobile resource endowments.

Finally, the organizational mode of exploiting the *O* advantages of firms must be considered. It is, at least, possible that differences in the structure of UK outward and inward direct investment in the 1960s might reflect the differences in the relative costs of (international) intermediate product markets and those of hierarchies in the sectors, or between the investing and recipient countries in question. Most outward investment, for example, involved the transfer of mature and codifiable technologies, where proprietary rights could be protected, and quality control assured. By contrast, a higher proportion of inward investment involved idiosyncratic or non-codifiable technologies for which there were no or highly imperfect cross-border markets; in consequence, to appropriate fully their economic rent, the owning firm perceived it had to internalize their transfer. Moreover, the economies of size, scope and organizational synergy tended to be pronounced in sectors in which foreign subsidiaries were well represented, relative to those in which UK MNEs tend to be concentrated.[2]

A NEW INTERNATIONAL DIVISION OF LABOUR

During the 1960s, although there was some concern about the effects of outward investment on the balance of payments and of inward investment on competition, market structure and technological capability,[3] there was not much anxiety about the MNEs as vehicles for relocating domestic economic activity or for determining the pattern of employment and output across countries. Partly this reflected the macro-economic climate of the day and partly the fact that few MNEs yet operated globally integrated product or sourcing strategies.

The slowing down of economic growth and increase in unemployment in Europe, the opening up of the Far Eastern economies, the move towards closer economic integration in Europe – and to a lesser extent in Latin America and Asia – the increasing ease with which organizations could be managed at a distance, and the spread of multinationalization *per se*, have quite dramatically affected the MNEs' role in structural change. While the MNEs' strength as producers of technology, particularly of advanced technology, continues undiminished, they have attracted most recent attention as agents in determining what kinds of technology are transferred to which countries to produce what products to be sold in which markets. As a result of the increased geographical diversification of activity under common ownership, and the closer relationships between firms at different stages of production processes, countries have become related to each other in a new international division of labour, which, if not actively engineered by MNEs, has been largely orchestrated and utilized by them.

In such a division of labour, the structure of international production is determined by MNE hierarchies competing among themselves, rather than by independent buyers and sellers at arm's-length prices. Efficiency and success are judged from a corporate standpoint rather than from that of the countries in which the corporations produce. In such conditions, industrial restructuring by MNEs may link one economy with another in ways unacceptable to either or both. In such cases, the role of international hierarchies is less that of resource transferors, or tutors in resource usage, and more that of allocators of economic activity to meet their global goals. Moreover, the process of adjustment may bring its own problems and require a modification in government economic strategies.

THE IMPACT OF NEW TECHNOLOGY

The arrival of the new technologies of the last decade is likely to have no less a far reaching effect. Over the years, technological change has become less activity- or customer-specific. Nowhere is this better seen than in the fields of telematics and biotechnology, in which tremendous strides are now being made. The micro-chip, the latest generation of computers, robotics, laser technology and optic fibres have multitudinous applications. Yet because equipment systems and techniques can be used jointly by firms engaged in related activities, there are good reasons for such firms to be linked to each other in the production chain. This is leading to hierarchical galaxies, with a pivotal group of firms (which control the key technologies) being surrounded by satellite suppliers and customers. In the case of information technology, the core firms are sometimes the computing and sometimes the telecommunications giants; in biotechnology, the battle for supremacy is divided between the food processing, chemical and pharmaceutical enterprises, but its uses extend from pollution control and mineral extraction to health care and agriculture.

Because most technological developments are transmittable across national boundaries, and different stages of the value-added chain have different locational configurations, the globally integrated MNE is in a strong position to capitalize on them. This may show itself in a regional or global marketing policy (that is, the development of a world product mandate) or in the international sourcing of components and raw materials. It certainly adds to the need for flexible production systems, low inventories, the integration between computer-aided design and manufacturing processes. All these developments are highly capital- and/or technology-intensive and only pay off if international markets can be captured. As a consequence, if countries (particularly smaller countries) wish to be in the van of progress, they need to generate their own MNEs and/or encourage the formation of national or international corporate alliances. This suggests that the MNEs of the 1990s will pose new challenges and opportunities to national governments and require a conscious re-examination of their technological and industrial policies.

THE STRUCTURAL IMPACT OF MNEs IN THE 1960s AND 1970s: SOME THEORETICAL CONSIDERATIONS

Multinational enterprises may affect the economic structure of the countries in which they operate in a number of ways. First, by the resources they transfer, and the control exerted over these and the local resources they acquire, they can directly affect the strategy, performance, and conduct of their foreign affiliates, while indirectly they may affect other firms, for instance, by linkages, example and competitive stimulus. Second, by their choice of activity they may influence the way resources are allocated. Third, by their internalization of product and factor markets they may impinge on both domestic and international market structures. Fourth, over time, the way they respond to changes in supply or demand conditions may influence the adaptive capabilities of the economies in which they operate. Fifth, by their mode of entry (takeover of green-field investment) and their global strategies, they may modify both market structure and the nationality of ownership of firms.

How far is it possible to identify an optimum economic structure for a country? This is exceedingly difficult, as the goals of government are multiple and extend well beyond the quest for economic efficiency. Many countries exercise some control over inward and outward direct investment for social or political reasons. A short run improvement in industrial composition may not necessarily be beneficial in the long run; neither does it follow that all groups in the community will gain, or gain to the same extent. In practice, there are trade-offs in goals and priorities which can be resolved only by political judgement and action. What happens if an improved structure leads to more unemployment? Is less national autonomy in decision taking an acceptable price to pay for more efficiency, and so on?

All first-year students reading economics are taught the conditions under which trade is beneficial. The well-known principle of comparative advantage holds good only under very restrictive conditions, for example, the existence of perfect competition, full employment, and immobility of factor services, and is concerned only with efficiency goals. The principle also assumes that the economic structures of the trading countries are different from each other, and ignores the role of technology, learning by doing and improvements in human capital in restructuring resource availability and usage. Few of these conditions apply in the modern world economy, though some are more relevant in (or between) some countries and/or sectors than in others. In particular, all sorts of obstacles and rigidities inhibit the speedy and efficient reallocation of resources required, while internal markets established by hierarchies may create entry barriers to countries seeking to cultivate new areas of comparative advantage. Governments, too, may play positive, as well as negative, roles in the creation and use of resources.

Since MNEs themselves engage in trade, and especially of intermediate products such as technology, it seems reasonable to suppose that their role in restructuring might be explained and evaluated using trade type analyses. Certainly they control or have access to resources which may not be easily available to uninational firms. Since they usually operate in several nation-states, and produce many products and processes, they are in a favoured position to respond to economic and technical change or take advantage of it; indeed, in many respects their affiliates are like countries trading with each other.

A Normative Proposition

Let us next turn to consider the UK's situation by making a proposition drawn from our understanding of trade theory. The proposition is that foreign MNEs producing in the UK should be encouraged to steer resources to, or help better to utilize resources in, sectors in which the UK is perceived to have, or is likely to develop, a comparative advantage. By contrast, UK MNEs should help steer activities away from the UK which require immobile resources in which the home country's comparative advantage is declining, but which can be put to good use by other countries, using the entrepreneurship, management, technology and organizational skills of firms of the home country. Here, one would expect foreign and domestic MNEs to operate in different industrial sectors; in such cases, foreign capital would substitute for domestic capital but the net result would be an improvement in national productivity. Quite a bit of MNE activity in and out of the UK fits in well with this kind of proposition – particularly that of a North–South orientation.

Increasingly, however, MNEs are also engaging in activities which cannot be evaluated in this way. Like trade, international production often takes place in different countries in similar sectors. Indeed three-quarters of all foreign direct investment is undertaken by advanced-country MNEs in other advanced countries, and most of this is in sectors in which there is a substantial amount of intra-industry specialization. Such specialization is usually undertaken to take advantage of economies of scale and scope and, because of the advantages of common governance, is usually conducted within MNEs.

The sectors in which MNEs operate are often capital-, technology- or information-intensive. They are also those which produce a wide range of processes or products springing from a common or generic technological or marketing base. Their market structure is characterized by oligopoly and usually international oligopoly. Over the years, their degree of multinationalization has dramatically increased and their strategy has become increasingly global. Already vertically and horizontally integrated across national boundaries, the latest technological developments are causing them to become centres of new galaxies. It is the presence of the subsidiaries of these firms which might seem to offer host countries access to advanced technology, but some fear that this could turn out to be a Trojan horse. At the same time, to keep up with their competitors in world markets, these same countries may need to generate their own MNEs. This inevitably results in the inter-penetration of markets and a growth in intra-industry trade. According to Kenichi Ohmae (1985), the scale of research and development necessary to maintain a leading competitive position in the knowledge-intensive manufacturing and service sectors requires firms in those sectors to have a marketing or production presence in each of the main industrial markets – the so-called 'triad' of the USA, Western Europe and Japan. From time to time, the country-specific characteristics of firms come to the fore, but, for the most part, competition is based on firm-specific product, production and marketing strategies.

Policy recommendations are more difficult, especially for small industrial countries, the wealth of which rests on their human capital and skills. Often specialization within sectors or close collaboration with foreign firms is the only alternative to opting out of the technological race altogether. Most larger countries have a wider range of choices, as they can opt for a policy of self-sufficiency; Japan is an obvious exception. For medium-sized countries like the UK, we believe the situation calls for a broader based strategy which encompasses both the courtship of inward investment as an example and a stimulus, and the encouragement of domestic MNEs to penetrate foreign markets and ensure the innovatory bases on which their future competitive prowess rests. Equally important, the government has a role in providing the infrastructure and the incentives to promote the kind of foreign investment which is most suitable to the long-term development of its indigenous resources, especially human capital, and in combating unfair competition from abroad. In the short term, some help in revitalizing and restructuring indigenous firms or sectors may be called for – especially where the prospects for the UK are favourable, but because of market failure, for example, in the capital market, UK-owned firms are unable to catch up with foreign competition without external assistance. We shall return to these issues later in this chapter.

MEASURING THE IMPACT OF MNEs ON UK INDUSTRIAL STRUCTURE

Before considering the data we have regarding the impact of MNE activity on the industrial structure of the UK, let us briefly summarize the methodology followed. There have been two main approaches to evaluating the impact of MNEs on national economies. The first is the *alternative position* or *counter-factual* approach which tries to measure the effect of FDI on foreign production as the difference between the actual impact and that which it is hypothesized would have occurred in its absence. Such an approach was used by Reddaway in the 1960s to evaluate the effects of outward direct investment on the GNP of the UK (Reddaway, Potter and Taylor, 1968). The second, which in many ways involves similar reasoning to the first, is the *comparative factual* approach: this seeks to compare the activities of MNEs with those of their non-MNE competitors, arguing that the difference between the two may be attributable to the multinationality of the former. This methodology was used by Cohen (1975) in a study of the export performance of US and indigenous firms in South Asia. The advantages are obvious: actual data are available and a comparison of, or changes in, performance can be made. But the pitfalls are many, not least that of isolating the 'multinational' effect from other differences between the two groups of firms. Moreover, to draw any policy conclusions, for example with respect to encouraging or discouraging inward or outward investment, implicitly assumes that the marginal and average impact is the same, and that the real opportunity cost lies in the ownership of activity rather than in its direction. Finally, this approach assumes just one 'alternative position'.

Nevertheless, we shall adopt this second approach. First, we shall review the main structural characteristics of inward and outward production financed by investment in 1971 and 1979, compared with that of UK-owned companies in the UK, and (where data permit) changes in these between these two years. Second, we shall examine the statistical relationship between a number of structural variables and the sectoral distribution with manufacturing industry of three types of production:[4] (1) production of foreign-owned firms in the UK; (2) the foreign production of UK MNEs; and (3) the production of UK firms (including the UK-based MNEs) in the UK. Ideally we would have liked to have separated the UK production of UK MNEs from that of UK uninational firms, but the data do not allow us to do this. The purpose of this exercise is to compare the significance of the three groups of firms on economic structure. By itself, of course, any statistical association does not tell us anything about the direction of causation; we also accept that the level of significance of each variable may be influenced by other variables not included in the equation, and that there may be some multicollinearity between the independent variables.

We tackle the causation problem in the following way. First it could be argued that if, for example, foreign MNEs *respond* to a change in, say, revealed competitive advantage (RCA) in a more positive and significant way than domestic firms, this will have an impact on future RCA. It is possible to test the impact of whether the activities of the MNEs lead or lag structural change by examining the relationship between the relative change in production between 1971 and 1979 and the value of structural parameters at the beginning and the end of the period. This a later section of the chapter seeks to do.

The sources of the statistics used are set out in the Appendix to this chapter. Suffice it at this point to say that they embrace all UK-owned firms and foreign affiliates engaged in manufacturing production from official statistics, and a selection of 188 of the largest UK MNEs covering an estimated 95 per cent of the value of overseas manufacturing investment. Data specially provided by the Department of Trade and compiled from company accounts enable us to classify the first two groups of firms by 44 minimum list headings; from an examination of the company accounts of UK MNEs, we have classified these latter firms by 29 headings.

Table 13.2 sets out some of the structural characteristics of the three groups or firms under consideration. For each characteristic we wished to establish the proportion of the total output of the three groups which was in sectors with below or above the average value of the characteristic. For example, while 44.2 per cent of the sales of indigenous firms was in sectors in which the RCA trade competitiveness of the UK was below average, the corresponding proportion for foreign affiliates and the foreign activities of UK MNEs were 37.9 per cent and 26.0 per cent respectively. The conclusions of Table 13.2 are self-evident. They suggest, a priori, that there are important differences in the structural characteristics of the groups, and hence that there is likely to be a distinctive impact on these characteristics arising from the nationality of ownership of UK-based companies and/or geographical involvement of UK-owned firms.

THE STATISTICAL TESTING

Let us now list some specific propositions about the interaction between MNEs and economic structure.

Allocative Impact

We have suggested this may vary according to the type of MNE activity, the existing technical and allocative efficiency of UK-owned firms and the extent to which extra or imperfect market forces affect resource allocation. But first let us take a neo-classical type proposition.

Table 13.2 Comparisons between industrial distribution of sales of UK and MNE-related companies and selected structural characteristics, 1979 and 1971–79

		UK firms in UK (UK)	Foreign affiliates in UK ($FMNE_{UK}$)	UK MNEs abroad (UK MNE_f)
Allocative efficiency (1979)				
(1) Trade competitiveness	BA	44.2	34.9	26.0
(RCA)	AA	49.2	59.4	61.7
(2) Labour productivity	BA	54.0	37.7	25.5
(LP)	AA	45.5	62.2	73.9
(3) Capital labour ratio	BA	69.1	42.7	38.7
(K/L)	AA	30.4	57.2	61.7
(4) Skill intensive ratio	BA	72.8	70.6	75.8
(NO/OWB)	AA	26.7	29.3	24.4
(5) Advertising ratio	BA	81.3	81.0	87.0
(A/S)	AA	16.1	14.2	12.8
(6) Concentration ratio	BA	48.0	31.6	19.4
(C)	AA	51.5	68.5	80.9
(7) Economies of scale	BA	72.5	76.4	64.2
(SP)	AA	27.0	23.5	36.1
Sectoral efficiency (1979)				
(8) Relative labour productivity	BA	58.8	48.7	39.0
	AA	34.1	49.1	57.3
(9) Relative total factor productivity	BA	55.1	47.0	37.4
	AA	37.5	48.9	48.0
(10) Relative skill intensity	BA	55.1	66.9	38.1
	AA	44.0	32.6	47.1
Adaptive efficiency (1971–79)				
(11) Growth in sales	BA	62.4	51.4	42.9
	AA	37.1	48.5	57.4
(12) Change in trade competitiveness	BA	50.5	50.0	30.9
	AA	45.4	46.0	57.6
(13) Change in labour productivity	BA	89.7	58.1	67.4
	AA	9.8	41.8	32.9
Other ratios				
(14) Intra-industry trade (1979)	BA	23.8	19.0	10.8
	AA	35.1	51.8	48.8
(15) Intra-firm trade (1977)	BA	49.5	20.3	37.3
	AA	26.1	56.4	48.2

Notes: BA and AA = % of manufacturing sales of firms in sectors with a performance ratio below or above the unweighted arithmetic mean.
For definitions of variables see the Appendix.

Proposition 1. Relative to UK-owned firms producing in the UK, foreign-owned MNEs will produce in those UK sectors which are the most internationally competitive, while the production of UK firms abroad will favour those sectors in which the UK is the least internationally competitive.[5]

This proposition is intended to test the extent to which inward and outward direct investment, relative to the UK production of indigenous firms, is concentrated in sectors in which the UK economy is comparatively advantaged.

$$RCA = 1.03 - \underset{(1.46)}{0.0305}\, UK_i + \underset{(1.18)}{0.0221}\, FMNE_{UK} - \underset{(0.77)}{0.116}\, UKMNE_f \qquad (1) \qquad (n = 28)$$

$$RCA = 0.951 - \underset{(1.06)}{0.0245}\, UK_i + \underset{(1.14)}{0.161}\, FMNE_{UK} \qquad (1a) \qquad (n = 44)$$

The relationship set out in equations (1) and (1a)[6] lends some support to this proposition. In 1979, compared with a negative, though insignificant, association between the ability of manufacturing sectors to compete in foreign markets, and the distribution of domestically produced output of UK-owned firms (UK_i), there was a positive, though insignificant, association between RCA and the sectoral distribution of foreign affiliates ($FMNE_{UK}$). Indeed, in that year, 63 per cent of the output of such affiliates was in sectors in which the RCA was greater than 1, compared with 44 per cent of UK firms. In other words, relative to their indigenous competitors, foreign MNEs *are* more inclined to invest in sectors in which UK international competitiveness is above average.

The absence of any significant position relationship between RCA and $FMNE_{UK}$, in either of the two variants of the equation[7] set out, is explained by some major exceptions. In the office machinery and computer sectors, for example, the RCA ratio was 0.92, while the foreign participation ratio was 3.1; by contrast, the corresponding figures for bricks, pottery and glass were 1.21 and 0.33. While in some cases such discrepancies reflect the level of disaggregation,[8] in others, even in narrowly delineated sectors, they occur for more substantive reasons. Two of these deserve special mention. The first is that the RCA ratio is based on sales rather than value-added data and does not distinguish between cases in which imports and exports compete with each other and those in which they complement each other. In resource-based sectors such as non-ferrous metals, timber and food-processing, the latter is the more likely as imported semi-processed goods are necessary ingredients of the final output of a product. While RCA measures based on gross exports overcome this difficulty, they tend to overstate competitiveness in that they take no account of imports of similar products. The second is that in some sectors – noticeably those in which there is international oligopolistic rivalry – the prevalence of inward FDI cannot be separated from that of outward FDI. In such cases, firm-specific ownership characteristics rather than locational forces dominate the cross-hauling of international production which is as likely to be complementary as substitutable between countries.

The first equation also shows that, as far as outward direct investment is concerned, there is no suggestion that this is more concentrated (relative to the domestic activities of UK firms) in sectors in which the UK is comparatively *disadvantaged*. However, omitting oil refining and timber and furniture, the rank correlation coefficient between RCA and the industrial distribution of $UKMNE_f$ is –0.37, and significant at a 10 per cent level. Other research (Dunning and Walker, 1982) has demonstrated that outward direct investment is significantly correlated with *domestic* competitiveness, that is, it tends to be concentrated in those sectors which record above average productivity and profitability. That the relationship between the foreign activities of UK MNEs and lack of international competitiveness is not closer may again reflect the fact that, in some sectors, exports and outward direct investment complement, rather than substitute for, each other. Some MNEs find it profitable to exploit their *O* advantages to some countries via exports and others via foreign production, while, *ceteris paribus*, products at later stages of the product cycle are more likely to be produced abroad than those at earlier stages of the cycle. This is particularly likely to be so in the case of vertical *inter*- or horizontal *intra*-industry trade. We shall return to this point later.

The second proposition relates to the extent to which MNEs are, in some sense, better allocators of resources between sectors than uninational firms. Here, much depends on in which sectors the MNEs perceive they have an advantage over their foreign competitors and whether the productivity advantages originate from the possession or use of mobile or immobile resource endowments. If the former, then both outward and inward investment may be concentrated in similar sectors; if the latter, for example, in resource-based sectors, the structure of the two may be different. The proposition set out seeks to test the latter view. We take two measures of allocative efficiency: productivity and profitability.

Proposition 2. Relative to UK-owned firms producing in the UK, foreign-owned MNEs will produce in those UK sectors which are of above average productivity or profitability, while the production of UK firms abroad will favour sectors which are of below average productivity or profitability in the UK.

The only index of productivity which is readily available is the gross value-added per head ratio, though ideally one would like to have used a total productivity index.[9] Equations (2) and (2a) suggest that this proposition is upheld for inward direct investment but not for the foreign activities of UK

MNEs. Indeed $UKMNE_f$ is significantly more concentrated in above average productivity sectors than is $FMNE_{UK}$; by contrast, domestic investment by UK firms is significantly concentrated in below average productivity sectors. Both regressions suggest that MNEs prefer to invest in high-productivity sectors; this may also reflect the fact that, in the case of the UK, there is a lot of investment cross-hauling leading to intra-industry production. Finally, it would appear that exports and FDI are most likely to complement each other in above average labour productivity sectors.

$$LP = 8253 - \underset{(424)^{**}}{3195\ UK_i} + \underset{(1.8)}{1158\ FMNE_{UK}} + \underset{(6.4)^{**}}{3159\ UKMNE_f} \qquad (2) \qquad (n = 29)$$

$$LP' = 8773 - \underset{(3.32)^{**}}{2946\ UK_i} + \underset{(7.78)^{**}}{4229\ FMNE_{UK}} \qquad (2a) \qquad (n = 44)$$

(Associations which are significant at a 10 per cent level are denoted by an asterisk * and those significant at a 5 per cent level by two asterisks ** in the above and subsequent equations.)

The equations on the relationship between profitability and resource allocation portray a similar picture. Defining π as the profit/gross sales ratio, both $FMNE_{UK}$ and $UKMNE_f$ are seen to be positively, though not significantly, associated with profitability, while UK_i is negatively associated with π.

$$\pi = 18.4 - \underset{(1.64)}{0.796\ UK_i} + \underset{(0.68)}{0.280\ FMNE_{UK}} + \underset{(0.17)}{0.054\ UKMNE_f} \qquad (2b) \qquad (n = 29)$$

$$\pi' = 16.9 - \underset{(1.60)}{0.637} + \underset{(1.59)}{0.388} \qquad (2c) \qquad (n = 44)$$

Allied to the second proposition are two others to do with the direction of MNE activity towards capital- or technology-intensive sectors or those in which product quality, consistency and reliability are important competitive advantages. These latter industries, mainly supplying branded consumer goods (or inputs to same), may be expected to generate above average by advertising to sales expenditure. In this case, one is identifying *O*-type advantages which apply irrespective of whether they are being exploited by trade or production. One might then expect one and/or other of the advantages to be positively related to both $FMNE_{UK}$ and $UKMNE_f$.

Proposition 3. Relative to UK-owned firms producing in the UK, foreign-owned MNEs will produce in UK sectors which record an above average (1) net capital expenditure per employee (K/L), (2) non-operative/operative wage bill

NO/OWB, and/or (3) advertising/sales ratio (A/S); UK firms abroad will also produce in these sectors, although the sub-sectors of their particular strengths will probably differ.

Equations (3) and (3a) show that, unlike UK firms producing in the UK, both foreign affiliates of foreign MNEs and UK MNEs abroad concentrate in capital-intensive sectors, and in both cases significantly so. There is a positive but insignificant association between inward MNE activity and the skill-intensity ratio (see equations (4) and (4a)), but the reverse relationship applies to UK firms producing both in the UK and abroad. There was a very weak negative association between A/S and inward and outward MNE activity (see equations (5) and (5a)), but relative to the domestic production of UK firms, such activity is geared more to sectors supplying branded consumer goods in which quality control is perceived to be especially important.

$$K/L = 852 - \underset{(3.59)^{**}}{242\ UK_i} + \underset{(2.1)^{*}}{121\ FMNE_{UK}} + \underset{(6.05)}{269\ UKMNE_f} \qquad (3) \qquad (n = 29)$$

$$K/L' = 829 - \underset{(2.67)^{**}}{207\ UK_i} + \underset{(8.05)^{**}}{383\ FMNE_{UK}} \qquad (3a) \qquad (n = 44)$$

$$NO/OWB = 77.3 - \underset{(1.64)}{5.09\ UK_i} + \underset{(0.74)}{1.97\ FMNE_{UK}} - \underset{(0.6)}{1.24\ UKMNE_f} \qquad (4) \qquad (n = 29)$$

$$NO/OWB' = 68.3 - \underset{(1.44)}{3.87\ UK_i} + \underset{(0.59)}{0.97\ FMNE_{UK}} \qquad (4a) \qquad (n = 44)$$

$$A/S = 3.27 - \underset{(1.44)}{0.346\ UK_i} - \underset{(0.01)}{0.003\ FMNE_{UK}} - \underset{(0.14)}{0.024\ UKMNE_f} \qquad (5) \qquad (n = 29)$$

$$A/S' = 3.03 - \underset{(1.53)}{0.339\ UK_i} - \underset{(0.08)}{0.011\ FMNE_{UK}} \qquad (5a) \qquad (n = 39)$$

The final proposition in this section concerns the impact of market structure. Here the suggestion is that one of the main advantages of MNEs *qua* MNEs is the ability to exploit the advantages of international division of labour and the economies of synergy of multiple operations; that is, to capture economies internal to the MNE, but external to the individual affiliates of MNEs. If this is so, MNEs are likely to be attracted to sectors which have economies of firm size or those in which the concentration ratio is above average.

Proposition 4. Relative to UK-owned firms producing in the UK, both foreign affiliates in the UK and UK MNEs abroad will concentrate in sectors in which the competition is oligopolistic, as reflected by an above average concentration ratio (C) and/or where size of enterprise confers some productivity advantage (Sp).

Equations (6) and (6a) show that the first part of this proposition is generally supported, but that the association between $FMNE_{UK}$ and $UKMNE_f$ and C is statistically insignificant. Equations (7) and (7a) reveal that while UK firms at home and abroad tend to concentrate in sectors in which the largest firms record above average labour productivity, this is not so with $FMNE_{UK}$; indeed, if anything, the reverse seems to be the case. Excluding the oil-refining sector, the positive association between Sp and $UKMNE_f$ becomes significant at a 1 per cent level, but the association between Sp and UK_i becomes negative at near 5 per cent level.

$$C = 56.4 - \underset{(1.14)}{1.93}\ UK_i + \underset{(0.1)}{0.15}\ FMNE_{UK} + \underset{(0.9)}{1.00}\ UKMNE_f \qquad (6) \qquad (n = 29)$$

$$C' = 50.0 - \underset{(0.78)}{1.14}\ UK_i + \underset{(1.69)}{1.52}\ FMNE_{UK} \qquad (6a) \qquad (n = 44)$$

$$Sp + 1.13 + \underset{(0.38)}{0.0130}\ UK_i - \underset{(1.23)}{0.0362}\ FMNE_{UK} + \underset{(1.09)}{0.0246} \qquad (7) \qquad (n = 29)$$

$$Sp' = 1.15 + \underset{(0.30)}{0.081}\ UK_i - \underset{(0.57)}{0.0095}\ FMNE_{UK} \qquad (7a) \qquad (n = 44)$$

The conclusion of the above statistical exercises is that the interaction between a number of indices of UK economic structure and the distribution of UK manufacturing activity by the affiliates of foreign MNEs and that of UK MNEs abroad is generally different from that of UK-owned firms in the UK, and that the direction of the difference is such as to suggest that the UK's involvement in international production has made a positive contribution to domestic allocative efficiency.

Technical Impact

We now turn to examine some propositions concerning the extent to which activities of MNEs are related to the technical or sectoral efficiency of UK production. The literature strongly suggests that, locational considerations apart, MNEs will invest in those sectors in which they perceive they have the most technological and other advantages over their indigenous competitors. It may therefore be reasonable to hypothesize that these advantages may result in higher productivity ratios – particularly labour productivity ratios – as many of the advantages are capital- or technology-intensive and labour-saving.

Proposition 5. Relative to that of UK firms in the UK, production by foreign MNEs in the UK is likely to be concentrated in industries in which the productivity of the foreign affiliate is highest relative to the domestic firms, while the foreign production of UK firms is likely to be concentrated in sectors where domestic firms have a productivity advantage over their foreign competitors.

Acknowledging the usual caveats of any measure of the performance of firms – and particularly that between MNEs, or parts of MNEs, and the total activities of uninational firms – we consider two such indices. The first is the relative net output per man year in the UK (RLP) of foreign affiliates;[10] and the second an index of relative total factor productivity of foreign affiliates (RTP).[11] Equations (8) and (9) show that there is some evidence to support proposition 5, but that the association is more pronounced using the RLP than the RTP measure.[12]

$$\underset{}{RLP} = 1.30 - \underset{(1.65)}{0.0396\ UK_i} + \underset{(0.39)}{0.0081\ FMNE_{UK}} + \underset{(2.99)^{**}}{0.0476\ UKMNE_f} \qquad (8) \qquad (n = 27)$$

$$RLP' = 1.34 - \underset{(1.55)}{0.491} + \underset{(2.93)^{**}}{0.0571} \qquad (8a) \qquad (n = 41)$$

$$RTP = 1.07 + \underset{(0.11)}{0.0019\ UK_i} - \underset{(0.45)}{0.0071\ FMNE_{UK}} + \underset{(1.85)}{0.0235\ UKMNE_f} \qquad (9) \qquad (n = 27)$$

$$RTP' = 1.09 - \underset{(0.00)}{0.0001\ UK_i} + \underset{(1.27)}{0.0139\ FMNE_{UK}} \qquad (9a) \qquad (n = 42)$$

The detailed statistics reveal that in 34 out of 41 sectors, foreign affiliates record a higher labour productivity than UK-owned firms, and in 30 out of 41 sectors a higher total productivity. Moreover, equation (8a) clearly shows that, relative to UK_i, $FMNE_{UK}$ favour sectors in which their *O* advantages are the most pronounced.[13] However, of greater interest, and contrary to expectations, is the highly significant *positive* association between outward direct investment and RLP. One possible explanation suggested by earlier equations is that there is some complementarity between different forms of foreign involvement, and that *firm-* rather than *country*-specific *O* advantages explain the presence of MNEs in certain sectors. It would also seem that UK firms are relatively more profitable overseas in industries in which the UK is most internationally competitive.[14] For example, in 1979, 62 per cent of the foreign sales of UK companies was in sectors in which the normalized RCA ratio was above average for manufacturing industry. Data on other structural variables for each of the three categories are not available to make other comparisons of technical efficiency. However, earlier published information on the comparative export propensity between all UK firms and US subsidiaries in 1973/74 (Dunning, 1976) suggests that, while in 22 of the 36 manufacturing sectors for which data are available, the export/sales of US subsidiaries exceeds that of all UK firms, there is significant correlation between the normalized share of the sales of US subsidiaries and differences in export propensity.

Adjustment Impact

There are various ways in which the efficiency at which resources are reallocated might be evaluated. We deal first with changes in market growth.

Adaptation to market needs

To what extent do foreign MNEs invest in growth sectors or in those in which the UK is becoming more internationally competitive? How do the affiliates of UK MNEs adjust to market changes relative to UK firms in the UK? The hypothesis to be tested is that the *O* advantages of MNEs enable them to be better choosers of growth sectors or to create growth, and/or allow them to redirect their attention to those sectors which are becoming more productive and/or internationally competitive.

Proposition 6. Relative to UK firms, foreign MNEs are more concentrated in growth sectors, while they adjust to changes in market demand better than UK firms. Depending on their position in the product cycle and the relative significance of O and L advantages, UK firms overseas will invest in sectors in which the UK's international competitive position is deteriorating.

We present four pairs of equations. The first pair – (10) and (11) – relate the sectoral shares of gross sales of the three groups of firms in 1979 to two measures of market growth, that is, growth of UK *output* (GUK) and growth of UK *demand* plus exports (GUKX); the second pair – (12) and (13) – the share of the *change* (Δ) in production between 1971 and 1979 of UK-based firms divided by the share of the production in 1971 of these sectors (UK_i and $FMNE_{UK}$)[15] to these same measures.

$$GUK = 319 - \underset{(1.6)}{12.1}\, UK_i + \underset{(1.41)}{913}\, FMNE_{UK} + \underset{(1.5)}{7.53}\, UKMNE_f \qquad (10) \qquad (n = 29)$$

$$GUK' = 327 - 12.0\ UK_i + 16.0\ FMNE_{UK}$$
$$(2.02)^{*} \quad (4.4)^{**} \qquad (10a) \qquad (n = 44)$$

$$GUKX = 349 - 11.7\ UK_i + 7.90\ FMNE_{UK} + 8.13\ UKMNE_f$$
$$(1.80) \quad (1.28) \quad (1.64) \qquad (11) \qquad (n = 27)$$

$$GUKX' = 354 - 13.3\ UK_i + 16.1\ FMNE_{UK}$$
$$(2.62)^{*} \quad (5.33)^{**} \qquad (11a) \qquad (n = 42)$$

$$GUK = 95 + 112\ \Delta\ UK_i + 107\ \Delta\ FMNE_{UK} + 23.7\ \Delta\ UKMNE_f$$
$$(349)^{**} \quad (0.87) \quad (0.72) \qquad (12) \qquad (n = 17)$$

$$GUK' = 109 + 23.8\ \Delta\ UK_i + 195\ \Delta\ FMNE_{UK}$$
$$(1.79) \quad (4.28) \qquad (12a) \qquad (n = 37)$$

$$GUKX = 233 + 89.5\ \Delta\ UK_i + 26\ \Delta\ FMNE_{UK} + 27.1\ \Delta\ UKMNE_f$$
$$(2.32)^{*} \quad (0.17) \quad (0.70) \qquad (13) \qquad (n = 17)$$

$$GUKX' = 219 + 16.1\ \Delta\ UK_i + 122\ \Delta\ FMNE_{UK}$$
$$(1.18) \quad (2.59)^{*} \qquad (13a) \qquad (n = 36)$$

The equations suggest that foreign firms in the UK and UK firms abroad are distinctly more inclined to invest in growth sectors than are UK firms in the UK, and that is particularly noticeable when growth includes exports from the UK (GUKX). In equations (10a) and (11a) the $FMNE_{UK}$ coefficient seems to be positively significant at the 1 per cent level, but foreign production by UK MNEs is positively, but not significantly, related to growth. However, the bivariate correlation coefficients between the $FMNE_{UK}$ and $UKMNE_{UK}$ and the growth of the UK market plus exports work out at + 0.567 and + 0.653, and both are significant at a 1 per cent level. While 67 per cent of UK production by foreign affiliates in 1979 was in sectors which recorded above average rates of growth between 1971 and 1979, the corresponding proportion for indigenous firms was 32 per cent.

Between 1971 and 1979, foreign affiliates in the UK increased the value of their output at more than twice the rate of indigenous firms in the UK.[16] Moreover, as equations (12) and (13) show, there was also a tendency for foreign affiliates (relative to the UK competitors) to increase their market share in sectors which were growing fastest; indeed, the correlation coefficient between GUK' and $FMNE_{UK}$ in equation (12a) was + 0.631 and significant at a 1 per cent level.

Over a slightly shorter period (1972/3–1979) the output of UK firms abroad grew relative to that of the domestic production by UK firms in 14 of 17 sectors.

There was some tendency for domestic and foreign growth by UK MNEs to be complementary to each other and rank correlation between the two variables was + 0.29, but excluding drink and tobacco + 0.45.

Adaptation to structural change

The next set of propositions examines the extent to which MNEs and other firms adapt their output to changes in economic structure. We shall take indices of such change for the period 1971–79:

1. changes in RCA;
2. changes in labour productivity;
3. changes in non-operative/operative wage bill;
4. changes in the labour productivity gap between foreign affiliates and indigenous firms;

and follow the methodology adopted in testing Proposition 7.

Proposition 7. Relative to UK firms producing in the UK, foreign affiliates of MNEs will produce in sectors in which (1) the RCA ratio has most improved, (2) productivity has most increased, (3) the human capital content has most increased, and (4) the productivity gap between affiliates and indigenous firms has (relatively) increased.

In the case of the foreign production of UK MNEs one might predict a positive relationship between its sectoral distribution and (2) and (3) and a negative relationship between that distribution and (1) and (4).

And a dynamic version of Proposition 7:

Proposition 8. Relative to UK firms producing in the UK, foreign affiliates of MNEs may be expected to increase their share of production in sectors in which (1) the RCA ratio has most improved, (2) productivity has most increased, (3) the human capital content has most increased, and (4) the productivity gap between affiliates and indigenous firms has (relatively) increased.

The predictions for the activities of UK MNEs abroad follow those set out in Proposition 8.

The set of equations (14)–(16) and (17)–(21)[17] set out below suggest a mixed interaction between MNE involvement and structural change.

$$\Delta RCA = -0119 + \underset{(0.37)}{0.060\, UK_i} - \underset{(3.02)^{**}}{0.438\, FMNE_{UK}} + \underset{(3.41)^{**}}{0.0398\, UKMNE_f} \qquad (14) \qquad (n = 28)$$

$$\Delta LP = 3.76 - 0.273\ UK_i + 0.150\ FMNE_{UK} + 0.183\ UKMNE_f$$
$$(3.04)^{**} \quad (1.96)^{*} \quad (3.1)^{**} \qquad (15) \quad (n = 29)$$

$$\Delta LP' = 3.88 - 0.282\ UK_i + 0.330\ FMNE_{UK}$$
$$(3.37)^{**} \quad (6.45)^{**} \qquad (15a) \quad (n = 44)$$

$$\Delta NO/OWB = 1.11 - 0.006\ UK_i + 0.012\ FMNE_{UK} - 0.013\ UKMNE_f$$
$$(0.58) \quad (1.3) \quad (1.84) \qquad (16) \quad (n = 29)$$

$$\Delta RLP = 1.13 - 0.0300\ UK_k + 0.0759\ FMNE_{UK} - 0.0505\ UKMNE_f$$
$$(0.86) \quad (2.39)^{*} \quad (2.0)^{*} \qquad (17) \quad (n = 26)$$

$$\Delta RCA = -0.396 + 0.186\ \Delta UK_i + 0.117\ \Delta FMNE_{UK}$$
$$(2.85) \quad (0.64)$$
$$-0.004\ \Delta UKMNE_f$$
$$(0.08) \qquad (18) \quad (n = 13)$$

$$\Delta RCA' = -0.553 + 0.0439\ \Delta UK_i + 0.363\ \Delta FMNE_{UK}$$
$$(1.25) \quad (3.0)^{**} \qquad (18a) \quad (n = 36)$$

$$\Delta LP = 2.41 + 2.73\ \Delta UK_i - 1.49\ \Delta FMNE_{UK} + 0.297\ \Delta UKMNE_f$$
$$(3.6)^{**} \quad (0.51) \quad (0.38) \qquad (19) \quad (n = 13)$$

$$\Delta NO/OWB = 1.24 - 0.048\ \Delta UK_i - 0.26\ \Delta FMNE_{UK}$$
$$(0.86) \quad (0.12)$$
$$+ 0.071\ \Delta UKMNE_f$$
$$(1.23) \qquad (20) \quad (n = 13)$$

$$\Delta RLP = 1.21 + 0.068\ \Delta UK_i - 0.291\ \Delta FMNE_{UK} + 0.12\ \Delta UKMNE_f$$
$$(0.66) \quad (0.74) \quad (0.12) \qquad (21) \quad (n = 13)$$

$$\Delta RLP' = 1.61 + 0.123\ \Delta UK_i - 0.700\ \Delta FMNE_{UK}$$
$$(1.98)^{*} \quad (3.27)^{**} \qquad (21a) \quad (n = 37)$$

For example, UK MNEs appear to be increasing their foreign activities in areas where the UK's RCA is increasing, while the reverse is the case for foreign affiliates in the UK (see equation (14)). On the other hand, both UK firms and foreign affiliates in the UK seem to be redirecting their output to sectors in which RCA is improving (see equations (18) and (18a)). Whereas UK MNEs tend to favour sectors in which labour productivity has risen the most, the opposite is the case for UK firms in the UK (see equations (15) and (15a)). However, this latter group of firms appears to be redirecting its output towards sectors with rising productivity (see equation (19)). No relations of any significance emerge between changes in the skill-intensity ratio and the distribution of output of MNEs *vis-à-vis* UK firms in the UK. Changes in the productivity gap (favouring $FMNE_{UK}$ seem to be positively and significantly associated with the distribution of output of foreign affiliates, but negatively associated with that of UK firms abroad (see equation (17)). On the other hand, UK firms producing in the UK have adjusted their output towards industries in which RLP is rising, while the opposite has occurred in the case of foreign affiliates in the UK (see equations (21) and (21a)).[18]

MNEs and the Organization of Transactions

There is one other structural aspect of MNEs which requires consideration. This concerns the role of MNEs as co-ordinators of separate economic activities across national boundaries, and the effect this has on domestic, that is UK, economic structure. While it is an inherent feature of MNEs that they internalize international intermediate product markets, they may also impinge on such markets *within* a country and on final goods traded between countries. This market-replacing effect is inadequately captured in the statistics but may have far-reaching implications both on the type of economic activity carried out and on its determinants. Received theory would suggest that relative to non-MNEs, MNEs will tend to concentrate in sectors in which there are the most opportunities for minimizing transaction costs. Data on such market-replacing activities are extremely limited. However, it might be reasonably argued that the greater the degree of product or process diversification within MNEs, and the more they practise product or process specialization between countries, the more likely the structural impact of MNEs will be of concern to those countries that do not wish to identify themselves with the resulting international division of labour. We illustrate from just two aspects of internalization: (1) vertical integration in the UK, and (2) international product or process specialization between different parts of the same MNE in different countries.

Proposition 9. To minimize transaction costs or capitalize on market failure, UK affiliates of foreign MNEs and/or UK MNEs abroad, relative to UK firms producing in the UK, will tend to concentrate in sectors which are vertically integrated (VAR), or are increasing their integration (ΔVAR), and/or, within an international context, offer opportunities for intra-industry (IIT) and/or intra-firm trade (IFT).

$$\underset{}{VAR} = 37.8 - \underset{(0.29)}{0.203\ UK_i} - \underset{(0.9)}{0.391\ FMNE_{UK}} \qquad (22) \qquad (n = 44)$$

$$\Delta VAR = 1.95 - 0.542\ UK_i + 0.403\ FMNE_{UK}$$
$$\qquad (5.03)^{**} \qquad (6.1) \qquad\qquad (23) \qquad (n = 44)$$

$$ITT = 0.838 = 0.0279\ UK_i + 0.0126\ FMNE_{UK} - 0.0016\ UKMNE_f$$
$$\qquad (1.4) \qquad (0.96) \qquad (0.15) \qquad (24) \qquad (n = 22)$$

$$IFT = 39.2 - 2.51\ UK_i + 5.20\ FMNE_{UK} - 2.74\ UKMNE_f$$
$$\qquad (3.45)^{**} \qquad (2.34)^{**} \qquad (25) \qquad (n = 22)$$

These propositions are tested in equations (22) to (25).[19] We consider the results of each form of internalization separately.

Vertical integration

There is no evidence that the affiliates of foreign-based MNEs are more vertically integrated in their UK activities than are indigenous firms (see equation (22)). In 1979, foreign affiliates in the UK recorded a higher net/gross output ratio than their UK competitors in 17 out of 40 sectors and a lower ratio in 22 sectors. Neither is there any suggestion that the foreign participation ratio is highest in sectors with the highest value-added ratios. However, within industries, broadly interpreted, it would appear that foreign affiliates do concentrate in sectors with above average ratios (the main exception is oil). The degree of vertical integration in both foreign and domestic firms has changed little in the 1970s, but equation (23) suggests quite strongly that, in sectors in which foreign affiliates are most markedly represented, vertical integration has *fallen* either absolutely or relatively to indigenous firms. One reason for this may be that there is increasing specialization within sectors of products supplied by MNEs across national boundaries. The intra-industry trade equation (22) suggests there is a positive but insignificant association between ITT and the foreign participation ratio; excluding the $UKMNE_f$ variable increases the observations to 37, and the significance of the $FMNE_{UK}$ variable to 1.68. On the other hand, equation (25) shows there is a significant positive association between the propensity of foreign affiliates to engage in intra-firm trade and the sectoral distribution of their output. The association goes in the opposite direction for UK MNEs, but all the data suggest that UK-related MNE activity is likely to have had as much, if not a greater, effect on market-replacing activities between the UK and the rest of the world, than within the UK.

International product specialization

Regrettably, intra-industry data are rarely presented in sufficient detail to allow us to separate *vertical* from *horizontal* transactions. But again casual empiricism suggests that both UK and foreign-based MNEs are increasingly viewing Europe as a single market, and engaging in intra-plant product specialization.

Inter alia, this is confirmed by the propensity of MNEs to concentrate in sectors in which the trade intensity of the UK is increasing. Between 1971 and 1979, the value of imports plus exports to total manufactured goods produced in the UK of all firms rose from 36 per cent to 50 per cent. However, in sectors in which foreign-based MNEs had a participation ratio of 1 or more, the average rise was from 44 per cent to 74 per cent. A rank correlation between the $FMNE_{UK}$ ratio in 1979 and change in trade intensity between 1971 and 1979 was + 0.424. Data on changes in intra-industry trade ratios and the distribution of MNE activity tell the same story. Both foreign affiliates and UK MNEs abroad are strongly concentrated in sectors in which the intra-industry trade ratio rose the sharpest between 1971 and 1979; this is not the case with domestic production of UK firms. That these latter sectors happen to be those in which MNEs are more likely to adopt a global strategy, and maintain a 100 per cent equity interest, suggests growing internalization of economic activity across national boundaries *vis-à-vis* that within national boundaries. This is an important conclusion which has far reaching policy implications; these are taken up in the final section of this chapter.

Product diversification

Data on industrial diversification are extremely limited but what there are[20] do not support the proposition that MNEs, either absolutely or relative to non-MNEs, tend to concentrate in sectors which are themselves diversified; indeed, compared with an average diversification index[21] for the leading MNEs in 1981 of 24.3, petroleum, automobiles, and office equipment – three of the most international of sectors – recorded ratios of 12.6, 16.9, and 20.5 respectively. And while it might be expected that enterprises, in a particular industry, which are the most multinational will be more diversified than non-MNEs, partly because they are larger and partly because they operate in different economic environments, in any one country, the range of output of their affiliates may well be less than that of indigenous firms. But the very fact that an affiliate is linked with an enterprise which is more diversified than its indigenous competitors may give it a competitive edge. Certainly there are several examples leading the diversification of many sectors, such as drink, tobacco, and chemicals in the last five years; unfortunately as far as the UK is concerned, there are no recent data on diversification trends to enable us to go beyond this casual empiricism.[22]

POLICY IMPLICATIONS

The previous sections have demonstrated that, in a variety of ways, MNEs have had an impact on UK economic structure different from that of UK indigenous firms producing in the UK (including the UK output of UK MNEs). This is a reflection both of the differences in the configuration of the *OLI* advantages facing MNEs and the way in which they have translated these into conduct and performance. Despite the imperfections of data, there are strong suggestions that the *O* advantages of MNEs have assisted the UK's economic restructuring in the 1970s towards higher allocative and technical efficiency; and that MNEs have adjusted to changing *L* advantages of UK resource endowments rather more positively than uninational indigenous firms. However, one cost of the greater internationalization of the UK economy may have been the loss of some structural autonomy on the part of the UK, as MNEs may encourage more corporate internalization between different parts of their operations and less sectoral or cross-sectoral integration within the UK. This may have the effect of reshaping both market and economic structure and, in so far as the common ownership of separate production affiliates matters, is relevant to the pattern of resource allocation. There is insufficient evidence to suggest whether or not this kind of impact on structure has worked to the long-term advantage of the UK economy; much depends on the international market structure in which MNEs compete and the signals given to them by various governments. There can, however, be little doubt that, by promoting structural interdependence between national markets, MNEs have made the UK economy more vulnerable to changes in international demand and supply conditions.

What should UK government policy be towards MNE activity? What modifications of existing policies are needed? Clearly, much depends on how far it is considered that foreign ownership and/or control of domestic resource allocation matters, and on one's judgement of the possible risk of being dependent on external economic and political forces. In practice, too, much will rest on the domestic macroeconomic policies pursued and particularly those relevant to structural change. What also seems to be increasingly likely is that, at least as far as investment within the OECD is concerned, internationalization of some industries by some form of cross-border alliances will continue. The important question is to ensure that, where it is thought appropriate, a country's own firms can survive and compete with foreign firms. This inevitably requires governments to re-examine their role in producing the right economic environment and their means of achieving that goal. For it is a fact that as MNEs have become more footloose in their choice of markets to exploit and/or sites from which to produce, the influence of government-related locational variables has become more important. These range from import controls to encourage import-substituting investment, to providing the right educational, technological, and telecommunications infrastructure, and to aiding firms in newer sectors in the restructuring process.

The fact that the kind of impact we have attributed to MNEs has been associated with their increasing involvement in the UK economy suggests that the market may itself be the main adjustment mechanism. Why then should any government intervention be required, other than to ensure the market works properly? The answer lies in the divergence between private and social economic welfare and the very specific impact which MNEs have on this divergence. It is well accepted that in conditions where governments seek only economic goals, and in the absence of externalities or structural market imperfections, a *laissez-faire* policy might be appropriate. In a modern industrialized economy, however, particularly one subject to rapid technological change and faced with all kinds of institutional rigidities and structural disequilibria, this is an extremely unlikely situation, as indeed is the belief that the only role of governments is a negative one. Indeed, in the long run, this could be worsened by foreign firms, which might be equipped to overcome the market failure, gaining a monopoly position and creating an even more unacceptable market position. Governments have the responsibility for positive interventionism whenever there are costs and benefits which it is not reasonable to expect individual firms to bear. In the past this included the provision of roads and public utilities. Today the modern equivalents include air transport and international data-transmitting facilities.

To what extent is the growing internationalization of the UK economy arising from MNE activity in the long-term interests of the UK? The data set out in this chapter present a mixed picture. On the one hand they suggest that MNEs have aided the restructuring of UK industry in a way consistent with both its revealed comparative advantage and its domestic efficiency; on the other, MNEs appear to inject an additional element of economic vulnerability, in the sense that they increase the interdependence of the UK with the rest of the world. In particular, let us examine the proposition that such internationalization may reduce the freedom of action on the part of the UK to restructure the economy as it thinks fit. The argument takes as its starting point the tendency of MNEs, particularly in advanced economies, to encourage more corporate internalization between different parts of their operations in different countries, but to reduce sectoral integration within these countries. This may have a variety of consequences, arising out of the conflict of interests between the global objectives of international hierarchies and the more domestically oriented goals of the UK government.

This is clearly demonstrated in the area of technology creation and dissemination, where not only may the innovatory activities on the part of MNEs be centralized in the home country, but the control which they exercise over the purchasing requirements of their affiliates throughout the world may have far reaching effects on the technological capabilities of suppliers in different countries. Thus, for example, while the presence of Japanese firms in the UK has undoubtedly raised the productivity of the assembly of colour television sets, any monopolization by them of this gain would be more than outweighed if (1) their greater efficiency forced UK competitors out of the industry, (2) they chose to import most of their high value electronic components from Japan and (3) the Japanese market were closed to UK component suppliers. In the last case, there could be considerable spin-off effects on the UK economy as the fall in the demand for electronic components might weaken the ability of the industry to supply other purchasers with this product. Here the UK government has a positive role to play, in keeping a watching brief on the strategy of inward investors, in ensuring (where it considers appropriate) effective domestic competition, and in trying to persuade the Japanese government to open its markets to British products.

A further concern is the effect which MNE activity may have on the de-industrialization of the UK economy. This arises from the fact that the increasing international mobility of capital management and technology is resulting in *absolute* locational advantage replacing *comparative* locational advantage as a paradigm influencing the location of economic activity. Where this new disposition is decided by private capital in promotion of its own goals, it does not follow that the resulting distribution of output will be consistent with that which the countries in which MNEs operate are seeking. This new international division of labour is certainly accelerating the relocation of some industrial sectors from older to newer industrialized countries, although the current generation of computer-related technological advances is causing the return of some of these activities, so as to be closer to upstream or downstream production.

Within the industrialized world, while there is no a priori reason to suppose that the UK should be more adversely affected than any other country the fact remains that within Europe, at least, the deployment of MNE-related activity in the UK has expanded *least* in recent years. This is mainly due to the poor rates of return on corporate capital in the UK, itself partly attributed to the strength of organized labour. Multinationals have the flexibility to counteract such frictions by transferring output or increases in output across national boundaries; and, as Dunning 1988b, Chapter 10 shows, over the past two decades, UK investment, especially in labour-intensive sectors, has increasingly preferred a Contintental European to a UK location.

There seems little doubt that the growth of corporate integration in Europe and the UK's accession to the EEC have reduced the freedom of the UK government to control the activities of both UK MNEs and foreign affiliates in the UK. While affiliates may be regarded as hostages, in the last resort, they have the power to withdraw their investment, or switch new investment away from the UK. This reduces the power of the government to introduce policies specifically adverse to MNEs; on the other hand, by more general policies it can affect the structure of outward and inward investment to make it better serve its long-term goals.

For many years now, successive UK governments have adopted a broadly non-discriminatory and liberal policy towards inflows and outflows of direct investment. The main exception is the *ad hoc* negotiating stance on large new inward investments, particularly with respect to local sourcing requirements, as illustrated in the Nissan case. But there is little evidence that UK governments have consciously taken the growth of international corporate integration into account in the framing of their industrial trade or technological strategies. The implication of a no-action or *laissez-faire* approach is that the allocation of economic activity, both within the UK and between the UK and the rest of the world, by UK and foreign MNEs, is consistent with the objectives of national aspirations.

In spite of the beneficial effects of MNE activity set out in this chapter, we question whether this is the case. We believe there are signs of MNEs linking the UK economy with the economies of other industrialized countries in ways which require some changes in (or changes in emphasis of) UK policy. We are not fully persuaded, for example, that, in the absence of positive action on the part of the UK authorities, MNEs will site their activities in the UK in a way consistent with the UK's long-term interests. To encourage this it is not only necessary for the private sector to offer the right kind of economic climate, but also that the technological, social and educational infrastructure should be at least as attractive as that offered by other countries. This is not primarily a question of special tax or other inducements to foreign investors. Numerous surveys have shown that investors, domestic and foreign alike, regard other supply side factors as much more important in influencing locational choice. These include availability of the right kinds of manpower at competitive wages; supportive (including university) research facilities; a well-motivated and co-operative labour force; first-rate telecommunication and transport provisions; a good network of suppliers; a consistent, well-articulated and publicized industrial strategy; and a sympathetic climate for growth and innovation. In addition, UK MNEs, in their attempt to be competitive in world markets, look for government encouragement and strength in negotiating with foreign governments over unfair or ill-considered trading practices.

However self-evident the above points may seem, it is clear that, in the view of both foreign and UK MNEs, the UK is not offering the locational attractions that it might. Let us take the wave of Japanese investment in the UK as an example. Most recent investment by Japanese firms has been to supply the European market with products previously exported from Japan. The UK has been preferred as a location to other countries of Europe, not primarily because of fiscal or other incentives, but because of the quality and costs of labour, excellence of infrastructure and for cultural and language reasons. Similarly, firms which – particularly in the high technology sectors – have chosen Germany or the Low Countries have done so because of the perceived higher quality and better motivated labour (particularly electronic engineers), the excellence of the telecommunication facilities and the economic and industrial strategy of the governments. Much of what has been written applies to UK outward investment as well. The recent fortunes of the UK motor industry have been such that not only do foreign MNEs prefer the Continental to a UK location but UK component supplies have followed in their wake – at the expense of employment in the Midlands. Government support to British Leyland has helped, but an economic environment stimulating the application of modern computer-controlled manufacturing and design techniques in the UK would do much more.

On the other hand, governments need to be aware of some of the challenges of inward investment. Japanese MNEs are participating in Europe as part of a long-term worldwide strategy. Their aim is to dominate such sectors as electronics and motor vehicle manufacturing. However much the UK may gain in the short term through more employment in Japanese subsidiaries, if they act as a Trojan horse, not only by driving out competition but also through their design policies, and their insistence that purchases should be made from Japanese component suppliers (or their affiliates in the UK), a lot of high value-added activity will be lost to the UK. This is possibly the most serious structural challenge, which is being exacerbated by the problems faced by UK firms penetrating the Japanese market (either by export or local production). Again, the UK government has a catalytic and positive role to play, both by assisting its own firms to combat the competition and through its negotiating tactics with the Japanese.

CONCLUSIONS

Space precludes our giving further examples. The main message of this chapter is a simple yet important one. The growing internationalization of business, and the interpenetration of technologically advanced industries among industrialized countries, is making new demands on individual governments – and particularly those in integrated markets such as the EEC. Because of the footloose nature of MNE activity, and the increasing role played by mobile factors of production in the production process, the location of industrial activity is increasingly obeying the dictates of absolute, rather than comparative, advantage. At the same time, the role of governments is crucial in influencing the attractions of a particular location by the provision of infrastructure and appropriate macroeconomic policies. In the nineteenth century such intervention mainly took the form of the provision of public utilities, the foundation for the prosperity of industry which was largely locked into its existing location. In the late twentieth century their equivalents are airports, motorways, telecommunications, technical colleges and universities and an efficient economic system, which have to be at least as attractive as those offered by other governments to retain and attract an increasingly mobile population of firms.

Naturally, not all societies can attract all kinds of investment, which is why most countries, particularly smaller ones, need a selective technological, industrial and trade policy. Japan is the classic example of a case in which government and industry can work together to promote a positive and yet well-articulated policy towards both inward and outward MNE activity. The UK policy-makers could well learn from this experience, if they wish to use MNEs as servants rather than masters in their bid for efficient and harmonious restructuring.

NOTES

1. See e.g. Dunning (1958); Reddaway, Potter and Taylor (1968); Steuer et al. (1973).
2. It is interesting to observe, for example, that joint ventures and non-equity agreements between UK and overseas firms were considerably more competent relative to 100 per cent owned equity investments than between US and overseas firms.
3. This latter concern was most forcibly articulated by Jean-Jacques Servan Schreiber, and led to deliberate and sustained efforts by the EEC in the 1970s to build up a strong European counter-presence to US firms in high technology sectors.
4. We would be the first to accept that changes in the distribution of activity *between* manufacturing and the service sector in the UK have been at least as significant as those *within* manufacturing industry. Unfortunately, data on MNE activity in the service sector are extremely limited.
5. Competitiveness is measured by revealed comparative advantage (RCA). RCA is defined as $1 + (Xi - Mi)/(Xi + Mi) \div 1 + (Xt - Mt)/(Xt + Mt)$ where X = exports, M = imports, i a particular sector, t = all sectors.
6. In this, and in later relationships, we test the association of inward MNE activity together with outward MNE activity and separately from it. This is because we have 44 observations for the former and only 29 for the latter.
7. Defined as the proportion of the total sales of foreign affiliates accounted for by a particular sector divided by the corresponding share of all UK enterprises of that sector.
8. As the extent of foreign participation may not be evenly distributed *within* the sectors.
9. Similar to the one used in testing Proposition 7. See also the Appendix to this chapter, below.
10. RLP = net output per head of foreign affiliates divided by net output per head of indigenous firms.
11. See the Appendix for definition.
12. This suggests that the relatively higher labour productivity of $FMNE_{UK}$ is at least partially offset by a lower capital productivity.
13. One major exception being other clothing where RTP of foreign affiliates in the UK was 188 while their participation ratio was 0.10.
14. For example, in terms of price cost margins, the rank correlation between the industrial distribution of the outward capital stake (1) and (2) net output per head and (3) profitability of the outward capital stake in 1971, 1974 and 1978 varied from + 60 to + 0.94 and in every case it was significant at a 5 per cent level (Dunning and Walker, 1982).
15. For example, taking a sector j

$$UK_{ij} = \frac{UK_{ij}1979 - UK_{ij}1971}{UK_{it}1979 - UK_{it}1979} \div \frac{UK_{ij}1971}{UK_{it}1971}.$$

16. The growth of output of foreign affiliates was 446.5 per cent compared to that of indigenous firms (in the UK) of 195.0 per cent. Between 1972/3 and 1979, the output of UK firms abroad rose by an estimated 275.1 per cent.

17. We have set out the two (independent) variable equations only when the statistical significance of one or more of the variables is improved.
18. This is further evidence of narrowing of the spillover effect of inward investment in the UK and the productivity gap between foreign affiliates and UK firms.
19. A dynamic version of Proposition 9 was also tested. This supported the findings of Proposition 9 but revealed no new relationships.
20. As reviewed in Stopford and Dunning (1983); Dunning and Pearce (1985).
21. The percentage of sales in other than the industry to which firms are classified.
22. For a more thorough examination of the interaction between the geographical and industrial diversification of MNEs see Pearce (1983).

APPENDIX: SOURCES OF DATA

The Independent Variables

Data on the sectoral distribution of output (gross sales) of indigenous firms in the UK (UK_i) were obtained from the *Censuses of Production* 1971 and 1979. The gross sales of indigenous firms are equal to gross sales of UK enterprises less those of the subsidiaries of foreign-owned firms. Data on the sales of foreign affiliates ($FMNE_{UK}$) were obtained from the same censuses, supplemented by additional data provided by the Business Statistics Office. Data on UK firms abroad ($UKMNE_f$) for 1979 were calculated by the author directly from the accounts of 188 of the largest UK MNEs accounting for between 90 per cent and 95 per cent of all UK-foreign direct investment. The data were then checked for consistency with those on UK assets owned abroad published triennially by the Department of Trade (in *Business Monitor* M4). Data for UK MNEs for 1972/3 were derived from Houston and Dunning (1976).

The Dependent Variables

Many of the data on production-related variables were obtained from the *Censuses of Production* 1971 and 1979. This includes: (1) labour productivity (LP) (net output ÷ total employment); (2) profitability (π) (gross output – gross value-added ÷ gross output); (3) skill ratio (NO/OWB) (non-operative wage bill ÷ operative wage bill); (4) concentration ratio (C) (percentage of gross output accounted for by five largest enterprises); (5) size effect (Sp) (average productivity of the largest two groups of enterprises in any sector ÷ by the average productivity of the rest of the sector); (6) output growth (GUK) (growth of gross output in UK 1971/1979); (7) the value-added ratio (VAR) (gross value-added ÷ gross output). The advertising ratio (AS) (advertising/sales) was obtained from data published in the *Census of Production*, 1968. The relative total productivity index (RTP) which attempts to measure the efficiency of $FMNE_{UK}$ relative to that of UK_i is obtained by calculating (for 1979) the formula:

$$\frac{WL + \pi S}{W*L + \pi*S} \text{ for } FMNE_{UK}$$

where W = wage bill, L numbers employed, π the profit/sales margin, S = sales of $FMNE_{UK}$ and W* + π* the wage bill and profit/sales margin for UK_i. Separate calculations were made for non-operative and operative wages. The formula essentially relates to the actual value-added of $FMNE_{UK}$ to the opportunity cost of the resources used; as a proxy for this opportunity cost the payments to the same quantity of comparable factor services by indigenous firms is used. For further details, see Dunning (1971).

For the main trade-related variable (RCA) as defined on p. 370, data were provided by the Department of Trade Statistics Division and are similar to those used to produce import and export ratios published by *Economic Trends*. The variable GUKX estimates the total demand for goods (UK-produced goods and imports) plus exports, and is derived from the same source, as were data for the ratio intra-industry trade (IIT). The intra-firm trade ratio (IFT) was derived from data published by the UK Department of Commerce (1981). As a proxy for this latter variable we took the imports from a proportion of total US imports in 1977 accounted for related parties (e.g. US affiliates abroad) as published in Helleiner (1981).

REFERENCES

Cohen, B.I. (1975), *Multinational Firms and Asian Exports* (New Haven: Yale University Press).

Dunning, J.H. (1958), *American Investment in British Manufacturing Industry* (London: Allen & Unwin).

Dunning, J.H. (1971), *Studies in International Investment* (London: Allen & Unwin).

Dunning. J.H, and Pearce, R.D. (1985), *The World's Largest industrial Enterprises, 1962–1983* (Farnborough: Gower).

Dunning, J.H. and Walker, P. (1982), *The Competitiveness and Allocative Efficiency of UK Manufacturing Industry and Foreign Direct Investment*, Reading: Reading University (mimeo).

Helleiner, G.K. (1981), *Intrafirm Trade and the Developing Countries* (London: Macmillan).

Houston, T. and Dunning, J.H. (1976), *U.K. industry abroad*, London: Financial Times.

Pearce, R.D. (1983), 'Industrial diversification amongst the world's leading multinational enterprises', in M.C. Casson (ed.), *The Growth of International Business* (London: Allen & Unwin), pp. 140–79.

Reddaway, W.B., Potter, S.J. and Taylor, C.T. (1968), *The Effects of UK Direct Investment Overseas; Final Report* (Cambridge; Mass.: Cambridge University Press).

Steuer, M.D. et al. (1973), *The Impact of Foreign Direct Investment in the United Kingdom* (London: HMSO).

Stopford, J.M. and Dunning, J.H. (1983), *Multinationals: Company Performance and Global Trends* (London: Macmillan).

14. Governments and the macro-organization of economic activity: a historical and spatial perspective*

INTRODUCTION

The optimal role of governments[1] in the organization of economic activity has long been a subject of intense – and sometimes passionate – controversy. Yet a study of the writings of the leading scholars of the past two centuries reveals that these have reflected not only their personal ideologies, and the economic and institutional milieu of the time in which they lived, but the particular issues addressed by them. Indeed, while not wishing to underestimate the real differences of opinion among social scientists about the rationale for, and the appropriate content of, government involvement in the creation and management of resources within their jurisdiction, it is, nevertheless, possible to identify a distinct evolutionary pattern of scholarly thinking, and the reasons for it.

This chapter has two main tasks. The first is to trace the lineage of academic writings since the time of Adam Smith, on the respective roles of markets, hierarchies, inter-firm alliances, and governments as modes of organizing economic activity in a capitalist economy; and also to analyse why, and in what ways, economists, political scientists, and organizational theorists have differed in their interpretation of the optimal role of governments. The second is to examine the implications of the internationalization, and more recently the globalization, of economic activity for the governance of resource creation and deployment, and the extent to which national administrations and supra-national regimes need to modify their agendas and policy prescriptions in the light of the growing mobility of many tangible and intangible assets. The chapter will further argue that changing patterns of demand and technological advances – especially as they have impacted on the coordinating and transaction costs of value-added activity, and on the institutions and cultural infrastructure underpinning such activity – have critically affected the merits of alternative modes

* From *Review of International Political Economy*, **4**(1) (1997): 42–86. Reprinted as Chapter 1 in J.H. Dunning (ed.), *Governments, Globalization and International Business*, Oxford: Oxford University Press (1997), pp. 31–72.

of economic organization; and that, over the years, the optimal combination of these modes has undergone a marked change.

The chapter proceeds in the following way. The next section examines the main historical thrust of thinking about the economic legitimacy of democratically elected governments over the past 200 years. The following section deals with some of the main justifications for government intervention set out in the literature; and the next goes on to present an evaluation of these justifications. The chapter then proceeds to analyse the implications of the spatial widening of value-added activity; and suggests that such widening, and, in particular, the emergence of the globalizing economy, is significantly affecting 'best-practice' organizational arrangements for both the creation and the deployment of organizing domestic resources.

AN EVOLUTIONARY APPROACH TO ECONOMIC ORGANIZATION

In taking a bird's-eye view of the economic organization of democratic societies over the past two centuries, it is useful to distinguish between two quite different functions which governments may perform. The first is as an initiator and overseer of the economic system,[2] which sets the legal and institutional framework within which the resources and capabilities in its jurisdiction are created and deployed; and as an arbitrator as and when disputes arise between economic agents.[3] The second is as an owner of assets, and as a *participator* in, or *influencer* of, the way these assets are utilized. The former functions are the special and unique responsibility of governments;[4] the latter can frequently be undertaken by either public or private institutions. Much of the changing attitudes of scholars towards government intervention over the past two centuries reflects their perceptions of the appropriate balance between these two roles and their interface with other institutions in achieving societal goals.

We begin by offering a schema – set out in Table 14.1 – which identifies three stages in the evolution of market-based capitalism, which we have called respectively *entrepreneurial*, *hierarchical*, and *alliance* capitalism. While the nomenclature and the timing of the stages may be open to question, there can be little doubt that the macro-economic and organizational[5] environment for the management of physical and human resources has dramatically changed over the past 200 years. In particular, the increasing complexity and specialization of economic activity, the growing interdependence of many intermediate product markets, the accelerating movement towards an information- and innovation-driven economy, the widening territorial boundaries of firms, the increasing significance of created assets (e.g. human skills and technological

Table 14.1 Some features of the three ages of capitalism

	Phase 1 Entrepreneurial capitalism (1770–1875)	Phase 2 Hierarchical capitalism (1875–1980)	Phase 3 Alliance or flexible capitalism (1980–?)
Markets	Small and fragmentary, local and national: mainly competitive	National or international: increasingly oligopolistic	Regional and global: dynamic and more competitive
Specialization	Simple and modest, based mainly on distribution of natural assets	Becoming more complex: both national and international	Extensive and interdependent: the paradox of an increasing global division of labour based on location of created assets, together with the sub-national specialized clusters of economic activity
Key resources	Natural assets, e.g. fruits of the land and relatively unskilled labour	Physical and some knowledge capital	Tangible assets, e.g. infrastructure and technological capacity Intangible assets, e.g. human competence and knowledge, information, organizational and learning capability
Mobility of assets	Little except for finance capital, and some emigration	Gradually increasing via MNE operations	Substantial mobility of *firm-specific* created assets. But less mobility of some *location-specific* created assets
Organization	Factory, small firms	Large integrated corporate hierarchies	More inter-firm alliances, single firm heterarchies, corporate networks
Production system	D form, batch	M form, mass or scale	Innovation driven: flexible
Government role	Limited involvement: active role confined to provision of public utilities, fiscal policy and social welfare	Growing intervention: growth in welfare providing services. In inter-war years considerable protectionism	More systemic and market enabling: less regulation of individual markets
Government structure	Local/national legislation	National legislation, limited supranational institutions	Greater plurality of governmental forms, especially at sub-national and supra-national levels
International activities	Classical trade, very little foreign production	Market and natural resource seeking FDI: growth of intra-industry trade	Substantial efficiency and strategic asset-seeking FDI: more cross hauling of FDI and growth of cross-border strategic alliances
Cross-border integration	Of product and finance markets	Fluctuating: cf. inter-war years with early post-Second-World-War period	Increasing, through corporate and regional integration
Hegemonic power	UK	USA	No single country

capacity) in the value-adding process, the evolvement of new institutions and organizational forms, and a re-evaluation of cultures and behavioural norms have all impacted on the costs and benefits of alternative resource allocative systems, and, in particular, the relative advantages of markets, firms, and governments as modes of governance.

At the time of Adam Smith, and the emergence of *entrepreneurial* capitalism, production was mainly undertaken by relatively small, single-activity family firms; and most transactions were conducted at arm's-length prices between independent buyers and sellers. For the most part, the division of labour was elemental, and markets were independent of one another and spatially limited. Firms made relatively little use of created assets in the production process. The institution of political democracy was still in its infancy.

In such conditions it was not surprising that the market was the favoured signal for, and modality of, resource allocation, as the transaction and coordinating costs associated with it were insignificant, particularly when compared with those of hierarchies;[6] while, public administrations had neither the experience nor the motivation to organize economic activity efficiently. It was not surprising, either, that the dominant scholastic paradigm which emerged at that time was that of *laissez-faire*; and this was so, not because markets were thought to be perfect, but because the disbenefits of non-market intervention were perceived to be so much greater than the benefits.[7]

The century which followed, which we have called *hierarchical* capitalism, saw the emergence of the multi-activity firm and the gradual internalization by corporations of a range of intermediate product markets. While, frequently, such internalization – or, in the case of inter-firm cooperative agreements, quasi-internalization – helped circumvent endemic failure and enabled the economies of common governance of inter-related activities to be better exploited, it also led to sub-optimal market structures and to unacceptable business practices; hence the justification for government intervention to counteract structural distortions.

Economists also began to justify an interventionist role by national governments on other grounds. Already, following on the writings of Alexander Hamilton (1751–1804) and Frederick List (1798–1846),[8] a new school of political economists was asserting that nations seeking to 'catch up' in the development process needed some temporary protection against their established competitors if they were properly to exploit their dynamic comparative advantages.[9] Faced, too, with some of the downsides of nineteenth-century capitalism, scholars were arguing for governments to shelter the less fortunate members of society by taking a more active role in promoting social welfare – for example, by such means as the Factory Acts (1819–1901) and Poor Laws (1782–1834) in the UK. As economic activity became more complex, and an increasing number of products took on the form of public goods, governments saw fit to engage in some activities which, at the time, the private sector was not prepared to undertake – and yet which were market-facilitating and welfare-enhancing. Examples include the construction of a wide range of infrastructural facilities – including canals, roads, and railroads – all of which involved a high ratio of fixed to variable costs of production and had extremely long pay-back periods.

In the present century, additional aspects of the macro-organizational role of governments have been recognized in the literature. The concept of externalities and the distinction between social and private costs and benefits were especially highlighted by Alfred Marshall (1920) and A.C. Pigou (1932), while the severe unemployment in industrial economies for much of the inter-war years led other economists, notably J.M. Keynes (1936), to urge for more positive interventionism by national governments, which, they believed, was critical if the benefits of the market system were to be fully realized.

At the same time, a different group of scholars was pointing to the increasing costs of coordinating economic activity (Commons, 1924, 1934), and to those associated with technological advances and other structural changes (Schumpeter, 1934, 1942; Beveridge, 1944). While some economists of this era[10] distinguished between systemic and structural market failures, there was no real attempt to evaluate the alternative ways of coping with the former. This was because, until the writings of Ronald Coase, the role of transaction costs in determining the organization of economic activity had not been incorporated into mainstream economic theory.[11]

Moreover, there was little scholarly discussion of the role of governments as overseers of the organization of economic activity, and of how the economic system, for which they were responsible, might require adaptation because of the changing circumstances. Because of this, the debate between the interventionists and the champions of the 'free' market system became polarized; and it was, indeed, the failures of increasing socio-economic government intervention – which, perhaps, reached its peak in the third quarter of the twentieth century – that led to a renaissance of market-based economics, so vigorously propounded by Friedrich Hayek, Milton Friedman, James Buchanan, and Robert Lucas. Indeed, given the contemporary economic environment, one may be tempted to conclude that, not since the time of Adam Smith (1723–90), has liberal economics so dominated political actions.[12]

Yet, it may be that not all is as it seems. It is one thing to argue that, within a modern capitalist economy, market forces should play a more decisive role as a mechanism for resource allocation. It is, however, quite another to argue that, by themselves, such forces are sufficient to ensure the efficient organization of the economic system of which they are part – particularly in the knowledge-based and globalizing economy of the 1990s. It is quite clear that, along with the liberalization of individual markets, and the regulation of many value-added activities, new (or revitalized) organizational forms are emerging. Within the framework of an innovation-driven market economy, too, there is room for a plurality of organizational arrangements. Indeed, in such an economy, cooperation – for example, between firms and their suppliers, between the research and development (R&D) and manufacturing departments of a firm, between labour and management, and between the private and public sector – is often a critical ingredient of economic success. Hence, the term alliance capitalism[13] has been coined to reflect the kind of socio-institutional structure now emerging in market-based economies.

The two distinctive features of alliance capitalism are its emphasis, first, on the partnership between the various organizational modes of resource allocation, and, second, on the role assigned to government as the overseer of the economic system and the ultimate arbitrator of the functions undertaken by both private and public institutions. Of course, it is recognized that governments, on behalf of their constituents, may have other objectives; and, indeed, as a society becomes more prosperous, the trade-offs between further economic growth and other goals may change.[14] But, having said this, the economic and social milieu of the 1990s is such that, even if the role of government as a direct participator in national economies is declining, its function as (i) a creator and sustainer of the institutional, legal, and commercial infrastructure, (ii) a fashioner of value systems and ideologies, and (iii) a provider of a focal point or consensus around which resource allocative decisions can be coordinated is becoming more, rather than less, critical (Chang, 1994). Indeed, it is our contention that not only are the costs of supervising a systemic market-based economy rising all the time, but the role of government in affecting decisions taken by the main organizing entities in individual market transactions continues to be a decisive one. The following sections will elaborate on this thesis in some detail.

One other aspect of alliance capitalism, which will be discussed more fully later in this chapter, is the growing structural integration of the world economy. *Inter alia*, this is leading to a network of cross-border collaborative agreements, not only between firms of different nationality, but between firms and foreign governments, between national governments, and between interest groups and participants in the value-added process located in different countries. Such alliances may be both market-facilitating and market-distorting. However, one of the consequences of the globalizing economy is the renewed attention now being given to intergovernmental cooperation and supra-national regimes, as a means of reducing or circumventing undesirable market distorting practices of both firms and national governments. Moreover, this is occurring not only in the field of cross-border commerce, but in several other areas of macro-organizational policy which affect the disposition of resources and capabilities between and within nation states.

A TYPOLOGY OF APPROACHES TO ECONOMIC ORGANIZATION

Any attempt to classify the writings of past and contemporary scholars on the organization of economic activity is bound to be subjective, and to reflect the purposes for which it is being made. In this chapter I shall identify *six* different perceptions of the role of government (and for the most part national government) in a market-oriented economy. I would also observe that the great majority of scholars have confined their attention to the organization of economic activity within the context of either a closed economy or one in which cross-border trade is mainly conducted at arm's-length prices between independent parties.[15] Only since the 1970s, for example, have the implications of the activities of multinational hierarchies been explicitly analysed and a later section will consider some of these.

I now turn to discuss the lineage of academic scholarship associated with these six approaches, each of which, apart from the first, may be viewed as departures from a perfectly competitive market situation, as perceived by classical and neoclassical economists. For the most part, too, the approaches presume that the extent and form of government involvement are dependent on the extent and character of market imperfections – although, until recently, rarely has any attempt been made to assess whether or not the intervention by government is more cost effective than the market it replaces.[16] For the most part, too, academic research has concentrated on the role of government as controller, regulator, participator or influencer of *particular kinds* of resource disposition, rather than as an initiator and supervisor of the system by which all resources are created and deployed.

Although it is possible to identify a trajectory of scholarly research about the merit of alternative organizational modes, most of the philosophies, theories, and policy prescriptions articulated cannot be divorced from the particular circumstances of their time. For example, although Adam Smith is usually portrayed as an ardent supporter of free markets, his analysis of the situations in which government intervention is justified – if modified to embrace the institutional, technological, and social environment of the late twentieth century – suggests that he was fully aware of the role of governments as overseers of an economic system in which market forces might flourish. Indeed, a close reading of Smith's analysis of the functions of government is quite consistent with the tenets of modern institutional economics; and the fact that their systemic activities were less in evidence than they are today largely reflects the relative simplicity of eighteenth-century economic life, as compared with its contemporary equivalent. Similarly, while, in the context of the US economy of the 1990s, the views of Frederick List might be considered highly protectionist, in the context of that of the German economy of the 1830s, they are entirely in accord with that part of contemporary transaction-cost theory which argues for the need of extra-market action to facilitate the restructuring of an economy in line with its comparative dynamic advantage.

Let me now discuss the lineage of the six approaches to the role of government.

The Philosophical/Ideological View on how Economic Activity should be Organized

This view essentially reflects that of the nature of society and the 'right' (rather than the most efficient) way to organize economic activity. Scholars who prescribed such views rarely sought to offer a rigorous economic defence for them. The Mercantilists of the sixteenth and seventeenth centuries, for example, believed that the political and economic interests of the state should be the primary justification for economic activity; and, not surprisingly, accorded the rulers of the state direct responsibility for advancing this goal. The two centuries which followed saw a reaction to the Mercantilist philosophy, which was spearheaded by Quesnay (1694–1774) and the French Physiocrats, who believed in the natural law or the 'natural' order of things. Their economic principles were encapsulated in the classic maxim '*laissez faire et laissez passer, le monde va de lui-même*' or 'let do and let alone and the world goes by itself'. To the Physiocrats the role of the state was to regulate affairs to follow the natural order 'ordained by God and susceptible to the discovery of man'. They maintained that 'governments should never extend their influence in economic affairs beyond the minimum absolutely essential to the protection of life and property and the maintenance of freedom of contracts' (Ferguson, 1938, p. 50).

Although philosophical and ideological elements were also contained in the writings of some of the English classical and neoclassical scholars – for example, David Hume (1711–76), Adam Smith, Jeremy Bentham, and Ludwig von Mises (1881–1973)[17] – the growing sophistication of societies over the last 200 years, which *inter alia* has reflected the increasing dependence on the upgrading of human skills and physical capacity – has tended to lessen the appeal of this kind of approach. However, as a direct result of the less desirable social consequences of the industrial revolution, a new school of thought – which might be dubbed the social welfare school of economics – emerged. The founder of this school was a French historian, Jean Charles Simonde de Sismondi (1773–1843).[18] To begin with, Sismondi was an admirer of Adam Smith, but, in his later writings, he vigorously attacked wealth accumulation both as an end in itself and for its detrimental effect on the poor.

After Sismondi, the course of social economics took two distinct paths. The first was that of *socialist* economics, which urged the collective ownership of property and an active, participatory role of the state in all aspects of economic affairs. Such an approach to economic organization was initially explored by French and English social reformers such as Claude Saint-Simon (1760–1825), Jean Louis Blanc (1811–82), and Robert Owen (1771–1858), and by the German state socialists such as Johann Rodbertus (1805–75) and Ferdinand Lassalle (1825–64), but most extensively, and fervently, by Karl Marx (1818–83).

The second path was that of *welfare* economics, which, while firmly rooted in classical and neoclassical theoretical analysis, was built around the concept of the social welfare of the community (rather than the economic self-interest of individual) and the distribution (in addition to the size) of the national dividend. Hints of scholarly dissatisfaction with the hedonism of Jeremy Bentham, and a realization that the theory of competitive markets did not allow for the less welcome extra-market diseconomies of consumption and production, were first explicitly mentioned in the writings of Henry Sidgwick (1838–90).[19] However, it was Vilfredo Pareto (1848–1923) and A.C. Pigou who provided the intellectual apparatus for identifying the situations in which the social costs and benefits of economic activity might diverge from those resulting from free-market transactions; and of how governments might intervene to optimize – or come near to optimizing – the marginal social net product.

The writings of both Pareto and Pigou – and indeed that of Marx before them – cannot solely be classified to the philosophical–ideological approach to economic organization. Indeed, with the growing complexity of most Western societies and the development of more rigorous economic and social analysis, most scholars came to adopt a less polemical course of reasoning. For example, notwithstanding his contempt for the self-interest promoted by the free enterprise system, and his belief that class warfare would eventually lead to its destruction, several of the writings of Karl Marx foreshadowed not only the kind of state-guided capitalism currently favoured by many East Asian countries, but the critical role played by institutions in determining the success or failure of free markets.

In more recent years, there has been some resurgence in the ideological aspects of economic organization – mainly as a result of the practical failures of dogmatic socialism. The 'high priests' of the unfettered market in the second half of the present century have been Friedreich von Hayek and Milton Friedman. Indeed, given the post-1945 economic and political milieu, it may be reasonably argued that Hayek – in advancing his philosophy of contractarianism[20] – was even more ideologically attuned to personal liberty and against state interventionism than Adam Smith himself. Having experienced the ultimate consequences of fascist-style governments in the inter-war years, Hayek was apprehensive, lest, in the aftermath of the Second World War, socialism would engulf large parts of Europe and pose a serious challenge to capitalism and to civil liberty.

While acknowledging the concerns of Hayek, other economists of his generation did not share his confidence in either the efficiency or the social justice of the market economy. In particular, in the 1960s and 1970s, the theoretical and ideological insights of Nicholas Kaldor, Albert Hirschman, and Raúl Prebisch were used by policy-makers in both developed and developing countries to justify a whole series of market-interventionist policies. However, as it turned out, far from advancing social welfare, such policies frequently inhibited the economic restructuring and growth on which such welfare depended.

The Cost–Benefit View of Alternative Organizational Forms

There are several variants of this view. Most begin with the presumption that, in a situation of perfect competition, markets are the best instrument for allocating scarce resources, and the only justification for external intervention is that, in one way or other, markets fail to perform in a Pareto-optimal fashion. Again, I would observe that those presumptions make no explicit reference to the costs of setting up and sustaining the efficient working of either particular markets or the market system as a whole.

Yet, as I shall argue later in this chapter, it is the systemic costs and benefits of coordinating economic activity that have become such an important component of the total resource allocative process in recent years; and that, quite frequently, the process can best be achieved by a partnership between alternative organizational entities. A review of scholarly research over the past two centuries suggests that five kinds of market imperfections stand out above all others; and it is the presence of these imperfections which has usually led to a discussion of the appropriate role of government in counteracting their adverse affects. I shall briefly discuss each of these in turn.

Structural market distortions

Perhaps the most widely accepted interventionist role of government is to restrict or counteract any actions on the part of the participants in a market to inhibit the efficient operation of competitive forces. The most obvious case is that of monopolistic or monopsonistic pricing behaviour, but there are many other instances when, through restricting entry into goods or factor markets, or by engaging in excessive product differentiation or anti-competitive practices, sellers (or buyers) might behave in a socially unacceptable fashion.

Such a need for government action has been well recognized by economists since Adam Smith first maintained that the state had a duty to protect the general public from 'extortionate practices',[21] and from the innate selfishness of competing businessmen. At the same time, Smith was quick to denounce any market-distorting behaviour on the part of the state itself. While there remains little disagreement among economists about the need to minimize both private and public structural market imperfections, there is less consensus on the merits and demerits of the alternative organizational arrangements for promoting dynamic allocative efficiency, or those which might best accommodate plant or firm specific economies of scale. Other areas for dispute over the ideal market structure include the trade-off between the benefits of the risk diversification and common governance of related activities, and the opportunities that a domestic multi-activity or multinational enterprise (MNE) may have for engaging in cross-subsidization, transfer price manipulation, and other business practices not available to the single-activity enterprise.

The recent explosive growth in strategic alliances – particularly cross-border alliances – is creating an additional dilemma for competition policy. On the one hand, the alliances may enable the participating firms to be more competitive in global markets; on the other, they may better enable the collaborating firms to crowd out smaller competitors, and/or reduce the contestability of markets. Such trade-offs as these are becoming more, rather than less, prolific in the contemporary globalizing economy – and, as several economists have observed[22] – are requiring national governments, regional authorities, and supranational regimes to reconsider their anti-trust and competition policies, which were originally formulated in a very different economic environment.

Externalities and social welfare

Most contemporary studies of economic organization tend to address the causes of endemic, rather than those of structural, market failure. Endemic market failure refers to the inability of markets to perform in a Pareto-optimal way because of intrinsic market impurities, rather than because of any distorting behaviour of the participants of the market. The rest of this section will consider some of these from a historical perspective.

The idea that a particular market transaction may affect individuals or institutions, other than those engaging in the transaction – that is, that give rise to externalities and a divergence between private and social costs and benefits – dates back to the time of David Hume, Adam Smith, and Jeremy Bentham. According to Rostow (1990, p. 49), Hume and Smith were 'acutely conscious of external economies that governments should assure were exploited and external diseconomies that government should prevent'. Bentham held that, if it could be shown that government action enhances the happiness of the community more than it diminishes it, then such action would be justified (Ekelund and Hebert, 1975, p. 111). In spite of his defence of an individualist utilitarian creed, John Stuart Mill (1806–73) took a similar view. He argued that, on humanitarian grounds, it was the state's responsibility to redress the increasing divergence between social and (private) economic welfare, which he believed had been brought about by the industrial revolution.

The implications of wider and deeper levels of economic specialization for extra-market activities, and the possible divergence between the private and social benefits of market forces were well recognized by Alfred Marshall. Here a quote from his classic work (Marshall, 1920, p. 241) is worth repeating:

> The development of the organism whether social or physical involves an increasing sub-division of functions between its separate parts on the one hand, and on the other a more intimate connection between them. Each part gets to be less and less self-sufficient, to depend for its well being more and more on other parts, so that any disorder in any part of the highly developed organism will affect other parts also.

Although Marshall is also credited as being the father of welfare economics,[23] it was his one-time student and successor to his Chair of Economics at Cambridge University – A.C. Pigou (1877–1959) – who formalized the conditions in which extra-market intervention might be necessary to ensure that competitive market transactions were to advance the wider social good. However, although, in principle, wherever there are externalities to a particular economic activity, there may be a case for increasing or reducing that activity or redistributing some of its costs and/or benefits, this does not necessarily mean that action by public authorities is the best way for this to be achieved. Indeed, over the past century, perhaps the main mode of overcoming the failure of markets to capture the externalities of transactions has been for business enterprises to internalize these markets.

Clearly, however, there are instances – particularly in the provision of public goods – where governments may well be the most suitable organizational mode. This has been acknowledge by almost all scholars from the time of Smith, J.S. Mill, and John McCullogh (1789–1864) onwards. McCullogh, for example, was particularly critical of the principle of *laissez-faire* when it came to the social functions of government, and referred to it as savouring 'more the policy of a parrot than of a statesman or philosopher' (McCullogh, 1848, p. 156).

It is, however, worth observing that, in the absence of serious economic analysis, it is not possible to evaluate the optimal role of government either in reconciling social and private costs and benefits or in the provision of public goods. Some services which in the nineteenth century were best supplied by governments are now at least as well provided by private enterprise;[24] while others, which have become too costly for even groups of firms to produce and which generate enormous externalities, may now be best supplied by public authorities – or public authorities jointly with private corporations. One can, however, point to the need for governments in their overseeing role to take more account of the increasing interdependency of economic activities. One may also observe that, as certain social issues (e.g. those to do with the environment) have risen on the political agenda, the efficacy of traditional resource-allocative mechanisms has been further questioned.

The issue of structural unemployment

Economists have always recognized that it is the unique and critical task of governments to engage in responsible and efficient macro-economic management, even though – at least since the abolition of the gold standard in 1925 – there has been much controversy over how this task can be best done. Although this chapter is primarily concerned with macro-organizational issues, the question of the role of the appropriate macro-economic arrangements for dealing with unemployment is worthy of some attention – especially since (so we would argue!), in modern times, an increasing proportion of unemployment is due to dynamic structural forces rather than to any overall deficiency in the demand for goods or services.[25]

For most of the nineteenth- and early twentieth-century economists were almost exclusively concerned with structural unemployment. Adam Smith, Jeremy Bentham, and Saint-Simon each advocated the use of public works to reduce the jobless population; while John McCullogh was one of the first economists to argue for the provision of unemployment assistance. By the mid-nineteenth century there was also some acknowledgement that governments can play a role in the upgrading of a country's human and physical resources. John Stuart Mill, for example, strongly believed that government had a duty to provide general education to reduce economic and social inequities, and to prepare men and women for their duties as 'intelligent consumers and trained producers' (Ferguson, 1938). This theme was later echoed in the writings of Robert Owen, Karl Marx, Alfred Marshall, and Henry Sidgwick.

The seminal contribution of J.M. Keynes to macro-economic theory and policy-making is germane to our interests in so far as he believed that, unaided, market forces could not always ensure the full and efficient employment of resources, and that government intervention might be necessary to achieve this goal. At the same time, Keynes did not challenge the market system *per se*. He argued, as did the Austrian economists before him, that any inability of the market properly to perform its functions was not a reflection of the system itself – that is, of endemic market failure – but rather the result of the failure of governments properly to execute their own responsibilities. In particular, Keynes argued that, in the inter-war years, neither the UK nor the US government was efficiently managing its fiscal and monetary affairs; and that, were they to do so, then markets would operate in textbook fashion.

In short, although in one sense Keynes was a traditional neoclassicist, in another he posed a great challenge to *laissez-faire* orthodoxy. Moreover, to the extent that he argued that governments may sometimes be justified in extending their macro-economic boundaries to embrace issues of competition, education and science, and industry, they were eagerly (although often incorrectly) seized on by the policy-makers of the day – and particularly by Franklin D. Roosevelt – as an excuse for more widespread state involvement in economic affairs.

Indeed, throughout the 1930s, and in the early post-war period, the Keynesian paradigm formed the basis for macro-economic policy in most Western countries.

Keynes was mainly concerned with unemployment caused by lack of effective demand.[26] Only peripherally did he concern himself with structural unemployment, although he clearly recognized that rigidities in the factor and product markets could impede the successful implementation of his policy prescriptions. The significance of these rigidities was first explored in depth by William Beveridge – a scholar and social reformer who was the architect of the modern welfare state in Britain. In his view, the central weakness of the unplanned market economy was its incapacity not only to generate sufficient and steady demand for its products, but to cope with a 'local misdirection of demand' and 'the disorganization of the labour market' (Beveridge, 1944, p. 28). However, unlike Keynes, Beveridge believed that demand-side fiscal and monetary policies were not enough to cure unemployment, and particularly that caused by technological change. Such unemployment, according to Beveridge, was a reflection of the failure of markets efficiently to adjust to changes in supply-and-demand conditions. While in some cases this was due to structural impediments – for example, on the part of firms or organized labour – in others it was not. In these latter instances, Beveridge recommended government intervention – for example, introducing worker-retraining schemes, encouraging the occupational and geographical mobility of labour, providing additional risk capital, and fostering the relocation of industry.

While Beveridge's policy prescriptions were most certainly more interventionist than those of Keynes, many of them, like those of the Cambridge economists, were intended to facilitate the efficient workings of markets, rather than to replace them. However, the distinction between these two rationales for intervention were obscured by both policy-makers and academic scholars. Partly, this was because the dynamic and static functions of market forces had been insufficiently distinguished. This, itself, reflected the fact that economists at the time gave little real attention to technological change as an endogenous variable affecting economic welfare, and one which, by definition, is incompatible with a situation of perfect competition.

And, of course, more than anything else, it has been technological change which has challenged the full employment policies of governments in the post-war period, and particularly since 1970; and it has been the inability or unwillingness of individuals and firms to bear the social costs of technological change that has led economists to urge governments (on behalf of the communities they represent) to help absorb such costs. This responsibility has been embraced more fully by some governments than by others. This reflects partly the differing ability of governments to shoulder the costs of such change, and partly their political or ideological differences in the need for such intervention.

The interaction between technological change and the structure of economic activity was first seriously articulated by Karl Marx, although several classical economists (e.g. J.S. Mill and J. McCullogh) had anticipated it. According to Marx, the historical development of economies proceeds in a stepwise progression from feudalism to capitalism, and then to socialism, and is fashioned by the interplay between institutional and technological forms. In particular, he argued that history was a series of class struggles, and that each class put its own interests above the national interests (Olson, 1965). This, he concluded, was bound to lead to the self-destruction of capitalism. Governments might attempt to compensate for the deficiencies of the market system; but, in the end, 'it was socially impossible for a government to set things right' (Heilbroner, 1965, p. 140). To Marx, the only answer was a Communist state.

Marx had only a rudimentary understanding about the economics of technical change in a capitalist society. It was left to Joseph Schumpeter (1883–1950) to explain the ways in which innovations impacted on economic organization. He coined the expression 'creative destruction' to describe a situation in which innovations led to the obsolescence of existing products and ways of doing things, and hence structural shifts in demand-and-supply conditions. More than any other economist, Schumpeter explicitly distinguished between the static and dynamic components of market failure. While he rejected Marx's diagnosis of capitalistic ills, he did believe that increasingly rapid technological change would necessitate a bigger and more influential role for national governments, if the benefits of such change were to be exploited at minimum social costs. In Schumpeter's writings, too, we also see the distinction between the social and private consequences of innovatory activities, and the notion that firms may under-invest in R&D as they cannot fully appropriate the gains of their innovations. As economic organization has become increasingly innovation-driven, the need for a sympathetic institutional environment to minimize structural adjustment costs has become more urgent. The contributions of Nat Rosenberg, Christopher Freeman, Keith Pavitt, Richard Nelson, and Stanley Winter in the 1970s and 1980s in adding to our knowledge on these issues is particularly noteworthy.[27] In this respect, it is also clear that the actions taken by governments both to encourage their own firms to innovate new products and to minimize the costs of structural adjustment have been one of the main ingredients of their post-war success. But, like Keynes, by and large, the economists justifying such government intervention have done so on the basis that it is necessary to *facilitate* the market system rather than to *replace* it.

Institutions, transactions, and coordination costs

Perhaps the most thought-provoking – and certainly the least understood – contribution to our understanding of the economics of organization has been that which focuses on the *transaction* and *coordination* costs of economic activity, rather than on the *production* or *transformation* costs. Here, the thesis is a deceptively simple one. In conditions of perfect competition, the transaction and coordinating costs of using the market as a mode of allocating scarce resources are zero. This is because the information necessary to engage in economic activity is assumed to be complete; there is no uncertainty attached to contracts, and there is no interaction between buyers and sellers, except at the point of contract completion. It is further presumed that there are no externalities to market transactions and, in consequence, there is no incentive for firms to capture the economies of common governance. This scenario of perfect knowledge and no uncertainty reduces the role of organizations, other than markets, to that of a black box. In perfect market conditions, *homo economicus* reigns supreme.

The practical unreality of these assumptions provided the initial challenge to English classical economics by a group of French and German scholars.[28] Strongly influenced by Hegelian philosophy, they questioned the idea of economic determinism, the universality of classical doctrines and the strategy of individualistic self-interest. Essentially, they argued that any study of economic phenomena had to be set within a particular historical, institutional, and spatial context which might vary over time and space; and, that, because of this, an inductive method of scientific approach was at least as relevant as its deductive counterpart.

The belief that the efficiency of economic organization cannot be separated from the institutional framework of which it is part spawned a new branch of economic thought in the nineteenth century, which has had a chequered influence. Two distinct strands may be identified. The first – to which we give only passing attention[29] – is what might be called a *socio-organizational* variant, the modern inheritors of which are scholars interested in the sociology of organization and institutions, and of the way individuals and interest groups may influence the decisions taken by public agencies. The lineage of this group of scholars dates back to Karl Marx; and among its most vociferous contemporary exponents is Mancur Olson (1965, 1979, 1982).

The other stream of thought is more evolutionary, and focuses the impact of institutions on the costs and benefits of coordinating economic activity. The premise is that, as economic development proceeds, the costs of organizing production and exchange increases. The question of interest is not why markets fail, but under what conditions alternative forms of governance may be more cost-effective. In their analysis, however, most institutionalists make no presumption that the visible hand of hierarchies and governments is necessarily preferable to the *invisible* hand of markets.

While Smith and Ricardo fully recognized that the specialization of value-added activities might lead to productivity gains in the deployment of resources, neither paid any attention to its effects on the volume and complexity of transactions. In particular, they made no attempt to explore such concepts as asset specificity, bounded rationality, opportunistic behaviour, information asymmetry, and the economies (and diseconomies) of the common governance of related activities. While Smith recognized that the classical duties of government became more extended as the society 'advanced in civilization', it was a French sociologist, Émile Durkheim (1893), who first provided the analytical underpinnings to the German historical school.

Durkheim's thesis was that the hallmark of 'elevated' societies was the increased specialization of production and exchange. In particular, he argued that this required a reappraisal of the 'existing processes of government involvement' both in the provision of legal and social institutions and in the minimization of the costs of market transactions. Durkheim identified several such pervasive market failures. These included the presence of externalities and spillovers,[30] the difficulty of coordinating an increasingly sophisticated infrastructure of public goods, the need for a tighter protection of property rights, a reduced coincidence of ideologies and values brought about by a separation of tasks, and an increasing differentiation between managerial information and cognitive frames.

Durkheim's views had relatively little impact on orthodox economic thinking in the years before the First World War, which tended to be dominated by the Austrian School of economists.[31] It did, however, strike a sympathetic chord with a group of US scholars who were questioning some of the socio-cultural foundations of neoclassical economics, and particularly its failure to recognize the need for institutional adaptation to the technological and organizational changes. Although Thorsten Veblen (1857–1929)[32] is commonly regarded as the leader of this school, the later writings of Wesley Mitchell (1874–1948) and John Commons (1862–1945) were more influential. Commons, in particular, developed a theory of collective action by the state (and other non-market institutions) which he saw as essential to an understanding of the realities of economic life. Commons focused on the *transaction* as the vehicle for organizing resource usage, and for the building of institutions. In his analysis, he took an interdisciplinary and a dynamic perspective. He foresaw that, as economic activity became more complex and highly specialized, and as human beings and institutions gained in experience and learning, then so did both the costs and benefits of transactions.

Although Commons failed to make inroads into traditional mainstream economic theory before the First World War,[33] he did provide the intellectual backing for some of the welfare reforms initiated by the US federal government in the 1930s. It was, however, left to a British economist – Ronald Coase – to provide the theoretical underpinning of the contemporary revival of institutional economics. Coase, himself, was not an institutionalist, nor, indeed, did he have much to say about the role of government in economic affairs. But, in his seminal essay on the theory of the firm, Coase (1937) not only explained why competitive markets may not always be the most cost-effective way of translating goods and services; he also identified the situations in which market failure could best be overcome by firms, replacing (i.e. internalizing) the market by administrative fiat.[34]

Over the last half century, the theory of market failure has been extended and refined by several economists following in the tradition of Coase, and by behaviourists such as Herbert Simon (1947, 1959) and organizational scholars such as Oliver Williamson (1975, 1985). In principle, there is no reason why the methodologies devised to evaluate the choice between markets and hierarchies as modes of resource creation and deployment should not be extended to that between governments and markets, or between governments and hierarchies. But, until recently, however, economists have been reluctant to do so. One exception has been Coase himself (1960), who analysed the various ways in which negative externalities of market transactions may be overcome by private or public administrative fiat. More specifically,

> The problem is one of choosing the appropriate social arrangement for dealing with the harmful effects. All solutions have costs and there is no reason to suppose that government regulation is called for simply because the problem is not well handled by the market or the firm. Satisfactory views on policy can only come from a patient study of how, in practice, the market, firms and governments handle the problem of harmful effects. (Coase, 1960, p. 18)

In the last 20 years or so, economists and organizational scholars have given more attention to evaluating the costs and benefits of alternative organizational forms. Mancur Olson, for example (1965, 1979), has proposed a theory of economic organization based on the concept of fiscal equivalence.[35] Like Coase and J.M. Clark (1923) before him, Olson concentrates his attention on the problem of negative environmental externalities. Another group of scholars – for example, Charles Wolf (1988), Robert Wade (1988), Joseph Stiglitz (1989), and Ann Krueger (1990) – have attempted to formalize the conditions under which governments might successfully intervene either to replace or to facilitate other organizational arrangements; and also to analyse the costs of non-market failure. Among the limitations of direct government intervention identified by these scholars, are – to quote my own words –

> The rent seeking activities of powerful pressure groups; the magnification of market failures (e.g. with respect to the supply of environmental or social products) by the news media or other politically motivated interests; the inability of governments to attract the best talents (due *inter alia* to ineffective incentive systems); the lack of commercial expertise and bounded rationality of public decision takers; the pursuance of non-economic (especially ideological) goals by politicians; the inadequacy of market related performance indicators which may lead to the establishment of sub-

> optimal standards (e.g. with respect to budgets, investment and control of information flows); the high-time discount (or short-termism) of political decision takers; the lack of market pressures to minimize X inefficiency, especially in the case of public monopolies; uncertainties and ambiguities inherent in the provision of goods and services, which are in the domain of governments, e.g. defense equipment, educational and health services; and the lack of a coordinated system of governance (cf. with that in case of private hierarchies); and the difficulty of adjusting policies and institutional structures to quickly meet the needs of technological and economic change. (Dunning, 1994, p. 30)

In a recent analysis of the political economy of industrial policy, Ha-Joon Chang (1994) treats all costs of state intervention as transaction costs. Such costs, he argues, are justifiable as long as they yield net benefits exceeding those offered by the market or by market-based hierarchies. In addition to the rationale for government intervention to advance the efficiency of particular markets, Chang – like the present author (Dunning, 1994) – suggests that governments can help lower the transaction and coordination costs of the economic *system* by ensuring that the activities of private and public institutions are suited to the needs of the day. This they may do by fostering an ethos and value system among contracting agents which reduce the gains from opportunism; and, by encouraging an ambience of inter-firm cooperation wherever such cooperation is likely to lead to a more socially acceptable allocation of resources and capabilities.

Perhaps the most interesting facet of Chang's work is his recognition that an 'exit' approach to the failure of markets, or of governments, efficiently to coordinate economic activity is not always the first best strategy.[36] The fact that markets fail does not necessarily warrant their replacement by hierarchies or governments. The fact that there are political constraints on governments to perform efficiently does not mean that they should take no corrective action. Sometimes, indeed, 'exiting' from a problem may create more problems that it alleviates. On those occasions, a 'voice' strategy to reduce the costs (or to increase the benefits) of political failure may be the preferable response. But, this, according to Chang, almost certainly requires a reconfiguration of the institutional design of government.

A good example of institutional redesign is the reaction of Japanese firms to market failure. Rather than internalize the markets (an 'exit' response), they have tended to pursue a strategy of reducing the coordinating costs of markets by way of inter-firm cooperative alliances, and by the Japanese government providing market-facilitating facilities.[37]

Research into the ways in which governments, in their capacity of overseers of the wealth-creating activities within their jurisdiction, can help advance these by reducing the structural costs of readjustment and the X inefficiency of non-market organizational modes is still in its infancy. But, in the tradition of Marx and Commons, scholars such as Douglass North are encouraging scholars to refocus their attention on the role of institutions in affecting the efficiency of market-based economic systems.

The focus of North's work (e.g. North 1981, 1990, 1993) is on the increasing transaction costs of twentieth-century society.[38] These, he asserts, are the direct result of technological and organizational advances, and their impact on institutional arrangements. But North goes beyond Durkheim (1964) in identifying the coordination costs which result from the increasing complexity of economic activity. He suggests that, as national economies have become richer, goods and services with a high transaction cost component have become increasingly important. Although he accepts that some product and process innovations (e.g. the computer and satellite communications) have helped reduce transaction costs and macro-level market failures, he believes that most have caused them to increase. While he observes that, in the private sector, the response to such failures has been the development of more efficient hierarchies and/or inter-corporate alliances,[39] he suggests that extra-market organizational modes (e.g. public institutions) have, in general, been much less successful in adapting to the demands made on them.

North is ambivalent about the impact of national government involvement on institutional design.[40] While arguing that the shift in the locus of decision-making of economic organization from economic to political has adversely affected a country's productivity and competitiveness (North, 1993), he also contends that governments can play a positive role in encouraging the institutions within their ambience of responsibility to react to (and, in some cases, actively to facilitate) structural change in a way which is consistent with the societal good. In his writings North takes an incremental approach to economic development. He believes that the trajectory of change is set by the character of established institutions and their ability to adjust to change in the most cost-effective way. To use his own words:

> Well specified and enforced property rights, decentralized political and economic decision taking and effective competition have been the underlying institutional structure for the organizational changes allowing modern economies to reap the productivity gains of the technology. (North, 1993, pp. 14, 18)[41]

However, in echoing Durkheim's views a century earlier, North then goes on to argue that many technological and organizational advances are undermining traditional institutions built upon informal restraints – and especially the family, personal relationships, and repetitive individual exchanges. In their place, new institutions have emerged, which have given rise to new transaction costs. North believes that those societies whose governments have fostered the institutional environment by which economic agents are able to take advantage of the new technological advances (e.g. by reducing uncertainty, encouraging flexible economic organizations, releasing creative entrepreneurial talent, and minimizing environmental volatility) are those which are best equipped to succeed in the contemporary world economy.

Technology and organizational change

Although an earlier section gave some attention to the dynamics of structural change, we shall complete our historical survey by briefly considering the role of non-market institutions as facilitators or inhibitors of that change. In general, the consensus of scholarly opinion is more sympathetic to a participatory role of government in assisting or reducing the adjustment costs of change than in affecting the static allocation of resources. Thus, it is not surprising that one of the first scholarly pleas for government intervention was made by a German economist, Frederick List;[42] and that this was because he viewed the existing system of free trade between nations to be market-distorting and argued from the perspective of the long-term economic advantages of the German economy. In his belief that countries passed through various stages of development, he justified some degree of import protection by latecomer nations. This was not because of any static misallocation of resources in the German economy, but because German firms needed some temporary alleviation from established foreign manufacturers if they were to restructure their value-added activities in line with their potential or dynamic comparative advantages.[43]

It was not, however, until well after the second generation of major technological advances had occurred in the third quarter of the nineteenth century that the issue of dynamic market imperfections gained the attention of mainstream economists. Basically, the argument was that not only were the costs of structural adjustment sometimes too great for unaided markets to bear;[44] but that the social benefits of such adjustments were often greater than the private benefits. Although the germs of a dynamic theory of organizational structure had earlier been voiced by such scholars as Ricardo, J.S. Mill, Saint-Simon, and the socio-economic theorizing of Marx, it was not until Schumpeter explicitly identified innovation, or, as he put it, 'new combinations of productive means', as the main driver of economic change, that the properties of dynamic markets were properly identified.[45] Like Marx, Schumpeter believed that technological progress would lead to instabilities in production and exchange, demand new organizational structures, and encourage more influential governments. However, unlike Marx, he did not regard innovations as a catalyst for the demise of market-based capitalism. Rather, he perceived them as vehicles for a reconfiguration of the established institutional norms, embedded value systems, and the traditional exchange patterns between the main organizational entities.[46]

Schumpeter, then, was essentially concerned with the structural forces underlying and influencing economic development, and with the ways in which institutions might adjust to these forces. In particular, he doubted that, unaided, free markets could offer the necessary inducements for firms, consumers, and workers to undertake the changes needed; and that governments might need to intervene to ensure that the social net benefits of restructuring were optimized. In contemporary economic parlance, Schumpeter's analysis can be expressed in terms of the transaction and coordination costs of innovation-led development, which, he observed, do not occur in any predictable pattern.

Later scholars have built upon Schumpeter's ideas and related organizational change to a series of long-term technological trajectories. Carlota Perez (1983), for example, has identified a series of time-related clusters of radical innovations which, she claims, have been watersheds in the economic evolution of countries. However, unlike Schumpeter, she believes that the long waves between these watersheds – as, for example, identified by Nikolai Kondratiev (1926) – are not primarily the result of economic forces, but rather the manifestation of the 'harmonious or disharmonious behaviour of the total socio-economic and institutional system'. In her view, quantum leaps in the best-practice frontier of value-added activity (Perez, 1983, p. 358) require shifts not only in the techno-economic organization of economic activity, but in the socio-institutional fabric of society. In a later contribution with Christopher Freeman, Perez explores the institutional changes forced by the first industrial revolution (*circa* the late 1700s) and those of the second (*circa* the late 1800s) and goes on to argue that the global economy is currently undergoing a third industrial revolution as a result of a constellation of radical innovations in computers, electronics and telecommunications (Freeman and Perez, 1988).

The analysis of Perez and the Sussex economists[47] not only fits in very nicely with the ideas of Douglass North. It is also complementary to the writings of such economists as Nelson and Winter (1982),[48] which are primarily directed to examining the behavioural responses of institutions to innovatory change. Issues such as the appropriate incentives or penalties to encourage organizational adjustments, and the implications of new technological trajectories for organizational learning, routines, search processes, path dependencies, the distribution of information and capabilities, and inter-firm transaction costs, are at the core of contemporary debate. These and related issues are being increasingly explored in the literature, and are discussed in more detail in the following chapters. They are mentioned here, partly because, they are among the most germane to our understanding of the micro- and macro-organization of resource allocation; and, also to emphasize that scholarly analysis is currently being conducted in a very different socio-institutional environment to that in which earlier economists framed their ideas.

CONCLUSIONS OF THE HISTORICAL REVIEW

The general conclusion of our historical review is that past scholars have had a considerable amount to say about the way in which market-based capitalist economies are, and should be, organized. I do not wish to minimize the differences between their opinions or their policy prescriptions, but it is, none the less, the case that their writings often address very different aspects of the role of governments.

A number of specific conclusions can be drawn. Let me highlight six of these. *First, wherever economic activity involves transaction and coordination costs, it is not possible to formulate an optimum mix of alternative organizational modes which are universally applicable.* Much depends on the circumstances facing particular countries at the time. As Chang (1994, p. 135) has sagaciously observed:

> neither the market, nor the state, nor any other economic institution is perfect as a coordination mechanism. Each institution has its costs and benefits, and is therefore better than others under certain conditions and worse under other conditions. This means that different countries facing different conditions can, and should have different mixes of the market, the state and other institutions. And in fact ... even economies that are usually lumped together as 'capitalist' or 'market' economies have been based on substantially different institutional mixes.

A similar view is expressed by Aronson and Ott (1991, p. 525), who write:

> Some (countries) will assign more functions to government than others will, and some will have a stronger taste for public services than others will. Moreover, the allocation of responsibilities between different levels of government will also vary, with some countries relying more on the central government than others. The differences exist because groups have different political systems, because the demographic forces at work differ, because countries differ in income and wealth and because people differ in their preferences for publicly supplied goods and services.

Second, in retrospect, it is clear that the main thrust of historical research has been to evaluate alternative organizational arrangements in terms of their impact on market failure. Only in the last half century has attention been given to the *endemic* benefits and disbenefits of alternative modes of governance, as are primarily reflected in the costs of such governance and of the synergistic interaction between North-type institutions.

Third, and allied to the second conclusion, differences among scholars have strongly reflected the time-frame of their analyses. For example, most of the ideas and prescriptions of the classical economists about the role of governments tended to assume that the wealth of a nation rested in its *natural* resources, which, apart from population, were perceived to be largely fixed.[49] Later, the historical, institutional, and Schumpeterian schools all viewed the evolution of economies in terms of their ability to *create* new assets and capabilities, notably technology, capital, human skills, and managerial expertise. It was in the production and dissemination of these assets, and in their ability to adjust to changing factor and product markets, that economists now saw the ingredients of growth. Thus if, for example, one takes a longitudinal view to market-based capitalism (Stiglitz, 1989), it can be demonstrated that, in the early stages of development, governments play a critical function in setting up a market system and providing assets of a public-goods character (e.g. social infrastructure) to enable the efficient production of privately financed goods and services. Assuming the absence of major innovations, the role of governments may then be expected to decline – particularly where there is little uncertainty, and few economies of scale or externalities of production or consumption. But, then, as economic growth becomes more dependent on technological and organizational innovations, and as these involve increasingly large expenditures on human resource development and supportive physical infrastructure, the systemic functions of government again become important; even though, in some areas, its role as a producer and regulator might decrease.[50] The next section of this chapter will suggest that the emergence of a globally, or regionally, integrated world economy is also requiring a re-examination of the role of national governments in domestic resource allocation.

Fourth, although the debate on the optimal structure of organizational arrangements still remains heavily overloaded with value judgements, over the last 50 years it has taken on a more objective or technical character. Although most obviously demonstrated in the management of macro-economic affairs, the need for a more coherent and holistic governance of the macro-organization of economic activity is becoming increasingly recognized.[51] But there is a long way to go. While there is a plethora of writings on the organizational structures of corporations, and on how these may need to be modified in the light of technological advances and globalization,[52] the study of the governance of government remains in its infancy. The transaction-costs paradigm, as applied to the management of hierarchies and inter-firm alliances, has yet to be applied to that of government-related institutions; and there remain major differences in the structures of authority in the private and public sectors (Shultz 1979).[53]

Fifth, until quite recently, scholars have generally opined that, governments, in their intervention in organization of economic activity, have been more likely adversely to affect economic welfare than to advance it, although the scope and depth of the adversity has varied according to particular circumstances of the time. Very gradually, however, as society has become more complex, the role of government has been more positively acknowledged. Today, in many – especially East Asians – societies, governments and markets work in close association with each other; and, in its 1992 annual report, the World Bank emphasized the complementarity between the two forms of organizational arrangements. Again, the exact nature of the partnership between the public and private sectors partly depends on the nature of the production or transaction functions being undertaken,[54] but perhaps the most notable feature of the successful market-oriented economies of recent years has been the ways in which governments and markets systemically interact with each other, rather than on the extent to which one or the other produces or exchanges (or influences the production or exchange of) particular goods and services.

According, for example, to Amsden, Kochanowicz, and Taylor (1994), the primary reason for the failure of Eastern European countries to develop a market-based economy in the last five years is that they have chosen to adopt an Anglo-Saxon type of capitalism which, while suited to the needs of nineteenth-century England and the UK, has 'resulted in high social costs and low rates of return when applied to the project of restructuring Eastern Europe under the competitive conditions of technologically advanced twentieth century capitalism' (Amsden et al., 1994, p. 2). This, the authors suggest, is in marked contrast to the East Asian (including Chinese) model of economic development which has long recognized the need to adapt the structure of its market-based capitalism to the unique characteristics of its own institutions.

Sixth, the views of scholars about the efficacy of alternative organizational forms – and particularly of the role of government – strongly reflects the particular issues being addressed; and these have varied greatly over time and space. Take, for example, the economic justification of government intervention. In the mid-nineteenth century it was largely directed to protecting the emerging industries of the (then) newly industrializing nations against the abuses of the factory system from foreign competition. In the late nineteenth century, with the growing power and concentration of big business (especially) in the USA, attention shifted to anti-trust policy. In the inter-war years the rationale of government intervention was directed to reducing unemployment, while, in the 1940s, attention switched to the need for social reform. Growing environmental concerns in the 1970s further intensified the plea for government involvement, while in the 1980s and 1990s the role of government in fostering competitiveness by a range of market-facilitating and strategically related policies became the 'flavour of the month'!

THE SPATIAL DIMENSION OF THE ORGANIZATION OF ECONOMIC ACTIVITY

In the historical analysis, I have largely ignored the spatial dimension of economic activity. This was not deliberate, but rather a reflection of the fact that, for the most part, scholars – including some of the most recent contributors to the debate – have given little attention to the ways in which the geography of value-added activity and markets may affect the optimal governance of resource allocation. The one exception to this statement is the consideration given by economists to the consequences of trade in goods and services on the role of governments, but even here, until very recently, it had been assumed that such inter-country transactions are conducted between independent parties at arm's-length prices (Dunning, 1995).

How exactly – if at all – does the widening of the territorial boundaries of economic activity affect the way societies organize the disposition of their natural and created assets? If division of labour is limited by the extent of the market, does it matter if that market is a foreign, rather than a domestic, one? Is it of any consequence if resources and capabilities are mobile across national borders? Should one be interested in where firms undertake their R&D activities? If, as Douglass North and others have asserted, institutions critically affect the costs of structural adjustment, does it make any difference if these institutions are foreign-owned? And, what if the externalities of market transactions primarily affect individuals and organizations in foreign rather than in home countries?

It is questions such as these about which we will offer some general thoughts. We shall do so by considering the determinants of economic organization first in a *closed* economy, which we define as one completely isolated from the rest of the world; second, in a *partially open* economy, which is one in which there are cross-border transactions, but which primarily take the form of arm's-length trade in goods and services; and, third, in a *fully open* economy, which we shall identify as an economy which is structurally integrated with the rest of the world, and one in which there is a plurality of economic transactions, including FDI by MNEs and a range of collaborative ventures (UNCTAD, 1993; Dunning, 1994).

A Closed Economy

The main feature of a closed economy is the equivalence between political and economic space. This reflects the fact that the resources and capabilities originate or are created, and are deployed within the domain of particular nation states. Both product and factor markets are exclusively domestic, and there is no cross-border trade, investment, or migration. Economic agents – including national governments – are assumed to be completely unaffected by the behaviour of their counterparts in other nation states.

In such circumstances, the costs and benefits of alternative organizational arrangements and the optimal structure of such arrangements are entirely determined by the structure of domestic resources and capabilities, and by consumer tastes. More particularly, the rationale and consequences of government intervention are influenced by the configuration of the transaction and coordination costs of alternative modes of governance, and of how these may be affected by indigenous supply or demand-induced changes.

A Partially Open Economy

Assume, now, some transactions take place between economic agents located in different countries. What impact is this likely to have on the costs and benefits of alternative domestic organizational forms – and in particular the role of government? Since external transactions are presumed to be entirely governed by market forces, it is the degree to which markets are imperfect, or are perceived to lead to less than optimal domestic resource allocation, that will determine the extent to which extra-market activities are undertaken.

In such circumstances, governments might step in and, by a variety of policy instruments (e.g. tariffs, quotas, subsidies, etc.), affect the quality, composition, and terms of trade. Such intervention might be either market-facilitating or market-distorting. It may seek both to counteract anti-competitive behaviour by foreign buyers or sellers, and/or by international cartels, and to promote import-substituting policies in the belief these may protect or advance its domestic industries.

Much, of course, will depend on the kinds of coordinating and transaction costs which are specific to cross-border trade. Protectionism, for example, is a response to foreign competition, which has been historically justified by the inability of the country's domestic markets efficiently to adjust to structural change. By contrast, as firms seek to sell to, or buy from, less familiar territories, the costs of market search, uncertainties about future supply conditions, and imperfect knowledge about the tastes of foreign consumers are all likely to increase their transaction costs. Sometimes, other kinds of markets (e.g. insurance and futures markets) may help modify these risks; in others, particularly where political risk is involved, governments may choose to initiate or subsidize insurance or investment-guarantee schemes. In still other cases, the social benefits of cross-border information-gathering and dissemination may justify the role of public authorities as information brokers.[55] National administrations may also act to ensure that their environmental or cultural objectives are not impeded by the trade in certain goods or services, while exposure to foreign competition, particularly in sectors of burgeoning comparative advantage, may require a more focused attention by governments on reducing the costs of structural adjustment. Clearly, too, macro-economic policies may need to be modified or extended to embrace the issues relating to balance of payments and the external value of the currency, but consideration of these is outside the brief of this chapter.[56]

In short, the opening-up of an economy to international trade is likely to pose new problems for the organization of domestic resources. It may help reduce structural market imperfections and better enable an economy to promote its comparative advantage and benefit from scale economies. It may also lead to more endemic market failure by adding to the transaction and coordination costs of domestic economic activity.

A review of both the historical and contemporary literature on international trade reveals that relatively little attention has been given to the interaction between different forms of economic organization and international trade regimes. This is primarily because most trade theorists have adopted (and still adopt) a neoclassical perspective to evaluating the costs and benefits of trade, and regard institutional issues of secondary importance. Strategic trade theory (see e.g. Krugman, 1986, 1991) has introduced an industrial-organizational and behavioural perspective into trade theory, but its main emphasis has been on structural market distortions. Although the consequences of endemic market failure[57] and the role of institutions in affecting the optimum level and pattern of trade have been explored by such scholars as Lipsey and Dobson (1987) and the present author (Dunning, 1995), there is much work still be done.

A Fully Open Economy

It is, however, the macro-organizational consequences of being part of a fully open and structurally integrated economy that is the main focus of interest of this chapter. Because of space limitations, this chapter will confine its attention to FDI – and particularly integrated FDI – as the main vehicle by which economies are linked to each other.[58] According to the UN (UNCTAD, 1995), there are more than 38 500 corporations which engage in FDI; these now account for one-third of the non-agricultural world output; and about the same proportion of this amount is produced outside their home countries.

Much has been written about the features of the emerging global economy,[59] but we would emphasize four in particular. These are:

1. the increasing mobility of firm-specific resources and capabilities – especially knowledge-related assets – across national boundaries;
2. the growing significance of cross-border transactions which are either intra-firm, or between firms with ongoing cooperative agreements;
3. the dramatic reduction in long-distance transportation and communication costs and of the psychic and cultural barriers between countries;
4. the growing importance of location-bound assets, notably an educated labour force and a sophisticated physical infrastructure, in influencing the siting of the value-added activities by MNEs.

Closely associated with globalization – and sometimes fashioning its rationale and its shape – have been a series of far-reaching technological and organizational advances. Three particular characteristics of such advances may be identified.

1. Apart from the experiences of a few developing countries rich in natural resources, economic progress is being increasingly conditioned by the abilities of private institutions – sometimes in conjunction with public institutions – to innovate new assets, and to upgrade the efficiency at which these may be utilized with their existing resources and capabilities.
2. Not only do a rising proportion of created assets contain a strong 'public-goods' element, but the market for them is highly imperfect; in addition, they frequently have multiple uses – i.e. are not sector specific. Such assets include an educated labour force, technological capability, and a sophisticated legal and commercial infrastructure.
3. Since there is some suggestion that globalization is encouraging some convergence in the economic structure, at least among high- and medium-income countries (Williamson, 1995), it follows that the way in which a nation's physical and human assets are organized becomes a critically important determinant of a nation's economic performance. Moreover, in so far as governments, as overseers and participants in the resource creative and allocative process, play any role at all, their actions in affecting the competitiveness of firms located within their domain are likely to affect that performance.

To what extent is the globalization of economic activity likely to affect the ways in which national economies organize their resource creation and deployment? How far does it require a reappraisal of established institutional modes? What are the likely costs and benefits of markets, hierarchies, inter-firm alliances, and governments as organizing arrangements on a fully open economy? What are likely to be the consequences of globalization for inter-government relations?

In a previous volume (Dunning 1997b) we explored these propositions in some depth. The basic issue relates to the impact of the extension of economic space[60] on the costs and benefits of the interaction between economic agents – be they interactions in the production or exchange process. In so far as transformation, coordination, and transaction costs of alternative modes are affected, then so will be the appropriate structure of organizational arrangements and most likely, too, the configuration of the socio-institutional system.

In the historical section of this chapter, we used the concept of market failure to examine the costs and benefits of alternative modes of governance. We concluded that no one mode was intrinsically preferable to another as a vehicle for coordinating economic activity; and that the optimum combination of modes was likely to vary across both time and space.

It is possible to adopt a similar approach in examining the impact of the increasing porosity of national boundaries. Here our review of received literature can be brief as it has only been in the last 35 years that scholars have given serious consideration to the interaction between FDI and the domestic macro-organizational strategies of governments. One is, however, permitted some glimpses of the views of past scholars. The Mercantilists, for example, favoured government support for outbound investment[61] as long as it helped provide raw materials for, or increase employment in, the home country. Adam Smith was less enthusiastic about the benefits of capital exports, although he recognized that, when they promoted the agricultural development of the recipient countries, they could also be to the advantage of sending countries. Ricardo was generally opposed to foreign investment, fearing that it would be at the expense of its domestic counterpart.[62] J.S. Mill did not agree. Writing in 1848, he argued that capital exports could help arrest the declining profitability of domestic capital, and provide the home country with cheaper food and raw materials, as well as access to new markets.

In their writings, all the classical economists took it for granted that there was only limited mobility of capital across national boundaries – although Mill recognized that, as capital became more cosmopolitan, customers and institutions would converge and suspicion of foreigners would diminish. For the most part, they also assumed that the allocation of international economic activity was largely based on the distribution of *natural* resources – although both Smith and Ricardo acknowledged the possible role of innovation in promoting economic growth. Later in the nineteenth century, economists such as Bagehot and Marshall accepted the increasing significance of portfolio capital exports. However, they strongly believed that these were best organized through the brokerage of the international capital market.

At the same time, economists were beginning to explore the consequences of tariffs and other trade barriers, not only for the location, but also for the organization of value-added activity. In Germany, for example, there was a lively debate on the relative merits of FDI and international cartels[63] as cross-border organizational arrangements; while Marx was not slow to speculate on how his theory of the internalization of labour markets might be applied to the transnationalization of capital. By contrast, in the USA, the institutionalists confined their analysis to domestic issues, although the origins of hierarchical capitalism – as later recounted by Alfred Chandler (1962, 1977) – were no less relevant in explaining the initial territorial expansion by US firms.

During the inter-war years, Bertil Ohlin (1933) made a seminal contribution by extending location theory into the international arena; while J.H. Williams (1929, p. 203) not only recognized the growth of FDI as a modality of international commerce, but was prepared explicitly to state that enterprises undertaking such investment provided 'an organic interconnection of international trade, movement of productive factors, transport and market organization'. However, neither economists nor the location theorists of the time – for example, Weber (1929) and Hotelling (1929) – embraced the costs and benefits of alternative organizational modes in their analyses. Of the few scholars who did this, special mention may be made of Alfred Plummer (1934), whose work on international trusts paved the way for a discussion of cross-border market failure, which is now a cornerstone of the theory of the MNE.

In the light of the severe unemployment in the inter-war years, it is surprising that more attention was not given to the social costs and benefits of outbound or inbound FDI. Keynes, although generally sceptical of the advantages of portfolio capital exports (Keynes, 1924), had little to say about the territorial expansion of firms;[64] and, while the protectionist policies of governments in the 1930s most certainly took account of the likely consequences for capital inflows, academic scholars made few pronouncements on the subject.[65] There were also some murmurings – particularly in countries becoming heavily reliant on FDI (e.g. Canada and Australia) – about the impact of inbound MNE activity on economic sovereignty.

During the Second World War and for the first part of the post-1945 period, governments of most developed countries intervened in the workings of the free market both to limit outward direct investment and to encourage inward direct investment. Initially, this action was justified on balance-of-payments grounds, but subsequent theorizing by McDougall (1960) and Jasay (1960), and some empirical research on the profitability of home and foreign investment (Dunning, 1970), upheld the contention that the marginal social product of FDI was frequently less than that of its domestic equivalent – i.e. there were external costs to FDI. However, later research by Reddaway, Potter, and Taylor (1968) and Bergsten, Horst, and Moran (1978) questioned these findings. Not only did they argue that FDI might bring a whole range of benefits to the investing companies and home countries beyond any profits earned[66] (e.g. a feedback of technical knowledge, additional exports, and so on), but, in the absence of such investment, the overall competitive position of the investing firms might be disadvantaged. The Brookings study, in particular, asserted that, if foreign (and more particularly US) direct investment was not advancing the welfare of the home country as much as it should, this was probably due to market-distorting economic policies on the part of home or host governments, or to the anti-competitive behaviour of the investing firms. The authors were the first not only to examine the ways in which outbound FDI might require some modification to domestic macro-organizational policies, but also to suggest new instruments (e.g. investment guarantee schemes), which might reduce cross-border guarantee imperfections in product and factor markets.

In retrospect, the analysis of Bergsten, Horst, and Moran and its policy prescriptions were highly prophetic of much of the contemporary debate about the impact of globalization on domestic institutions and macro-organizational structures. In particular, their plea for a more systemic evaluation of the effects of MNE activity, and for a strengthening of international rules to head off conflicts among nations, was both original and highly pertinent. At the same time, the study lacked the analytical foundation for analysing the suitability of the respective organizational modes in coping with the effects of the internationalization of production. Moreover, at the time, few MNEs were operating an integrated strategy towards their foreign operations; in consequence two of the key benefits of cross-border hierarchies – namely, the specialization and common governance of interrelated activities and the spreading of environmental risk and volatility (Kogut, 1985) – were given only passing attention.

It was left to a following generation of scholars interested in explaining the increasingly rapid growth of FDI and MNE activity to provide the theoretical insights on these issues. Essentially, they did so by internationalizing the market-failure paradigm. The writings of scholars such as Stephen Hymer, J.C. McManus, Mark Casson, Peter Buckley, Alan Rugman, Jean-François Hennart and many others are not the subject of this chapter.[67] But, their methodology of approach – which has since been extended to explain the growth of cross-border non-equity alliances – is highly relevant to our understanding of how a fully open economy may affect the optimal organization of domestic activities. There are, for example, specific market failures associated with cross-border value-added activities; and almost all of these reflect the additional transaction and coordination costs and/or benefits of producing in different political, institutional, and cultural environments. Thus, on the one hand, the opening-up of national boundaries to FDI might reduce structural imperfections in domestic markets. Similarly, corporate and regional integration may lessen the need for national government regulation of domestic activities. On the other hand, the global competitiveness of enterprises is increasingly dependent on the efficient provision of complementary assets which governments are frequently best suited to supply – or, at least, to oversee.

I have already observed in the historical analysis that scholars have increasingly come to stress not only the importance of the transaction and coordination costs of economic activity, but also the need for flexible institutions and organizational modes. This is changing the role of government – making it sometimes more important, sometimes less important,[68] and sometimes changing its character completely. Frequently, too, the impact of change has been industry and/or issue specific. Thus, while, for example, US government intervention in agriculture has been long accepted,[69] it has been viewed with a great deal of suspicion in the service and manufacturing sectors, where most of the activities of the world's most globalized firms are concentrated (Kozul-Wright, 1995).

Similarly, it might be argued that the widening territorial boundaries of economic activity bring their own particular transaction or coordinating costs. These costs largely arise because of the very diverse institutions involved in transactions. More specifically, they reflect the additional complexities of human interaction arising from different educational backgrounds, languages, cultures, ideologies, and social objectives. Likewise, even within market-based economies, the institutional framework and the perceptions of the role of governments, hierarchies, and markets themselves differ – together with a reaction to failure of organizational failure.[70] Finally, the structures of the organizational modalities may vary. In consequence, so will the degree to which such modalities complement or compete with each other.[71]

In the past two decades, a substantial amount of literature has been concerned with the response of governments to the growing significance of the cross-border activities of firms, and the acknowledgement that the key assets to wealth creation – namely, technology, entrepreneurship, and organizational skills – are often highly mobile across national boundaries. But, while the quicksilver nature of these assets have widened the arena of market-based organizational modalities, including private hierarchies, the domain of national governments has remained mainly unchanged. It is this growing dichotomy between the boundaries of economic and political jurisdiction which is necessitating a re-appraisal of the institutional framework of national economic systems. Sometimes, this means a reorientation of the overseeing roles of governments; and sometimes, of their role as conflict managers and as stabilizers of last resort (Panic, 1995); and sometimes of their regulatory, participatory or advisory roles. But, sometimes, it also suggests that governments – like firms – should engage in cross-border alliances to exchange information and ideas and, where appropriate, to coordinate policies.

The advent of globalization is, then, not only demanding that governments reconsider their functions, *vis-à-vis* those of other organizational modes, but on how they interact with each other. Yet, because the interests of the constituents of government are primarily nationalistic, such interaction tends to be adversarial, rather than cooperative. Although some progress had been made towards the coordination of inter-governmental macro-economic policies, this is not the case with most macro-organization policies. And, this is primarily because – using Douglass North's language – the transaction costs of the necessary institutional changes are currently perceived to outweigh the perceived benefits; or, to put it more bluntly – governments prefer to compete rather than to cooperate with each other. As globalization proceeds, the trade-offs between the benefits of inter-government competition and cooperation, and indeed of the role and organization of supra-national economic regimes, may well be expected to change.[72]

A Final Footnote

In evaluating the views of social scientists about the macro-economic organizational framework of market-oriented economies, scholarly thought may well be entering a new phase. This is partly the outcome of a new generation of technological advances and the increasing structural integration of markets, hierarchies, and government policies across geographical space; and, partly because, since the mid-1970s, there has been a wave of new thinking among economists, organizational theorists, and business analysts on the role of institutions and organizational modes in strategic decision-taking. Although it is my personal opinion that a dynamic interpretation of the transactions–institutions paradigm probably offers the most fruitful avenue for further research, there can surely be little question that the topic of macro-economic organization is, itself, worthy of more study than it has so far had.

The challenges to interpret the implications of the institutional framework of the late twentieth century are at least as daunting as those facing past scholars in their search to understand the macro-organizational implications of the introduction of the factory-based system at the end of the eighteenth century, and the advent of hierarchical capitalism at the end of the nineteenth century. Yet, alongside the evolvement of market-based capitalism have been advances in the intellectual content of scholarly research. Perhaps the main contribution of the classical and neoclassical economists was to further our understanding about the nature of markets as an economic phenomena; while that of the institutionalists was (and is) to emphasize the significance of institutions as both economic and social phenomena. But, apart from the writings of socialists, there have been only fragmentary attempts systematically to explore the role of government in an industrial society; and even fewer rigorously to analyse the interaction between different economic agents. With the advent of an arsenal of new theoretical tools, and a growing appreciation of the need to adopt a holistic and interdisciplinary approach to the study of organizational arrangements and structures, these lacunae in scholarly thinking are gradually being closed.

ACKNOWLEDGEMENTS

I wish to express my appreciation to Alison McKaig-Berliner of Rutgers University, for her valuable research assistance in the preparation of this chapter. I am also indebted for the exchange of ideas I have had with another of my past Ph.D. students, Timo Hämäläinen.

NOTES

1. I use the term governments to embrace all forms of polity – be it at a local, regional, national, or supra-national level.
2. On behalf of the constituents which it represents.

3. Or, in Milton Friedman's words, 'to do something the market cannot do for itself ready to determine, arbitrate and monitor the rules of the game' (Friedman, 1962, p. 27).
4. According to Ekelund and Hebert (1975, p. 476), these unique functions include the making of laws that embrace contracts and property rights and the power to coin money. As an umpire, the state provides the functions associated with the police, courts, and monetary authorities.
5. By macro-organizational policies I mean policies of governments designed to affect the structure rather than the level of economic activity which is undertaken within their jurisdictional domain.
6. The concept of limited liability had yet to be introduced.
7. For example, classical economists believed that *laissez-faire* was not so much about allowing efficient markets to work as it was about not allowing powerful governments to take control (Steiner, 1953).
8. In the case of each of the nineteenth-century scholars named, rather than our citing their writings, the reader is invited to consult Sills (1968) for a brief biography and compilation of their major works.
9. It is pertinent to note there are traces of these thoughts in Smith's writings. Indeed, he argued for the granting of monopolies to infant industries and to those businesses attempting to establish international trade linkages (Smith, 1776, bk iv, ch. 11).
10. That is, the first and second quarters of the twentieth century.
11. Indeed, the real influence of Coase on micro-economic thought was not apparent until the 1970s.
12. Or, at least, did so until the early 1990s.
13. Also called 'relational', 'collective', and 'cooperative' capitalism (see Lazonick, 1992; Dunning, 1994).
14. However, in some cases, social and economic goals may be complementary to each other. Examples include some environmental protection schemes and expenditures on health care.
15. What I shall refer to later as a partially open economy.
16. But see e.g. Wade (1988), Wolf (1988), and Chang (1994).
17. Noticeably the concept of utilitarianism, which viewed laws as being man-made, and, as such, were to be evaluated by their degree of social utility (Robbins, 1953).
18. For a review of Sismondi's writings, see Gide and Rist (1915).
19. Although before that, David Hume, Adam Smith, Jeremy Bentham, and John Stuart Mill were well aware of the concept of externalities.
20. In the words of Ha Joon Chang (1994, p. 14), contractarianism is 'a position that no other person or authority can impose his/her or its own ethical judgement on the individual, since the individual knows best what his situation is and what his best option in that situation is'. Any interference with the making of individual decisions is seen as violating the innate right to freedom of the individual. According to this view, individuals (or firms) should be left free to make their own contracts and should not be coerced into any transaction however beneficial it may appear to an outsider.
21. For example with respect to state monopolies, bounties, embargoes, and high tariffs (Smith, 1776; Ferguson, 1938). Both J.S. Mill and Henry Sidgwick also advocated government action to curb monopolistic abuses.
22. See particularly Graham and Richardson (1996), Graham (1996), (1997).
23. According to Blaug and Sturgess (1983, p. 252), Marshall's decision to take up economics originated in a moral purpose, and one general conclusion of his early writings was that a redistribution of income from rich to poor would increase overall satisfaction. In his subsequent writings, the great neoclassicist fully recognized that state interference in free markets might be necessary in order to promote the maximum satisfaction of society (Ekelund and Hebert, 1975).
24. McKenzie and Lee (1991) give various examples. They include the postal service, several public utilities, and some highways.
25. More correctly, perhaps, one should say that the natural rate of unemployment has been increasing and that this is due to the inability of economies speedily to absorb or restructure those unemployed as a result of structural change.

26. According to Stein (1988, pp. 46–8), Keynes believed that what he was prescribing did not confer additional powers to the state, but rather 'new rules for exercising the traditional and inescapable powers of government'. The state simply had to get its monetary and fiscal policy right. Therefore, the structural reforms called for by Communism and Fascism as radical alternatives to the free-market mechanism at the time were not needed to cure its systemic ills.
27. For a review of contemporary theories of technical change, see Dosi et al. (1988) and Freeman and Soete (1990); for a review of the interaction between technical change and international trade, see Dosi et al. (1990); and for a review of some of the organizational implications of technical change, see Dosi et al. (1992).
28. Led by Wilhelm Roscher (1817–94).
29. Not because we consider it unimportant, but because it takes us far outside the domain of economics or even political economy.
30. In his own words (which can be compared with those of Marshall on p. 54): 'When society is made up of segments, whatever is produced in one of the segments has little chance of re-echoing in the others as the segmental organization is strong. The cellular system naturally lends itself to the localization of social events and their consequences. This is no longer true when society is made up of a system of organs. According to their mutual dependence, what strikes one strikes the others and thus every change even slightly significant takes a general intent' (Durkheim, 1964, p. 223).
31. Notably Friedrich von Mises (1851–1926), Eugen von Bohm-Bawerk (1851–1914) and Karl Menger (1840–1921). The Austrian economists attributed most market failures to government intervention and to the existence of government created impediments to the coordinating process of the market system. In their opinion, disturbances did not arise from some intrinsic attribute of the exchange process itself, but rather from factors exogenous to the process – and more especially from government intervention (Barry, 1991, p. 81). One exception to this view was that of Adolph Wagner (1835–1917), who, like Durkheim, saw an increasing role for the state in education, public health, transport and communications, and public utilities.
32. Better known for his analysis of conspicuous consumption.
33. This was possibly because his focus of interest was primarily directed to legal and social, rather than economic, issues.
34. In particular, Coase emphasized such transaction costs of using markets as 'discovering what the relevant prices are' and 'negotiating and concluding a separate contract for each exchange transaction'.
35. To quote directly from Olson (1979, p. 184): 'What is the necessary condition for a jurisdiction to deal optimally with an environmental problem? The necessary condition is that the domain of the environmental problem must match the boundaries of the political jurisdiction. There must be what I like to call "fiscal equivalence". The taxing or regulating area must match the benefit area. If the argument I have made here is correct, we should see in the world about us various developments that would suggest a tendency, however faint, in the direction of fiscal equivalence.'
36. The concept of 'entry' and 'voice' responses to economic problems was first introduced by Albert Hirschman (1970) to explain the reactions of nation states to threats to their sovereignty. Borrowing from Hirschman's terminology, we can identify two reactions to the presence of market or government failure. The first is to 'exit' when action is directed to finding some alternative organizational route (e.g. by internalizing market or eliminating government intervention). The second is a 'voice' strategy where efforts are made to improve the efficiency of the existing organizational arrangements (e.g. by reducing information asymmetries and opportunism between buyers and sellers, or by streamlining the governance of government).
37. Although we do not imply that the role of Japanese government was (or is) always market supporting!
38. As demonstrated, e.g., by Wallis and North (1986). Becker and Murphy (1992) argue that the degree of division of labour in a modern economy is ultimately limited by the costs of coordinating specialized workers who perform complementary, but increasingly complex, tasks.
39. Although it should be emphasized that, as long as there is effective competition between hierarchies, this organizational form is entirely consistent with free-market principles.

40. North (1993, p. 3) defines institutions as 'humanly devised constraints imposed on human interaction. They consist of formal values, informal constraints (norms of behavior, conventions and self-imposed conduct) and the enforcement characteristics of both. In short, they are the structure that humans impose on their dealings with each other.'
41. North (ibid.) quotes from a study by Christiansen and Haverman (1981) which suggests that US federal regulations may have been responsible. However, he also argues that the indirect impact of regulations in terms of increasing uncertainty and foregone production might be even greater – particularly in the Third World.
42. Earlier Alexander Hamilton had made much the same plea for protectionism against European imports into the USA.
43. For a contemporary view of the interventionist policies pursued by the US government, particularly in the first half of the nineteenth century, see Kuttner (1991) and Kozul-Wright (1995).
44. *Inter alia*, this reflected the growing fixed costs of production, the longer time for returns on these outlays to be generated, the rising externalities of markets, and the growing transaction and coordination costs of economic activity.
45. In the first part of the 1900s, serious attention began to be given to the inabilities of the capitalist system. These were two main streams of thought. The first was essentially concerned with cyclical fluctuations in economic activity and the possible imbalances of aggregate supply and demand. The second was concern with the long-run effects on technological change on economic and social structure.
46. Hence the expression 'creative' destruction. It will also be observed that Schumpeter's reaction to technological process was more 'voice'-oriented than that of Marx.
47. Notably, Christopher Freeman, Keith Pavitt, and Luc Soete.
48. See, too, some pertinent contributions by Chesnais (1982, 1988), and various authors in Dosi et al. (1988) and OECD (1992).
49. See especially the work of Thomas Malthus (1776–1836). However, both Smith and Ricardo were interested in explaining its determinants of economic progress.
50. For some alternative views of economists and organizational scholars on the reasons for this and why relationships between the public and private sectors have been more adversarial in the USA and the UK than in continental Europe and Japan, see Chandler (1990), Steiner (1953), Galbraith (1994), and Shultz (1979).
51. See e.g. Chapters 8 and 13 of Dunning (1997).
52. See e.g., Bartlett and Ghoshal (1989) and Hedlund (1993).
53. It also varies according to the rationale for and form of government intervention. Compare, for example, the effects of anti-trust legislation, environmental legislation, corporation taxation, and R&D subsidies as an import protection on domestic firms and markets (McConnell, 1980).
54. As has already been suggested, in different countries and at different time periods, the costs and benefits of the different organizational arrangements will change.
55. The Japanese government, for example, puts a major effort into understanding the competition, institutions, technologies, and consumer preferences in foreign markets. It has established a worldwide market-intelligence system that produces and disseminates vast amounts of information for private and public policy-makers.
56. But see some remarks by Susan Strange in Dunning (1997), pp. 132–46.
57. Particularly, those to do with externalities, structural adjustment, counteracting trade-distorting practices of other countries, information asymmetries, uncertainties, and learning by doing.
58. Data reveal that the value of foreign sales of MNEs in 1992 exceeded that of non-agricultural exports; and, over the past 15 years, FDI has increased at twice the rate of exports (UNCTAD, 1995).
59. See, e.g., Chapter 5 by Stephen Kobrin and Chapter 16 by John Stopford in Dunning (1997), the literature surveyed in Dunning (1994), and Nunnenkamp et al. (1994).
60. Political space may effectively be enlarged or reduced by the splitting-up or merging of countries.
61. Particularly when undertaken by the chartered trading companies.
62. At the same time, Ricardo was reluctant to recommend government action, as he believed that there were natural institutional checks on capital exports. In particular, he maintained

that capital owners (in the first part of the nineteenth century) would be 'loath to take the risk of allowing the capital to go out of their immediate control'; or, if they accompanied their capital, to forsake their homeland and submit themselves to strange regimes and unfamiliar laws, even with the prospects of more favourable returns (Ricardo, 1911, p. 83). The antecedents of the contemporary theory of FDI and international production are traced in Dunning et al. (1986).

63. See e.g. the writings of Levy (1911) and Hilferding (1910).
64. Although, in various of his writings, he acknowledged that the free movement of capital and goods could undermine the power of national fiscal policy and, more generally, erode national sovereignty.
65. An exception was the Canadian economist Jacob Viner.
66. *Inter alia*, this was because, while the taxation on profits earned by the foreign subsidiaries would accrue to the host country, that of domestic investment would accrue to the home country.
67. These are described in some detail in Dunning (1993) and Caves (1996).
68. All too frequently, importance is measured by the percentage of government expenditure to GNP. But, this is an extremely poor measure of the effectiveness of government as an organizational instrument. The Japanese experience demonstrates that effective government intervention does not have to be expensive. Even excluding defence expenditure, Japan has one of the lowest ratios of government expenditure to GDP, yet the Japanese government has probably had a more critical influence on market forces than any of its foreign counterparts.
69. That is, in the form of price-support schemes, subsidies to farming, R&D, and guaranteed returns on investment.
70. In Japan, for example, the 'voice' strategy of dealing with both market and political failure is more widely practised than the 'exit' strategy.
71. Cf., e.g., the adversarial business–government mentality in the USA and the UK over the last century with that of the more conciliatory and high-trust business–government relationships in Germany and Japan.
72. For a recent examination of the impact of international integration on the role of national governments, see Panic (1995). In his contribution, Panic identifies four possible responses of national governments to the emergence of globalization of the world economy, namely (i) try to reverse the process of globalization by insulating their economies from those of the rest of the world, (ii) cooperate in a way that the consequences of their policies are similar to those which might have been achieved by a supra-national authority, (iii) engage in political integration with nation states transpiring some of their authority to a regional or supra-national regime, and (iv) let the market mechanism reconcile any conflicts which might arise among national governments or between themselves and supra-national regimes. Panic thinks that an amalgam of these responses is the most likely scenario to emerge in the next decade or so; and, as a result, the framing and implementation of distinctive national economic policies will become more, rather than less, difficult (Panic, 1995, esp. pp. 67–74).

REFERENCES

Amsden, A., Kochanowicz, J., and Taylor, L. (1994), *The Market Meets its Match: Restructuring the Economies of Eastern Europe* (Cambridge, Mass.: Harvard University Press).

Aronson, J.R., and Ott, A.F. (1991), 'The Growth of the Public Sector', in D. Greenaway, M. Bleaney, and I.M.T. Stewart (eds.), *Companion to Contemporary Economic Thought* (London: Routledge), 523–46.

Barry, N.P. (1991), 'Austrian Economics: A Dissent from Orthodoxy', in D. Greenaway, M. Bleaney, and I.M.T. Stewart (eds.), *Companion to Contemporary Economic Thought* (London: Routledge), 68–87.

Bartlett, C.G., and Ghoshal, S. (1989), *Managing across Borders: The Transnational Solution* (Boston: Harvard Business School Press).

Becker, G.S., and Murphy, K.M. (1992), 'The Division of Labour: Coordinating Costs and Knowledge', *Quarterly Journal of Economics*, **107**/4: 1138–59.

Bergsten, C.F., Horst, T., and Moran, T. (1978), *American Multinationals and American Interests* (Washington: Brookings Institution).

Beveridge, W.H. (1944), *Full Employment in a Free Society* (London: Allen & Unwin).

Blaug, M., and Sturgess, P. (1983) (eds.), *Who's Who in Economics: A Biographical Dictionary of Major Economists 1700–1981* (Cambridge, Mass.: MIT Press).

Caves, R. (1996), *Multinational Firms and Economic Analysis* (rev. edn.; Cambridge: Cambridge University Press).

Chandler, A.D., Jr. (1962), *Strategy and Structure: The History of American Industrial Enterprise* (Cambridge, Mass.: MIT Press).

Chandler, A.D., Jr. (1977), *The Invisible Hand: The Managerial Revolution in American Business* (Cambridge, Mass.: Harvard University Press).

Chandler, A.D., Jr. (1990), *Scale and Scope: The Dynamics of Industrial Capitalism* (Cambridge, Mass.: Harvard University Press).

Chang, H.J. (1994), *The Political Economy of Industrial Policy* (New York: St Martin's Press).

Chesnais, F. (1982), 'Schumpeterian Recovery and the Schumpeterian Perspective – Some Unsettled Issues and an Alternative Interpretation', in H. Giersch (ed.), *Emerging Technologies: Consequences for Economic Growth, Structural Change and Employment* (Tübingen: J.C.B. Mohr).

Chesnais, F. (1988), 'Multinational Enterprises and the International Diffusion of Technology', in G. Dosi, C. Freeman, R. Nelson, G. Silverberg, and L. Soete (eds.), *Technical Change and Economic Theory* (London: Pinter Publishers).

Christiansen, G., and Haverman, R.H. (1981), 'Public Regulations and the Slowdown in Productivity Growth', *American Economic Review*, **80** (May), 355–61.

Clark, J.M. (1923), *Studies in the Economics of Overhead Costs* (Chicago: University of Chicago Press).

Coase, R.H. (1937), 'The Nature of the Firm', *Economica*, NS 4 (November), 386–405.

Coase, R.H. (1960), 'The Problem of Social Cost', *Journal of Law and Economics*, **3**: 1–10.

Commons, J.R. (1924), *The Legal Foundations of Capitalism* (Madison: University of Wisconsin Press; repr. 1957).

Commons, J.R. (1934), *Institutional Economics* (Madison: University of Wisconsin Press; repr. 1959).

Dosi, G., Freeman, C., Nelson, R., Silverberg, G., and Soete, L. (1988) (eds.), *Technical Change and Economic Theory* (London: Pinter Publishers).

Dosi, G., Pavitt, K., and Soete, L. (1990), *Technical Change and International Trade* (New York: Harvester Wheatsheaf).

Dosi, G., Giannetti, R., and Toninelli, P.A. (1992) (eds.), *Technology and Enterprise in a Historical Perspective* (Oxford: Oxford University Press), 119–63.

Dunning, J.H. (1970), *Studies in International Investment* (London: Allen & Unwin).

Dunning, J.H. (1993), *Multinational Enterprises and the Global Economy* (Wokingham: Addison-Wesley).

Dunning, J.H. (1994), *Globalization, Economic Restructuring and Development* (The 6th Prebisch Lecture; Geneva: UNCTAD).

Dunning, J.H. (1995), 'What's Wrong – and Right – with Trade Theory?', *International Trade Journal*, **9/2**: 153–202.

Dunning, J.H. (ed) (1997), *Governments, Globalization and International Business* (Oxford: Oxford University Press).

Dunning, J.H., Cantwell, J., and Corley, T.A.B. (1986), 'The Theory of the Multinational Enterprise: Some Historical Antecedents', in P. Hertner and G. Jones (eds.), *Multinationals: Theory and History* (Farnborough: Gower Press), 19–41.

Durkheim, E. (1964), *The Division of Labor in Society* (New York: The Free Press) (originally published in German in 1893).

Ekelund, R.B., Jr., and Hebert, R.F. (1975), *A History of Economic Theory and Method* (New York: McGraw-Hill Book Company).

Ferguson, J.M. (1938), *Landmarks of Economic Thought* (New York: American Business Fundamentals).

Freeman, C., and Perez, C. (1988), 'Structural Crises of Adjustment: Business Cycles, and Investment Behavior', in G. Dosi, C. Freeman, R. Nelson, G. Silverberg, and L. Soete (eds.), *Technical Change and Economic Theory* (London: Pinter Publishers).

Freeman, C., and Soete, L. (1990) (eds.), *New Explorations in the Economics of Technical Change* (London: Pinter Publishers).

Friedman, M. (1962), *Capitalism and Freedom* (Chicago: University of Chicago Press).

Galbraith, J.K. (1994), *A Journey Through Economic Time: A Firsthand View* (Boston: Houghton Mifflin Co.).

Gide, C., and Rist, C. (1915), *A History of Economic Doctrines* (London: George G. Harrap).

Graham, E.M. (1996), *Global Corporations and National Governments* (Washington: Institute for International Economics).

Graham, E.M. (1997), 'Should there be multilateral values as on foriegn direct investment?' in Dunning, J.H. (ed.) *Governments, Globalization and International Business* (Oxford: Oxford University Press), pp. 481–506.

Graham, E.M., and Richardson, J. D. (1996), *Global Competition Policy* (Washington: Institute for International Economics).

Grestchmann, K. (1991), 'Analysing the Public Sector: The Received View in Economics and its Shortcomings', in F.-X. Kaufman (ed.), *The Public Sector: Challenge for Coordination and Learning* (Berlin: Walter de Gruyter).

Hämäläinen, T.J. (1994), 'The Evolving Role of Government in Economic Organization' (mimeo; Newark: Rutgers University).

Hedlund, G. (1993) (ed.), *TNCs and Organizational Issues: UN Library on Transnational Corporations* (London: Routledge).

Heilbroner, R.L. (1965), *The Worldly Philosophers: The Lives, Times and Ideas of the Great Economic Thinkers* (New York: Simon & Schuster).

Hilferding, R. (1910), *Finance Capital: A Study of Latest Phase of Capitalist Development* (Eng. trans.; London: 1981).

Hotelling, H. (1929), 'Stability in Competition', *Economic Journal*, **29**: 41–57.

Jasay, A.E. (1960), 'The Social Choice between Home and Foreign Investment', *Economic Record*, **38**: 105–13.

Keynes, J.M. (1924), 'Foreign Investment and the National Advantage', *The Nation and The Athenaeum*, **35** (August), 584–7.

Keynes, J.M. (1936), *The General Theory of Employment Interest and Money* (London: Macmillan).

Kogut, B. (1985), 'Designing Global Strategies: Profiting from Operational Flexibility', *Sloan Management Review*, **26** (Fall), 27–38.

Kondratiev, N. (1926), 'The Long Waves in Economic Life', *Review of Economics and Statistics*, **17**.

Kozul-Wright, R. (1995), 'The Myth of Anglo-Saxon Capitalism: Reconstructing the History of the American State', in H.-J. Chang and R. Rowthorn (eds.), *The Role of the State in Economic Change* (Oxford: Oxford University Press), 81–113.

Krueger, A.O. (1990), 'Economists' Changing Perceptions of Government', *Weltwirtschaftliches Archiv*, **126**: 417–31.

Krugman, P. (1986) (ed.), *Strategic Trade Policy and the New International Economies* (Cambridge, Mass.: MIT Press).

Krugman, P. (1991), *Rethinking International Trade* (Cambridge, Mass.: MIT Press).

Kuttner, R. (1991), *The End of Laissez Faire* (New York: Alfred A. Knopf).

Lazonick, W. (1992), 'Business Organizational and Competitive Advantage: Capitalist Transformations in the Twentieth Century', in G. Dosi, R. Gianetti, and P. A. Toninelli (eds.), *Technology and Enterprise in Historical Perspective* (Oxford: Oxford University Press).

Levy, H. (1911), *Monopoly and Competition: A Study in English Industrial Organization* (Eng. trans.) (London: Macmillan).

Lipsey, R.G., and Dobson, W. (1987), *Shaping Comparative Advantage* (Ontario: Prentice Hall for C.D. Howe Institute).

McConnell, J.W. (1980), *Ideas of the Great Economists* (2nd edn., New York: Barnes & Noble Books).

McCullogh, J. (1848), *Treatise on the Succession to Property Vacant by Death* (London: Rongmar, Brown, Green & Longmans).

McDougall, G.D.A. (1960), 'The Benefits and Costs of Private Investment from Abroad', *Economic Record*, **36**: 13–35.

McKenzie, R.B., and Lee, D.R. (1991), *Quicksilver Capital* (New York: The Free Press).

Markusen, A., (1994), *Sticky Places in Slippery Space: The Political Economy of Post-War Fast Growth Regions* (Rutgers University Working Paper No. 79; New Brunswick Center for Urban Policy Research).

Marshall, A. (1920), *Principles of Economics* (8th edn., London: Macmillan).

Mill, J.S. (1848), *Principles of Political Economy* (London: J.W. Parker); ed. with introduction by Jonathan Riley (Oxford: Oxford University Press, 1994).

Nelson, R.R., and Winter, S.G. (1982), *An Evolutionary Theory of Economic Change* (Cambridge, Mass.: Belknap Press of Harvard University Press).

North, D. (1981), *Structure and Change in Economic History* (New York: Norton).

North, D. (1990), *Institutions, International Change and Economic Performance* (Cambridge: Cambridge University Press).

North, D. (1993), 'Institutions, Transaction Costs and Productivity in the Long Run' (paper presented to Eighth World Productivity Congress, Stockholm, May).

Nunnenkamp, P., Gundlach, E., and Agarwal, J. (1994), *Globalization of Production and Markets* (Tübingen: J.C.B. Mohr).

OECD (1992), Organization for Economic Cooperation and Development, *Technology and the Economy* (Paris: OECD).

Ohlin, B. (1933), *Inter-Regional and International Trade* (Cambridge, Mass.: Harvard University Press; rev. edn., 1967).

Olson, M. (1965), *The Logic of Collective Action: Public Goods and the Theory of Groups* (Cambridge, Mass.: Harvard University Press).

Olson, M. (1969), 'Fiscal equivalence', *American Economic Review* (May), 479–87.

Olson, M. (1979), 'On Regional Pollution and Fiscal Equivalence', in H. Siebert, I. Walter, and K. Zimmermann (eds.), *Regional Environmental Policy: The Economic Issues* (New York: New York University Press), 181–6.

Olson, M. (1982), *The Rise and Decline of Nations: Economic Growth, Stagflation, and Social Rigidities* (New Haven: Yale University Press).

Panic, M. (1995), 'International Economic Integration and the Changing Role of National Governments', in H.-J. Chang and R. Rowthorn (eds.), *The Role of the State in Economic Change* (Oxford: Oxford University Press).

Perez, C. (1983), 'Structural Change and Assimilation of New Technologies in the Economic and Social Systems', *Futures*, **15** (October), 357–75.

Pigou, A.C. (1932), *The Economics of Welfare* (4th edn., London: Macmillan).

Plummer, A. (1934), *International Combines in Modern History* (London: Pitman).

Reddaway, W.B., Potter, S.T., and Taylor, C.T. (1968), *The Effects of UK Direct Investment Overseas* (Cambridge: Cambridge University Press).

Ricardo, D. (1911), *The Principles of Political Economy and Taxation* (first pub. 1817; republished with introduction by Donald Winch, London: J.M. Dent, 1992).

Robbins, L. (1953), *The Theory of Economic Policy* (London: Macmillan).

Rostow, W.W. (1990), *Theories of Economic Growth from David Hume to the Present: With a Perspective on the Next Century* (New York: Oxford University Press).

Schumpeter, J.A. (1934), *The Theory of Economics Development* (New York: Harper & Row).

Schumpeter, J.A. (1942), *Capitalism, Socialism and Democracy* (New York: Harper & Row).

Shultz, G.P. (1979), 'The Abrasive Interface', *Harvard Business Review* (November–December), 93–7.

Sills, D.L. (1968) (ed.), *International Encyclopaedia of the Social Sciences*, 18 vols. (London: Macmillan).

Simon, H.A. (1947), *Administrative Behavior* (New York: Macmillan).

Simon, H.A. (1959), 'Theories of Decision Taking in Economics and Behavioral Science', *American Economic Review*, **49**: 255–83.

Smith, A. (1776), *The Wealth of Nations* (repr. 1910, London: Everyman's Library).

Stein, H. (1988), *Presidential Economics: The Making of Economic Policy from Roosevelt to Reagan and Beyond* (2nd edn., Washington: American Enterprise Institute for Public Policy Research).

Steiner, G.A. (1953), *Government's Role in Economic Life* (New York: McGraw-Hill Book Co. Inc.).

Stiglitz, J. (1989), *The Economic Role of the State* (Oxford: Basil Blackwell).

UNCTAD (1993), United Nations Conference on Trade and Development, *World Investment Report: Transnational Corporations and Integrated International Production* (New York: United Nations).

UNCTAD (1994), *World Investment Report 1994: Transnational Corporations, Employment and the Workplace* (New York: United Nations).

UNCTAD (1995), *World Investment Report: Transnational Corporations and Competitiveness* (New York: United Nations).

Wade, R. (1988), 'The Role of Government in Overcoming Market Failure in Taiwan, Republic of Korea and Japan', in H. Hughes (ed.), *Achieving Industrialization in East Asia* (Cambridge: Cambridge University Press).

Wallis, J.J., and North, D.C. (1986), 'Measuring the Transaction Sector in the American Economy, 1870–1970', in S.L. Engerman and R.E. Gallman (eds.), *Long-Term Factors in American Economic Growth* (Chicago: University of Chicago Press).

Weber, A. (1929), *Über den Standort der Industrien*, trans. as *The Theory of Location of Industries* (Chicago: University of Chicago Press).

Williams, J.H. (1929), 'The Theory of International Trade Reconsidered', *Economic Journal*, **39**: 195–209.
Williamson, J.G. (1995), Globalization, Convergence and History (NBER Working Paper No. 5259; Cambridge, Mass.: NBER).
Williamson, O.E. (1975), *Markets and Hierarchies, Analysis and Antitrust Implications* (New York: The Free Press).
Williamson, O.E. (1985), *The Economic Institutions of Capitalism* (New York: The Free Press).
Wolf, C.J. (1988), *Markets or Governments* (Cambridge, Mass.: MIT Press).
World Bank (1991), *World Development Report* (Oxford: Oxford University Press).

15. Globalization: the challenge for national economic regimes*

INTRODUCTION

The role of government, as an organizing force in a global market economy, is coming under increasing scrutiny. Yet, in spite of a widespread eagerness to contain or reduce the extent of governmental intervention in the management of domestic resource allocation, it remains a fact that the countries which have recorded the most impressive economic performances over the past three decades are those whose governments have exerted a strong and positive influence over all aspects of commercial affairs.[1]

This chapter addresses just one, but an increasingly important, aspect of this enigma, viz. the implications of the globalization of business activity for the economic sovereignty of individual nation states. In particular, it considers the implications of the globalization of business activity for the organization and management of location bound human and physical assets. Its main thesis is that the pace and direction of technological, political and institutional change, especially as it has affected the extent and character of international transactions, is demanding a systemic recasting of the traditional role of national governments as custodians of the economic welfare of the citizens within their jurisdiction.

Central to this thesis is the premise that, as a result of the dramatic growth in the cross-border linkages forged by multinational enterprises (MNEs), the latitude for autonomous and purely domestic oriented actions on the part of the governments of nation states – that is to say actions which only affect the constituents of those states and not those of others – is being severely curtailed. Increasingly, too, national authorities – particularly those of the advanced industrial countries – are competing with each other for a share of the world's supply of technological and organizational capacity, and for the global economic rents of international production. Given this scenario, both the economic sov-

* Revised version of a booklet of the same title published in Dublin by the Economic and Social Research Institute. Also published as Chapter 11 in J.H. Dunning, *Globalization at Bay*, London and New York: Routledge (2001), pp. 331–56.

ereignty of governments and the efficacy of their policy instruments for affecting domestic wealth-creating activities are being called into question.[2]

This chapter will be divided into three parts. The first part will briefly outline the main features of the global economy now emerging, and the reasons why globalization is likely to continue for the foreseeable future. The second part discusses the implications of globalization – and, in particular, the cross-border activities of MNEs – for governments, and for the organization of economic activity for which they are responsible. The third part of the chapter is more normative in that it speculates a little about what some of the responses of national governments should be to globalization. Although, clearly, these responses will vary between countries according, for example, to their size, industrial structures, institutional regimes, cultures and stages of development, we believe there are some general implications for the behavior of all governments; and it is to these, rather than the more country specific consequences of globalization, which this chapter addresses.

THE MAIN FEATURES OF ECONOMIC GLOBALIZATION

As Chapter 2 of this volume has shown, while scholars and business practitioners continue to debate the meaning of the terms 'global business' and the 'global economy', there is less disagreement about globalization as a process towards the widening of the extent and form of cross-border transactions; and of the deepening of the economic interdependence between the actions of globalizing entities – be they private or public institutions or governments – located in one country and those of related or independent entities located in other countries.

The shallowest form of globalization – if that is not a misnomer for the term – is where an economic entity in one country engages in arm's-length trade in a single product with another economic entity in one other country. The deepest form of globalization – and it is here we can most easily distinguish globalization from other forms of internationalization – is where an economic entity transacts with a large number of other economic entities throughout the world; where it does so across a network of value-added chains;[3] where these exchanges are highly co-ordinated to serve the worldwide interests of the globalizing entity; and where they consist of a myriad of different kinds or forms of transactions.

In practice, few firms – or for that matter countries – engage in either the shallowest or the deepest forms of globalization. However, it is possible to identify a number of firms or countries which are towards the bottom or top of the globalization spectrum. More to the point of our present thesis, however, is the almost universal trend towards the deeper internationalization of economic activity. The structure of the world economy is, indeed, very different today than it was even a generation ago.[4] In particular, three features may be emphasized. First, the significance (and scope) of all kinds of cross-border transactions has greatly increased. For example, as a proportion of world gross national product (GNP), such transactions have more than doubled since 1970.[5] Second, the value of the foreign production of firms, i.e. production financed by foreign direct investment (FDI), and that arising from cross-border strategic alliances – both of which are deeper forms of internationalization than that of arm's-length trade – now considerably exceeds that of trade.[6] And third, there is a variety of signs that the organization of international transactions, particularly among the largest MNEs, has become both more systemic and geographically integrated (UNCTAD, 1993, 1999).

It is, of course, true that the pace and pattern of globalization has been very uneven among firms, sectors and countries. Indeed, since many of the features of globalization just described are principally applicable to members of the triad nations, some scholars (Morrison, Ricks and Roth, 1991; UNCTAD 1991, 1999; Rugman, 2002) have argued that the term regionalization better describes the current stage of development. This may well be the case; certainly, intra-regional transactions of all kinds in Europe, America and Asia have risen faster than inter-regional transactions. It is also true that certain parts of the world, notably sub-Saharan Africa, have been relatively unaffected by globalization.

Finally, since globalization has been largely driven by events in the industrialized nations, it is understandable that – up to now, at any rate – its greatest impact should have been felt in these countries. But, like ripples in a pond, regionalization tends to spread, initially to the immediate hinterland of the developed countries, but then further as this hinterland generates its own momentum of growth. Neither should one overlook the surge of autonomous development within certain parts of the developing world – particularly in East Asia and parts of Latin America. Indeed, international transactions involving developing countries have risen faster in the last decade than those internal to the triad countries (UNCTAD, 1999). The critical issue – to which we shall return later in this chapter – is whether regionalization will develop into a form of regionalism (a kind of extended nationalism, with all that this implies) or is a step – a phase – in the globalization process.

EXPLAINING GLOBALIZATION

As Richard Lipsey (1997) and others have demonstrated, the movement towards globalization is essentially technology driven.[7] Admittedly, the tremendous growth in all forms of international transactions over the last two or more decades could not have taken place without the introduction of new organizational structures within and between firms; or the widespread restitution of the market system by many national economies;[8] or, indeed, without the removal of many obstacles to intra-regional or international trade. But, these events, together with the dramatic reduction in the time and cost of traversing space, have, themselves, been accelerated by techno-electronic innovations, notably the advent of the Internet, and their impact on the competitive pressures on corporations to seek out new markets and conclude cross-border coalitions with other firms.

However, perhaps the most critical distinction between the globalizing economy of the turn of the millennium and the international economy of the last century rests in the nature of income generating assets. In 1900, the international division of labor was primarily based on the spatial distribution of natural resources, such as the fruits of the earth and untrained or semi-trained human capital. Today, the capabilities of a country to produce wealth rests increasingly on the extent to which it can create new resources or assets – such as information, technological capacity, management techniques and organizational competence. Particularly, in the triad nations, where there is slow population growth, it is the upgrading of the quality of human and physical assets and the more efficient use of existing assets – both natural and created – which is the critical determinant of economic progress.

Consider, for a moment, some of the implications of the growing importance of created, relative to natural, assets in the wealth producing process. First, by definition, created assets have to be produced. Unlike natural resources, they are not God-given; they are man-made and, in the case of many created assets (e.g. a university, an airport and the knowledge embodied in a new drug), they are very costly – both in terms of human and physical capital – to produce.

Second, because of their intangibility, many created assets are locationally mobile – although the degree of their mobility may rest on the quality and cost of other, or complementary, assets, e.g. transport and communication facilities. Most kinds of knowledge, information, professional skills, entrepreneurial talents and organizational principles acknowledge few national borders, even though there may be considerable costs incurred in transferring or diffusing these assets between different cultures (Kogut and Parkinson, 1993). The 'quicksilver' character of both financial and real assets is in marked contrast to the spatial fixity of many natural assets – a fact which helped shape the Ricardian and neo-classical theories of trade.

Third, created assets tend to be firm specific, i.e. proprietary to the firms producing them. In consequence, the market for created assets is likely to be much more imperfect than that for natural assets. Often created assets are the result of successful innovations; but, for every successful innovation, there are many more which are unsuccessful. To encourage firms to bear the risks and uncertainties inherent in innovatory activities, and to prevent the free-riding by competitors of successful innovations which cost little to reproduce, society – or, more specifically, government on behalf of society – has introduced various devices, e.g. the patent system, either to counteract such market failures or to reduce their net social costs.

Fourth, the markets for created assets tend to become more imperfect as and when they cross national boundaries. This is because the territorial expansion of firms into different political, institutional and cultural regimes is likely to raise the transaction costs of using such markets. Examples include the monitoring of quality control, the protection of proprietary rights, and the reduction of information asymmetries. Indeed, the desire to lower cross-border transaction costs and to exploit the cross-border economies of internal governance is one of the main reasons for the recent rapid growth of MNE activity which has, itself, helped sustain, or advance, globalization.

Fifth, the conditions under which created assets are produced and marketed are often strongly influenced by national governments – and much more so than in the case of natural assets. Sometimes, this is because governments – be they federal or state, central or local – are the main providers of the assets; primary and secondary educational services, roads and airports are examples. Sometimes it reflects the quality of the legal and commercial infrastructure they help provide; sometimes it is a direct result of the economic strategies and policies they pursue; and sometimes it is because of the general business climate and entrepreneurial ethos they foster. Several writers, notably Wallis and North (1986) and North (1993), have shown that, over the last century, government influenced production and transaction costs and benefits have become a more important component of the total costs of economic activity; and particularly so in those of knowledge intensive manufacturing and service sectors, which are the fastest growth points in the contemporary world economy.

The net result of all these characteristics of created assets – which, to repeat, though primarily a consequence of technological change, are also affected by the way in which economic agents respond to them – is that the determinants of the international division of labor and of the optimum distribution of a nation's resources and assets are more affected by the behavior of hierarchies – and especially multinational hierarchies – and that of national governments, than that of unregulated market forces.

The globalizing economy, then, is, first and foremost, an expression of a new international division of labor. This new division of labor is based increasingly on the way in which countries and firms are able to engineer the production of new income generating assets, and to combine these with location bound natural resources – the quantity and quality of which, itself, is influenced by the policies and strategies of governments.[9] It also comprises a network of imperfect intermediate product markets which is frequently under the common governance of multi-activity enterprises. The key wealth-creating actor in this scenario is the MNE, which is also the main determining institution of the spatial distribution of created assets. By internalizing the market for the intermediate products it wishes to acquire or use, and co-ordinating its markets throughout the world, it brings about a different pattern of resource allocation than by that which would have been dictated by purely external transactions.

MULTINATIONALS AND NATIONAL GOVERNMENTS

The relationship between international companies and national governments has always been an uneasy, if not a schizophrenic, one. This is primarily because, while MNEs normally aim to maximize the economic rent on their global activities, governments are more concerned with maximizing the value-added created by MNEs, and particularly that part which is retained within their national boundaries. Moreover, because of their wider locational options, MNEs are frequently perceived to possess more bargaining power than national governments. Frequently, in the past, MNEs have been targeted for criticism by host countries for attempting to extract an unacceptably large share of the value added they – the MNEs – have helped create; or for not engaging in the kind of economic activity which is perceived to be in the best long-term interests of the country. Similarly, home countries have been anxious lest MNEs should export jobs, worsen the balance of payments or, by transferring technology to foreign competitors, inhibit the upgrading of their own resources and capabilities.

At the same time, both host and home governments well recognize the benefits which MNE activity may confer. To host countries, MNEs bring new technologies, management skills, access to markets and organizational capabilities. They may inject new entrepreneurial cultures, competitive stimuli and working procedures. By their procurement practices and marketing and distribution techniques, they may help elevate the capabilities of their suppliers and raise the productivity of their industrial customers. To home countries, MNEs may not only earn valuable investment income and open up new markets, but they are the principal means of tapping into and monitoring the competitive advantages of foreign firms and countries.[10]

The last 100 years is a story of the ambivalent and shifting attitudes of governments (particularly host governments) towards the perceived costs and benefits of MNE activity. In retrospect, a kind of Kondratieff long-wave cycle seems to have been at work. Inbound investment has been particularly welcomed at times of strong market oriented economic growth, and when the need for the innovating and competitiveness enhancing qualities of FDI has been especially marked. Such was the case in the late nineteenth and early twentieth century, the 1960s and for most of the past two decades.

By contrast, it has been less enthusiastically acclaimed when the perceived need for its unique qualities has been less pressing, and where host governments have been pursuing market distorting or self-reliant economic policies; or where there has been a particular sensitivity to the strategic or cultural impact of MNE activity. The inter-war years and the 1970s saw one or other of these attitudes holding strong and, there is some suggestion that in the early 2000s, some of the earlier concerns are reasserting themselves,[11] reflected, for example in the less than cordial response by some US interest groups. Similarly, but we shall not do more than mention these, there have been periods, dating back at least to the first part of the nineteenth century, when the attitude of governments towards outbound MNE activity has been very restrictive.[12]

For the most part, however, the reactions of governments in the 1990s to MNE activity fall into the first category. According to a study published by UNCTAD (UNCTAD, 1999), of 895 changes in the investment regimes of countries between 1991 and 1998, 843, or 94.2 percent, were favorable to FDI. Korea is the latest example of a country which has completely liberalized its policies towards inbound FDI since the economic crisis of the late 1990s (UNCTAD, 1999).

Of the several reasons for the change in governmental attitudes toward MNE activity since the 1970s, two deserve especial mention. The first is the reconfiguration of economic growth and structural unemployment in countries of the world, which, coupled with the implementation of new labor and materials saving technologies and the increased mobility of intangible assets, has added to the pressure on countries to seek the ingredients of competitiveness and growth from wherever they can. The second factor is the opening up and development of new territories – especially in East Asia and Central and Eastern Europe – which has meant that the locational options open to MNEs have widened. These options have occurred at a time when global competitive pressures have compelled enterprises – especially MNEs – to be more adventurous in seeking out the most cost efficient locations for their value-added activities, and to form an increasing number and variety of cross-border alliances.

At the same time, there has been some reprioritization of the objectives of governments. From an emphasis on socially enhancing domestic goals in the 1960s and 1970s, the lenses of governments have been refocused towards identifying and deploying every means by which global competitiveness of their firms and their location bound resources may be enhanced; although the renewed quest for cultural autonomy and the growing resurgence of ethnic fruitions and tribalistic sentiments within nation states (possibly a reaction to the trend towards the harmonization of economic values) may well demand much more attention by governments in the next two decades or more.[13]

In so doing and in recognizing the innate mobility of many created assets, national authorities have begun to accept that, to best achieve their social objectives, they have to offer at least as attractive locational opportunities for the production and marketing of goods and services as do their main competitors; and to ensure that their domestic macro-economic and organizational policies are such that both their own and foreign firms are induced to invest in upgrading the kind of value activities best suited to the dynamic comparative advantages of their indigenous resources and capabilities.

Most certainly, one of the mistakes many national governments made in the 1970s and early 1980s was to try to force MNEs and their affiliates to accept the mould of established economic policies, and to exact penalties from those who did not. Often, the imposition of further market distorting programs not only did more harm than good, but soured the relations between MNEs and governments. Today it is recognized that in a world which is technologically *force majeure*, becoming economically interdependent and, for the most part, driven by international capitalism, the pursuance of domestic policies which are out of line with those of one's major competitors, is an unaffordable luxury. But – and this is a point worth stressing – although, in the 1980s, the inappropriateness of some government strategies was becoming sharply exposed by the activities of MNEs, such activities were not the primary cause. MNEs do, indeed, respond to the imperatives of the globalizing marketplace. But, although they are the main agents of change, they do not alone determine the consequences and shape of that change. This responsibility is shared by the macro-economic and organizational systems devised and implemented by governments, and by international economic regimes, e.g. the WTO, the World Bank and the IMF. In considering, then, the shift currently taking place in national government policies towards MNEs, it is necessary to look beyond the determinants and outcome of the latter's activities – and toward the implications of the globalizing economy *per se*.

THE CHANGING ROLE OF NATIONAL GOVERNMENTS

We have suggested that globalization – and its main enabling vehicle – the telematics revolution – is dramatically encapsulating space, and by so doing, is linking national economies in a way undreamed of by our forefathers. In addition, since economic growth is increasingly dependent on the enhancement and disposition of created, rather than natural assets, it follows that there is much more inter-country competition for the former and their products than for the latter and their products.

At the time of David Ricardo, i.e. the early years of the nineteenth century, it was possible to draw a clear dividing line between the foreign and domestic economic policies of national governments. As regards the former, the debate largely centered about the merits of protectionism in those cases where foreign competition was perceived to be damaging – or potentially damaging.

Not surprisingly, the stance taken by countries rested on their relative pecking orders in the development stakes; and also the lobbying power of firms from those sectors most likely to be adversely affected by trade liberalization. But, in general, the 'near' free traders – like the UK – asserted that each country should efficiently produce those goods and services which required resources in which they possessed a comparative advantage, and exchange those for others requiring resources in which they were comparatively disadvantaged. The preferred organizational route for achieving this goal was the unfettered market, with national administrations only intervening when the market was thought to operate inefficiently or unfairly, or where the barriers to entry into socially beneficial economic activities were too high for private investors to bear.

However, with one major exception, resources and capabilities were assumed to be location bound within national borders. Since, too, domestic firms could not 'escape' from unwelcome fiscal, macro-economic and micro-management policies – nor foreign firms be tempted to take advantage of more favorable policies – the only constraint on the behavior of governments was that of the demands of foreign countries and the supply capabilities of foreign producers via trade; and even here the connection was an indirect one. The one exception was that of finance capital – the one created asset that was able to flow freely across national boundaries. Hence, the argument later put forward by economists such as Robert Mundell (1957) that trade in capital and goods were largely substitutable for each other. In such a scenario, national governments could pursue domestic economic and social policies largely independent of each other without fear that these policies would provoke undesirable reactions by other governments. And, in point of fact, for much of recent economic history, such policies have differed greatly both between countries, and in the same country at different periods of time.

In the globalizing world of the early 2000s, the options open to national administrations are much more constrained. Primarily because of the easy movement of the critical wealth-creating assets, and the fact that there is more intensive competition among nation states to produce similar goods and services than once there was, the domestic economic strategies of national governments are more closely intertwined than once they were. This is because of the widening choice of the owners of the mobile assets as to the location of their production and usage. Thus, in pursuance of legitimate domestic objectives, if the government of one country imposes too high a corporation tax, firms – be they domestic or foreign – may decide to relocate their value-added activities in another country where taxes are lower; or, in considering where to site their new plants, firms may choose that country with the least burdensome environmental constraints, or whose government pursues the most favorable industrial policy, or which offers the most advanced telecommunication facilities or the most attractive tax breaks for R&D activities. Indeed, as several studies ably summarized in UNCTAD (1996) have shown, anything and everything a government does which affects the competitiveness of those firms which have some latitude in their cross-border locational choices must come under scrutiny. In such cases, the boundaries of domestic economic jurisdiction become blurred. And, because of this, one of the critical assumptions underlying the behavior of any government – viz. its autonomy in the framing and implementation of its economic strategy – is no longer valid. The mould is broken; it needs to be recast.

The last 20 or more years have seen a growing recognition by the leading industrial nations of the need for some co-ordination in their macro-economic policies to avoid counter-productive domestic monetary and fiscal policies, and to cushion the adverse affect of shocks to an increasingly volatile international financial system. Though the Group of Seven has had some success in this area – and, indeed, it may be argued that the decisions of this informal group of leaders has exerted more influence on the domestic macro-economic policies of the triad nations than the actions of more formal supra-national regimes, e.g. EEC, World Bank, etc. – the recent fragility of European currencies vividly demonstrates some of the difficulties of maintaining a unified exchange mechanism, where the member countries vary in economic well-being or are faced with different economic and social needs. When the crunch comes, national interests always seem to triumph over regional or international interests.

More recently, attempts to widen the terms of reference of the WTO, notably to embrace issues relating to FDI, labor standards and intellectual property rights are perhaps, the most explicit acknowledgement – at least by some governments – that their domestic economic programs can and do affect the playing field of international transactions; and that market distorting micro-management policies may be as damaging to the level and direction of world trade as any tariff or non-tariff barriers.[14] Once again, as in many other issues – notably the initiation of EC 1992 – MNEs, through such institutions as the European Round Table UNICE (Union of Industrial and Employers' Confederation) (and the Transatlantic Business Dialogue (TABD))[15] have played a critical role. More than most other economic agents, they – the MNEs – understand the implications of the gamut of legislation and policies – designed by governments to advance their own political and economic goals – not just on their own competitive position in international markets, but on how, in turn, these measures may induce a reaction from other governments.

The idea that governments, like corporations – on behalf of their constituents – compete with each other for resources and markets, and that, like corporations, they may behave as oligopolists in their rent seeking activities, is one which has, so far, gained only limited intellectual support. This is particularly so among neo-classical economists who believe that firms are the sole wealth creators in society; and that the role of government is simply (sic) to provide the legal and commercial backdrop to the market allocative mechanism, which alone and unaided, should provide the signals as to what should be produced, how it should be produced, who should produce it and where it should be produced. The idea of a UK, US or Ireland Ltd smacks too much of corporatism, and of the kind of economic interventionism which, in the past, has proved to be less effective than the imperfect markets which it sought to replace. In particular – so it is argued – the experiences of mainland China and Central and Eastern Europe over much of the previous century have shown that there is an unacceptable face of government just as there is an unacceptable face of the market place.

Yet, there can be no escaping the fact that in our complex and interdependent global village, markets do not always operate costlessly.[16] Neither can one deny that in social democracies, the government of the day is accountable to the electorate for its conduct of the economy, just as it is responsible for defence, law and order, the environment and public administration, and for the welfare of the less able and most disadvantaged members of society. Indeed, there is a parallel between the task of the elected authority to protect its citizens against military conquest or unacceptable political intervention and that of the sustenance of its economic security.[17] In conditions of economic isolation, this latter task is a minimal one. In the textbook world of a simple division of labor, perfect markets, immobile resources and complementary trade and production, there is little need for governments to intervene with the decisions of producers and consumers. But this is not the global economic scenario at the turn of the millennium. Countries and firms are intricately linked with each other. Resources are mobile. Governments do compete with each other. The division of labor is making for more, rather than less, interdependence of economic activities and more, rather than less, asset specificity. And markets do not always perform in the way that neoclassical economists like to think they should.

The literature on the rationale of government intervention to overcome or mitigate the inability of markets to fully optimize economic welfare is substantial and growing. It is also quite recent, although many of the justifications for government intervention date back to the time of A.C. Pigou and beyond. Economists today argue that there are three main reasons why governments may wish to intervene in markets.[18] The first – and one which will not be addressed in any detail in this chapter – is to achieve goals other than the efficient use of resources – notably to advance social, political or cultural mores – which the market system, is not (and never was), set up to achieve. This form of intervention by government is only relevant in the present context in so far as the money spent on the attainment of social goals may be at the cost of maintaining or upgrading a country's competitiveness in international markets, and, hence, the resources available to support social objectives in a future period of time. In other words, the competitiveness of US, British, German or Irish firms relative to their foreign competitors in period 1 will – in part at least – determine how much the US, British, German or Irish governments can afford to spend on social welfare in period 2.

The right, or optimum, balance of allocating a country's resources and capabilities between wealth-creating and other welfare-enhancing activities cannot be decided on economic grounds alone; moreover it is likely to be highly country specific. However, in comparing the economic performances of nations over the last 20 to 30 years, several studies have pointed to the very different emphasis to the creation and the distribution of wealth and social capital by the US and UK governments, compared with that given by the Japanese and German governments.[19] We will write no more on this issue, save to observe that the growing imperative of countries to be competitive in world markets – to maintain, let alone advance the living standards of their constituents – is requiring an increasing proportion of their resources to be directed to competitive enhancing activities; and it is this realization which is compelling some administrations to reappraise some of their spending programs and the means of financing them.

The second, and least controversial, reason why governments intervene in markets is because they perceive that the terms and conditions of exchange are being distorted by the conduct of one or more of the participants in the market – or of foreign governments. Such structural market impurities essentially result from the monopolistic, or monopsonistic behavior, on the part of producers, labor unions or consumers, although sometimes the desire to eradicate these distortions gets confused with the debate of whether some markets, e.g. those for education, housing, rail transport and health should perform a social as well as an economic function. *Inter alia*, this ambivalence of objectives explains why state run sectors are often uncompetitive. Here the concept of the social market economy becomes relevant, although in recent years, this concept has been widened to embrace societal goals which seek to balance the benefits of economic liberty with those of personal and social responsibility (Novak, 1998).

National governments possess a plethora of instruments to deal with structural market failures – most of which are directed to making markets more contestable, and to inhibiting one group of participants from exploiting such economic power as they may have at the expense of other groups. Anti-trust policies represent the kernel of such instruments. Insofar as the globalization of economic activity intensifies competition between firms, the intervention of governments may be less necessary. But, more relevant is the fact that technological and organizational advances are shifting the main locus of inter-firm rivalry from being intranational to being international.

At the same time, market structures are becoming more complex as firms both compete and collaborate with each other. The growth of cross-border acquisitions and mergers (A&Ms) and strategic business alliances has been one of the most dramatic phenomenon of the last decade (UNCTAD, 2000). Such alliances as the design and production of a supersonic aircraft, or a new generation of computers, are usually intended to accomplish a very specific purpose and, while some observers are concerned lest they are an excuse for monopolistic behavior, the general consensus is that many help protect or advance the global competitive positions of the participating firms.

Several European governments are currently encouraging transatlantic alliances between small to medium-size firms. However, the point we wish to underline is that one government's attitude – *vis-à-vis* that of another government competing for the same resources – towards the increased oligopolistic structure of trans-national production and the conclusion of cross-border A&Ms and alliances, may decisively affect both the incentive and capabilities of its domestically based firms to service foreign markets, and the locational options open to foreign based MNEs (or increase their investments) in that country. The mould of competition policy which is suitable to a closed economy may need to be recast in a global economy. At the same time, to discourage governments from using their competition policies to achieve goals other than those consistent with efficient markets, some kind of supra-national surveillance may be necessary where other governments are promoting economic strategies which are structurally distorting. We shall return to this point a little later.

Let us now turn to the third justification for governments to intervene in the way markets allocate resources, and one which globalization is forcing a major reassessment of the whole ethos of their macro-organizational strategies. This is to overcome, or to counteract, endemic or pervasive market failure. There are two kinds of such failure. The first reflects the costs required to create and sustain an efficient market. Economists refer to these costs as transaction costs; but, *de facto*, they include all expenditures which have to be incurred to ensure that the buyers and sellers in the market have the knowledge and incentives to behave as they would in a situation of perfect competition.

The second kind of endemic market failure arises from the fact that contrary to the assumptions of neo-classical economic theory, individual markets – be they product, labor or financial markets – are not always self-contained, independent entities, but are complementary to, and interdependent of, each other. The main implication of this interdependence is that a particular transaction may affect, for good or bad, the welfare of individuals or institutions other than those involved in that transaction. These are the so-called externalities of markets. Sometimes in their evaluation of the efficiency of markets, analysts distinguish between private costs and benefits (i.e. those incurred or enjoyed by the transacting parties to an exchange) and social costs and benefits, viz. those enjoyed by the wider community. To give just one example: it has been calculated (by some economists)[20] that the average social returns to research and development exceed those appropriated by the investing firms by 50 percent–100 percent.

The literature provides countless examples of situations in which endemic market failure is likely to flourish. Broadly speaking, these fall into two main groups. The first relate to characteristics of the goods or services being transacted; and the second to the conditions under which they are exchanged. Of the former, products whose production requires assets with a high level of specificity (or start-up) to variable costs of production (i.e. capital or technology intensive products); products the demand for which or supply of which is inelastic, uncertain or unstable; products, the supply of which is subject to substantial economies of scale or whose value rests on strict quality control; products which are more valuable if they are used jointly with other products; and products the output or use of which generates substantial external economies or costs (e.g. environmentally sensitive products).

As to market specific transaction costs, these are frequently the outcome of imperfections in interpersonal relationships, information asymmetries, moral hazard and inappropriate macro-organizational policies. They include country related political and economic uncertainties; the inadequacy of the legal or regulatory system with respect, e.g. to contract enforcement and protection of property rights; exchange risks; unacceptable or misunderstood business practices; undemanding consumer attitudes towards product improvement and quality; abrasive work and worker–management relationships; and the failure of government to adequately acknowledge or cope with endemic market failure.

It may not have escaped the reader's notice that the products which possess the characteristics just identified – or, to put it another way, when produced and sold through the market, incur substantial relational and transaction costs – are the output of created assets. They are also products which are currently predominantly supplied by large firms – though, due to the advent of electronic markets and the opportunities offered by strategic alliances, are likely to be increasingly provided by small to medium-size corporations; and the conditions of their production are markedly influenced by the actions of national governments. They are products the supply of which tends to increase proportionately as a country moves along its development path. They are also trade and FDI intensive; while the markets for them vary in their degree of imperfection according to the location of the participants involved. Finally, they are the products at the forefront of globalization, which, to be produced efficiently, often require the use of complementary assets.

Some of the responses to market failure – both by the market participants and by extra market institutions have been set out elsewhere (Dunning 1992, 1997, and Chapter 2 of this book). Here, we would simply reiterate three of the more important. The first is for firms to internalize intermediate product markets by the vertical integration of value chains or the horizontal diversification of products or processes. Such action may either lower or increase economic welfare, depending on whether it is prompted by the desire of the internalizing firms to raise economic efficiency or to advance monopoly power. An example of the former kind of exit strategy is where a hierarchy internalizes a market to lower its transaction costs or to exploit the economies of scale or scope. This is likely to be welfare raising, especially where the firm is faced with competition in the less idiosyncratic factor or intermediate goods markets, and in the final goods or services markets. On the other hand, a hostile takeover could be prompted by the desire of the acquiring firm to eliminate a competitor and engage in market distorting practices.

The second response to market failure is for the participants in the market – sometimes assisted by non-participants – to try to reduce that failure. For example, quality variation and an inability of subcontractors to adhere to delivery dates might be reduced by a closer and more productive working relationship between the buying firms and their suppliers; while, by reducing macro-economic uncertainties and removing market inhibiting governmental practices, e.g. discriminatory purchasing procedures, transaction costs might be lowered. These are all examples of 'voice' strategies to market failure emphasized by Hirschman (1970) in his writings.

The third solution is for governments or some other extra-market institutions (e.g. groups of firms) to counteract the intrinsic deficiencies of the market by offering producers and consumers inducements to behave as if a perfect market existed. Examples include the provision of tax concessions and subsidies to increase the private benefits of R&D and training to the level of their social benefits; improving information about the export opportunities for small firms; setting up investment guarantee schemes to protect outbound MNEs against political risks; making certain that patent legislation and procedures properly reflect the needs of innovators; assisting the market in its provision of risk capital – especially for projects which are likely to generate social benefits and are long-term in their gestation – and ensuring, directly or indirectly, that the transaction or 'hassle' costs of doing business – e.g. industrial disputes, inadequate transport and communication facilities and time-consuming bureaucratic controls, are kept to the minimum.

While it is possible to cite many other examples of endemic market shortcomings, most reduce to the presence of X inefficiency of one kind or another. There is, however, another aspect of market failure which economists are apt to neglect, mainly because they tend to assume human beings behave in a consistent and rational manner and are only interested in the pursuance of wealth. But – one might question – is this a realistic interpretation of why individuals and institutions engage in market transactions? Organizational theorists question this, and talk about the bounded rationality and opportunistic behavior of producers and consumers; and about the *homo psychologicus* of cognitive psychology as compared with the *homo economicus* of economics.[21]

We consider extending this idea of psychological man to the mentality or culture of wealth-creating activities by countries and corporations. Even the most cursory glance at the ways in which (say) the Arab countries and the Germans conduct day to day business; or the attitudes of the Japanese and Nigerians to inter-firm relationships and contractual obligations; or the ethos of work and leisure of the Taiwanese and Greeks; or the perceived personal and social morality of workers, business managers and governments of the Koreans, Chileans and Russians – or the cross-border operational and organizational strategies of Nissan and Toyota or Motorola and Texas Instruments – reveals wide differences in the culture or ideology of wealth-creating behavior. As Chapter 2 of this volume has shown, the globalizing economy is unearthing a new importance to concepts such as trust, forbearance and reciprocity; and of informal, rather than formal, organizational forms in affecting national competitiveness, and, hence, the disposition of resources and capabilities.

The extent to which the culture of wealth-creating behavior is an intrinsic characteristic of a country or corporation or can be shaped by exposure to other cultures, by decree or economic pressure, or by a reorientation of personal or business values, is debatable. So indeed, is the question of which, if any, moral virtues can be considered absolute or universal (Fukuyama, 1999). At the same time, there can be little doubt that the forces of globalization are compelling firms and governments to review their respective roles in influencing mental attitudes towards wealth-creating activities. Whether we like it or not, the trade-offs between these and other activities, such as leisure pursuits, are changing; and, whether we like it or not, to a large extent, they are being set by countries which value competitiveness the highest. The grasshopper's attitude to life is fine as long as the grasshoppers do not aspire to the living standards of the ant. The trouble is that most of us want to retain our lifestyles of work and leisure, but also enjoy all the material benefits of our economically more successful neighbors.

Here, again, I believe governments have a critical role to play, both as information providers to their constituents about the real costs of not being competitive in an open world economy; and in helping to create a culture or psychology of economic behavior which encourages, rather than discourages, competitiveness. Much more contentious is the extent to which some culturally related business or work practices are perceived to be the 'unacceptable face of competitiveness'; or, how far the promotion of the twin goals of wealth creation and social justice are mutually consistent? Why should British, or American, or Dutch textile workers be expected to have their wages or working conditions reduced to the level nearer their counterparts in Bangladesh or Sri Lanka – or lose their jobs? Although the question of harmonizing cross-country cultures of work, wealth-creating activities and social needs is not yet on the political agenda of countries, it is not far below the surface, and is likely to become an increasing talking point as globalization impels governments to reappraise their attitudes on this issue.

Of course, the culture of economic behavior does not start or end with the work ethic. A no less – and perhaps, a more important consideration – and one which is in line with the principle of comparative dynamic advantage – is for a country threatened by low labor cost competitiveness to upgrade or restructure its resource usage and efficiency. Governments again can play a decisive part not just by providing the right kind of market-enabling incentives and structural adjustment assistance (Ozawa, 1987), but by encouraging – and be seen to be encouraging – an ethos of entrepreneurship and innovation; a readiness by enterprises to anticipate and take advantage of technical and economic change; and an appreciation by workers of the need for job restructuring and retraining.

If what has been written is familiar to most economists and business scholars, we do not think it is generally acknowledged. And this, primarily, is because the average Westerner's perception of the appropriate tasks of government is 50 to 100 years out of date. Part of the reason is, most certainly, a cultural or ideological one – compare, for example, a Christian with an Islamic or Confucian viewpoint of such issues as personal initiative, authority and collective responsibility; but, part is because Western governments have not seen the need to, or have had the political will to, recast the mold of their economic responsibilities. Some recent contributions by scholars have urged governments to reappraise their policies[22] – but these are not helped by analysts who continue to preach a minimal role for governments, or encourage a 'them' and 'us' attitude between private firms and the public sector, with the former being perceived as the wealth creators and the latter as the profligate spenders of that created wealth.

The core economic task of government as an enabler or facilitator of wealth creation is not yet appealing to most people. The reality – as opposed to the idea – of a partnership between government, firms and individuals in enhancing competitiveness is only now starting to take root in Europe and North America. The suggestion that the globalized economy demands a fundamental rethink of the 'how,' 'why' and 'wherefore' of the organization of government, as it does of firms is still not generally supported. For the most part, political scientists and economists either assert that governments should not involve themselves at all in macro-organizational affairs, or that they should play a direct and activist interventionist role in shaping or manipulating markets to better meet perceived social and economic needs.

Yet, *de facto*, the rhetoric of government ministers is often far removed from the practice. To take one example; in her time as Prime Minister, Mrs Thatcher constantly applauded the virtues of the free market. Yet, a reading of her record suggests that she was one of the most interventionist of Prime Ministers – if one uses the word interventionist to include any and every action taken by a government which might affect the competitiveness of the resources under its jurisdiction. But somehow, either out of ignorance, lethargy, or for some reason best known to themselves, right-wing politicians seem reluctant to acknowledge that such actions as tax hikes, environmental regulations, a new educational curricula, attitudes towards monopolies, investment in roads, energy policies, regional development, health care programs, industrial relations legislation and the finance of universities – all affect competitiveness just as much as direct intervention (mainly via industrial policy) in the allocation and use of resources. And certainly, there seems little appreciation of how these policies interact with each other; hence, there is no holistic or systemic approach to them.

We would not want to press our critique of Western governments too far. In several countries – noticeably the UK and the US – there is a growing recognition that the globalizing economy is compelling an upscaling of industrial competitiveness on the political agenda, and a reappraisal of traditional macro-organizational strategies. Issues such as training, the funding of R&D, information and advice for small businesses, competition policy, attitudes towards inward investment, new road and rail links and so on are being increasingly viewed and evaluated in terms of their perceived impact on competitiveness. But, for the most part, most of the action so far taken by Western governments has been *ad hoc*, unco-ordinated and fragmentary; and as an 'add-on' to existing policies, rather than part of a systemic remolding of the organizational structure of decision taking so that it may best embrace the challenges and opportunities of a globalizing economy.

To some extent, the problem is educating the decision takers in government. Here, the fault partly lies with the academic community. We have just not got over the message that there is a fundamental difference between the kind of government action necessary to help overcome endemic market failure and to facilitate the upgrading of resources and capabilities, and that which seeks to replace or modify the behavior of firms in the belief that central planning can do a better job in advancing economic and social welfare than can markets. We have not got over the message that, to optimize their efficiency and response to market signals, firms require the availability of created assets and a wealth-creating ethos which only governments can provide. We have not got over the message that increasingly what governments do and how they do it, is much more important than how much government involvement should there be!

To some extent, too, the problem is one of re-forming opinions and attitudes towards the role of governments. We need a new vocabulary to promote the image of government as a public good rather than as a necessary evil. We need a 'perestroika' of government. We need to recognize that, just as 'Fordism' is an outdated method of organizing work, so the kind of government interventionism appropriate to a 'Fordist' environment is outdated. And, just like the emerging managerial structure of twenty-first century firms, we need governments to be lean, flexible and anticipatory of change. The new paradigm of government should eschew such negative or emotive sounding words as 'command', 'intervention', 'regulation', and replace them by words such as 'empower', 'steer', 'co-operative', 'co-ordination' and 'systemic'. Moreover, not only must governments recognize the need for a much more integrated and holistic system of organizing their responsibilities, which demands a 'spider's web' rather than a 'hub and spoke' relationship between the various decision taking departments and the core of government, viz. the cabinet of the Prime Minister or President (Dunning, 1992); but, for all those affected by governments, and particularly the ordinary taxpayers, to take a more positive view of the benefits which only the former can produce.

It is not the purpose of this chapter to suggest how the organization of governments should change to accommodate the kind of remolding we have articulated. But, this issue is now very much being considered in the literature. For example, Douglas Hague (Hague, 1993) has identified four ways in which institutions – be they public or private – can re-engineer themselves, viz. by coercion, contagion, coaching and learning. While the latter three are usually more acceptable agents of change than the first; in practice, as demonstrated by the East Asian crisis of the late 1990s, such change usually has to wait until some kind of crisis coerces action.

At the same time we would not wish to imply that actions taken by national governments to overcome or reduce market failure are costless, or that such actions are necessarily the most cost effective way of achieving that objective.[23]

More generally, it is possible to identify the kind of situations which favor government intervention of one kind or another. Table 15.1, which is derived and adapted from Robert Wade's evaluation of the role played by national administrations in fostering the economic development of Japan, Taiwan and Korea (Wade, 1988) sets out some of these situations, and the ways in which they may help reduce the transaction costs of governance.

While the data in Table 15.1 are fairly self-explanatory, and provide a set of guidelines for governmental intervention, they have not yet been subject to rigorous scrutiny by scholars. The globalizing economy may well enhance the need for such a scrutiny, as it increases the costs of misinformed or inappropriate government action.

MULTILATERAL ACTION

We cannot end this chapter without at least the briefest of mentions of the implications of globalization for the existing supra-national regimes of governance;

Table 15.1 Some examples of situations in which governments might successfully contain their own organizational costs

Intervention or form of government intervention	Consequences for the reduction of government related transaction costs
• The enhancement of national competitiveness by market facilitating measures; and publicly promoting this objective • The containment of interventionist policies to activities severely hampered by market failures • A holistic approach to the co-ordination of complementary policies and institutional mechanisms • An ethos of consensus and co-operation between private and public policy makers, e.g. with respect to mutually beneficial goals and the means by which goals can best be achieved • The recruitment of the most talented and well-motivated individuals for public sector employment, e.g. by offering competitive working conditions and encouraging initiative and entrepreneurship • The insulation of the policy making process from the strongest (and most undesirable) pressure groups • The presence of a national ethos or mentality of the need to be competitive and create wealth. Partly, this embraces a 'communitarian' culture and partly one which encourages personal initiative, entrepreneurship, scientific specialization and competition • The absence of strong sectoral interest groups, e.g. farmers and left-wing labor groups, which might press for interventionist measures by governments other than those which are market facilitating	• Reduces effectiveness of rent seeking special interest groups • Increases work effort of public agents • Makes policy trade-offs easier to identify and solve • Clarifies policy makers' task and reduces problem of bounded rationality • Reduces likelihood of sub-optimization • Captures economies of scope in governance and increases intra-organizational information flows and learning • Reduces transaction costs of interaction between representatives of private and public sector • Increases knowledge of public decision takers • Reduces chance of uninformed or biased media coverage in forcing governments into ill-advised or hasty decisions • Likely to inhibit the pursuance of sub-optimal goals and to reduce bounded rationality and opportunism and use of inefficient production technologies • Reduces the effectiveness of rent seeking by special interest groups, and relieves the policy making process from the pressure of day to day politics • Favors co-ordination of strategies and policies of public and private organizations and reduces the sub-optimization problem in the public sector • Reduces possibility of ideological conflicts and undue emphasis being placed on the redistribution of incomes as a (short-term) social good

Sources: Wade (1988), Stiglitz (1989), Grestchmann (1991), Hämäläinen (1994).

although some of the relevant issues have been dealt with in Chapter 2 of this volume. If our thesis that governments are increasingly competing with each other for resources and markets to maintain or increase their living standards is correct; and, if *de facto*, such competition tends to be oligopolistic, then there is a real danger that the strategic rent seeking measures taken by individual governments might lead to a situation not unlike the 'beggar my neighbor' restrictive trade policies of the inter-war years. For the last 40 years, GATT – and latterly the WTO – has helped set the rules of the game for trade. But, today the playing field of international competition is structured very differently. As we have argued in this chapter, it embraces many policy instruments of governments, which as much affect the capabilities of nations to trade and compete with each other, just as much as the conditions underlying trade *per se*.

And, it is in pursuance of industrial, technology, taxation and competition strategies to advance national interests where the level of the playing fields is currently the most uneven. Again, *inter alia*, because of their unique business cultures, different countries have different interpretations of the fairness or otherwise of government interventions; hence – to give just one example – the strategic initiative talks between Japan and the US have been designed to try to reconcile some of the differences between the two nations in their interpretations of the legitimacy of government enabling measures.

The next decade is likely to see much written about the remoulding of international institutions such as WTO, the World Bank, IMF and the UN so that they can better cope with the problems of globalization – including those occasioned by the dictates of MNEs – which cannot easily be tackled or solved at a national, or even a regional, level. Several scholars, notably Joseph Stiglitz (1998), have argued the need for a new paradigm of economic growth and development to replace that of the Washington consensus of the late 1980s.[24] Again, the role of national governments in championing their own causes will be a critical one. But, just as we have argued in this chapter, the kinds of restructuring of the organization of markets and firms demanded by globalization is impelling national governments to redesign their world of governance, so, too, the functions and authority of international institutions may need to be reconsidered if globalization is to offer the fullest possible benefits – which a free exchange of people, goods and services demands.

NOTES

1. The concept of strong and positive government does not necessarily imply there should be substantial government intervention in economic affairs. For example, an IMF study of East Asia's experience suggests there is little evidence to suggest that even 'selective' interventionism is correlated with superior growth performance. Instead, high domestic savings and investment rates, an emphasis on the upgrading of human capital, flexible labor markets and

an unrestricted access to foreign resources, capabilities and markets are among the shared factors in the success of the Asian economies (Ostry, 1993). However, it is our contention that, by their macro-economic and organizational strategies, governments may play a critical role in influencing the value of these, and other, competitive enhancing variables.

2. Teece (1992) has pleaded for a re-evaluation of the role of the *corporation* in the light of the global economy; our analysis argues for a similar reconceptualization of the role of government; see also Dunning (1997).
3. There are various other expressions which, like globalization, are difficult to define precisely. Interdependence and integration are two of these.
4. Some writers, e.g. Drucker (1989), even trace the evolution of the globalization of economic activity back to the thirteenth century.
5. In the US, for example, the percentage of GDP accounted for by trade rose from 7 percent to 12 percent between 1970 and 1996, while that accounted for by the stock of inward and outward direct investment increased from 4.2 percent to 9.4 percent. (See Appendix A.2.7 of Chapter 2 of this volume.)
6. Latest figures published by UNCTAD (1999) suggest that in 1998, the sales of the foreign affiliates of MNEs amounted to $11.4 trillion compared with that of trade of goods and non-factor services of $6.7 trillion.
7. We use the word technology to embrace all forms of assets which make for the more efficient development of resources and capabilities.
8. McKenzie and Lee (1991), for example, argue that the fall of Communism in Central and Eastern Europe was triggered by economic, rather than political, forces and, in particular, by the former's impact on increasing inter-firm competition and reducing cross-border psychic distance between the countries of the world.
9. Chapters 3 and 4 of Dunning (2001) explore these and related issues in more detail.
10. The role of MNEs in upgrading the competitive advantages of both home and host countries is described by several writers in a special edition of *Management International Review*, edited by Alan Rugman and published in spring 1993. See also the annual World Investment Reports of UNCTAD, especially UNCTAD (1995, 1999).
11. As documented for example in Vernon (1998).
12. These are more fully described in Dunning (1993a).
13. For example, John Naisbitt has argued that, in the next 20 years or so, the number of sovereign states will dramatically increase from around 200 to upwards of 500 (Naisbitt, 1994).
14. At the same time, as explained in Chapter 2 of this volume, other governments and several non-governmental organizations, are generally opposed to the enlargement of the WTO's agenda – at least in so far as that agenda is (or is perceived to be) dominated by the interests of developed nations and by those of the larger MNEs.
15. See Dunning (2001), Chapter 10.
16. This was recognized by Émile Durkheim in 1893, when he stated that increasing internationalization and division of labor in a society – the hallmarks of economic progress – leads to the 'accumulation of government tasks' (Durkheim, 1964, pp. 219–26).
17. Indeed, in the past, many wars have been fought to preserve or advance such security.
18. The literature on this subject is extensive. Much of it is summarized in Dunning (1997). See also Ostry (1990), Stopford and Strange (1991) and Prakash and Hart (1999). For an analysis of the changing balance between the role of governments, hierarchies and markets as economic development proceeds, see Stiglitz (1989), Dunning (1993b), Hämäläinen (1994), and Porter (1998).
19. See particularly the annual *World Competitive Yearbook* issued by IMD, Lausanne, Switzerland; and the writings of Francis Fukuyama, e.g. Fukuyama (1995, 1999).
20. See especially Aaron and Schultze (1992).
21. As, for example, explored by Williamson (1992).
22. See especially those identified by various authors in Dunning (1997).
23. Among the possible failures of direct government intervention to successfully overcome the deficiencies of the market, one might mention the rent seeking activities of powerful pressure groups; the magnification of market failures (e.g. with respect to the supply of environmental or social products) by the news media or other politically motivated interests; the inability

of governments to attract the best talents (due *inter alia* to ineffective incentive systems); the lack of commercial expertise and bounded rationality of public decision takers; the pursuance of non-economic (especially ideological) goals by politicians; the inadequacy of market related performance indicators which may lead to the establishment of sub-optimal standards (e.g. with respect to budgets, investment and control of information flows); the high time discount (or short-termism) of political decision takers; the lack of market pressures to minimize X inefficiency, especially in the case of public monopolies; uncertainties and ambiguities inherent in the provision of goods and services, which are in the domain of governments, e.g. defense equipment, educational and health services; and the lack of a co-ordinated system of governance (cf. with that in the case of private hierarchies); and the difficulty of adjusting policies and institutional structures to quickly meet the needs of technological and economic change. For a more detailed examination of these and other factors which might lead to excessive or inappropriate governmental intervention or the sub-optimal provision of public goods and services, see for example Wolf (1988), Grestchmann (1991), Stiglitz (1989), Hämäläinen (1994), and Dunning (1997).

24. For a recent summary of some of the issues involved in promoting the appropriate supranational governance as a public good in its own right see Levy (1999). For an earlier exposition of the changing role of governments in a global economy see Ostry (1990), Preston and Windsor (1992) and Graham (1992).

REFERENCES

Aaron, H.J. and Schultze, C.L. (eds) (1992), *Setting Domestic Priorities: What Can Government Do?*, Washington: The Brookings Institution.

Audretsch, D.B. (1989), *The Market and the State*, New York and London: Harvester Wheatsheaf.

Bergsten, C.F. and Graham, E.M. (1992), 'Needed: New rules for foreign direct investment,' *International Trade Journal* **VII**, pp. 15–44.

Colclough, C. and Manor, J. (eds) (1991), *States or Markets*, Oxford: Clarendon Press.

Cowles, M.G. (1993), 'The rise of the European multinational,' *International Economic Insights* **IV**, July/August, pp. 15–18.

Drucker, P. (1989), *The New Realities*, Washington: Library of Congress.

Dunning, J.H. (1988), *Multinationals, Technology and Competitiveness*, London: Allen and Unwin.

Dunning, J.H. (1992), 'The global economy, domestic governance, strategies and transnational corporations: interactions and policy recommendations,' *Transnational Corporations* **1**, December, pp. 7–45.

Dunning, J.H. (1993a), *Multinational Enterprises and the Global Economy*, Wokingham, England and Reading, MA: Addison-Wesley.

Dunning, J.H. (1993b), *The Globalization of Business*, London and New York: Routledge.

Dunning, J.H. (ed.) (1997), *Governments, Globalization and International Business*, Oxford: Oxford University Press.

Durkheim, E. (1964), *The Division of Labor in Society*, New York: The Free Press (reprinted from original monograph in 1893).

Fukuyama, F. (1995), *Trust: The Social Virtues and the Creation of Prosperity*, New York: The Free Press.

Fukuyama, F. (1999), *The Great Disruption*, London: Profile Books.

Grestchmann, K. (1991), 'Analyzing the public sector: The received view in economics and its shortcomings,' in Kaufman, Franz-Xaver (ed.), *The Public Sector: Challenge for Coordination and Learning*, Berlin: Walter de Gruyter.

Guisinger, S.E. and associates (1985), *Investment Incentives and Performance Requirements*, New York: Praeger.

Hague, D.C. (1993), *Transforming the Dinosaurs*, London: Demos.

Hämäläinen, T.J. (1994), 'The evolving role of government in economic organization,' Newark: Rutgers University (mimeo).

Hirschman, A. (1970), *Exit, Voice and Loyalty*, Cambridge, MA: Harvard University Press.

Kogut, B. and Parkinson, D. (1993), 'The diffusion of American organizing principles to Europe,' in Kogut, B. (ed.), *Country Competitiveness, Technology and the Organization of Work*, Oxford: Oxford University Press, pp. 179–202.

Krueger, A.O. (1990), 'Economists' changing perceptions of government,' *Weltwirtschaftliclies Archiv* **126**, pp. 417–31.

Lipsey, R.G. (1987), 'Globalization and national government policies; an economist's view.' in Dunning, J.H. (ed.), *Governments, Globalization and International Business*, Oxford: Oxford University Press, pp. 73–113.

Lodge, G.C. and Vogel, E.F. (1987), *Ideology and National Competitiveness: An Analysis of Nine Countries*, Boston: Harvard Business School Press.

Management International Review, Spring 1993. Special edition on Michael Porter's *Diamond of Competitive Advantage*, edited by Alan Rugman, 33, No. 2.

McKenzie, R.B. and Lee, D.R. (1991), *Quicksilver Capital*, New York: The Free Press.

Morrison, A.J., Ricks, D.A. and Roth, K. (1991), 'Globalization versus regionalization: which way for the multinational?,' *Organizational Dynamics* **19** (3), Winter, pp. 17–29.

Mundell, R. (1957), 'International trade and factor mobility,' *American Economic Review* **47**, pp. 321–35.

North, D. (1993), 'Institutions, Transaction Costs and Productivity in the Long Run', Paper presented to Eighth World Productivity Congress, Stockholm, May.

Novak, M. (1998), *Is there a Third Way*? London Institute of Economic Affairs, Health and Welfare Unit Choice in Welfare, No. 46.

Ostry, J. (1993), *Selective Government Interventions and Economic Growth: A Survey of the Asian Experience and its Applicability to New Zealand*, Washington: IMF (Paper on Policy Analysis and Assessment).

Ostry, S. (1990), *Governments and Corporations in a Shrinking World: Trade and Innovation Policies in the United States*, Europe and Japan, New York and London: Council on Foreign Relations.

Ozawa, T. (1987), 'Can the market alone manage structural upgrading? A challenge posed by economic interdependence,' in Dunning, J.H. and Usui, M. (eds), *Structural Change, Economic Interdependence and World Development*, Vol. 4, London and Basingstoke: Macmillan, pp. 45–62.

Porter, M. (1998), 'The microeconomic foundations of economic development in World Economic Forum,' *Global Competitiveness Report 1998*, Geneva World Economic Forum.

Preston, L.E. and Windsor, D. (1992), *The Rules of the Game in the Global Economy*, Boston and London: Kluwer.

Rugman, A. (2002), 'Multinational enterprises and the end of global strategy,' in Dunning, J.H. and Mucchielli, J.L. (eds), *Multinational Firms: The Global–Local Dilemma*, London and New York: Routledge.

Scott, B.R. and Lodge, G.R. (eds) (1985), *US Competitiveness in the World Economy*, Boston: Harvard Business School Press.
Stiglitz, J. (1989), *The Economic Role of the State*, Oxford: Basil Blackwell.
Stiglitz, J. (1998), *Towards a New Paradigm of Development*, Geneva. The 9th Prebisch Lecture, UNCTAD.
Stopford, J. and Strange, S. (1991), *Rival States, Rival Firms*, Cambridge: Cambridge University Press.
Teece, D.J. (1986), 'Transaction cost economics and the multinational enterprise,' *Journal of Economic Behavior and Organization* **1**, pp. 21–45.
Teece, D.J. (1992), 'Competition, cooperation and innovation,' *Journal of Economic Behavior and Organization* **7**, pp. 1–25.
UNCTC (1991), *Government Policies and Foreign Direct Investment*, New York: UN sales No. E91 II A 20.
UNCTAD (1991), *World Investment Report 1991: The Triad in Foreign Direct Investment*, New York and Geneva: UN.
UNCTAD (1993), *World Investment Report 1993: Transnational Corporations and Integrated International Production*, New York: UN.
UNCTAD (1995), *World Investment Report 1995: Transnational Corporations and Competitiveness*. New York and Geneva: UN.
UNCTAD (1996), *Incentives and Foreign Direct Investment*, New York and Geneva: UN.
UNCTAD (1999), *World Investment Report 1999: Foreign Direct Investment and the Challenge of Development*, New York and Geneva: UN.
UNCTAD (2000), *World Investment Report 2000: Cross Border Mergers and Acquisitions and Development*, New York and Geneva: UN.
Wade, R. (1988), 'The role of government in overcoming market failure in Taiwan, Republic of Korea and Japan,' in Hughes, H. (ed.), *Achieving Industrialization in East Asia*, Cambridge: Cambridge University Press.
Wallis, J.J. and North, D.C. (1986), 'Measuring the transaction sector in the American economy; 1870–1970,' in Engerman, S.L. and Gallman, R.E. (eds), *Long-term Factors in American Economic Growth*, Chicago: University of Chicago Press.
Wilkins, M. (1989), *Foreign Investment In The United States*, Cambridge, Mass.: Harvard University Press
Williamson, O.E. (1992), 'The evolving science of organization,' Berkeley: University of California, Business and Public Policy Working Paper 53.
Wolf, C.J. (1988), *Markets or Governments*, Cambridge, Mass.: MIT Press.

Subject index

Name index